GENETIC ALGORITHMS
AND THEIR APPLICATIONS:
Proceedings of the
Second International Conference on
Genetic Algorithms

July 28-31, 1987
at the
Massachusetts Institute of Technology
Cambridge, MA

Sponsored By

American Association for Artificial Intelligence

Naval Research Laboratory

Bolt Beranek and Newman, Inc.

John J. Grefenstette
Naval Research Laboratory
Editor

Psychology Press
Taylor & Francis Group

New York   London

First Published by
Lawrence Erlbaum Associates, Inc., Publishers
365 Broadway
Hillsdale, New Jersey 07642

Transferred to Digital Printing 2009 by Psychology Press
270 Madison Ave, New York NY 10016
27 Church Road, Hove, East Sussex, BN3 2FA

ISBN 0-8058-0158-8 cloth edition

ISBN 0-8058-0159-6 paperback edition

Publisher's Note
The publisher has gone to great lengths to ensure the quality of this reprint
but points out that some imperfections in the original may be apparent.

ACKNOWLEDGEMENTS

On behalf of the Conference Committee, it is my pleasure to acknowledge the support of our sponsors: the American Association for Artifical Intelligence, the Navy Center for Applied Research in Artificial Intelligence at the Naval Research Laboratory, and Bolt Beranek and Newman, Inc. The Committee also appreciates the cooperation of Dr. Edwin H. Land. I would personally like to thank the other members of the Conference Committee for their conscientious efforts as referees. Stewart Wilson deserves special thanks for handling the local arrangements.

John J. Grefenstette
Program Chair

Conference Committee

John H. Holland	University of Michigan (*Conference Chair*)
Lashon B. Booker	Navy Center for Applied Research in AI
Dave Davis	Bolt Beranek and Newman
Kenneth A. De Jong	George Mason University
David E. Goldberg	University of Alabama
John J. Grefenstette	Navy Center for Applied Research in AI (*Program Chair*)
Stephen F. Smith	Carnegie-Mellon Robotics Institute
Stewart W. Wilson	Rowland Institute for Science (*Local Arrangements*)

CONFERENCE PROGRAM

TUESDAY, JULY 28, 1987

5:00 - 9:00   REGISTRATION: *Lobby, McCormick Hall*

7:00 - 9:00   WELCOMING RECEPTION: *Courtyard, McCormick Hall*

WEDNESDAY, JULY 29, 1987

8:00   REGISTRATION: *Room 10-280*

9:00   OPENING REMARKS: *Room 10-250*

9:20 - 10:40   GENETIC SEARCH THEORY

10:40 - 11:00   COFFEE BREAK

11:00 - 12:00   ADAPTIVE SEARCH OPERATORS I

12:00 - 2:00   LUNCH

THURSDAY, JULY 30, 1987

6:30 - 10:00   CONFERENCE BANQUET: *New England Clambake*

FRIDAY, JULY 31, 1987

9:00 - 10:20   APPLICATIONS I

10:20 - 10:40   COFFEE BREAK

10:40 - 12:00   APPLICATIONS II

12:00 - 2:00   LUNCH

2:00 - 3:20   PANEL DISCUSSION: GA's and AI

3:20 - 3:40   COFFEE BREAK

3:40 - 5:00   INFORMAL DISCUSSION AND FAREWELL

FINITE MARKOV CHAIN ANALYSIS OF GENETIC ALGORITHMS

David E. Goldberg and Philip Segrest

The University of Alabama
Tuscaloosa, AL 35487

ABSTRACT

A finite Markov chain analysis of a single-locus, binary allele, finite population genetic algorithm (GA) is presented in this paper. The Markov analysis is briefly derived and computations are presented for two kinds of problems: genetic drift (no preference for either allele) and preferential selection (one allele is selected over the other). Approximate analyses are presented to explain the detailed Markov analysis. These computations are useful in choosing parameters for artificial genetic search.

INTRODUCTION

Genetic algorithms (GAs) are receiving increasing application in a variety of search and machine learning problems. These efforts have been greatly aided by the existence of theory that explains what GAs are processing and how they are processing it. The theory largely rests on Holland's exposition of schemata (1968, 1975), his bridge to the two-armed bandit problem (1973, 1975), his fundamental theorem of genetic algorithms (1973, 1975), and later works by several of his students (Martin, 1973; De Jong, 1975; Bethke, 1981). All of these works have necessarily made bounding assumptions: population sizes have been assumed to be infinitely large, probability limits have been estimated by relatively crude limits, and in some cases genetic operators have even been modified to facilitate the analysis. As a result, there is still a need for more exact analysis of genetic algorithm behavior using finite populations and realistic analytical models of genetic operators.

In this paper, we perform a Markov chain analysis of a one-locus, two-operator (reproduction and mutation) genetic algorithm acting upon a finite population of haploid binary structures. Specifically, we calculate the expected time of first passage to various levels of convergence under different selection ratios and mutation rates.

To understand the Markov chain analysis and its application, we first develop an analysis of genetic drift: convergence in finite populations under no selective pressure. Understanding this phenomenon is useful in explaining why finite GAs make convergence errors at relatively unimportant bit positions. We then examine expected GA performance at different levels of selective pressure assuming a deterministic fitness function. This analysis permits calculation of the selective pressure required to reduce the probability of selecting the wrong bit to some known level. We also discuss how these results and their extension may be used for designing and sizing finite GAs.

STOCHASTIC ERRORS IN FINITE GENETIC ALGORITHMS

As simple three-operator genetic algorithms have been used in a wider array of search and machine learning applications (Goldberg & Thomas, 1986), a number of objections have been voiced concerning their performance. Chief among these objections is the occurrence of premature convergence (De Jong, 1975). Premature convergence is that event where a population of structures attains a high level of uniformity at all loci without containing sufficiently near-optimal structures. Two reasons have been given for this undesirable form of convergence: a problem (with its chosen coding) can itself be GA-hard, or the finite GA can suffer from stochastic errors.

GAs may diverge because a problem is inherently difficult for a three-operator GA. Such problems have been called GA-hard (Goldberg, 1983), and Bethke (1981) has proved that GA-hard problems exist using Walsh function computation of schema averages. Reordering operators based on natural precedent have been suggested (Holland, 1975; Goldberg & Lingle, 1985) as one remedy for such problems, especially those where building blocks are not linked tightly enough to permit the three-operator GA to find near-optimal points. Despite the possibility of GA-hardness, Bethke's study and an extended schema analysis of the minimal deceptive problem (Goldberg, 1986) suggest that it is more difficult to construct intentionally misleading (GA-hard) problems than was previously thought. Furthermore this notion --that GA-hard problems are relatively hard to construct--is empirically supported by the widespread success of simple GAs across a spectrum of problems. Nonetheless, the study of GA-hard problems and the design of operators to circumvent the difficulty remain important open areas of research activity.

The other major source of convergence difficulty in genetic algorithms results from the stochastic errors of small populations. These errors may themselves be divided into two types: errors in sampling and errors in selection. A pollster makes a sampling error when he selects a sample size which is too small to achieve the accuracy he desires. He also commits a sampling error when the sample he selects is not representative of the population as a whole. Genetic algorithms may make similar sampling errors when either the strings representing important schemata are not present in sufficient numbers or the individuals present are not representative of the whole similarity subset. Sampling errors in small populations in this way prevent the proper propagation of the correct (above average) schemata, thereby circumventing the expected and desired action predicted by the schema theorem (Holland, 1975).

Errors of selection are harder to understand because their disruptive effects are counterintuitive. A simple example will help clarify the problem. Suppose we have a population of 50 single-locus structures containing 25 ones and 25 zeros. Suppose further that we select a new population from the old population by choosing 50 new members one at a time using selection with replacement (where once picked, an individual is placed back in the sampled population). Since we are picking each new member with probability 1/50, and since there are currently 25 ones and 25 zeros, the expected number of ones and zeros is still 25 and 25 respectively; however, because the selection process is fairly noisy, we shouldn't expect to retain exactly the same 25/25 split. In fact, the probability of exactly that division is only $P(25/25) = \binom{50}{25}(0.5)^{50} = 0.1123$. Therefore it is reasonably likely the population will fall away from this initial starting point. In the next generation, the new population becomes the new initial condition with the expected number of ones and zeros determined by the new state. This process continues, and in finite time for a finite population, the population converges to all ones or all zeros. Once converged there is no way to get back any of the missing material (unless we permit some mutation, a possibility we will consider later).

Geneticists have long recognized that finite populations do converge in this manner even when there is no selective advantage for one allele over another. This error of selection is so important it has been given a special name, genetic drift. Selection errors can accumulate, causing a drift to one allele or the other. By itself, genetic drift is bad enough. After all, if the environment has no preference for one allele or another, we might like a GA to preserve both of them (perhaps we would even like the GA to preserve them in relatively equal numbers). Genetic drift insures that this won't happen unless we take special action to encourage this

behavior (see Goldberg & Richardson, this volume). To make matters worse, these errors of selection can cause a genetic algorithm to converge to the wrong allele when the environment does prefer one allele over the other, especially when that selective advantage is relatively small. The analysis of these difficulties is our main concern in the remainder of this paper. We consider first the case of no selection pressure--genetic drift --followed by analysis of cases with varying degrees of selective pressure.

MARKOV CHAIN ANALYSIS OF GENETIC DRIFT

Discrete and continuous models of genetic drift have received attention in the literature of mathematical biology (Crow & Kimura, 1970); however, many of these analyses contain additional details of biological reality that are not always of interest to genetic algorithmists. De Jong (1975) presents computer simulations of genetic drift in the context of simple GAs, showing graphs of the relationship between expected first passage time to varying convergence levels as a function of population size and mutation rate. In this section, we calculate these quantities more exactly using the mathematics of Markov chains (Kemeny & Snell, 1960).

Markov Chains

Suppose we have a sequence of random variables s_0, s_1,..., and suppose the possible values for these random variables are drawn from the set (0, 1,..., N). We think of the random variables s_t as the state of some system at time t: more precisely, the system is in state i at time t if $s_t = i$. If at each time t there is a fixed probability p_{ij} that the system will be in state j at time t+1 when the system was in state i at time t, we say the sequence of random variables forms a Markov chain. The fixed quantities p_{ij} are said to be transition probabilities:

$$p_{ij} = P(s_{t+1}=j \mid s_t=i)$$

Markov chains may be classified by the types of states they contain. States that may not be reached as a process goes to infinity are said to be transient states. Those that may be reached as time marches on are said to be ergodic states (non-transient). In this paper, we will only be interested in those Markov chains that contain a particular type of ergodic state: an absorbing state. A state is said to be absorbing if once entered it may never be left. For any state i, this is true if and only if the following condition holds:

$$p_{ii} = 1$$

We have already seen examples of absorbing states in our earlier description of genetic drift: we recognize the all-zeros and all-ones states as absorbing states, because once we get to either one of them we can never leave. A chain with at least one absorbing state and no ergodic states

2

other than absorbing states is said to be an absorbing Markov chain.

The states of an absorbing Markov chain may be renumbered to obtain a transition probability matrix P in the following canonical form (Kemeny & Snell, 1960):

$$P = \left(\begin{array}{c|c} I & 0 \\ \hline R & Q \end{array} \right)$$

where I is an identity matrix and 0 is a matrix of all zeros. The submatrices Q and R are used to calculate important properties of an absorbing chain.

Genetic Drift without Mutation

To illustrate the construction of a transition probability matrix, we turn to the genetic drift problem at hand. Suppose we have a population of N ones and zeros. We let state 0 be that situation where we have all zeros and we let state N be that case where we have all ones (no zeros), and in general we let state i be that state with exactly i ones. Thus we have a total of $N+1$ states, $i = 0, 1, \ldots, N$, that together represent all possible conditions within the population. Then if we assume random selection of exactly N new population members with replacement, we may calculate the elements of our drift transition probability matrix P_d as follows:

$$P_d = \left(P_{ij} \right)_{drift} = \binom{N}{j} \left[\frac{i}{N} \right]^j \left[1 - \frac{j}{N} \right]^{N-j}$$

These calculations are provably correct, because at each state i, we have a probability of selecting a one $p_{one} = i/N$; further, the probability of getting to state j (j ones) is binomially distributed with probability p_{one} and size N. In this matrix, the states 0 and N are both absorbing states because $p_{00} = p_{NN} = 1$. Thus, it is a simple matter to obtain the canonical form of the matrix shown above. In particular, we are interested in the Q matrix which may be obtained simply by stripping off the first and last rows and columns of the original P_d matrix.

The Q matrix may then be used to calculate the expected number of visits n_{ij} to any transient state j starting in the transient state i (the N matrix):

$$N = (I - Q)^{-1}$$

We won't belabor the details leading to this calculation here; however, the desired N matrix may first be written as an infinite matrix geomet-

ric series in Q. Thereafter, the closed form calculation may be obtained in a manner similar to that used in summing an infinite scalar geometric series.

The total expected time in transit to any one of the absorbing states starting in state i--we call this the transit time τ_i--may easily be calculated as a row sum over the ith row of the N matrix:

$$\tau_i = \sum_{j=0}^{N} n_{ij}$$

The τ_i values may then be used to calculate the expected time to absorption given any initial starting conditions. If we assume an initial population chosen uniformly at random, the probability of being in a state i initially--we call this π_i--is binomially distributed as follows:

$$\pi_i = \binom{N}{i} \left(\frac{1}{2} \right)^N$$

The expected time to an absorbing state, the quantity $t_{absorbed}$, may then be calculated as the dot product of the initial state probability vector π_i and the transit time vector τ_i:

$$t_{absorbed} = \sum_{i=0}^{N} \tau_i \pi_i$$

These calculations suggest a straightforward procedure for calculating the expected time until either the all-ones state (state N) or all-zeros state (state 0) is reached, but what can we do if we are interested in calculating the time of first passage to some level of convergence other than 100 percent? We may calculate such quantities quite simply by replacing all rows in the P_d matrix within a desired percentage of convergence by identity rows: $p_{ii} = 1$ and $p_{ij} = 0$ for $i \neq j$. This bit of chicanery makes the once-transient states absorbing states, and the procedure described above may be used on a now-reduced Q matrix to determine expected first passage times to the particular level of convergence.

These computations are carried out for convergence levels of 60%, 70%, 80%, 90%, and 100%. The expected time of first passage is calculated for populations ranging from $N=10$ to $N=100$. Computations have been performed in APL to exploit that language's facility with vector and matrix operations. Figure 1 displays the expected first passage time versus population size at different convergence levels. The relationship between passage time and population size at a given level of convergence is strikingly linear. Although we may expect the passage time to grow with increased population size, it is not at all obvious why that growth is linear.

3

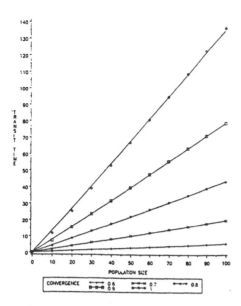

$$\sigma = \sqrt{Np_{con}(1-p_{con})}$$

This operation yields the following approximate expression for the number of generations to a particular level of convergence:

$$t_{convergence} \propto \left[\frac{(2p_{con}-1)^2}{4p_{con}(1-p_{con})} \right] N$$

Thus we have reasoned that the expected transit time increases linearly with population size. As with many approximate models, the derived proportionality constant is mainly useful an indicator of order of magnitude. The simple model does help explain why the slopes of lines of successively higher convergence proportion increase faster than the proportion itself.

Genetic Drift with Mutation

To combat the undesired convergence of genetic drift in simple GAs, mutation rate increases are often suggested. To investigate the effect of mutation on expected times of convergence we continue our Markov chain analysis by including mutation in our overall probability transition matrix.

With mutation included, we view the overall probability transition matrix P_o as the product of the drift matrix P_d developed earlier and a mutation probability transition matrix P_m:

$$(P_o) = (P_d)(P_m)$$

To develop the mutation transition probability matrix, we need to select from a number of possible mutation models. We may perform a single mutation with probability p_m, replace the individual in the original population, and then perform a sequence of N such operations (we call this mutation with sequential replacement). We may also mutate (again with probability p_m) population member by population member (mutation without replacement). We develop the transition probability matrices for both types of mutation.

The transition probability matrix for mutation with sequential replacement may be developed quite simply. A single mutation permits a shift in state by one step (either one more one or one less one). Thus, the single mutation transition probability matrix P_{ms} is tridiagonal, and its elements may be specified as follows:

$$P_{i(i+1)} = \left(1 - \frac{i}{N}\right)p_m$$

$$P_{ii} = 1 - p_m$$

Figure 1. Genetic drift Markov chain computation of expected first passage time versus population size at different convergence levels with no mutation.

To understand this better, we appeal to a simpler but related stochastic model: the gambler's ruin problem. In the gambler's ruin problem, a gambler with a fixed stake D places successive one dollar wagers on the outcome of a coin toss. In our version of the game we assume that the coin is fair, $p_{winning} = p_{losing} = 0.5$. The game ends when the gambler either loses all his money or attains a goal value value A. All this is interesting, but how is it at all related to the genetic drift problem? We may view the genetic drift problem as a gambler's ruin problem where we drift toward either ruin (all zeros) or reward (all ones). In the real genetic drift problem, our range of outcomes on a given "gamble" is not binary; however, by using an average step size per generation we may calculate an approximate form for the genetic drift solution using the simpler gambler's ruin model.

Fortunately, the expected duration of the gambler's ruin problem is a well-known computation (Feller, 1968). Under the assumptions above, the expected number of coin tosses to ruin or reward may be calculated as E(number of coin tosses) = D(A-D). In our problem, the stake amount is given by $N(p_{con}-0.5)$ (the distance to ruin or reward at a particular convergence level, p_{con}); the desired accumulation to quit (assuming equal distances) is twice the stake amount. To place these quantities in terms of numbers of generations, we divide both terms (D and A-D) by the average number of steps taken per generation. This quantity is simply the standard deviation of the expected number of ones (or zeros) per generation:

$$P_{i(i-1)} \quad = \quad \left(\frac{i}{N}\right)P_m$$

$$P_{ij} \quad = \quad 0, \quad \text{otherwise}$$

The overall mutation transition probability matrix under sequential replacement may then be taken as the product of N single mutation matrices:

$$\left(P_m\right)_{\text{sequential replacement}} = \left(P_{ms}\right)^N$$

The transition probability matrix for mutation without replacement may also be calculated. Although the computation is more cumbersome, the extra effort is worthwhile as mutation without replacement is a more faithful model of mutation as it is implemented in most GAs. To calculate the transition probability matrix for mutation without replacement, we recognize a simple fact. To go up in state value by, for example, two ones, we must have exactly two more zeros change to ones than we have ones change to zeros. If we sum over all the possible occurrences where this is true we obtain the elements of the transition probability matrix. For $j \geq i$ (where we shift to a state with more ones) we obtain the elements of the transition probability matrix as follows:

$$P_m \quad = \quad \left(P_{ij}\right)_{\text{mutation no replacement}}$$

$$= \sum_{k=0}^{\ell} \binom{i}{k}\binom{N-i}{k+j-i} P_m^{2k+j-i}(1-P_m)^{N-2k-j+i}$$

where $\ell = \min(i, N-j)$

A similar expression may be derived for the case where $j \leq i$ (a transition occurs to a state with fewer ones). Because mutation without selection is a better model of mutation as performed in real GAs, we adopt it in all subsequent computations.

We perform similar calculations as in the case without mutation. Expected passage times are plotted versus population size (log-log scale) at different mutation rates in Figures 2 and 3. These graphs are presented for convergence levels of 100% and 80% respectively. Increasing mutation probabilities increase the expected time of first passage to a particular level of convergence as we expect.

CONVERGENCE UNDER PREFERENTIAL SELECTION

The genetic drift cases demonstrate the problem of undesirable convergence when the environment has no preference for one allele over another. In this section, we examine the rate of convergence when there is a preference for a particular allele. We also calculate the probability that the allele we converge to is the correct allele.

We assume that a one allele receives an environmental reward of f_1 and a zero allele

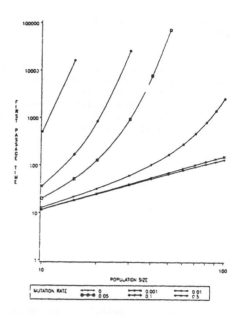

Figure 2. Genetic drift Markov chain computation of expected first passage time versus population size at 100 percent convergence level with different mutation probabilities.

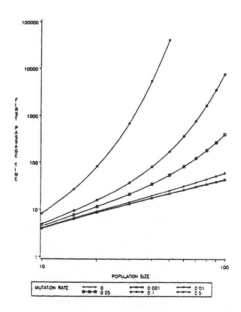

Figure 3. Genetic drift Markov chain computation of expected first passage time versus population size at 80 percent convergence level with different mutation probabilities.

receives an environmental reward of f_0. These rewards are assumed to be stationary and deterministic, and the rewards are given in the ratio $r = f_1/f_0$. In the genetic drift cases of the last section the overall transition probability matrix was the product of the drift matrix and the mutation matrix. Under preferential selection, we must replace the drift

5

matrix by a reproduction matrix that accounts for the differential pressure toward one allele or another.

We may account for the added pressure toward a particular allele by recognizing that the probability of selecting a particular one is $f_1 / \sum f$, and therefore the probability of selecting a one from the population is the number of ones times the probability of selecting a particular one:

$$p_1 = \frac{i \cdot f_1}{\sum_{\text{all } s} f(s)}$$

$$= \frac{f_1}{i \cdot f_1 + (N-i) f_0}$$

$$= \frac{r \cdot i}{r \cdot i + (N-i)}$$

where the sum in the denominator is take over all structures s. With this selection probability, the transition probability matrix for reproduction (P_r) may be calculated:

$$P_r = \left(P_{ij} \right)_{\text{reproduction}}$$

$$= \binom{N}{j} \left(\frac{i \cdot r}{i \cdot r + (N-i)} \right)^j \left(\frac{N-i}{i \cdot r + (N-i)} \right)^{N-j}$$

The probability of going from a state with i ones to a state with j ones is binomially distributed with the selection probability a function of the state i and the fitness ratio r. Notice that the reproduction matrix reduces--as it must--to the drift matrix as r goes to one.

Using the same procedure as before, we may calculate the expected time to some level of convergence; however, in the case where the environment is not indifferent to the two alleles, we are not simply interested in knowing when we expect to converge. We are also interested in knowing the probability that we converge to the allele with higher fitness. Fortunately we may obtain this probability in a straightforward manner using our fundamental N matrix and the R matrix.

The probability of starting in a transient state i and going to absorbing state j--we call this the B matrix, (b_{ij})--may be obtained as the product of the fundamental matrix N and the R matrix:

$$B = NR$$

That this is so may be reasoned directly (Kemeny & Snell, 1960). Any time we are in transient state k, we have probability r_{kj} of going to absorbing state j; however we will be in state k assuming we have started in state i a total of n_{ik} times. To finish the computation, we simply realize that we must sum over all the transient states k leading to state j. This is precisely the computation represented by the matrix product above.

With the probability b_{ij} of going from a starting transient state i to a final absorbing state j thus calculated, it is a simple matter to obtain the probability of being in a final state j--the probability α_j--as time goes on assuming initial state probabilities π_i. We simply add the initial probability of being in state j to the sum of the probabilities of getting from all transient states i--call this the set T--to the particular absorbing state j:

$$\alpha_j = \pi_j + \sum_{i \in T} \pi_i b_{ij}$$

Having calculated the probability of ending up in a particular absorbing state, we now may find the probability of convergence to the correct allele, $P_{correct}$, by summing the α values over the desired absorbing states--call this set A':

$$P_{correct} = \sum_{i \in A'} \alpha_i$$

We calculate the expected time to 100 percent convergence and the probability that the convergence is correct for varying r values at different population sizes. These results are plotted in Figures 4 and 5 respectively. To put these results in perspective, we consider the expected performance in a large population and compare those results to the exact study of finite populations.

The schema theorem (Holland, 1975) tells us what to expect in a large population. Under reproduction only, the proportion of ones P_1 grows according to the following equation:

$$P_1^{t+1} = \left[\frac{r}{(r-1) P_1^t + 1} \right] P_1^t$$

where the superscript t is a generation index. For r values near 1 this equation reduces to a geometric progression in r:

$$P_1^t = (r^t) P_1^0$$

Taking the natural logarithm of both sides we obtain the following relationship for the time to a given proportion of ones:

$$t = \frac{\ln \left(P_1^t / P_1^0 \right)}{\ln r}$$

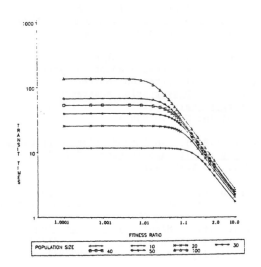

Figure 4. Markov chain computation of expected first passage time versus fitness ratio r for reproduction cases to 100 percent convergence level with different population sizes.

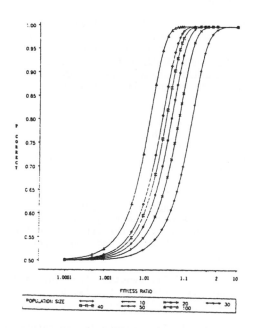

Figure 5. Markov chain computation of probability of correct convergence versus fitness ratio r for reproduction cases to 100 percent convergence level with different population sizes.

On a plot of log(t) versus log(log r) this curve plots as a straight line with negative slope. Referring to Figure 4, at high enough r values we notice this straight line behavior. At small r values the curve levels out and approaches the constant value predicted by the genetic drift computations. We may derive an approximate r value where this divergence should occur with a little physical reasoning. During a given genera-

tion we expect an increase in ones approximately equal to $N(r-1)P_1{}^t$. On average, the increase or decrease of ones due to selection noise is simply the standard deviation σ. When the noise is of the same order of magnitude or greater than the expected increase, we should expect divergence between simplified model and the finite model. This divergence should occur at values of r predicted by the following relationship:

$$r-1 \le \sqrt{\frac{1-P_1{}^t}{N P_1{}^t}}$$

When the population is half ones and half zeros, this equation says that the large population result becomes suspect when the excess fitness (r-1) is less than the inverse of the square root of the population size. This relationship explains the decreasing break point value (between drift-like and convergent behavior) with increasing population size as can be seen in both Figures 4 and 5. At values of r beneath this critical value, the expected time results flatten, and the probability of converging to the correct allele starts to fall dramatically.

Similar calculations may be performed for reproduction with mutation. As in the genetic drift case, we take the overall transition probability matrix as the product of two matrices; here, we multiply the reproduction transition probability matrix by a mutation matrix (without replacement) as follows:

$$(P_o) = (P_r)(P_m)$$

We perform expected first passage time calculations as before. In Figure 6, we graph first passage time versus r for different mutation probabilities p_m at a population size N=50. Using our previous physical analysis, we expect the finite analysis to approach the bounding analysis for r-1 values greater than sqrt(1/50) = 0.1414. This holds true for small p_m values; however, as the mutation probability grows, the expected time grows beyond that predicted by the bounding analysis. That this should occur may be reasoned intuitively. If the expected net loss of good alleles due to mutation starts to exceed the expected increase in good alleles from reproduction, the process loses its ability to converge as quickly. This point occurs when the following condition holds true:

$$r-1 \le \left[\frac{2P_1{}^t-1}{P_1{}^t}\right]p_m$$

When the excess fitness (r-1) is of the same order or less than the mutation, the GA will take a longer time to converge, because mutation is adding errors faster than the reproduction can erase them. This shows up in Figure 6 as succes-

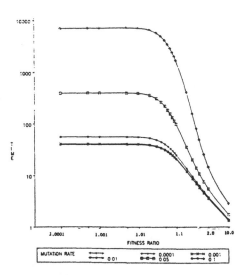

Figure 6. Markov chain computation of expected first passage time versus fitness ratio r for reproduction and mutation cases to 90 percent convergence with N=50 and different mutation levels.

sively higher mutation rates cause the expected time curves to break away from the bounding analysis results more quickly.

CONCLUSIONS

In this paper, we have analyzed the performance of one-locus, two-operator (reproduction and mutation) genetic algorithms with finite populations of haploid structures using finite Markov chains.

The results in particular and the Markov chain analysis in general are useful in understanding the performance of finite GAs commonly in use. These results and their extension should be useful in sizing populations appropriately, selecting proper mutation rates, and choosing rates of selection in scaling procedures.

ACKNOWLEDGEMENTS

This material is based upon work supported by the National Science Foundation under Grant MSM-8451610.

REFERENCES

Bethke, A. D. (1981). Genetic algorithms as function optimizers. (Doctoral dissertation, University of Michigan). Dissertation Abstracts International, 41(9), 3503B. (University Microfilms No. 8106101)

Crow, J. F., & Kimura, M. (1970). An introduction to population genetics theory. New York: Harper and Row.

De Jong, K. A. (1975). An analysis of the behavior of a class of genetic adaptive systems. (Doctoral dissertation, University of Michigan). Dissertation Abstracts International, 36(10), 5140B. (University Microfilms No. 76-9381)

Feller, W. (1968). An introduction to probability theory and its applications (Vol. 1, 3rd ed.). New York: Wiley.

Goldberg, D. E. (1983). Computer-aided gas pipeline operation using genetic algorithms and rule learning (Doctoral dissertation, University of Michigan). Dissertation Abstracts International, 44(10), 3174B. (University Microfilms No. 8402282)

Goldberg, D. E. (1986). Simple genetic algorithms and the minimal deceptive problem (TCGA Report No. 86003). Tuscaloosa: University of Alabama, The Clearinghouse for Genetic Algorithms.

Goldberg, D. E., & Lingle, R. (1985). Alleles, loci, and the traveling salesman problem. In J. J. Grefenstette (Ed.), Proceedings of an International Conference on Genetic Algorithms and Their Applications (pp. 154-159). Pittsburgh: Carnegie-Mellon University.

Goldberg, D. E., & Thomas, A. L, (1986). Genetic algorithms: A bibliography 1962-1986 (TCGA Report No. 86001). Tuscaloosa: University of Alabama, The Clearinghouse for Genetic Algorithms.

Holland, J. H. (1968). Hierarchical descriptions of universal spaces and adaptive systems (Technical Report ORA Projects 01252 and 08226). Ann Arbor: University of Michigan, Department of Computer and Communication Sciences.

Holland, J. H. (1973). Genetic algorithms and the optimal allocations of trials. SIAM Journal of Computing, 2(2), 88-105.

Holland, J. H. (1975). Adaptation in natural and artificial systems. Ann Arbor: The University of Michigan Press.

Kemeny, J. G., & Snell, J. L. (1960). Finite Markov Chains. Princeton: Van Nostrand.

Martin, N. (1973). Convergence properties of a class of probabilistic adaptive schemes called sequential reproductive plans. (Doctoral dissertation, University of Michigan), Dissertation Abstracts International, B-3747B. (University Microfilms No. 74-3685)

AN ANALYSIS OF REPRODUCTION AND CROSSOVER IN A BINARY-CODED GENETIC ALGORITHM

Clayton L. Bridges and David E. Goldberg

The University of Alabama
Tuscaloosa, AL 35487

ABSTRACT

The foundation of genetic algorithm (GA) theory--the so-called schema theorem or fundamental theorem of genetic algorithms--provides a lower bound on the expected number of representatives of a particular schema (similarity subset) in the next generation under various genetic operators. In this paper, assuming a large population of binary, haploid structures of known distribution, processed by fitness proportionate reproduction, random mating, and random, single-point crossover, an exact expression for the expected proportion of a particular string (or representatives of a particular schema) in the next generation is calculated. This derivation is useful in analyzing the expected performance of simple GAs.

INTRODUCTION

Over the past two decades, the application of genetic algorithms (GAs) to search and machine learning problems in science, commerce, and engineering has been been made possible by a number of theoretical developments (Holland, 1973, 1975; De Jong, 1975; Bethke, 1981). Without these theories, it is doubtful that many of us would have made much sense of our computer simulations or experiments; this speculation is supported by the experience of genetic algorithm prehistory. We need only recall some of the evolutionary schemes that resorted to mutation-plus-save-the-best strategies (Box, 1957; Bledsoe, 1959; Friedman, 1959; Fogel, Owens, & Walsh, 1966) to remember that shots in a darkness without schemata or the fundamental theorem (Holland, 1975) can be frustrating experiences indeed. Because of the usefulness of theory to progress in genetic algorithm research, there is still a pressing need to improve our understanding of the foundations-- the theoretical underpinnings--of genetic algorithms and their derivatives.

In this paper, we extend the fundamental theorem of genetic algorithms to exactitude. Specifically, we derive a complete set of equations describing the combined effects of reproduction and crossover on a large population of binary, haploid structures. These equations may be used to determine the correct expected performance of a genetic algorithm on a given problem with specified coding; they may be used for calculating the correct expected propagation of a set of competing schemata; they may also be used for estimating disruption or source probabilities for particular strings or particular schemata in a specified population of structures.

In the remainder of the paper, we develop our extended analysis in three steps. We reexamine the fundamental theorem of GAs (the schema theorem), calculate an exact expression for the probability of disruption due to crossover, and calculate the expected gain of individuals due to mating and crossover by others.

THE FUNDAMENTAL THEOREM OF GENETIC ALGORITHMS

The fundamental theorem of genetic algorithms (Holland, 1975) calculates a bound on the expected number, m, of schemata (similarity templates), H, in successive generations, t, under the action of reproduction and crossover (other operators are often included in the calculation; we choose to focus on reproduction and crossover alone):

$$m(H, t+1) \geq m(H, t)\frac{f(H)}{\bar{f}}\left[1 - p_c \cdot \frac{\delta(H)}{\ell-1} \right]$$

In this equation, ℓ is the string length, p_c is the probability of crossover, and δ is the schema defining length (the distance between its outermost defining positions). In words, the schema theorem tells us that a particular schema H receives trials according to the ratio of schema fitness to population average fitness as long as the schema is not unduly disrupted by crossover. The average fitness of a schema f(H) may be calculated by summing over all strings s_i representatives of H at time t:

$$f(H) = \frac{\sum_{\{i | s_i(t) \in H\}} f_i}{m(H, t)}$$

We note that the theorem is an inequality--a lower bound. Our main goal in this paper is to transform the bound to an equality. To do this, it is helpful to look at a full schema conservation equation in broad outline:

$$m(H,t+1) = m(H,t)\frac{f(H)}{\bar{f}}\left[\ 1-p_cp_d\ \right]$$

$$+ \text{[gains from crossing]}$$

The increase due to reproduction is multiplied by the probability of the schema surviving a cross (one minus the product of the crossover probability p_c and the probability of disruption p_d). For completeness we must also include possible gains from mating and crossover of other strings.

Hidden within this broad outline are the two items that prevent the schema theorem from providing an exact analysis. First, we usually calculate a crude upper bound on the probability of disruption p_d due to crossover: the usual term $\delta(H)/(\ell-1)$ assumes that the schema is destroyed every time a cross falls within its defining length. This is a conservative assumption because it ignores the possibility of getting back the same material from a particular mate. Second, the schema theorem ignores all sources of schemata from crosses of strings containing different competing schemata. In crossover, one schema's loss is another's gain. Although these terms may seem small and somewhat beside the point, a recent study (Goldberg, 1986) has shown that inclusion of these terms in an extended schema analysis permits the prediction of convergence of a simple genetic algorithm on a problem specifically designed to cause the GA to diverge (the minimal, deceptive problem). As such, these terms deserve more of our attention. We first look at the probability of disruption due to crossover.

DISRUPTION DUE TO CROSSOVER

In this section we calculate the probability of disruption of a string due to the set of all possible crosses. To do this, we define some useful symbols and terms.

We take S as the set of all possible binary strings of length ℓ; there are 2^ℓ such strings. Furthermore, we index the set S so S_j is the the jth member of S, where j goes from 0 to $2^\ell-1$. As a convenience, we choose our indexing scheme so the decoded value of our string is equal to the index value j. We note that we are working in terms of strings, and the schema theorem is written in terms of schemata. We continue here to work with strings as the equations are easier to derive and understand; however, keep in mind that we ultimately want to come back to a particular set of competing schemata. We do this in a later section.

We define arbitrary string variables B, Q, and R; these may take on any value in S. We also permit ourselves to refer to their individual positions by subscripted lower case letters:

$$B = b_0b_1\ldots b_{\ell-1}$$

Thus b_j is the boolean variable representing the jth position of a string of length ℓ.

Before we proceed with the derivation of the probability of disruption, we convert the schema theorem to proportion form. Suppose reproduction is operating by itself. In this case, we only have the first part of the schema theorem:

$$m(B,t+1) = m(B,t)f(B)/\bar{f}.$$

If we divide both sides of the equation by the population size N, and if we define P_B^t to be the proportion of the string B in the population at time t, we obtain the following equation for the expected proportion in the next generation (or the mating pool) under the action of reproduction alone:

$$P_B^{t+1} = P_B^t\cdot\frac{f_B}{\bar{f}}$$

where f_B is the fitness of string B and $\bar{f}$ is the average fitness of the population as given by the following expression:

$$\bar{f} = \sum_{i=0}^{2^\ell-1} P_i^t f_i$$

Of course, we are currently interested in calculating the crossover disruption term that reduces the above expression by a factor $1-p_cp_d$ where p_c is the probability of crossover and p_d is the probability of disruption; however, we envision the GA acting in two phases: a selection phase followed by a mating and crossover phase. Therefore it is useful to define the expected proportion of string B under reproduction alone. We shall use this quantity in our calculation of the probability of disruption p_d. We call this important intermediate quantity R_B^t the reproductive proportion:

$$R_B^t = P_B^t\frac{f_B}{\bar{f}}$$

To calculate the probability of disruption to a given string B under crossover, we need to know which strings will disrupt B and which won't. Clearly a string that is different from another string by a single bit cannot fail to return a copy of the original string among the two strings produced by the cross. For example, suppose we have two strings B and B' which differ at position 3 (the bar is used to indicate a complementary bit position):

$$B = b_0b_1b_2b_3b_4$$
$$B' = b_0b_1b_2\bar{b}_3b_4$$

Every possible cross produces a copy of B. On the ·

other hand, strings with two or more bits of difference must (for at least one cross site) disrupt one another. Consider the two strings with three different bits:

$$B = b_0 b_1 b_2 b_3 b_4$$
$$B' = b_0 \bar{b}_1 \bar{b}_2 \bar{b}_3 b_4$$

In this case, disruption occurs if a cross falls between the two outermost bits of difference (between positions 1 and 3). These two outermost bits--we call them sentry bits--are important in the analysis of disruption, because we need only consider their location when deciding how two strings will disrupt one another. We can use this information to create a general scheme for analyzing mutual disruption:

Region	begin	middle	end
Length	x	$\delta+1$	$\ell-\delta-x-1$
Characteristics	-	$\bar{b}*\ldots*\bar{b}$	-

Here we have divided the string into three regions: the beginning, the middle, and the end. In the beginning and ending regions, the strings under consideration must have the same bit values as string B. The middle region is bounded by sentry bits (the b's) where the string B is different from its prospective mate. Bit positions other than the sentry positions are marked with *'s, the usual don't care or wild card symbol used in schema analysis; we may properly use the don't care symbol here, because it really does not matter where we cross between sentry bits. Every such cross is disruptive. To quantify the disruption we define a number of useful variables. We take δ ($\delta \epsilon [1, \ell-1]$) as the defining length of the middle region; this is also the number of possible cross sites. Separately we recognize that the length of the middle section (including both sentries) is $\delta+1$. We define x ($x \epsilon [0, \ell-\delta-1]$) as the length of the beginning region; it also is the position of the first sentry bit. Finally, we recognize that the length of the final section is the remaining portion that causes the total to sum to ℓ: $\ell-\delta-x-1$.

To facilitate our disruption computation, we define a middle function $M = M[B, \delta, x]$. The middle function is a subset generator, generating a similarity subset according to the following schema:

$$M[B, \delta, x] = b_0 \ldots b_{(x-1)} \bar{b}_x * \ldots * \bar{b}_{(x+\delta)} b_{(x+\delta+1)} \ldots b_{(\ell-1)}$$

We may now use the middle function M to calculate the probability of disruption of a given string B. This probability is the sum over all strings of the product of proportions and defining lengths:

$$P_d(B) = \left[\sum_{\delta=1}^{\ell-1} \frac{\delta}{\ell-1} \cdot \sum_{x=0}^{\ell-\delta-1} \sum_{\{j | S_j \epsilon M[B, \delta, x]\}} R_j^t \right]$$

The use of the middle function M insures that we count each string only once. This may be confirmed by removing the δ and R factors and simply using the summation to count the number of such crosses. After clearing the expression, we find that there are $2^\ell-\ell-1$ crosses that match the M function. This quantity may be reasoned independently as the total number of strings less the number of one-bit mismatches (these don't disrupt) and the string B itself (a zero-bit mismatch).

STRING GAINS FROM CROSSOVER

Just as we are interested in detailing the losses from crossover, so are we interested in knowing the potential gain from other string crosses. We may construct a template to precisely identify when this occurs. Specifically, we consider the construction of a string B from two strings Q and R as follows:

Region	begin	middle	end
Length	α	σ	ω
Q Characteristics	$*\ldots*\bar{b}$	-	-
R Characteristics	-	-	$\bar{b}*\ldots*$

We now demand that the Q string be identical to B in the middle and end regions, and we require the R string to be identical to B in the beginning and middle sections. This time around we post sentries outside the middle region, and when we cross between the sentries we obtain a copy of the desired string B as one of the products of the cross. To make our summation a bit easier we define several important quantities.

The quantity α ($\alpha \epsilon [1, \ell-1]$) is the length of the beginning region in string Q. The quantity ω ($\omega \epsilon [1, \ell-\alpha]$) is the length of the ending region in R, and σ ($\sigma = \ell-\alpha-\omega$) is the length of the middle region.

We define formal string functions to specify the strings they may cross to yield B. We call the two functions the beginning function $A[B, \alpha]$ and the ending function $\Omega[B, \omega]$. The beginning function is a subset generator as follows:

$$A[B, \alpha] = **\ldots**\bar{b}_{(\alpha-1)} b_\alpha \ldots b_{(\ell-1)}$$

The ending function generates subsets as follows:

$$\Omega[B, \omega] = b_0 \ldots b_{(\ell-\omega-1)} \bar{b}_{(\ell-\omega)} **\ldots**$$

The probability that these two strings will cross to give B is dependent on the value of σ, the length of the region where they are the same. If $\sigma = 0$, then there is only one site where the strings can cross to yield B. In general there are a total of $\sigma+1$ cross sites; therefore, the probability that a cross will give B is given by the expression:

11

$$\frac{\sigma+1}{\ell-1}$$

We may now calculate the expected proportion gain P_g of strings B from crosses by all other strings as follows:

$$P_g(B) = \frac{1}{2}\binom{2}{1}P_c \cdot$$

$$\sum_{\alpha=1}^{\ell-1}\sum_{\omega=1}^{\ell-\alpha}\frac{\sigma+1}{\ell-1}\left[\sum_{\{j\,|\,S_j\,\epsilon\,A[B,\alpha]\}}R_j^t\left[\sum_{\{k\,|\,S_k\,\epsilon\,\Omega[B,\omega]\}}R_k^t\right]\right]$$

We multiply by 2 because there are two ways to pick Q and R. We divide by two because only half the products of the cross are B strings.

THE COMPLETE EQUATION

With both disruptions and gains now calculated, it is a straightforward matter to write the expected proportion of strings B in generation t+1 under both reproduction and crossover:

$$P_B^{t+1} = R_B^t\left[1 - P_c\left[\sum_{\delta=1}^{\ell-1}\frac{\delta}{\ell-1}\cdot\sum_{x=0}^{\ell-\delta-1}\sum_{\{j\,|\,S_j\,\epsilon\,M[B,\delta,x]\}}R_j^t\right]\right]$$

$$+ P_c\left[\sum_{\alpha=1}^{\ell-1}\sum_{\omega=1}^{\ell-\alpha}\frac{\sigma+1}{\ell-1}\left[\sum_{\{j\,|\,S_j\,\epsilon\,A[B,\alpha]\}}R_j^t\left[\sum_{\{k\,|\,S_k\,\epsilon\,\Omega[B,\omega]\}}R_k^t\right]\right]\right]$$

EXTENSION TO SCHEMATA

So far we have confined our analysis to individual strings. We often want to examine the expected propagation of a set of competing schemata over some specified bit positions. To do this in our current scheme requires only minor modifications to our equations.

To interpret the extended equations in schemata, we first index the sums over the o fixed positions (where o is the schema order or the number of fixed positions) instead of the ℓ positions in the string (we do use ℓ in the denominator of the disruption probability, however). Next, we introduce a function $\Delta(x,\delta)$ to account for the possibly unequal spacing of the fixed positions. For example, if we are interested in the order 3 competing schemata defined by the template f***f*f (where the f indicates a fixed position, a 0 or a 1) at x=0 and δ=1, the defining length function may be calculated as Δ=4-0=4. Since the x values only run through the consecutive fixed positions, at x=1 (the middle fixed position) we find Δ(1,1)=2. With such a function defined, we may rewrite our disruption probability for a schema H as follows:

$$P_d(H) = \left[\sum_{\delta=1}^{o-1}\sum_{x=0}^{o-\delta-1}\frac{\Delta(x,\delta)}{\ell-1}\sum_{\{j\,|\,S_j\,\epsilon\,M[H,\delta,x]\}}R_j^t\right]$$

Here we interpret S_j as a member of the set of schemata sharing the same o fixed positions as H. Also, R_j is interpreted as the reproductive proportion of the schema S_j.

Thus we are able to extend the computation of the probability of disruption to schemata using the same middle function M through careful indexing and the introduction of a function that tracks unequal defining bit spacing. Similar modification may be introduced in the expected gain proportion computation, P_g.

CONCLUSIONS

In this paper, we have derived an equation for the expected propagation of strings in a genetic algorithm under reproduction and crossover, and we have shown how such a derivation can be extended to schemata. The computation is exact within the assumptions of the analysis (large populations, uniformly random mating, and randomly chosen cross sites). The equations may be used for the analysis of specific problems and codings or it may be used to quantify disruption in populations of strings or schemata of known distribution. The equations should further our understanding of the detailed operation of genetic algorithms.

ACKNOWLEDGEMENTS

This material is based upon work supported by the National Science Foundation under Grant MSM-8451610.

REFERENCES

Bethke, A. D. (1981). Genetic algorithms as function optimizers. (Doctoral dissertation, University of Michigan). Dissertation Abstracts International, 41(9), 3503B. (University Microfilms No. 8106101)

Bledsoe, W. W. (1961, November). The use of biological concepts in the analytical study of systems. Paper presented at the ORSA-TIMS National Meeting, San Francisco, CA.

Box, G. E. P. (1957). Evolutionary operation: A method for increasing industrial productivity. Applied Statistics, 6(2), 81-101.

De Jong, K. A. (1975). An analysis of the behavior of a class of genetic adaptive systems. (Doctoral dissertation, University of Michigan). Dissertation Abstracts International, 36(10), 5140B. (University Microfilms No. 76-9381)

Fogel, L. J., Owens, A. J., & Walsh, M. J. (1966). Artificial intelligence through simulated evolution. New York: John Wiley.

Friedman, G. J. (1959). Digital simulation of an evolutionary process. General Systems Yearbook, 4, 171-184.

Goldberg, D. E. (1986). <u>Simple genetic algorithms and the minimal deceptive problem</u> (TCGA Report No. 86003). Tuscaloosa: University of Alabama, The Clearinghouse for Genetic Algorithms.

Holland, J. H. (1973). Genetic algorithms and the optimal allocation of trials. <u>SIAM Journal of Computing</u>, <u>2</u>(2), 88-105.

Holland, J. H. (1975). <u>Adaptation in natural and artificial systems</u>. Ann Arbor: The University of Michigan Press.

REDUCING BIAS AND INEFFICIENCY IN THE SELECTION ALGORITHM

James Edward Baker

Vanderbilt University

Abstract

Most implementations of Genetic Algorithms experience sampling bias and are unnecessarily inefficient. This paper reviews various sampling algorithms proposed in the literature and offers two new algorithms of reduced bias and increased efficiency. An empirical analysis of bias is then presented.

1. Introduction

Genetic Algorithms (GAs) cycle through four phases[4]: evaluation, selection, recombination and mutation. The selection phase determines the actual number of offspring each individual will receive based on its relative performance. The selection phase is composed of two parts: 1) determination of the individuals' expected values; and 2) conversion of the expected values to discrete numbers of offspring. An individual's expected value is a real number indicating the average number of offspring that individual should receive. Hence, an individual with an expected value of 1.5 should average, 1 1/2 offspring. The algorithm used to convert the real expected values to integer numbers of offspring is called the sampling algorithm. The sampling algorithm must maintain a constant population size while attempting to provide accurate, consistent and efficient sampling. These three goals lead to the bias, spread and efficiency measures described below:

1) **bias** -- Bias is defined to be the absolute difference between an individual's actual sampling probability and his expected value[3]. To ensure proper credit assignment to the represented hyperplanes, the expected values should be sampled as accurately as possible. The optimal, zero bias is achieved whenever each individual's sampling probability equals his expected value.

2) **spread** -- Let f(i) be the actual number of offspring individual i receives in a given generation. We define the "spread" as the range of possible values for f(i). Furthermore, we define the "Minimum Spread" as the smallest possible spread which theoretically permits zero bias. Hence, the Minimum Spread is one in which

$$f(i) \in \left\{ \lfloor ev(i) \rfloor, \lceil ev(i) \rceil \right\}$$

where $ev(i)$ = expected value of individual i.

Whereas the bias indicates accuracy, the spread indicates precision. Hence the spread reveals the sampling algorithm's consistency.

3) **efficiency** -- It is desirable for the sampling algorithm not to increase the GAs' overall time complexity. GAs' other phases are $O(LN)$ or better, where L = length of an individual and N = population size.

All currently available sampling algorithms fail to provide both zero bias and Minimum Spread[3]. Yet an accurate sampling algorithm is crucial. All of the GAs' theoretical support presupposes the ability to implement the intended expected values. How much the existing inaccuracies have affected the GAs' performance is unknown. However, inaccuracies of sufficient magnitude to alter performance should be either understood or eliminated. This paper offers an empirical analysis of one of the most common sampling algorithms[5] -- Remainder Stochastic Sampling without Replacement--and introduces two new sampling algorithms designed to reduce or eliminate these inaccuracies.

Section 2 reviews and compares previously proposed sampling algorithms. Section 3 introduces an improved sampling algorithm which can be partially executed in parallel. Section 4 introduces a sampling algorithm of zero bias, Minimum Spread and optimal $O(N)$ time complexity. Section 5 presents an empirical analysis of these algorithms and section 6 provides a summary and conclusions.

2. Previous Work

The basic characteristics of various sampling algorithms[3] are presented in Table 1. The first four algorithms are stochastic and involve basically the same technique:

-- Determine **R**, the sum of the competing expected values.
-- 1-1 map the individuals to contiguous segments of the real number line, [0..**R**), such that each individual's segment is equal in size to its competing expected value.
-- Generate a random number within [0..**R**).
-- Select the individual whose segment spans the random number.
-- Repeat the process until the desired number of samples is obtained.

This technique is commonly called the "spinning wheel" method. It is analogous to a gambler's spinning wheel with each wheel slice proportional in size to some individual's expected value. This technique is typically implemented in $O(N^2)$ time, but can be implemented in $O(NlogN)$ by using a B-tree.

In "Stochastic Sampling with Replacement", the "spinning wheel" is composed of the original expected values and remains unchanged between "spins". This provides zero bias yet virtually unlimited spread -- any individual with expected value > 0 could be chosen to fill the entire next population. "Stochastic Sampling with partial Replacement" prevents this. In this algorithm, an individual's expected value is decreased by 1.0 each time he is selected. (If the expected value becomes negative, it is set to 0.) This modification provides an upper bound of $\lceil$expected value$\rceil$ on the spread. However, this upper bound is achieved at the expense of bias. Furthermore, a reasonable lower bound is not provided.

Remainder sampling methods reduce the spread further. A remainder sampling method involves two distinct phases. In the integral phase, samples are awarded deterministically based on the integer portions of the expected values. This phase guarantees a lower bound of $\lfloor$expected value$\rfloor$ on the spread. The fractional phase then samples according to the expected values' fractional portions.

In "Remainder Stochastic Sampling with Replacement", the fractional expected values are sampled by the "spinning wheel" method. The individual's fractions remain unaltered between "spins", and hence continue to compete for selection. This sampling algorithm provides zero bias and the greatest lower bound on the spread, yet it provides virtually no upper bound. Any individual with an expected value fraction > 0 can obtain all samples selected during the fractional phase. "Remainder Stochastic Sampling without Replacement", (RSSwoR), provides Minimum Spread. This remainder algorithm also uses the "spinning wheel" for the fractional phase. However, after each "spin", the selected individual's expected value is set to zero. Hence, individuals are prevented from having multiple selections during the fractional phase. Unfortunately, although this is a commonly used sampling algorithm, it is biased by favoring smaller fractions[2].

A "Deterministic Sampling" algorithm is suggested and used by Brindle[3]. In this remainder algorithm's fractional phase, the individuals with the largest fractions are selected. The result is a minimum sampling error for each generation, yet a high overall bias. Since overall accuracy in approximating the expected values is crucial to the applicability of the GAs' current theory, high bias is considered unacceptable. Hence, "Deterministic Sampling" is not widely used.

3. Remainder Stochastic Independent Sampling

In a spinning wheel algorithm, selection is based on the relative expected values of those competing. This relativity is unnecessary since the expected values themselves are population normalized. Furthermore, this relativity is causing the bias-spread tradeoff and the $O(NlogN)$ time complexity. (If the selected individuals are not inhibited in future competitions, then there is little spread limitation. However, if they are inhibited, subsequent selection is biased.)

In "Remainder Stochastic Independent Sampling" (RSIS), the fractional phase is performed without use of the error-prone "spinning wheel". RSIS independently uses each fractional expected value as a probability of selection. This is accomplished by *traversing* the population and stochastically determining whether each individual should be selected:

"C" Code Fragment for RSIS

```
/* Integral Phase */
NumSelected = 0;
for (i=0; i<N; i++)
    for ( ; ExpVal[i] >= 1.0; ExpVal[i]--)
    {   SelectInd(i);
        NumSelected++;
    }
/* Fractional Phase */
for (i=0; NumSelected<N; )
{   if (ExpVal[i] > Rand())
    {   SelectInd(i);
        ExpVal[i] = 0;
        NumSelected++;
    }
    if (++i == N) i=0;
}
```

Where Rand() returns a random real number uniformly distributed within the range [0..1].

The code for RSIS is noticeably less complex than typical implementations of sampling and much less than $O(NlogN)$ algorithms. Although the fractional phase is potentially an infinite loop, probabilistically it completes after one traversal of the population and is only $O(N)$. Empirical studies indicate that it rarely proceeds beyond the second traversal --

averaging only 0.017% over a variety of expected value distributions. Hence a modified algorithm which randomly selected the remaining sample(s) after two traversals would be heuristically appropriate.

An individual can not be selected more than once during the fractional phase, since the selected individual's expected value is set to zero. Hence this remainder sampling algorithm has Minimum Spread. However, some bias is present in RSIS. This bias occurs if a second population traversal is necessary and is similar to that found in latter stages of a spinning wheel algorithm without replacement. However, the overall bias of RSIS will be much less since, typically, most of the samples are obtained in the zero biased, first traversal. Note that "positional bias" may occur if the individuals are ordered. However, in a remainder sampling algorithm, the population is shuffled to prevent excessive cloning. Hence, this potential bias does not exist.

The selection phase of GAs requires some sequential processing, both in obtaining and sampling the expected values. However, the GAs' evaluation, recombination and mutation phases can be executed in full parallel. Hence, increases in the parallel nature of the selection phase may eventually prove useful. RSIS is the only acceptable sampling algorithm which can be partially executed in parallel. The fractional phase can be performed in full parallel but must precede the O(N) sequential, integral phase.

"C" Code Fragment for Partially Parallel RSIS

```
/* sample fractions in full parallel */
/* copy population and mark selected ind.s */
/* code of jth processor */
parbegin
   NextPop.Ind[j] = CurrPop.Ind[j];
   NextPop.flag = (ExpValFract[j] > Rand());
parend;

/* sample integers sequentially */
/* overwrite unmarked individuals first */
k = 0;            /* pointer to NextPop */
set = 1; /* availability flag */
for (i=0; i<N; i++)
   for ( ; ExpVal[i] >= 1.0; ExpVal[i]--)
   {  while ( NextPop.flag[k] == set )
         if (++k == N) k = set = 0;
      NextPop.Ind[k++] = CurrPop.Ind[i];
   }
```

In the parallel fractional phase, the current population is copied into the next population and the selected individuals are marked with a

1. This mark indicates the positions' unavailability. During the integral phase, the unmarked positions will be filled first. Two potential problem conditions exist: the fractional phase may select too few or too many individuals. If too few are selected, then some unmarked individuals will not be overwritten during the integral phase and hence will be considered selected. This is equivalent to a standard RSIS implementation employing random selection on the second traversal. (If this proves undesirable, a sequential, stochastic, second traversal could easily be performed.) If fractional selection choses too many individuals, then integral selection will require additional positions. However, ⌊expected value⌋ must be guaranteed to maintain Minimum Spread. Thus, some individuals selected during the fractional phase must be replaced. This replacement does not alter the performance characteristics of RSIS, since sequential RSIS would not have chosen these extra individuals in the first place. In either case, Minimum Spread is maintained and the low bias of RSIS remains uneffected.

4. Stochastic Universal Sampling

"Stochastic Universal Sampling" (SUS) is a simple, single phase, O(N) sampling algorithm. It is zero biased, has Minimum Spread and will achieve all N samples in a single traversal. However, the algorithm is strictly sequential.

"C" Code Fragment for SUS

```
ptr = Rand();
for ( sum=i=0; i<N; i++)
   for (sum += ExpVal[i]; sum > ptr; ptr++)
      SelectInd(i);
```

On a standard spinning wheel, there is a single pointer which indicates the "winner". SUS is analogous to a spinning wheel with N equally spaced pointers. Hence, a single spin results in N "winners". Since the sum of the population's expected values = N, the pointers are exactly 1.0 apart. Thus an individual is guaranteed ⌊expected value⌋ in samples and no more than ⌈expected value⌉. Hence, SUS has Minimum Spread. Furthermore, in a randomly ordered population, an individual's selection probability is based solely on the initial spin and the magnitude of his expected value. Hence, SUS has zero bias. Like remainder sampling algorithms, the population must be shuffled before crossover. Therefore, positional bias can not exist in SUS, either. (Note that, in general, any number of samples, n, can be obtained by letting ptr range within [0..N/n) and incrementing it by N/n after each selection.) In a sequential environment, SUS seems to be the optimal sampling algorithm. In the next section, an empirical analysis of RSIS and SUS is presented.

5. Empirical Analysis

This analysis investigates the severity, direction and progression of bias in RSSwoR, sequential RSIS and SUS. The severity is important from an implementation standpoint. Although bias can be proven theoretically[2], it is of less interest if it does not alter performance. The direction of the bias indicates which individuals are favored and the progression indicates when the bias occurs. Since we are concerned only with the sampling algorithm, a full execution of GAs is not necessary. Rather, we simply maintain a population of expected values. This allows a single expected value distribution to be sampled, repeatedly. We use linear distributions specified by the parameter MAX. Given $1.0 \leq$ MAX ≤ 2.0, the expected values' range is $(2-$MAX$..$MAX$)$, see Figure 1.

Bias Severity

The severity of the bias is given by its average actual affect on selection, ie. by the number of individuals not selected that should be, or visa versa. The "Fertility Factor", (FF), is defined to be the percentage of the population selected to reproduce[1]. The FF indicates the number of distinct individuals that are selected. Therefore, the difference between the experimentally observed FF and the theoretically expected FF[2] indicates the severity of the bias. In Experiment 1, the sampling algorithms are executed 1,000,000 times for each of ten MAX values between 1.1 and 2.0. The average FFs of each sampling algorithm are compared in Figure 2. Figure 3 presents the bias severity, the difference between the experimental and theoretical FFs.

Clearly RSSwoR is severely biased. It has been empirically shown that in GAs, expected values seldom exceed 1.2[1]. Yet for such a case (MAX = 1.1) approximately 3% of the total population is erroneously not selected. Thus, for N=100, an average of 3 individuals are lost due to bias during each generation. The bias in RSIS is much less severe. For N=100, RSIS averages losing only 1 individual due to bias in every 3 generations. This is an order of magnitude better than RSSwoR. The zero bias expected for SUS is empirically supported by this experiment. Note that, Experiment 1 simply indicates favoritism between two groups: those selected in the integral phase versus those not selected in the integral phase. Hence, some decline in the bias severity as MAX$\rightarrow$2.0 is due to the increasing similarity between these group's fractions, see Figure 3.

Bias Direction

We define an individual's "Bias Factor" as the ratio of his actual sampling probability to his expected value. By comparing Bias Factors, we can characterize the direction of the bias, ie. what type of individuals are favored? Since bias only occurs in the fractional phase and the integral phase is deterministic, the Bias Factors will be based solely on the fractional expected values. In Experiment 2, each sampling algorithm is executed 10,000,000 times with MAX = 1.1. This MAX value is chosen to closely resemble a typical expected value distribution. The actual sampling frequencies of each fractional expected value are obtained and used to calculate the Bias Factors plotted in Figure 4. Note that for MAX = 1.1 the fractional expected values form a split range (0 .. 0.1) and (0.9 .. 1.0).

RSSwoR and RSIS favor smaller fractions. Furthermore, the Bias Factor monotonically decreases with increasing fractional magnitude. Both of these results can be proven theoretically[2]. Experiment 1's indication of the sampling algorithms' relative bias is also confirmed, as is its affect on the FF. (In this example, individuals with small fractions have expected values in the range (1.0 .. 1.1). Hence, they are selected during the integral phase. A favorable bias toward these individuals will decrease the FF, see Figure 1. Furthermore, as MAX increases, these fractions increase, thereby decreasing the bias severity, see Figure 3.) Experiment 2 indicates that SUS does not favor any individuals and hence, is empirically zero biased.

Bias Progression

Is the bias constant throughout the fractional selection phase or does it vary? This is important both in understanding the bias and for systems where the generation gap, (fraction of the population replaced during each generation), is less than 1.0. To determine the progression, we must know the sampling probability each individual experiences whenever each sample is taken. This is obtained by recording *when* each selected individual is sampled. Long term averages reveal Bias Factors for each selection cycle, ie. the Bias Factor each individual experiences whenever the 1st selection is made, whenever the 2nd selection is made, etc. In Experiment 3, the sampling algorithms are executed 10,000,000 times with MAX = 1.1 and the Bias Factors are determined. Due to the unwieldy amount of data, only two arbitrarily chosen, representative individuals are compared: the fifth smallest fraction (0.009) and the fifth largest fraction (0.991). Figure 5 presents these individuals' Bias Factors, though some stochastic fluctuation is still evident.

Clearly, the bias in RSSwoR gets progressively worse. This is intuitive -- as more fractions are removed from the "spinning wheel", the bias increases. For RSIS the zero bias of its first population traversal is evident in Figure 5. The second population traversal has constant bias, however it depends upon the number and nature of the first traversal's samples. Hence the apparent steady, late increase in RSIS bias is misleading. It is a direct result of the variable length of the zero biased, first traversal of the population. As a consequence of the increase during latter selections for both RSSwoR and RSIS, the amount of overall bias is strongly dependent upon the generation gap. This dependence upon the generation gap may in fact have affected previous determinations of optimal generation gap settings[4,6]. Due to the simultaneity of SUS -- all N samples are simultaneously determined by the single random number generated -- the concept of a sample cycle is inapplicable.

6. Conclusions

The commonly used sampling algorithm RSSwoR is severely biased and is O(NlogN). Whereas efficiency is always desirable, accurate performance (zero bias) is crucial. Hence, two new sampling algorithms are presented. The first algorithm, RSIS, has Minimum Spread, optimal O(N), and an order of magnitude less bias than RSSwoR. Furthermore, it can be partially implemented in parallel. The second algorithm, SUS, has Minimum Spread, optimal O(N), and zero bias. Yet it can only be implemented sequentially.

Empirical evidence is presented that reveals the relative bias of these three sampling algorithms. The Bias Factors are found to decrease monotonically with increasing expected values. The Bias Factors in RSSwoR are also found to grow steadily worse as an increasing number of selections are made. For RSIS, zero bias is maintained throughout the algorithm's first traversal, yet increases sharply for later traversals. This results in bias occurring only for the last few selections. SUS is shown to be zero biased for all individuals.

The SUS algorithm is an optimal sequential sampling algorithm. Its use enables GAs, for the first time, to assign offspring according to the theoretical specifications. How much the bias has affected the GAs' ability to perform, is unknown. Since the bias reduces the actual FF, its removal will impede convergence. Thus, the bias should improve performance on simple, unimodal functions and worsen performance on others. This has not been empirically verified, but will be thoroughly analyzed in [2]. Since simple functions are not the domain for which GAs are most useful, a degradation in their performance is not of great concern. Hence, in sequential environments, GAs should employ the SUS algorithm. It will sample performance on more difficult functions. If a parallel environment is available, RSIS may prove valuable, especially if a generation gap < 1.0 is desired.

Acknowledgements

I would like to thank Dr. John J. Grefenstette for directing me toward this research area and for numerous discussions of GAs in general. Furthermore, I would like to thank Dr. J. Michael Fitzpatrick for his substantial assistance on the theoretical proofs of bias in RSSwoR.

References

1. J. E. Baker, *Adaptive selection methods for genetic algorithms*, Proc. International Conf. on Genetic Algorithms, Ed. J. J. Grefenstette, Carnegie-Mellon University, Pittsburgh, PA, pp.101-111 (July 1985).

2. J. E. Baker, *Balancing diversity and convergence in genetic search*, Ph.D. Thesis, Computer Science Dept., Vanderbilt University, Nashville, TN, (September 1987), (expected).

3. A. Brindle, *Genetic algorithms for function optimization*, Ph.D. Thesis, Univ. of Alberta, Alberta (1981).

4. K. A. DeJong, *Analysis of the Behavior of a class of genetic adaptive systems*, Ph.D. Thesis, Dept. Computer and Communication Sciences, Univ. of Michigan (1975).

5. J. J. Grefenstette, *A user's guide to GENESIS*, Tech. Report CS-84-11, Computer Science Dept., Vanderbilt Univ., Nashville, TN, (August 1984).

6. J. J. Grefenstette, *Optimization of control parameters for genetic algorithms*, IEEE Transactions of Systems, Man, and Cybernetics, SMC-16(1), pp.122-128 (1985).

Sampling Method	Bias	Spread	Cost	Parallelability
Stochastic with Replacement	zero	unlimited $0 \rightarrow N$	O(NlogN)	None
Stochastic with Partial Replacement	medium	upper bounded $0 \rightarrow \lceil ev \rceil$	O(NlogN)	None
Remainder Stochastic with Replacement	zero	lower bounded $\lfloor ev \rfloor \rightarrow \lfloor ev \rfloor + R$	O(NlogN)	None
Remainder Stochastic without Replacement	medium	minimum $\lfloor ev \rfloor, \lceil ev \rceil$	O(NlogN)	None
Deterministic	high	minimum $\lfloor ev \rfloor, \lceil ev \rceil$	O(NlogN)	None
Remainder Stochastic Independant Sampling	low	minimum $\lfloor ev \rfloor, \lceil ev \rceil$	O(N)	Fractional Phase
Stochastic Universal Sampling	zero	minimum $\lfloor ev \rfloor, \lceil ev \rceil$	O(N)	None

Table 1 -- Comparison of Sampling Methods

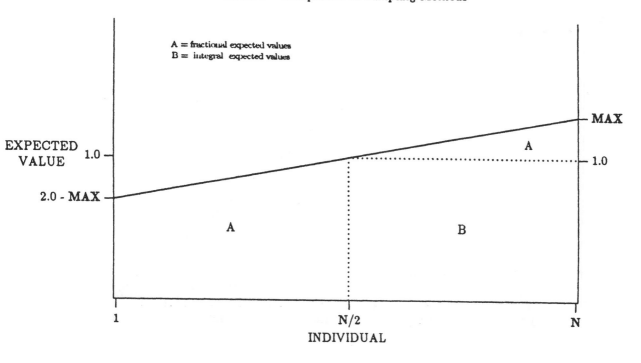

Figure 1 -- Expected Value Distribution

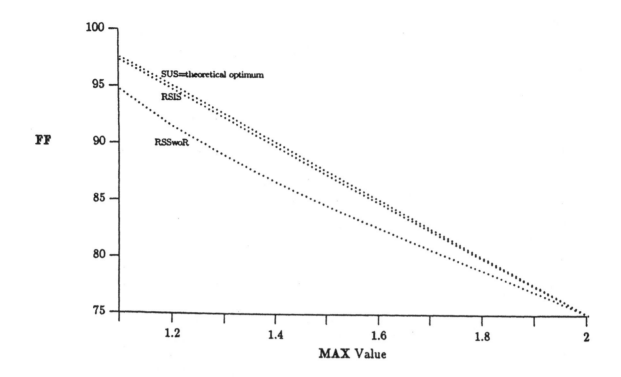

Figure 2 -- Observed **FFs**

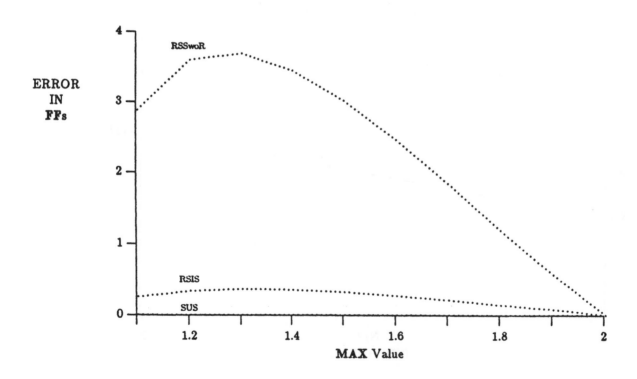

Figure 3 -- Bias Severity

20

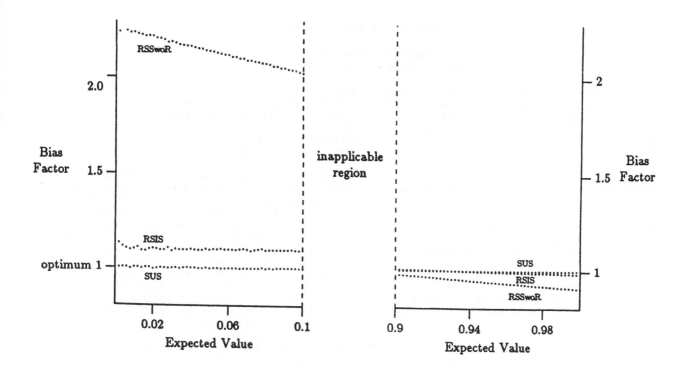

Figure 4 – Bias Direction
(Optimal Bias Factor = 1.0)

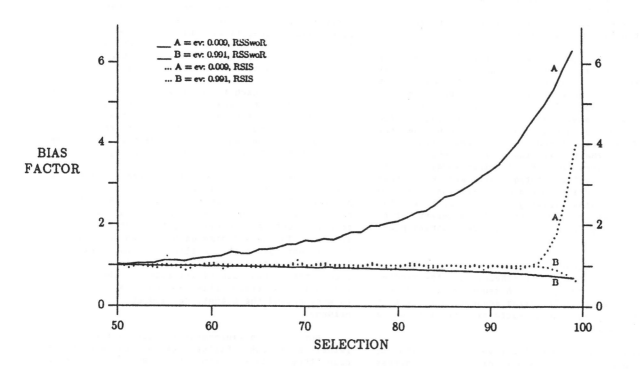

Figure 5 – Bias Progression
(Optimal Bais Factor = 1.0)

Thomas H. Westerdale
Birkbeck College, University of London

Abstract --We examine the bucket brigade in a simple illustrative production system. We employ a penalty scheme to produce an interpretable bucket brigade reward scheme. The result is a reward scheme that looks like a genetic scheme with altruism added.

1. INTRODUCTION: A PRODUCTION SYSTEM VIEWED AS A RAILWAY

We shall investigate the action of certain reward schemes in a simple illustrative production system and environment. The system consists of seven productions: h, b, c, d, e, f, and g. I call the set of productions that can fire in the current time unit the eligibility set. It is of course a function of environment state. Our eligibility situation can be summarized with a simple diagram -- see Fig. 1.

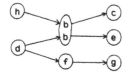

System and Environment
Fig. 1

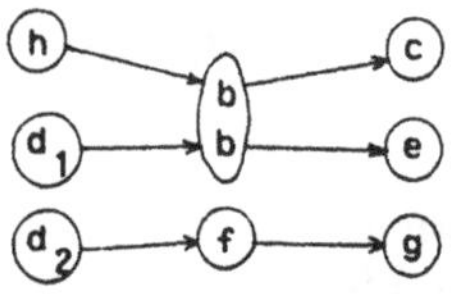

With Station d Split
Fig. 2

After each production fires, the eligibility set is the set of those productions it is connected to by arrows. The possible firing sequences are the left to right paths in the figure.

The figure looks like a railway map, where the productions are stations. Trains on this railway always move from west to east. The stations can be seen to form three groups: the western, central, and eastern group. The railway layout is on a cylindrical planet and so trains leaving eastern stations proceeding eastwards, pass around the far side of the planet and appear on the western edge of the map. Their next stop will be one of the western stations, h or d. In other words, emanating from each eastern station there are two arrows (not shown) pointing to h and d. Station b has two platforms. Trains arriving from h arrive at the northern platform and they always depart for c. Trains arriving from d arrive at the southern platform and they always depart for e.

On a trip around the planet, a train takes one of three routes: the northern, hbc; the middle, dbe; or the southern, dfg. A sequence of productions is a permissible firing sequence just if that sequence is a sequence of successive stations on a possible railway journey.

With every train that arrives at station c, the railway company is paid payoff μ(c), whereas with every train that arrives at station e the company is paid μ(e), and with every train that arrives at station g the company is paid μ(g). These three fares are fixed and unchanging. Arrivals at western and central stations yield no such income, no payoff.

Attached to each station is a positive real number called the station's availability. When a train has a decision to make as to which track to take (as for example when it leaves station d) then it makes a probabilistic choice from among the stations in the eligibility set, chosing with probabilities proportional to the stations' availabilities. (Systems in which the driver's choice is deterministic [1] are more common in practice, but harder to analyze. We shall not discuss them, but see section 7 for a comment on their rationale and analysis.) It will be the job of the reward scheme to adjust the availabilities in an attempt to maximise company income per unit time. For example, if μ(g) is very high then the reward scheme will want to have a high availability of f.

When the reward scheme increases a station's availability we say the station has been rewarded. The amount of the increase is the station's reward.

2. TWO RAILWAY REWARD SCHEMES

Our simple system and environment has a periodicity of 3. Reward schemes discussed in this paper will be specifically designed to handle systems and environments which have a periodicity of 3. We have discussed elsewhere [2,3] the handling of more general systems and environments.

Scheme A: Each train keeps a record of the stations it passes through while crossing the map from west to east. When the train arrives at an eastern station, the payoff received is added to the availabilities of the last three stations the train has passed through.

Scheme A is not a subgoal reward scheme, so its analysis is comparatively easy. (I said "comparatively". See the analysis in [2].) Bucket brigade schemes, on the other hand, are subgoal reward schemes. Let us move directly to a bucket brigade scheme. In this scheme each station holds a certain amount of cash, called its cash balance. Every time a train arrives at a station, that station sends a hundredth of its cash to the station from which the train arrived. Thus cash moves east to west around the planet, carried by the "bucket brigade".

But the cash management at eastern stations is rather different. Eastern stations throw away the cash they receive from the bucket brigade.

Instead, when a train arrives at an eastern station x, the cash balance of x is incremented by the payoff $\mu(x)$.

Scheme B simply sets the availability of each station equal to its cash balance.

In Scheme A, trains coming from h end up at c, and their payoff, $\mu(c)$, rewards station h, but does not reward station d. In Scheme B that payoff rewards d as well. In other words, cash traveling through station b can change platforms, whereas trains cannot.

Under the bucket brigade, the cash balances of the stations will fluctuate around an "equilibrium value", at which the expectation of cash inflow per train arrival is equal to the expectation of the cash outflow. For any station x, we write $\bar{x}$ to mean the equilibrium value of the cash balance of x. Thus we have $\bar{c} = 100 * \mu(c)$, $\bar{e} = 100 * \mu(e)$, $\bar{g} = 100 * \mu(g)$, and $\bar{f} = \bar{g}$.

For analysis purposes, it is sometimes useful to modify the bucket brigade as follows: All payoffs are multiplied by 100, and when a train arrives at a station, that station sends its whole cash balance (rather than only a hundredth) to the station from which the train arrived. This modification produces what we will call the modified bucket brigade. The equilibrium cash balances are unchanged by the modification.

Scheme B looks interesting, but it is never used and it is clearly wrong. In fact it is clearly wrong in even simpler systems and environments. Suppose for example that there is no northern route on the map, that there are no stations h and c and that station b has only one platform. Then we have both $\bar{f} = \bar{g}$ and $\bar{b} = \bar{e}$. Suppose that $\mu(g) = 2 * \mu(e)$, so that $\bar{f} = 2\bar{b}$. Then the trains leaving d take the route to f about twice as often as the route to b. As they do this, more and more evidence piles up that the f route is the better route, but instead of sending more and more trains to f, the system keeps sending about a third of its trains to b.

3. A MORE BIOLOGICAL BUCKET BRIGADE

In biologically motivated systems one generally sets the reward proportional to payoff. That is, the change in availability is proportional to payoff. This is the case in Scheme A. But in Scheme B, the cash balances are proportional to payoff, so the cash balances ought not to be the availabilities, but rather ought to be the change in the availabilities. So we have

Scheme C: Each station keeps two numbers, its cash balance and its availability. The cash balances are maintained exactly as in Scheme B. The availabilities are updated as follows: Every time a train arrives at a station, that station's availability has added to it the product of K and the station's cash balance.

(K is a small positive constant.)

It is Scheme C, not Scheme B, which we should have been comparing to Scheme A. If we use the modified bucket brigade, then Schemes C and A are almost identical. If we look at the east to west path followed by any penny in the modified bucket brigade, we can see that if the penny could not change platforms at b then Scheme C would be just like Scheme A.

Let us look more carefully at what happens in Scheme C. Note that $\bar{h} = \bar{b}$ whatever the availabilities. The value of $\bar{b}$ depends on the availabilities, since these determine the ratio between the number of trains passing through the northern platform of b and the number of trains passing through the southern platform of b.

Let us let the station name without the tilde stand for the availability of that station. It should be clear from context whether it is the station or its availability that is meant.

To obtain a formula for $\bar{b}$ in terms of availabilities, we need to know the proportion of trains that go through h, and the proportion that go through d. We define $q = h + d$, the total availability of the western stations. We define $H = h/q$ and $D = d/q$. The capital letters can be thought of as normalized availabilities, or under certain circumstances, as probabilities. Similarly for the central stations we let $r = b + f$, $B = b/r$, and $F = f/r$. There are three routes for trains going from west to east, and their probabilities are H for route hbc, DB for route dbe, and DF for route dfg. The first two routes go through b and so it is easy to see that $\bar{b} = (H\bar{c} + DB\bar{e})/(H + DB)$. Similarly, $\bar{d} = B\bar{b} + F\bar{f}$. The $\bar{b}$ is the equilibrium value of the cash balance of b for the given availabilities. The cash balance will fluctuate around this value $\bar{b}$ provided the availabilities are held constant.

They will of course be changing, but we assume slowly. Thus we can approximate the behavior of the system by the usual continuous deterministic model in which we think of the trains as fluids and the tracks as pipes, the volume of fluid flowing through a pipe reflecting the average number of trains passing along that track. Under Scheme C the availability of, for example, f increases by $K\bar{f}$ (on average) every time a train enters f. Thus f', the rate of change of the availability of f, is $K\bar{f}$ times the rate at which trains enter f. If n trains leave the western stations per hour on average, then there are on average nDF of these passing through f and so $f' = K\bar{f}nDF$, in our continuous model. By the same reasoning, there are $nH + nDB$ trains passing through b on average, so $b' = K\bar{b}n(H + DB)$. We can similarly calculate h' and d'. Then, defining $\bar{q} = H\bar{h} + D\bar{d}$ and $\bar{r} = B\bar{b} + F\bar{f}$, and using ordinary differential calculus, we can obtain the other rates in Table 1.

So what does Table 1 tell us about Scheme C? Not a lot, I'm afraid. Perhaps the three routes,

$$h' = KnH\bar{h} \qquad\qquad H' = (1/q)KnHD(\bar{h} - \bar{d})$$
$$d' = KnD\bar{d} \qquad\qquad D' = (1/q)KnHD(\bar{d} - \bar{h})$$
$$b' = Kn(H + DD)\bar{b} \qquad B' = (1/r)KnF((H + DB)\bar{b} - DB\bar{f})$$
$$f' = KnDF\bar{f} \qquad\qquad F' = (1/r)KnF(DB\bar{f} - (H + DB)\bar{b})$$
$$q' = Kn\tilde{q}$$
$$r' = Kn\tilde{q}$$

Table 1: Rates for Scheme C

hbc, dbe, and dfg can be thought of as three geno-types with respective fitnesses $\tilde{c}$, $\tilde{e}$, and $\tilde{g}$. There would need to be some fancy recombination rules.

Let's look at the three routes under Scheme C. The proportion of trains on the three routes is H, DB, and DF, respectively. The changes in these three are easily calculated. H' we have already: $(DF)' = (1/q)KnDF(H\bar{f}-H\bar{b})+(1/r)KnDF(DD\bar{f}-H\bar{b}-DB\bar{b})$; and $(DB)' = (1/q)KnDB(H\bar{f}-H\bar{b})+(1/r)KnDF(H\bar{b}+DB\bar{b}-DB\bar{f})$. This doesn't look very helpful.

4. AN ATTEMPT AT STATION SPLITTING

Let's try to go part way toward separating our system into the three routes, part way toward thinking of it in a genetic manner. It looks as if a fork like that at d can be treated as if it were two stations d_1 and d_2, with trains from d_1 going only to b and trains from d_2 going only to f. See Figure 2. A train leaving an eastern station goes to h, d_1, or d_2 according to the 3 availabilities of those stations.

The hope is that Fig. 2 will behave just as Fig. 1 did if $d_1 = dB$ and $d_2 = dF$. Unfortunately, this doesn't work. $D_1' = (1/\tilde{q})KnDFDB(\bar{b} - \bar{f})$, if we represent it in Fig. 1 quantities, and $D_2' = (1/q)KnDF(H + DB)(\bar{f} - \bar{b})$. If our splitting of station d really results in an equivalent system, then D_1' should equal our Fig. 1 (DB)', and D_2' should equal our Fig. 1 (DF)'. Even when $r = \tilde{q}$ these quantities are not equal. When $r = q$ we have
$(DF)' = (1/q)KnDF((H + DB)(\bar{f}-\bar{b}) - H\bar{b})$,
$(DB)' = (1/q)KnDFDB(\bar{b}-\bar{f}) + (1/q)KnDH(B\bar{f} + (F-B)\bar{b})$,
and $D_2' - (DF)' = (1/q)KnDFH\bar{b}$.

5. THE PENALTY SCHEME

Looking at $D_2' - (DF)'$, we see that the Fig. 1 dfg route seems to be getting less reward than it should. It looks as if cash from b has something to do with the discrepancy. If we look at b' and f' in Table 1, we can see what might be causing the problem. b' is too big. The availabilities b and f are used by trains leaving d. Under Scheme C, all those irrelevant trains leaving h proceed on to b and boost its availability. Clearly the H in the formula for b' does not belong.

This is part of a more general problem. A sensible reward scheme penalizes a production when-ever it is a member of the eligibility set. Other-wise, there is no incentive for a production to take itself out of the eligibility set when there

is little likelihood of its doing good. I have pro-posed, in a non-bucket-brigade context, that when a production is rewarded, its reward is then sub-tracted from all the members of the eligibility set in proportion to their availabilities [2]. If we do this we obtain the rates given in Table 2.

$$h' = KnHD(\bar{h} - \bar{d}) \qquad H' = (1/q)KnHD(\bar{h} - \bar{d})$$
$$d' = KnHD(\bar{d} - \bar{h}) \qquad D' = (1/q)KnHD(\bar{d} - \bar{h})$$
$$b' = KnDBF(\bar{b} - \bar{f}) \qquad B' = (1/r)KnDBF(\bar{b} - \bar{f})$$
$$f' = KnDBF(\bar{f} - \bar{b}) \qquad F' = (1/r)KnDBF(\bar{f} - \bar{b})$$
$$q' = 0$$
$$r' = 0$$

Table 2: Rates for Scheme C with Penalties

We can now go ahead and derive as before
$(DB)' = KnDF((1/q)HB(\bar{f} - \bar{b}) + (1/r)DB(\bar{b} - \bar{f}))$, and
$(DF)' = KnDF((1/q)HF(\bar{f} - \bar{b}) + (1/r)DB(\bar{f} - \bar{b}))$.
Splitting station d and using the penalty scheme gives
$$D_1' = (1/q)KnDBDF(\bar{b} - \bar{f}) \qquad\text{and}$$
$$D_2' = (1/q)KnDF(1 - DF)(\bar{f} - \bar{b}) \;.$$

It is now easy to show that to have (DB)' = D_1' and (DF)' = D_2' it is necessary and sufficient that r = d. The penalty scheme was developed for a non-subgoal reward scheme like Scheme A, but is applied here to a bucket brigade. And its applica-tion suddenly makes sense of the equations: The availabilities b and f are for the use of trains leaving d. One will be able to split d just if the availabilities of b and f add up to the availabi-lity of d. I questioned [4] whether the penalty scheme made sense in the bucket brigade context. Evidently it does.

On the other hand, the penalty scheme doesn't really allow station splitting. With the penalty scheme, r is constant, so keeping d = r means d can't be rewarded. Since q is also constant, that means h can't be rewarded either. That's no good.

6. RESTORING THE PENALTY

The penalty scheme was developed [2] as a practical equivalent to a biologically motivated scheme which instead of penalizing productions inside the eligibility set, rewards productions outside it. The biologically motivated scheme can be thought of as identical to the penalty scheme except that after penalizing, the penalty is restored as follows: All the stations of the current locus (the geographical region at which the train is arriving: west, central, or east) are rewarded by the total penalty in proportion to their availability. The penalized eligibility set is a subset of the locus, so for the locus as a whole, the penalty is restored.

There are two obvious ways of implementing this scheme. One is by making the reward, then penalizing across the eligibility set, and then distributing the restoration across the whole locus. Another more suggestive, but much noisier implementation is as follows. When a train arrives at a station, calculate the reward (K times the station's cash balance), but don't give it to that deserving station necessarily. Choose an arbitrary station from the same locus (choose with probabilities proportional to availabilities). If the chosen station is outside the eligibility set, give the reward to the chosen station. If the chosen station is inside the eligibility set, give the reward instead to the deserving station.

Table 3 gives the rates for Scheme C with restored penalties.

$$h' = KnH\bar{h} \qquad\qquad H' = (1/q)KnHD(\bar{h} - \bar{d})$$
$$d' = KnD\bar{d} \qquad\qquad D' = (1/q)KnHD(\bar{d} - \bar{h})$$
$$b' = KnB\bar{b} \qquad\qquad B' = (1/r)KnDF(\bar{b} - \bar{f})$$
$$f' = KnF(H\bar{b} + D\bar{f}) \qquad F' = (1/r)KnDF(\bar{f} - \bar{b})$$
$$q' = Kn\bar{q}$$
$$r' = Kn\bar{q}$$

Table 3: Rates for Scheme C with Restored Penalties

If we use Table 3 to calculate $(DB)'$ and $(DF)'$, and if we ask what is necessary for these to equal D_1' and D_2' respectively after station splitting, we come up with the ridiculous requirement that $D = 1$. Why should this be so? Can we make any sense of Table 3?

7. ALTRUISM

If we set $r = q$, then Table 3 makes sense. We can think of a population of size $q * q$, consisting of individuals of the four genotypes (see Table 4). The number of individuals in the population of genotype hb is simply the product hb, and the same for the other genotypes. So the population is in Hardy-Weinberg equilibrium.

We can view the operation of the scheme as follows. Each time unit, n genotypes are chosen at random from the population. Each of these genotypes is then run as follows. It is given to a train driver who runs his train west to east, using the genotype as a prescription to tell him which track to take when the tracks fork. When the train arrives at the eastern station, the payoff ($\mu(c)$, $\mu(e)$, or $\mu(g)$) is passed to the modified bucket brigade, which runs it back east to west. Table 4 shows the routes back west that the payoff can take, and for each route, Table 4 shows which stations can be rewarded.

The top line of the table says that when hb is the genotype, the payoff will be $\bar{c}$ (since the train will go by the northern route). The payoff has two possible routes back west, via b and h or via b and d. (Remember, money can change platforms at b.) Whether it goes from b to h or from b to d depends on where the next train entering b comes from. The probability that it comes from h is clearly $H/(H + DB)$. We can see that if it follows the route via b and h, it has a chance to make one reward to a central station (when it is at b and a train arrives at b) and one to a western station (when it is at h and a train arrives at h). Now in

geno-type	Pr	payoff	routes of payoff	Pr	rewards to	Pr
hb	HB	$\bar{c}$	hb	H/(H + DB)	hb	B
					hf	F
			db	(DB)/(H + DB)	db	1
hf	HF	$\bar{c}$	hb	H/(H + DB)	hb	B
					hf	F
			db	(DB)/(H + DB)	db	1
db	DB	$\bar{e}$	hb	H/(H + DB)	hb	B
					hf	F
			db	(DB)/(H + DB)	db	1
df	DF	$\bar{g}$	df	1	df	1

Pr = probability

Table 4: Payoff Routes and Rewards

rewarding the central station, b will be the deserving station, whereas the chosen station will be b with probability B, and f with probability F. The eligibility set is {b}, so if f is chosen the reward goes to the chosen station f, whereas if b is chosen the reward goes to the deserving station b. In rewarding the western station, h will be the deserving station, whereas the chosen station will be h with probability H and d with probability D. The eligibility set is {h,d}, so whether h or d are chosen, the reward will in any case go to the deserving station h. Thus if the payoff follows the route via b and h, the reward will go to h and b with probability B, and to h and f with probability F. This is summarized in the first two entries in each of the last two columns of the table.

Table 4 can be used to calculate the rates. In each time unit, n trains run from west to east, so for example to get h' we need only run down the second to the last column, choosing all entries containing an h. For each of these entries, we multiply together K, n, the reward in column 3, and the three probability columns. We then sum the results. The rates we so obtain are those given in Table 3.

There is a certain strange uniformity in Table 4. The last four columns have identical entries for the genotypes hb, hf, and db. In other words, these three genotypes distribute their reward identically. So we can simplify Table 4 to Table 5.

genotype	payoff	rewards to	probability
hb	$\bar{c}$	hb	(hb)/(hb + hf + db)
hf	$\bar{c}$	hf	(hf)/(hb + hf + db)
db	$\bar{e}$	db	(db)/(hb + hf + db)
df	$\bar{g}$	df	1

Table 5: Reward Distribution

The last column of Table 5 is the product of columns five and seven of Table 4. Table 5 tells us that when hb is the genotype, the payoff is $\bar{c}$ and this reward is given to one of the genotypes hb, hf, or db, according to the probabilities in the last column.

So we can think of the four genotypes in our

population as being grouped into two nations. One nation consists of all those individuals whose genotypes are hb, hf, or db. The other nation consists of all those whose genotypes are df. Each genotype has a value (Table 5 column 2). If the scheme were a straightforward genetic scheme, the number of children per time unit of each individual would be K times that individual's value, and then complete recombination would take place. In this scheme, however, each individual altruistically hands his payoff to an arbitrary individual which he selects at random from his own nation. Thus the payoff determines the number of children of the arbitrary recipient rather than of the donor. Of course the payoff does at least remain within the same nation. So our system can indeed be divided into two parts, but evidently not in the way we intended.

The system seems to exhibit genuine altruism and not simply kin selection [5]. Each genotype would do better for its genes if it didn't give away its payoff. Group selection is taking place, the nations being the groups.

Suppose we remove from the scheme the altruistic handing over of payoff, giving us a straightforward genetic scheme. If we had begun not with Scheme C, but with Scheme A, and if we had added the penalties and then the restorations to Scheme A, then the scheme we would have ended up with would have been that straightforward genetic scheme. Thus it is the altruism that distinguishes Scheme C from Scheme A. It is altruism when the pennies change platforms at station b.

To what extent can the previous analysis be performed in a more complex system and environment? The short answer is that I don't know. Elimination of the periodicity does not seem to me to present the more serious problem. It is the introduction of fancier railway branching that looks the more worrying. Suppose for example that there were an additional route hjk in the extreme arctic. Then how could alleles specify choices both for drivers leaving h and for those leaving d? I suggested in [2] that to handle more complicated branchings, the alleles should be orderings of the stations at a given locus. That trick might work.

In many published systems [1] the train driver makes a deterministic rather than a probabilistic choice when the track forks. The rationale is that since a higher cash balance will ultimately lead to a very much higher availability, we can forget about availabilities and ask the driver to always head for the station with the higher cash balance. Such a system relies on noise to shake the system out of non-maximal equilibria. Analysis is difficult because results depend on assumptions regarding noise. Such an analysis is not attempted here.

8. CONCLUSIONS

By a continual process of modifying our bucket brigade scheme and trying to make sense of it, we have arrived at a scheme which has a simple description in one simple system and environment. This scheme employs a system of penalties. It looks like a genetic scheme with altruism added.

The sequence of analyses and changes reported here are genuinely in the order I followed, but with the false trails removed. I really did try the Scheme C first with no penalty, and was puzzled by the messy equations. I had previously used the penalty scheme in a non subgoal reward context [2], but I genuinely forgot about it and so was led astray. The nature of my difficulties reminded me of it, and it seemed to work. I had previously [4] wondered whether the penalty scheme made sense in a subgoal reward context. I'm convinced now that it does. If I had used it from the first, I wouldn't be so sure.

If we had tried different modifications we would have ended up with a different scheme, and perhaps if we had been cleverer we could have made sense of some of the schemes we rejected as nonsensical. Still, what we have shown is that we can ask our questions rigorously enough that the answer can (and frequently does) come out "no". That we can be forced by the facts into an explanation different from the one we intended is an indication that we are doing more than merely making qualitative generalizations. But perhaps not very much more.

References

1. J. H. Holland, "Escaping Brittleness: the Possibilities of General Purpose Learning Algorithms Applied to Parallel Rule Based Systems", pp. 593-623 in *Machine Learning II*, ed. T. M. Mitchell, Morgan Kaufmann, Los Altos, Calif. (1986).

2. T. H. Westerdale, "A Reward Scheme for Production Systems with Overlapping Conflict Sets", *IEEE Trans. Syst., Man, Cybern.* Vol. SMC-16(3), pp.369-383 (May/June 1986).

3. T. H. Westerdale, *An Automaton Decomposition for Learning System Environments*, Submitted.

4. T. H. Westerdale, "The Bucket Brigade is not Genetic", in *Proceedings of an International Conference on Genetic Algorithms and their Applications*, ed. John J. Grefenstette, Carnegie-Melon University, Pittsburgh (1985).

5. John Maynard Smith, *The Theory of Evolution*, Penguin, Harmondsworth, Middlesex, England (1966).

SCHEMA RECOMBINATION IN A PATTERN RECOGNITION PROBLEM

Irene Stadnyk *

Theoretical Division

Los Alamos National Laboratory

Los Alamos, NM 87545. †

Abstract

A simple pattern recognition problem is presented, where a population of binary strings evolves under the genetic algorithm as it tries to match and recognize another population of binary strings. Sampling is used in the genetic algorithm to do matching, which determines fitness, and crowding, which allows subpopulations to form that recognize different pattern strings. To understand what subpatterns the recognizer strings chose as the regularities in the patterns and how these are organized as recognition improves, the theory of schemata is applied to the resulting recognizer string population. The schemata that are formed by recombining other schemata and mutating them with a low level of noise emerge in a default hierarchy. This hierarchy has general properties that apply to any knowledge representation used in such a pattern recognition system.

1 Introduction

Adaptive systems require a dynamic memory in which to store information about the environment. The memory must be organized in such a way so that relevant information can be retrieved quickly and can be used to predict states of the environment based on the current states. Feedback from the environment should be used to have the system learn: the memory should be updated using the feedback so that it can make more accurate predictions in the future, even with partial or noisy information about the environment. The memory's predictions are also used to determine the performance or behavior of the system.

The adaptive system builds its memory by trying to find regularities in the environment that occur in more than one environmental state or occur frequently in the environment. These regularities based on similarity and repeateability are then used to form equivalence classes of environmental states that are then used to organize the memory. These form the basis of the learned model of the environment stored on memory.

In a population of adaptive systems, another requirement can be placed on the memory. The memory must be capable of being transmitted from one system to another. That is, a code representing instructions on how to build a functioning memory must be transmitted to the another system. The code consists of discrete units, which are transmitted in some partial sequential order. Once the code is formed, it does not change but rather is subjected to pressures of selection. It is transmitted throughout the population based on its fitness. It is not clear how the transmitted code is decoded and how it affects the structure and information represented in the receiving memory.

Adaptive system memories have been described in the paradigm of adaptive networks. Adaptive networks include autocatalytic networks of chemical reactions [3], the idiotypic network in the immune system [10], classifiers under the Bucket Brigade Algorithm [9], and nets abstracted from these systems [4]. Transmittable adaptive memories include self-reproducing "organsims" in cellular automata [12] and genetic algorithms [8].

This paper presents a model of an adaptive system based on genetics, which has a memory consisting of binary bit strings. The transmittability of the memory is not discusses since presumably the binary strings can be transmitted in a sequence of discrete bits. However, the organization of a memory consisting of binary strings is studied as the binary strings evolve under a genetic algorithm. The system with this memory is a simple pattern recognizer, based on pattern recognition in the immune system. The system's memory is a population of recognizer strings which try to recognize many pattern strings in parallel by picking out regularities in the pattern strings. The genetic algorithm generates new recognizer strings according to fitness. The fitness of each recognizer string is determined by how many bits it matches of how many pattern strings. Recognizer strings with above average fitness reproduce, and of those, the ones with higher fitness produce more offspring. Thus, recognizers that contain "subpatterns" or substrings of one or more pattern strings will prolifer-

---

*Permanent address: EECS Department, The University of Michigan, Ann Arbor, MI 48109.

†Arpanet address: ims@lanl.gov.

ate through the population. These subpatterns are the schemata that the recognizer population contains and that the genetic algorithm implicitly manipulates. Initial runs of this model show that these schemata evolve into a default hierarchy.

2 The Problem

This pattern recognition problem has been motivated by the pattern recognition that occurs in the immune system. In the immune system[5], one population of antibodies (recognizers) tries to recognize any antigens (patterns) that might invade an organism. By recognizing the antigens, the antibodies tag the antigens, which will then be killed and removed by other cells. The antibodies are formed from gene libraries. From experimental data, we see that these initial antbodies undergo a high rate of mutation once an anitgen is found in the organism. This implies that the initial antibodies must contain some initial structure that can simply be mutated to quickly produce an antibody that recognizes the new antigen. Also, this structure must have been transmitted through the gene libraries. What structure might exist in the gene libraries that have evolved to produce antibodies that are good at recognizing antigens?

In order to study what structure might be found in the gene libraries, a model has been built and simulated which represents the antibodies (recognizers) and antigens (patterns) as binary strings of a fixed length. Several constraints have been put on this model which will be used to study the structures that might occur in the gene libraries. The gene libraries are implicitly represented in this model by the antibodies for which they code. The model constraints are evolutionary constraints, pattern recognition constraints, and covering constraints. The evolutionary constraints have been implemented by the genetic algorithm described in the next section.

The pattern recognition problem is defined as follows:

Population A_r of binary strings of length l recognizes a binary string $x \epsilon$ population A_p of binary strings of length l,
where $|A_r| > |A_p|$ if and only if
$\exists$ a non-empty $S \subseteq A_r$ such that
$\forall x' \epsilon S$

$$\sum_{i=0}^{l-1}((\neg(x \uparrow x') \gg i)\&1) \geq T,$$

where $\uparrow$ is the XOR operator, $\gg$ is the shift-right operator, $\&$ is the bitwise AND operator, and T is an integer threshold. Thus, a population A_r of recognizer strings recognizes a pattern string when there is at least

one recognizer string that has the same bit values in at least T bit positions.

T in the immune system has been experimentally found to be between six and eight amino acids, but in this conceptual model T has been set to five bits, though this can easily be changed. Also, in the real immune system the antibodies form three dimensional configurations so that any T or more positions can try to match the antigen. In the current model, this translates to letting any bit position value of the recognizer string match any other bit position value of the pattern string within the limits of the configuration possibilities. Since the configurations of real antibodies are not known yet, this idea has been abstracted to simply allowing any T bit position values to match with the values in the *same* bit positions in the pattern string. Also, two bit values match if they are not only in the same position in the binary string, but also if they are the same values. In the real immune system, matches occur between complementary values rather than identical values. In this simple model, this does not make a difference. However, if the model were to incorporate the fact that antibodies can match other antibodies as well (where self-recognition and loop creation are important), then complementary matching would have to be the rule. However, in the current model, antibodies as recognizers evolve as they try to match the antigens or patterns, regardless of what other recognizers the recognizer string may match.

Another way of looking at the pattern recognition problem is in terms of schemata. Schemata represent subsets of binary strings by picking out certain bit positions that must have a certain bit value, where the rest of the bit positions can have either value[8]. For instance, the string 011 is contained in schemata 0##, #1#, ##1, 01#, 0#1, #11, 011, and ###, where the #-sign indicates that for that position the schema will accept any value. In this model, the defining bits of a schema would represent those bit values that match between a recognizer string and a pattern string.

The theory of how schemata are manipulated under the genetic algorithm can be used to understand how the recognizer strings are evolving. Since each binary string is a member of 2^l schemata, between 2^l and 3^l *schemata* are implicitly tested and recombined by the genetic algorithm each generation or time step as the *strings* get tested and recombined with respect to their fitnesses. The strings reproduce in proportion to their fitness. Schemata can also be thought of as having fitnesses based on the average of the fitnesses of the strings that are members of that schema. Then as Holland has shown[8], the schemata also reproduce in the population in proportion to their fitnesses. Each schema is implicitly manipulated in the strings that are members of that schema, where the strings are explicitly manipulated by the genetic operators. What this means for the current pattern recognition problem is that if the genetic algorithm finds one schema in the recognizer population with at least T defining bits that match with a pattern, then the recognizer population recognizes that pattern string. Also, as the genetic algorithm manipulates *schemata* at an exponential rate to find useful ones that match patterns in the pattern population, it also finds recognizer *strings* at an exponential rate to match and recognize the patterns.

The covering problem can simply be stated as follows:

Population A_r covers population A_p

if and only if

$\forall x \epsilon A_r \exists$ a non-empty $S \subseteq A_p$

such that

$\forall\ x' \epsilon S,\ x'$ recognizes x.

That is, every pattern string in the pattern population should be recognized by at least one recognizer string.

The runs of this model should at least be able to show that the recognizer population can evolve under the genetic algorithm to recognize a pattern string as well as cover the pattern population. Once parameter settings and reproduction strategies have been found that give this result, the schemata in the evolving recognizer population can be studied to determine how the recognizer population as a whole organizes information about the patterns as it discovers recognizers to recognize the patterns.

3   The Model

The parameter values for the genetic algorithm are set as follows.

The length of the strings is

$$l = 36$$

bits.

To determine the size of the recognizer population, the length of the schemata one expects to find must be taken into account. Based on recognition in the immune system, the model should be able to let schemata with five or six defining bits develop in the recognizer population. To see what schemata we can expect to find in the recognizer population, we can use a corollary of John Holland's Theorem 6.2.3 [8] that

$$\varepsilon < \frac{2n}{l}$$

where ε is the error due to crossover (which may break an instance of a schema), n is the the number of defining bits in the schemata one is interested in, and l is the string length. Since $l = 36$, the error for a schema of length 1 is < 0.056, $2 < 0.12$, $3 < 0.17$, $4 < 0.23$, $5 < 0.28$, $6 < 0.34$, and so on. In order for the recognizer population to be able to search for schemata with

$n = 6$ defining bits, of which there are $2^n = 2^6 = 64$, the recognizer population size should be about 64 as an upper bound. Schemata with more defining bits might still be found. The recognizer population size has been set to

$$recognizer population size = 50$$

which is still much greater than $2^5 = 32$ and close to $2^6 = 64$, where the error rate is about 0.3, about as high as the genetic algorithm can tolerate. The initial strings in the recognizer population are created at random.

The pattern population size has been chosen to be

$$pattern population size = 1$$

for one set of runs, and

$$pattern population size = 10$$

for another set of runs to see if the recognizer population can recognize just one string as well as cover several pattern strings. The population is initialized with random strings that do not change over time.

The point mutation rate has been set as low background noise,

$$point mutation rate = 2$$

two point mutations per time step, where the mutated bits are chosen at random.

The crossover rate has been set to

$$crossover rate = \frac{1}{3} \cdot recognizer population size$$

so that in each generation $\frac{1}{3}$ of the recognizer strings are chosen as parents, thus producing that many new strings, and replacing that many old strings. The parents are chosen probabilistically with respect to fitness so that the algorithm results in reproduction with emphasis (on fitness)[8]. Schemata with above average fitness have new copies or samples of them generated in the recognizer population in accordance with the theorem that guarentees minimal performance loss.

Several fitness functions have been considered. With fitness equal to the average number of matching bits of the recognizer string to every pattern string, fitness generally does not increase monotonically nor exponentially as claimed should happen with crossover[8]. To encourage the recognizer strings to evolve with as many consecutive bits matching a pattern string as possible so that it is less likely that the schema of matching bits will be broken by crossover, fitness has been chosen to be

$$f(x) = \frac{\sum_{j=1}^{msample} \sum_{i=1}^{\#j matches} \frac{m_j(i)}{2^{-m_j(i)}(l - m_j(i) + 1)}}{msample}$$

where x is a recognizer string, msample is *matchsample*, $m_j(i)$ is the number of consecutive bit matches between the ith set of consecutive bit matches in string x and the jth pattern string in sample s_m, $\#jmatches$ is the number of consecutive bit match sequences between string x and the jth pattern string, and l is the length of the strings. For example, if $x = 01101$ and $s_m = \{11100, 00101\}$, then $m_1(1) = 3$, $m_2(1) = 1$, $m_2(2) = 3$, and

$$f(x) = \frac{3}{2^{-3} \cdot 3} + \frac{1}{2^{-1} \cdot 5} + \frac{3}{2^{-3} \cdot 3} = 16.4.$$

The *matchsample* is the size of the sample s_m of strings chosen from the pattern population. The sample s_m, rather than all of the strings in the pattern population, is used to compute fitness. Using this sample helps subpopulations emerge in the recognizer population, as in Booker's simulation [1]. Subpopulations are necessary if all of the patterns are to be recognized by the recognizer population.

The combinatorial bias of the probability of finding m matching bits between two strings, $\frac{1}{2}^m(l - m + 1)$, has been removed by dividing the number of matches by the bias to get the unbiased fitness that would make all lengths of matches equally likely to occur when based on fitness. The probability of finding a match between two bits is $\frac{1}{2}$. For m bits, it is $\frac{1}{2}^m$. Since these bits are consecutive, there are $(l - m + 1)$ ways that they can be chosen in a string of length l. Therefore, a sequence of m consecutive matching bits occurs with a probability of $\frac{1}{2}^m(l - m + 1)$ in a string of length l. Dividing by this probability is equivalent to putting more emphasis on longer schemata since the dominating term of $2^{m_j(i)}$ increases exponentially with the length of the substring, $m_j(i)$.

Several replacement strategies have been tried for determining which recognizer strings get replaced by the new offspring strings created by crossover. Choosing a string probabilistically with respect to $\frac{1}{fitness}$ eventually gives rise to a homogeneous population consisting of one highly fit string. Choosing a string that most closely matches the new string, a "crowding" strategy, never allows the fitness to go up since the child too often replaces its parent and thus schemata do not increase in proportion to their fitness as they should. A similar strategy, first tried by DeJong [2] and later by Booker [1] where the closest matching string is chosen from a small random *sample* of the recognizer population does not do much better than the first strategy. A strategy which works well is one which chooses a small sample of recognizer strings, s_c, of size *crowdsample* probabilistically with respect to $\frac{1}{fitness}$. Then from this sample, the string which most closely matches the new string is chosen to be replaced. With this strategy, the recognizer population fitness increases and does not yield a homogeneous recognizer population. The *crowdsample* is determined by how many copies of a schema one wants.

A sample of size n would on average include recognizer strings in all schemata that are present in $\frac{1}{n}$ of the recognizer population. Thus, n subpopulations are allowed to coexist in the recognizer population since any subpopulation cannot contain more than $\frac{1}{n}$ recognizer strings. Since the replacement strategy uses fitness to determine which strings to replace, it is consistent with the reproduction with emphasis plan. That is, schema with below average fitness will have copies or samples removed so that their sample size decreases and makes room for an increase in the number of above average schema. Thus, this strategy generally replaces the string with the lowest fitness and which is in the same subpopulation as the new string.

The algorithm to find schemata actually finds a small sample of all schemata present in a string population. The sampling is designed to find the more useful schemata (building blocks) that evolve under the genetic algorithm rather than all of the schemata present in a population. The algorithm to find these schemata is:

1. Choose a sample, s_1, of the population in which want to find schemata (e.g. n most fit strings).

2. Find the schemata in each string in sample s_1. For each string in sample s_1:

   (a) Get a random sample, s_2, from the population.

   (b) Check string against each string from s_2 to find which bits match.

   (c) Record schemata which appear between string and each string in s_2 with matching bits no more than two bits apart (otherwise you have a separate schema).

   (d) Do not store duplicates.

   (e) Store schema frequency, sf, by running through all the strings in s_2 again.

3. Check to see what schemata are present randomly. For each string in sample s_1:

   (a) Use same random sample s_2 as in 2a).

   (b) Count the number of matches at each bit between the string and every string in s_2.

   (c) If

   $$sf < \prod_{i=1}^{\#definedbits} \frac{\#matches_i}{|s_2|}$$

   where sf is the schema frequency, $\#matches_i$ is the number of matches found in 2b) for bit i defined in schema, then remove the schema from the list.

30

For example, let $s_1 = \{0110100011\}$ and $s_2 = \{1110011101, 0101010101\}$. For step (2),
$$s_{11} \cap s_{21} = \#110\#\#\#\#\#1$$
with schemata
$$\#110\#\#\#\#\# \text{ of frequency } \tfrac{1}{2} \text{ and}$$
$$\#\#\#\#\#\#\#\#\#1 \text{ of frequency } \tfrac{2}{2}$$
and
$$s_{11} \cap s_{22} = 01\#\#\#\#0\#\#1$$
with schemata
$$01\#\#\#\#\#\#\#\# \text{ of frequency } \tfrac{1}{2} \text{ and}$$
$$\#\#\#\#\#\#0\#\#1 \text{ of frequency } \tfrac{1}{2}.$$
For step (3), the number of matches at each bit is
$$(1)(2)(1)(1)(0)(0)(1)(0)(0)(2).$$
Then for schema
$$\#110\#\#\#\#\#, \tfrac{1}{2} < \tfrac{2 \cdot 1 \cdot 1}{2} \text{ so remove this schema,}$$
$$\#\#\#\#\#\#\#\#\#1, \tfrac{2}{2} \geq \tfrac{2}{2} \text{ so keep this schema,}$$
$$01\#\#\#\#\#\#\#\#, \tfrac{1}{2} < \tfrac{1 \cdot 2}{2} \text{ so remove this schema,}$$
and
$$\#\#\#\#\#\#0\#\#1, \tfrac{1}{2} < \tfrac{1 \cdot 2}{2} \text{ so remove this schema.}$$

For the schemata in the pattern population, both samples are the entire pattern population. That is, all useful pattern schemata that can be located by the algorithm are found and counted. For the recognizer population, the $(\tfrac{1}{3} \cdot recognizer\, population\, size) = n$ most fit strings are chosen for the first sample, s_1, and the same size sample is chosen for the second random sample, s_2. So recognizer schemata occuring in $\tfrac{1}{n}$ of the recognizer population are located this way in every time step. Rather than being explicitly represented anywhere in the model, the schemata so-located are printed out at every time step so that they can be analyzed.

This model for pattern recognition is very similar to, though implemented differently from, Booker's genetic algorithm simulation[1]. In that simulation, the classifier system learns useful categories or taxa (the conditions of the classifers) for one or more categories in the environment, where the categories are generating input messages to the system. The taxa are equivalent to schemata though there are fewer of them in a classifier string than in the recognizer binary bit string. The binary bit string messages are equivalent to binary bit pattern strings that the classifers and recognizers, respectively, are trying to match.

The matchscore that he uses, called M_3, is defined for a taxon x and message (binary bit string) x' as
$$M_3(x) = \begin{cases} 1 & \text{if } x \text{ and } x' \text{ match identically} \\ \frac{l-n}{l^2} & \text{otherwise} \end{cases}$$
where n is the number of mismatched bit values and l is the length of the strings. This function is linear with slope $-\tfrac{1}{l^2}$ except for the case of all defining bits matching where M_3 returns the value 1 rather than $\tfrac{1}{l}$. This jump when the optimal solution is reached ensures that a good taxon is never lost from the population. On the other hand, the fitness function in the model just

presented is an exponential curve which increases the fitness exponentially with each additional matching bit rather than just a big jump when the perfect match is found. The fitness function encourages bit by bit additions to matching schemata whereas the matchscore encourages this but really emphasizes the final perfect match. The fitness function is also more apt to keep schemata of all lengths in the population in case the pattern strings in the environment change so that the recognizer population can quickly build a matching recognizer from a few schemata. Matchscore just tries to match the categories in the current environment.

In the pattern recognition model, there are no mating restrictions, unlike Booker's simulation where two strings can mate only if they match the same message. Mating in the new model is probabilistic with respect to fitness, which is computed with respect to a sample of pattern strings. Thus, higher fitness implies that the recognizer string matches more pattern strings out of its sample which implies that there is a good chance that two mating strings both match at least one same pattern string, like a probabilistic mating restriction. This chance is equal to $1 - \frac{(a-m)(a-m-1)\cdots(a-2m+1)}{(a)(a-1)\cdots(a-m+1)}$, where a is the pattern population size and m is $matchsample$. For instance, in this model the chance would be $\tfrac{17}{24}$ where $a = 10$ and $m = 3$. Thus, the recognizer population can find the near-optimal points representing the pattern strings and still incorporate new strings with new schemata for each time step.

Crowding is also implemented similarly to Booker's simulation. The $\frac{1}{fitness}$, equivalent to $\frac{1}{strength}$, is used to pick out a $sample$ of strings to delete based on which string best matches the new string. This is similar to Booker's crowding scheme where taxation and a tax rebate lower the strength of strings in a subpopulation that has reached its "carrying capacity". Then the strings with lower strength, are more likely to get removed, just as strings in the new model with lower $fitness$ and higher $\frac{1}{fitness}$ are more likely to get removed. Since fitness is noisy, there are recognizer strings in each subpopulation with lower fitness that will probably get removed; if the subpopulation is of size $\tfrac{1}{n}$, then these strings with lower fitness will appear in the sample and get chosen to be replaced. Also, in the current model, using a sample size equal to the number of desired subpopulations is simpler to implement than Booker's scheme where the system keeps track of which taxa are relevant to what message, unless the relevance criterion is such that it can be calculated for each subpopulation rather than every individual taxon.

Thus, the recognizer population in the pattern recognition model, just like the classifiers in Booker's model, can also find the near-optimal points representing the pattern strings and still incorporate new recognizer strings with new schemata for each time step.

4   Results

Preliminary runs have found parameter settings with which the recognizer population increases its fitness (equal to the sum of the fitnesses of each recognizer string) as shown in the following $log_{10}(fitness)$ vs. *time* plot. Increasing fitness implies that the recognizer population is matching one or more pattern strings at more bits.

To test the model's ability to solve the recognition problem, fifty recognizer strings have been run under the genetic algorithm to get them to match one pattern string. The population fitness does increase exponentially (Figure 1) until it reaches the maximum population fitness possible when about ninety percent of the recognizer strings match the pattern string at every bit position. The other ten percent match at almost every bit.

To test the model's ability to solve the covering problem, a run where fifty recognizer strings try to recognize ten pattern strings has been tried. The fitness of the recognizer population does increase fairly monotonically (Figure 2). The listing of pattern schemata found in the final recognizer population shows that all pattern schemata with five or fewer defining bits have also been found in the final recognizer population. Also, upon closer inspection of the recognizer population, a recognizer string can be found for each pattern string such that the recognizer string matches the pattern string at no fewer than five bit positions. Thus, the recognizer population recognizes and covers all of the pattern strings.

With what sample sizes does this genetic algorithm solve the recogntion and covering problems? How does the recognizer population evolve with these parameter settings?

It turns out to be critical that the value for *matchsample* be less than the size of the pattern population. That is, fitness for each string must be computed with respect to only a few patterns and with respect to different patterns each time step for a given recognizer string. If all patterns are used to determine the fitness of a recognizer string, then the entire recognizer population ends up matching only one pattern as it reaches maximum possible value for fitness.

There are several reasons why *matchsample* should be just a portion of the pattern population size. First of all, the computations to determine fitness are done faster if only a few patterns are used for the calculation.

Secondly, each recognizer uses the same sample of patterns to compute its fitness, namely all of the patterns. Thus, the first pattern with a longer schema found in the recognizer population will be the one matched by all of the recognizers over time. That schema will increase the fitness exponentially of the recognizer containing it with respect to the fitnesses of the other recognizers. That recognizer's descendents will take over the

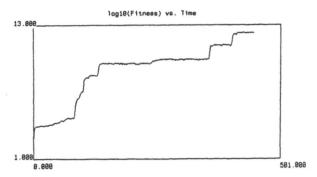

Figure 1. $patternpopulationsize = matchsample = crowdsample = 1.$

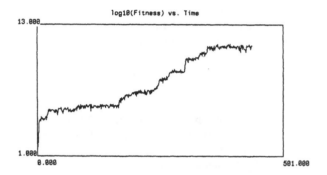

Figure 2. $patternpopulationsize = crowdsample = 10, matchsample = 3.$

entire recognizer population to match that one pattern. Thus, in order to cover all of the patterns, a different sample of patterns must be used to calculate fitness for each recognizer string.

Thirdly, and most importantly, sampling is the counterpart in this model of collision dynamics. One recognizer can try to recognize only a few patterns at any one time in real physical space. Modelling this accurately models the fact that this system is far from equilibrium most of the time where changes in the system are most likely to increase rather than decrease order in the system. That is, new schemata introduced into the recognizer population will get their numbers increased with respect to their fitness and give rise to new recognizer strings as they get distributed throughout the recognizer population. Otherwise, with non-noisy fitness, these new schemata would be ignored and eventually be removed from the recognizer population as one recognizer string containing one longer schemata was the only one with surviving descendent strings.

The other sample size for which the value turns out to be critical is *crowdsample*. With *crowdsample* = 10 (equal to *patternpopulationsize* in this case), a schema will be replaced if it is in $\frac{1}{10}$ of the recognizer population. This allows more room for other schemata to occur and distribute in $\frac{1}{10}$ of the recognizer population. If *crowdsample* is less than that, for example if it set to 3, then the fitness of the recognizer population increases but only recognizes about three of the patterns.

With *crowdsample* = 10, as in the second run described, it was found that the recognizer population maintains a high number of schemata at all times, keeping the number of recognizer schemata around 100 ± 25 each time step. By maintaining such diversity in the recognizer population, all pattern schemata of 5 or fewer defining bits are found by the genetic algorithm along with a few schemata with even more defining bits. This is also due to the *recognizerpopulationsize* parameter. Theory predicts that when there are 2^n schemata of length n, a population of size $2^5 = 32$ or greater should be able to search these. A population of size 50, where $2^5 < 50 < 2^6$, does this plus finds a few other longer schemata. One of these longer schemata, not in the initial recognizer population, has been created by putting together two shorter schemata that increase in frequency enough to form the longer schema, which then increases in frequency. The shorter schemata decrease in frequency since they have been incorporated into the longer schema. Thus, we see the beginning of a default hierarchy forming[7][9]. First shorter, more general schemata are tested against the environment, and then the useful ones are used to build longer, more specific schemata that predict the environment (or in this case cover the strings in the pattern population even more accurately). With a larger population, more of the longer schemata should emerge.

5 Conclusion

The recognition and covering constraints are the minimal ones that the current model can satisfy. It does this by taking two shorter schemata and applying crossover to the strings of those schemata to form a new longer schema. This longer schema is a combination of the two shorter ones and is in a string that matches a pattern at more bits. Thus, a default hierarchy is emerging in the recognizer population. Mutation also can create such longer schemata and fitter strings but only one more bit will match an pattern. The one additional matching bit does not increase the fitness of the string nor the number of recognizer strings to match pattern strings as much as recombination does. However, these results are based on preliminary runs and need to be quantified more precisely before more specific conclusions can be made.

There are still many questions to study about this pattern recognition model.

1. How is the default hierarchy of schemata represented in the recognizer string population? Are there recognizer strings that contain several shorter pattern schemata and some recognizer strings with longer schemata? In terms of knowledge representation[6], is the representation fine-grained with longer, more specific schemata or coarse-grained with more general schemata? Is the entire emerging default hierarchy maintained in the recognizer population?

2. Do distinct subpopulations evolve in the recognizer population with respect to the patterns or other criteria such as regularities in the pattern strings? Does each recognizer string contain schemata for one pattern or for more than one pattern? If the *patternpopulationsize* is increased, will the system no longer be able to pick out all of the regularities which may no longer come from one pattern but may include several patterns? How will this depend on the *recognizerpopulationsize*?

3. How do the schemata in the recognizer population change when the initial pattern population is changed? And if one of the parameter values is changed? What if the fitness function is changed to give maximum fitness value when T bits match?

4. Are *matchsample* and *crowdsample*, which maintain diversity in the recognizer population, also resulting in suboptimal fitnesses for the recognizers that cover the patterns? That is, does it become impossible for perfect matches to evolve for each pattern? Is this somehow an adaptive advantage even if it is not a performance advantage? How can their values be set by some feedback mechanism based on regularities found and the resulting fitness, so that the recognizer population can continue to recognize and cover a pattern population that is changing its size and strings over time?

5. Is the final recognizer population robust to changes in the pattern population? Will the recognizer population fitness decrease alot quickly if an original pattern is replaced with a new and different pattern string? Will the entire recognizer population have to re-evolve to redistribute the pattern schemata it has, lose the ones no longer in the pattern population, and acquire new ones?

Various tools still need to be built to analyze the evolution of schemata and the default hierarchy in the recognizer population. For instance, since the schema finding algorithm only finds a sample of the schemata present in the pattern population, a reasonably-sized phylogenetic tree can be plotted over time based on what pattern schemata in the recognizer strings give rise to which new and possibly longer pattern schemata in new recognizer strings. The frequency of each pattern schemata in the recognizer population (equal to the number of recognizer strings with that pattern schemata) could be plotted over time and used with the phylogenetic tree to trace the development of the default hierarchy.

The frequencies of the schemata can also be studied with analytical tools developed for understanding dynamical systems. Every schemata changes its frequency (equal to the number of strings in the population belonging to that schema) in the population with respect to the probability

$$P_s(t+1) = \frac{M_s(t+1)}{M} = \hat{f}_s(t) \cdot \varepsilon_s \cdot M_s(t)$$

where schema s has an average expected fitness $\hat{f}_s(t)$ at time t, $M_s(t)$ is the number of strings in the recognizer population that are elements of schema s, M is the total number of strings in the fixed sized recognizer population, and ε_s is an error term created by having a schema instance get broken up by a crossover point or mutation. The size of the recognizer population and the sample sizes also affect the number of schemata and the number of their instances that are possible to have in the recognizer population. Thus, the schemata dynamics can be studied under different parameter settings for the population and sample sizes, and the affects of fluctuations occuring when new schemata are introduced into the recognizer population by crossover, mutation, or changes in the pattern population can also be studied.

Once the structure and evolution of the default hierarchy is better understood, this pattern recogniton model can be used to study the structural evolution of memory in other physical and biological systems that do pattern recognition. The features of the particular system can be assigned to the bits of the pattern and recognizer strings. Then one can study how the recognizer strings of that system's memory are structured with respect to the regularities in the patterns the system is trying to recognize.

For instance, in modeling the immune system, experimental evidence can be used to set up the fitness function and parameter values to be more realistic with real immune systems and to see if the model results in antibodies with similar characteristics as those found in the experiments. Some experimental studies have shown that one antibody can recognize more than one antigen (called "multi-specificity" in immunology) [13]. Such an antibody is a generalist. Other evidence shows that when new antigens are introduced, new antibodies are created by an increased rate of point mutations. The affinity of these new antibodies for new antigens increases ten-fold over a short period of time, indicating that the antibodies become very specific at recognizing the antigens [14]. Thus, some sort of default hierarchy is developing in the immune system. What is the nature of this default hierarchy if the fitness function and paramters are set to correspond to actual numbers used and seen in these experiments? What antibodies result if the intial antibodies are ones that have evolved in this pattern recognition model and can only undergo mutation in the future when presented with a new antigen? How might a network of such antibodies compensate for any shortcomings of the antibody population which can no longer undergo crossover?

Also, in a letter recognition system, letter patterns can be represented with line features of different lengths, angles, and positions. Could this model then generate a default hierarchy to recognize the letter or letters? How could it recognize the same letters if they are written in a different style?

In cognitive science, a concept is represented by a prototype developed from a set of instances. The nature of the prototype with respect to the properties of the instances is not yet clearly understood, but the instances do not necessarily all share some set of property values which might then be the prototype. Rather, each instance shares one or more property values with one or more other instances in the set [11]. Translated into the pattern recognition model, the recognizer population can try to match the instances in the environment where the prototype would appear as the more general schema that persists over time and is not just used to build one specific schema. On the other hand, the prototype might turn out to be some piece of the default hierarchy distributed over several recognizer strings. How would this correspond to any experimental data that has been collected by psychologists on the nature of prototypes? What kinds of prototypes are actually communicated in these experiments (i.e. trasmitted verbally to the experimenter)?

By understanding the organization of the default hierarchy in the recognizer strings, the memories of other pattern recognition systems evolving under a genetic algorithm can be analyzed as well. A system that tries to recognize patterns in the environment and then builds an internal model or memory of those patterns must use some definition of similarity to cluster the patterns into classes. If this system also transmits its internal model by a code representing how to reconstruct that model, then this system is a good candidate to be cast in and analyzed by this pattern recognition model.

6   Acknowledgements

This work has been performed under the auspices of the U.S. Department of Energy. I would like to thank John H. Holland for his guidance and ideas about genetic algorithms and modelling, Chris Langton for his comments on modelling artificial life, and Alan Perelson, Doyne Farmer, and Norman Packard for their valuable insights into the structure and dynamics of biological and physical systems.

References

[1] Booker, L.B. 1985, "Improving the Performance of Genetic Algorithms in Classifier Systems". Proceedings of an International Conference on Genetic Algorithms and Their Applications, Pittsburgh, Pennsylvania : Carnegie-Mellon University.

[2] DeJong, K.A. 1975, "Analysis of the Behavior of a Class of Genetic Adaptive Systems". PhD Dissertation, Ann Arbor : The University of Michigan.

[3] Farmer, J.D., Kauffman, S.A., and Packard, N.H. 1987, "Autocatalytic Replication of Polymers". Physica 22D, pp. 50-67.

[4] Farmer, J.D., Kauffman, S.A., Packard, N.H., and Perelson, A.S. 1987, "Adaptive Dynamic Networks as Models for the Immune System and Autocatalytic Sets". Annals New York Academy of Sciences.

[5] Farmer, J.D., Packard, N.H., and Perelson, A.S. 1986, "The Immune System, Adaptation, and Machine Learning". Physica 22D, pp. 187-204.

[6] Feldman, J.A. 1986, "Neural Representation of Conceptual Knowledge". TR189, Dept. of Computer Science, Rochester, NY : The University of Rochester.

[7] Goldberg, D.E. 1983, "Computer-aided Gas Pipeline Operation Using Genetic Algorithms and Rule Learning". PhD Dissertation, Ann Arbor : The University of Michigan.

[8] Holland, J.H. 1975, Adaptation in Natural and Artificial Systems. Ann Arbor, Michigan : The University of Michigan Press.

[9] Holland, J.H. 1985, "Escaping Brittleness: The Possibilities of General Purpose Learning Algorithms Applied to Parallel Rule Base Systems". Machine Learning II, Ch. 20, Los Altos, CA : Morgan Kauffman.

[10] Jerne, N.K. 1974, "Toward a Network Theory of the Immune System". Annals of Immunology (Inst. Pasteur) 125C : 373.

[11] Kaplan, S. 1986, Neural Models, Course Notes, Ann Arbor : The University of Michigan.

[12] Langton, C.G. 1984, "Self-Reproduction in Cellular Automata". Physica 10D, pp. 135-144.

[13] Rosenstein, R.W., Musson, R.A., Armstrong, M.Y.K., Konigsberg, W.H., and Richards, F.F. 1972, "Contact Regions for Dinitrophenyl and Menadione Haptens in an Immunoglobulin Binding More Than One Antigen". Proceedings of the National Academy of Science, USA, Vol. 69, No. 4, pp. 887-881.

[14] Wysocki, L.J., Manser, T., and Gefter, M.L. 1986, "Somatic Evolution of Variable Region Structures During an Immune Response". Proceedings of the National Academy of Science, USA, Vol. 83, pp. 1847-1851.

An Adaptive Crossover Distribution Mechanism for
Genetic Algorithms

J. David Schaffer
Amy Morishima

Philips Laboratories
North American Philips Corporation
Briarcliff Manor, New York

ABSTRACT

This paper presents a new version of a class of search procedures usually called genetic algorithms. Our new version implements a modified string representation that includes special punctuation used by the crossover recombination operator. The idea behind this scheme was abstracted from the mechanics of natural genetics and seems to yield a search procedure wherein the action of the recombination operator can be made to adapt to the search space in parallel with the adaptation of the string contents. In addition, this adaptation happens "for free" in that no additional operations beyond those of the traditional genetic algorithm are employed.

We present some empirical evidence that suggests this procedure may be as good as or better than the traditional genetic algorithm across a range of search problems and that its action does successfully adapt the search mechanics to the problem space.

1. Background

A genetic algorithm is an exploratory procedure that is able to locate high performance structures in complex task domains. To do this, it maintains a set (called a population) of trial structures, represented as strings. New test structures are produced by repeating a two-step cycle (called a generation) which includes a survival-of-the-fittest selection step and a recombination step. Recombination involves producing new strings (the offspring) by operations upon one or more previous strings (the parents). The principle recombination operator was abstracted from knowledge of natural genetics and is called crossover. Holland has provided a theoretical explanation for the high performance of such algorithms [5] and this performance has been demonstrated on a number of complex problem domains such as function optimization [3, 4] and machine learning [6, 8, 9].

The action of the traditional crossover is illustrated in figure 1.

Starting with two strings from the population†, a point is selected between 1 and L-1, where L is the string length. Both strings are severed at this point and the segments to the right of this point are switched. The two starting strings are usually called the parents and the two resulting strings , the offspring. Taking the metaphor one step further, we will call this operation a mating with a single crossover event. In all previous work with which we are familiar, the crossover point is chosen with a uniform probability distribution.

The motivation for our new crossover operator sprang from some properties of this traditional operator. Specifically, it has a known bias against properly sampling structures which contain coadaptive substrings that are far apart. In metaphorical terms, we might call them genes which are far apart on the chromosome. The reason is not difficult to grasp intuitively. The farther apart the genes are, the higher the probability that a uniformly selected random crossover point will fall between them causing them to be passed to different offspring. We observe that this crossover operator requires only knowledge of the string length; it pays no attention to its contents. Furthermore its action is nonadaptive. It performs the same way in every generation.

In contrast to this, what we know of Nature's genetic crossover activity suggests that the location of crossover events may be quite sensitive to the contents of the chromosome [1]. There are many activities in this microworld which involve the initiation of an action by the binding of an enzyme to a specific base-sequence. We were motivated to design a crossover mechanism which would adapt the distribution of its crossover points by the same survival-of-the-fittest and recombination processes already in place. We reasoned that it should do so by the use of special punctuation marks introduced into the string representation for this purpose. The operation envisioned for this new crossover was to proceed by "marking" the site of each crossover event in the string in which it occurred. Thus if the search space had the characteristic that crossovers at particular loci were consistently associated with inferior offspring, then they would die out, taking their markings with them. The converse was also hoped for. If no consistent relation existed to be exploited, then a

---

† We will show all strings as bit strings, but this is not a requirement imposed by the algorithm.

```
PARENTS
     0000000
     1111111
          |___ crossover point -- selected randomly with
                                  a uniform distribution
OFFSPRING
     0001111
     1110000
```

Figure 1. The action of the traditional crossover operator. The two parent strings are shown as all zeros and ones for clarity.

random allocation of markings was expected. In this, we were reminded of speculation by Lenat that modern gene pools may contain accumulated heuristics to guide genetic search as well as an accumulation of well-adapted expressible genes [7].

The idea of punctuation in the strings used by a genetic algorithm was first proposed by Holland [5], but this proposal was for a different purpose than that proposed here.

The rest of this paper will present, the mechanics of our new crossover operator, some empirical results indicating that superior performance can indeed be achieved with it, and some data exhibiting properties of its behavior.

2. Mechanics

In this section we will explain the mechanics of operation of our new crossover operator. We address how the crossover punctuation is coded, how an initial distribution is generated, how this distribution affects the crossing over of the functional parts of the strings, how the punctuation marks themselves are passed on to the offspring, and how a linkage is established between individual punctuation marks and the functional substrings with which they are associated.

The representation is straightforward. To the end of each chromosome (string of bits interpretable as a point in the search space) we attach another bit string of the same length. Thus any string representation previously used with a traditional genetic algorithm can be employed in our scheme simply by doubling its length. The bits in the new section are interpreted as crossover punctuation, 1 for yes and 0 for no (i.e. 1=crossover, 0=no crossover). The loci in the punctuation (second) part of the string correspond one-to-one with the loci in the functional (first) part of the chromosome. Thus it is natural to think of these two parts of the chromosome as interleaved. Punctuation mark i tells whether crossover is or is not to occur at locus i. In figure 2, the punctuation marks are shown as "!" in the functional string.

It is common practice when beginning a genetic search to initiate a population of strings by randomly generating bits with equal probability for zero and one. We follow this practice for the functional string, but the

```
THE CHROMOSOME

     0 1 1 0 0 0 1 1 0 0 0 1 0 0 1 0 0 0 0 0
     _____/ _____/
       expressible         crossover
          string          punctuation
          L = 10            L = 10

MAY BE INTERPRETED AS

     0 1!1 0 0 !0 1 1 0 0
        |       |
        |_____|___ i.e. crossover here
```

Figure 2. The string representation of chromosomes with crossover punctuation marks.

probability of generating a one in the punctuation string is designated P_{so} and is set externally. The influence of this variable was studied empirically.

```
BEFORE CROSSOVER

mom:   a a a a a a a!b b b b b b b
pop:   c c c c!d d d d d!e e e e

AFTER CROSSOVER

kid1:  a a a a d d d b b b e e e e
kid2:  c c c c!a a a!d d!b b b b
```

Figure 3. The action of punctuated crossover.

The mechanics of crossover governed by these punctuation marks is illustrated in figure 3. The bits from each parent string are copied one-by-one to one of the offspring from left to right. When a punctuation mark is encountered in either parent, the bits begin going to the other offspring (a crossover). When this happens, the punctuation marks themselves are also passed on to the offspring, just before the crossover takes effect. Thus we may think of the marks as being linked to the functional bit string to the left of its locus. A little experimentation with pencil and paper should serve to give the reader a sense of the redistribution possibilities of this process. Some parental distributions will result in all the punctuation marks being passed to one of the offspring and none to its sibling, while others will redistribute clumped distributions. When an offspring fails to survive the fitness-based selection step in its generation, its punctuation marks die with it. Thus, the dynamics of the distribution of these marks in the gene pool should reflect an accumulating experience about where is or is not a good place to crossover the genetic material in the pool.

The action of the mutation operator has traditionally been employed as a low level (i.e. small probability) defense against premature convergence of the gene pool. It seems consistent with our metaphor to allow the mutation operator equal access to the entire chromosome, both functional and punctuation parts. A few experiments supported this belief.

3. Empirical Evidence

We selected the task domain of function optimization (minimization) to test the capabilities of this new genetic algorithm and a set of five scalar-valued functions which has been used in the past to test genetic algorithms. These functions provide a range of characteristics of search problems and are summarized in table 1. Recently Grefenstette has found a configuration of the traditional genetic algorithm which performs consistently better on this function set than any previously known. [4]. We will use his results (which we will call BTGA for best traditional genetic algorithm) as a benchmark.

TABLE 1
Functions Comprising the Test Environment

Fcn	Dimensions	Space Size	Description
f1	3	1.0×10^9	parabola
f2	2	1.7×10^6	Rosenbrock's saddle
f3	5	1.0×10^{15}	step function
f4	30	1.0×10^{72}	quadratic with noise
f5	2	1.6×10^{10}	Shekel's foxholes

We adopted Grefenstette's strategy of setting a genetic algorithm to optimize a genetic algorithm (GA) in order to locate a good set of parameter values for our new procedure (a "meta-search"). The meta-level GA was a traditional GA that allowed vector-valued fitness (one dimension for each of the five functions) called VEGA [8]. The parameter set searched at this level included: population size, crossover rate, mutation rate, P_{zo}, and scaling window. The performance measure was online average function value (i.e. an average of all trials in a run of 5000 function evaluations). For more details on these matters the reader is referred to Grefenstette's paper and its predecessors.

Since the performance of BTGA on each of the individual functions was not previously published, we first estimated this by running a BTGA on each one five times (n) with different random seeds. The results are given in table 2.

The results of the Meta-search revealed that the genetic algorithm with punctuated crossover (GAPC) performed well for the whole set of functions at the

TABLE 2
Performance of Best Traditional Genetic Algorithm on Test Functions

Function	mean	s.d.	n	global optimum
f1	1.664	.1900	5	0
f2	25.16	4.497	5	0
f3	-27.78	.2111	5	-30
f4	24.28	1.383	5	0
f5	30.78	2.148	5	≈ 1

following parameter settings: population size = 40, crossover rate = 0.45, mutation rate = 0.002, P_{zo} = 0.04, and scaling window = 3. Estimates of the performance of GAPC comparable to those for BTGA are given in table 3 along with results of two-tailed t-tests of the mean differences between them.

TABLE 3
Performance of Genetic Algorithm with Punctuated Crossover on Test Functions and a comparison with the Best Traditional Genetic Algorithm

Function	mean	s.d.	n	t-test	significance
f1	1.111	.1706	5	4.84	.01
f2	17.22	3.279	5	3.19	.05
f3	-27.90	.5907	5	0.42	ns
f4	20.32	1.320	5	4.63	.01
f5	14.81	1.475	5	13.71	.001

These results clearly show the superiority of GAPC. It statistically outperforms BTGA on four of the five functions and, is no worse on the other (f3). We believe the reason for this latter result lies in a floor effect. Both GAs find good solutions very quickly on f3 so that the online average rapidly approaches the global optimum. There is simply insufficient room for improvement to allow for a statistical difference. We believe the same explanation applies to the finding that no significant differences were noted between BTGA and GAPC when offline average was used as a criterion.

4. Characterization of GAPC Search

There are a number of questions about the realization of the performance characteristics we envisioned when this scheme was designed. Specifically, does the distribution of crossover marks adapt to the task environment in a meaningful way, is the process stable (i.e. does the number of punctuation marks in the population tend to vanish or saturate), and how many crossovers per mating does it settle upon (if it does settle)? In this section we present some evidence related to these questions that was collected while monitoring the searches reported above.

We define the population distribution of punctuation marks at time t as the sum of the punctuation bits at each locus across all the individuals in the population.

$$p_{zo}(l,t) = \sum_{i=1}^{popsize} punct_i(l,t) \qquad (2)$$

The total number of punctuation marks in the population is then

$$T_{zo}(t) = \sum_{l=1}^{L} p_{zo}(l,t) \qquad (3)$$

Figure 4 shows a time history of $p_{zo}(l,t)$ for 200 generations of one search of function f1. The x-axis is chromosome locus and the y-axis is both $p_{zo}(l,t)$ and time (generations). The vertical separation between successive generations is equal to popsize (i.e. the number of individuals in the population) so that, a locus at which every member of the population has a punctuation mark, will appear as a peak which just reaches the baseline of the line above. This figure shows that the initial distribution is flat since the random initialization of the punctuation marks does not favor one locus over any other. As time progresses, however, some loci tend to accumulate more punctuation marks than others. The location of these concentrations changes with time; a peak may appear and remain prominent for some generations only to die out as others emerge. The distribution of punctuation marks does indeed seem to adapt as the gene pool adapts.

Figure 5 shows a plot of $T_{xo}(t)$ for the same run. Also shown are the $\max p_{xo}(l,t)$ and $\min p_{xo}(l,t)$. Although the total seems to be growing with no sign of stabilizing, the population is far from saturated†, the minimum remains zero until the last few generations and the maximum concentration at any one locus never exceeds 30 out of the possible 40 (i.e. popsize).

a) generations 0 – 99

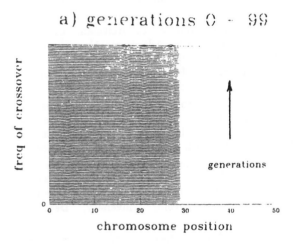

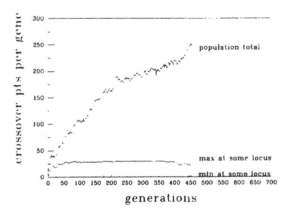

Figure 5. How the numbers of punctuation marks change with time. These data were from one search on f1, and were typical.

Figure 6 shows the average number of crossover events occurring per mating. This simple counting can be misleading, however, since the gene pool is converging as the generations progress. Note that when a crossover event swaps gene segments which are identical, it is an unproductive crossover event. When these events are discounted, we were surprised to see that the number of "productive" crossover events per mating remained nearly constant. What is more, the level at which this statistic holds appears to correlate strongly with L. See table 4. These results are not dissimilar to results reported by DeJong when experimenting with multiple crossover points [2]

b) generations 100 – 199

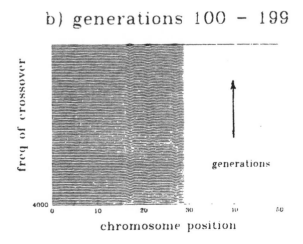

TABLE 4
Time-averaged "Productive" Crossovers per Mating

Function	chromosome length	crossovers
f1	30	1.49
f2	24	0.87
f3	50	2.02
f4	240	8.64
f5	32	1.65

Figure 4. A time history of the distribution of punctuation marks for one run on f1.

† Saturation would mean a punctuation bit at every one of the *popsize* × L (40 × 30 = 1200) possible locations.

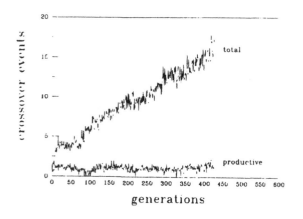

Figure 6. Total and "productive" crossover events per mating for one run on f1.

5. Conclusions

We have described a modified knowledge representation and crossover operator for use with genetic search. Its design was driven by intuition abstracted from Nature's mechanisms of crossover during meiosis. Experiments indicate that it performs as well or better than a traditional GA for a set of test problems, that exhibits a range of search space properties. Experiments on other test problems are continuing.

The distribution of crossover events evolves as the search progresses and the statistics of "productive" crossover events per mating indicate steady search effort even in the face of a converging gene pool. These statistics seem to correlate with chromosome length and are consistent with previous results.

We remain cautiously optimistic that continued experimentation will strengthen these conclusions and will lead to a robust approach to adaptive knowledge representation.

Acknowledgement

We wish to acknowledge the valuable contributions of D. Paul Benjamin to the conception of this project and to discussions of its implications.

References

1. B. Alberts, D. Bray, J. Lewis, M. Raff, K. Roberts and J. D. Watson, *Molecular Biology of the Cell*, Garland Publishing, Inc., New York, 1983.

2. K. A. De Jong, Analysis of the Behavior of a Class of Genetic Adaptive Systems, Ph.D. Thesis, Department of Computer and Communication Sciences, University of Michigan, 1975.

3. K. A. De Jong, Adaptive System Design: A Genetic Approach, *IEEE Transactions on Systems, Man & Cybernetics SMC-10*,9 (September 1980), 566-574.

4. J. J. Grefenstette, Optimization of Control Parameters for Genetic Algorithms, *IEEE Transactions on Systems, Man & Cybernetics SMC-16*,1 (January-February 1986), 122-128.

5. J. H. Holland, *Adaptation in Natural and Artificial Systems*, University of Michigan Press, Ann Arbor, MI, 1975.

6. J. H. Holland and J. S. Reitman, Cognitive Systems Based on Adaptive Algorithms, in *Pattern-Directed Inference Systems*, D. A. Waterman and F. Hayes-Roth (editor), Academic Press, New York, NY, 1978.

7. D. B. Lenat, The Role of Heuristics in Learning by Discovery: Three Case Studies, in *Machine Learning*, R. S. Michalski, J. G. Carbonell and T. M. Mitchell (editor), Tioga, Palo Alto, CA, 1983.

8. J. D. Schaffer, Some Experiments in Machine Learning Using Vector Evaluated Genetic Algorithms, Ph.D. Thesis, Department of Electrical Engineering, Vanderbilt University, December 1984.

9. S. F. Smith, Flexible Learning of Problem Solving Heuristics Through Adaptive Search, *8th International Joint Conference on Artificial Intelligence*, Karlsruhe, Germany, August 1983.

GENETIC ALGORITHMS WITH SHARING FOR MULTIMODAL FUNCTION OPTIMIZATION

David E. Goldberg, The University of Alabama,
Tuscaloosa, AL 35487

and

Jon Richardson, The University of Tennessee
(formerly at The University of Alabama),
Knoxville, TN 37996

ABSTRACT

Many practical search and optimization problems require the investigation of multiple local
optima. In this paper, the method of sharing
functions is developed and investigated to permit
the formation of stable subpopulations of different strings within a genetic algorithm (GA),
thereby permitting the parallel investigation of
many peaks. The theory and implementation of the
method are investigated and two, one-dimensional
test functions are considered. On a test function
with five peaks of equal height, a GA without
sharing loses strings at all but one peak; a GA
with sharing maintains roughly equally sized subpopulations clustered about all five peaks. On a
test function with five peaks of different sizes,
a GA without sharing loses strings at all but the
highest peak; a GA with sharing allocates decreasing numbers of strings to peaks of decreasing value as predicted by theory.

INTRODUCTION

Genetic algorithms (GAs) are finding increasing application in a variety of problems across a
spectrum of disciplines (Goldberg & Thomas, 1986).
This is so, because GAs place a minimum of requirements and restrictions on the user prior to
engaging the search procedure. The user simply
codes the problem as a finite length string, characterizes the objective (or objectives) as a black
box, and turns the GA crank. The genetic algorithm then takes over, seeking near-optima primarily through the combined action of reproduction
and crossover. These so-called simple GAs have
proved useful in many problems despite their lack
of sophisticated machinery and despite their total
lack of knowledge of the problem they are solving.
Yet as their usage has grown, several objections
to their performance have arisen. Simple GAs have
been criticized for sub-par performance on multimodal (multiply-peaked) functions. They have also
been criticized for so-called premature convergence where substantial fixation occurs at most
bit positions before obtaining sufficiently near-
optimal points (Cavicchio, 1970; De Jong, 1975;
Mauldin, 1984; Baker, 1985).

In this paper, we examine the first of these
maladies and propose a cure borrowed from nature.
In particular, our herbal remedy causes the formation of niche-like and species-like subdivision of
the environment and population through the imposition of sharing functions. These sharing functions help mitigate unbridled head-to-head competition between widely disparate points in a search
space. This reduction in competition between distant points thereby permits better performance on
multimodal functions. As a side benefit we find
that sharing helps maintain a more diverse population and more considered (and less premature) convergence. In the remainder of this paper, we review the problem and past efforts to solve it; we
consider the theory of niche and speciation
through Holland's modified two-armed bandit problem, and we compare the performance of a genetic
algorithm both with and without the sharing function feature. Finally we examine extensions of
the sharing function idea to permit its implementation in a wide array of problems.

MULTIMODAL OPTIMIZATION, GENETIC DRIFT, AND A SIMPLE GA

The difficulty posed by a multimodal problem
for a simple genetic algorithm may be illustrated
by a straightforward example. Figure 1 shows a
bimodal function of a single variable: $f(x) = 4(x-0.5)^2$ coded by a normalized, five-bit binary
integer. In this problem, the two optima are lo-
cated at extreme ends of the one-dimensional
space. If we start a genetic algorithm with a
population chosen initially at random and let it
run for a large number of generations, our fondest
hope is that stable subpopulations cluster about
the two optima (about 00000 and 11111). In fact
if we perform this experiment, we find that the
simple GA eventually clusters all of its points
about one peak or the other.

Why does this happen? After all, doesn't the
fundamental theorem of genetic algorithms (Holland, 1975; De Jong, 1975; Goldberg, 1986) tell us
that exponentially increasing numbers of trials
will be given to the observed best schemata? Yes
it does, but the theorem assumes an infinitely
large population size. In a finite size popula-

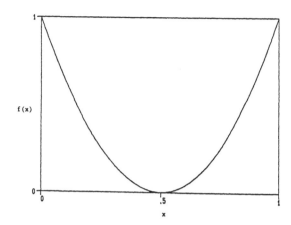

Figure 1. Bimodal function with equal peaks.

tion, even when there is no selective advantage for either of two competing alternatives (as is the case for schemata 11*** and 00*** in the example problem) the population will converge to one alternative or the other in finite time (De Jong, 1975; Goldberg & Segrest, this volume). This problem of finite populations is so important that geneticists have given it a special name, genetic drift. Stochastic errors tend to accumulate, ultimately causing the population to converge to one alternative or another.

The convergence toward one optimum or another is clearly undesirable in the case of peaks of equal value. In multimodal problems where peaks of different altitudes exist, the desirability of convergence to the globally best peak is not so clear cut. In Figure 2 we see a bimodal function with unequal peaks: $f(x) = 2.8(x-0.6)^2$ with a five-bit normalized coding. If we are interested in obtaining only the global optimum, we should not mind the eventual convergence of the population to the leftmost point; however, this convergence is not always guaranteed. Small initial populations may allow sampling errors which overestimate the schemata of the rightmost points thereby permitting convergence to the wrong peak. Furthermore, in real world optimization we are often interested in having information about good, better, and best solutions. When this is so, it might be nice to see a form of convergence that permits stable subpopulations of points to cluster about both peaks according to peak fitness.

In either of these cases, we can argue for more controlled competition and less reckless convergence than is possible when we work with a simple, tripartite (reproduction, crossover, and mutation) genetic algorithm. For these reasons we turn to the theory of niche and speciation to find an appropriate model for naturally regulated competition.

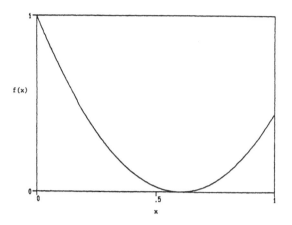

Figure 2. Bimodal function with unequal peaks.

THEORY OF SPECIES AND NICHE

The results of our initial gedankenexperimente (thought experiments) with simple GAs and multimodal functions are somewhat perplexing when juxtaposed with natural example. In our problem with equal peaks, the simple GA converges on one peak or the other even though both peaks are equally useful. By contrast, why doesn't nature converge to a single species? In our second problem with unequal peaks, we notice that the simple GA again converges to one peak, usually--but not always--the "correct" peak. How, when faced with a somewhat less fit species, does nature choose to limit population size before resorting to extinction? In both cases, nature has found a way to combat unbridled competition and permit the formation of stable subpopulations. In nature, different species don't go head to head. Instead they exploit separate niches (sets of environmental features) in which other organisms have little or no interest. In this section, we need to bridge the gap between natural example and genetic algorithm practice through the application of some useful theory.

Although there is a well-developed biological literature in both niche and speciation, its transfer to the arena of GA search has been limited. Like many other concepts and operators, the first theories directly applicable to artificial genetic search are due to Holland (1975). To illustrate niche and species, Holland introduces a modification of the two-armed bandit problem with distributed payoff and sharing. Let's examine his argument with a concrete formulation of the same problem.

Imagine a two-armed bandit as depicted in Figure 3. In the ordinary two-armed bandit problem (Holland, 1975; De Jong, 1975), we have two arms, a left arm and a right arm, and we have different payoffs associated with each arm. Suppose we have an expected payoff associated with the left arm of $25 and an expected payoff associated with the right arm of $75; in the standard two-armed bandit, we are unaware initially which arm pays the higher amount, and our dilemma is to min-

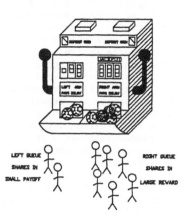

Figure 3. Sketch of the two-armed bandit with queues and sharing.

imize our expected losses over some number of trials. In this form, the two-armed bandit problem puts the tradeoffs between exploration and exploitation in sharp perspective. We can take extra time to experiment, but in so doing risk the possible gain from choosing the right arm, or we can experiment briefly and risk making an error once we choose the arm we think is best. In this way, the two-armed bandit has been used to justify the allocation strategy adopted by the reproductive plans of simple genetic algorithms.

This is not our purpose here. Instead we examine the modified two-armed bandit problem to put the concepts of niche and species in sharper focus. In the modified problem, we further suppose that we have a population of some number of players, say 100 players, and that each player may decide to play one arm or the other. If at this point we do nothing else, we simply create a parallel version of the original two-armed bandit problem where we expect that all players eventually line up behind the observed best (and actual best) arm. To produce the subdivision of species and niche, we introduce an important rule change. Instead of allowing a full measure of payoff for each individual, individuals who choose a particular arm are now forced to <u>share</u> the wealth derived from that arm with other players queued up at the arm. At first glance, this change appears to be quite minor. In fact, this single modification causes a strikingly and surprisingly different outcome in the modified two-armed bandit.

To see why and how the results change, we first recall that despite the different rules of the game, we still allocate population members according to payoff. In the modified game, an individual will receive a payoff which depends on the arm payoff value and the number of individuals queued up at that arm. In our concrete example, an individual lined up behind the right arm when all individuals are lined up behind that same arm receives an amount $75/100 = $0.75. On the other hand, an individual lined up behind the left arm

when all individuals are queued there receives $25/100 = $0.25. In both cases, there is motivation for some individuals to shift lines. In the first case, a single individual changing lines stands to gain an amount $25.00 - $0.75 = $24.25. The motivation to shift lines is even stronger in the second case. At some point in between we should expect there to be no further motivation to shift lines. This will occur when the individual payoffs are identical for both lines. If N is the population size, m_{right} and m_{left} are the number of individuals behind the right and left queues, and f_{right} and f_{left} are the expected payoff values from the right and left arms respectively, the equilibrium point may be calculated as follows:

$$\frac{f_{right}}{m_{right}} = \frac{f_{left}}{m_{left}}$$

In our example, this complete equalization of individual payoff occurs when 75 players select the right arm and 25 players select the left arm, because $75/75 = $25/25 = $1.

This problem may be extended to the k-armed case directly, and the extension does not change the fundamental conclusions at all: the system attains equilibrium when the ratios of arm payoff to queue length are equal (Holland, 1975). The incorporation of forced sharing causes the formation of stable subpopulations (species) behind different arms (niches) in the problem. Furthermore, the number of individuals devoted to each niche is proportional to the expected niche payoff. This is exactly the type of solution we had hoped for when we considered the bimodal problems of Figures 1 and 2. Of course the extension of the sharing concept to real genetic algorithm search is more difficult than the idealized case implies. In a real genetic algorithm there are many, many arms and deciding who should share and how much should be shared becomes a non-trivial question. In the next section we will examine a number of current efforts to induce niche and species through indirect or direct sharing.

A BRIEF REVIEW OF CURRENT SCHEMES

A number of methods have been implemented to induce niche and species in genetic algorithms. In some of these techniques the sharing comes about indirectly. Although the two-armed bandit problem is a nice, simple abstract model of niche and species formation and maintenance, nature is not so direct in divvying up her bounty. In natural settings, sharing comes about through crowding and conflict. When a habitat becomes fairly full of a particular organism, individuals are forced to share available resources.

Cavicchio's (1971) dissertation study was one of the first to attempt to induce niche-like and species-like behavior in genetic algorithm search. Specifically, he introduced a mechanism he called preselection. In this scheme, an offspring replaces the inferior parent if the offspring's fitness exceeds that of the inferior parent. In this way diversity is maintained in the population because strings tended to replace strings similar to themselves (one of their parents). Cavicchio claimed to maintain more diverse populations in a number of simulations with relatively small population sizes (n=20).

De Jong (1975) has generalized preselection in his crowding scheme. In De Jong crowding, individuals replace existing strings according to their similarity with other strings in an overlapping population. Specifically, an individual is compared to each string in a randomly drawn subpopulation of CF (crowding factor) members. The individual with the highest similarity (on the basis of bit-by-bit similarity count) is replaced by the new string. Early in the simulation, this amounts to random selection of replacements because all individuals are likely to be equally dissimilar. As the simulation progresses and more and more individuals in the population are similar to one another (one or more species have gotten a substantial foothold in the population) the replacements of individuals by similar individuals tends to maintain diversity within the population and reserve room for one or more species. De Jong has had success with the crowding scheme on multimodal functions when he used crowding factors CF=2 and CF=3. De Jong's crowding has subsequently been used in a machine learning application (Goldberg, 1983).

Booker (1982) discusses a direct application of the sharing idea in a machine learning application with genetics-based, classifier systems. In classifier systems, a sub-goal reward mechanism called a bucket brigade passes reward through a network of rules like money passing through an economy. Booker suggests that appropriately sized subpopulations of rules can form in such systems if related rules are forced to share payments. This idea is sound and has been forcefully demonstrated in Wilson's recent work with boolean function learning (Wilson, 1986); however, it does not transfer well to function optimization, because unlike classifier systems, there is no general way in function optimization to determine which strings are related.

Shaffer (1984) has used separate, fixed size subpopulations in his study of vector evaluated genetic algorithms (VEGA). In this study, each component of the vector (each criterion or objective measure) is mapped to its own subpopulation where separate reproduction processes are carried out. The method has worked well in a number of trial functions; however, Shaffer has expressed some concern over the procedure's ability to handle middling nondominated individuals--individuals that may be Pareto optimal but are not extremal (or even near extremal) along any single dimension. Furthermore, although the study does use separate subpopulations, it is unclear how the same method might be applied to the more usual single-criterion optimization problem.

A direct exploration of biological niche theory in the context of genetic algorithms is contained in Perry's (1985) dissertation. In this work, Perry defines a genotype-to-phenotype mapping, a multiple-resource environment, and a special entity called an external schema. External schemata are special similarity templates defined by the simulation designer to characterize species membership. Unfortunately, the required intervention of an outside agent limits the practical use of this technique in artificial genetic search. Nonetheless, the reader interested in the connections between biological niche theory and GAs may be interested in this work.

Grosso (1985) also maintains a biological orientation in his study of explicit subpopulation formation and migration operators. Multiplicative, heterotic (problems with diploid structures where a heterozygote is more highly fit than the homozygote) objective functions are used in this study, and as such, the results are not directly applicable to most artificial genetic search; however, Grosso was able to show the advantage of intermediate migration rate values over either isolated subpopulations (no migration) and panmictic (completely mixed) subpopulations. This study suggests that the imposition of a geography within artificial genetic search may be another useful way of assisting the forming diverse subpopulations. Further studies are needed to determine how to do this in more general artificial genetic search applications.

Although he has not directly addressed niche and species, Mauldin (1984) has attempted to better maintain diversity in genetic algorithms through his uniqueness operator. The uniqueness operator arbitrarily returns diversity to a population whenever it is judged to be lacking. To implement uniqueness, Mauldin defines a uniqueness parameter k_u that may decrease with time (similar to the cooling of simulated annealing). He then requires that for insertion in a population, an offspring must be different than every population member at a minimum of k_u loci. If the offspring is not sufficiently different, it is mutated until it is. By itself, uniqueness is little more than a somewhat knowledgeable (albeit expensive) mutation operator. That it is useful in improving offline (convergence) performance is not unexpected. Grefenstette (1986) has recently supported the notion of fairly high mutation probabilities (p_m = 0.01 to 0.1) when convergence to the best is the main goal. It is interesting to note that uniqueness combined with De Jong's crowding scheme worked better than either operator by itself (Mauldin, 1984). This result suggests that maintaining diversity for its own sake is not the issue. Instead, we need to maintain appropriate diversity--diversity that in some way helps cause (or has helped cause) good strings. In the next section, we show how we can maintain appropriate diversity through the use of sharing functions.

SHARING FUNCTIONS

In attempting to induce species, we must either directly or indirectly cause intraspecies sharing, but we are faced with two important questions: who should share, and how much should be shared? In natural systems, these two questions are answered implicitly through conflict for finite resources. Different species find different combinations of environmental factors--different niches--which are relatively uninteresting to other species. Individuals of the same species use those resources until there is conflict. At that point, they vie for the same turf, food, and other environmental resources, and the increased competition and conflict cause individuals of the same species to share with one another, not out of altruism, but because the resources they give up are not worth the cost of the fight. It might be possible to induce similar conflict for resources in genetic optimization. Unfortunately, in many optimization problems, there is no natural definition of a resource. As a result, we must invent some way of imposing niche and speciation on strings based on some measure of their distance from each other. We do just this with what we have called a <u>sharing function</u>.

A sharing function is nothing more than a way of determining the degradation of an individual's payoff due to a neighbor at some distance as measured in some similarity space. Mathematically, we introduce a convenient metric d over our decoded parameters x_i (the decoded parameters are themselves functions of the strings $x_i = x_i(s_i)$):

$$d_{ij} = d(x_i, x_j)$$

Alternatively, we may introduce a metric over the strings directly:

$$d_{ij} = d(s_i, s_j)$$

In this paper, we use a metric defined over the decoded parameters x_i (phenotypic sharing); later on, we briefly consider the use of metrics defined over the strings (genotypic sharing). However we choose a metric, we define a sharing function <u>sh</u> as a function of the metric value sh = sh(d) with the following three properties:

1. $0 \leq sh(d) \leq 1$, for all d

2. $sh(0) = 1$

3. $\lim_{d \to \infty} sh(d) = 0$

Many sharing functions are possible. Power law functions are convenient:

$$sh(d) = 1 - \left(\frac{d}{\sigma_{share}} \right)^{\alpha}, \quad d < \sigma_{share}$$
$$= 0, \quad \text{otherwise}$$

In this equation, σ_{share} and α are constants, and Figure 4 displays power law sharing functions with α values equal to one, greater than one, and less than one.

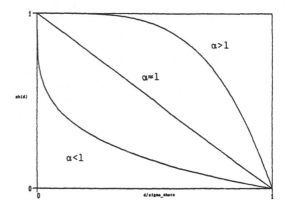

<u>Figure 4</u>. Power law sharing functions sh=sh(d).

Once we have selected a metric and a sharing function, it is a simple matter to determine a string's realized or shared fitness. We define a string's shared fitness f' as its potential fitness divided by its niche count m_i':

$$f_i' = \frac{f_i}{m_i'}$$

The niche count m_i' for a particular string i is taken as the sum of all share function values taken over the entire population:

$$m_i' = \sum_{j=1}^{N} sh(d_{ij}) = \sum_{j=1}^{N} sh(d(x_i, x_j))$$

Note that the sum includes the string itself. Thus, if a string is all by itself in its own niche ($m_i' = 1$), it receives its full potential fitness value. Otherwise the sharing function derates fitness according to the number and closeness of neighboring points.

RESULTS

We evaluate the use of sharing functions through computational experiments on two multi-modal problems. The first function is a periodic function with five peaks of equal magnitude:

$$f_1(x) = \sin^6(5.1\pi x + .5)$$

We compare the performance of a simple genetic algorithm with stochastic remainder selection, crossover, no mutation, and no sharing to the performance of the same GA with sharing. We use a triangular sharing function ($\alpha=1$) with $\sigma_{share} = 0.1$; the metric d is taken as the absolute value of the difference between the string x values. Length 30 binary strings are decoded as unsigned binary integers and normalized by the constant $2^{30}-1$. Genetic algorithm parameters have been held constant across all runs as follows:

Probability of mutation $p_m = 0.0$

Probability of crossover $p_c = 0.8$

Population size = 50

Maximum number of generations = 100

We seek methods that maintain appropriate diversity without introducing arbitrary diversity through mutation or other means. Therefore, we have set the mutation probability to zero to put the sharing function technique to its most stringent test: if appropriate diversity can be maintained without mutation, we should expected similar or better (off-line) performance when mutation is present.

Runs with and without sharing are started from the same population generated uniformly at random. After 50 generations the run without sharing has lost all points at two peaks as shown in Figure 5. By contrast, the run with sharing has stable subpopulations roughly equal in size at all five peaks as shown in Figure 6. Similar graphs at generation 100 are shown in Figures 7 and 8. Note how the run without sharing (Figure 7) has completely converged to a single peak even though there is no selective advantage for any peak. By contrast, the run with sharing remains committed to stable subpopulations clustered about each peak. This latter result is especially remarkable considering that no mutation has been used. With no mutation, once an allele is lost at a particular locus, there is no way to get it back. The existence of stable subpopulations about each peak shows how the sharing function maintains appropriate diversity--the necessary, sometimes competing building blocks--required to exploit all five peaks.

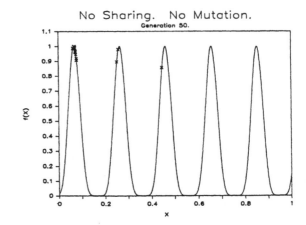

Figure 5. GA without sharing concentrates points at three peaks after 50 generations on function f_1 (equal peaks).

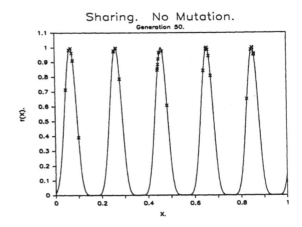

Figure 6. GA with sharing distributes points to all five peaks after 50 generations on function f_1 (equal peaks).

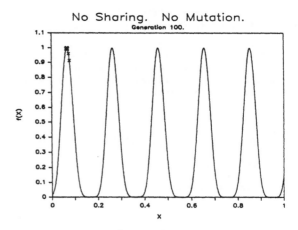

Figure 7. GA without sharing concentrates all points on a single peak after 100 generations on function f_1 (equal peaks).

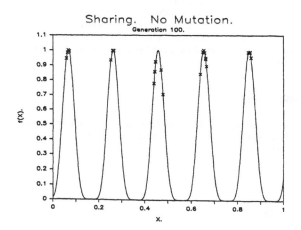

Figure 8. GA with sharing continues to distribute points among all five peaks after 100 generations on function f_1 (equal peaks).

The second test function $f_2(x)$ has five peaks with decreasing peak magnitude as given by the following equation:

$$f_2(x) = f_1(x) \cdot e^{\left[-4\ln2 \frac{(x-0.0667)^2}{0.8^2} \right]}$$

We make comparisons of the two GAs, with and without sharing, using the same parameters and string coding as before. Specifically, we compare the two cases at generation 100. By that time, the genetic algorithm without sharing has allocated all of its trials to the highest peak as shown in Figure 9. By contrast, the GA with sharing forms stable clusters of points about four of the five highest peaks with cluster size roughly proportional to peak fitness as shown in Figure 10. This is the kind of performance we predicted earlier, except for the lack of strings at the lowest peak. To understand why this has occurred we briefly return to the theory of sharing presented earlier.

From our earlier discussion, we expect a stable equilibrium to form when the following equations hold true:

$$\frac{f_i}{m_i'} = \frac{f_{i+1}}{m_{i+1}'}$$

for all niches i, and

$$\sum_{i=1}^{M} m_i' = N$$

where M is the number of niches and N is the population size. It may be shown that this set of equations predicts proportions of niche members as the ratio of niche fitness to the total fitness. On function f_2, we expect a total number of trials to be allocated to the lowest peak as follows:

$$50*0.075/(0.075+0.22+0.5+0.85+1.0) = 1.42$$

In other words, we expect approximately one individual to remain at that peak, and we should not be surprised that no strings cluster there. If we want to maintain a subpopulation at such a low peak, our theory suggests that we need a larger population to overcome the unavoidable errors of stochastic sampling and selection.

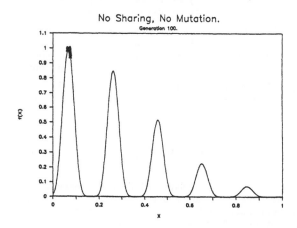

Figure 9. GA without sharing concentrates all points on highest peak (at generation 100) on function f_2 (decreasing peaks).

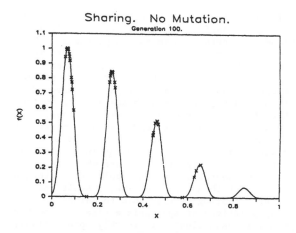

Figure 10. GA with sharing distributes points to all but lowest peak (at generation 100) on function f_2 (decreasing peaks). Lowest peak has expected population size of only one member, not enough to overcome selection and sampling errors.

EXTENSIONS

The method of sharing functions is not limited to one-dimensional problems. Sharing functions may be evaluated using any reasonable metric that includes any number of problem parameters. Additionally, there is no reason to limit the method to phenotypic sharing (where the measures are calculated based on differences in the phenotype--the decoded problem parameters). As an alternative, sharing functions may be evaluated using the genotype (the string) directly. In this form, the Hamming distance (the number of different bits) may be an especially useful metric.

In many cases, there may be no need to perform the sharing calculations as precisely as has been implied by the above equations. With the full formulation, $\binom{N}{2}$ sharing function evaluations are required (N^2 if symmetry is not exploited) to calculate the niche count values m_i exactly. This level of computation may be reduced by taking a random sample of k ($k \ll N$) share function values and extrapolating the mean. If the mean of the k share function evaluations for string i is μ_i and the population is of size N, then the following formula provides a reasonable way to estimate the niche count m_i':

$$m_i' = (N-1)\mu_i + 1$$

Although this approximate niche count method has not been tested, Monte Carlo sampling techniques have been adopted in at least one other GA study with success (Grefenstette & Fitzpatrick, 1985). There is every reason to suspect that cheaper, approximate niche count estimates may be used without excessive performance degradation.

CONCLUSION

In this paper, we have developed a method for improving the performance of genetic algorithms in multimodal function optimization problems. This method uses <u>sharing functions</u> to induce artificial analogs to the natural concepts of niche and species, thereby permitting the formation of stable, non-competing subpopulations of points surrounding important peaks in the search space. The method has been tested on two multimodal functions, one with peaks of equal size and one with peaks of decreasing size. In both cases, the genetic algorithm with sharing is able to maintain stable subpopulations about significant peaks while an identical GA without sharing is unable to maintain points at more than a single peak. Additionally, the GA with sharing is also able to maintain stable subpopulations of appropriate size: the number of points in each cluster is roughly proportional to the peak fitness value. This automatic allocation of resources in a reasonable fashion should not only be transferable to other multimodal optimization problems, it should help in maintaining appropriate diversity in genetic algorithms with-

out resorting to mutation and mutation-like operators that unnecessarily degrade on-line performance. These proof-of-principle results should permit the extension of these methods to other larger and more complex problems of genetic optimization.

ACKNOWLEDGEMENTS

This material is based upon work supported by the National Science Foundation under Grant MSM-8451610.

REFERENCES

Baker, J. E. (1985). Adaptive selection methods for genetic algorithms. In J. J. Grefenstette (Ed.), <u>Proceedings of an International Conference on Genetic Algorithms and Their Applications</u> (pp. 101-111). Pittsburgh: Carnegie-Mellon University.

Booker, L. B. (1982). Intelligent behavior as an adaptation to the task environment. (Doctoral dissertation, Technical Report No. 243. Ann Arbor: University of Michigan, Logic of Computers Group). <u>Dissertations Abstracts International</u>, <u>43</u>(2), 469B. (University Microfilms No. 8214966)

Cavicchio, D. J. (1970). <u>Adaptive search using simulated evolution</u>. Unpublished doctoral dissertation, University of Michigan, Ann Arbor.

De Jong, K. A. (1975). An analysis of the behavior of a class of genetic adaptive systems. (Doctoral dissertation, University of Michigan). <u>Dissertation Abstracts International</u>, <u>36</u>(10), 5140B. (University Microfilms No. 76-9381)

Goldberg, D. E. (1983). Computer-aided gas pipeline operation using genetic algorithms and rule learning (Doctoral dissertation, University of Michigan). <u>Dissertation Abstracts International</u>, <u>44</u>(10), 3174B. (University Microfilms No. 8402282)

Goldberg, D. E. (1986). <u>Simple genetic algorithms and the minimal deceptive problem</u> (TCGA Report No. 86003). Tuscaloosa: University of Alabama, The Clearinghouse for Genetic Algorithms.

Goldberg, D. E., & Thomas, A. L. (1986). <u>Genetic algorithms: A bibliography</u> (TCGA Report No. 86001). Tuscaloosa: University of Alabama, The Clearinghouse for Genetic Algorithms.

Grefenstette, J. J. (1986). Optimization of control parameters for genetic algorithms. <u>IEEE Transactions on Systems, Man, and Cybernetics</u>, <u>SMC-16</u>(1), 122-128.

Grefenstette, J. J., & Fitzpatrick, J. M. (1985). Genetic search with approximate function evaluations. In J. J. Grefenstette (Ed.), _Proceedings of an International Conference on Genetic Algorithms and Their Applications_ (pp. 112-120). Pittsburgh: Carnegie-Mellon University.

Grosso, P. B. (1985). _Computer simulation of genetic adaptation: Parallel subcomponent interaction in a multilocus model._ (Doctoral dissertation, University of Michigan, University Microfilms No. 8520908).

Holland, J. H. (1975). _Adaptation in natural and artificial systems._ Ann Arbor: The University of Michigan Press.

Mauldin, M. L. (1984). Maintaining diversity in genetic search. _Proceedings of the National Conference on Artificial Intelligence,_ 247-250.

Perry, Z. A. (1984). Experimental study of speciation in ecological niche theory using genetic algorithms. (Doctoral dissertation, University of Michigan). _Dissertation Abstracts International, 45_(12), 3870B. (University Microfilms No. 8502912)

Shaffer, J. D. (1984). _Some experiments in machine learning using vector evaluated genetic algorithms._ Unpublished doctoral dissertation, Vanderbilt University, Nashville.

Wilson, S. W. (1986). _Classifier system learning of a boolean function_ (Research Memo RIS-27r). Cambridge: Rowland Institute for Science.

THE ARGOT STRATEGY:
ADAPTIVE REPRESENTATION GENETIC OPTIMIZER TECHNIQUE

Craig G. Shaefer

Rowland Institute for Science, 100 Cambridge Parkway, Cambridge, MA 02142

Abstract

The ARGOT method is a search system that "learns" a strategy appropriate to the problem being solved. It accomplishes this through dynamic adaptation of its internal representation of the current trial solutions, reducing or eliminating the context sensitivity normally associated with this choice of representation. When applied to function optimization problems, ARGOT, in effect, "learns" a method of solution similar to the global homotopy techniques, techniques that utilize the derivative information available in function optimizations but which do not easily become 'stuck' in local extrema as do most 'hill-climbers'. The ARGOT strategy may, moreover, be applied in more general contexts to classes of problems other than function optimizations. For instance, when applied to combinatorial optimizations (*e.g.*, Traveling Salesman Problems which do not contain derivative information and thus usually evade solution by 'hill-climber' methods), ARGOT "learns" a strategy that may be described as a 'divide-and-conquer' method.

Section: 1. Introduction

The ARGOT Method is a search algorithm designed in a manner flexible enough to allow it to learn its own strategies for searching parameter spaces. The ARGOT algorithm employs the standard genetic algorithm as its basis and hence utilizes chromosomes composed of bit strings to represent, in some fashion, the trial parameters of the search space. ARGOT differs from the Standard Genetic Algorithm Optimizer (SGAO) through insertion of an intermediate mapping between the chromosome space and the solution space. It is this mapping that translates the chromosomes into their proper trial parameters, and instead of this mapping being a fixed one, it dynamically changes based upon internal measurements over the chromosome population. In effect, the translation mapping generalizes and stores information about the current trial solutions determined through the normal hyperplane analysis being carried out by the usual crossover, mutation, and selection operators of the SGAO. One view of the SGAO is as a Darwinian evolution scheme where random mutations occur with selection of the fittest for further reproduction and mating. From this viewpoint, the SGAO would not be called a learning algorithm but rather an evolutionary one. ARGOT, on the other hand, not only employs this Darwinian evolution of the chromosome population, but also utilizes information from the current trial solutions to modify the translation mapping between the chromosomes and the parameter space.

This transfer of information from the parameter space into the intermediate mapping is Lamarkian in nature and thus provides the mechanism by which ARGOT can generalize from its trial solutions and thereby 'learn' a strategy for solving a particular problem. By a 'learned strategy', we mean that the translation mapping displays behaviors and properties during the solution phase of a problem that mimics the behaviors and properties observed during the solution phase of some other known algorithm. When ARGOT behaves in a particular fashion, we would say that it has learned a particular strategy. It is important to note that ARGOT has not imposed a particular search strategy upon the search process, as is typical for most algorithms, but rather the translation mapping has learned its own strategy. A demonstration of this capability is that, in practice, ARGOT 'discovers' differing strategies when it is applied to different problems.

ARGOT's ability to adapt its internal representation provides it with certain advantages over other algorithms as well as alleviates some of the disadvantages inherent in the SGAO. In particular, the problem of premature or rapid convergence is usually a serious one for genetic algorithms.[1] The chromosome population of ARGOT, however, never undergoes convergence. Even after the solution has been determined, the chromosome population is still 'fresh' and continues searching for further refinements to the estimated solution. In addition, the "Hamming cliff" problem[2] that arises when using a binary coding scheme for the chromosomes is eliminated by ARGOT.[3] In fact, ARGOT works equally well whether employing the typical binary code or a Gray code for the chromosomes.[4] ARGOT also alleviates a large part of the sensitivity of the SGAO upon the particular values choosen for its internal variables. This insensitivity will be illustrated by the extended range of mutation rates available to ARGOT. We discuss these advantages in subsequent sections.

The next section provides a brief description of the ARGOT strategy[5] while the final section provides test results from the ARGOT program.[6]

Section: 2. Adaptive Representation Genetic Optimizer Technique

The ARGOT strategy consists of a substructure, roughly equivalent to the SGAO, that employs crossover, mutation, and selection to perform the standard, implicitly parallel, hyperplane analysis, plus numerous triggered operators which modify the intermediate mapping that translates the chromosomes into the trial parameters.

These triggered operators are controlled through three types of internal measurements performed upon the chromosome population or the population of trial solutions. Population measurements are employed by numerous other algorithms, and here we list just a few examples. The clustering optimization algorithms employ statistical measurements over the past trial solutions in order to direct future trials.[7] Specific heat measurements have been suggested to control the annealing schedule[8a] of Simulated Annealing techniques and the step sizes.[8b] For genetic algorithms, Baker uses a 'super-individual' criterion for switching between different selection operators in an attempt to alleviate premature convergence of the gene pool,[1] and Wilson's usage of the thermodynamic entropy of a classifier system to appropriately switch off the crossover operator as the trial estimates near the actual solution.[9]

The three types of population measurements calculated by ARGOT are: (i) convergence measurements (e.g., the uniformity of the chromosomes at a particular locus) on the chromosomes, (ii) positioning measurements (relative average position of the current trials to their roving boundaries) of the trial parameters, and (iii) variance measurements (e.g., the 'breadth' of the trial parameter distributions relative to the roving boundaries) of the trials across the current parameter search space. These measurements are made for each gene of the chromosome and employed to triggered a given operator when appropriate for a specific gene. The triggered operators include ones that alter the resolution of a gene (number of bits used to represent a parameter) and ones that shift, expand, and contract the intermediate mapping between chromosomes and parameters.

In order to describe this mapping, we first introduce "roving" boundaries that limits the trials of a parameter in the function optimization problem to the interval between the two roving boundaries. As the name implies, the roving boundaries allow the range for the trial parameters to move, contract, and expand in ways that ultimately lead to restricting the ARGOT algorithm to search regions near the true solutions. That is, instead of the optimizer continually exploring a fixed parameter domain, that domain, in effect, "climbs the hill" as the population converges towards the true parameter values. These roving boundaries thus eliminate the possibility that the nearest trial parameter is not equal to one of the true parameter values, since shifting the boundary could always bring the trial parameter values closer to the true value. In addition, as the chromosome population begins to converge for a given parameter, that parameter's domain can then be contracted, thus restricting the search to smaller and smaller neighborhoods of the true parameter values. In addition to the roving boundaries, each parameter also has a set of "brick wall" boundaries defining an interval within which the roving boundaries must always remain. These 'brick wall' boundaries provide a method for applying inequality constraints upon the parameter

values of problem.

There are four primary classes of triggered operators employed to implement the intermediate mapping of these roving boundaries. Later, we will add other classes of triggered operators to the ARGOT strategy, but for now we consider only those operators which directly modify the roving search domains: Contraction/-Expansion, Increase/Decrease Resolution, Shift Right/-Left, and Dithering.

Let us give a synopsis of the strategies that are employed by ARGOT and reasons explaining their use. In what follows, we will limit our discussion to a single parameter in a function optimization problem, but the same reasoning applies to all parameters. If the chromosome population for that parameter has converged, i.e., the bit representations across the population of chromosomes for that gene are almost identical, then it is assumed that the hyperplane analysis has correctly evaluated the parameter and since there are no further bits (hyperplanes) to be found, the resolution for that parameter is increased (more bits are added to that parameter's gene) in order that ARGOT may perform a finer search of the parameter space. If the chromosomes are not uniform for a gene, i.e., highly random bit representations, then it is assumed that the hyperplanes are not being efficiently evaluated and thus the resolution is decreased. That is, the number of bits along the chromosome dedicated to that particular parameter is reduced thus leading to a coarser set of trial parameters. This in effect "clumps" the previous finer resolution into a coarser set of trials $,\{p_{ji}\}$, and thus raises the convergence measure (increases uniformity) for that parameter. As the convergence increases above a defined threshold, the resolution is increased. The second component of the strategy entails determining where the current trial parameter value is located relative to the current roving boundaries. As the trial parameter value approaches one of the roving boundaries, then the parameter range is shifted in an attempt to better center the trial parameter. This is a means for the roving parameter boundaries to follow the trial parameter value as it moves to its true value. In addition, if the convergence measure of the parameter is an intermediate range, it is assumed that the genetic operators are still evaluating the hyperplanes and thus the resolution is not altered but rather both of the roving boundaries are dithered (shifted by random small increments). This is an attempt to randomly shift the trial parameter values so that one may come in coincidence with, or at least come closer to, the true parameter value and thus allow the chromosome population to converge on that value. The third component entails determining whether the trial parameters are sharply or widely distributed within the current roving boundaries. If the distribution is sharp, then the roving boundary interval is contracted in size thereby following the argument that the chromosome population, after translation, is concentrating its efforts in a smaller domain that the current roving domain, hence the roving domain should be contracted. Similarly, if the trials are broadly distributed, then the chromosomes have not narrowly concentrated their search efforts and thus the roving domain should be expanded in size. Therefore, as the current chromosome population begins to converge on a given trial parameter value, the resolution of the search is increased as well as the search domain being contracted, thus allowing the ARGOT operators to "hill climb" to the true parameter value by increasing the resolution of the search and narrowing the neighborhood over which the search is being done. ARGOT's policy thus insures that better trial parameters will not be missed at the same time it is zeroing in on the solutions at ever increasing accuracies.

Besides these primary operators that modify the chromosome to parameter space mapping, there are several secondary operators which increase the efficiency of searching the parameter space. These include a Metropolis mutation operator that accepts a bit mutation based upon the change in payoff to the chromosome after mutation. If the payoff decreases (gets better in our convention) the mutation is always accepted, but if the payoff increases then it is sometime accepted and sometimes rejected. The probability of acceptance is forms Boltzmann weighted distribution over the increase in payoff. In addition to this Metropolis sampling operator, ARGOT also includes two Annealing Schedule operators that, when triggered by population measurements, are able to implement an automatic annealing schedule. Hence, if the chromosomes are reaching an 'equilibrium state' then the metropolis temperature is lowered, otherwise when the chromosomes are in a nonequilibrium state it is assumed that one should be searching more of the sample space and hence the temperature in raised.

A homotopy (local search) operator is also switched on whenever the chromosome population has largely converged to a particular trial value. The reasoning is that after convergence the best trial solution is most likely within the "basin of attraction" of the global solution and hence a local search technique will quickly proceed towards it.

These secondary operators are not necessary for ARGOT to find solutions, but they sometimes speed the rate of discovery and learning. The secondary operators also allow for comparisons between alternate algorithms, such as Simulated Annealing, and the ARGOT method.

Section: 3. Test Problems and Results

We have applied the ARGOT strategy to a series of both function optimization and combinatorial optimization problems. Seven of these test cases are from a previously defined set of global optimization problems.[10] Having been designed specifically to compare the accuracy and efficiency of various algorithms these artificial problems are easier to solve than most optimizations stemming from practical problems. There

are two primary reasons for the relative ease with which these problems may be solved: (i) they are Lipschitzian in character, and (ii) they have large "basins of attraction" surrounding their global minima. Being Lipschitzian, one can easily calculate the number of samples, either probabilistic or deterministic that are needed to assure that a global minimum will not escape between the trial points. This ability to calculate the sample size is of primary importance to probabilistic algorithms as well as any algorithm that endeavors to mesh the search space. Unfortunately, practical optimizations arising in modelling problems are usually not Lipschitzian. Thus probabilistic and meshing routines have difficulties solving the non-Lipschitzian optimizations stemming from model fitting problems. The second characteristic, (ii), relates to local homotopy, or quasi-Newton, techniques. These local deterministic techniques divide the search space into basins of attraction. If the initial trial solution lies within a specific basin then the local technique will ultimately find the minimum contained within that particular basin. This minimum may be either a local minimum or the global minimum. Consequently, if the global minima have relatively large basins of attraction when compared with the local minima then the local homotopy techniques have a correspondingly large probability of finding the global minima over the local minima. For these seven test problems the smallest basin of attraction surrounding a global minimum was 20% of the hypervolume of the entire search space. For this particular case, then 20% of randomly chosen initial trials followed by a local homotopy technique would lead to the determination of the global optimum. Again, this is uncharacteristic of most practical optimization problems for which the basin of attraction surrounding the global minimum is typically a very small fraction of the sizes of the basins of attraction surrounding local minima. ARGOT easily located all of the global minima for these seven test problems. Because of the simplicity of these artificial problems along with the relative ease with which ARGOT found their global solutions, we next chose to apply ARGOT to two additional and more difficult problems from functional optimization which stem from fitting a mathematical problem to a physical situation. The first of these entails solution to a system of nine nonlinear simultaneous equations based upon a model of transistor behavior.[11] In contrast to the Price CRS algorithm which required five user interventions to find what appears to be a local minimum for this problem, the ARGOT system located a global minimum after calculating only one-tenth the number of function evaluations and *without* user intervention. Although the sizes of the basin of attraction for the global minima of this problem are unknown, probabilistic samples indicate that they are considerably less than one percent of the search space hypervolume.

To better illustrate the power of the ARGOT strategy for difficult problems we chose a second problem, called the A_1 problem, stemming from the fitting of a model to experimental data and employing the Directed

Trees Method. We chose this problem for several reasons. Although trajectory minimization methods employ function gradient information, there seems to be no known method which makes efficient use of all function and/or gradient evaluations performed during each line minimization. The Directed Trees Method, however, implements a strategy designed to utilize all of this information. This is accomplished by incorporating evaluation and gradient information into a global model of the function being optimized. The second reason for choosing the A_1 is that it is a difficult one, being both non-Lipschitzian as well as having two degenerate global minima with very small "basins of attractions" relative to the total search space. In addition, the very nature of the solution of the A_1 problem makes this a difficult test case for many algorithms. In particular, the solution consists of two bimodal and two unimodal parameters. The two bimodal parameters produce doubly degenerate global minima with symmetric basins and therefore one would hope that an unbiased algorithm would be able to locate both of these minima with equal likelihood. In addition, the functional dependencies upon these four parameters differ widely. As mentioned earlier, the A_1 is non-Lipschitzian, which means that there are no bounds on the derivatives of the function with respect to some of these parameters. A consequence of this is that the basins of the global minima make up a very small fraction of the total search space. Also, the Jacobian matrix over these four parameters is near singular, and thus elementary Newton-like methods fail for algorithmic reasons. Hence we studied the A_1 problem with a global homotopy method that does not fail for singular Jacobians and found that in less than one percent of randomly chosen starting points, this method was capable of locating a global minimum. Even though global homotopy methods are designed not to fail for singular Jacobians, these techniques still employ gradient information and provides an explanation for their failure on the A_1 problem. The reason stems from the fact that one of the unimodal parameters has a very broad functional dependency. The partial derivatives with respect to this parameter are thus extremely small which leads to large elements in the inverse of the Jacobian. These large elements are translated by the global homotopy techniques into very large steps being taken along the calculated trajectories resulting in divergence. We also studied this problem by probabilistic methods including random search (Monte Carlo) and the Simulated Annealing methods. The second unimodal parameter has an extremely sharp functional dependency which results in the basins of attraction for the global minima being very small relative to the basins for the local minima. Consequently, probabilistic methods as well as composite methods have a difficult time locating the global minima for this problem. The non-Lipschitzian nature of this problem also leads to the unusual property that the more data points one employs in the least-squares fit, the more difficult it is to locate the global minima. We will return to the specific cases comparing the Monte Carlo, Simulated Annealing, SGAO, and ARGOT methods to this problem but first let us briefly describe the general framework available within the ARGOT strategy.

Since the ARGOT system allows any of the operators to be switched on or off, then other algorithms may be implemented within ARGOT. For instance, switching off all operators excepting mutation and increasing the mutation rate to 0.5 implements a Monte Carlo (MC) search strategy. If only a single chromosome is employed with the Metropolis mutation operator, then a Simulated Annealing (SA) approached is obtained. Composite strategies are also available. For example, with 200 chromosomes and Metropolis mutation, population measurements may be employed to automate the annealing schedule *via* the temperature lowering and raising operators. Of course, all ARGOT operators may be switched off leaving crossover, mutation, and selection of the SGAO. The important point of the general framework of the ARGOT system is that all of these alternate strategies are searching identical chromosome spaces and hence may be compared not only qualitatively but also quantitatively.[12]

The A_1 problem is derived from fitting a model function to a set of data points employing least squares differences between the data and their predicted values. In particular, the following equation provides the payoff function for the A_1 problem: $\sum_{i=1}^{k} \{ x_{13}^2 a_i^4 + 2 x_6 x_{13} a_i^3 + (x_6^2 + 2 x_5 x_{13}) a_i^2 + 2 x_5 x_6 a_i + x_5^2 + x_{10} - a_i^2 - a_i - 1 \}$, where k is the number of data points.

We studied multiply cases employing a range of input data points, the a_i. These included samples of from 50 to 200 data points on various intervals ranging from -10 to 10. Both uniformly distributed samples over these intervals as well as randomly chooses points were tested. To some test cases white noise was added to the data. In all of the tests ARGOT found the global solutions of this problem, which consist of the two degenerate minima: $(x_5, x_6, x_{10}, x_{13}) = (1/2, 1, 3/4, 0)$ and $(-1/2, -1, 3/4, 0)$. Comparisons of ARGOT with MC, SA, and SGAO were performed with 150 uniformly distributed data points without any added noise. Thus, at the true global minima, the payoff function has a value of 0. (With noise added to the data, the payoff is positive.) Each parameter was restricted to the interval $[-25, 25]$ and tests were halted at 3000 generations, unless the global minima were discovered earlier.

These comparison studies yielded three general regimes of resolution for which qualitatively different solutions are found by MC, SA, and SGAO. The first regime consists of resolutions for the parameters which are too small, roughly all resolutions below 12 bits per parameter. In this regime, the trial parameters are too coarse, allowing the true solutions to 'slip' in between the trials. In this regime only local minima were obtained by each of the standard algorithms. The second regime is one of medium resolutions, from 12 to 15 bits per pa-

53

rameter, for which the SGAO was able to locate global minima on a few of the tests, but these global minima were shifted from their true positions because the trials were too coarse. See the 12 bit entries in Table 2. In this regime MC only located local minima while the SA algorithm found a shifted global minimum on one occasion. The third regime consists of the high resolutions, from 16 to 20 bits per parameter, where the trials are now very finely spaced and hence the global minima do not 'slip between the cracks'. But in this regime none of the standard algorithms found the global minima but rather they became 'stuck' in local minima. Presumably this is due to the vast size of the search space at these higher resolutions. In effect, the SGAO can not effectively search such large spaces to locate the global minima before premature convergence of the chromosome population occurs. Table 1 lists the sizes of the search spaces, $S(\Re^4)$, for a few of the resolutions, l_j, considered in these tests. Since a single generation of each of the algorithms samples equivalent numbers of points in this space, the $\%/t$ column gives the percentage of the space searched in every generation. The $Payoff_0$ column lists the payoff that corresponds to the trial solution which lies closest to one of the true global minima. From this column note that at a resolution of 4 bits per parameter, the payoff for the "nearest" trial is quite large (the global minima 'slip' between the trials) which results in only local minima being found. At a resolution of 20 bits, however, the "nearest" payoff is quite small and consequently a very good estimate of the true solutions are theoretically possible, but now the percent of the search space sampled per generation is so small that the global minima are missed and again only local minima are found. Table 2 provides the theoretical and the best solutions found by the various techniques at various resolutions. The last row of this table lists one of the solutions located by the ARGOT method. The resolution, l_j, is not given for ARGOT since ARGOT alters the parameters resolutions dynamically and independent of each other during a solution. Over the course of the ARGOT solution, however, the average resolution per parameter was approximately 4 bits.

The lower resolution employed by ARGOT during its solution leads to an increase in search efficiency over the SGAO. This is because low resolution means that the order, or length, of the hyperplanes needed to solve the problem is lower for ARGOT than for the SGAO. This results in an additional advantage for ARGOT. Since mutation typically limits the order of the hyperplanes that the SGAO can develop (mutation disrupts long hyperplanes), the SGAO fails for large mutation rates (typical rates are less than 0.001). ARGOT, on the other hand, does not require high-order hyperplanes to solve a problem and therefore can tolerate a much larger mutation rate without failing (up to 0.05). The low resolution and high mutation rate act symbiotically to greatly enhance the search efficiency of ARGOT. This occurs because the lower resolutions per parameter means the size of search space is much smaller and

consequently the higher allowed mutation rates actually provide a means of effectively sampling this small search space. This is in contrast with the SGAO which simply uses mutation as an 'insurance policy' against allele loss since the lower allowed mutation rates cannot efficiently sample the much larger search spaces.

The figures at the end of this paper provide graphs of the roving boundaries and best population estimates of the parameters for the A_1 problem as a function of generation number. Note for this case the initial roving boundaries were all set to $[4.95, 5]$. These intervals do not even include the global solutions to the problem, but the ARGOT method is still capable of adjusting the roving boundaries to find the true parameters. When a modified Newton-Raphson with Marquardt parameter method was applied to the A_1 problem starting with the same 200 initial points as the ARGOT method, not one of the 200 runs succeeded in finding a global minimum. Most ended by diverging and a few runs succeeded in halting at local minima. Note that the ARGOT 'best' estimates for the x_5 and x_6 parameters 'jumps' between the two global minima before it settles onto one of them. This behavior is typical for multimodal parameters and gives a clear indication of mulimodality. Also, note that the 'broad' x_{10} parameter has correspondingly large roving boundaries while the 'sharp' x_{13} parameter has very narrow roving boundaries. In effect, ARGOT learned a strategy of solution similar to global homotopy methods.

When ARGOT was employed to solve the Traveling Salesman Problem (TSP)[13] for 10 to 50 cities, the strategy found by ARGOT was to initially make rearrangements of large clusters of cities and then gradually reduce the 'size' of the clusters ultimately concluding with making just local rearrangements of the tour path. This strategy is a 'divide-and-conquer' one.

Section: 4. Acknowledgements

We would like to express our appreciation to Kenneth De Jong for supplying Pascal code for a standard genetic algorithm optimizer. We also thank Stewart Wilson for numerous very insightful discussions concerning genetic algorithms.

Section: 5. References

[1] Baker, J.E. in "Proceedings of an International Conference on Genetic Algorithms and their Applications"; Carnegie-Mellon University, July 24, 1985.

[2] Bethke, A.D. "Genetic algorithms as function optimizers"; Ph.D. Thesis; University of Michigan. 1980.

[3] A simple argument employing the resolution operators illustrates how ARGOT avoids the "Hamming cliff". Shaefer, C.G. "The Context Insensitivity of the ARGOT Method". Rowland Institute Report: RIS 42r; May, 1987.

[4] A Gray code, while removing the "Hamming cliff" problem, causes the hyperplane analysis to become inefficient and thus is not used with the SGAO. ARGOT, though, does not suffer from this disadvantage stemming from the Gray code.

[5] For further information, see Shaefer, C.G. "The ARGOT Strategy"; Rowland Institute Report: RIS 40r; May, 1987.

[6] A detailed account of the operators and population measurements of ARGOT is provided in Shaefer, C.G. "The ARGOT Program"; Rowland Institute Report: RIS 42r; May, 1987.

[7] Price, W.L. "A controlled random search procedure for global optimization" in "Towards Global Optimisation 2"; Dixon, L.C.W. and Szegö, G.P. (eds.); North-Holland, Amsterdam, **1978**; p 71.

[8a] Kirkpatrick, S.; Gelatt, C.D.; Vecchi, M.P. *Science* **1983**, *220*, 671.

[8b] Vanderbilt, D. and Louie, S.G. *J. Comput. Phys.* **1984**, *56*, 259.

[9] Wilson, S.W. "Classifier System Learning of a Boolean Function"; Rowland Institute Report: RIS 27r; February, 1986.

[10] Dixon, L.C.W. and Szegö, G.P. "The global optimization problem: An introduction." In "Towards Global Optimisation 2"; Dixon, L.C.W. and Szegö, G.P. (eds.); North-Holland, Amsterdam, **1978**; p 1.

[11] Price, W.L. "A controlled random search procedure for global optimization" in "Towards Global Optimisation 2"; Dixon, L.C.W. and Szegö, G.P. (eds.); North-Holland, Amsterdam, **1978**; p 71.

[12] Shaefer, C.G. "General Framework of the ARGOT System"; Rowland Institute Report: RIS 41r; May, 1987.

[13] We employed an extension of Stephen Smith's (Thinking Machines Corporation, Cambridge, MA) tour representation for the ARGOT TSP tests. (private communication)

Tables and Figures

Search Spaces at Different Resolutions			
l_j	$S(\Re^4)$	$\%/t$	$Payoff_0$
4	2^{16}	$10^{-0.5}$	3.05×10^5
5	2^{20}	$10^{-1.7}$	6.97×10^4
9	2^{36}	$10^{-6.5}$	1.42×10^3
14	2^{56}	$10^{-12.6}$	4.15×10^1
20	2^{80}	$10^{-19.8}$	1.34×10^0

Table 1 l_j = Number of bits per parameter (resolution); $S(\Re^4)$ = Number of points in search space; $\%/t$ = Percent of solution space searched per generation; $Payoff_0$ = Theoretical payoff for the 'nearest' trial solution

Comparisons of Solutions at Different Resolutions					
l_j	x_5	x_6	x_{10}	x_{13}	$Payoff$
12$\star$	0.49449	0.99511	0.75091	0.60997×10^{-2}	160.3725
12†	0.32356	0.99511	0.92185	0.60997×10^{-2}	116.7395
14‡‡‡	0.551	0.813	12.12	0.46×10^{-1}	1073.4
20$\star$	0.49999	1.00000	0.74999	-0.22888×10^{-4}	1.3384
20†	-4.68133	-0.66591×10^{-1}	-19.71969	-0.70215×10^{-1}	264.298
20‡‡	1.551	-0.080	-4.129	-0.678×10^{-1}	1432.4
$\mathcal{A}$	0.5000001	1.0000000	0.7499999	-0.23817×10^{-5}	0.00914

Table 2 $\star$ = Theoretical 'nearest' trial solution; † = SGAO; ‡ = MC, ‡‡ = 10^7 points, ‡‡‡ = Best MC; $\mathcal{A}$ = ARGOT, on average, uses $l_j \approx 4$

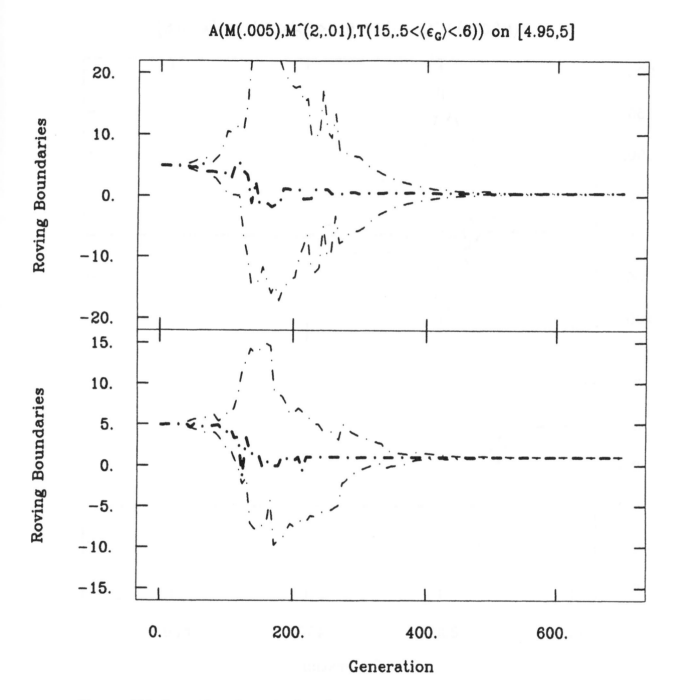

Figure 1 This figure plots the roving boundaries and best estimates for the two bimodal parameters of the A_1 Problem: $x_5 = \{-.5, .5\}$ (upper) and $x_6 = \{-1, 1\}$ (lower). Note that the best estimates of the parameters, the **bold** lines, undergo early 'switching' between the two possible global solutions.

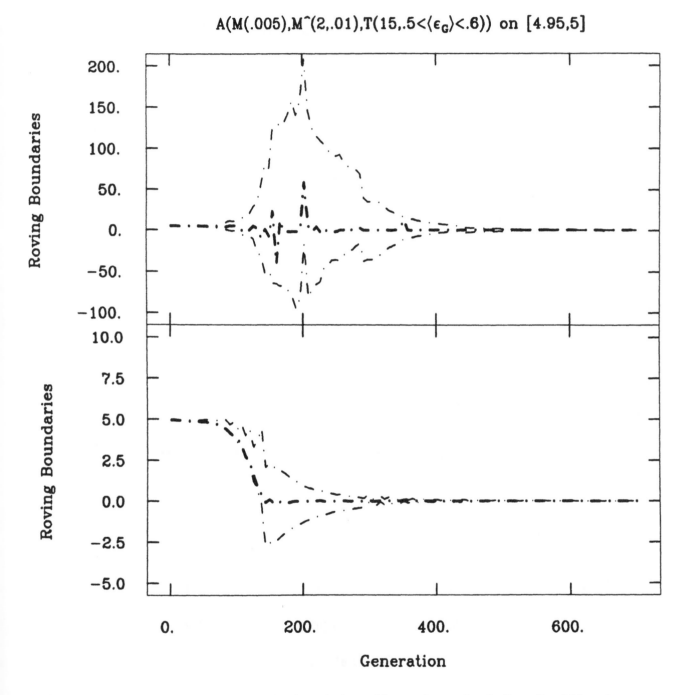

A(M(.005),M^(2,.01),T(15,.5<⟨ε_G⟩<.6)) on [4.95,5]

Figure 2 This figure plots the roving boundaries and best estimates for the 'broad' and 'sharp' parameters of the A_1 Problem: $x_{10} = .75$ (upper) and $x_{13} = 0$ (lower). Note the differing scales of the two graphs and how the broad parameter has very large roving boundaries while the sharp parameter has extremely narrow roving boundaries.

NONSTATIONARY FUNCTION OPTIMIZATION USING GENETIC ALGORITHMS WITH DOMINANCE AND DIPLOIDY

David E. Goldberg and Robert E. Smith

Department of Engineering Mechanics
The University of Alabama
Tuscaloosa, AL 35487

ABSTRACT

This paper investigates the use of diploid representations and dominance operators in genetic algorithms (GAs) to improve performance in environments that vary with time. The mechanics of diploidy and dominance in natural genetics are briefly discussed, and the usage of these structures and operators in other GA investigations is reviewed. An extension of the schema theorem is developed which illustrates the ability of diploid GAs with dominance to hold alternative alleles in abeyance. Both haploid and diploid GAs are applied to a simple time varying problem: an oscillating, blind knapsack problem. Simulation results show that a diploid GA with an evolving dominance map adapts more quickly to the sudden changes in this problem environment than either a haploid GA or a diploid GA with a fixed dominance map. These proof-of-principle results indicate that diploidy and dominance can be used to induce a form of long term distributed memory within a population of structures.

INTRODUCTION

Real world problems are seldom independent of time. If you don't like the weather, wait five minutes and it will change. If this week gasoline costs $1.30 a gallon, next week it may cost $0.89 a gallon or perhaps $2.53 a gallon. In these and many more complex ways, real world environments are both nonstationary and noisy. Searching for good solutions or good behavior under such conditions is a difficult task; yet, despite the perpetual change and uncertainty, all is not lost. History does repeat itself, and what goes around does come around. The horrors of Malthusian extrapolation rarely come to pass, and solutions that worked well yesterday are at least somewhat likely to be useful when circumstances are somewhat similar tomorrow or the day after. The temporal regularity implied in these observations places a premium on search augmented by selective memory. In other words, a system which does not learn the lessons of its history is doomed to repeat its mistakes.

In this paper, we investigate the behavior of a genetic algorithm augmented by structures and operators capable of exploiting the regularity and repeatability of many nonstationary environments.

Specifically, we apply genetic algorithms that include diploid genotypes and dominance operators to a simple nonstationary problem in function optimization: an oscillating, blind knapsack problem. In doing this, we find that diploidy and dominance induce a form of long term distributed memory that stores and occasionally remembers good partial solutions that were once desirable. This memory permits faster adaptation to drastic environmental shifts than is possible without the added structures and operators.

In the remainder of this paper, we explore the mechanism, theory, and implementation of dominance and diploidy in artificial genetic search. We start by examining the role of diploidy and dominance in natural genetics, and we briefly review examples of their usage in genetic algorithm circles. We extend the schema theorem to analyze the effect of these structures and mechanisms. We present results from computational experiments on a 17-object, oscillating, blind 0-1 knapsack problem. Simulations with adaptive dominance maps and diploidy are able to adapt more quickly to sudden environmental shifts than either a haploid genetic algorithm or a diploid genetic algorithm with fixed dominance map. These results are encouraging and suggest the investigation of dominance and diploidy in other GA applications in search and machine learning.

THE MECHANICS OF NATURAL DOMINANCE AND DIPLOIDY

It is surprising to some genetic algorithm newcomers that the most commonly used GA is modeled after the mechanics of haploid genetics. After all, don't most elementary genetics textbooks start off with a discussion of Mendel's pea plants and some mention of diploidy and dominance? The reason for this disparity between genetic algorithm practice and genetics textbook coverage is due to the success achieved by early GA investigators (Hollstien, 1971; De Jong, 1975) using haploid chromosome models on stationary problems. It was found that surprising efficacy and efficiency could be obtained using single stranded (haploid) chromosomes under the action of reproduction and crossover. As a result, later investigators of artificial genetic search have tended to ignore diploidy and dominance. In this section we examine the mechanics of diploidy and dominance to understand their roles in shielding alternate solutions from excessive selection.

Most studies of genetic algorithms to date have considered only the simplest genotype found in nature, the haploid or single-stranded chromosome. In this simple model, a single-stranded string contains all the information relevant to the problem we are considering. While nature contains many haploid organisms, most of these tend to be relatively uncomplicated life forms. It seems that when nature wanted to build more complex plant and animal life it had to rely on a more complex underlying chromosomal structure, the diploid or double-stranded chromosome. In the diploid form, a genotype carries a pair of chromosomes (called homologous chromosomes), each containing information for the same functions. At first, this redundancy seems unnecessary and confusing. After all, why keep around pairs of genes which decode to the same function? Furthermore, when the pair of genes decode to different function values, how does nature decide which allele to pay attention to? To answer these questions, let's consider a diploid chromosomal structure where we use different letters to represent different alleles (different gene function values):

AbCDe
aBCde

At each position (locus) we have used the capital form or the lower case form of a particular letter to represent alternative alleles at that position. In nature, each allele might represent a different phenotypic characteristic (or have some nonlinear or epistatic effect on one or more phenotypic characteristics). For example, the B allele might be the brown-eyed gene and the b allele might be the blue-eyed gene. Although this scheme of thinking is not much different from the haploid (single-stranded) case, one difference is clear. Because we now have a pair of genes describing each function, something must decide which of the two values to choose because, for example, the phenotype cannot have both brown and blue eyes at the same time (unless we consider, as nature sometimes does, the possibility of intermediate forms, but we shall not concern ourselves with that possibility here).

The primary mechanism for eliminating this conflict of redundancy is through an operator which geneticists have called <u>dominance</u>. At a particular locus, it has been observed that one allele (the dominant allele) takes precedence (dominates) over the other alternative alleles (the recessives) at that locus. More specifically, an allele is dominant if it is <u>expressed</u> (it shows up in the phenotype) when paired with some other allele. In our example above, if we assume that all capital letters are dominant alleles and all lower case letters are recessive, the phenotype expressed by the example chromosome pair may be written:

AbCDe ----> ABCDe
aBCde

At each locus we see that the dominant gene is always expressed and that the recessive gene is only expressed when it shows up in the company of another recessive. In the geneticist's parlance we say that the dominant gene is expressed when heterozygous (mixed, Aa --> A) or homozygous (pure, CC --> C) and the recessive allele is expressed only when homozygous (ee --> e).

The mechanics of diploidy and dominance seem relatively clear. On a more abstract level, we can think of dominance as a genotype-to-phenotype mapping. Yet, if we continue to ponder the nature and action of diploidy and dominance, they are really quite bizarre. Why does nature double the amount of information carried within the genotype and then turn around and cut by half the quantity of information it uses? On the surface this seems wasteful and unnecessarily tedious. Yet, nature is no spendthrift, nor is she given to whimsy or caprice. There must be good reason for the added redundancy of the diploid genotype and for the reduction mapping of the dominance operator.

Actually, diploidy and dominance have long been the object of genetic study, and numerous theories and explanations of their role have been put forth. The theories which make the most sense in the context of artificial genetic search hypothesize that diploidy provides a mechanism for remembering alleles and allele combinations which were previously useful and that dominance provides an operator to shield those remembered alleles from harmful selection in a currently hostile environment. In a natural context, we can understand the need for both a distributed long term memory and a means of protecting that memory against rapid destruction. Over the course of the evolution of life on Earth, the planet has undergone many changes in environmental conditions. From hot to cold and back to moderate temperatures, from dark to light to somewhere in between, there have been dramatic and rapid shifts in environmental conditions. The most effective organisms have been those able to adapt most rapidly to the changing conditions. Animals and plants with diploid or polyploid structure have been those most capable of surviving, because their genetic constitution did not easily forget the lessons learned prior to previous environmental shifts. The redundant memory of diploidy permits multiple solutions (to the same "problem") to be carried along with only one particular solution expressed. In this way, old lessons are not lost forever, and dominance and dominance change permit the old lessons to be remembered and tested occasionally.

An often cited example of the long term memory induced by diploidy and dominance can be found in the shifts in population balance of the peppered moth in Great Britain during the industrial revolution. The wild form (and originally the dominant form) of this lepitopteran had white wings with small black specks. Prior to the Industrial Revolution, this coloration was effective camouflage against birds and other beasts of prey in the moth's natural habitat, lichen-covered trees. In the middle of the nineteenth century, black forms were caught in the neighborhood of industrial towns. Careful experiments by Kettlewell (Berry, 1972) showed that the speckled version was advantageous in the pristine setting, while the melanic (dark) form was advantageous in the industrial environment where pollution had killed off the lichen covering the tree trunks. It turned out that the melanic forms were controlled by a single dominant gene, implying that a shift in dominance occurred. When the industrial revolution shifted the balance of power toward the darkened form, the darkened form became dominant and the speckled form was held in abeyance. Note that the melanic form was not a new invention; this was no case of fortuitous mutation magically concocting the needed form. Instead, the black form had been invented earlier, perhaps in response to forests where lichen was naturally suppressed. When the by-products of industry caused the lichen to disappear, the melanic form was sampled more frequently and then evolved to the dominant form. With this alternate solution held in the background, the peppered moth was easily able to adapt rapidly to the selective pressures of its changing environment.

In this example we see how diploidy and dominance permit alternate solutions to be held in abeyance--shielded against over selection. We also see how dominance is no absolute state of affairs. Biologists have hypothesized and proven that dominance itself evolves. In other words, the dominance or lack of dominance of a particular allele is itself under genic control. Fisher (1958) theorized that dominance at a particular position (locus) along a chromosome is actually determined by another modifier gene at another locus. This implies that dominance is an evolving feature of the organism, subject to the same search procedures as any other feature. If a particular allele is favored by selection, it will spread more rapidly if it is dominant. A modifier gene therefore enhances the spread of the gene being modified. This in turn enhances the spread of the modifier. If the two genes are closely linked, this positive feedback quickly propagates both the favored allele and the modifier in the population.

But what sets the dominance of the modifier gene? In order to avoid infinite regress, we recognize that a gene can have more than one effect on the phenotype. In fact, an allele can have several major effects on the phenotype while it affects the dominance at one or more other loci. The presence of such multiple effects is known as pleiotropy. We will use a simple form of pleiotropic modifiers (one with the modifier always attached to the gene it modifies) in experiments with a diploid GA representation suggested by Hollstien (1971) and Holland (1975).

In the next section, we examine the diploidy-dominance schemes used in artificial genetic search to see how they incorporate diploid structure, dominance, and the evolution of dominance.

DIPLOIDY AND DOMINANCE IN GENETIC ALGORITHMS, AN HISTORICAL PERSPECTIVE

Some of the earliest examples of practical genetic algorithm application contained diploid genotypes and dominance mechanisms. In Bagley's early (1967) dissertation, a diploid chromosome pair mapped to a particular phenotype using a variable dominance map coded as part of the chromosome itself (Bagley, 1967, p. 136):

Each active locus contains, besides the information which identifies the parameter to which it is associated and the particular parameter value, a dominance value. At each locus the algorithm simply selects the allele having the highest dominance value. Unlike the biological case where partial dominance may be permissible (resulting, for example, in speckled eyes), our interpretation demands that only one of the alleles of the homologous loci be chosen. The decision process in the case of ties (equal dominance values) involves position effects and is somewhat complicated so that it will be necessary to outline the process in some detail.

The introduction of a dominance value for each gene allowed this scheme to adapt with succeeding generations. Unfortunately, Bagley found that the dominance values tended to fixate quite early in simulations thereby leaving dominance determination in the hands of his somewhat complicated and arbitrary tie-breaking scheme. To make matters worse, Bagley prohibited his mutation operator from operating on his dominance values, thereby further aggravating this premature convergence of dominance values. Additionally, Bagley did not compare haploid and diploid schemes, and in all of his cases the environment was held stationary. In the end, the convergence of dominance values at all positions led to an arbitrary random choice dominance mechanism and inconclusive results.

Rosenberg's (1967) biologically-oriented study contained a diploid chromosome model; however, since biochemical interactions were modeled in detail, dominance was not considered as a separate effect. Instead, any dominance effect in this study was the result of the presence or absence of a particular enzyme. The presence or absence of an enzyme could inhibit or facilitate a biochemical reaction, thus controlling some phenotypic outcome.

Hollstien's study (1971) included diploidy and an evolving dominance mechanism. In fact Hollstien described two simple, evolving dominance mechanisms and then put the simplest to use in his study of function optimization. In the first scheme, each binary gene was described by two genes, a modifier gene and a functional gene. The functional gene took on the normal 0 or 1 values and was decoded to some parameter in the normal manner. The modifier gene took on values of M or m. In this scheme 0 alleles were dominant when there was at least one M allele present at one of the homologous modifier loci. This resulted in a dominance expression map as displayed in Figure 1.

	OM	Om	1M	1m
OM	0	0	0	0
Om	0	0	0	1
1M	0	0	1	1
1m	0	1	1	1

Figure 1. Two-locus evolving dominance map from Hollstien (1971).

Hollstien recognized that this two-locus evolving dominance scheme could be replaced by a simpler one-locus scheme by introducing a third allele at each locus. In this triallelic scheme, Hollstien drew alleles from the 3-alphabet $\{0, 1, 2\}$. Here the 2 played the role of a dominant "1" and the 1 played the role of recessive "1." The dominance expression map he used is displayed in Figure 2.

	1	0	1_0
1	1	1	1
0	1	0	0
1_0	1	0	1

Figure 2. Single-locus, triallelic dominance map from Hollstien (1971) and Holland (1975).

The action of this mapping may be summarized by saying that both 2 and 1 map to "1", but 2 dominates 0 and 0 dominates 1. Holland (1975) later discussed and analyzed the steady state performance of the same triallelic scheme, although he introduced the clearer symbology $\{0, 1_0, 1\}$ for Hollstien's $\{0, 1, 2\}$.

The Hollstien-Holland triallelic scheme is the simplest practical scheme suggested for evolving dominance and diploidy in artificial genetic search. With this scheme, the more effective allele becomes dominant, thereby shielding the recessive. Minimum excess storage is required (half a bit extra per locus) and furthermore, dominance shift can easily be handled as a mutation-like operator, mapping a 2 to a 1 (a 1 to a 1_0 using Holland's notation) and vice versa. Despite the clarity of the scheme, Hollstien's results with this mechanism were mixed. Although his Breed Type III simulations maintained better population diversity (as measured by population variance) than did his haploid simulations, there was no significant overall improvement of either average or ultimate performance. This seems surprising until we recognize that his test bed only contained stationary functions. If the role of dominance-diploidy is shielding or abeyance, we should only expect significant performance differences between haploid and diploid genetic algorithms when the environment changes with time.

Brindle (1981) performed experiments with a number of dominance schemes in a function optimization setting. Unfortunately, their has been some question as to the validity of this study's test functions and codings (K. A. De Jong & L. B. Booker, personal communication, 1986). Furthermore the study ignored previous work in artificial dominance and diploidy, and a number of schemes developed were without basis in theory and without biological precedent.

Specifically, Brindle considered a total of 6 schemes:

1. random, fixed, global dominance
2. variable, global dominance
3. deterministic, variable, global dominance
4. choose a random chromosome
5. dominance-of-the-better chromosome
6. haploid-controls-diploid individual dominance

The second and third schemes make local dominance decisions based on global population knowledge. The use of global information is questionable since the primary beauty of both natural and artificial genetic search is their global performance through local action. Once global operators are inserted, this attractive feature is destroyed. This is no small matter if we are ultimately concerned with efficient implementation of these methods on parallel computer architectures.

Of the remaining schemes, only the the sixth scheme suggested by Brindle uses an adaptive dominance map like those in Hollstien's (1971) and Bagley's (1967) earlier work; however, this scheme completely separates the dominance map (the modifying genes) from the normal chromosome (the functional genes) as an added haploid chromosome.

This separation effectively destroys linkage between the dominance map and the functional genes.

In addition to the problems with the dominance schemes and test functions, Brindle's work, like studies before, considered only stationary functions. This is a common thread running through all previous genetic algorithm studies of dominance and diploidy. If dominance and diploidy do act to shield currently out-of-favor solutions from excessive selection, use of these operators in static environments is unlikely to show any performance gain when compared to a haploid GA. In the next section, we further buttress the case for dominance and diploidy as abeyance--long term memory--mechanisms through an analysis of schema propagation under these operators.

THEORY OF DOMINANCE AND DIPLOIDY

Before analyzing the specific effects of dominance and diploidy, we briefly review the notion of schemata and the fundamental theorem of genetic algorithms. The cornerstone of all genetic algorithm theory is the realization that GAs process schemata (schema-singular, schemata-plural) or similarity templates. Suppose we have a finite length binary string, and suppose we wish to describe a particular similarity. For example, consider the two strings A and B as follows:

$$A = 1 \ 0 \ 1 \ 1 \ 1$$
$$B = 1 \ 1 \ 1 \ 0 \ 0$$

We notice that the two strings both have 1's in the first and third position. A natural shorthand to describe such similarities introduces a wild card or don't care symbol, the star *, in all positions where we are disinterested in the particular bit value. For example, the similarity in the first position can be described as follows:

$$1 \ * \ * \ * \ *$$

Likewise, the similarity in the third position may be described with the shorthand notation

$$* \ * \ 1 \ * \ *$$

and the combined similarity may be described with *'s in all positions but the first and third:

$$1 \ * \ 1 \ * \ *$$

Of course, these schemata or similarity templates do not only name the strings A and B. The schema 1**** describes a subset containing $2^4 = 16$ strings, each with a one in the first position. The more specific schema 1*1** describes a subset

of $2^3 = 8$ strings, each with ones in both the first and third position.

We notice that not all schemata are created equal. Some are more specific than others. We call the specificity of a schema H (the number of fixed positions) its order, o(H). For example, o(1****) = 1 and o(1*1**) = 2. Some schemata have defining positions spaced farther apart than others. We call the distance between a schema's outermost defining positions its defining length, δ(H). For example, the defining length of any one-bit schema is zero:

$$\delta(1****) = \delta(**1**) = 0.$$

On the other hand, the defining length of our order-two schema example may be calculated by subtracting the position indices of the outermost defining positions:

$$\delta(1*1**) = 3-1 = 2.$$

These properties are useful in the fundamental theorem of genetic algorithms, otherwise known as the schema theorem. Under fitness proportionate reproduction, simple crossover, and mutation, the expected number of copies m of a schema H is bounded by the following expression:

$$m(H, t+1) \geq m(H,t) \cdot \frac{f(H)}{\bar{f}} \left[1 - p_c \cdot \frac{\delta(H)}{\ell-1} - p_m \cdot o(H) \right]$$

In this expression, the factors p_m and p_c are the mutation and crossover probabilities respectively, and the factor f(H) is the schema average fitness which may be calculated by the following expression:

$$f(H) = \frac{\sum_{s_i \in H} f(s_i)}{m(H,t)}$$

The schema average fitness f(H) is simply the average of the fitness values of all strings s which currently represent the schema H. Overall, the schema theorem says that above average, short, low-order schemata are given exponentially increasing numbers of trials in successive generations. Holland (1975) has shown that this is a near-optimal strategy when the allocation process is viewed as a set of parallel overlapping, multi-armed bandit problems. We will not review this matter in detail here. Instead, we need to look at how dominance and diploidy modify expected schema propagation.

To see the effect of dominance and diploidy on schema propagation, we recognize that the schema theorem still applies: however it is useful to separate the physical schema H from its expression H_e(H). Of course the expression of a schema is a function of the schema, its range of mates, and the dominance map in use. Recognizing all this, we may rewrite the schema theorem in somewhat clearer form:

$$m(H,t+1) \geq m(H,t)\frac{f(H_e(H))}{\bar{f}}\left[1 - p_c\frac{\delta(H)}{\ell-1} - o(H)\ p_m\right]$$

Everything remains the same, except the average fitness of the schema H, f(H), is replaced by the average fitness of the expressed schema $H_e(H)$, $f(H_e(H))$. In the case of a fully dominant schema H, the average fitness of the physical schema always equals the expected average fitness of the expressed schema $H_e(H)$:

$$f(H) = f(H_e(H))$$

In the case of a dominated schema H, the hope is that the average fitness of the expressed schema is greater than or equal to the average fitness of the physical schema:

$$f(H_e(H)) \geq f(H)$$

This situation is most likely to occur when the dominance map itself is permitted to evolve. If the average fitness of the allele as expressed is greater than its fitness when homozygous, then the currently deleterious, dominated schema will not be selected out of the population as rapidly as in the corresponding haploid situation. This is how dominance and diploidy shield currently out-of-favor schemata.

To make this argument more quantitative, let's consider a simple case where only two alternative, competing schemata may be expressed, one dominant and the other recessive. Physically, we can think of this as representing either two alternate alleles at a particular locus, or two multi-locus schemata that have come to dominate a particular set of loci. In either case, we assume that the dominant alternative is expressed whether heterozygous or homozygous, and we assume that the recessive alternative is expressed only when homozygous. Rearrangement of the schema growth equation permits us to calculate the proportion of recessive alleles, P_r^t, in successive generations, t. If we assume that there are only two alternatives and the dominant form has a constant expected fitness value of f_d and the recessive form when expressed has a constant expected fitness value of f_r, the proportion of recessives expected in the next generation may be calculated as follows:

$$P_r^{t+1} = P_r^t\ K\left[\frac{P_r^t + r(1-P_r^t)}{(P_r^t)^2 + r[1-(P_r^t)^2]}\right]$$

where $r = f_d/f_r$, and K = crossover-mutation loss constant.

A similar equation may be derived for the haploid case where the deleterious alternative (we will still call this recessive even though it no longer recesses) is always expressed when present in a haploid structure:

$$P_r^{t+1} = P_r^t\ \frac{K}{P_r^t + r(1-P_r^t)}$$

Proportion ratio (P_r^{t+1}/P_r^t) and proportion versus time graphs are plotted for haploid and diploid cases in Figures 3 and 4. From Figure 3 we note that for a comparable proportion of alleles, the haploid case always destroys more recessives (always has a smaller proportion ratio) than the corresponding diploid case. Of course, this does not imply that the diploid case has a low on-line performance measure. In fact, the sampling rate remains low (proportional to P^2) for the poor (recessive) alleles in the diploid case.

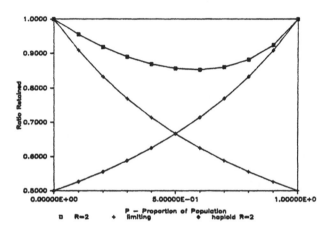

Figure 3. Expected ratio of recessives proportion P_r^{t+1}/P_r^t versus P_r^t, for haploid (r = 2), diploid (r = 2), and limiting diploid (r = ∞).

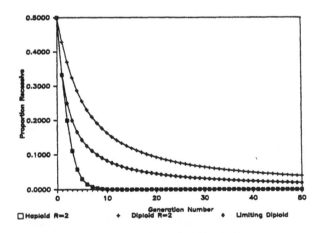

Figure 4. Proportion of recessives alleles P_r^t versus generation t for haploid (r = 2), diploid (r = 2), and limiting diploid (r = ∞).

The previous analysis clearly demonstrates the long term memory induced by diploidy and dominance. Because of this effect we also expect that mutation should play even less of a role in the operation of a diploid genetic algorithm. Holland (1975) has presented an analysis of the steady state mutation requirements of diploid structures as compared to haploid structures. We reproduce his arguments to understand the ergodic performance of these mechanisms.

For a haploid structure under selection and mutation it may be shown that the proportion of recessive alleles in the next generation P_r^{t+1} is related to the proportion in the current generation, P_r^t by the following equation:

$$P_r^{t+1} = (1-\epsilon)P_r^t + p_m(1-P_r^t) - p_mP_r^t$$

Here we have the sum of three terms, the proportion due to selection, the source of alleles from mutation and the loss of alleles from mutation. The ϵ factor is the proportion lost due to selection and other operator losses. At steady state,

$$P_r^{t+1} = P_r^t = P_{ss}.$$

Solving for p_m, we obtain the following equation:

$$p_m = \frac{\epsilon P_{ss}}{1 - 2P_{ss}}$$

This equation suggests that the final steady state proportion of alleles is directly proportional to the mutation rate (with large ϵ and small P_{ss}).

For a diploid structure under selection and mutation it may be shown that the proportion of recessive alleles in the next generation is related to the number in the current generation by the following equation:

$$P_r^{t+1} = (1-2\epsilon P_r^t)P_r^t + 2p_m(1-2P_r^t)$$

At steady state we obtain a relationship between the required mutation rate and the steady proportion of recessive alleles:

$$p_m = \epsilon P_{ss}^2/(1-2P_{ss})$$

For small steady state proportions of recessive alleles, $P_{ss} \ll 1$, this equation suggests that the mutation rate required to keep a certain proportion of recessive alleles around is proportional to the square of the proportion. Of course, the presence of the same proportion of alleles in the diploidy case does not mean that they will be sampled as frequently. Although the same proportion is present, they are sampled as the square of their proportion. This underlines the need for occasional dominance changes so stored alleles may be sampled in the current context.

EXPERIMENTAL RESULTS

To investigate the behavior of a genetic algorithm with dominance and diploidy, we compare three schemes: a simple haploid GA, a diploid GA with a fixed dominance map (1 dominates 0) and a diploid GA with an evolving dominance map (Hollstien-Holland triallelic scheme). We apply all three GAs to a 17-object, blind, nonstationary 0-1 knapsack problem where the weight constraint is varied in time as a periodic step function.

The 0-1 knapsack problem is an NP-complete problem of operations research where we maximize the total value of a subset of objects (selected from a set of N possible objects) that we place in a knapsack subject to some maximum load or weight constraint. More mathematically, we associate a value v_i and a weight w_i with the ith object. The problem may then be stated as follows:

$$\max \sum_{i=1}^{N} v_i x_i$$

subject to the weight constraint

$$\sum_{i=1}^{N} w_i x_i \leq W.$$

Here the x_i variables take on the values 1 or 0 as the object is in or out of the sack respectively, and W is the maximum permissible weight.

Table 1

17-Object 0-1 Knapsack Problem Parameters

Object Number i	Object Value v_i	Object Weight w_i
1	2	12
2	3	5
3	9	20
4	2	1
5	4	5
6	4	3
7	2	10
8	7	6
9	8	8
10	10	7
11	3	4
12	6	12
13	5	3
14	5	3
15	7	20
16	8	1
17	6	2
Total:	91	122

We have adopted weights and values from the literature (Gillett, 1976) as shown in Table 1, but we have made the problem more difficult along two dimensions. First, as with most GAs, the problem is presented to the GA blindly. In other words, the algorithm has no knowledge of the problem structure or problem parameters. It is forced to exploit high performance similarities in the problem coding. Second, since we are primarily interested in observing the long term memory induced by dominance and diploidy, we have introduced a nonstationarity in our problem to test this capability. In particular we cause the weight constraint to vary as a step function between two values: 80% and 50% of the total object weight. The weight is shifted between the two values at 15 generation intervals (a total period of 30 generations).

We code the problem as we did in an earlier set of haploid-only experiments (Goldberg & Smith, 1986). The 17 x_i values are concatenated position by position to form a 17-bit string. In the diploid cases a second homologous string is carried along, and in the triallelic case three different alleles (1, 1_0, 0) are permitted at each locus within each homologous string. The constraint inequality is adjoined to the problem with an external penalty method where weight violations are squared and multiplied by a penalty coefficient, $C_{penalty} = 20$. Negative fitness values that result from the application of the penalty function are set to zero.

Optimal solutions to the problem at both weight constraints have been calculated using standard methods. In the 80% constraint case, the optimal sack value is 87 and the optimal string is 01111101111111111 (low object number to high object number from left to right). In the 50% constraint case, the optimal sack value is 71 and the optimal string is 01101101111111011.

All three GAs have been coded in Pascal and executed on IBM PCs. The details of the haploid GA are similar to those covered elsewhere. In the diploid GAs, we need to discuss one important implementation detail: the appropriate place to perform crossover. In nature, crossover occurs during the pachytene stage of the first prophase during meiosis. For GAs the important point to keep in mind is that the cross occurs (if it does) between the homologous chromosomes of a mature individual. This detail has been overlooked by some genetic algorithmists; however, it is important, because the cross within a viable individual is a less risky affair than a cross of chromosomes from random individuals (the usual haploid GA cross). There is always the possibility that when stripped of its current context (the new genome's homologous complement) that a few recessive alleles will be expressed with possible negative results; however, the new chromosome (regardless of a cross) did at least make it to adulthood in some context. In a way we may think of this as a safe cross.

As a benchmark we examine the performance of a simple haploid GA on the oscillating knapsack problem. We select GA parameters as follows:

crossover probability $p_c = 0.75$,

mutation probability $p_m = 0.001$,

and population size N = 150.

These parameters are held constant throughout all simulations (both haploid and diploid), and stochastic remainder selection (Booker, 1982) is used throughout.

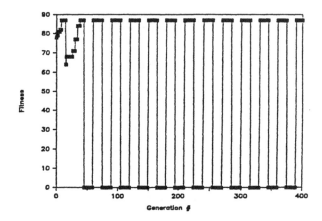

Figure 5. Haploid GA best-of-generation results.

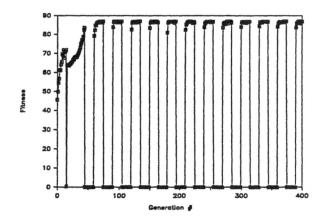

Figure 6. Haploid GA generation average results.

Figure 5 shows the best-of-generation results with the haploid GA. Starting from a randomly generated population, the haploid GA quickly decides on the solution with the higher fitness value (the 80% weight constraint case), and thereafter each oscillation to the other problem (50% constraint) causes a crash to infeasible, low fitness solutions. This same set of circumstances is reflected in the generation average results as shown in Figure 6. These results are not unexpected as earlier experiments with haploid GAs in nonstationary problems (Pettit & Swigger, 1983) also were unable to track changing environmental conditions.

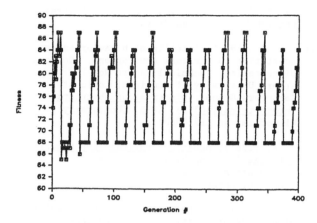

Figure 7. Diploid GA with fixed dominance map (1-dominates-0) best-of-generation results.

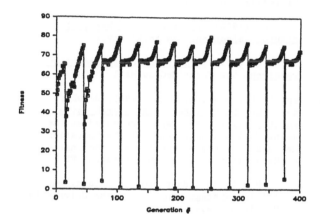

Figure 8. Diploid GA with fixed dominance map (1-dominates-0) generation average results.

observations underscore the need for evolving dominance maps.

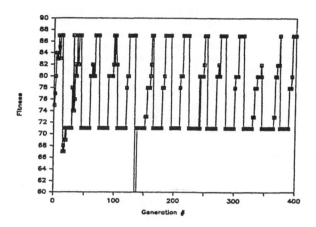

Figure 9. Diploid GA with evolving dominance map (triallelic scheme) best-of-generation results.

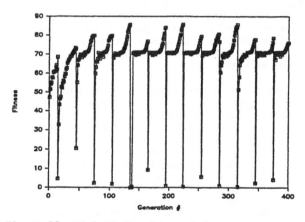

Figure 10. Diploid GA with evolving dominance map (triallelic scheme) generation average results.

We perform a diploid experiment with a fixed dominance map (where 1 dominates 0 at all loci). In Figure 7 (best-of-generation results) we see that the existence of diploidy and dominance enables better switching capability under the same sudden shifts than was obtained in the haploid run. Similar improvement is noted in the generation average results (Figure 8). It is important to note that once the algorithm has searched under the influence of both weight constraint values, it instantly recovers a near optimal lower valued solution when the next shift occurs; however, repeated searching must be performed to attempt to find a higher valued solution. Also, the lower-valued (50% constraint) optima is never discovered. These inadequacies are a direct consequence of the problem representation coupled with the fixed dominance map. A knapsack with a higher weight constraint requires more objects to be put in the optimal bag (with more 1's in the string). As the simple 1-dominates-0 map can only hold 0's in abeyance, the GA is able to hold only light knapsack building blocks in abeyance. Therefore, the GA cannot memorize the higher-valued (80% constraint) solution. This disruption also retards overall performance of the algorithm. These

In the third and final experiment, we execute the triallelic diploid GA. Figures 9 and 10 show best-of-generation and generation average results respectively. The triallelic scheme with an evolving dominance map demonstrates better tracking of time-varying optima than either the haploid or fixed dominance schemes: the algorithm is able to discover and retain both optima. Despite the fact that the higher-valued solution is periodically unacceptable (overweight), the population retains the information necessary to quickly rediscover this solution in the majority of the problem cycles. Other important features of the triallelic diploid GA's performance occur at generation 135, and in the last 3 sets of cycles near the end of the run. At first glance these points seem to show drastic performance failures, but further inspection shows desirable memory-like activity at work. At generation 135, the algorithm has completely converged on the higher-valued (80% constraint) optima, and the population fitness collapses after the weight constraint shifts; in the following generation, the alleles necessary to construct the lower-valued optima are brought out of abeyance (through expression in their homozygous form), and the algorithm recovers the optimal solution for the 50% weight constraint case. Near the end of the run, the GA does not find the higher-valued optima for two consecutive cycles; after rediscovering this optima in generation 375, however, the solution is quickly recalled in the following cycle. These are important demonstrations of the triallelic diploid GA's ability to recover solutions from its past

CONCLUSIONS

We have examined the use of diploidy, dominance, and evolving dominance maps in genetic algorithm search. We have found these mechanisms to be an effective means of inducing a form of long term distributed memory within a population of structures.

Specifically, we have examined the theory and implementation of these mechanisms. The schema theorem has been extended to distinguish between a physical schema and its expression. The theory suggests that evolving dominance permits currently deleterious alleles to become recessive thereby providing an extra element of shielding against excessive selection.

Computational experiments have shown the superiority of diploidy over haploidy in a nonstationary knapsack problem. A 17-object, 0-1 knapsack problem with an oscillating weight constraint has been optimized using three GAs: haploid, diploid with a fixed dominance map, and diploid with an evolving dominance map. Both diploid schemes were better able to satisfy the switching requirements of the nonstationary environment than was the haploid scheme. The diploid scheme with the evolving dominance map was better able to quickly serve both optima as the environment changed than was the diploid scheme with the fixed map. These proof-of-principle results demonstrate the effectiveness of diploidy, dominance, and evolving dominance maps as a means of achieving faster response to severe environmental nonstationarities.

ACKNOWLEDGEMENTS

This material is based upon work supported by the National Science Foundation under Grant MSM-8451610. The second author gratefully acknowledges assistantship support from the Rochester Products Division of General Motors.

REFERENCES

Bagley, J. D. (1967). The behavior of adaptive systems which employ genetic and correlation algorithms. (Doctoral dissertation, University of Michigan). Dissertation Abstracts International, 28(12), 5106B. (University Microfilms No. 68-7556)

Berry, R. J. (1972). Genetics (2nd ed.). Liverpool: English Universities Press.

Booker, L. B. (1982). Intelligent behavior as an adaptation to the task environment. (Doctoral Dissertation, Technical Report No. 243. Ann Arbor: University of Michigan, Logic of Computers Group). Dissertation Abstracts International, 43(2), 469B. (University Microfilms No. 8214966)

Brindle, A. (1981). Genetic algorithms for function optimization. Unpublished doctoral dissertation, University of Alberta, Edmonton, Canada.

De Jong, K. A. (1975). An analysis of the behavior of a class of genetic adaptive systems. (Doctoral dissertation, University of Michigan). Dissertation Abstracts International, 36(10), 5140B. (University Microfilms No. 76-9381)

Fisher, R. A. (1958). The genetical theory of natural selection. New York: Dover.

Gillett, B. E. (1976). Introduction to operations research. New York: McGraw-Hill.

Goldberg, D. E., & Smith, R. E. (1986, October). AI meets OR: Blind inferential search using genetic algorithms. Paper presented at the Joint National Conference of the Operations Research Society of America and The Institute of Management Sciences, Miami Beach, FL.

Holland, J. H. (1975). Adaptation in natural and artificial systems. Ann Arbor: The University of Michigan Press.

Hollstien, R. B. (1971). Artificial genetic adaptation in computer control systems. (Doctoral dissertation, University of Michigan). Dissertation Abstracts International, 32(3), 1510B. (University Microfilms No. 71-23, 773)

Pettit, E., & Swigger, K. M. (1983). An analysis of genetic-based pattern tracking and cognitive-based component tracking models of adaptation. Proceedings of the National Conference on Artificial Intelligence, 327-332.

Rosenberg, R. S. (1967). Simulation of genetic populations with biochemical properties. (Doctoral dissertation, University of Michigan). Dissertation Abstracts International, 28(7), 2732B. (University Microfilms No. 67-17,836)

Syslo, M. M., Deo, N., & Kowalik, J. S. (1983). Discrete optimization algorithms with Pascal programs. Englewood Cliffs, NJ: Prentice-Hall.

GENETIC OPERATORS
FOR HIGH-LEVEL KNOWLEDGE REPRESENTATIONS

H. J. Antonisse
K. S. Keller

The MITRE Corporation, McLean, VA
April, 1987

ABSTRACT

The genetic algorithm has been demonstrated as an effective learning and discovery technique for a large class of problems. Despite its promise, however, the algorithm has not found wide acceptance among members of the artificial intelligence community at large. Our contention is that this is due to the representations used in genetic algorithm research. These representations are extremely simple, while much of the progress in artificial intelligence has been supported by highly expressive, relatively complex representations. In this paper we discuss the the adaptation of the genetic operators to a representation that captures the salient features of the description and processing of knowledge typical of high-level knowledge representation systems.

1. Introduction

Learning is any process by which a system improves its performance through modification of its behavior.[1] The capacity for learning is a key element of intelligent behavior in living organisms, yet one that is almost totally absent in present intelligent artifacts such as computer programs. However, as we attempt to build increasingly sophisticated problem-solving behavior into computers, the flexibility and adaptability afforded by learning approaches to problem-solving will become increasingly essential for success.

The genetic algorithms (GA) community has been engaged for well over a decade in research in automated learning and discovery.[2,3] This work has led to a number of impressive successes in the solution of difficult problems.[4,5,6] The approach is particularly interesting in its use of two powerful metaphors by which computation is organized -- the economy metaphor in the bucket brigade algorithm, and the metaphor of natural selection and evolution in the genetic algorithm proper. Yet this approach has failed to make significant inroads to the artificial intelligence (AI) community. We believe this is primarily due to three closely related factors: (1) the need to simulate very large numbers of generations in the GA to reach convergence on good problem solutions; (2) the need for great speed in the simulation in order to produce the numbers of generations needed in a reasonable time; and (3) the representation of the basic units of the GA as vectors, typically bit strings so that a large proportion of the possible solutions can be represented by any population of strings.

AI is characterized in large part by its attention to highly expressive knowledge representations. The theoretical advantage of the bit-string representation is disavowed in most AI research programs. Many programs depend on logically tagged data structures that are intended to be interpreted directly as human cognitive models of a domain. The mechanisms which exploit those knowledge representations tend to be adequately fast for decision aids and other interactive programs, but are very much slower than the speeds demanded of GA algorithms in the past. However, the speed at which learning is achieved may not need to be as fast for knowledge-based systems as has been needed for GA research and previous GA applications. The GA typically starts with little knowledge of correct solutions, and does much of its work converging on good approximate solutions. In contrast, knowledge-based systems are knowledge-engineered precisely to embody good solutions at the outset of their operational deployment. Moreover, such systems are expected to have a fairly long operating life-span. Consequently, for many AI applications it is reasonable to trade the speed of the bit-string GA for a slower genetic processes based on the more complex representations found in typical knowledge-based systems.

2. Project Objectives and Organization of the Paper

This paper describes work conducted as part of a machine learning project at MITRE. The overall objective of the project is to improve the performance capacity of knowledge-based systems by imbuing such systems with an ability to learn from their "experience". For an automated system to exhibit learning it must (at some level) be able to evaluate its performance to determine whether its behavior is adequate to its tasks, and it must be able to modify its behavior if not. For a knowledge-based system the modification, and therefore the evaluation, must occur at the knowledge level, since that is the level at which the system was designed to be open to modification. In the context of such a system, we interpret "experience" to mean 1) that which the system is told by the knowledge engineer, 2) the system's input data stream, and 3) the introspective examination of the knowledge base, data base, and system results by the system itself. In such knowledge-based systems, the bucket brigade is appropriate as an evaluation mechanism of system performance, the GA as a discovery algorithm for system improvements over the long term of the life of the system. We have explored the utility of the bucket brigade algorithm for knowledge evaluation in traditional rule-based application systems[7] and for one variant of rule-based inference under uncertainty.[3]

The principle problem which we are addressing in this paper is the generation of legal rules within a high-level rule representation language. We reconsider the GA in light of representations widely used by the mainstream AI community. In the past the GA has been applied to high-level problems by developing a representation for the problem that can be mapped to an underlying GA vector representation.[6,9,10] The mapping has followed two paths, often called the "Michigan" and "Pittsburg" approaches to the GA after the schools at which their respective research teams established each approach. The Michigan approach views the GA as working as a process internal to a system, so both evaluation and modification occur in the context of a simple system adaption, to its environment. The Pittsburgh approach views each represented individual in the GA as an entire system, for instance a possible rule-base, which is in competition with other systems to establish itself in an environment.[12] Our work can best be understood as that part of the "Michigan" tradition concerned with mapping GA approaches to complex representations internal to a system.

The GA has in the past been applied to existing high-level representations indirectly, through the creation of mapping functions to interpret GA results at the representation level.

We are engaged by the other side of the problem. Given a knowledge representation, we are asking how we might modify the genetic operators to accommodate that representation. We believe the representation we have chosen is sufficiently general to be of interest to a wide audience. We hope that, in turn, the computing paradigm represented by the GA will be fruitfully applied within the traditional computing approaches in AI, and in increasing numbers of real-world AI applications. Finally, we hope to clarify the relationship and relative utility of GA approaches to other learning and discovery techniques in the field.

The rest of the paper is organized as follows. Section 3.0 describes our representation. In Section 4.0, we reconsider the operators that form the heart of the GA from the point of view of the representations of Section 3.0. We point out some issues raised by this work in Section 4.0, and conclude the section and the paper with a description of the status of this work and the expected activities in this area for the next year.

3.0 The Knowledge Representation

We represent knowledge in two forms: the "static" knowledge and vocabulary of the system, in our case an object description and datatype language

expressed as a taxonomy of the terms of interest, and the "procedural", dynamic knowledge of the system expressed by pattern-invoked condition-action production rules. Our description of these forms will be a slight simplification of the actual representations in our system. The simplifications are aimed at avoiding the difficulties of explaining aspects of production systems that don't bear directly on the adoption of GA operators to the representation.

The conceptual content of the system is expressed at four levels corresponding to the components of the rule language. They are **objects** and their characteristics or attributes, such as $object_1$ and (location of $object_1$); **relations** among objects and their characteristics; expressed in clauses such as (is-within-distance (location of $object_1$) (location of $object_2$) distance); **conditionals**, which are the relations on those clauses that constitute rule left-hand sides, e.g., (AND $clause_1$ $clause_2$); and the rules themselves, which express inferential relations with conditionals as antecedents, such as IF (AND $clause_1$ $clause_2$) THEN assert ($clause_2$).

3.1 Objects

The objects are organized in a taxonomy of types of objects, thus every object can be characterized by its class membership as well as the properties attached to it. Properties of a class* are inherited by all members of the class. An example object definition hierarchy appears in Figure 1.

Figure 1

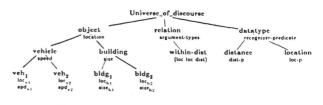

Concept representation: Objects

The leaves of the tree are instantiated objects, each of which has a set of characteristics as specified by the class of objects to which it belongs.

The leaves of the tree are instantiated objects, each of which has a set of characteristics as specified by the class of objects to which it belongs.

3.2 Relations

Relations are expressed in prefix notation, with the relation name followed by an ordered list of arguments wrapped in parenthesis. The arguments are *typed*, the available datatypes being provided by the concepts defined at the time the relation is defined. Relations and datatypes are represented

---

* The collection of properties of a class are the necessary and sufficient conditions for membership in that class.

as terms in the concept language in the same way that objects are, with properties and class membership. A relation may be expressed among constants or variables of the appropriate types, with the use of variables in relations providing quantification. An instantiated relation, one with all constants in its arguments, takes on a value (true or false for predicates, a member of the function range for functions). Figure 2 illustrates a relational form, a relation with free variables, and an instantiated relation.

Figure 2

Concept representation: Relations

$(Relation_1 \ concept\text{-}type_1 \ concept\text{-}type_2 \ ...)$

$(within\text{-}distance \ ?location_1 \ ?location_2 \ ?distance)$

$(within\text{-}distance \ (location \ vehicle_1) \ (location \ vehicle_2) \ 10ft)$

3.3 Conditionals

The left-hand side of a rule expresses a predicate relation among a set of propositional clauses. The predicate relation forms the condition under which the rule can be applied. There are three types of propositional clause: *short term memory* elements (STM), *associations*, and *predicates*. We give these special attention because of their roles in the left-hand side of inference rules. STM are used to introduce an arbitrary number of new variables into the conditional part of a production rule. Facts that are expressed to the system in such a way as to legally bind to (unify with) all the variables of a STM pattern are said to match that pattern. Variables must be bound in the datatype of the corresponding relation argument. Variables may also be *constrained* to be any subtype of the relation argument's datatype, as defined in the concept hierarchy. Variables bound to values in one STM must be bound in the same way whenever the variable is mentioned in another proposition of the left-hand side.*

Associations introduce a single new variable into the left-hand side by binding that variable to the value of a function call. The function's arguments must all be constants or previously bound variables. Association clauses function to set up variable bindings for the clauses.

Predicates are the only other type of clause directly expressed in the left-hand side. They introduce no new variables. As with functions in association clauses, all the predicate's arguments must be constants or bound variables.

---
* One might think of a list of possible bindings being carried from left to right across the list of propositions, such that at any break between propositions one can construct the bindings so far. We will use such a view in describing GA operators in the representation in Section 4.0, below.

The propositions of the conditional part of a rule are considered in some relation to each other, and the values of the propositions combined according to that relation. The combination operator collects and combines the values of the clauses of the left-hand side. For simplicity we consider only combination operators "and" and "or". "Not" is viewed as a relation that may appear as a proposition in the conditions (where "and" and "or" may also appear, recursively). Any clauses that mention variables bind those variables to appropriate values. Bindings remain in effect over the entire scope of the rule. Figure 3 illustrates one possible form of a conditional.

Figure 3

Concept representation: Relations in rule left-hand sides.

$(combination\text{-}operator$
$(STM\text{-}relation_1 \ ?var_1 \ constant_1)$
$(STM\text{-}relation_2 \ ?var_2 \ constant_2 \ constant_3)$
$(Associate \ ?var_3 \ (function_1 \ ?var_2 \ constant_4))$
$(predicate_1 \ ?var_3 \ ?var_2))$

3.4 Production Rules

Figure 4 illustrates a typical rule in our system. The rule's conditional clause contains the combination operator "And", indicating that all participating clauses must be true for this rule to be a candidate for firing. Each participating clause in the conditional denotes a relation whose *value* plays a part in the combination method. (Associate clauses are not participating clauses in these relations). The matching of the rule's left-hand side makes it a candidate for taking its right-hand side action and it is added to the conflict set.

Figure 4

Concept representation: rules.

$IF \quad (AND \quad (Rel_1 \ ?var1 \ const_1)$
$\qquad\qquad\qquad (Rel_2 \ ?var1 \ const_2))$
$THEN \quad (DO \quad (Action_1 \ ?var1))$

The actions a rule can take fall into three categories, adding STM elements to working memory, deleting such elements from working memory, or evaluating an arbitrary function. No new variables are bound on the right hand side, and all variables mentioned are bound to the the corresponding values of their bindings on the left-hand side. For example, a constant $Const_3$ bound to *?var1* such that both $(Rel_1 \ ?var1 \ const_3)$ and $(Rel_1 \ ?var1 \ const_2)$ are true results in $(Action_1 \ const_2)$ taking place.

3.5 Rule Grammar

The system described should be naturally expressible by a context-sensitive grammar, since each
category is systematically well-formed and each
depends on context information (e.g. variable
bindings) provided by previous rule elements. Such
a grammar would provide a formal framework for
describing the construction of legal rules, including variable binding decisions, as derivation
trees. We are preparing such a grammar to support
a version of crossover for this rule representation. Its role is described in section 4.5,
below.

3.6 Control

The minimal control structure for a production
system consists of a three-step cycle, plus an
initial action taken by a "prime mover" (typically
the user). The "mover" adds a working memory
element to the database of facts on which the
system operates, simulating what would otherwise be
control cycle. In the second step the resultant
set of candidate rules to fire, the *conflict set*,
is computed. Step three consists of a rule being
chosen and firing.* The rule may add or delete
elements of working memory, initiating a new
cycle. The conflict set is updated with the new
set of matched rules, and so on. The system halts
when the conflict set is empty at the end of a
cycle.

We have described a pattern-invoked, strongly
datatyped knowledge representation. The representation is typical of a well-organized AI application system based on such tools as OPS-like rule
interpreters and FRL-like declarative representation systems. In the next section we discuss the
implications of adopting GA type learning and
discovery algorithms to such systems.

4. Genetic Operators for Pattern-invoked, Datatyped Representations

The genetic algorithm simulates evolution and
natural selection over a population of individuals
in an artificial environment. The population is
usually represented as a set of simple production
or rewrite rules such as the one illustrated in
Figure 5.

---

* If several rules are chosen for firing simultaneously we have a parallel system. Since we are
concerned, in this paper, with the manner of
automated rule construction, and not (directly)
with the results of inference using those rules, we
needn't concern ourselves with the issues parallelism normally raises. Such issues may need to be
raised in considering how to control the application of the GA operators, but, except for the
comments on Section 5.0, that is beyond the scope
of this paper.

Figure 5

Bit-string representation of productions.

| 0 | 0 | 1 | # | 1 | 0 | # | 0 | → | 0 | 0 | 1 | 1 | 1 | 0 | # | 0 |

Abstractly, the bit-string represents the possible
states of the world. Each position of the string
may be thought to correspond to an independent
proposition about the world, so all strings of 0's
and 1's correspond to particular possible world
states. A "don't care" character, "#", is introduced to make it possible to refer to sets of
possible world states. In the context of a bit-
string production rule, a left-hand side string
represents the (set of) state(s) in which the rule
may rewrite the world-state as its right-hand
side. For example, in Figure 5, a world-state of
00101010 would be rewritten by the rule as
00111010.

Below we consider how to express the operators
developed in this representation in the language of
relations described in the last section. We will
first describe the operator of interest in terms of
the bit-string manipulations it performs. We then
consider mechanisms which carry out an analogous
operation in pattern-invoked, datatyped representations. We do not consider modifications at the
object level, which is considered the primitive
level of the system -- analogous to bit positions
and values in the bit-string representation. Nor
do we consider the rule level, since considerations
of the relation and conditional levels suffice and
can be trivially extended to include the right-hand
sides of rules (no new variables being introduced
there). We don't mean to imply that modifications
in the action parts of rules are uninteresting,
just that the mechanics of those modifications can
be understood completely analogously to modifications of the left-hand sides of rules.

The operators we consider are generalization,
specialization, mutation, inversion, and crossover. Because of the importance of hierarchical
concept representations in many AI systems, the
issues in concept specialization and generalization
have been the concern of a large part of the
machine learning community. We therefore treat
them separately, even though specialization and
generalization are, strictly speaking, sub-species
of mutation.

4.1 Generalization

Generalization is achieved in the bit-string
representation by changing a "0" or "1" to a "don't
care" symbol ("#"). The utilization of "#" within
the condition of a bit-string production provides
an opportunity for that production to apply to more
world states. It is used as a global pattern-
matching variable. Figure 6 shows an example of a
bit-string production being generalized by switching the 0 in position 1 for a # in position 1.

Figure 6

Generalization of Rule in Figure 5.

Old rule:

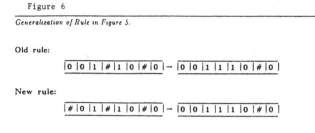

New rule:

4.1.1 Generalization at relation level

Instantiated relations in the rule language can be generalized completely analogously to the bit-string operation by changing a literal to a variable. Due to the strong typing of our relational language, constraints apply to those variables. A variable might be bound to any member of the class to which the literal belongs, or to any member of a superclass of the literal, up to the datatype of the relation argument that the literal was instantiating. For instance, the instantiated relation *(location-of bldg₁)* can be generalized by replacing the reference to a specific building by reference to a class of buildings or objects, such as *(location-of ?bldg)* or *(location-of ?object)*, but not just any element of the universe of discourse. Notice that *(location-of ?vehicle)* is *not* a generalization of, e.g., *(location-of ?building)*.

A very similar mechanism can be brought to bear to affect generalization at a slightly higher level. The relation language itself is defined in a taxonomy in which a particular relation may have parent relations of which they are specializations. Such parent relations would have the same or fewer parameters of the same or more general types. Generalizing a relation directly would require, at most, removing one or more arguments from the previous relation's argument list.

4.1.2 Generalization of conditionals and productions

Generalization can also be achieved by removing clauses from the conditional, thereby removing a requirement for invoking the right-hand side action. Removal of an entire clause has to be handled with care because of the interaction of variable binding among conditional clauses and the actions of the rule. If a clause introduces a set of variables, subsequent references to those variables must be purged from the rule. The easiest way to do this is to simply remove all clauses with such references, but one might also replace such variables with variables of the same class introduced elsewhere in the conditional. So dropping the first clause of the conditional in Figure 3 would necessitate either the removal of clause 3 and then clause 4(!), or it would require changing ?var₁ in clause 3 to, e.g., ?var₂ from clause 2. On the other hand, dropping clause 4 could be done without further adjustments because it introduces no new variables.

If we keep to the analogy that generalization of a literal or a variable is like "0" or "1" turned into "#", it's difficult to see what analogy to make of generalization at the relation level, unless it is something like turning some pattern of "0"'s and "1"'s into a pattern of "#"'s. The difficulty of finding a GA analog seems rooted in the richly layered representation inherent in the relation-based approach, whereas the simple description of the GA presented here is for only one level of process. Although it is possible to organize layered GA processes, it is a particular strength of most AI representations that they do so naturally. The price for such expressiveness, apparent here, is in the degree of complexity of operations on such representations.

4.2 Specialization

The specialization operator in a bit-string operation changes a "don't care" symbol to a literal value of 1 or 0. The example in figure 7 shows the fourth position of the condition specialized to a 1 value. This restricts the application of this rule to fewer possible world states.

Figure 7

Specialization of Rule in Figure 5.

Old rule:

New rule:

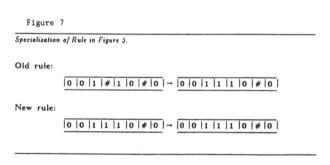

4.2.1 Specialization at relation level

The mechanics of specialization in relations is very similar to generalization. Rules can be specialized by filling variable positions with literal values that have a type of the corresponding relation arguments (a constructor being used to generate a legal literal value based upon its type in the class hierarchy), by constraining the variable to be of a subtype of the type at which it is presently constrained, or by replacing the relation with a subspecie of the relation.

4.2.2 Specialization at conditional level

Another method of specialization is the addition of clauses in the left-hand side of the rule. In the simple case the new clause does not introduce any new elements, it only further constrains the conditions of the rule's applicability. However, when new variables are introduced by a STM or associate clause, the clause will do little useful work unless at least one of the newly introduced variables is mentioned elsewhere in the rule.* Therefore, specialization by clause introduction needs to be tied to the existing clauses through an existing variable or must be complemented by another process other clauses to effect such a tie.

4.3 Mutation

Mutation is very similar to specialization and generalization in that it is conceptually a local operator that transforms individual elements of a rule construct. In the bit-string representation this transformation consists of replacing a "1" with a "0" and vice versa, see figure 8.

Figure 8

Mutation of Rule in Figure 5.

Old rule:

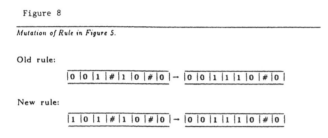

New rule:

4.3.1 Mutation at relation level

In the production rule representation, mutation is constrained by the same datatyping considerations as specialization and generalization. It produces value changes based upon the type of the argument corresponding to the selected position, but, as opposed to those two operators, it seeks sibling concepts for the new variable or constant. Recall the instantiatied relation *(location-of bldg$_2$)* that was generalized by replacing the reference to a specific building by reference to a superclass of the building. A mutation on that clause would be, for instance, *(location-of ?vehicle)*, which, as was pointed out in the discussion of generalization above, is *not* a generalization of the instantiated relation.

4.3.2 Mutation at conditional level

Mutation of the relation expressed by the clause can be viewed as the removal of a clause from the conditional followed by the addition of a new clause. Notice that in a fully articulated concept graph, the relation expressed by the new clause must be, at some level, a sibling or cousin relation to the original. One might use this to provide a metric and control regimen for the degree of mutation in a rule .

---

*This is by no means always the case. Sometimes variables are introduced to test for some general condition to decide if an action should be taken, resulting in a rule like IF *(STM ?var$_2$)* THEN DO *(action constant$_1$)*.

4.4 Inversion

The inversion operator of the GA produces an end for end reversal of positions in the condition of a rule. It can be applied as a mutation operator during the running of the system, or as a crossover/mutation operator applied during reproduction. The example in figure 9 shows the basic notion behind inversion.

Figure 9

Inversion of rule in Figure 5.

Old rule:

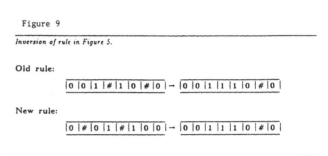

New rule:

4.4.1 Inversion at relation level

Because of the strict ordering of arguments within relations, inversion cannot be in general achieved unless the types of the relation's arguments are symmetrical. Under any other circumstances, inversion would result in illegally formed clauses.

4.4.2 Inversion at conditional level

The production system as described restricts ordering of clauses according to the introduction of variables. Inversion of the clauses in the conditional would presumably destroy some of the dependencies of that variable introduction scheme, requiring renaming and rethreading of variables through the inverted clause set. Without an explicit relation between, say, the clauses in a rule and the actions to be taken in a plan, it's difficult to see the point of inversion. Given the variable set for a rule, it shouldn't make any semantic difference in what order the clauses are expressed.

4.5 Crossover

The crossover operator is the workhorse modification operator of the GA. It is also an operator which doesn't have direct analog in the "traditional" machine learning literature. The example in figure 10 shows two rules being crossed over after they were chosen as mates. A locus (denoted by the cut) determines how much of Rule1 and how much of Rule2 will be used. In this example, Rule1 provides the first 3 positions of the new rule with Rule 2 providing the remaining positions.

4.5.1 Crossover at relation level

It is not immediately obvious that crossover makes sense for relations. In fact, the argument typing requirements are often cited as the cause for crossover's inapplicability in this domain.

Figure 10

Crossover of rule in Figure 5 and another rule.

Rule1:

| 0 | 0 | 1 | # | 1 | 0 | # | 0 | → | 0 | 0 | 1 | 1 | 1 | 0 | # | 0 |

Rule2:

| 1 | 1 | # | # | # | 0 | 1 | 0 | → | 0 | 0 | 1 | 1 | 1 | 0 | # | 0 |

cut! 1st half of Rule 1, 2nd half of Rule 2

New rule:

| 0 | 0 | 1 | # | # | 0 | 1 | 0 | → | 0 | 0 | 1 | 1 | 1 | 0 | # | 0 |

Figure 11

Crossover Operator: Problems.

Rule1:

Cut > ·········· IF   (AND $(Rel_1 \ ?var1 \ const_1)$

                     $(Rel_2 \ ?var1 \ const_2)$) <

        THEN   (DO $(Action_1 \ ?var1)$))

Rule2:

Cut > ·········· IF   (AND $(Rel_3 \ ?varA \ ?varB)$ <

                     (Pred ?varA)

                     $(Assoc \ ?varC \ (function \ ?varB))$

        THEN   (DO $(Action_2 \ ?varC)$)

New Rule:

        IF   (AND $(Rel_1 \ ?var1 \ const_1)$

                     (Pred ?varA)

                     $(Assoc \ ?varC \ (function \ ?varB))$

        THEN   (DO $(Action_2 \ ?varC)$)

However, there is a way in which crossover might be applied (the locus of crossover chosen) even within strongly datatyped relations when two rules are being crossed. This requires two modifications of the system we have so far described: (1) the system should be described by same context-sensitive rule grammar that formally delineates what is legal at all the levels as described in Section 3.5, (2) all rules should be described by a datastructure that indicates the derivation tree through the grammar followed in the construction of the rule. A rule can be cut at any point, but each part of the rule must carry a copy of its (partial) derivation. Crossover can then be performed by any two rule fragments whose derivations complete each other. That is, the cut results not only in the splitting of a rule into two fragments, but the tagging of each cut end of the fragment, the left-hand side with the partial derivation tree down to the cut. The right-hand side with the subtree starting at the art. The unification of the derivations produces the new rule. This process is obviously more complex than the other operators considered thus far and we are presently trying to specify a grammar for our system that will form the basis of the derivation path datastructure.

4.5.2 Crossover at conditional level

Figure 11 illustrates a naive view of crossover when the cut occurs between clauses in the conditional. Rule1 and Rule2 are two hypothetical rule mates. Their combination via crossover produces a rule that mentions a variable in its action that is not well-founded; ?varC is supposed to be bound to (function ?varB), but ?varB is unbound in New Rule). Moreover, ?varA is also unfounded, and neither ?varA nor ?var1 are doing any work that is obviously related to the action to be taken.

Our first implementation of crossover attempted to achieve crossover for conditions, and initial experience to test some intuitions. It promoted modification only among rules with the same goal or class of goals. A rule was naively produced. It then went through one round of generalization, in which variables of the same type with different names were unified and one round of specialization in which variables of predicates and associative relations are given literal values if they are not were bound by the STM relations. Predicates without any variables (only literals) or associative relations whose variable is not used by predicates or assertions, were expunged from the rule condition because of their useless computational expense.

Our present approach (until we work out the grammar-based one) is to view crossover as a repeated generalization by clause removal on the rule that is to provide the action side of the new rule (e.g., Rule2 in Figure 11), followed by a repeated specialization by clause addition on the resulting generalized rule. The clauses added in the specialization process are those before the cut in the rule that is to provide the first part of the new rule (e.g., Rule1 in the figure). The characterization is rough because the conditional is bound together by the combination operator. We mutate the combination operator of the generalized intermediate form of the rule (derived from Rule2) to the combination operator of the rule providing the specialization clauses (Rule1).

5. Issues and Future Work

At least two issues are raised by the representational adaptations we are attempting. Firstly, are we still discussing computation within a *genetic* metaphor if we accept this representation? Secondly, how are these operators to play in AI systems, what kind of control regimen should they operate under, and is that genetic? We discuss these issues very briefly here.

5.1 The Genetics Metaphor

An important issue raised by this work is whether the metaphor of genetic recombination is not completely lost when one goes to such high-level representations. The integrity requirements on the variable bindings makes it difficult to view rules as suitable material for local genetic recombination operators. When the legality requirement is enforced the way we have described, the whole operation of adapting GA

75

techniques seems driven by a priori representation characteristics. The result has been an adaptation that may seem ad hoc, from the GA perspective.

A much more satisfactory solution seems to be at hand if the entire production system can be described in a formal grammar. In that context genetic recombination re-emerges much more clearly as a metaphor for the process, although the operators are much more complex than usually described in the GA literature. Perhaps an analogy of such operators to the role of RNA is appropriate. A glimpse of this approach appears in the discussion of crossover within relations, above.

5.2 Control

Having constructed a set of operators to generate changes to a rule base, we are now confronted with the heart of the machine learning problem, how to control system modification operators. A (perhaps crucial) element of the GA is the probabilistic control of recombination of elements in a gene pool of some sort, leading to new generations of the overall system. In real world applications of knowledge-based systems, the effort expended on knowledge engineering, the expectation that system changes will be incremental, and the hope that they will be well-understood seems to argue against directly incorporating the GA approach to control in such systems. Yet the GA approach may represent an aspect of control that *must* be present in a system (in some form) for it to exhibit the capacity for discovery.

5.2 Future Work

We have described issues in the application of the GA to pattern-based production systems. We are currently implementing the operators described so we may explore those issues. The system in which this approach is being explored is implemented on a Symbolics 3670. It runs the bucket brigade as a knowledge evaluation mechanism, and has demonstrated auto-modification of its behavior using the bucket brigade alone. We are presently exploring variations on the competitive learning scheme exemplified by the bucket brigade, as well as rule generation strategies as exemplified the genetic operators. Generalization, specialization, and a version of crossover are implemented, and, at present, invoked on a per-rule basis depending on a rule's performance.

Next year's work is aimed at quantitatively assessing these approaches through controlled machine learning experiments. We expect to pay particular attention to the GA control strategy as process for generating effective new rules in competition with other such processes. We will attempt to implement operators in a meta-level rule representation to begin to provide explanation of rule derivations and justification of system modifications.

6. References

1. Simon, H. A., "Why Should Machines Learn?," Machine Learning, an Artificial Intelligence Approach, R. S. Michalski, J. G. Carbonell, and T. M. Mitchell, Eds., Tioga Publishing Co., Palo Alto, CA, 1983.

2. Holland, J. H., "Adaptation in Natural and Artificial Systems", University of Michigan Press, Ann Arbor, MI, 1975.

3. DeJong, K. A., "Genetic Algorithms: a 10 year perspective", Proc. Int. GA Conf., pp. 169-177, 1985.

4. Goldberg, D. E., "Computer-aided gas pipeline operation using genetic algorithms and rule learning", Ph.D. Thesis, University of Michigan, Ann Arbor, MI, 1975.

5. DeJong, K. A., and Smith, T., "Genetic Algorithms Applied to Information Driven Models of US Migration Patterns", IEEE Trans. on Systems, Man and Cybernetics, 10,9, Sept. 1980.

6. Grefenstette, J. J., Gopal, R., Rosmaita, B. J., and VanGucht, D., "Genetic Algorithms for the traveling salesman problem", Proc. Int. GA Conf., pp. 160-168, 1985.

7. H. J. Antonisse and K. S. Keller, "Dynamic Evaluation of Imprecisely Specified Knowledge," Proc. Digital Avionics Systems Conf. (Fort Worth, TX, 1986).

8. H. C. Tallis and H. J. Antonisse, "Evaluation of Intelligence Fusion Rules Using the Bucket Brigade", submitted for publication.

9. Cramer, N. L., "A representation for the adaptive generation of simple sequential programs", Proc. Int. GA Conf., pp. 183-185, 1985.

10. Smith, D. "Bin packing with adaptive search", Proc. Int. GA Conf., pp. 202-206, 1985.

11. Forrest, S., "Implementing semantic network structures using the classifier system", Proc. Int. GA Conf., pp. 24-44, 1985.

TREE STRUCTURED RULES IN GENETIC ALGORITHMS

Arthur S. Bickel
Riva Wenig Bickel

Department of Computer and Information Systems
Florida Atlantic University
Boca Raton FL 33432

ABSTRACT

We apply genetic algorithm techniques to the creation and use of lists of tree-structured production rules varying in length and complexity. Actions, conditions and operators are randomly chosen from tables of possibilities. Use of the techniques is facilitated by the notions of time delay and dependency in performing tests or observations and by accounting for indeterminate test results.

GENES, a general program, can adapt to a variety of systems by changing the contents of the various tables to accomodate the domain of a particular problem and by substituting a library of appropriate cases.

INTRODUCTION

The genetic algorithm is an iterative adaptive search technique which has been applied successfully to learning systems having large search spaces and to problems which cannot easily be reduced to closed form. Holland, who originated the notion of computer constructs which mimic natural adaptive mechanisms, noted that in order to apply this technique, the subject to be treated must be capable of being represented by some data structure and the solutions must be capable of being evaluated and ranked (1,2).

APPLICATION TO EXPERT SYSTEMS

Conventionally in genetic algorithm implementations, the rules containing the expertise have been expressed in the form of bit strings of fixed length. This approach works quite well in terms of the ease of applying the genetic operators - mutations may turn a 0 to a 1 or to some other symbol taken from a similar simple alphabet; crossovers are implemented by randomly choosing two crossover points along the string and exchanging the information between those two points. However there are many problems which cannot be easily expressed in terms of a simple alphabet, and still be amenable to the genetic operators (see, e.g. work on the traveling salesman problem (3, 4)). The commonly used dual valued alphabet is especially troublesome for two reasons. First, since the number of possible actual interpretations is unlikely to be a power of two, some interpretations will be redundant, weighting the possible choices unevenly. Secondly, some mutations would be extremely unlikely, e.g. 000 would probably not mutate to 111. These problems are both eliminated by having each decisional element be an index into an appropriate table. Choices for each position and changes due to point mutations are then made merely by randomly chosing one of the possible indices into that table.

Schaffer and Grefenstette (5), building upon the LS-1 learning system originated by Smith (6), used a data structure where each expert was not an individual rule but, rather, an entire set of rules, in order to deal with multi-objective learning. These rule sets were of fixed length, although all the rules might not necessarily be used. But there may be insufficient flexibility in solving difficult classes of problems where the expert is composed of linear data structures of fixed length, since practicable computer expert systems are often presented as a system of non-linear rules (7). These rules tend to be of the form:

IF condition [{and|or condition}] THEN action

where the action may be either an attempt to obtain more information on the system (an action rule), or a terminal decision in the nature of deciding the answer to the presented problem (a decision rule).

CREATING AN EXPERT GENERATOR

We created GENES, a program to develop expert systems. Each expert in our system consisted of a linked list of rules, each rule parsed syntactically as a tree structure. The actual number of rules in each linked list was randomly determined via an average length parameter passed to the program upon its initiation. The number of rules allowed was optionally bounded.

A different program parameter determined the maximum number of nodes for each rule. The minimal possible value was one, this single node being an action node - which would mean that some prescribed action (randomly chosen from a table of possible actions) would always be carried out. One type of action was the undertaking of a specific additional test or observation; the other possible action was a final determination as to the state of the system - e.g. if the expert was a prospector, then this might be that a given mineral exists at a certain location in recoverable concentrations.

There was only one action node per rule. Additional nodes each represented a possible condition precedent to carrying out the action, linked by boolean operators (again, randomly chosen). Conditions precedent nodes are of the form:

IF {test-result-yields RELATIONAL OPERATOR scalar quantity}.

As an example, if the expert created were a chemist, a possible node might be "if melting point > 180.51 degrees". In creating (but not in evaluating) the expert, booleans, relational operators, possible tests, and possible range of results were all randomly chosen from a permissible domain of actions, conditions

{IF (NOT ((C1 = 2) AND (C4 > 3)) OR (C2 >= 12)) THEN A1} ->

{A5} ->

{IF ((C5 = TRUE) OR NOT (C1 <> 17)) THEN A1}

Figure 1

Statements within {} indicate a single set of rules Statements beginning with C are conditions
Statements beginning with A are actions
-> indicates the linking of rules which are evaluated in order

and values appropriate to the area of expertise desired for the system. Figure 1 shows a possible rule set for an unspecified expert.

APPLYING THE GENETIC OPERATORS TO THE EXPERT POPULATION

Three types of genetic operators were applied to the population of experts - mutation, crossover and inversion. The tree structured nature of each rule called for some modifications to the way these operators normally deal with fixed length strings of bits.

Mutation was performed as an operation upon a single rule. A number of varieties of mutation were possible and the type of mutation occurring in each given case was chosen randomly from the list of possibilities, as was the rule to be mutated and the node of the rule at which the mutation would occur. The simplest type of mutation was a point mutation. This involved the change of one operator to another (e.g., > becoming >=). It was also possible for an operand of either a condition or an action type to be exchanged with another (e.g., in a chemical setting boiling point becoming melting point or 450 degrees might become 200). A third possibility is exemplified by the exchange of an OR for an AND or the addition or deletion of a NOT in the boolean expression. The last mutation possible was the addition or deletion of a rule or a portion of a rule - the latter being equivalent to a randomly selected branch of the parse tree.

The next simplest genetic operation was an order inversion. Each inversion was carried out on a single set of rules. This involved randomly choosing, via the MOD operator, two points along a rule set of given length, and then exchanging the order of rules that existed between the two points. This operation did not affect the rules themselves but, rather, the order in which they were evaluated. The possible effects of inversion were twofold. First, the firing of an earlier rule (that is conditions evaluating positively so that an action is taken) could cause later rules to evaluate differently. With a new ordering, given preconditions now may or may not exist. Second, due to rule evaluation halting once a decision rule fired, new rules might come under consideration or old ones might not now be reached.

The most complex genetic operator used involved crossover. Crossover, in this system, occurred at points between rules, and involved exchanges of identical amounts of genetic material (in terms of number of rules) between experts. Because the rule sets of each of the pair of experts chosen to undergo crossover were unequal in length, one point for crossover was chosen to be MOD the length of the shorter expert and one MOD the longer expert. If both values turned out to be less than the length of the shorter rule set then a double crossover occurred: a central list of rules was exchanged between the two and both experts retained their original size. If only one point was less than the shorter rule set, then only a single crossover occurred, with the tail end of the shorter expert now grafted on to what was once the longer one, and vice versa. Both offspring of each inversion survived. Figures 2a and 2b demonstrate the two types of crossovers.

```
R1A--R1B--R1C-I-R1D--R1E--R1F-I-R1G--R1H--
R1I--R1J--R1K

R2A--R2B--R2C-I-R2D--R2E--R2F-I-R2G
```

crossover of rule sets 1 & 2 yield

```
R1A--R1B--R1C-I-R2D--R2E--R2F-I-R1G--R1H--
R1I--R1J--R1K

R2A--R2B--R2C-I-R1D--R1E--R1F-I-R2G
```

DOUBLE CROSSOVER - CROSSOVER POINTS INDICATED BY I

Figure 2a

```
R1A--R1B--R1C--R1D-I-R1E--R1F--R1G--R1H--
R1I--R1J--R1K

R2A--R2B--R2C--R2D-I-R2E--R2F--R2G
```

crossover of rule sets 1 & 2 yield

```
R1A--R1B--R1C--R1D-I-R2E--R2F--R2G

R2A--R2B--R2C--R2D-I-R1E--R1F--R1G--R1H--
R1I--R1J--R1K
```

SINGLE CROSSOVER - CROSSOVER POINT INDICATED BY I

Figure 2b

THE ROLE OF THE CRITIC

Experts, naturally, relate to some field of expertise. The general set of problems which these experts were to solve involved a set of related problems, where a number of different tests could be undertaken in order to determine some information about the system. The goal of each expert was to generate the proper set of tests, in proper order, so that the correct solution for each presented problem would be obtained at a minimal cost in terms of testing expenses.

The role of the critic was to apply each expert's rule set, in order, (and repeatedly if necessary), to each member of a library of actual cases, and to obtain thereby some figure of merit for each expert. If the conditions precedent in the rule were met, then the rule fired and the action called for was taken. If the rule action called for an observation about the case, information might be unmasked, and the expert's state of knowledge increased (but only if the information was available in the actual library case). Of course costs may have been incurred in making such observations. These costs could involve time, money, or injury to the subject being observed. Results might be inconclusive or even unavailable.

Rule evaluation ceased when a decision rule fired. If the entire rule set was evaluated without a decision rule firing, then the set was reevaluated from its beginning (and at an additional cost), because the results of earlier fired rules were likely to have provided additional information that could result in different rules firing on subsequent passes. A maximum number of passes were allowed in order to ensure termination. A valuation of the expert's merit vis a vis that particular problem was made, and then the next problem in the set was presented to it, and so on. Obviously, the larger and more varied the set of problems, the more sophisticated and discriminating the expert.

Creation of a library of problems under direct program control can be a tedious and error-prone process. In order to facilitate both entry of and changes to the problem set, GENES allowed creation of the problem set via the normal Unix(TM) vi editor, and then fed the error-free result to the program.

In our trial system we were interested in evaluating our experts on a dual basis. One consideration was how often they reached the correct result. The other was how little cost was expended in reaching this result. An apportionment between these two factors is clearly a value judgment that must be made for each particular expert system. Thus each expert accrued a certain cost in its decision making, that being the sum of dollar costs incurred in running tests, degradation costs in the case of environmental misfortunes (e.g. a damaged drill in the instance of oil exploration) and penalties for bad evaluations. The merit of each expert was inversely related to the costs it incurred.

TIME DEPENDENT EVALUATIONS

Because the system we were studying was one where time was a factor, we introduced the notion of time dependency to our evaluations of the goodness of each expert. Many of the tests which could be performed by the experts would not yield immediate results. While such answers were pending other tests might or might not be undertaken, depending upon the rules (where actions might or might not be dependent upon previous test results).

Time dependency required that the entire rule set for each expert be reevaluated repeatedly, because new tests might be ordered once earlier test results came in. In many existing systems such delay involves additional daily overhead costs, so these costs were factored into the testing costs for each expert where appropriate.

A related notion was persistence, persistence being a quality associated with tests whose results do not change meaningfully over short intervals. In order to prevent the repeated ordering of such tests, they were each assigned a persistence value which was decremented with time. If a rule required that a test be done when that test showed a non-zero persistence value, the rule was ignored.

It should also be noted that there was a possibility that test results might be equivocal. To simulate this possibility, the individual problems in the sets presented were issued certain flags representing both the current and possible results of tests and observations that the expert might make. Thus, for example, in a medical situation, the patient's sex might generally be immediately knowable, the results of a blood culture would be available in 24 hours, but meaningful results of a CAT scan might actually turn out to be unobtainable. Because there was no prohibition on the repetition of rules within an expert's repertory, however, the CAT scan could be repeated and might show results the second time.

HANDLING CONVERGENCE

Researchers in the genetic algorithm field have repeatedly noted the difficulty of fine tuning the parameters in order to obtain results along the desired results. The algorithm shares this rather nasty

fact with other types of computer programming: "what you ask for is what you get" (See, e.g., (8)). Due to the emphasis upon getting the correct result as compared to the cost of arriving at that result, the population of experts tended to converge rapidly to a rather homogeneous solution set, wherein a high percentage of the problem sets tested were solved properly, but at less than optimum cost. Rapid convergence is a common problem in these types of systems and has been solved in various ways (9). The solution used in GENES was to consider the system to have converged if the sum of all the expert scores remained within a narrowly bounded interval over several consecutive iterations.

If the system was judged to have converged, then a percentage of the population was replaced by newly generated experts, thereby providing a major influx of genetic material into the system.

PARAMETERS FOR GENETIC OPERATIONS

Rates of mutation, inversion and crossover, as compared with just plain duplication, were tunable parameters, as was the population size. Typically, rates in the range recommended by Grefenstette (10), namely a 30 percent crossover rate, 3 percent mutation rate, 5 percent inversion rate, and a 40 percent generation gap, were found to give good results and were used. Variations in these rates affected the time it took to reach a good solution, but did not effect the goodness of that solution. Other typical variable values were a population of experts set at 50 and 50 maximum rules; this was with 13 possible actions that could be taken and 12 possible tests-to-be-done where the possible variations for the bound of each test-to-be-done were extremely large since the constants chosen were from a continuous rather than a discrete population (e.g. temperature > 102.45). This, along with the variable number of branches in each rule and the variable number of rules in each set, makes the size of the search space difficult to estimate. It certainly is not small.

Using these parameters, the choice of which experts were to undergo each procedure was made via the weighted roulette wheel. In all cases at least one copy of the expert with the best value was retained.

RESULTS

The GENES model, we tested at least on a small scale, converged in approximately 2000 iterations with a population size of 30, or in 8 iterations with a population size of 50, to results which appear optimal in that the correct decisions were made for all nine problems presented and at a reasonably low cost. This required no excessive or duplicative testing. Due to the very large possible variation of rules, there did, however, seem to be some strange rules that remained in the best expert's rule sets. These rules tended not to make a great deal of sense, but they did not actually affect the system as their very weirdness assured that they either always or never fired. Thus the rule interpreted as "if the patient's temperature is less than 120.3 degrees discover if abdominal pain is present", is practically equivalent to stating "always check for abdominal pain".

Additionally, it should be noted that all rules following one that resulted in a decision being made were never evaluated, so they did not actually contribute to the rule set, although they did provide genetic material to succeeding generations and might be activated during inversion.

FURTHER DIRECTIONS

This system is currently being examined with promising results in two areas of expertise.

The first area that we are investigating is the minimization of hospital costs during patient diagnostic evaluations in a prospective reimbursement environment. The simple environment we are studying is a rule set appropriate to a patient admitted with suspected gall bladder disease. The expert in this system should be able to arrive at a correct diagnosis using minimal hospital resources in terms of tests and time. It should be noted that this system does not involve interpretation of tests, but only the suggests the order of testing, as a function of previous results.

The second system under study involves server activation and deactivation in queueing problems. Costs here include both activation and use of the server, with the goal being minimization of costs, while providing adequate service to the queue under varying server loads.

A back end interpreter to translate the rule sets into terms understandable by semi-expert users is also under consideration.

ACKNOWLEDGMENT

The authors wish to acknowledge the assistance of Neal Coulter for his many helpful suggestions.

BIBLIOGRAPHY

1. John H. Holland. Outline for a Logical Theory of Adaptive Systems. In Essays on Cellular Automata, Edited by Arthur W. Burks. University of Illinois Press (1970).

2. John H. Holland, "Adaptation in Natural and Artificial Systems". Univ. Michigan Press, Ann Arbor (1975).

3. David E. Goldberg and Robert Lingle, Jr., Alleles, Loci, and the Traveling Salesman Problem, Proceedings of an International Conference on Genetic Algorithms and Their Applications, John J. Grefenstette, ed. (1985) pp 154-159.

4. John Grefenstette et al, Genetic Algorithms for the Traveling Salesman Problem, Proceedings of an International Conference on Genetic Algorithms and Their Applications, John J. Grefenstette, Ed. (1985) pp 160-165.

5. J. D. Schaffer and John Grefenstette, Multi-Objective Learning Via Genetic Algorithms, International Joint Conference on Artificial Intelligence (9th 1985) pp 593 - 595.

6. S. F. Smith, Flexible Learning of Problem Solving Heuristics Through Adaptive Search, International Joint Conference on Artificial Intelligence (8th 1983) 422 - 425.

7. A.J. Tomas and A. Th. Schreiber, HERMAN Computer Aided Medical Decision Making, Artificial Intelligence in Medicine, I. De Lotto, M. Stefanelli, Ed. North-Holland 1985, pp 1 - 9.

8. K. De Jong, Genetic Algorithms: A 10 Year Perspective, Proceedings of an International Conference on Genetic Algorithms and Their Applications, John J. Grefenstette, ed. (1985) pp 169 - 177.

9. J. E. Baker, Adaptive Selection Methods for Genetic Algorithms, Proceedings of an International Conference on Genetic Algorithms and Their Applications, John J. Grefenstette, ed. (1985) pp 101 - 111.

10. John Grefenstette, Optimization of Control Parameters for Genetic Algorithms, IEEE Transactions on Systems, Man, and Cybernetics, (Vol. SMC 16 No. 1 Jan/Feb 1986) pp 122 - 128.

GENETIC ALGORITHMS AND CLASSIFIER SYSTEMS: FOUNDATIONS AND FUTURE DIRECTIONS

John H. Holland

The University of Michigan

Abstract

Theoretical questions about classifier systems, with rare exceptions, apply equally to other *adaptive nonlinear networks* (ANNs) such as the connectionist models of cognitive psychology, the immune system, economic systems, ecologies, and genetic systems. This paper discusses pervasive properties of ANNs and the kinds of mathematics relevant to questions about these properties. It discusses relevant functional extensions of the basic classifier system and extensions of the extant mathematical theory. An appendix briefly reviews some of the key theorems about classifier systems.

Classifier systems are examples of a broad class of systems sometimes called *adaptive nonlinear networks* (ANNs, hereafter). Broadly characterized, classifier systems, and ANNs in general, consist of a large number of units that (1) interact in a nonlinear, competitive fashion, and (2) are modified by various operators so that the system as whole progressively adapts to its environment. Typically an ANN confronts an environment that exhibits perpetual novelty and it can function (or continue to exist) only by making continued adaptations to that environment. Because ANN/environment interactions are complex, except in artificially constrained cases, an ANN usually operates far from equilibrium. ANNs form the core of areas of study as diverse as cognitive psychology, artificial intelligence, economics, immunogenesis, genetics, and ecology.

Foundations.

Classifier systems are quite typical ANNs so that questions about classifiers, suitably translated, are typically questions about ANNs and vice versa. To carry out the translation it is necessary to identify the counterparts in other ANNs of the message-processing rules, called *classifiers*, that are the units of classifier systems. For example: In genetics, the counterparts are chromosomes; in game theory and economics, they are (rule-defined) strategies; in immunogenesis, antigens; in connectionist versions of cognition, (formally-defined) neurons; and so on. Under such translation it is relatively easy to identify a range of important theoretical questions that apply to classifier systems in particular and ANNs in general:

[These questions, and some of the ensuing discussions, are presented assuming that the reader has some familiarity with Holland et al. [1986] or Holland [1975]. There is simply not enough room here to define the terms; a reader familiar with the literature concerning some other ANN should be able to make the relevant translation in most cases.]

(1) What parameters and operators favor the emergence of stable hierarchical covers such as default hierarchies, internal models, and the like (via an increased diversity of units and progressively more complicated interactions between them)?

(2) Are the familiar "ecological" interactions -- parasitism, symbiosis, competitive exclusion, etc. -- a common feature of all parallel, nonlinear competitive systems?

(3) Are multi-functional units (units that can serve in several contexts) the major stepping-stone employed by all ANNs in making adaptive advances?

(4) What environmental conditions favor recombination, imprinting, triggering, and other constrained or biased procedures for generating new trials (rules, chromosomes, organizational structures, etc.)?

(5) What environmental conditions favor

tracking vs. averaging, exploration vs. exploitation, etc.?
(6) What combinations of operators yield
implicit parallelism?

Traditional mathematics with its reliance
upon linearity, convergence, fixed points, and
the like, seems to offer few tools for studying
such questions. Yet, without a relevant
mathematical framework, there is less chance
of understanding ANNs than there would be of
understanding physical phenomena in the
absence of guidance from theoretical physics. A
mathematics that puts emphasis on combinatorics and competition between parallel
processes is the key to understanding ANNs.
What seems startling when one uses differential
equations, where the emphasis is on continuity, is comonplace in a programming or
recursive format, where the emphasis is upon
combinatorics. (Consider, for example, the
chaotic regimes that are so unexpected in the
context of differential equations, but are an
everday occurrence, in the guise of biased
random number generators, in the programming context.)

Because classifier systems are formally
defined and computer-oriented, with an
emphasis on combination and competition, they
offer a useful test-bed for both mathematical
and simulation studies of ANNs. We already
have some theorems that provide a deeper
understanding of the behavior of classifier
systems (see the Appendix), and simulations
suggest a broader class of theorems that
delineate the conditions under which internal
models (q-morphisms) emerge in response to
complex environments (Holland [1986b]).

By putting classifier systems in a broader
context, we can bring to bear relevant pieces
of mathematics from other studies. For
instance, in mathematical economics there are
pieces of mathematics that deal with (1)
hierarchical organization, (2) retained earnings
(fitness) as a measure of past performance,
(3) competition based on retained earnings, (4)
distribution of earnings on the basis of local
interactions of consumers and suppliers, (5)
taxation as a control on efficiency, and (6)

division of effort between production and
research (exploration versus exploration).
Many of these fragments, mutatis mutandis,
can be used to study the counterparts of these
processes in other ANNs.

As another example, in mathematical
ecology there are pieces of mathematics dealing
with (1) niche exploitation (models exploiting
environmental opportunities), (2) phylogenetic
hierarchies, polymorphism and enforced
diversity (competing subsystems), (3) functional convergence (similarities of subsystem
organization enforced by environmental
requirements on payoff attainment), (4)
symbiosis, parasitism, and mimicry (couplings
and interactions in a default hierarchy, such
as an increased efficiency for extant generalists
simply because related specialists exclude them
from some regions in which they are
inefficient), (5) food chains, predator-prey
relations, and other energy transfers (apportionment of energy or payoff amongst
component subsystems), (6) recombination of
multifunctional co-adapted sets of genes (recombination of building blocks), (7) assortative
mating (biased or triggered recombination), (8)
phenotypic markers affecting interspecies and
intraspecies interactions (coupling), (9) "found-
er" effects (generalists giving rise to specialists),
and (10) other detailed commonalities such as
tracking versus averaging over environmental
changes (compensation for environmental
variability), allelochemicals (cross-inhibition),
linkage (association and encoding of features),
and still others. Once again, though
mathematical ecology is a young science, there
is much in the mathematics that has been
developed that is relevant to the study of other
nonlinear systems far from equilibrium.

The task of theory is to explain the
pervasiveness of these features by elucidating
the general mechanisms that assure their
emergence and evolution. Properly applied to
classifier systems, or to ANNs in general, such
a theory militates against ad hoc solutions,
assuring robustness and adaptability for the
resulting organization. One of the best ways to
insure that the mechanisms investigated are
general is "to look over your shoulder"

frequently to see if the mechanisms apply to all ANNs. This view is sharpened if we pay close attention to features shared by all ANNs:

(1) *Hierarchical organization*. All ANNs exhibit an hierarchical organization. In living systems proteins combine to form organelles, which combine to form cell types, and so on, through organs, organisms, species, and ultimately ecologies. Economies involve individuals, departments, divisions, companies, economic sectors, and so on, until one reaches national, regional, and world economies. A similar story can be told for each of the areas cited. These structural similarities are more than superficial. A closer look shows that the hierarchies are constructed on a "building block" principle: Subsystems at each level of the hierarchy are constructed by combination of small numbers of subsystems from the next lower level. Because even a small number of building blocks can be combined in a great variety of ways there is a great space of subsystems to be tried, but the search is biased by the building blocks selected. At each level, there is a continued search for subsystems that will serve as suitable building blocks at the next level.

(2) *Competition*. A still closer look shows that in all cases the search for building blocks is carried out by competition in a population of candidates. Moreover there is a strong relation between the level in the hierarchy and the amount of time it takes for competitions to be resolved -- ecologies work on a much longer time-scale than proteins, and world economies change much more slowly than the departments in a company. More carefully, if we associate random variables with subsystem ratings (say fitnesses), then the sampling rate decreases as the level of the subsystem increases. As we will see, this has profound effects upon the way in which the system moves through the space of possibilities.

(3) *Game-like system/environment interaction*. An ANN interacts with its environment in a game-like way: Sequences of action ("moves") occasionally produce *payoff*, special inputs that provide the system with the wherewithall for continued existence and adaptation. Usually payoff can be treated as a simple quantity (energy in physics, fitness in genetics, money in economics, winnings in game theory, reward

in psychology, error in control theory, etc.) It is typical that payoff is sparsely distributed in the environment and that the adaptive system must compete for it with other systems in the environment.

(4) *Exploitation of regularities*. The environment typically exhibits a range of regularities or *niches* that can be exploited by different action sequences or *strategies*. As a result the environment supports a variety of processes that interact in complex ways, much as in a multi-person game. Usually there is no super-process that can outcompete all others so an ecology results (domains in physics, interacting species in ecological genetics, companies in economics, cell assemblies in neurophysiological psychology, etc.). The very complexity of these interactions assures that even large systems over long time spans can have explored only a minuscule range of possibilities. Even for much-studied board games such as chess and go this is true; the not so simply defined "games" of ecological genetics, economic competition, immunogenesis, CNS activity, etc., are orders of magnitude more complex. As a consequence the systems are always far from any optimum or equilibrium situation.

(5) *Exploration vs. exploitation*. There is a tradeoff between *exploration* and *exploitation*. In order to explore a new niche a system must use new and untried action sequences that take it into new parts (state sets) of the enviroment. This can only occur at the cost of departing from action sequences that have well-established payoff rates. The ratio of exploration to exploitation in relation to the opportunities (niches) offered by the environment has much to do with the life history of a system.

(6) *Tracking vs. averaging*. There is also a tradeoff between "tracking" and "averaging". Some parts of the environment change so rapidly relative to a given subsystem's response rate that the sub-system can only react to the average effect; in other situations the subsystem can actually change fast enough to respond "move by move". Again the relative proportion of these two possibilities in the niches the subsystem inhabits has much to do with the subsystem's life history.

(7) *Nonlinearity*. The value ("fitness") of a given combination of building blocks often cannot be predicted by a summing up of values assigned to the component blocks. This nonlinearity (commonly called *epistasis* in genetics) leads to co-adapted sets of blocks (*alleles*) that serve to bias sampling and add additional layers to the hierarchy.

(8) *Coupling*. At all levels, the competitive interactions give rise to counterparts of the familiar interactions of population biology -- *symbiosis*, *parasitism*, *competitive exclusion*, and the like.

(9) *Generalists and specialists*. Subsystems can often be usefully divided into *generalists* (averaging over a wide variety of situations, with a consequent high sampling rate and high statistical confidence, at the cost of a relatively high error rate in individual situations) and *specialists* (reacting to a restricted class of situations with a lowered error rate, bought at the cost of a low sampling rate).

(10) *Multifunctionality*. Subsystems often exhibit multifunctionality in the sense that a given combination of building blocks can usefully exploit quite distinct niches (environmental regularities), typically with different efficiencies. Subsequent recombinations can produce specializations that emphasize one function, usually at the cost of the other. Extensive changes in behavior and efficiency, together with extensive *adaptive radiation*, can result from recombinations involving these multifunctional founders.

(11) *Internal models*. ANNs usually generate implicit internal models of their environments, models progressively revised and improved as the system accumulates experience. The systems *learn*. Consider the progressive improvements of the immune system when faced with antigens, and the fact that one can infer much about the system's environment and history by looking at the antigen population. This ability to infer something of a system's environment and history from its changing internal organization is the diagnostic feature of an implicit internal model. The models encountered are usually *prescriptive* -- they specify preferred responses to given environmental states -- but, for more complex systems (the CNS, for example), they may

also be more broadly *predictive*, specifying the results of alternative courses of action. The relevant mathematical concept of a model of process-like transformations is that of a *homomorphism*. Real systems almost never admit of models meeting the requirements for a homomorphism ("commutativity of the diagram"), but there are weakenings, the so-called *q-morphisms* (*quasi-homomorphsms*). The origin of a hierarchy can be looked upon as a sequence of progressively refined q-morphisms (specifically q-morphisms of Markov processes) based upon observation.

Functional Extensions.

The foregoing questions and commonalities, together with some of the problems already encountered in simulations, have already suggested extensions of the standard definitions (as in Holland [1980]) of classifiers systems.

One important change involves the way bids are used in determining the winners of competititions for activation. The standard way of doing this is to calculate a *bid* = [bid ratio]*[strength]. Under this arrangement, the local fixed points of classifiers are such that a generalist and a specialist active in the same situations will come to bid the same amount (because the strength of the generalist increases to the point of compensating for its smaller bid ratio, see the Appendix). This goes against the dictum that specialists should be favored in a competition with generalists. To compensate for this an *effective bid* is calculated by reducing the *bid* in proportion to the generality of the classifier producing the bid. The *effective bid* is then used in determining the probability that the classifier generating it is one of the winners of the competition. If the classifier wins it must pay the bid, *not* the effective bid, to its suppliers under the bucket brigade. Thus, the local fixed points are not changed, but specialists *are* favored in competition with generalists. This change goes a long way toward reducing instabilities in emergent default hierarchies. (We are still exploring the effects in simulations and, at the level of theory, the resulting modifications in global fixed points).

A related change concerns the method of determining a classifier's probability of producing offspring, its fitness, under the genetic algorithm. The higher strength of a generalist at its local fixed point greatly favors it in the production of offspring, and simulations indicate that this overbiases the evolution of the system toward the offspring of generalists. The simplest way of compensating for this is to make the fitness proportional to [bid ratio]*[strength] rather than strength alone. In intuitive terms, this makes the fitness proportional to the classifier's potential for affecting the system (its bid can be thought of as a "phenotypic" effect), rather than its reserves (strength is a quantity determined by its "genotypic" fixed-point). We have yet to carry out an organized set of simulations based on fitness so-determined.

Simulations have also revealed two other effects worth systematic investigation. The first of these is the "focussing" effect of the size of the message list (see R. Riolo's paper in this Proceedings). In effect, a small message list forces the system to concentrate on a few factors in the current situation. Clearly there is the possibility of making the size of the message list depend upon the "urgency" of the situation. For example, during "lookahead" the message list's size can be quite large to encourage an exploration of possibilities, while at "execution" time the size can be reduced to enforce a decision. Clearly, the system can use classifiers to control the size of the message list. This makes the size dependent upon the system's "reading" of the current situation, and the "reading" is subject to long-term adaptive change under the genetic algorithm.

A second simple effect is to revise the definition of the environment, or equivalently the definition of the system's speed, so that typical stimuli persist for several time-steps. (This corresponds to the fact that the CNS operates rapidly relative to typical changes in its environment -- usually, milliseconds vs. tenths of a second.) The resulting "persistence" and "overlap" of input messages makes it much easier for the classifier system to develop causal

models and associative links (see below). As yet, to my knowledge, no simulations have been built along these lines.

At a much more general (and speculative) level, use of *triggered* genetic operators provides a major extension of genetic algorithms. Triggering amounts to invoking genetic operators with selected arguments, when certain pre-defined conditions are satisfied.

As an example of a triggering condition consider the following: "Only general classifiers that produce weak bids are activated by the current input message." When this condition occurs it is a sign that the system has little specific information for dealing with the current environmental situation. Let this condition trigger a cross between the input message and the condition parts of some of the active general rules. The result will be plausible new rules with more specific conditions. This amounts to a bottom-up procedure for producing candidate rules that will automatically be tested for usefulness when similar situations recur.

As another example of a triggering condition consider: "Rule C has just made a large profit under the bucket brigade." Satisfaction of this condition signals a propitious time to couple the profitable classifier to its stage-setting precursor. An appropriate cross between the message part of a rule C_0 active on the immediately preceding time-step -- the precursor -- and the condition part of the profit-making successor can produce a new pair of *coupled* rules. (The trigger is *not* activated if C_0 is already coupled to C). The coupled, offspring pair models the state transition mediated by the original pair of (uncoupled) rules. Such coupled rules can serve as the building blocks for models of the environment. Because the couplings serve as "bridges" for the bucket brigade, these building blocks will be assigned credit in accord with the efficacy of the models constructed from them. Interestingly enough, there seems to be a rather small number of robust triggering conditions (see Holland et al. [1986]), but each of them would appear to add substantially to the responsiveness of the classifier system.

Tags are particularly affected by triggering conditions that provide new couplings. Tags serve as the glue of larger systems, providing both associative and temporal (model-building) pointers. Under certain kinds of triggered coupling the message sent by the precursor in the coupled pair can have a "hash-coded" section (say a prefix or suffix). The purpose of this hash-coded tag is to prevent accidental eavesdropping by other classifiers -- a sufficient number of randomly generated bits in the tag will prevent accidental matches with other conditions (unless the tag region in the condition part of the potential eavesdropper consists mostly #'s). If the coupled pair proves useful to the system then it will have further offspring under the genetic algorithm, and these offspring often will be coupled to other rules in the system. Typically, the tag will be passed on to the offspring, serving as a common element in all the couplings. The tag will only persist if the resulting cluster of rules proves to be a useful "subroutine". In this case, the "subroutine" can be "called" by messages that incorporate the tag, because the conditions of the rules in the cluster are satisfied by such messages.

In short, the tag that was initially determined at random now "names" the developing subroutine. It even has a *meaning* in terms of the actions it calls forth. Moreover, the tag is subject to the same kinds of recombination as other parts of the rules (it is, after all, a schema). As such it can serve as a building block for other tags. It is as if the system were inventing symbols for its internal use. Clearly, any simulation that provides for a test of these ideas will be an order of magnitude more sophisticated than anything we have tried to date. Runs involving hundreds of thousands of time-steps and thousands of classifiers will probably be required to test these ideas.

Support is another technique that adds considerably to the system's flexibility. Basically, support is a technique that enables the classifier system to integrate many pieces of partial information (such as several views of a partially obscured object) to arrive at strong conclusions. Support is a quantity that travels *with* messages, rather than being a counter-flow as in the case of bids. When a classifier is satisfied by several messages from the message list, each such message adds its support into that classifier's *support counter*. Unlike a classifier's strength, the support accrued by a classifier lasts for only the time-step in which it is accumulated. That is, the support counter is reset at the end of each time-step (other techniques are possible, such as a long or short half-life). Support is used to modify the size of the classifier's bid on that time-step; large support increases the bid, small support decreases it. If the classifier wins the bidding competition, the message it posts carries a support proportional to the size of its bid. The propagation of support over sets of coupled classifiers acts somewhat like spreading activation (see Anderson [1983]), but it is much more directed. It can bring associations (coupled rules) into play while serving its primary mission of integrating partial information (messages from several weakly-bidding, general rules that satisfy the same classifier).

In addition to these broadly conceived extensions, there are more special extensions that may have global consequences, particularly in respect to increased responsiveness and robustness. One of these concerns a simple redefinition of classifiers. The standard definition of a 2-condition classifier requires that *each* condition be satisfied by some message on the message list, in effect an AND, requiring a message of type X and a message of type Y. It is a simple thing to replace the implicit AND with other string operators, e.g. a bit-by-bit AND or a binary sum of the satisfying messages, which is then passed through as the outgoing message. This extension has been implemented, but has not been systematically tested.

Other simple extensions impact the functioning of the genetic algorithm. It is easy to introduce, in the string defining a classifier, *punctuation marks* that bias the probability of crossover (say crossover is twice as likely to take place adjacent to a punctuation mark). These punctuation marks are not interpreted in executing the classifier, but they bias the form of its offspring under the genetic algorithm. Punctuation marks can be treated as alleles under the genetic algorithm, subject to mutation, crossover, etc., just as the other (function-defining) alleles. This ensures that the placement of punctuation marks is adaptively determined. Similarly one can introduce *mating tags* that restrict crossover to classifiers with similar tags; again the tags, as part of the classifier, can be made subject to modification and selection by the genetic algorithm.

Finally, there are two broad ranges of investigation, far beyond anything we yet understand either theoretically or empirically, that offer intriguing possibilities for the future. One of these stems from the fact that classifier systems are general-purpose. They can be programmed initially to implement whatever expert knowledge is available to the designer; learning then allows the system to expand, correct errors, and transfer information from one domain to another. It is important to provide ways of instructing such systems so that they can generate rules -- tentative hypotheses -- on the basis of advice. It is also important that we understand how lookahead and virtual explorations can be incorporated without disturbing other activities of the system. Little has been done in either direction.

The other realm of investigation concerns fully-directed rule generation. In a precursor of classifier systems, the *broadcast language* (Holland [1975]), provision was made for the generation of rules by other rules. With minor changes to the definition of classifier systems, this possibility can be reintroduced. (Both messages and rules are strings. By enlarging the message alphabet, lengthening the message string, and introducing a special symbol that indicates whether a string is to be interpreted as a rule or a message, the task can be accomplished.) With this provision the system can invent its own candidate operators and rules of inference. Survival of these meta-(operator-like) rules should then be made to depend on the net usefulness of the rules they generate (much as a schema takes it value from the average value of its carriers). It is probably a matter of a decade or two before we can do anything useful in this area.

Mathematical Extensions.

There are at least two broader mathematical tasks that should be undertaken. One is an attempt to produce a general characterization of systems that exhibit *implicit parallelism*. Up to now all such attempts have led to sets of algorithms that are easily recast as genetic algorithms -- in effect, we still only know of one example of an algorithm that exhibits implicit parallelism.

The second task involves developing a mathematical formulation of the process whereby a system develops a useful internal model of an environment exhibiting perpetual novelty. In our (preliminary) experiments to date, these models typically exhibit a (tangled) hierarchical structure with associative couplings. As mentioned earlier, such structures can be characterized mathematically as quasi-homomorphisms (see Holland et al. [1986]). The perpetual novelty of the environment can be characterized by a Markov process in which each state has a recurrence time that is large relative to any feasible observation time. Considerable progress can be made along these lines (see Holland [1986b]), but much remains to be done. In particular, we a need to construct an interlocking set of theorems based on:
(1) a more global set of fixed point theorems that relates the strengths of classifiers under the bucket brigade to observed payoff statistics;
(2) a set of theorems that relates building blocks exploited by the "slow" dynamics of the genetic algorithm to the sampling rates for rules at different levels of the emerging default hierarchy (more general rules are tested more often); and
(3) a set of theorems (based on the previous two sets) that detail the way in which various kinds of environmental regularities are exploited by the genetic algorithm acting in terms of the strengths assigned by the bucket brigade.

Appendix.

A simplified version of the fundamental theorem for genetic algorithms can be stated as follows (for an explanation of terms, see Holland [1975] or Holland [1986a]).

Theorem (*Implicit parallelism*). Given a *fitness function* $u: (0,1)^k \to Reals^+$, a *population* $B(t)$ of M strings drawn from the set $(0,1)^k$, and any *schema* $s \in (0,1,*)^k$ defining a hyperplane in $(0,1)^k$,

$$M_s(t+1) \geq u\hat{\ }_s(t)\epsilon_s M_s(t),$$

where $M_s(t+1)$ is the expected number of instances of s in $B(t+1)$,

$$u\hat{\ }_s(t) = \sum_{b \in s \text{ AND } b \in B(t)} u(b)/M_s(t),$$

is the average observed fitness of the instances of schema s in $B(t)$, and

$$\epsilon_s = (1-(k_s-1)P_{cross})/(k-1)),$$

is a "copying error" induced by crossover, where P_{cross} is a constant of the genetic algorithm (often $P_{cross} = 1$) giving the proportion of strings undergoing crossover in a given generation, and k_s-1 is the number of crossover points between the outermost defining symbols of $s \in (0,1,*)^k$.

Under interpretation, the implicit parallelism theorem says that the sampling rate for *every* schema with instances in the population is expected to increase or decrease at a rate specified by its observed average fitness, with an error proportional to its defining length.

Theorem (*Speedup*). The number of schemas processed with an error $< \epsilon$ under a genetic algorithm considerably exceeds M^3 for a population of size $M = 2^{\frac{1}{2}k'}$, where $\epsilon = k'/k$.

Theorem (*Bucket brigade local fixed-point*). If, under the bucket brigade algorithm, I_c is the long-term average income (after taxes) of a classifier C, and r_c is its bid-ratio, then its strength S_c will approach I_c/r_c.

Theorem (*q-morphism parsimony*; for definitions, see Holland et al. [1986]). A q-morphism of n levels, in which each successive level uses k or fewer additional variables to define exceptions to the previous level, and in which the rules at each level are correct over at least a proportion p of the instances satisfying them, requires no more than $\sum_j n_2{}^{jk}(1-p)^{j-1}$ rules. (A homomorphism defined on nk variables requires 2^{nk} rules). For n=10, k=2, p=0.5, the q-morphism requires fewer than 2^{12} rules, while a corresponding homomorphism would require 2^{20} rules; that is, the homomorphism would require at least 256 times as many rules as the q-morphism.

References.

Anderson, J. R. [1983]. *The Architecture of Cognition*. Cambridge, Massachusetts: Harvard University Press.

Holland, J. H. [1975]. *Adaptation in Natural and Artificial Systems*. Ann Arbor: University of Michigan Press.

Holland, J. H. [1980]. "Adaptive algorithms for discovering and using general patterns in growing knowledge-bases." *International J. Policy Analysis and Information Systems*, 4, 2. 217-240.

Holland, J. H. [1986a]. "Escaping brittleness: The possibilities of general purpose algorithms applied to parallel rule-based systems." Ch. 20 in *Machine Learning II*. (eds. Michalski, R. S., et al.). Los Altos: Morgan Kaufmann.

Holland, J. H. [1986b]. "A mathematical framework for studying learning in classifier systems." *Physica 22D* 307-317.

Holland, J. H., Holyoak, K. J., Nisbett, R. E., and Thagard, P. R. [1986]. *Induction: Processes of Inference, Learning, and Discovery*. Cambridge, Massachusetts: MIT Press.

Acknowledgments.

Much of the research reported here has been supported by the National Science Foundation, currently under grant IRI 8610225. The author also wants to thank the Los Alamos National Laboratory for a year (1986-87) as Ulam Scholar at the Center for Nonlinear Studies, a year to pursue his chosen research objectives without hinderances.

GREEDY GENETICS

by

G. E. Liepins & M. R. Hilliard
Oak Ridge National Laboratory, Oak Ridge, TN 37831*

Mark Palmer & Michael Morrow
University of Tennessee, Knoxville, TN 37996

ABSTRACT

The performance of conventional and PMX genetic algorithms as problem optimizers is compared with greedy algorithms coupled with genetic algorithms. Set covering, traveling salesman, and job shop scheduling problems form the basis for the comparison. Conventional and PMX genetic algorithms are suggested to be robust, although not particularly distinguished, optimizers for the class of problems studied in this paper. Greedy genetics are recommended only when the underlying greedy algorithm is powerful, but not optimal; it remains difficult to characterize when greedy genetics will outperform pure greedy algorithms.

INTRODUCTION

The goal of this research is to investigate whether the population diversity of genetic algorithms can be favorably used to ameliorate the myopic tendencies of the greedy algorithm; or in short, is a synergistic combination possible? (Greedy algorithms are best-first search algorithms with no backtracking -- see Lawler, 1976 and Nilsson, 1980.) This paper contrasts the performance of greedy genetics to conventional and PMX genetic algorithms. A comparison with established operations research algorithms and techniques such as simulated annealing awaits further experiments.

A criticism of conventional genetic algorithms as optimizers is that they fail to incorporate problem structure in their formulation. Their only tie to the specific function being optimized is through the reward structure. The incorporation of the greedy algorithm allows problem specific information to be used in the crossover operation.

Three classes of problems are studied: set covering, traveling salesman, and job shop scheduling. Not unexpectedly, results suggest that when the associated greedy algorithm is powerful (that is, a single application of the algorithm produces a generally "reasonable" solution), greedy genetics outperform conventional and PMX genetics. Conversely, when the greedy algorithm is weak, greedy genetics perform worse than conventional genetics. No definitive comparison can be drawn regarding the comparative performance of the pure greedy algorithm and greedy genetics. The lesson seems to be that the conventional and PMX genetic algorithms are robust; use greedy genetics only when there is good reason to believe that the underlying greedy is powerful but not optimal.

Conventional Genetics

Genetic algorithms were originally developed by Holland (1975). Follow-on research of their suitability as function optimizers has been completed by DeJong (1975) and Bethke (1980). The basic regimen contains five major features: (1) representation of the solution space as a binary string, (2) a critic (function evaluation), (3) reproduction, (4) crossover, and (5) mutation.

Hidden behind the conceptual simplicity of the genetic algorithm are a variety of parameters and policies such as crossover rate, mutation rate, and replacement policy -- all of whose settings affect performance (DeJong 1975; Liepins and Hilliard, 1986). With the parameters properly set, conventional genetic algorithms are robust and powerful when applied to multimodal real valued optimization problems (DeJong 1975; Bethke 1980). However, they are sorely inadequate for combinatorial optimization problems whose solutions require manipulation of permutations (problems such as the traveling salesman and job shop scheduling). Goldberg and Lingle (1985) modified the basic genetic algorithm to handle permutations by the introduction of the partially-mapped crossover (PMX). The example Goldberg and Lingle use to illustrate PMX considers two permutations of ten objects:

$$A = 9\ 8\ 4\ 5\ 6\ 7\ 1\ 3\ 2\ 10$$
$$B = 8\ 7\ 1\ 2\ 3\ 10\ 9\ 5\ 4\ 6$$

If two random numbers, say 4 and 6, are chosen as the crossover points for these two genes, then each is to be modified by the permutations (5 2), (6 3), and (7 10)

$$A = 9\ 8\ 4\ |\ 5\ 6\ 7\ |\ 1\ 3\ 2\ 10$$
$$B = 8\ 7\ 1\ |\ 2\ 3\ 10\ |\ 9\ 5\ 4\ 6$$

and the respective results become

$$A' = 9\ 8\ 4\ 2\ 3\ 10\ 1\ 6\ 5\ 7$$
$$B' = 8\ 10\ 1\ 5\ 6\ 7\ 9\ 2\ 4\ 3\ .$$

Goldberg and Lingle investigated survivability of o-schemata under PMS and then applied PMX to Karg and Thompson's ten city traveling salesman problem.

Greedy Genetics

Although they did not call it such, Grefenstette et al (1985) developed a greedy crossover for the traveling salesman problem:

1. For each pair of parents, pick a random city for the start.

2. Compare the two edges leaving the city (as represented in the two parents) and choose the shorter edge.

3. If the shorter parental edge would introduce a cycle into the partial tour, then extend the tour by a random edge.

4. Continue to extend the partial tour using steps two and three until the circuit is completed.

Grefenstette et al. applied their heuristic to a 50 city and a 100 city problem. Unfortunately, the results of Grefenstette et al. were not directly comparable to those of Goldberg and Lingle.

It might be expected that an analysis of schemata survivability (Goldberg, 1986) or a hill-climbing variant (Ackley, 1987) might be investigated for the greedy crossover. A little reflection suggests that the former is significantly more difficult than for PMX or traditional crossover operators. Alternating hill-climbing with genetic algorithms has produced successful results when interim populations suggested by the genetic algorithm provide good initial points for hill-climbing. However, the greedy algorithm (as implemented here) is not a "hill-climber", nor does it benefit from different starting points. On the other hand, Markov chain analysis (Goldberg and Segrest 1987) might provide insight into greedy genetics; such studies are expected to be pursued in later papers.

Implementation

The comparative analysis of conventional and greedy genetics was performed on three classes of problems: set covering (SCP), job shop scheduling (JSS), and traveling salesman (TSP). The genetic algorithm used was the Genesis system (Grefenstette 1986) modified to generate a single offspring for each crossover operation. This offspring replaced the most similar of its parents. (One offspring per crossover was mandated by the greedy genetics and was used in all crossover methods to insure comparability. Replacement of the most similar parent provided a simple yet efficient means of avoiding premature convergence-- a pervasive problem with greedy genetics.) Additional modifications were made to accommodate the integer coding underlying JSS and TSP. (No such modification was required for SCP.) PMX and greedy crossover operations were added to Genesis. A fixed population size of 75 was used for SCP and candidate solutions were represented as binary strings of length 25 (the SCP matrices were of dimension 50 x 25). A fixed population size of 50 was used for TSP and JSS for the majority of the experiments and the candidate solutions were represented as permutations of 15 objects (JSS and TSP problems involved 15 jobs and 15 cities, respectively). (Selected experiments were run with population sizes 100 and 250. The results differed little from those presented here.) Genesis parameters not explicitly discussed in the previous paragraphs were left at their default settings.

For each of the problem classes, a sample of problems were generated and the problems were attacked with both conventional and greedy versions of the genetic algorithm. Comparative performance of the best solution and trial at which it was achieved; as well as on-line, off-line, and average performance were all investigated. Golden and Stewart (1985) suggest a number of statistical tests to evaluate the relative performance of competing algorithms. They suggest the Wilcoxon signed rank test, the Friedman test, and an expected utility approach. Such tests are useful as confirmatory statistical analysis. However, the results of this paper are still considered preliminary and it is felt that little would be gained by additional statistical formalism.

Set-Covering

The set-covering problem (SCP) is NP-complete (Garey and Johnson 1979) and is often encountered in applications such as resource allocation (Revelle et al 1970) and scheduling (Marsten and Shepardson, 1981). Known solution techniques for SCP include such methods as integer programming; heuristic branch and bound; and most recently, Lagrangian relaxation with subgradient variations -- see Balas and Ho (1980) for a review of set covering solution techniques.

The usual representation of a set covering problem is as a zero/one matrix with a cost associated with each column. A set of columns is defined to cover the matrix if for each row of the matrix at least one of the columns of the set contains a '1' entry. The SCP objective is to find a minimal cost cover of the matrix as follows:

Let A be an $m \times n$ binary matrix and w_i, $i=1, \ldots, n$ non-negative costs.

$$\text{Minimize (over } \underline{\delta} \text{)} \sum_{i=1}^{n} w_i \delta_i$$

Subject to $A \underline{\delta} \geq \underline{1}$ where

a. $\underline{\delta} = (\delta_1, \ldots, \delta_n)^t$

b. $\underline{1}$ is an m-dimensional column vector of ones, and

c. each $\underline{\delta}_i$ is binary.

The genetic algorithm representation of SCP is straightforward: a candidate SCP solution is expressed as a binary string where a '1' in position i indicates that the ith column of the matrix is included in the solution. The reward is a large number M minus the sum of the cost of the columns used and a penalty function $P\eta$ for failure to cover:

$$R = M - \sum_{i=1}^{n} w_i \delta_i - P\eta$$

where δ_i and η are binary with $\eta = 0$ if the solution is a cover and $\eta = 1$ otherwise, and P is an appropriate scaling for the penalty. (The choice of the penalty scaling factor P is known to affect the performance of the genetic algorithm SCP performance, but will not be investigated in this paper.)

Each of single crossover, double crossover, and greedy crossover was investigated. The latter was defined as follows:

For every pair of parent genes,

1. Initialize the set S to be empty and the matrix A to be the original set covering matrix with columns $\{c_i\}$ and associated costs $\{w_i\}$.

2. For the unused columns and uncovered rows calculate the cost-ratio (cost/number-of-rows -covered = w_i/number-of-rows-covered).

3. Append to S the column (say column c) with the least cost that is included in one of the parents.

4. Strike column c and the rows covered by c from A and let this new matrix be A'.

5. If S is a cover or if no other columns are represented in the parents, stop. Otherwise, set A to A' and go to step 2.

The greedy SCP crossover is illustrated in Figure 1.

```
parent 1: 1 0 0 0 0   w1=5  w2=2  w3=5  w4=4  w5=2
parent 2: 0 1 1 0 0    0     1     1     1     1
                       1     1     1     0     1
initial selection      0     0     0     1     0
for child: column      1     0     0     1     0
2 with cost-ratio 1
___ 1 ___ ___ ___

                       second-stage cost-ratio
second
selection:  column 1  column 3  column 4  column 5
column 1      5          ∞          2         ∞
1 1 ___ ___ ___
```

Note: Column 4 was not selected because it was not represented in either parent.

Figure 1. Greedy crossover for SCP.

The experimental design for the set-covering problem involved matrix density as an additional parameter. (Matrix density for a zero-one matrix is the proportion of ones in the matrix.) Five test problems were generated for each of the (expected) densities ranging from 10% to 90%. The results are displayed below: Table 1 presents the relative success of each of the methods on each of the classes of the problems and Table 2 presents a problem by problem breakdown of the performance. Generation average performance and best of generation performance was displayed for representative matrices of 30% and 70% density in Figures 2-5.

PROBLEM DENSITY	CROSSOVER METHOD					
	one-point wins	ties	two-point wins	ties	greedy wins	ties
10				1	4	
20				1	4	1
30				2	3	2
40	1			1	?	1
50		2			3	2
60				1	4	1
70		1		2	3	2
80		2		2	2	3
90		1		1	3	2
Totals	1	6	1	10	29	14

Table 1. Relative SCP performance by problem density and crossover method.

The major conclusion that can be drawn from the SCP results is that the greedy genetics for the set-covering problem not only yield a better solution than either the pure greedy or conventional genetics, but that convergence to that solution is much more rapid than with conventional genetics.

Job Shop Scheduling

The JSS problem (just like the TSP) problem is a pure ordering problem. Since it is not guaranteed to result in an order, conventional crossover is not applicable to ordering problems unless the problems are formulated as a penalty function problem. Otherwise, mechanisms such as PMX must be used and the underlying genetic building blocks are the o-schemata. Bethke (1980) analyzed GA-hard functions using Walsh transforms, group characters of the group πZ_2, the n-fold Cartesian product of the group Z_2 with component-wise addition (Dym and McKean 1972). A natural extension of Bethke's work to the analysis of "GA-order-hard" functions might be based on the group representations of the symmetric group (Boerner 1963).

Three types of crossover operators were investigated for job shop scheduling: PMX, a weak greedy crossover, and a powerful greedy crossover. The job shop scheduling problem investigated was the simplest scheduling problem: a static queue of jobs with specified due dates and run times with no precedence constraints, a single server and minimal

		1 Pt. Best	Cross Trial	2 Pt. Best	Cross Trial	Greedy Best	Cross Trial	Pure Greedy[@]	Optimal
	1:	61.29	412	62.03	560	60.11	80	60.11	?
	2:	45.72	593	47.79	593	48.2	56	48.76	?
10%	3:	48.31	613	43.16	630	43.28	258	44.42	?
	4:	49.72	702	51.58	663	49.11	90	49.82	?
	5:	55.79	547	50.85	389	48.38	77	48.38	?
	1:	19.36	682	18.78	831	18.78	61	22.33	?
	2:	34.54	550	33.6	496	29.34	669	31.27	?
20%	3:	33.66	713	38.37	524	27.49	114	30.25	?
	4:	26.42	534	27.02	783	22.22	646	24.17	?
	5:	24.09	614	16.23	641	13.41	75	16.03	?
	1:	16.30	786	11.52	787	11.52	77	11.52	11.52
	2:	20.13	918	16.70	733	16.06	93	17.19	14.80
30%	3:	8.46	611	11.85	913	8.20	85	8.20	8.20
	4:	17.77	763	18.10	431	18.10	108	20.06	?
	5:	9.99	688	8.83	915	7.55	96	7.57	7.55
	1:	10.73	937	11.58	788	11.53	81	11.53	10.70
	2:	12.21	791	12.97	745	9.78	108	11.62	9.56
40%	3:	11.38	949	11.70	1006	7.50	95	7.50	7.50
	4:	7.99	523	6.45	633	6.45	96	6.82	6.42
	5:	17.95	631	15.26	612	13.31	104	16.00	12.64
	1:	3.62	703	5.45	623	2.86	78	3.62	2.86
	2:	4.38	378	5.40	434	4.38	79	4.38	4.38
50%	3:	8.07	855	11.16	684	7.57	81	7.57	7.57
	4:	6.10	992	·8.91	718	6.10	220	7.90	6.10
	5:	6.39	929	6.39	644	6.27	90	6.39	6.19
	1:	4.75	893	4.24	913	3.12	90	3.28	3.12
	2:	6.49	687	4.66	581	4.66	1014	5.23	4.66
60%	3:	6.14	723	6.14	962	5.86	77	5.86	5.31
	4:	5.15	799	3.64	795	3.63	82	3.63	3.63
	5:	6.93	493	4.05	779	3.77	76	5.12	3.77
	1:	4.78	645	4.49	607	4.49	107	5.76	3.96
	2:	3.42	663	2.15	795	1.76	94	2.04	1.76
70%	3:	2.31	547	2.31	729	2.31	76	2.31	2.31
	4:	5.21	727	3.00	610	2.64	97	2.78	2.64
	5:	0.96	473	0.96	540	0.61	77	0.76	0.61
	1:	0.92	728	2.09	802	0.92	78	0.92	0.92
	2:	2.03	426	2.03	922	2.03	92	2.69	2.03
80%	3:	3.89	442	3.41	548	2.25	85	2.92	2.25
	4:	4.85	545	5.46	922	4.13	80	4.18	3.70
	5:	3.58	819	2.59	686	2.59	80	3.58	2.59
	1:	3.08	887	0.62	551	0.62	76	0.78	0.62
	2:	0.66	979	1.19	787	0.66	86	0.68	0.66
90%	3:	0.73	851	0.54	815	0.51	79	0.72	?
	4:	3.82	667	3.81	532	3.65	80	5.20	3.65
	5:	1.33	738	2.34	825	1.04	76	1.04	1.04

[@] Greedy heuristic applied recursively until a cover is generated.

Table 2. Problem by problem SCP performance.

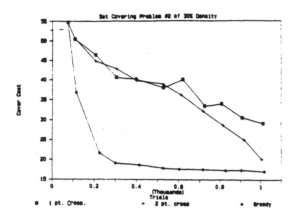

Figure 2. Generation average performance.

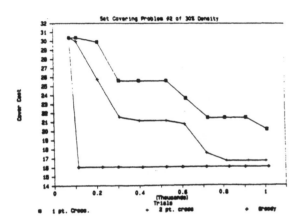

Figure 3. Best of generation.

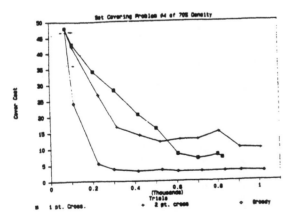

Figure 4. Generation average performance.

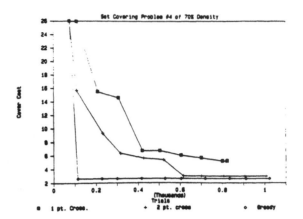

Figure 5. Best of generation

(signed) lateness as the criterion. (The more complicated job shop scheduling problem considered by Davis (1985) was not investigated.) A well known heuristic provides the optimal job schedule for this problem: "Order the queue according to increasing run times." The two versions of the greedy crossovers were based on weak and powerful heuristics, respectively. The powerful heuristic is the optimal heuristic previously discussed; the weak heuristic states "order the queue according to increasing difference between due date and run time"; that is, a job with an early due date and a long run time would be scheduled before a job with a late due date and a short run time. The greedy crossovers are implemented as follows:

1. For each parent pair, start at the first job (i=1).

2. Compare the two jobs at the ith position of the two parents and place the better (according to the heuristic being used) of the two in the child's ith position. If one of the jobs has already been placed in the child, then automatically pick the other. If both of the jobs have already been placed, then pick a job randomly from the yet unplaced jobs.

3. Repeat step 2, incrementing i, until all positions in the child string are defined.

Results from the job shop scheduling experiments are presented in Table 3 and generation average and best of generation performance for each of the crossover methods for a representative JSS problem are graphically presented in Figures 6 and 7. It is obvious that the strong greedy crossover dominates PMX, which in turn dominates the weak greedy crossover. Repeated application of the powerful heuristic (pure strong greedy) would yield the optimal schedule with an evaluation of 0.00.

	PMX		Weak	Greedy	Strong	Greedy
	Best	Trial	Best	Trial	Best	Trial
1:	40.84	825	124.41	314	0.00	514
2:	33.78	913	51.42	951	8.82	321
3:	29.74	938	57.71	948	2.27	397
4:	59.60	873	86.93	984	6.99	370
5:	27.22	861	55.94	972	2.75	576
6:	34.94	967	68.76	849	3.34	462
7:	20.90	689	71.71	926	2.20	938
8:	14.68	890	112.84	887	0.00	545
9:	53.60	695	101.93	923	2.20	881
10:	13.52	994	203.40	169	0.00	432
11:	28.99	946	74.98	711	0.00	416
12:	48.14	835	115.14	422	0.00	1005
13:	18.02	941	63.18	955	1.60	481
14:	17.57	701	80.20	967	1.24	720
15:	15.07	976	150.09	397	10.85	424
16:	7.93	946	136.03	492	2.23	599
17:	50.18	786	208.27	43	3.24	959
18:	31.35	1007	122.13	29	4.71	828
19:	25.97	904	184.46	281	2.49	344
20:	46.00	793	183.39	681	3.78	937

Table 3. Problem by problem JSS performance

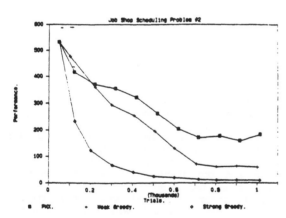

Figure 6. Generation average.

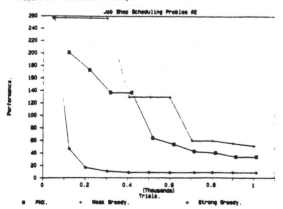

Figure 7. Best of generation.

Traveling Salesman Problem (TSP)

The traveling salesman problem (TSP) is another of the very difficult NP complete combinatorial ordering problems with a long history of interest. Few (1955) discovered a heuristic solution for the Euclidean problem with a guaranteed worst case performance of $\sqrt{2n} + 1.75$. Christofides (1976) discovered an elegant heuristic with a worst case error of 50% of optimal tour length. Karp (1977) showed that partitioning into subsets and concatenating optimal tours of each subset yields tours with expected percentage error approaching zero. Crowder and Padberg (1980) solved a 318 city tour to optimality, and Golden and Stewart (1985) reported excellent results for their CCAO heuristic. Of the many theorems and results relating to the TSP, two are of particular relevance to this paper.

Theorem 1 (Rosenkrantz, Stearns, and Lewis 1977). For every $r > 1$, there exist n-city instances of the TSP for arbitrarily large n obeying the triangle inequality such that $NN(I) > r \, OPT(I)$, where $NN(I)$ is the nearest neighbor optimal tour and $OPT(I)$ is the overall optimal tour.

problem #	nearest neighbor	pmx unanchored and seeded	pmx anchored and seeded	pmx anchored	greedy genetic seeded	greedy genetic
1	19484	19374[b]	18243[b]	23269	19211[b]	18243[ab]
2	16480[a]	16480[a]	16480[a]	18096	16480[a]	16480[a]
3	17673[a]	17673[a]	17673	22588	17673[a]	17815
4	15701	15626[b]	14837[b]	18495	14331[b]	14256[ab]
5	16219	16210[ab]	16219	18569	16219	16219
6	13613[a]	13613[a]	13613[a]	13613	13613[a]	13916
7	17400[a]	17400[a]	17400[a]	24578	17400[a]	17745
8	15067[a]	15067[a]	15067[a]	16714	15067[a]	15067[a]
9	19755	19755	10577[b]	25129	19555[ab]	19661[b]
10	21299	21299	20739[b]	23392	20778	19821[ab]
11	18034	17711[b]	17740[b]	22150	17364	17191[ab]
12	18587[a]	18587[a]	18587[a]	21998	18587[a]	19708
13	17078	17078	17078	21063	17078	15759[ab]
14	19535	19472[b]	19205[b]	23845	18581[ab]	18581[ab]
15	16052[a]	16052[a]	16052[a]	20856	16042[a]	16052[a]
16	21934	20228[b]	19897[b]	21442[b]	19253[b]	18971[ab]
17	16354	16354	16229[ab]	20352	16229[ab]	16354
18	21977	21977	21977	26089	21807a[b]	22668
19	17049	17006[ab]	17015[b]	22651	17049	18519
20	17869[a]	17869[a]	17869[a]	25119	17869[a]	17869[a]

Table 4. Problem by problem TSP performance

[a] best performance

[b] performance surpasses nearest neighbor

Theorem 2 (Papadimitriou and Steiglitz 1977). If A is a local search algorithm whose neighborhood search time is bounded by a polynomial of the problem representation, then if $P \neq NP$, A cannot be guaranteed to find a tour whose length is bounded by a constant multiple of the optimal tour even with an exponential number of iterations.

Theorem 1 is relevant to this paper because the standard against which the genetic algorithms are compared is the pure greedy algorithm, called the nearest neighbor solution in the operation research literature. The implication is that this standard itself could be poor.

Theorem 2 suggests that if the greedy genetic algorithm is a local search algorithm as is believed, then examples of tours can be found for which the algorithm performs arbitrarily poorly. Presumably, the same conclusions would hold for PMX.

The work presented here builds on that of Brockus (1983), Goldberg and Lingle (1985), and Grefenstette et al (1985). The results of those three studies were not directly comparable and it is interesting to ask how they compare. Moreover, none of the previous studies investigated the effect of seeding the initial populations, of anchoring the tours, or of stochastic variation due to different randomization.

Two types of crossover operators were investigated for the TSP: PMX and a modification of the greedy crossover of Grefenstette et al (1985). For the anchored case all members of the population were normalized to begin with the same starting city (city '1'). For the unanchored case this was not done and the starting cities were randomly chosen. For any two parents, the modified Grefenstette crossover (greedy crossover) produces a child according to the following specifications:

1. For a pair of parents, start at the first position (always the same city).

2. Choose the shortest edge leading from the current city (that is represented in the parents). If this edge leads to a cycle, choose the other edge. If this leads to a cycle, choose a random city that continues the tour.

3. If the tour is complete, stop; else go to 2.

The modified Grefenstette crossover will be called the greedy crossover and is always anchored in the results presented here. Both greedy crossover and PMX crossover were tested with seeded and unseeded initial populations. The seeded initial population included the fifteen optimal greedy algorithm generated tours (possibly including duplicates) beginning at each of the fifteen different cities. This subpopulation of fifteen was randomly extended to an initial population of fifty. The nearest neighbor tour was the best of the fifteen greedy algorithm generated tours. Results of the performance of the greedy and PMX crossovers are given in Table 4. Discouraging is the poor performance of the PMX with the unseeded population; only for one problem did it perform better than the nearest neighbor algorithm. Virtually no performance differential among the remaining variations of the genetic algorithm was observed; each performed somewhat better than the nearest neighbor. Perhaps surprisingly, the unseeded greedy genetic performed nearly as well as its seeded counterpart.

Relative performance between anchored and unanchored PMX and seeded and unseeded greedy crossover is presented in Table 5, where the 2 in the upper left hand corner indicates that the unanchored PMX performed better than the anchored PMX on two problems. The remaining entries are interpreted similarly. Apparently, no important differences are indicated. Figures 8 and 9 represent generation average performance and best of generation results for the fourth problem at 70% density.

Bethke (1980) has shown that for certain problems, genetic algorithms are unstable, that is, the solution determined seems to depend on genetic drift and on the randomization of the initial population and genetic mechanism. Tables 6 and 7 display the results of different randomization of initial populations and genetic mechanisms for the first problem at 10% density. Discouragingly, approximately 8% variation in performance can be noted for the greedy genetic as either initial population or genetic mechanism is randomized differently. The counterpart variations for the PMX are 13% and 17%, respectively. The implication seems to be that the TSP is a difficult problem for either the PMX or greedy genetics.

pmx unanchored and seeded	pmx anchored and seeded
2	6

greedy genetic seeded	greedy genetic unseeded
8	6

Table 5. Seeding and anchoring as factors in performance differential

population seed #	pmx	greedy genetic
1	22671	19636
2	22445	18243
3	21247	18733
4	22456	18771
5	24075	18858

Table 6. Random initial population seeds as a factor in performance differential

crossover seed #	pmx	greedy genetic
1	24029	19537
2	23244	20721
3	22167	20713
4	24074	20275
5	22427	19072
6	21460	20078
7	22898	19600
8	21628	19348
9	22671	19636
10	25125	20415

Table 7. Random seeds for GA mechanism as a factor in performance differential

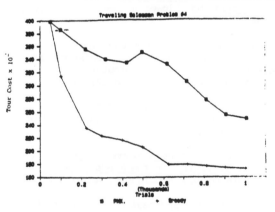

Figure 8. Generation average performance for unseeded initial population

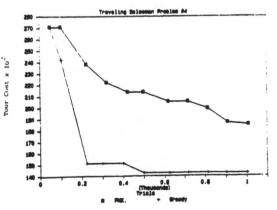

Figure 9. Best of generation for unseeded initial populations.

Conclusions and Future Research

Although little effort was made to optimize the algorithms investigated in this paper, the evidence suggests that greedy genetics can successfully make use of problem specific information whenever the underlying greedy algorithm is powerful. (The underlying greedy could be defined to be "powerful" whenever a single problem application of it results in a "reasonable" solution.) On the other hand, if the underlying greedy is misdirected, greedy genetics are less successful than traditional genetics. However, regardless of the power of the underlying greedy algorithm, greedy genetics often converge more rapidly that their conventional counterparts.

It appears that greedy genetics have their place in optimization and it would be interesting to extend this work to more realistic problems (such as job shop scheduling problems with precedence constraints and multiple servers) and to compare performance with more traditional optimization techniques. The variance in performance due to randomization. Markov chain results, extensions to Bethke's work, and proper penalty function formulations all deserve additional analysis.

RERERENCES

Ackley, D. H. (1987). A Connectionist Machine for Genetic Hillclimbing, Kluwer Academic Publishers, Boston, MA.

Balas, E. and A. Ho (1980). "Set Covering Algorithms Using Cutting Planes, Heuristics, and Subgradient Optimization: A Computational Study," Mathematical Programming 12, 37-60.

Bethke, A. D. (1980). Genetic Algorithms as Function Optimizers, Ph.D. Thesis, University of Michigan, Ann Arbor.

Boerner, H. (1963). Representations of Groups with Special Considerations for the Needs of Modern Physics, North Holland Publishers, Amsterdam.

Brockus, C. G. (1983). "Shortest Path Optimization Using a Genetics Search Technique", Proceedings of the Fourteenth Annual Modeling and Simulation Conference, Pittsburgh, PA. 241-5.

Christofides, N. (1976). Worst-Case Analysis of a New Heuristic for the Traveling Salesman Problem, Report 388, Graduate School of Industrial Administration, Carnegie Mellon University, Pittsburgh, PA.

Crowder, H. and M. W. Padberg. (1980). "Solving Large-Scale Symmetric Traveling Salesman Problems to Optimality, Management Science, 26, 495-509.

Davis, L., (1985). "Job Shop Scheduling with Genetic Algorithms," Proceedings of an International Conference on Genetic Algorithms and their Applications, Carnegie-Mellon University, Pittsburgh.

DeJong, K. A. (1975). An Analysis of the Behavior of a Class of Genetic Adaptive Systems," Ph.D. Thesis, University of Michigan, Ann Arbor.

Dym, H. and H. P. McKean (1972). Fourier Series and Integrals, Academic Press, New York.

Few, L. (1955). "The Shortest Path and the Shortest Road through n Points", Mathematika, 2, 141-144.

Garey, M. R., and D. S. Johnson, (1979). Computers and Intractability: A Guide to the Theory of NP-Completeness, Freeman, San Francisco.

Grefenstette, J. J., Gopal, B. J. Rosmaita, and D. V. Gucht, (July 1985). "Genetic Algorithms for the Traveling Salesman Problem," Proceedings of an International Conference on Genetic Algorithms and Their Applications, Carnegie-Mellon University, Pittsburgh.

Grefenstette, J. J., (April 1986). A User's Guide to GENESIS, Technical Report CS-84-11, Computer Science Department, Vanderbilt University, Nashville.

Goldberg, D. E. (1986). Simple Genetic Algorithms and the Minimal Deceptive Problem, The Clearinghouse for Genetic Algorithms, TCGA Report No. 86003, University of Alabama, Tuscaloosa.

Goldberg, D. E., and R. Lingle, (July 1985). "Alleles, Loci, and the Traveling Salesman Problem," Proceedings of a International Conference on Genetic Algorithms and Their Applications, Carnegie-Mellon University, Pittsburgh.

Goldberg, D. E., and P. D. Segrest, (to appear) "Finite Markov Chain Analysis of Genetic Algorithms", University of Alabama, Tuscaloosa.

Golden, B. L., and W. R. Stewart. (1985). Empirical Analysis of Heuristics in The Traveling Salesman Problem, Lawler et al (eds), John Wiley and Sons, 207-250.

Holland, J. H. (1975). Adaptation in Natural and Artificial Systems, University of Michigan Press, Ann Arbor.

Karp, R. M. (1977). "Probabilistic Analysis of Partitioning Algorithms for the Traveling Salesman Problems in the Plane, Math Operations Research 2, 209-224.

Lawler, E. L. (1976). Combinatorial Optimization: Networks and Matroids, Holt, Rinehart and Winston.

Lawler, E. H., J. K. Lenstra, A. H. G. Rinooykan, and D. B. Shmoys, (1985). The Traveling Salesman Problem, John Wiley and Sons.

Liepins, G. E., and M. R. Hilliard. (1986) "Representational Issues in Machine Learning", <u>Proceedings of the International Symposium on Methodologies for Intelligent Systems Colloquia Program</u>. Knoxville, TN. ORNL-6362.

Marsten, R. F., and F. Shepardson, 1981. "Exact Solution of Crew Scheduling Problems Using the Set Partitioning Model: Recent Successful Applications," <u>Networks</u>, Vol. 11, No. 2, pp. 165-177.

Nilsson, N. J. (1980). <u>Principles of Artificial Intelligence</u>, Tioga Publishing Company, Palo Alto, CA.

Papadimitriou, C. H., and K. Steiglitz. (1977) "On the Complexity of Local Search for the Traveling Salesman Problem". <u>SIAM</u> J. Comput.6, 78-83.

Revelle, C., D. Marks and J. C. Liebman (1970). "An Analysis of Private and Public Sector Facilities Location Models," <u>Management Science</u> 16, 12, 692-707.

Rosenkrantz, D. J., R. E. Stearns, and P. M. Lewis II, (1977). "An Analysis of Several Heuristics for the Traveling Salesman Problem", <u>SIAM</u> J. Comput. 6, 563-581.

INCORPORATING HEURISTIC INFORMATION INTO GENETIC SEARCH

Jung Y. Suh
Dirk Van Gucht

Computer Science Department
Indiana University
Bloomington, Indiana 47405
(812) 335-6429
CSNET: jysuh@indiana, vgucht@indiana

Keywords: Genetic Algorithms, Heuristics, Optimization Problems, Simulated Annealing, Sliding Block Puzzle, Traveling Salesman Problem.

Abstract
Genetic Algorithms have been shown to be robust optimization algorithms for (positive) real-valued functions defined over domains of the form R^n (R denotes the real numbers). Only recently have there been attempts to apply genetic algorithms to other optimization problems, such as combinatorial optimization problems. In this paper, we identify several obstacles which need to be overcome to successfully apply genetic algorithms to such problems and indicate how integrating heuristic information related to the problem under consideration helps in overcoming these obstacles. We illustrate the validity of our approach by providing genetic algorithms for the Traveling Salesman Problem and the Sliding Block Puzzle.

1. Introduction
Suppose we have an *object space* X and a function $f : X \to R^+$ (R^+ denotes the positive real numbers) and our task is to find a global minimum (or maximum) for the function f. In this paper, we will concentrate on *genetic algorithms*, a class of adaptive algorithms invented by John Holland [8], to solve (or partially solve) this problem.

Genetic algorithms differ from more standard search algorithms (e.g., gradient descent, controlled random search, hill-climbing, simulated annealing [9] etc.) in that the search is conducted using the information of a *population of structures* instead of that of a single structure. The motivation for this approach is that by considering many structures as potential candidate solutions, the risk of getting trapped in a local optimum is greatly reduced.

Genetic algorithms have been applied with great success by De Jong [4] to a wide variety of functions defined over object spaces of the form R^n, i.e., each structure x consists of n real numbers $x[1] \ldots x[n]$. Only recently have there been attempts to apply genetic algorithms to other optimization problems such has the Traveling Salesman Problem (TSP) [6, 7], Bin Packing [13], Job Scheduling [2, 3]. An important observation made by Grefenstette et.al. [7] was that to successfully apply genetic algorithms to such problems, heuristic information has to be incorporated into the genetic algorithm; in particular they proposed a heuristic crossover operator and showed the dramatic improvement as compared to crossover operators which did not such heuristic information. In this paper, we continue the efforts of [7]. In Section 2 we identify several problems which need to be overcome to successfully apply genetic algorithms to optimization problems other than the standard function optimization problems. In Sections 3 and 4 we illustrate the validity of our approach by providing genetic algorithms for the Traveling Salesman Problem and the Sliding Block Puzzle [12].

2. Design Issues of Genetic Algorithms
In this section, we outline the major obstacles in the design of genetic algorithms for optimization problems other than standard function optimization problems and suggest approaches to overcome them†.

2.1. The Representation Problem
As mentioned before, genetic algorithms have almost exclusively been applied to functions defined over object spaces of the form R^n. When we want to solve other optimization problems, such as combinatorial optimization problems, simple parametric representations of the structures can no longer be used. This suggests that the first step towards successfully applying genetic algorithms to these problems is to use a natural representation for the structures of the problem at hand. In particular, we suggest that the choice of such a representation allows for the definition of recombination operators which incorporate heuristic information of the problem. We thus imply that the selection of "good" representations and recombination operators are highly correlated (for a more detailed discussion of these issues we refer to [5]).

2.2. The Selection of Appropriate Recombination Operators and the Importance of Local Improvement
The power of applying genetic algorithms to functions defined over R^n is that the standard recombination operators, crossover and mutation, make intuitive sense in this problem. In other problem domains, however, this is not usually the case. Since the recombination step is critical for the success of a genetic algorithm, it is important to carefully select an appropriate set of recombination operators for such problem domains.

Early research on genetic algorithms [4, 8] was primarily concerned with operators which guarantee that (some) structural information of the structures to which they are applied is preserved. Examples of such recombination operators are the standard crossover, mutation and inversion operators used in function optimization. Grefenstette et.al. argued that such an approach does not carry over with similar success to the traveling salesman problem (TSP). They showed that considering recombination operators (in their case, only crossover operators) that merely preserve structural information results in poorly performing genetic algorithms (i.e., not much better than random search). They discovered however that it is possible and natural to incorporate heuristic information about the TSP into the crossover

---

† It should be noted that De Jong [5] and Grefenstette et.al. [7] already identified some of these problems.

operator and still maintain its fundamental property, namely: preservation of structural information of the structures to which the operator is applied. This resulted in a fairly successful genetic algorithm for the TSP, but certainly not an algorithm that is competitive with other approximation algorithms for the TSP (see [10]).

We claim that it is often the case that additional improvements can be gained if one incorporates even more heuristics about the problem into the recombination step of a genetic algorithm. Often, heuristics about problems are incorporated into algorithms in the form of operators which iteratively perform *local improvements* to candidate solutions. Examples of such operators can be found in gradient descent algorithms, hill climbing algorithms, simulated annealing, etc. We will argue that it is usually straightforward, and in fact, we think, essential if a competitive genetic algorithm is desired, to incorporate such local improvement operators into the recombination step of a genetic algorithm. An additional advantage of this approach is that it suggests a natural technique of blending genetic algorithms with more standard optimization algorithms.

2.3. Avoiding Premature Convergence

One of the major difficulties with genetic algorithms (and in fact with most search algorithms) is that sometimes premature convergence, i.e. convergence to a suboptimal solution, occurs. It has been observed that this problem is closely tied to the problem of losing diversity in the population. One source of loss in diversity is the occasional appearance of a "super-individual" which in a few generations takes over the population. One way of avoiding this problem is to change the selection procedure, as was demonstrated by Baker [1]. Another source of loss of diversity results from poor performance of recombination operators in terms of sampling new structures. To overcome such problems, we claim that the recombination operators should be selected carefully so that they can offset each others vulnerabilities (for a more detailed discussion of these issues, we refer to [1, 4, 7, 8]).

3. The Traveling Salesman Problem

In this section we show that solutions to the problems raised in Section 2 enable us to develop a genetic algorithm for the TSP.

The TSP is easily stated: Given a complete graph with N nodes, find the shortest Hamiltonian tour through the graph (in this paper, we will assume Euclidean distances between nodes). For an excellent discussion on the TSP, we refer to [10].

The object space X obviously consists of all Hamiltonian tours (tours, for short) associated with the graph, and f, the function to be optimized, returns the length of a tour.

As in [7], we represent a tour by its *adjacency representation*. It turns out that this representation allows us to easily formulate and implement heuristic recombination operators. In the adjacency representation, a tour is described by a list of cities. There is an edge in the tour from city i to city j if and only if the value in ith position of the adjacency representation is j. For example, the tour shown in Figure 1 is represented as (3 1 5 2 4).

We now turn to the most critical step of the design: the selection of appropriate recombination operators. We elected to have two such operators. The first operator is a slight modification of the heuristic crossover operator introduced by Grefenstette et.al. [7]. This operator constructs an offspring from two parent tours as follows: Pick a random city as the starting point for the offspring's tour. Compare the two edges leaving the starting city in the parents and choose the shorter edge. Continue to extend the partial tour by choosing the shorter of the two edges in the parents which extend the tour. If the shorter parental edge would introduce a cycle into the partial tour, check if the other parental edge introduces a cycle. In case the second

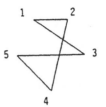

Figure 1. The tour (3 1 5 2 4).

edge does not introduce a cycle, extend the tour with this edge, otherwise extend the tour by a random edge. Continue until a complete tour is generated. It is in the selection of the shorter edges that we exploit heuristic information about the TSP; indeed, it seems likely that a good tour will contain short edges. The effect of the heuristic crossover operator is to "glue" together "good" (i.e., short) subpaths of the parent tours. (Notice also that it preserves structural information about the parent tours.) The problem with the heuristic crossover operator is that it leaves undesirable crossings of edges as illustrated in Figure 2 (see also Appendix 1). In other words, the heuristic crossover operates performs poorly when it comes down to fine-tuning candidate solutions. This motivated us to introduce a second recombination operator.

Whereas the heuristic crossover operator can be thought of as a global operator, the second recombination operator has a more local behavior and thus qualifies as a local improvement operator. It was introduced by Lin and Kernighan [11] and is called the 2-opt operator. The 2-opt operator randomly selects two edges (i_1, j_1) and (i_2, j_2) from a tour (see Figure 2) and checks if $ED(i_1, j_1) + ED(i_2, j_2) > ED(i_1, j_2) + ED(i_2, j_1)$ (ED stands for Euclidean distance). If this is the case, the tour is replaced by removing the edges (i_1, j_1) and (i_2, j_2) and replacing them with the edges (i_1, j_2) and (i_2, j_1) (see Figure 3). Actually, we use a more subtle variation of the 2-opt operator, inspired by recent work on *simulated annealing* for the TSP by Kirkpatrick et.al. [9]. In this variation there is a (small) probability (depending on a slowly decreasing temperature) that when $ED(i_1, j_1) + ED(i_2, j_2) \leq ED(i_1, j_2) + ED(i_2, j_1)$, the original tour is replaced using the previously described transformation †.

To make the description of our genetic algorithm complete, we need to describe three parameters:

a. **crossover rate**: this parameter indicates the amount of structures in the population which will undergo cross-

over.

b. **local improvement rate**: this parameter indicates the amount of structures in the population which will undergo 2-opt operations.

c. **2-opt rate**: if the graph under consideration has N nodes, each structure which is selected to undergo local improvement will undergo ($N \times$ **2 − opt rate**) 2-opt operations per generation.

The algorithm was stopped when the majority of the tours in the population were identical.

We tried our algorithm on a wide variety of (euclidean)

---

† It should be noted, however, that the performance of the algorithm with the simple 2-opt is usually only slightly worse than an algorithm that uses the simulated annealing version.

Figure 2. Tour with edges (i_1, j_1) and (i_2, j_2).

Figure 3. Tour with edges (i_1, j_2) and (i_2, j_1).

traveling salesman problems. In Figure 4, we show a selection of such problems.

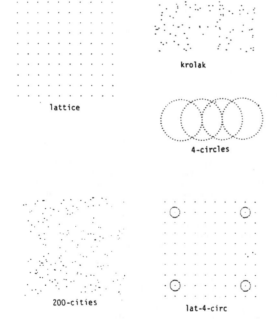

Figure 4. Five Traveling Salesman Problems

In Table 1, we show the results obtained by the algorithm of Grefenstette et.al. [7] for the following parameter settings: initial population = 100 randomly chosen tours, crossover rate = 50%, local improvement rate = 0%,

2-opt rate = not applicable. In Table 2, we show the results of a genetic algorithms which uses the local improvement operator with the following parameter settings: population size = 100 structures, crossover rate = 50%, local improvement rate = 50%, 2-opt rate = 0.1.

Table 1

Genetic Algorithm Without Local Improvement

TSP	Nodes	Optimum	Our Solution	Generations
krolak[10]	100	21282	25691	104
lattice	100	100	104.9	209
4-circles	200	24.67	39.0	300
lat-4-circ	200	112.56	139.2	286
200-cities	200	?	192.8	376

Table 2

Genetic Algorithm With Local Improvement

TSP	Nodes	Optimum	Our Solution	Generations
krolak	100	21282	21651	679
lattice	100	100	100	188
4-circles	200	24.5	24.5	218
lat-4-circ	200	112.56	113.3	669
200-cities	200	?	153.6	946

In Figure 5, we show the (best) tours obtained and the generation in which they were first found by the algorithm which uses local improvement. Clearly, the addition of a local improvement technique improves the performance (measured in terms of the tour length of the best tour obtained) of the algorithm dramatically. (In terms of extra resources, on average, the algorithm using local improvement required about 2.2 times more generations to obtain its best structure.) In fact, the results obtained by our algorithm are very competitive, again, in terms of the tour length of the best tour obtained, compared to results reported in the literature for other approximation algorithms for the TSP [9, 10]. (In Appendix 1, we give additional results.)

4. The Sliding Block Puzzle (SBP)

We now describe how the approach described in Section 2 can be used in the design of a genetic algorithm for a problem which is not usually thought of as a function optimization problem: the Sliding Block Puzzle [12]†.

Consider the initial board of the puzzle shown in Figure 6 and let the board shown in Figure 7 be a goal board (the empty tile is represented by the symbol 0).

```
 1  2  3  4
 5  6  7  8
 9  0 10 11
12 13 14 15
```

Figure 6. The Initial Board of a Sliding Block Puzzle.

```
 1  2  3  4
 6  9  0  8
 5 10  7 11
12 13 14 15
```

Figure 7. A Goal Board a Sliding Block Puzzle.

---

† In our implementation, we used 3×3 and 4×4 puzzles

krolak (21651)

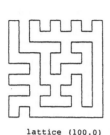

lattice (100.0)

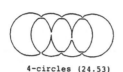

4-circles (24.53)

200-cities (153.67)

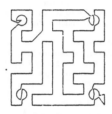

lat-4-circ (113.34)

Figure 5. Best Tours Obtained by a
Genetic Algorithm with Local Improvement.

The objective of the SBP is to reach the goal board starting from the intial board using a sequence of valid moves. There are four basic moves:

L: move the empty tile to the left.
U: move the empty tile upwards.
R: move the empty tile to the right.
D: move the empty tile downwards.

The only precondition required for applying a move is that it should not move the empty tile out of the board. For example, a sequence which transforms the board shown in Figure 6 into the board shown in Figure 7 is (L,U,R,D,R,U).

In order to apply genetic algorithms to the SBP, we need to formulate the problem as a function optimization problem. The object space X consists of all valid sequences of moves applicable to the initial board. Notice that the structures in X do not have a fixed length representation. Other research with genetic algorithms on object spaces with structures having variable length representations was done by Smith [14] who implemented a machine learning system (LS-1) using structures corresponding to production system programs.

In order to define f, the function to be optimized, we need to introduce some extra notation. We will denote the initial board by IB and the goal board by GB. Let $(x_1, \ldots, x_n)$ be a sequence of valid moves (i.e., an element of X), we denote by IB$(x_1, \ldots, x_n)$ the board which is obtained by applying the sequence of moves $(x_1, \ldots, x_n)$ to IB.

Consider the boards IB$(x_1, \ldots, x_n)$ and GB. For each tile (except the empty tile) in IB$(x_1, \ldots, x_n)$, compute the *Manhattan distance* between the tile's position in IB$(x_1, \ldots, x_n)$ and its position in GB. We define the *performance*$(x_1, \ldots, x_n)$ as the sum of all these Manhattan distances.

In our first attempt, we defined

$$f(x_1, \ldots, x_n) = performance(x_1, \ldots, x_n)$$

, but quickly discovered that a much better measure is

$$f(x_1, \ldots, x_n) = min\{performance(x_1, \ldots, x_i) | 1 \leq i \leq n\},$$

i.e., the value of a structure $(x_1, \ldots, x_n)$ is defined as the performance of the sub-sequence $(x_1, \ldots, x_i)$ whose corresponding intermediate board IB$(x_1, \ldots, x_i)$ comes closest to GB (it should be noted that computing $f(x_1, \ldots, x_n)$ can be done in $O(n)$). It should be clear that whenever $f(x_1, \ldots, x_n) = 0$, the sequence $(x_1, \ldots, x_n)$ contains a subsequence $(x_1, \ldots, x_i)$ which is a solution to the SBP. We now turn to the selection of the recombination operators.

The crossover process here is similar to that in the TSP. Suppose that two sequences of operators are given. We pick the first operator from each sequence. Apply each operator to the initial board to see which operator yields a new board closer to the goal board. Choose with high probability the operator which yields the closer board, i.e., the one with the better performance. Notice that it is here that we employ heuristic information about the Sliding Puzzle Problem, indeed, it seems likely that we should try to obtain intermediate configurations that get closer to the goal board. We do not always choose the better operator, however, because this may eventually lead to a bad sequence whose performance we can not improve as long as it starts with that particular operator. In short, we could get stuck in the local optimum. However, it is our assumption that in general it is more likely the case that selecting the better operator will contribute to constructing a good sequence. In case the two operators have the same performance, pick any of them randomly. Once the operator is chosen, it becomes the first operator of the new sequence and the board is updated accordingly. Now we pick the second operators of each sequence. Again, we will take the one with the better performance. It may however be the case that one or both of them is no longer legal, i.e., it pushes the empty tile off the edge of the board. This is possible because the operator chosen for the new sequence is not necessarily the one which preceded the current two operators. In case only one of the operators is illegal, choose the one which is legal. Otherwise, randomly generate a legal one. It becomes the second operator of the new sequence. Again update the board. This process is repeated until we reach the end of the two sequences.

The local improvement process is performed on a single structure. First randomly pick m positions $(0 \leq m \leq n)$ in the sequence. For the left-most position, make the corresponding board arrangement by applying the operators in the sequence preceding this position. Randomly generate a legal operator in that position and check if this new operator is acceptable by comparing it with the old operator using the boltzman distribution test (i.e., perform simulated annealing). This test goes as follows: Accept the new operator if it yields a board closer to the goal board than the old one does. Otherwise, accept it with the probability according to a boltzman distribution. If the temperature in the boltzman distribution is high, the new operator will be accepted with high probability, even if its performance is bad. If the temperature is low, the operator is accepted with less probability. (Temperature deceases exponentially. We chose the temperature $T = T_0 \rho^{gen}$, where T_0 is a initial temperature, $0 < \rho < 1$ and gen is the number of generations). If the new operator is accepted, it replaces the old one in the sequence. If not, the old one is kept. Now proceed scanning the given sequence to the right until the second initially chosen position at which local improvement will be performed is reached, checking if, along the way, any of the operators should be updated due to the replacement of the previous operator. If an operator has to be updated, replace it with a legal one. Repeat this process for all the initially chosen positions at which local improvement will be performed. Upon completion of this process, the whole new sequence is compared with the initial sequence and accepted according to the boltzman distribution test.

To overcome the difficulties of the non-fixed length representation of sequences, the genetic algorithm is embedded in a loop which periodically extends the length of the structures of the population under consideration. For example, we may start out with a population of sequences of length 10, apply the genetic algorithm to this population until a steady state is reached, then extend the sequences by randomly adding a fixed amount of valid moves to each sequence in the steady state population and resume the GA on the new population until a new steady state is reached. This extension process is continued until a solution or near-optimum solution is obtained.

The results of initial experiments are promising. Consistently we find solutions or near-optimum solutions using little computational time. In the case of the 3×3 sliding puzzle games, we always found a solution using the following parameter settings: `initial population = 20` randomly chosen structures of length 10, the extension of the structures when the algorithm reached a steady state was done in chunks of length 5, `crossover rate = 70%`, `local improvement rate = 30%`. In the case of 4×4 sliding puzzle games, the boards we reached (for difficult cases) are within 4 to 5 in Manhattan distance from the goal configuration, hence the majority of tiles are in place. Unfortunately, we seem to have trouble generating exact solutions for these puzzles. In Figure 8 we show a typical case of such a "difficult" puzzle. For this example, it takes 31 moves to transform the initial board into the goal board. In Figure 9, we show a board reached by a genetic algorithm using the following parameters: `initial population size = 50` randomly chosen structures of length 20, the extension of the structures when the algorithm reached a steady state was done in chunks of 10, `crossover rate = 70%`, `local improvement rate = 30%`. This board has a Manhattan distance of 4 from the goal board. In Appendix 2, we report additional results.

```
 1  2  3  4        10  1  6  2
 5  6  7  8         3  8 15  4
 9  0 10 11         9  7 13 11
12 13 14 15         5  0 12 14
```

Figure 8. The Initial and Goal Board of a 4×4-SBP.

```
10  1  6  2
 3  8 15  4
 5  7 13 14
 9  0 12 11
```

Figure 9. A Board Obtained by a Genetic Algorithm.

The fact that we only reached near-optimum solution was not totally unexpected since it is well known that genetic algorithms are excellent in finding near-optimum solutions (see the TSP above and [4]), but are usually not powerful enough to find exact solutions. However, we plan to fine-tune our current algorithm and expect, at least for the SBP, to overcome this problem.

5. Conclusion

We have identified several problems in generalizing genetic algorithms to optimization problems other than the standard function optimization problems. By addressing these problems we designed genetic algorithms for two well-known problems: the Traveling Salesman Problem, an example of a combinatorial optimization problem, and the Sliding Block Puzzle, an example of a puzzle problem studied in Artificial Intelligence. It turned out that the selection of a natural representation and the selection of heuristically motivated recombination operators is critical in the design of robust genetic algorithms for such problems. We believe that our approach is quite general and can be applied to many related problems.

Finally, it is worthwhile to mention that the "operator-oriented" approach used in the SBP is easily generalized to many other problems, thus rendering genetic algorithms applicable to such problems. As an example, in the standard function optimization problem (assuming that the arguments to the function are represented in binary code), we could define the following operators:
`Set(i,1)`: set the i-th position in the bitstring $00\ldots00$ to 1 and design heuristically motivated recombination operators which work on sequences of such operations. A similar approach could be taken for the TSP.

Acknowledgements
We would like to thank the referees for their insightful comments and criticisms which helped us to improve the paper.

6. References
[1] J. Baker," Adaptive Selection Methods for Genetic Algorithms", Proc. of an Int'l Conf. on Genetic Algorithms and Their Applications, pp. 101-111 (July 1985).
[2] L. Davis, "Job Shop Scheduling with Genetic Algorithms", Proc. of an Int'l Conf. on Genetic Algorithms and Their Applications, pp. 136-140 (July 1985).
[3] L. Davis, "Applying Adaptive Algorithms to Epistatic Domains", Proc. of 9th IJCAI, pp. 162-164 (Aug 1985).
[4] K.A. De Jong, "Adaptive System Design: a Genetic Approach", *IEEE Trans. Syst., and Cyber. Vol. SMC-10(9)*, pp. 556-574 (September 1980).
[5] K.A De Jong, "Genetic Algorithms: a 10 Year Perspective", Proc. of an Int'l Conf. on Genetic Algorithms and Their Applications, pp. 169-177 (July 1985).
[6] D.E. Goldberg and R. Lingle, "Alleles, Loci, and the Traveling Salesman Problem", Proc. of an Int'l Conf. on Genetic Algorithms and Their Applications, pp. 154-159 (July 1985).
[7] J.J. Grefenstette, R. Gopal, B.J. Rosmaita and D. Van Gucht, "Genetic Algorithms for the Traveling Salesman Problem", Proc. of an Int'l Conf. on Genetic Algorithms and Their Applications, pp. 160-168 (July 1985).
[8] J. Holland, *Adaptation in Natural and Artificial Systems*, Univ. of Michigan Press, Ann Arbor (1975).
[9] S. Kirkpatrick, C.D. Gelatt and M.P. Vecchi, "Optimization by Simulated Annealing", *Science Vol. 220(4598)*, pp. 671-680 (May 1983).
[10] E.L. Lawler, J.K. Lenstra, A.H.G. Rinnooy Kan and D.B. Shmoys (Ed), *The Traveling Salesman Problem*, John Wiley & Sons Ltd (1985).
[11] S. Lin and B.W. Kernighan, "An Effective Heuristic Algorithm for the Traveling Salesman Problem", *Operations Research* 1972, pp. 498-516.
[12] N.J. Nilsson, *Principles of Artificial Intelligence*, Tioga Publishing Company Palo Alto, California (1980).
[13] D. Smith, "Bin Packing With Adaptive Search", Proc. of an Int'l Conference on Genetic Algorithms and Their Applications, pp. 202-206 (July 1985).
[14] S.F. Smith, "Flexible Learning of Problem Solving Heuristics Through Adaptive Search", Proc. of 8th IJCAI (Aug. 1983).

APPENDIX 1

In this appendix we give some additional results concerning the Traveling Salesman Problem. The following is a description of the essential parameters and some terminology used in our experiments.

Population Size : The number of tours in a population at any given time.
Structure Length : The tour length.
Crossover Rate : The portion of population undergoing cross-over. The rest will undergo local improvement.
DECRATIO : If T is the current temperature used in annealing scheme, DECRATIO * T will be the new temperature.
** NOTE: the initial temperature is the 1% of average deviation of the initial population (0-th generation).
Trial : Each new computation of the tour length of tour counts as a trial.
INTERV : the number of trials after which the temperature is updated.
2-opt Rate : (2-opt Rate * Structure length) yields the number of 2-opt operations on a structure undergoing local improvement.

How to read a table.

Local Rate		0 %		10 %
lattice	exp. 1	111.1 (124; 6283)	100	(188;16910)
	exp. 2	108.6 (114; 5777)	100.8	(200;17706)
	exp. 3	104.9 (209;10545)	100	(207;18065)
	exp. 4	111.3 (139; 7013)	100	(237;22538)
	exp. 5	111.6 (125; 6346)	100.8	(163;13650)

The above table gives the results for the lattice TSP.
We conducted 5 experiments using two different 2-opt rates.
0 % Local Rate means that we are running cross-over only without using local improvement.
The description "exp. 1" stands for experiment 1.
The notation nnn.nn (ggg; tttt) indicates that we obtained the solution of length 111.1 after ggg generations which took tttt trials.

2. Kroisk

Population Size = 100
Structure Length = 100
Crossover Rate = 0.5
DECRATIO = 0.075
INTERV = 300

2-opt Rate		0 %		10 %
kroisk	exp. 1	25691 (104; 5298)	22193 (373;19135)
	exp. 2	26191 (236;11055)	22316 (386;30261)
	exp. 3	27259 (194; 9759)	21702 (403;31536)
	exp. 4	26852 (111; 5607)	21976 (627;49192)
	exp. 5	29727 (117; 5941)	21651 (679;49745)

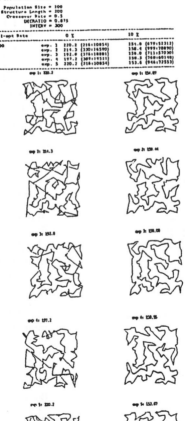

3. 4 Circles

Population Size = 100
Structure Length = 100
Crossover Rate = 0.5
DECRATIO = 0.075
INTERV = 300

2-opt Rate		0 %		10 %
4cir	exp. 1	40.1 (255;12805)	24.5 (118;17063)
	exp. 2	42.7 (176; 8675)	24.1 (140;18096)
	exp. 3	60.0 (173; 8717)	24.7 (145;19420)
	exp. 4	39.0 (300;15060)	24.7 (125;16623)
	exp. 5	39.3 (270;11055)	24.6 (159;17409)

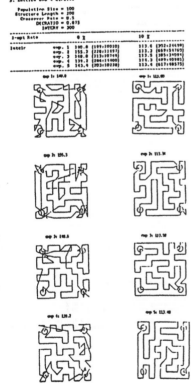

1. Lattice

Population Size = 100
Structure Length = 100
Crossover Rate = 0.5
DECRATIO = 0.075
INTERV = 300

2-opt Rate		0 %		10 %
lattice	exp. 1	111.1 (124; 6283)	100	(188;16910)
	exp. 2	108.6 (114; 5777)	100.8	(200;17706)
	exp. 3	104.9 (209;10545)	100	(207;18065)
	exp. 4	111.3 (139; 7013)	100	(237;22538)
	exp. 5	111.6 (125; 6346)	100.8	(163;13650)

4. 200 Random Points

Population Size = 100
Structure Length = 200
Crossover Rate = 0.5
DECRATIO = 0.075
INTERV = 300

2-opt Rate		0 %		10 %
200	exp. 1	220.2 (216;10854)	185.0 (879;52312)
	exp. 2	214.3 (330;16590)	158.4 (999;70870)
	exp. 3	192.0 (376;18801)	158.3 (713;57030)
	exp. 4	197.2 (307;19511)	158.3 (768;60190)
	exp. 5	220.2 (216;10854)	153.6 (966;72353)

5. Lattice and 4 Circles

Population Size = 100
Structure Length = 200
Crossover Rate = 0.5
DECRATIO = 0.075
INTERV = 300

2-opt Rate		0 %		10 %
lattcir	exp. 1	150.0 (199;10010)	113.4 (792;24690)
	exp. 2	155.3 (220;11197)	113.3 (669;51702)
	exp. 3	160.0 (213;10719)	113.5 (385;34091)
	exp. 4	139.2 (286;11400)	113.3 (689;40901)
	exp. 5	143.4 (203;10230)	113.3 (617;48575)

APPENDIX 2

In this appendix, we show some of the results
obtained for two 3x3 puzzles and one (difficult) 4x4 puzzle.

Population Size   : same as in appendix 1
Percent of Population
  undergoing
    cross-over   : same as in appendix 1
    simulated
    annealing   : same as in appendix 1

Annealing Schedule :

   temperature = (initial average deviation) *
                 (0.975 ** gen)

where gen denotes the number of generations
and ** denotes: raise to the power.

Note: The Local Improvement Rate is 20 % here
      but is not explicitly shown.

Extension Schedule

generation	length
0 - 5	10
after 5	20

This table indicates that, between the 0-th and the 5-th generation, the length of the structures is 10. After the 5-th generation, the structures are extended to have length 20.

1. 3 by 3 Sliding Puzzle

Population Size   : 20
Percent of Population
 undergoing cross-over   : 70 %
 undergoing simulated annealing   : 30 %

Annealing Schedule: Temperature = (initial average deviation) * (0.975 ** gen)
                    where gen denotes the generation.

Extension Schedule:

generation	length
0 - 5	10
after 5	20

Note: 0 stands for the empty tile.

init board	goal board	distance
** task 1 **		
1 2 3 / 4 0 5 / 6 7 8	1 2 5 / 6 3 8 / 4 7 0	6
** task 2 **		
1 2 3 / 4 0 5 / 6 7 8	2 3 5 / 1 4 8 / 0 6 7	8

Best Structure obtained in each experiment

experiment	distance from goal board	number of moves taken	number of trials taken
** task 1 **			
1	0 (solved)	14	less than 300
2	0 (solved)	14	less than 300
** task 2 **			
1	0 (solved)	8	less than 200
2	0 (solved)	8	less than 200

3. 4 by 4 Sliding Puzzle

Population Size   : 50
Percent of Population
 undergoing cross-over   : 80 %
 undergoing simulated annealing   : 20 %

Annealing Schedule: Temperature = (initial average deviation) * (0.975 ** gen)
                    where gen denotes the generation.

Extension Schedule:

generation	length
0 - 10	20
11 - 20	30
after 20	40

Note: 0 stands for the empty tile.

init board	goal board	distance
1 2 3 4 / 5 6 7 8 / 9 0 10 11 / 12 13 14 15	10 1 6 2 / 3 8 15 4 / 9 7 13 11 / 5 0 12 14	27

Best Structure obtained in each experiment

experiment	distance from goal board	number of moves taken	number of trials taken
1	4	29	less than 2000
2	5	30	less than 2000
3	4	31	less than 2000

task 1   task 2

exp. 1

USING REPRODUCTIVE EVALUATION TO IMPROVE GENETIC SEARCH AND HEURISTIC DISCOVERY

Darrell Whitley

Computer Science Department, Colorado State University, Fort Collins, Colorado 80523

ABSTRACT

In experiments using real valued features, the role of inversion and reproductive evaluation in genetic search is explored. In problems where ordering does not affect performance, inversion does more than change the linkage between features. It provides a type of non-destructive noise that helps crossover to escape local maxima. The search using inversion was consistently more efficient, finding more optimal and near optimal solutions. *Reproductive evaluation* involves determining which parents have produced the most valuable offspring and then allocating them more reproductive opportunities. Experiments indicate that reproductive evaluation can further speed up the genetic search process.

INTRODUCTION

Genetic search and learning algorithms provide a very efficient and general technique for discovering critical combinations of information. To date, most of the research in the area of genetic learning has emphasized one genetic operator: crossover. Crossover involves swapping the information in two lists at some breakpoint, resulting in the generation of two new lists. In learning applications these lists may be the condition parts of if-then production rules, complete rules containing both conditions and actions, or even lists containing complete rule sets. The term *schema* will refer to any information structure to which genetic operators are applied. Inversion, another genetic operator, rearranges the order of the elemental data items (features) comprising the schema. In problems where order does not alter the value of a schema, inversion can be used to change the "linkage" of features (Holland 1975:108). In other words, it changes which features are most likely to be passed on together during crossover by changing the proximity of features in a schema.

Research with algorithms using inversion has largely been abandon because most researchers now use a binary notation to represent features. A binary representation provides a minimal alphabet as well as a compact, efficient form of data. Because binary representations are positionally dependent it is not possible to do inversion unless additional data is stored to interpret the bit string.

A series of experiments were conducted to explore the role of inversion in genetic search. The results of these experiments indicate that when real valued features are used on problems where ordering does not affect the value of schemata, inversion does more than change the linkage between features. It provides a type of non-destructive noise that helps crossover to escape local maxima. Compared to tests using crossover alone, the search using inversion was consistently more efficient; optimal and near optimal solutions were found faster and more high-valued combinations of features were found.

These experiments also introduce a new way of evaluating information structures. In biological systems natural selection is not based on the immediate worth (i.e. performance rating) of an individual's genetic composition, but instead upon reproductive potential. "Survival of the fittest," a pre-Darwinian concept introduced by Herbert Spenser (Bohannan and Glazer 1973:5), in fact does not accurately describe the selection process as it occurs in biological systems. Genetic fitness is a function of reproductive fitness--survival, although a necessary condition for reproductive fitness, is only one factor that contributes to genetic fitness. Indeed in many species individual survival may be risked when the potential for reproductive payoff is substantial. The importance of reproductive potential is especially relevant to problems where ordering does not affect performance in that inversion changes the reproductive potential of schemata but does not change the performance of such schemata. Two schemata with the same features, but with different orderings of those features, have exactly the same performance potential but may have very different reproductive potentials.

A simple method referred to as *reproductive evaluation* is proposed. The experiments reported here suggest that crediting schemata for their reproductive potential indeed speeds up the search process. In the search space explored it was possible to have duplicate features and the order of features did not affect schema performance. Further research is needed in problem domains where the search process might display different characteristics. Some preliminary research has been done on the traveling salesman problem. In this problem duplicates are not allowed and the order of rules *does* affect performance, since the order indicates the sequence in which cities are visited (Goldberg and Lingle 1985, Grefenstette et.al. 1985). Preliminary results indicate that reproductive evaluation is also helpful in this domain.

Reproductive evaluation can be done as part of the credit assignment process employed by *bucket brigade algorithms*. It therefore may be employed to speed up the discovery of new and useful rules in a production system environment. As a side advantage, the same method proposed for reproductive evaluation can be utilized to evaluate other heuristics used to aid in rule generation. Such evaluation makes it possible to integrate heuristic discovery methods with genetic algorithms.

THE ROLE OF INVERSION IN GENETIC SEARCH

The genetic learning process normally begins with the random generation of a pool of rules. This set of rules is analogous to a "gene pool" in that it contains the entire set of features that the learning system "knows" about. The search problem selected is that of all possible 5 card poker hands--except that 5 of a kind is allowed. (Straights and flushes are also ignored to keep evaluation simple.) The evaluation function gives the worth of a hand. Experiments were conducted using fixed pool sizes of 100 hands and 500 hands. Search preceded for 200 and 500 cycles in different experiments, where a cycle involves the generation of one new hand. Hands are the schemata, with each hand being a list of 5 cards. Real card values are used as the features, so the list elements are positionally independent.

During genetic search, the generation of a new hand is considered a trial. Trials should be directed so that the genetic operators are usually applied to those hands which have the highest worth, yet also occasionally allocate trials to hands with lower worth to insure that potential sources of information are not overlooked. If a small number of schemata come to dominate the pool, the search quickly stagnates at a local maxima, a problem that results in premature convergence. There are several ways of dealing with the problem of duplicate schemata. DeJong (1975) experimented with a "crowding mechanism" where some subset of the population is selected at random and the schema in that subset most like the newly created schema is replaced. However, such a method does not preclude duplicates. Furthermore, duplicates affected the average worth of hands in the pool. For these reasons duplicates are simply disallowed. Booker (1985) describes other crowding mechanisms that limit the number of schemata by requiring them to share limited resources. When there are too many schemata their share of the resources dwindles and weaker schemata are deleted. When resources increase or when there are few schemata, they are more likely to survive and reproduce. In the poker problem, hands have a fixed evaluation, so varying resources are not a factor.

Holland (1975:75) has pointed out that there are 2 competing goals when one is allocating reproductive trails. First, we would like to allocate trials to exploit the observed best. Second, lesser ranking schemata should also be allocated reproductive trials to reduce the probability of error. By allowing lower ranked schemata to reproduce, the system may exploit information that is not found among the higher ranked schemata. If trials are allocated randomly, there is no bias toward the best (except a passive bias as lower ranked schemata are deleted). To bias reproductive trials toward higher ranked schemata an exponential distribution of trials was used. An exponential distribution of trials produces 2 positive effects. First, it allows high ranking schemata to reproduce most of the time, while still maintaining a stochastic selection process to allow lower ranking schemata to occasionally be selected. Second, the active bias toward the higher ranking schemata makes it possible to exploit information about reproductive potential. We want to actively bias reproductive trials toward the schema with the better reproductive evaluation. An exponential distribution of trials does this when schemata are ranked according to both performance and reproductive evaluation. Performance and reproductive evaluation were added together to produce the rank of a schema. After a new schema is generated it must be added to the pool, displacing some schema. An exponential distribution of replacement choices is again used, this time with the bias toward the low worth end of the pool. Thus, lower ranked schemata are replaced, but the process is not deterministic.

An exponential bias perhaps made the premature convergence problem more acute than allocating reproductive trials equally. But using reproductive evaluation can also help here. Without reproductive evaluation a schema may obtain and maintain a high rank so that it dominates the pool. The result can be an undue bias toward high ranking schemata. Using reproductive evaluation assures that a schema will not maintain a high rank unless it maintains a high reproductive potential. This means the system will be biased toward a small set of schemata only as long as they yield competitive offspring. The result is an informed distribution of trials and fewer duplicates.

The genetic search algorithm was run using 5 different initial pools of randomly generated schemata so that different searches could be observed and averaged. This is not, of course, a sufficient number of cases to draw any conclusions of a statistical nature but does allow hypotheses to be established for future research. On each run, a pool of 100 random hands was generated, then 200 new hands were created using the genetic operators. For each pool, 7 different variants of the search algorithm were tried: 1) search using just crossover, 2) search applying inversion 10% of the time (90% crossover), 3) search applying inversion 20% of the time (80% crossover), 4) search applying inversion 30% of the time (70% crossover), 5) search where inversion was applied after 10 crossover

attempts failed to produce a new, non-duplicate hand, 6) search where inversion was applied after 5 crossover attempts failed to produce a non-duplicate hand, and finally, 7) search where inversion was applied after 2 crossover attempts failed to produce a non-duplicate hand. A non-duplicate hand is one that does not have the same information in the same position as another. Allowing hands that have the same information, but in different positions is necessary since this is exactly the type of hand that results from inversion. The idea behind the last three variants of the algorithm is that inversion moves around, or "stirs," the information available for crossover. Randomly doing inversion some X percent of the time has the same effect and is perhaps preferable since doing inversion after crossover begins to fail actually places the search in a position of difficulty before any corrective action is taken.

Of the 7 variants of the search algorithms, 3 were superior. Success of these algorithms can be measured in 3 ways: 1) by the increase in the average worth of the pools, 2) by the discovery of optimal or near optimal hands, and 3) by the amount of effort the algorithms expended generating a non-duplicate hand. Effort refers to the number of duplicate hands that are generated and must be discarded. Effort is one measure of the efficiency of the search, since in generating 200 new hands, the system may generate 1000 duplicates. Thus a large portion of the search time can be spent generating useless information.

Using 20% or 30% inversion worked well. In those cases where 20% inversion was used the optimal solution was found 4 out of 5 times after generating on average 66 new hands--much less than 1/1000th of the search space. Applying inversion after 5 failed crossovers also did well. Search applying only crossover consistently performed the poorest in terms of average worth, and in 2 cases performance was dramatically worse. In 2 cases it did find the optimal solution, but did so later in the search (after generating 100 new hands). (In experiments preliminary to those just discussed, 5 different sets of initial hands were used. In these experiments 20% inversion and inversion after 5 failed crossovers did about the same, 30% inversion did not perform as well and crossover failed in every search to find the optimal solution, again with

2 dramatic failures. These results are not averaged with those discussed here because of slight differences in the programs.)

One of the problems with using only crossover is that each position in the list of features is isolated. Its erratic performance may be due to the fact that crossover cannot exploit all the information in the pool and may not be able to get at certain segments of information that develop in the hands. If the pool is viewed as a two dimensional array with each row being a hand and the features appearing in the columns, it means that information in one column cannot be accessed in another column by crossover. For example, it is possible that no ace card appears in the search pool as the first card of a hand. Such a coincidence makes it impossible to find the optimal solution (5 aces) when only crossover is used. In less extreme cases, it can mean that certain features are not as well represented in some columns, or positions, as they are others. This limits the amount of information that crossover has to work with and forces the search to prematurely reach a local maxima.

Inversion "stirs up" the columns and thereby "stirs up" the available information. It not only creates a new linkage between features, but also moves these newly linked segments around. For example, assume that 2 schema segments in two different schemata are both located at the rightmost end of the schemata. Crossover will never allow the two segments to be joined. However if one of these schemata is inverted and one segment is no longer located at the rightmost end, then it can be joined with the other segment during crossover. Inversion therefore does more than increase the linkage between features. It provides a constructive type of noise that moves around information without disrupting schema performance. In doing so it helps the search to avoid stagnation. (Simulated annealing, as used in neural networks, also employs noise to escape local maxima, but of course the noise used must be disruptive enough to achieve the desired effect. This is part of the reason learning proceeds so slowly using this method. (Ackley and Hinton 1985).)

REPRODUCTIVE EVALUATION

Using the same 5 pools the tests were run again, except this time reproductive evaluation was used in conjunction with performance ratings to rank hands. Two different kinds of credit were recorded for each hand: performance credit and reproductive credit. Performance credit, or worth, is the value of the hand, the same value used in the previous tests. Reproductive credit is calculated using the average worth of the offspring of a hand. That is, when a hand is chosen for reproduction its offspring are evaluated and the parent given reproductive credit. In the tests reported here, a newly created offspring's value is averaged in with the current reproductive credit that the parent already possesses. Reproductive credit is then added to the worth of the hand to determine its rank. Figure 1 provides a comparison of the previous results (using just performance evaluation) and those achieved using reproductive evaluation. The initial average for the randomly generated pool of hands was 244. Averages in the hundreds range roughly correspond to 2 of a kind, averages in the thousands to 3 of a kind, and in the 10 thousands range to 4 of a kind. At first glance it appears that using reproductive evaluation reduces performance, but Figure 2 shows that it increased performance in the early part of search, but lost ground after an optimal or near optimal hand was discovered.

Part of the problem is that using reproductive evaluation means that some hands will be saved which have below average performance, but which have significant reproductive value. In a small pool these hands lower the average performance of the search. The lower average performance is less significant during the early search since many low valued hands are still in the system and the growth that results from the rapid exploitation of unsearched space offsets the disadvantage of keeping hands with below average performance. One would expect this to be much less of a problem when a larger pool of hands is maintained. Tests that used a pool size of 500 and ran for 500 cycles support this idea. Without reproductive evaluation an average worth of 2497 was achieved with an effort of 1085 over 5 runs. Using reproductive evaluation an average worth of 2953 was obtained with an effort of 1101. In both cases 20% inversion was used. The cases that employed reproductive evaluation produced a higher average worth in the pool in every case. Also, in terms of high-valued hands found, the tests using reproduc-

ALGORITHM PEFORMANCE					
		REPRODUCTIVE EVALUTION			
		No		Yes	
CROSSOVER INVERSION		VALUE	EFFORT	VALUE	EFFORT
100%	0%	6138	1989	5672	2105
90%	10%	9288	2144	8189	1521
80%	20%	11881	1658	10369	1435
70%	30%	12258	2228	10800	1583
FAILED-CROSS		VALUE	EFFORT	VALUE	EFFORT
10		9981	1948	10155	1301
5		11231	2492	11702	1670
2		10186	4904	11606	3632

FIGURE 1. Comparison of results with and without the use of reproductive evaluation. Trials were run using 0%, 10%, 20% and 30% inversion as well as using inversion after 10, 5, and 2 failed attempts at crossover. VALUE refers to the resulting hand average. EFFORT refers to the number of duplicate hands that were generated.

FIGURE 2. A graph of search with and without reproductive evaluation. The dotted line shows that reproductive evaluation improved search in the early stages of the search process. The solid line line maps the performance of search without reproductive evaluation. Both of these cases used 20% inversion. The dashed line maps the search using just crossover. Note that this graph is a log graph.

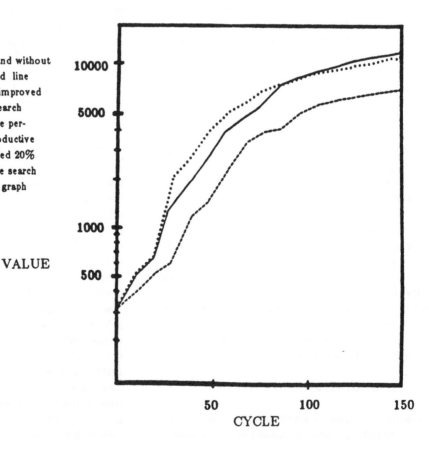

tive evaluation did so on average 38 cycles faster. The resulting averages for a pool size of 500 are of course lower than those obtained when a pool size of 100 was used. The seeming disparity in averages is partly an illusion in that hands which would have been pushed out of a pool of 100 are saved and pushed down in a pool size of 500.

THE TRAVELING SALESMAN AND REPRODUCTIVE EVALUATION

These experiments demonstrate that reproductive evaluation is effective in improving search for the poker problem. However, the poker problem is ideally suited to a combined use of crossover and inversion since duplicates are allowed and ordering does not affect performance. There are problems, such as the traveling salesman problem, that might be implemented as a genetic search problem with very different characteristics than the search space of all possible poker hands. In the traveling salesman problem ordering is very much related to performance, and duplicates are not allowed. Some preliminary work has been done using *just* inversion on this problem; an exponential bias was again used. Searches were conducted both with and without reproductive evaluation. The specific tour studied is a 10-city tour given by Karg and Thompson (1964). All tests were run for 400 cycles, with 1 new tour generated each cycle. The genetic algorithm was run 15 times using 15 different initial pools for each variant of the algorithm-- with and without reproductive evaluation. When reproductive evaluation was used the optimal tour was found 60% of the time (9 out of 15 cases) and the second optimal tour was found 80% of the time (12 out of 15) cases. Without reproductive evaluation the optimal tour was found only 40% of the time (6 out of 15 cases) and the second optimal tour was found 47% of the time (7 out of 15 cases). Using reproductive evaluation, the system also produced on average 23% fewer duplicates during the search process (Whitley and Davidson 1987).

Part of the reason that reproductive evaluation helps here is that it correctly directs the strong bias of the system toward good parent tours. If tours are in fact not good candidates for reproduction, then this will show up in the reproductive evaluation. So even though the use of an exponential bias does favor the schemata at the top, schemata may be devalued after reproducing a few times. In this way the bias toward high ranked schemata is mitigated by reproductive evaluation; the top of the pool changes as schemata are evaluated for reproductive potential. This phenomenon was much more evident in the traveling salesman problem than in the poker problem. Also, in the traveling salesman problem it was noticed that a large number of offspring will usually pull down the parent's reproductive rating because on average the offspring tend not to be as good as the parent, especially if the parent has a high performance rating. Furthermore, finding better offspring becomes more difficult as the average tour length gets closer to an optimal solution.

REPRODUCTIVE EVALUATION AND CREDIT IN PRODUCTION SYSTEMS

One of the problems in using genetic algorithms for learning applications is crediting rules for their performance. The action of a rule may not yield an immediate payoff, but may instead create a situation where another rule is able to fire and achieve positive (or negative) results. For example, a rule that allows a chess player to capture a piece has an obvious payoff, but several stage-setting moves must have previously been made to make such a payoff possible. This is known as the credit assignment problem. Holland has been able to deal very nicely with the problem of distributing credit in a production system, and it is worthwhile to relate his solution here. It will also provide a context in which to discuss ways of distributing reproductive credit in such an environment.

Obviously, if some rules post messages (or assert conditions) when they fire and some rules perform output actions when they fire, only those rules that perform output actions are going to directly receive a payoff for their actions. This is the credit assignment problem in a little different guise. In terms of a production system, a rule that posts messages to working memory has no means of receiving direct credit and so it is entirely dependent on sharing credit for its stage-setting role for output rules. To solve this problem Holland uses what he calls a *bucket brigade algorithm*. Holland (1986) offers the metaphor of a small economic system to describe it. When a rule fires it must pay those rules whose messages match some item on its condition list. A rule pays its predecessors by giving away some percentage of its own credit. The more credit it has accumulated, the better it is able to pay these preceding rules. If the firing rule performs an output action, it receives credit, or payoff, directly. If the firing rule posts a message, then it must re-accumulate credit by having its message used by other rules. Over time, rules that are part of a chain leading to positive payoff will accumulate credit relative to the amount of that payoff. Rules that are part of chains that do not lead to positive payoffs will lose credit as the loss of payoff negatively affects the ability of rules farther along in the chain to pay back those rules whose messages match items in its condition list. Much as in an economy, the effect of a payoff (or lack of it) does not have an immediate effect throughout the system. Holland also discusses the use of rules that define goals and remain active until some output action occurs that either achieves the goal or fails in an attempt to achieve the goal. This provides a kind of focus which can speed up the credit assignment process. Overall the bucket brigade algorithm provides a very elegant means of apportioning credit.

REPRODUCTIVE EVALUATION IN A BUCKET BRIGADE ENVIRONMENT

A means of achieving reproductive evaluation is outlined that can be used in conjunction with algorithms that use a bucket brigade to apportion credit. Some suggestions are also made as to how reproductive evaluation can be used to evaluate other kinds of heuristics that might be employed in conjunction with genetic operators.

In many ways reproductive evaluation is a heuristic method for improving genetic algorithms. However, reproductive evaluation is a primary part of biological evolution. In natural selection, genetic fitness is achieved not just by being well-adapted--the real issue is reproductive fitness. If ordering does not affect performance, then the inversion operator does not change the adaptive value of a rule, but rather its reproductive potential. In a natural system, those individuals with greater reproductive potential are more likely to pass on

their genetic information. To make full use of the inversion operator we need to allocate more opportunities to reproduce to those rules which in the past have produced good rules. This echoes a heuristic proposed by Douglas Lenat, "If a gene has mutated successfully several times in the past, then increase its chance of mutating in the next generations, and conversely" (Lenat 1983:294). The difference is that we do not want to mutate rules, but rather to cross rules, or do inversion. Still, the fundamental idea is there: if the genetic algorithm is considered a kind of heuristic search, we should be able to introduce rules that serve as metaheuristics for improving the efficiency of genetic search. Rules related to reproductive potential are particularly important. Reproductive evaluation provides the basis for such a heuristic.

Reproductive evaluation must be tied into the credit assignment process since this is how rule performance is evaluated. Those parent rules that produce viable new offspring must tap into the payoff scheme as outlined in the bucket brigade algorithm. Each rule could maintain a "created-by" arc that pipes credit from the bucket brigade payoff to the parent rules involved in its creation. By shuttling credit to parent rules, the "created-by" arc makes it possible to evaluate the reproductive potential of parent rules. Two kinds of credit would then be circulating in the system: performance credit and reproductive credit. This would of course come at some additional cost in terms of computation time, although the extra effort should not be dramatic. In any case, production systems, as Holland has pointed out, allow a high degree of parallelism. If one is using a bucket brigade algorithm, part of what happens when these rules fire is that they pay off those rules whose actions created conditions allowing them to fire. The "created-by" arc could fire in parallel with the "payoff" arc. Since the "created-by" arc may point to more than one rule, all rules would be credited in parallel.

The "created-by" arc not only makes it possible to distribute credit for reproductive evaluation, but also provides an elegant means for evaluating other heuristics. There is no need to simply assume heuristics work; a heuristic must earn its way or be removed. These heuristics can be expressed as special production rules that generate new rules when their condition lists are satisfied. Such rules could embody more cognitive kinds of heuristic rules about creating problem-domain rules, or could be the kinds of general heuristics outlined in Lenat's work. Such rules would bid for the right to fire (and thereby create a new rule) just like the problem-domain rules, except their measure of performance would be the reproductive credit they receive. Lenat's work indicates that previously useful heuristics may cease to be useful when the problem-domain shifts. By requiring heuristics to maintain a good credit rating it is guaranteed that existing rules are working to create useful problem-domain rules.

CONCLUSIONS

The research reported here suggests that reproductive evaluation can be an effective means of speeding up genetic search and learning. Reproductive evaluation, when used in conjunction with an exponential bias, focuses the search by biasing the allocation of reproductive trials toward schemata which are the most promising candidates for reproduction. If reproductive evaluation is not used, reproductive trials might be allocated randomly to existing schemata, or crowding mechanisms used to reduce or enlarge pool size in response to available resources--but only performance is considered.

This research emphasizes real valued features. It is not clear yet how reproductive evaluation will effect searches that use a binary notation. In languages using a notation that is binary at lower levels and multi-valued at higher levels, such as that used by Smith (1980), reproductive evaluation and inversion can be used to speed up the search process. Reproductive evaluation also provides a very effective means of merging genetic algorithms with other forms of heuristic discovery and learning.

REFERENCES

Ackley, D.H., Hinton, G.E., & Sejnowski, T.J.
1985 A Learning Algorithm for Boltzmann Machines. Cognitive Science 9:147-169.

Bohannan, P., and Glazer, M.
1973 High Points in Anthropology. New York: Knopf.

Booker, L.B.
1985 Improving the Peformance of Genetic Algorithms in Classifier Systems. Proc. International Conf. on Genetic Algorithms and their Applications. J. Grefenstette, ed.

DeJong, K.
1975 Analysis of the Behavior of a Class of Genetic Algorithms. Ph.D. dissertation. University of Michigan.

Goldberg, D. & Lingle, R., Jr.
1985 Alleles, Loci, and the Traveling Salesman Problem. Proc. International Conf. on Genetic Algorithms and their Applications. J. Grefenstette, ed.

Grefenstette, J., Gopal, R., Rosmaita, B., & Van Gucht, D.
1985 Genetic Algorithms for the Traveling Salesman Problem. Proc. International Conf. on Genetic Algorithms and their Applications. J. Grefenstette, ed.

Holland, John
1975 Adaptation in Natural and Artificial Systems. Ann Arbor: Univ. of Michigan Press.
1986 Escaping Brittleness: the Possibilities of General Purpose Learning Algorithms Applied to Parallel Rule-Based Systems. IN Machine Learning, Vol 2. R. Michalski, J. Carbonell and T. Mitchell, eds. Los Altos, CA: Morgan Kaufman.

Karg, R.L., and Thompson, G.L.
1964 A Heuristic Approach to Solving the Travelling Salesman Problem. Management Science, vol. 10, no. 2.

Lenat, D.
1983 The Role of Heuristics in Learning by Discovery: Three Case Studies. IN Machine Learning, Volume 1. R. Michalski, J. Carbonell and T. Mitchell, eds. pp: 243-306. Palo Alto, CA: Tioga.

Smith, S.
1980 A Learning System Based on Genetic Algorithms. Ph.D. dissertation. Department of Computer Science, University of Pittsburgh.

Whitley, D. & Davidson, H.
1987 The Role of Inversion in Genetic Search. Proceeding of the Rocky Mountain Conference on Artificial Intelligence.

TOWARD A UNIFIED THERMODYNAMIC GENETIC OPERATOR

David J. Sirag   Paul T. Weisser

United Technologies Research Center, East Hartford, CT 06108

Abstract

Controlling the rate of population convergence in the Genetic Algorithm can be difficult. Poor convergence behavior can prevent the Genetic Algorithm from discovering an acceptable solution. Work toward a unified thermodynamic operator has been undertaken to improve performance in ordering problems such as the Travelling Salesman Problem. The operator uses a model of genetic activity based on the Boltzmann distribution to allow control of convergence by a global temperature value as is done in Simulated Annealing.

Introduction

For analysis, the optimization tasks performed by the Genetic Algorithm (GA) can be grouped into two classes: value problems and order problems. Value problems are those problems, traditionally well suited to a GA representation, whose solutions can be naturally represented as a set of assignments of values to variables (in genetic terminology, the assignment of alleles to genes). Ordering problems are those problems, traditionally more difficult to represent, whose solutions are naturally represented as an ordered list of values (the assignment of genes to loci). Examples of problems in the GA literature which are naturally represented as ordering problems include the Travelling Salesman Problem (TSP), Job Scheduling, and Priority Assignment.

Diversity of individuals in the population is required to find good solutions with the GA. A new operator is presented within the framework of this extension that unifies crossover, inversion, and mutation operators with concepts from Simulated Annealing. The operator uses a "temperature" parameter to provide control of the genetic diversity in the population. Diversity can be introduced by raising the temperature. The GA works to remove the diversity when the temperature is lowered.

Ordering Problems

Ordering problems can be represented in the GA by encoding them in a way that allows them to be treated as value problems. This approach has several drawbacks. The first difficulty is that the encoded form of the solution may not retain information when the genetic operators are applied. Second, low order schemata may no longer contain important information about the solution. Third, the encoded form may change the problem so that legal solutions are omitted or illegal solutions are included. Fourth the encoding may increase the size of the solution space which must be searched because representations of permutations are inherently less dense than binary representations of the same length. Finally, the fitness of an encoded solution will typically be more expensive to compute because the individual must first be decoded.

A natural extension to the GA along the lines suggested by Holland's inversion operator [Ref. 1] allows the GA to be applied to ordering problems. Ordering problems can be accommodated more naturally by allowing the GA to compute the locus of each gene in addition to the allelles. The final order of the genes can then be interpreted directly as the desired permutation. This serves two purposes. In a value oriented problem it allows the GA to group the genes of a successful schema together. Second, in an ordering problem, the position of the gene in the individual can represent the ordering information required to solve the problem.

In mixed problems the value and ordering mechanisms can operate together. However, this problem will be larger than usual because the solution space of this mixed problem will be the product of the solution spaces of each of the separate subproblems. As an example of this last case consider assigning school busses to bus stops. The route to be taken can be represented by the order of the stops in the individual and the bus assigned to each stop can be represented by the value of the gene. For instance, parent-1 in Figure 1 represents a route in which bus 1 stops first at St. Charles, then at Ventnor, and so on...

PARENT-1

NAME	ST. CHARLES	PARK PLACE	VENTNOR	ATLANTIC	BOARDWALK
VALUE	BUS-1	BUS-2	BUS-1	BUS-2	BUS-3

PARENT-2

NAME	ST. CHARLES	ATLANTIC	VENTNOR	PARK PLACE	BOARKWALK
VALUE	BUS-1	BUS-3	BUS-3	BUS-1	BUS-2

OFFSPRING OF CROSSOVER AT POINT

NAME	ST. CHARLES	PARK PLACE	ATLANTIC	VENTNOR	BOARDWALK
VALUE	BUS-1	BUS-2	BUS-3	BUS-3	BUS-2

Figure 1. Crossover with mixed representation

This extended representation requires changes to the genetic operators to allow them to operate on individuals encoded in this way. Inversion can be implemented in this context simply by allowing it to invert the order of the genes in a substring of the individual without changing their alleles. Crossover can be extended in the following way: Select a crossover point in parent #1; Transcribe allele/gene pairs from parent #1 into the offspring up to the crossover point in the order found in parent #1; Complete the offspring by copying the remaining allele/gene pairs from parent #2 in the order in which they occur in parent #2 (Figure 1). Mutation is unchanged because the inversion and crossover defined above are sufficient to guarantee that no permutation will be permanantly lost from the population's potential search space.

Implemented System

We have implemented the Genetic Algorithm on a Symbolics Lisp Machine. The system uses the representation for individuals described just above. There are other aspects of the system that are "non-standard" as well. These will be described briefly below. These extensions were developed before our work on the thermodynamic operator. Because of their observed usefulness they have been retained in the current work.

In the standard GA each individual's fitness is evaluated by a single function. In contrast we allow multiple independent fitness measures. Individuals are chosen for breeding based on these measures with each measure used in a proportion defined by the analyst. One of the fitness measures is designated "primary". This is the parameter that is really being optimized. The other measures are "secondary" and are used to promote the presence of desireable characteristics within the population. For instance, in the TSP, the primary fitness is the length of the tour. A secondary fitness we have used is based on the number of cities that are connected to their nearest neighbor. The rationale is that although simply connecting each city to its nearest neighbor (a greedy solution) does not produce an optimal route, the optimal route does contain many nearest neighbor connections. The "nearest-neighbor" secondary fitness is intended to promote the presence of such connections in the population. The secondary measures are typically invoked much less frequently than the primary measure, perhaps about 20% of the time.

A copy of the current best individual as measured by each of the fitness measures is stored seperately from the main population. The "refresh" operator brings a copy of one of these current best individuals back into the population. This operator must be used sparingly (about 5%) because it can easily focus the population on a local minimum.

Both the secondary fitness functions and the refresh operator are intended to increase the GA's performance by maintaining diversity yet retaining important information in a smaller population.

We also use the heuristic crossover operator described by Greffenstette et al. [Ref 2]. Heuristic operators contain domain knowledge and bring this knowledge to bear during a crossover operation. The heuristic for the TSP described in [Ref. 2] is to choose the next city to be visited from either parent, whichever is closer to the last city transcribed. This provides a powerful performance boost for the GA in solving travelling salesman problems. Later, we suggest briefly a way to incorporate heuristic operators into the proposed thermodynamic scheme.

Convergence Rates

Goldberg and Lingle [Ref. 3] introduce order schemata (o-schemata) as the ordering analog to the traditional allele schemata (called a-schemata in Ref. 3). In ordering problems the o-schemata are building blocks for optimal orderings just as the a-schemata are building blocks for optimal variable assignments in value problems. The hope has been that operators could be discovered that sift through the o-schemata allocating trials to them optimally as is done with a-schemata. However, the effect of the extended genetic operators on o-schemata is not immediately apparent. For instance, the crossover operator described above is much more destructive of o-schemata than a standard crossover is to a-schemata [Ref. 4]. Put another way, the context sensitivity of o-schemata makes them fragile with respect to crossover.

Consider the extended crossover described above. A crossover point is chosen randomly. Then all of the genes to the left of this point are transcribed from the first parent. These genes define o-schemata retained from the first parent. The remaining unused genes are then transcribed to the offspring from the second parent. However, since the genes that have already been used must be skipped, the section of the offspring to the right of the crossover point will not be identical to a section in either parent. In general these genes define new o-schemata not present in either parent.

We call the expected number of schemata retained by an operator divided by the total number of schemata in an individual the retention ratio of the operator. We have estimated the retention ratios for the extended crossover and inversion operators described above. We find that as the length of the individual becomes very large, the o-schemata retention ratio for crossover approaches zero (most o-schemata are destroyed) while the o-schemata retention ratio for inversion approaches one (most o-schemata are retained). An example derivation of the o-schemata retention ratio for inversion is given in the appendix.

While the destructive behavior of crossover could be tempered by introducing a "breeding" operator that just copies a selected individual (retention ratios = 1) and the activity of inversion increased by taking more than one cut point per individual it is not clear what the most desirable retention ratios are or if they remain the same over the duration of the GA optimization process. What is needed is a control parameter for schemata retention that allows the amount of information retained by genetic activity to be varied continuously.

Simulated Annealing

Simulated annealing [Ref. 5] provides just such a parameter, the temperature. In simulated annealing solutions are evaluated on the basis of their "energy". Disordered states (inefficient solutions) have a higher energy than ordered states (efficient solutions). A single best solution is maintained, rather than a population of solutions as in the genetic algorithm. The probability that a newly generated solution is accepted as the current best solution depends on the temperature and relative energies of the current best and new solution as follows:

$$\text{if } (E_n < E_c) \quad p = 1$$
$$\text{if } (E_n > E_c) \quad p = \exp[(E_c - E_n)/kT] \quad \text{(eq 1)}$$

where E_n is the energy of the new solution and E_c is the energy of the current best solution.

Conceptually, the system must pay a price in terms of energy to transition to a state that is higher in energy than the current state. The energy required is supplied by the heat present in the system. Boltzmann's equation relates the temperature to the available energy. The equation is probabalistic rather than deterministic since the ambient temperature represents the average of a large number of small volumes. Even at a low ambient temperature the local temperature in a small volume might be very high. Boltzmann's equation gives the probability that a given amount of energy is available at a given temperature. In simulated annealing the temperature is set to a high value initially and then lowered according to an annealing schedule provided by the analyst.

There are reports that simulated annealing has enjoyed great success at the travelling salesman problem [Ref. 6]. These reports are difficult to assess, since performance numbers are not given.

In any event, it would be desirable to include some aspects of simulated annealing within the general framework of the genetic algorithm. In particular we desire to tie the schemata retention behavior of the standard operators (crossover, inversion and mutation) to a temperature parameter. This suggests a model for genetic operators as described in the following section. The model described is artificial in the sense that it is motivated by a need to control schemata retention in a computer program rather than by biological or physical processes.

Thermodynamic Operator

We consider a crossover operation between two parent individuals that have been selected from the population with probability proportional to their fitness. An offspring individual is constructed by transcribing the genes from the parents in such a way that o-schemata and a-schemata are partially preserved.

Transcription begins with the first gene of one of the parents. We imagine that it is energetically favorable to continue transcription from the same parent; it costs energy to switch transcription to the other parent. The energy available in the environment follows a Boltzmann distribution. If we call the energy at which transcription will switch to the other parent θ_c (the crossover threshold energy) then a switch will occur just when the energy available locally (which depends on the temperature) exceeds θ_c. This occurs with probability

$$\exp[-\theta_c/kT] \quad \text{(eq 2)}$$

where k is an arbitrarily chosen scaling constant. We assume k = 1. Transcription continues from the second parent until the crossover threshold energy is again exceeded. At high temperatures, transcription might switch back and forth between the parents many times. At low temperatures transcription might not switch at all resulting in a direct copy of the parent individual.

Inversion is modelled similarly. We imagine that the strings selected from each parent stand a chance of being rotated as they are transported from the parent to the offspring (see figure 2). Again, it costs energy to perform this rotation and this energy is supplied by the heat available locally. Thus, the probabilty of inversion is

$$\exp[-\theta_i/kT]$$

where θ_i is the inversion threshold energy. In some domains it may be desirable to model the fact that it requires more energy to rotate a longer string than to rotate shorter one. Due to the rotational symmetry in the travelling salesman problem we ignored this issue. That is, the distance from city-i to city-j is the same as the distance from city-j to city-i so that in this case, o-schemata wholly contained within the rotated string are not affected by the operation. In other cases, for instance bin packing, packing item-i before item-j will almost always result in a different fitness than packing item-j before item-i.

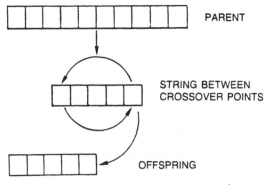

Figure 2. A string may be rotated

Thus inverting a longer string in the bin packing case should require more energy than inverting a shorter string.

Finally, mutation (of the allele) is treated similarly. We imagine that as each allele is transcribed there is a probability that its value will change. The probability of mutation is just

$$\exp\left[-\theta_i/kT\right]$$

Thus a thermodynamic operator is specified by a triple: $[\theta_c, \theta_i, \theta_m]$. The overall system temperature is varied according to an "annealing" schedule chosen by the analyst. As the temperature approaches zero, the probability that any of the thresholds will be exceeded also approaches zero, genetic activity ceases, and the schemata retention ratio approaches 1. As the temperature approaches infinity, schemata are retained only by chance and the algorithm becomes a random search. The operator therefore provides a retention ratio for o-schemata that is continuously variable from 0 to 1.

Implemented Operators

We have implemented the unified thermodynamic operator and use it in place of the basic genetic operators. Since the exponentiation operation in (eq 2) is computationally expensive, we calculate the expected number of genes to be transcribed at the current temperature before a crossover event occurs. This quantity is given by a geometric distribution [Ref. 7]:

$$N = \lceil \ln U/ \ln(1 - e^{-\theta/kT}) \rceil$$

where U is a uniform deviate in the interval [0,1]. The calculation is the same for crossover, inversion and mutation. These quantities should be recalculated if the temperature is raised.

In the thermodynamic framework refresh is implemented by allowing the operator to be defined by a 4-tuple $[\theta_c, \theta_i, \theta_m, r]$ where $0 < r < 1$. Normally, individuals are selected as parents with probability proportional to their fitness. The parameter, r, specifies the probability of using the saved copy of the current best individual instead. When there are secondary fitness measures one of the current best individuals is selected randomly. At high temperatures this individual is altered significantly through crossover with the second parent before being returned to the population but at low temperatures it tends to be copied directly into the population. An overview of the system is shown in figure 3.

Although we have not done so, it would seem that the heuristic operators could also be placed in the thermodynamic framework. (We use a heuristic operator which is seperate from the thermodynamic operator.)

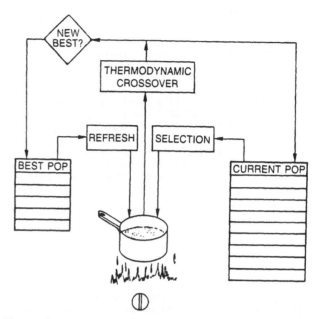

Figure 3. Overview of a system to implement the GA

The heuristic employed in [Ref. 2] for the travelling salesman problem is to choose the next city to be visited from the next available gene in either parent, whichever is closer to the last city transcribed. One could imagine, instead, evaluating the relative energies of the two choices as in simulated annealing and then using (eq 1) to make a choice. Thus, the less favorable alternative is more likely to be chosen at higher temperatures than at lower ones. This at least ameliorates the deterministic quality of the heuristic operator. An implementation difficulty for this idea is that there does not seem to be a way to avoid an expensive exponentiation operation at each gene during transcription.

Annealing Schedule

The overall performance of the GA using the thermodynamic operator is sensitive to the annealing schedule chosen by the analyst. The general strategy we have used is to start the system at a high temperature, drop the temperature fairly rapidly to a moderate range and then descend more slowly to a very low temperature. The process is then repeated with a slightly lower initial temperature. This can continue until the initial temperature becomes too close to the final temperature. Then the process can be repeated again starting from a high temperature (figure 4).

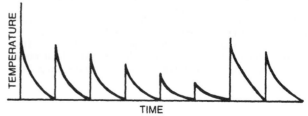

Figure 4. Temperature vs Time for a typical annealing schedule

The specific annealing schedule used for a 100 city problem is implemented by the routine shown in Figure 5. Two individuals are created and evaluated between each call to this update routine.

```
(Defun update-temp ()
  (cond ((> *temp* 115) (decf *temp* 1.0))
        ((> *temp* 100) (decf *temp* 0.2))
        ((> *temp* 50)  (decf *temp* 0.1))
        ((> *temp* 36)  (decf *temp* 0.05))
        (t (prog1 (setq *temp* *reset-temp*)
                  (if (< *reset-temp* 50)
                      (setq *reset-temp* 150)
                      (decf *reset-temp* 10))))))
```

Figure 5. A LISP routine to implement an annealing schedule

Test Cases

We have run many experiments with travelling salesman problems of various sizes. Some sample cases are exhibited in figures 5, 6, and 7. We have found that the use of thermodynamic crossover in conjunction with heuristic crossover provides a marked improvement over the use of the extended crossover operator alone or heuristic crossover alone. We have also found that thermodynamic crossover allows the reduction of the population to sizes much smaller than those indicated by Goldberg and Lingle [Ref. 3]. For instance, we use a population size of 12 - 15 individuals for a 200 city problem.

Other parameter settings used in the 100 city problem are as follows.

θ_c:	375.0
θ_i:	140.0
θ_m:	not applicable
refresh:	.07
initial temperature:	250.0

The annealing schedule shown in figure 5 was used. The heuristic crossover operator was invoked 25% of the time and thermodynamic crossover 75%. A population of size 12 was used.

In the following figures "Trials" is the number of individuals that have been evaluated. The fitness measure is in terms of the theoretical optimum value derived in [Ref. 8] and referenced in [Ref. 9]. The fitness quantity used is the optimum tour length divided by the actual tour length. Thus a fitness of .95 is about 5% above the theoretically predicted minimum tour. These results compare favorably with results presented by other researchers using the GA on the TSP, [Ref. 2] for example, both in terms of the required number fitness evaluations and the resulting route length.

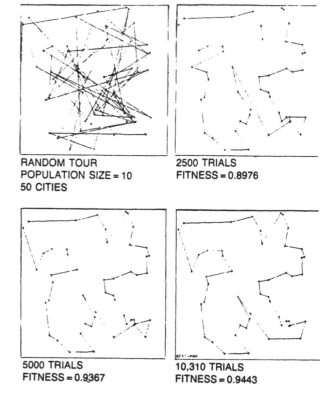

RANDOM TOUR
POPULATION SIZE = 10
50 CITIES

2500 TRIALS
FITNESS = 0.8976

5000 TRIALS
FITNESS = 0.9367

10,310 TRIALS
FITNESS = 0.9443

Figure 6. A 50 city problem

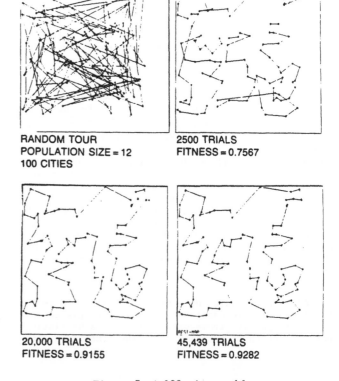

RANDOM TOUR
POPULATION SIZE = 12
100 CITIES

2500 TRIALS
FITNESS = 0.7567

20,000 TRIALS
FITNESS = 0.9155

45,439 TRIALS
FITNESS = 0.9282

Figure 7. A 100 city problem

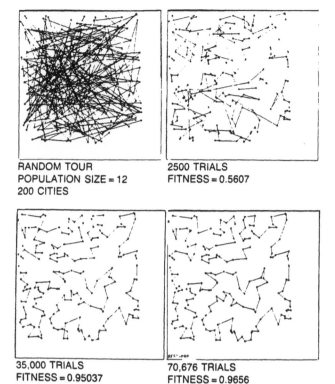

RANDOM TOUR
POPULATION SIZE = 12
200 CITIES

2500 TRIALS
FITNESS = 0.5607

35,000 TRIALS
FITNESS = 0.95037

70,676 TRIALS
FITNESS = 0.9656

Figure 8. A 200 city problem

Conclusion

Although the unified Thermodynamic Operator is not directly motivated by a theory of genetics or thermodynamics it provides an explicit control over population convergence. Empirically, it has been shown to increase performance through the use of an annealing schedule, a concept borrowed from Simulated Annealing. Analysis of the thermodynamic operator and a better understanding of the relationship between schemata retention and optimal convergence rates is expected to lead to even better performance by customizing the annealing schedule to the requirements of specific applications.

Appendix

0-Schemata Retention Ratio for Inversion

The inversion operator on an individual of length L selects two unique points A and B. The order of the genes between these points is reversed. To calculate the o-schemata retention ratio (the fraction of o-schemata retained by a typical application of the inversion operator) we first calculate the expected number of o-schemata retained and then divide by 2^L, the total number of o-schemata originally represented in the individual.

To calculate the expected number retained, E, we sum the product of the expected number retained

for each choice of A times the probability of choosing that value of A. Since all the values of A are equally likely (for all x,0<x<L+1, P(A=x) = 1/L) this multiplication can be moved outside the summation.

To calculate the expected number retained for a given A, E_A, we break this problem into two cases: the case where (A>B) and the case where (B>A).

$$E_A = P(A>B) \, E_{A>B} + P(B>A) \, E_{B>A}$$

Since all choices for B are equally likely:
$$P(A>B) = (A-1) \, / \, (L-1)$$
$$P(B>A) = (L-A) \, / \, (L-1)$$

$E_{A>B}$ can be calculated by summing the product of the actual number to be retained, when A and B are both known (and A>B), times the probability of that selection of A and B given A>B. Once again this probability is the same for all values of A and B given A>B (P = 1/(A-1)) so it can be moved outside the summation.

Finally, the number retained when A and B are known (and A>B) can be rewritten as the total number, 2^L, minus the number lost. Generally, any o-schemata using genes from the inversion region will be lost, so the number lost in an inversion between A and B can be shown to be $2^{(1+A-B)}-1$ (the number of o-schemata using genes between A and B).

A similar analysis will also work for the other half where B>A simply by reversing the roles of A and B and using P = 1/(L-A).

Assembling the expression described above leads to a complex expression which reduces to:

$$E = 2^L + 1 + 8/(L-1) + 8/L(L-1) - [8(2^L) \, / \, L(L-1)]$$

To get the retention ratio we must divide by 2^L:

$$R = 1 + (1/2^L) + [8 \, / \, 2^L(L-1)] + [8 \, / \, 2^L L(L-1)] - [8 \, / \, L(L-1)]$$

For large values of L it can be approximated by:

$$R = 1 - \frac{8}{L(L-1)}$$

which approaches 1 as L becomes very large.

From this analysis we can see that inversion will have a tendency to retain a large portion of the o-schemata, not allowing it to explore new schemata effectively. This could help to explain the generally poor performance of inversion in solving order problems cited by Goldberg and Lingle [Ref. 3].

Similar analysis of the other operators has shown that each one has different retention characteristics for o-schemata than for a-schemata.

References

1. Holland, J. H.: Adaptation in Natural and
    Artificial Systems. The University of Michigan
    Press, Ann Arbor, 1975.

2. Greffenstette, J., R. Gopal, B. Rosmaita, and
    D. Van Gucht: Genetic Algorithms for the
    Travelling Salesman Problem. Proceedings of an
    International Conference on Genetic Algorithms
    and their Applications, Pittsburgh, July 24-26
    1985, pp 160-168.

3. Goldberg, D. E. and R. Lingle, Jr.: Alleles,
    Loci, and the Travelling Salesman Problem.
    Ibid, pp 154-159.

4. De Jong K.: Genetic Algorithms: A 10 Year
    Perspecitve. Ibid, pp 169-177.

5. Kirkpatrick, S., C. D. Gelatt, and M. P.
    Vecchi: Optimization by Simulated Annealing.
    Science, Vol. 220, May 1983, pp 671-680.

6. Press, W. H., B. P. Flannery, S. A. Teukolsky,
    and W. V. Vetterling: Numerical Recipes, the
    Art of Scientific Computing. The Press
    Syndicate of the University of Cambridge,
    Cambridge, 1986, pp 326-334.

7. Knuth, D. E.: The Art of Computer Programming,
    Vol. 2. Addison-Wesley Publishing Co., Reading,
    MA, 1969, pp 116-117.

8. Beardwood,J., H. Halton and J. M. Hammersley:
    The Shortest Path Through Many Points. Proc.
    Cambridge Philosophical Society, Vol 55, 1959.

9. Bonomi, E. and J. Lutton.: The N-city
    Travelling Salesman Problem: Statistical
    Mechanics and the Metropolis Algorithm. SIAM
    Review, Vol. 26, No. 4, October 1984

TOWARDS THE EVOLUTION OF SYMBOLS[1]

Charles P. Dolan
Hughes AI Center and
UCLA AI Laboratory

Michael G. Dyer
UCLA AI Laboratory

Abstract

This paper addresses the dual problem of implementing symbolic schemata in a connectionist memory and of using simulated evolution to produce connectionist networks that operate at the symbolic level. Connectionist models may change the way we model symbols, and we take the view that a connectionist architecture that implements symbol processing must have a plausible evolutionary path through which it could have passed. A simulation methodology is introduced which allows symbolic models to be studied at the neural level without expensive computational numerical models. A model for schema processing is proposed and that model is shown to have a plausible evolutionary path using only mutation. The proposed model allows us to implement the memory model of CRAM, a model of learning and planning currently implemented entirely at the symbolic level, using distributed representations. We also propose a more general solution for using genetic algorithms to construct connectionist networks that manipulate explicit symbolic structures.

1. What do genetic algorithms have to offer connectionism?

The question of "what genetic algorithms have to offer connectionism" is an important one because we believe that genetic algorithms are not just another search method for finding a good set of weights in a high-dimensional non-linear weight space. Genetic algorithms may be part of a solution to the problem of representational opacity.

One problem in connectionist systems is that the representations they learn are often incomprehensible to humans. In the case of the NETtalk system for pronouncing English text (Sejnowski 1987) it was necessary to use multi-dimensional clustering techniques to find out what distinctions the hidden layer was making among the inputs. In Rumelhart and McClelland's system (1986) for learning the past tense of verbs, even though the system looked as though it was following rules, no rules could be found directly in the weights of the network. In both these systems, the back-propagation learning algorithm (Rumelhart *et al* 1986) learned non-intuitive mappings of symbols (English words) to actions.

It is our contention that a network that learns a specific task, but does so by constructing an opaque representation, may yield little to our understanding of human cognitive information processing. General intelligence will probably not be achieved by only picking statistically significant features of the environment[2]. To combat this tendency of connectionist systems we follow the principle of *intermodular transparency*. This principle states that modules always communicate with a fixed representation that can be given some symbolic interpretation. In the case of connectionist networks, the module communicate with patterns of activation. Inside the modules any representation at all may be used.

The problem we encountered is that there are no connectionist learning algorithms for performing search in the space of configurations of functional units. To attempt a solution to this problem we used a degenerate form of genetic search (Holland 1975), hill climbing, to search a small space of configurations and received encouraging results described in Section 9. This has led us to formulate the entire problem as a general genetic search problem using the representation described in Section 10. We have yet to show that genetic search yields reasonable structures, but the representation we have constructed shows some promise when measured against the representational issues set forth in (DeJong 1985).

---

[1] The second author is supported in part by the JTF program of the DoD, monitored by JPL, and by grants from the ITA Foundation and the Hughes Artificial Intelligence Center.

[2] In (Holland *et al* 1987) the point is made that the inductive inferences a system makes are highly dependent on the goals of the system, not just the regularities of the data.

2. Symbol processing in PDP networks

We adopt a functional approach modelling cognitive processes. For a given process we want to model, we design a complex architecture that models it. Then, piece by piece, we try to replace functional parts of the architecture with networks of simple units, as in parallel distributed processing (PDP) (Rumelhart and McClelland 1986) models. This approach simultaneously answers the questions of how to adapt symbolic models for PDP implementation and how to implement symbols in PDP models. The question which this approach does not answer satisfactorily is "How could these architectures have gotten there?" To answer this question we must provide a plausible evolutionary path through which an architecture could have developed. We hope that genetic algorithms will not only help us establish this path but will give a tool for exploring the space of possible architectures in a principled manner.

To more fully understand our approach it is helpful to see that distributed connectionist models fall on a continuum of functional structure. The continuum ranges from homogeneous to highly functional models. The homogeneous models such as (Rumelhart and McClelland 1986) have a large number of identical units and a uniform connection pattern among units. These networks use the same learning rule for all units and rely on emergent properties of these collections of units for modeling all cognitive behavior. The approach we are taking here is highly functional. In these models, the general spirit of connectionism is kept, but large portions of the network may lose the ability to develop emergent properties. In addition, these models also admit larger amounts of external control than other models and more than one type of unit. These are all simplifying assumptions that allow us to model symbolic processing. A more complete discussion of the various degrees of functionality can be found in (Dolan and Dyer 1987).

3. Symbolic schemata and hierarchical structure

Too understand why we want to embed symbolic structures in connectionist networks one has to see the importance the such structures have played in previous cognitive models. For example, symbolic schemata have been used extensively in story understanding under various names, such as scripts (Cullingford 1980) and MOPs (Schank 1982). Schema recognition is a fundamental operation in such systems. Figure 1 shows an example schema with some unfilled roles: waiter, owner, food, and payment. This schema is simplified and adapted from the restaurant script in (Cullingford 1980). The notation used in Figure 1 stresses that a schema-based representation can be implemented as a set of relations, one relation for each slot in the schema. Likewise, the constraints among the slots of the schema, which

constitute the structural description of the schema, can be represented as sets of relations.

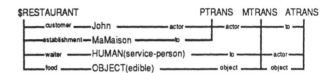

Figure 1 - Example schema, "the restaurant"

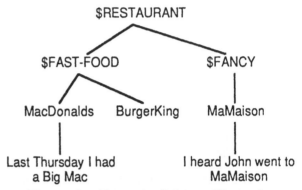

Figure 2 - Example Schema Hierarchy

In addition to having a rich structural description, symbolic schema are also often organized into a hierarchy such as the one shown in Figure 2. In these hierarchies, the most general schemata are located at the top with more specific schemata on the levels below. The leaves of the tree are instances of schemata that the program has encountered.

This organization supports two operations that give schema processing programs a great deal of their power. The first is inheritance. Once a situation is recognized as being an instance of a schema somewhere in the hierarchy, all the knowledge associated with that schema's super-classes is also available. The second is discrimination. Once a situation is recognized, the program can walk down the branches of the tree to see if the descriptions of anymore specific situations apply. Our approach to connectionist symbol processing is to directly implement features such as inheritance and discrimination at the neural level. This allows us to determine the value of such mechanisms when our models are implemented on physiologically more realistic hardware.

4. Symbol processing in CRAM

CRAM is a symbolic model of comprehension and learning from fables, with a schema-based memory (Dolan and Dyer 1986). CRAM has various components that use the schema-based memory: (1) a story comprehension system, (2) a planning system, (3) a symbolic learning system, and (4) an advice and adage-generating system. Such a model is ideal for testing a connectionist-style memory because the memory module must support these four diverse cognitive tasks. The memory model for CRAM is based primarily on three operations on schemata: (1) instantiation, (2) role binding, and (3) recognition.

For example, when CRAM notices that a character in a story has a particular goal, such as needing a secretary, and notices that the same character flatters a secretary, then CRAM needs to instantiate the schema for <offering someone a job> and bind all the correct roles. Role binding is different from binding in pattern matchers because it involves modifying the roles of schemata already instantiated in short term memory. For this reason we cannot use Touretsky and Hinton's solution (Touretsky and Hinton 1985) for production systems. For a discussion of role binding in connectionist memories see (Dolan and Dyer 1987).

5. Distributed symbols and relations

One way to think of symbols in distributed connectionist models is as "bit strings". These "bit strings" are not memory addresses, as are symbols in traditional implementations, but are feature vectors. An example of this is found in (McClelland and Kawamoto 1986) where each symbol is classified along a number of dimensions. A fixed number of bits is allocated to each dimension, one for each possible classification, and the bit string is formed from that set of features. As an example from (McClelland and Kawamoto 1986),

```
DIMENSIONS        FEATURES
GENDER            male,female,neuter
SIZE              small,medium,large
```

are the features, and the symbol mappings are

```
                   VECTORS
SYMBOLS           GENDER  SIZE
  John    -->     ( 100   001 )
  Mary    -->     ( 010   010 )
  Book    -->     ( 001   100 )
```

By constructing symbols this way, we ensure that symbols with similar meanings will have similar representations. Relations can then be formed from these symbols in a very straightforward manner, as in (Hinton 1981). Assume that we have defined the symbol "hit" for a relation as (100 100), then we can represent "John hit Mary" with (100001 100100 010010) for (ROLE1 REL ROLE2). This method of representation is compatible with the neutral/distributed and biased methods for intermodule communication.

Sets of relations of these units can be represented as a pattern of activation on a set of units using conjunctive coding (Hinton et al 1986). An example of such a representation is given in Figure 3. Here we allocate a cube of units where each dimension of the cube is the length of one symbol. Each unit in the cube represents a three-way conjunction of the features of the ROLE1, REL, and ROLE2 positions of a relation. In this way, multiple relations can be stored on the same set of units. This approach is similar to the design of the working memory for the production system in (Touretsky and Hinton 1985), except in that design, each element of the working memory was assigned a random subset of each of the possible symbols for the three positions in a relation. In our design, each unit in the working memory plays a very specific role in the semantic meaning of the relations stored in working memory.

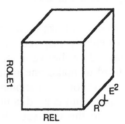

Figure 3 - Conjunctive coding of relations in working memory

6. Methodology

In order to understand the meanings of their symbols, symbolic researchers need a model of a network that allows them to study the interactions of micro-features and micro-inferences (Hinton et al 1986) while still being able to specify symbolic interactions at a relatively high level. The approach we propose here is to use a model of groups of idealized neurons. One useful side effect of this approach is that simulations are less complex compared to those of individual neurons. By making the objects of study functional groups of neurons, modelers can study architectural issues, but only after it has been shown that groups of units can be made to function in the desired way using detailed numerical simulations.

Using this method, we simulate a group of units, called a "unit-set", as an object that responds to messages in the sense of object-oriented programming. This is similar to the approach taken in (Eilbert and Salter 1986). Eilbert and Salter modeled each layer of the network as an object, and object parameters determined the probability of a particular unit exciting either the unit directly below it or some random unit in the next layer. In this way they were able to easily simulate complex hierarchical networks. In the Section 10 we describe a way of encoding a configuration of unit-sets that is suitable for use by a genetic algorithm.

Underlying this methodology is the idea that a network architecture can be judged by how well it minimizes three quantities: (1) the number of unit-sets, (2) the complexity of the control layer, and (3) the number of different messages used. We believe that symbolic processing can be accomplished with a small number of messages, including:

(1) SEND-OUTPUTS to trigger a unit-set to excite the unit-sets to which it is connected
(2) WINNER-TAKE-ALL to cause a mutually inhibitory unit-set to settle on a small number of active units
(3) REINFORCE to invoke reinforcement learning
(4) DECAY to cause a unit-set to decay the activation of each unit towards zero

Between unit-sets are weighted links (connections) of the type normally used in neurally inspired models. Static links are used to pass data between sub-networks. Modifiable links are used to make one unit-set learn to respond to a pattern of activation from another unit-set. In cases where a learning algorithm is used, a message of the appropriate type is sent to the unit-set. For units that learn by reinforcement, for example, the unit-set is sent a REINFORCE message. Active units within the unit-set have their links modified according to reinforcement (Barto *et al* 1981). The static links are used to implement the architecture and should be thought of as data paths. The modifiable links are used to store knowledge.

7. Evolving functional structure

Our methodology in studying distributed connectionism lends itself to answering questions pertaining to adaptation at the architectural level. If we assume a set of architectural building blocks, such as winner-take-all networks, hidden layers, conjunctive coding networks, and unit-sets for individual relations and symbols, then we can ask whether configurations of these building blocks convey some adaptive advantage over other configurations and what configurations of building blocks does some principled model of evolution lead us to postulate.

In order to discuss evolution of functional structure, we need an architecture from which to start developing that structure. An example of such an architecture is given in Figure 4. The task for the network is to learn to reproduce the patterns from the training set on the output units when excited by noisy versions of those patterns on the input units. If the training set is composed of non-linearly separable vectors then this is clearly a problem that requires hidden units. These hidden units are where we shall try to learn functional structure.

If we start with the network as described above, using a learning procedure such as back-propagation (Rumelhart *et al* 1986), the hidden units will learn to form features from the input patterns, and the output layer will learn to reproduce those patterns based on the features formed by

the hidden layer. The features that the network learns will depend on the width (i.e. number of units) of the hidden layer and to a large degree on chance, which is based on the order of presentation of the training set and the initial settings of the weights.

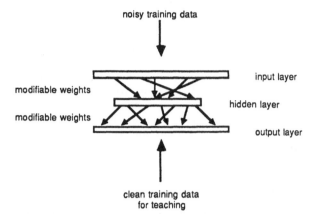

Figure 4 - Simple auto-associative network

As was shown in (Sutton 1986), search in the weight space is slowed by strict gradient descent. Because gradient procedures "creep" along a "bumpy" error surface they are not likely to come to rest with the same features that humans have. They are more likely to stop in some "pot hole", and if that pot hole allows the network to learn the training set without errors, the learning algorithm will not get out. Also there is no reason to expect that the features that people see in the training data are better than the "pot holes" in terms of the error surface.

We believe that general intelligence does not emerge from a single network of interconnected units. In order to learn large symbolic structures of the type that people use, specific architectures will be required. Such networks would have fewer stable states but would, we hope, generalize faster and would reach generalizations that are closer to those that people make.

Unfortunately, there *currently* are no algorithms along the lines of back-propagation that learn functional structure. There is, however, a process in nature, evolution, which does yield functional structure. The is also a class of algorithms, genetic algorithms (Holland 1975), which are idealizations of evolution and have been shown to be effective for high-dimensional, non-linear adaptive problems. These algorithms have been applied to such problems as adaptive control (see (DeJong 1985) for a summary) and the traveling salesman (Goldberg and Lingle 1985; Grefenstette *et al* 1985).

As a first attempt at search in the space of configurations of functional units we used an algorithm that is a degenerate form of a genetic search algorithm, which uses a population of 2, one genetic operator, mutation, and for each generation chooses the most fit structure and a mutation of that structure for the next generation. In terms of Holland's characterization for reproductive plans (1975), this one is[3]:

$$R_1(P_{crossover}=0, P_{inversion}=0, P_{mutation}=1, <1>)$$

Even with this simple degenerate case of genetic algorithms we were able to get improved performance from the network. This seems to indicate that for some problems, such as the one described in Section 9, search at the level of configurations of functional units is very important. Search for network structure at the link level, such as that demonstrated in (Ackley 1985), will yield learning that is too slow to operate on an evolutionary time scale. Also, this type of learning will yield systems which do not have intermodular transparency. It is better to assume a basic level of architectural organization, and then search for a solution at that level. Thus, we can evolve systems that are highly fit. This approach also agrees with the basic assumption of genetic search, that search occurs in the space of the genotype (genetic code), not the phenotype (physical manifestation of the organism). To require that individual links are coded for in the genotype would mean that the genetic code is the size of the network, and this is clearly not the case with people.

The proper measure of fitness for an architecture is how well it learns the training set. A fit architecture must be able to deal with noisy inputs, should be stable, and should learn fast. In addition an architecture should be flexible enough to be put in a different environment from that which formed it and still perform well. In our experiment we used a measure of fitness for a structure A in an environment E as below:

$$\mu_E(A) = a/e + b/(e_T + 1)$$

where T is the time the network is allowed to learn, e is the total number of errors the network makes, and e_T is the number of errors the network produces at the end of a run. The constants, a and b, are used to weight these two measures of network efficiency and in the experiment described in Section 9 they are both set to 1.

8. An architecture for schema processing

In this section we present an architecture for schema processing that performs the functions of schema recognition, instantiation and role binding. The central component of the architecture is the working memory. The working memory is a set of units that conjunctively code sets of relations, such as the one in Figure 3. The full architecture is shown in Figure 5. The schema memory performs the functions of recognition and instantiation. The procedural memory could be implemented a number of ways, as

a connectionist production system (Touretsky and Hinton 1985), as a classifier system (Holland and Reitman 1978), or as a symbolic production system. The full architecture is described more fully in (Doland and Dyer 1987).

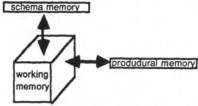

Figure 5 - Schema processing architecture

Figure 6b shows the details of the schema memory. The memory is composed of many winner-take-all cliques. Each clique discriminates a mutually exclusive set of possible schemata based on the contents of working memory. In addition to recognizing schema, each unit in the cliques also excites the units in working memory to instantiate the remainder of the schema. In addition to the connections to the working memory, the cliques are connected to each other. These links implement inheritance and discrimination. Part of the tree in Figure 6a is shown in the schema memory of Figure 6b. Strong positive weights, shown in the figure as think black lines from the subclass-units to super-class units, implement inheritance. Weak links, shown in the figure as thin black lines from the super-class units to the sub-class units, implement discrimination. Once a super-class is active, it slightly activates all of its sub-class units in the same clique. If there is enough additional evidence in working memory to activate any of the sub-classes the one with the most evidence wins. This structure can also implement exception handling. To override a default, a strong negative weight, shown in the figure as a thick gray line, is formed between sub-class and the super-class to be overridden.

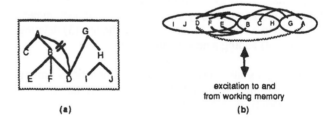

Figure 6 - An example schemata in memory

It is clear that this organization can be "wired up" to recognize and instantiate schema according to their symbolic definitions. What is not clear is how plausible this architecture is. The question we must answer is how this architecture got there. In the next section we describe an experiment in simulated evolution that shows that this architecture is very plausible.

---

[3]This can also be characterized as simple hill climbing.

9. An experiment in the evolution of structure

To test the plausibility of this architecture we designed an experiment to see if simulated evolution would arrive at anything similar to the architecture in Figure 6b. In genetic search algorithms, a genotype is defined from which phenotypes can be constructed. A population of the genotypes is then put in a pool and altered using genetic operations such as crossover, inversion, and mutation (Holland 1975). Differential reproduction based on estimated fitness, combined with recombination using crossover allows the system to search through the space of coadapted alleles with provable efficiency. In our experiment we used a population of two, a single organization of the network and one mutation of it, and determined which was most fit. The winner of the competition moved on to the next generation. The reason for not using a large gene pool is that we were only interested in finding a plausible evolutionary path.

9.1 Experimental design

The unit of mutation in our experiments is the winner-take-all clique. Within each clique, only the unit with the strongest activation is allowed to fire. In addition, each unit in a clique has an adaptive threshold. If the unit does not fire often enough, it lowers its threshold; if it fires too often, it raises its threshold. A unit decides whether or not it is firing "enough" based on the number of reinforcement cycles the network has gone through since it last fired. The effect of the adaptive threshold is to make each clique try to maximize its information-carrying capacity. If a unit is either not firing at all or firing all the time, it is not carrying any information.

It would be easy to define a genotype for this architecture by letting a certain number of genes code for the number of cliques and other genes for the relative distribution of clique sizes. However, for this experiment we define four types of mutation directly on the architectural phenotype[4]: (1) splitting a clique, (2) merging two cliques, (3) deleting a clique, (4) adding a new clique with two units.

Since cliques also have modifiable connections among each other, these four mutations allow the system to form a wide variety of architectures.

To ensure that the system does not simply learn an architecture that is tuned to a specific input set, for each generation we use a new training set. The only thing in common among all training sets is that they are all tree structured. For example, we might want a network that

---

[4] Because the mutations are performed at the level of functional blocks, this can be considered as search in the space of the genotype. Section 10 details a representation that allows search directly in the space of the genotype.

was able to handle trees of depth 3 and width 4, so each generation we generated a random tree of depth 3 where the branching fact varied from 0 to 4 at each node. For example, the some of the training set for the tree shown in Figure 6a is shown in Figure 7.

```
          Feature vector          Examples
     A B C D E F G H I J
1.  (1 0 1 0 0 0 0 0 0 0)            C
2.  (0 1 0 1 0 0 1 0 0 0)            D
3.  (0 0 0 0 0 0 1 1 0 1)            J
```

Figure 7 - An example of hierarchical features

For example, to represent a member of the class C as in test vector 1, turn on bit C and turn on bit A, because A is super-class of C, but never turn on bit B because B and C are in mutually exclusive sub-classes of A. Likewise, to represent a member of class F as in test vector 2, we turn on the bits on the path from F to the root: F, B, and A. To represent a member of class D, as in test vector 2, we turn on the bits for D, B, and G but not A because there is a cancellation link from D to A.

A set of features such as these were presented to a network such as the one in Figure 4 where the hidden layer was structured as a set of cliques. In addition, noise was added to the training vectors by flipping bits. The average number of bits flipped was proportional to the depth of the trees being learned. For 2 level trees it was 1 bit, for 4 levels, 2.

The experiments started with a hidden layer with just one clique. The clique was large enough to discriminate among a set of feature vectors from an "average bushy" tree of the desired depth. In this case we were trying to evolve an architecture for learning trees of depth three. The rationale for starting with a single large clique is that this structure works extremely well in an environment with no noise and with a training set whose size perfectly fits the width of the hidden layer.

We used learning to evaluate the fitness of the various architectures. Competitive learning (Rumelhart and Zipser 1986) was used to modify the weights from the input to the hidden layer and the weights among the cliques. Hebbian learning (Hebb 1949) was used to modify the weights from the hidden layer to the output layer. We wanted to select for three features of the learning performance: speed, stability, and accuracy. To select for speed, we only allowed the networks ten iterations through the training data. Considering the fact that noise was introduced, this was not a large number of trials. To select for stability and accuracy we kept track of two quantities during a given generation: the total number of errors a network made and the current performance. At the end of ten iterations, the networks were compared; if a network had lower scores on both counts it moved on to the next generation. If the decision was split, then it was settled at random.

9.2 Results
By watching the performance of various organizations we were able to derive some rules of thumb for predicting the fitness of an architecture. These observations are not quantitative, but serve to illustrate why one particular organization had a selective advantage over another.

Flat organizations (i.e. a single, wide clique) are extremely efficient. However, they are unstable and very susceptible to noise. Very often, noise will force the competitive learning algorithm to change the encoding from the input layer to the hidden layer, and this will undo all the learning performed between the hidden and output layers.

It is easy to construct an organization of binary cliques that exactly mirrors the hierarchy. This structure is efficient and extremely stable, but if the tree changes substantially in the next generation, a finely-tuned structure will not perform well. Organizations with lots of structure do extremely well. A good mix of various clique sizes allows the organization to perform well in a wide range of environments (i.e. all trees of depth three and branching factor 0-4).

9.3 Analysis
In general we found that networks tended to mutate towards increasing complexity. Since flat organizations are not particularly robust, a mutation in which a new clique is added will increase stability and will therefore be selected for. The mutation that adds another small clique gives only a small advantage if any, but allows the organization to mutate to one in which two small cliques combine. This yields a large advantage over multiple small cliques or one single, wide clique.

One unfortunate feature of this method is that the environment can kill off a promising line of evolution by accident. As a network is growing into a very complex organization, with many cliques of various sizes, if the training set for a particular generation is very bushy it may overload the capacity of the network to learn the structure of the tree. In these cases, a flat architecture with the same number of units will be more fit, since it can encode one training example on each unit of the hidden layer. This is a case of a representational boundary as described in (DeJong 1985). Because of that fact, the first architectures to evolve are often large, flat, single-clique architectures. Once these cliques split, however, they form very robust hierarchical architectures. It seems quite difficult for the system to develop hierarchical architectures from the start by incrementally adding more and more cliques. The reason is that the intermediate stages of such a development are subject to extinction by difficult environments.

10. A proposal for genetic search in the space of functional structure
The primary problem in any genetic algorithm is choosing the representation. DeJong (1985) has identified several issues that need to be addressed in choosing a representation. One is the problem of schema[5] that confer above-average performance: (1) do they exist?, and (2) are they at all preserved by the genetic operators? A second one is the problem of representational boundaries: are there representations which confer above-average performance, but which cannot be improved upon without a radical change in genotype? Although it is possible to devise such an encoding for the simple structures described in Section 9, it is difficult to devise a fixed encoding which would be capable of describing structures such as the one shown in Figure 5.

A solution to these problems may be found in adaptive codings as suggested in (Holland 1975). In that formulation, complex productions are expressed as strings of a ten member alphabet, which has a rather complex interpretation scheme, and a reproductive plan is run on that representation. A similar, but more elegant formulation is found in (Holland and Reitman 1978) in which each production is a bit string from the alphabet {1,0,#}, where # stands for "don't care". Productions are matched against and post bit-patterns to a blackboard whose contents also determine the actions of the system (in our case which unit-sets to create and how to connect them). A further refinement of this formulation called classifier systems along with the bucket-brigade algorithm (Holland et al 1987) allows credit (fitness) to be apportioned among a chain of productions responsible for producing a structure of above-average fitness. The genetic algorithm is then run either by treating an entire set of productions as a genotype, as in (Smith 1983), or by using each production as a genotype as in (Holland and Reitman 1978). In the second option the production system is treated as a population and the strength of a rule is its measure of fitness.

This style of representation holds great promise for our task because these classifier systems can be used to compute almost anything (anything if we give them an infinite blackboard). However, we must be cautious of DeJong's pitfalls for genetic algorithms (1985). To begin with, we structure the condition and action parts of a production's bit vector with the following fields,

```
(block-type,x1,y1,z1,unit-type,
 projection-type,x2,y2,z2,link-type,
 tag)
```

---

[5]The word schema is used in two different ways in this paper, to indicate a complex symbolic structure and to indicate a set of alleles on a genotype as in (Holland 1975). All previous references have been to the first meaning. All subsequent ones shall be to the second.

This indicates a functional block of a certain type (e.g. relation vector, symbol vector, relation cube, or hidden layer of a particular size) at location (x_1, y_1, z_1) with a certain type of units (e.g. linear threshold, with or without refractory period, etc.), projecting with a certain pattern (e.g. random, one-to-one, or layered) to a block at location (x_2, y_2, z_2) using a link with a particular learning rule (e.g. reinforcement or back-propagation). This same format is used both to test for blocks and to assert the existence of blocks onto the blackboard. The tag field can be used to link arbitrary productions.

Now we can attempt an informal evaluation of this representation in terms of DeJong's metrics. Taking the position that either individual productions or the entire system is a genotype, we can see that the position codes constitute fairly robust schema. However, they convey no particular advantage until combined with a particular block type, and they make even stronger schema when combined with a projection to another location. For example, a production with #'s in the positions for both sets of (x,y) coordinates would create a layer of identical unit sets, each one connected to the unit set either above or below it depending on the values of the z coordinates. Now, however, we are talking about schemata almost as long as the genotype if we use individual productions in population. Clearly, we need to use the first option, i.e. the entire production system as a genotype, to make such a linkage viable. With this method there is also a possibility that the message field can be used to form linkages between productions. These linkages, however, will be extremely weak unless we can use inversion to strengthen them.

This representation looks like it will have interesting representational boundaries. First, it is not clear whether most random genotypes will even produce a configuration with two connected functional blocks. Second, once there are a set of productions represented in the population which produce a structure with a certain fitness, it is not likely that an operation which modifies those productions will result in improved fitness. It is much more likely that it will completely inhibit the creation of the structure and result in much lower fitness. This conforms very well to our notion of how epistasis[6] should work in functional evolution. It is much more likely that productions will be found which add other structures on top of the ones already found to be useful. This is similar to the situation found in the evolutionary development of the brain. The structures found in higher organisms are built on top of those found in lower organisms (Kolb and Whishaw 1980).

---

[6]Epistasis is the phenomena, in genetics, of a reaction that depends on several enzymes, and will not proceed until all the enzymes are present.

In order to test this representation, we propose three steps. First, we will continue working with hand-coded networks of functional units, but restrict our attention to networks that can be compactly represented by a production system. Second, we will take those same representations and see what other systems are constructible from them, since classifier systems can be non-deterministic (when a classifier matches more than one element of working memory or when more than one classifier matches). Last, using a corpus of symbolic manipulation tasks, such as story comprehension and question answering, we will test the ability of a genetic algorithm to construct neural-like networks which can process symbolic structures.

11. Current status

The architecture for the schema memory is currently implemented in Scheme on a workstation. The model has been integrated with a long term schema-based memory and a procedural memory implemented serially at the bit-level. The system can currently understand fragments of one-paragraph stories. The largest network we have simulated so far stores six schemata with approximately seven relations each. The relations are represented with eight bits for each symbol. A more complete description of this system can be found in (Dolan and Dyer 1987).

12. Conclusions

We have found that search in the space of configurations of sub-networks can yield a network that learns human-like generalizations. The resulting architecture learns fast, and forms the same type of hierarchical structures that are formulated as symbolic models in humans. By using this approach we can now evaluate various symbolic models at the micro-feature level, to see if their symbolic representations hold up under a detailed analysis.

We now have a hope of using true genetic search in the space of configurations to find architectures for general intelligence. This would probably not be the case if we could not have shown that simple hill climbing in a simple case was able to yield a network that out-performed the simplest flat network.

13. References

Ackley, D. H. (1985). A Connectionist Algorithm for Genetic Search. *Proceedings of the First International Conference on Genetic Algorithms and their Applications*, 121-135.

Barto, A. G., Sutton, R. S., and Brouwer, P. S. (1981). Associative search networks: A reinforcement learning associative memory. *Biological Cybernetics*, 40, 201-211.

Cullingford, R. E. (1981). SAM, in R. C. Schank and C. K. Riesbeck (Eds) *Inside Computer Understanding: Five Programs Plus Miniatures*. Lawrence Erlbaum Associates.

DeJong, K. (1980). Genetic Algorithms: A 10 Year Perspective. *Proceedings of the First International Conference on Genetic Algorithms and their Applications*, 169-177.

Dolan, C. P. and Dyer M. G. (1986). Encoding Knowledge for Planning, Learning, and Recognition, in *Proceedings of the Eighth Annual Conference of the Cognitive Science Society*, 488-499.

Dolan, C. P. and Dyer, M. G. (1987). Symbolic Schemata in Connectionist Memories: Role Binding and the Evolution of Structure. UCLA AI Laboratory Technical Report, UCLA-AI-87-11.

Eilbert, J. L. and Salter, R. M. (1986) Modeling Neural Networks in Scheme. *Simulation*, 46(5), 193-199.

Goldberg, D. E. and Lingle R. (1985). Alleles, Loci, and the Traveling Salesman Problem. *Proceedings of the First International Conference on Genetic Algorithms and their Applications*, 154-159.

Grefenstette, J. J., Rajeev, G., Rosmaita, B. J., and Van Gucht, D. (1985). Genetic Algorithms and the Traveling Salesman Problem. *Proceedings of the First International Conference on Genetic Algorithms and their Applications*, 160-168.

Hebb, D. O. (1949). *The organization of behavior*. Wiley.

Hinton, G. E. (1981). Implementing Semantic Networks in Parallel Hardware, in G. E. Hinton and J. A. Anderson (Eds), *Parallel Models of Associative Memory*. Lawrence Erlbaum Associates.

Hinton, G. E., McClelland, J. L., and Rumelhart, D. E. (1986). Distributed Representation, in D. E. Rumelhart and J. L. McClelland (Eds) *Parallel Distributed Processing*, Volume 1. MIT Press.

Holland, J. H. (1975). *Adaptation in Natural and Artificial Systems*. University of Michigan Press.

Holland, J. H. and Reitman, J. S. (1978). Cognitive Systems Based on Adaptive Algorithms, in D. A. Waterman and F. Hayes-Roth (Eds) *Pattern-Directed Inference Systems*. Academic Press.

Holland, J. H., Holyoak, K. J., Nisbett, R. E., and Thagard, P. R. (1987). *Induction: Processes of Inference, Learning, and Discovery*. MIT Press.

Kolb, B. and Whishaw, I. Q. (1980). *Fundementals of Human Neuropsychology*. W. H. Freeman and Compandy.

McClelland, J. L. and Kawamoto, A. H. (1986). Mechanisms for Sentence Processing: Assigning Roles to Constituents, in J. L. McClelland and D. E. Rumelhart (Eds) *Parallel Distributed Processing*, Volume 2. MIT Press.

Rumelhart, D. E., Hinton, G. E., and Williams, R. J. (1986). Learning Internal Representations by Error Propagation, in D. E. Rumelhart and J. L. McClelland (Eds) *Parallel Distributed Processing*, Volume 1. MIT Press.

Rumelhart, D. E. and McClelland J. L.(1986). *Parallel Distributed Processing*, Volume 1. MIT Press.

Rumelhart, D. E. and Zipser, D. (1986). Feature Discovery by Competitive Learning, in D. E. Rumelhart and J. L. McClelland (Eds) *Parallel Distributed Processing*, Volume 1. MIT Press.

Rumelhart, D. E. and McClelland J. L. (1986). On Learning the Past Tenses of English Verbs, in J. L. McClelland and D. E. Rumelhart (Eds) *Parallel Distributed Processing*, Volume 2. MIT Press.

Schank, R. C. (1982). *Dynamic memory: A theory of reminding and learning in computers and people*. Cambridge University Press.

Sejnowski, T. J. (1987). From Signals to Symbols in Connectionist Networks. Lecture at UCLA, May 1987.

Smith, S. F. (1983). Flexible learning of problem solving heuristics through adaptive search. *Proceedings of the Eighth International Joint Conference on Artificial Intelligence*, 422-425.

Sutton, R. S. (1986). Two Problems with Back Propagation and Other Steepest-descent Learning Procedures for Networks. *Proceedings of the Eighth Annual Conference of the Cognitive Science Society*.

Touretsky, D. S., and Hinton, G. E. (1985). Symbols Among the Neurons: Details of a Connectionist Inference Architecture. *Proceedings of Ninth International Joint Conference on Artificial Intelligence*, 239-243.

SUPERGRAN: A connectionist approach to learning, integrating genetic algorithms and graph induction

G. Deon Oosthuizen

Dept. of Computer Science, University of Strathclyde
26 Richmond Street, Glasgow G1 1XH, Scotland

Abstract

The operation of genetic algorithms is based on the recurrent selection of strings of values according to their usefulness to the system and the subsequent creation of new strings, by application of genetic operators, in an effort to obtain more appropriate strings. A learning algorithm, based on a connectionist approach to knowledge representation, can be used to supervise and enhance the application of genetic operators on the basis of analysing the underlying features of the strings.

The genetic algorithm generates new strings. The learning algorithm utilises the strings to induce new concepts (schemata) and these are used to advise the genetic algorithm, which in turn produces new strings.

Combining the learning capabilities of the two components results in a versatile system that is able to *digest eagerly* and *adapt gracefully*.

Introduction

The application of genetic algorithms has already delivered very interesting results in various areas, including optimization [Grefenstette 1986], cognitive modelling [Holland & Reitman 1978], classification and control [Holland 1986]. Genetic algorithms have two inherent characteristics that make them highly suitable for learning by discovery: on the one hand, sufficient variability is maintained to prevent convergence to local optima. On the other hand, categorization and recombination yields powerful implicit parallelism.

Yet, the overall process is based on the appropriateness of strings. The underlying relations and dependencies between features are not dealt with directly in the generation of new strings.

We employ another learning method, the GRAND algorithm for GRAph iNDuction[1] developed by the author [Oosthuizen *et al.* 1987b], to supplement the genetic operators by providing knowledge about the underlying relations and dependencies between features. The aim is to use "deep" knowledge to direct the application of the genetic operators and thereby to enhance the performance of the overall process.

Since we are concerned with learning systems, we shall devote our attention to the application of genetic algorithms to the class of message-passing rule-based systems called *classifier systems* [Holland 1986], also referred to as Holland classifiers [Schrodt 1986]. We shall use the term *classifier system* to refer to a total learning system consisting of a rule base, an apportionment of credit algorithm and in particular a genetic algorithm. Although we shall use the terminology employed in that context, the ideas described here are applicable to the broader class of optimization procedures called genetic algorithms. Thus, our use of the term *string* refers to the members of the *population*, applying to the condition/action part of a classifier (or their concatenation), but also to a structure or vector in other optimization procedures.

In this paper we describe how, by combining the inductive capabilities of

---

[1] graph induction = induction by graphic representation and graph manipulation

genetic algorithms and graph induction, we obtain a competent learning system. We describe the system by first looking at the role of schemata in classifier systems. We then describe the method of graph induction in the context of classifier systems. Subsequently, we introduce the idea of a *supervised classifier system*. Finally, we highlight the characteristics of the integrated system, called SUPERGRAN, as well as some crucial implementation considerations.

Schemata

Schemata play a central role in the application of genetic algorithms. They are used as building blocks from which new strings are constructed, and are also used (as *tags*) to facilitate sophisticated transfer of knowledge from one situation to another [Holland 1986]. Schemata are basically generalized descriptions of categories of strings. A schema is expressed as a string containing particular symbols in particular positions, indicating that all strings in that category have similar symbols in the equivalent positions. Unspecified positions, i.e. positions that "don't matter" are filled with *'s. In classifier systems, schemata define subsets of the space of possible conditions or actions, i.e. subsets of the space of possible strings. A schema thus constitutes a *characteristic description* for a set of strings. We shall merely refer to a schema as a description of a set. The schema also serves as an identifier for a set of strings. We shall therefore sometimes just speak of a schema, when referring to the set it represents.

In the method described here, schemata are employed in an additional role. Information (already captured in schemata) regarding the composition of the "best" strings in the current population, is used directly, and forms the basis for concept generation and clustering. The kind of string categorization described here is based on the combination of features present in schemata and strings, and is therefore different from the use of *tags*, which also results in schema classification/string clustering. Tags relate schemata on the basis of the temporal sequences of categories [Holland 1986]. We consider the non-temporal association of schemata, based on their inherent properties.

Graph Induction

Graph induction evolved from research regarding the connectionist approach to knowledge representation. The method thus originated against the background of a study of the learning capabilities of connectionist architectures, i.e. systems in which connections - rather than memory cells - are the principle means of storing information. Such systems employ vast networks of very simple processors, functioning in a massively parallel way. This accounts for the graphic basis of our method. We will expand on the significance of the connectionist approach in a later section. We now describe the method in the context of its application to classifier system schemata.

Each individual position in a string (*genotype*) can assume more than one value (*allele* - taken from the standard terminology of genetics). Each allele can be considered to define an entire category of its own, i.e. the class of all strings in the population containing allele x in position y, say. Similarly, each allele can be used to identify a set of strings. If we compute the intersection of two such sets, we obtain a third set which is identified by the co-occurrence of two alleles. This third set can be conveniently described by a schema containing only the two alleles involved and *'s in all other positions.

We can now represent this situation graphically as illustrated in fig. 1. An upward arrow represents a subset relationship. If two arrow-ends meet - an intersection is implied. Fig. 1 represents the fact that the set identified by the schema 01* contains the intersection of the sets identified by the schemata *1* and 0**. Fig. 2 shows that the sets identified by the schemata *0* and *1* (we shall refer to them as 1-allele schemata), are contained in the set *#*.

Fig 3. shows some other intersections that may be formed. This notation can be extended to represent any combination of any number of alleles - i.e. the intersection of any

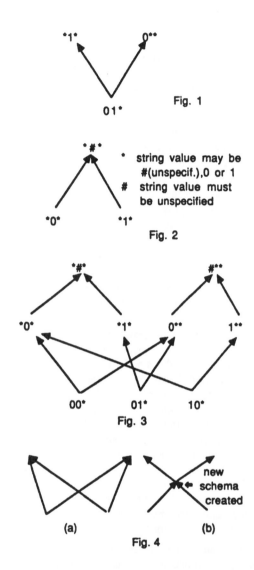

Fig. 1

* string value may be
#(unspecif.),0 or 1
string value must
be unspecified

Fig. 2

Fig. 3

(a)   (b)

new
schema
created

Fig. 4

member of the population is assigned to its own set - i.e. a special kind of schema containing no *'s. This schema can then be accurately described in terms of the intersection of k other sets, where k is the length of the string. These k sets will belong to the abovementioned level of 1-allele schemata. The result is a two-level graph: the top level containing the 1-allele schemata and the bottom level containing the k-allele schemata.

In essence the GRAND algorithm now does the following. The graph structure is restricted in such a way that it adheres to the rule that the intersection of any two sets in a graph must be contained in a single set. This means that a configuration like the one in fig. 4a (referred to as a distributed intersection) is changed to the one in fig. 4b. This results in a policy of consistent data factoring. If the tranformation is applied to fig. 5, the configuration of fig. 6 is obtained. Taking into account the fact illustrated in fig. 2 and applying the basic principles of set theory, we find that fig. 6 can once again be transformed, resulting in fig. 7.

$$000 \cup 100 = (0^{**} \cap {}^{*}00) \cup (1^{**} \cap {}^{*}00) \text{ - fig. 6}$$
$$= (0^{**} \cup 1^{**}) \cap {}^{*}00$$
$$= \#^{**} \cap {}^{*}00 \qquad \text{as in fig. 7}$$

The significance of the GRAND algorithm is that it maintains a regime of maximal schema integration. Maximally common schemata (sets) are identified and strings are clustered together accordingly. By close inspection one finds that the application of above transformation rule corresponds to the generalization rules introduced by Michalski in his theory of inductive learning [Michalski 1983]. The different generalization rules described by Michalski manifest as different variants of semantic network configurations. This is an interesting result, because it implies that the application of above transformations to the network structure represents learning. As changes occur in the world of interest, nodes and relations are constantly added and removed, transformations are continuously triggered, and new schemata (concepts) are formed. Consequently, we obtain what could be described as a "self-learning" network.

group of sets. These newly obtained sets can in turn be intersected at random to form further new sets - each described by its own schema. Thus we obtain a graph consisting of tangled hierarchies of schemata, categorizing groups of strings.

The sets thus created contain strings from the population. Some schemata may therefore represent empty sets. Our convention is to create and retain schemata (nodes in the graph) only when they are needed, i.e. for non-empty sets. At the lowest level, every

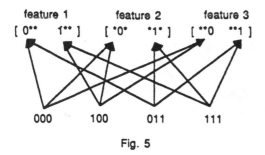

Fig. 5

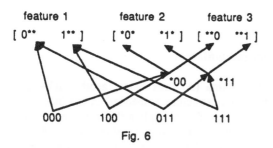

Fig. 6

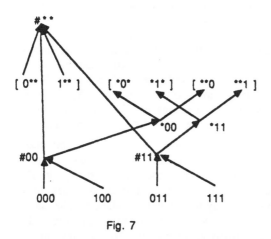

Fig. 7

Graph induction has been applied to published examples as processed by packages based on Quinlan's ID3 algorithm for learning from examples, and produced similar results. (In some cases the results were better.) It has also been shown [Oosthuizen 1986] that in principle they imply an extention of Lebowitz' "similarity-based generalization" method of learning from observation [Lebowitz 1986]. Thus, GRAND embodies various inductive learning strategies, in particular learning from examples, learning from observation and conceptual clustering.

Supervised Classifier System

The application of the GRAND algorithm makes a graph structure highly sensitive to similarities between strings. The consequent effect is the rapid identification of any such similarities and the creation of new categories characterizing these similarities. Thus, we obtain an automized string classification and clustering mechanism. Employing this mechanism, string "fitness" can now be judged on more general "feature" levels rather than on the string level itself. The objective is to discover more easily and to make it more transparent, what aspect of a string it is that makes it a "good" string - and then to be able to concentrate on that aspect. A similar argument holds for the "bad" aspects of a string.

The above effects can be obtained as follows:

For each schema set Q, we store its current number of members, as well as the current average value of v(Ci), the "fitness" of the individual strings Ci that are members of Q. In each case, the stored value pertains to the terminal nodes (i.e. strings) of the tree below a particular node (schema) of which the node is the root. However, not all the strings in the population are taken into account. To improve the efficiency of the method, only the best performing 50%, for example, of the population is used. As strings in this best performing group are replaced by new ones, some schemata might eventually become redundant on the basis of not having any members, and are then removed from the graph.

Enhancement of crossover operation

Let us say two schemata exhibit above average "strength", neither is a subset of the other (like schema B and schema E in fig. 8), and both represent an adequate number of strings. Such a situation would indicate that the two schemata represent two clusters of strings. It would now be sensible to apply the crossover operation to strings within the same schema (cluster) in the hope to discover stronger variations within this schema. This corresponds

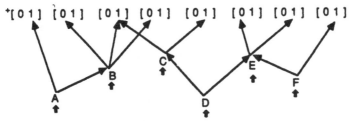

$^+[01]\quad[01]\quad[01]\quad[01]\quad[01]\quad[01]\quad[01]\quad[01]$

↑ = sets that might have individual strings as their members

+ because of lack of space we use [0 1] to represent e.g. [**0***** **1*****]

Fig. 8

to what has been done in other applications of genetic algorithms. The only difference is that the schemata used here are systematically selected schemata and maximal within clusters.

When the crossover operator is applied to strings from different dominant schemata (e.g. schemata B and E), then we would like to retain the features that characterize each. Consequently, we introduce a *pattern-crossover* (as opposed to the known part-crossover defined by a crossover point). The pattern-crossover is achieved by replacing the alleles in a string from schema E with the characterizing features of schema B and vice versa. This effects the combination of the eminent features of both schemata.

Once again, we are concerning ourselves with characteristics already present in contemporary genetic algorithms and playing a major role in their behaviour. Genetic algorithms already preserve good schemata and generate new instances for them. We are just building upon the existing characteristics, trying to enhance their effect by focussing them on the relevant elements of strings.

A genetic algorithm, by definition, preserves the best strings from a population. Only the best of these are entered into the induction graph and only the most common features of "strong" schemata are selected for recombination by means of a pattern-crossover. Thus, the pattern-crossover combines the most common alleles from strings that are already proven winners.

Supervised mutation

If one schema (A) falls below another schema (B) in a tree structure embedded in the induced graph (see fig. 8), it implies that schema A is a subset of B. It also implies that schema A is more specific than schema B and therefore contains characteristic features not present in schema B. Now, if

$$av(A) > av(B),$$

where $av(Q)$ is the average strength of the strings in Q, it means that the extra features in A actually improve the "fitness" of its strings. Since these strings are also incorporated in B, it means that some of the strings in B´ (=B-A), i.e. those in B which are not in A, did not fare so well.

We now use a *supervised mutation* operation to combine the extra features present in A with those of the strings in B´. Thus, we are spreading proven qualities in a controlled way to a larger population. The same effect can be obtained by applying the pattern-crossover operation to strings in A and B, respectively. Since the characteristic features of B is contained in A, this operation will have no effect on strings in A.

If the opposite situation holds, i.e.

$$av(B) > av(A),$$

then similarly, supervised mutation can be used to create new strings not having the distinguishing features of A. This might give rise to other schemata under B, i.e. specializations of B, if the newly introduced features correspond to others already present in another string in B.

Clearly, the application of above operations should be dependent on a defined minimum value for D, where

$$D = abs (av(A) - av(B)),$$

the difference of the average fitness of strings in A and B. In other words, if the superiority of one of the schemas is not evident, the operation might be superfluous.

Application

It is envisaged that the standard genetic operators (mutation, inversion, etc.) would be applied as usual to maintain the variability of the population and thereby to guard against overemphasis of a given kind of schema. The supervised operations described above should be applied in a constrained manner, to prevent distortion of the well balanced search process. The role of the graph induction is seen primarily in speeding up convergence once a possible optimal solution area has been spotted, by applying knowledge obtained from significant discoveries in immediate subsequent string generation. An appropriate mix of standard and supervised operations should, however, prevent premature convergence to suboptimal solutions.

SUPERGRAN

The account given above, amounts to the system represented in fig. 9. However, the concept acquisition and generalization capabilities of GRAND enables SUPERGRANd to conduct two learning strategies in parallel. Whilst the genetic induction mechanism ensures flexibility (internally), SUPERGRAN can also digest information from an external source (see fig. 10). Strings volunteered to the system are added to the population. Such strings are given a high initial strength and are therefore immediately absorbed into the induction graph. Strings volunteered are either *specific* - corresponding to examples - or *general* - corresponding to rules. If the added strings are of significance, GRAND, in its advisory role, will trigger immediate adjustments to the mixture of features in the new strings created by the genetic algorithm.

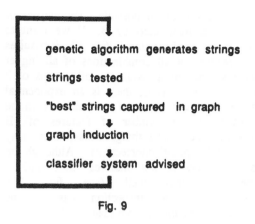

Fig. 9

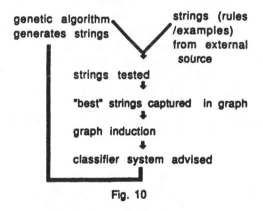

Fig. 10

SUPERGRAN is currently being implemented.

Graph Induction and Connectionism

As mentioned earlier, graph induction originated from a study of the knowledge representation capabilities of massively parallel connectionist networks.

Although the basic idea behind graph induction - the restructuring of a graph into a "canonical" form - is quite straightforward, its application poses a computational problem, illustrated in fig. 11. Let us say a certain schema A is described by 6 features (e-j) and another schema B is added to the graph. According to the graph induction rule, fig. 11 has to be transformed to the configuration in fig. 12. But, recognizing distributed intersections like those at A and B, requires the inspection of the conjunction of all possible combinations of pairs of sets intersected by B. If we want to arrive at the configuration in fig. 12, it requires the inspection of all combinations of all higher order conjunctions as well, i.e. of groups of 3 sets, 4 sets, etc. Thus, there is an exponential increase in the number of conjunctions to be inspected as the number of features of B increases. To make things worse, sets may have 'semi-explicit' intersections. Although the sets themselves do not intersect, their indirect descendents may well (see fig. 13). Consequently, the inspection has to be conducted to depths of more than one level.

McGregor & Malone [1982a,1982b] developed a set processing machine that is able to operate on vast quantities of data items (nodes). Subsequently software as well as hardware implementations (prototypes) have been created as part of the low level functions of the FACT Expert Database System [McGregor & Malone 1983]. The hardware version of the system, known as Generic Associative Memory (GAM), dynamically

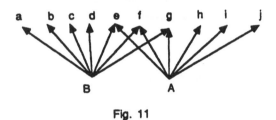

Fig. 11

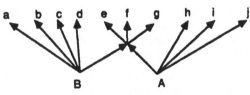

Fig. 12

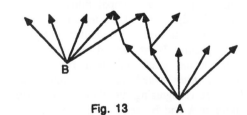

Fig. 13

constructs networks to process set data in a massively parallel fashion which makes processing speed not highly dependent on the depth of the network. These systems are described in detail elsewhere.

The core operation of this set processing system, involves the *closure* of a set (node). The *upward closure* of a node includes the node itself as well as all nodes "above" it in the network, i.e. following the arrows. The *downward closure* includes all nodes below. The determination of the intersection of closures is implemented as a hardware function [Oosthuizen *et al.* 1987a].

As mentioned above, transformations are triggered by the detection of distributed intersections. The GAM closure operation is ideal for the detection of distributed intersections and especially semi-explicit distributed intersections in complex networks (i.e. where the distributed intersections exist at levels lower than the immediate descendents of the two nodes involved).

The use of the GAM closure operation in principle eliminates the distinction between explicit and semi-explicit intersections. Because of its inherent parallelism, the closure operation is also virtually independent of the width of the "tree" involved - i.e. whether a particular node has 2 or n descendants (where n >> 2). Furthermore, the intersection of closures of two nodes like A and B in fig. 11 is (1) a primitive operation in GRAND and (2) executed in a minimal amount of time.

Although the abovementioned computation problem does not affect current small scale prototype learning systems, GAM ensures the feasibility of the application of graph induction as a general purpose learning method.

Concluding Remarks

Although dependencies between features (attributes) are dealt with implicitly in the induction graph, we have not made explicit use of them. Functional dependencies can be used to make further inductive inferences. (Functional dependencies can be inferred from mappings between sets - information already captured in the graph.)

SUPERGRAN exploits the interaction between two learning methods: the genetic algorithm generates strings and thereby creates examples which are used by the graph induction method to generate schemata and highlight underlying properties. "Champions" are identified among features or combinations of features and used to advise the genetic discovery mechanism on where to look for "better" strings. Thus, a higher degree of coherence is established between the event of a significant discovery, or underlying trend, and the present exploration of the search space.

By incorporating the whole population in the induction graph, the induction graph becomes a knowledge base to the system. In that way, the learning process becomes fully integrated with the knowledge representation function of the cognitive system. (The notation used in the induction graph in fact constitutes a knowledge representation model based on Generic Associative Sets [Oosthuizen *et al.* 1987b].)

Acknowledgements

I am indebted to the members of the IKBS working group (in particular to Michael Odetayo) for their stimulating discussions and to Jesus Christ, the Origin of all knowledge.

References

Grefenstette, J.J. [1986] Optimization of Control Parameters for Genetic Algorithms. IEEE Transactions on Systems, Man, and Cybernetics. Vol. SMC-16, No. 1, January/February.

Holland, J.H. [1986] Escaping Brittleness: The Possibilities of General Purpose Algorithms Applied to Parallel Rule-Based Systems. In Machine Learning: An Artificial Intelligence Approach Vol. 2 by Michalski, R.S., Carbonell, J.G., Mitchell, T.M. (Eds.) Morgan Kaufman.

Holland, J.H., Reitman, J.S. [1978] Cognitive Systems based on adaptive algorithms. In Pattern-Directed Inference Systems by Waterman, D.A., Hayes-Roth, F. (Eds.), Academic Press.

Lebowitz, M. [1986] UNIMEM, a general learning system: An overview. Proceedings of ECAI-86, Brighton, England.

McGregor, D.R., Malone, J.R. [1982a] Generic Associative Hardware. Its Impact on Database Systems. Proceedings IEE Colloquium on Associative Methods & Database Engines, May 1982.

McGregor, D.R., Malone, J.R. [1982b] Generic Associative Memory, G.B. Patent No. 8236084.

McGregor, D.R., Malone, J.R. [1983] The Fact System - a Hardware- oriented approach. In DBMS A Technical Comparison - State of the Art Report. Maidenhead; Pergamon Infotech pp 99-112.

Michalski, R.S. [1983] A Theory and Methodology of Inductive Learning. Artificial Intelligence, Vol. 20 pp. 111-161.

Oosthuizen, G.D. [1986] A Paradigm for Automatic Learning. Internal FACT 24/86. University of Strathclyde, Scotland.

Oosthuizen, G.D., McGregor, D.R., Henning, M., Renfrew, C. [1987a] Parallel Network Architectures for Large Scale Knowledge Based Systems. Proceedings of First Workshop of the British Special Interest Group on Knowledge Manipulating Engines (SIGKME). Reading, England. January 1987.

Oosthuizen, G.D., McGregor, D.R., Malone, J.R. [1987b] The Use of a Simple Connectionist Architecture for Matching and Learning. Internal Report FACT 2/87. University of Strathclyde, Scotland.

Schrodt, P.A. [1986] Predicting international events. BYTE, November.

PARALLEL IMPLEMENTATION OF GENETIC ALGORITHMS IN A CLASSIFIER SYSTEM

George G. Robertson
Thinking Machines Corporation

Abstract

Genetic Algorithms are the primary mechanism in Classifier Systems [16] for driving the selective evolution of rules (learning) to perform some specified task. The Classifier System approach to machine learning, in particular, and Genetic Algorithms, in general, are inherently parallel. Implementations of Classifier Systems and Genetic Algorithms to date have mostly been done on conventional serial computers. Because of this serial bottleneck, researchers have been able to study only relatively small problems. The advent of commercially available massively parallel computers, such as the Connection Machine system [10], now make parallel implementations of these inherently parallel algorithms possible, and make it possible to begin studying these algorithms on larger task domains. This paper describes an implementation of Genetic Algorithms in a Classifier System on the Connection Machine.

Classifiers Systems and Machine Learning

Classifier Systems represent one basic approach to learning by example. Two other approaches are symbolic rule-based systems and Connectionist Network systems. These approaches, and the inherent parallelism in them, are compared and contrasted with Classifier Systems below. This provides a framework for machine learning in which to place Classifier Systems, and suggests the ease of implementation for each approach on massively parallel computers.

Symbolic rule-based systems attempt to model high (symbolic) level cognitive processes. A good example is the SOAR problem-solving architecture being studied at Carnegie-Mellon University (Newell), Stanford University (Rosenbloom), and Xerox PARC (Laird) (see [18, 19, 20]). SOAR is an architecture for problem solving and learning, based on heuristic search in problem spaces and chunking. It is based on a modified version of the OPS5 Production System architecture [5]. Although SOAR shows promise as an approach to learning, it does not appear to be a good candidate for massively parallel computers.

Gupta [8] has done studies of parallelism possible in symbolic production systems and found that systems with more than thirty or so processors would not be effectively utilized. Most of the traditional AI work in machine learning (see Michalski et all [22]) also operates at the symbolic level and is perhaps even less easily parallelized than SOAR.

Connectionist Network approaches to learning began with the work on Perceptrons by Rosenblatt [28] (also see Minsky and Papert [24]). New ways of dealing with the problems that they encountered have recently been studied, including work on Boltzmann Machines [1], Back Propagation networks [29, 30, 31], work by Klopf [17], Barto [2], Grossberg [7], Feldman [4], Hinton [12], and Minsky [23]. These systems model low level neural processes, with long-term knowledge represented as strengths (or weights) of the connections between simple neuron-like processing elements. The Boltzmann Machines introduce a stochastic process to avoid the pitfalls of local minima in learning behavior. Back Propagation networks have successfully been used to learn to recognize symmetries in visual patterns [31], as well as to learn a speech synthesis task [30]. In this latter task a corpus of text and its phonetic translation is used as the example for learning. A fixed initial structure (a three level Connectionist Network) begins with random link and node threshold weights and over time learns the proper weights to translate the text into understandable phoneme streams. These systems are well-adapted to massively parallel systems: in fact, Back Propagation and Boltzmann Machines have been implemented on the Connection Machine system.

Classifier Systems attempt to model macroscopic evolutionary processes with Genetic Algorithms and natural selection. Holland's early work on Genetic Algorithms [15] has recently led to numerous research efforts and application of Classifier Systems to a number of task domains (see [6, 13, 14, 25, 26, 36, 37]) This approach shares some properties with both the symbolic rule-based and Connectionist Network approaches. It is rule-based, but the rules are low level message passing rules (below the symbol level). A symbolic level can be added on top of Classifier Systems (see Forrest's work [6]). Like Boltzmann Machines, Classifier Systems use a stochastic process to avoid local minima in learning behavior. They use Genetic Algorithms to replace weak rules (those not contributing or contributing incorrectly to the problem solution) with offspring of strong rules. Unlike the Back Propagation approach, which requires predefined layers of networks, the Classifier System approach does not require any predefined structure (although one can be provided if desired, in the form of an initial set of rules). Because of the nature of the rules, messages, and the match cycle, this approach is very well-adapted to massively parallel computers.

To date, work on all of these approaches has taken place primarily on conventional serial computers with simulators. Because the speed of these serial simulators depends directly on the size of the problems being solved, only small examples have been used to test these ideas. The massive parallelism and dynamic reconfigurability of the Connection Machine offers a chance to implement and evaluate the Connectionist Network and Classifier System approaches to learning on much larger (and more realistic) task domains. The speed of the parallel versions of these systems is nearly independent of the size of the problems being solved.

Parallelism on the Connection Machine

Most computer programs consist of a control sequence (the instructions) and a collection of data elements. Large programs have tens of thousands of instructions operating on tens of thousands, or even millions of data elements. There are opportunities for parallelism in both the control sequence and in the collection of data elements. In the control sequence, it is possible to identify threads of control that could operate independently, and thus on different processors. This approach is known as "**control parallelism**", and is the method used for programming most multiprocessor computers. The primary problems with this approach are the difficulty of identifying and synchronizing these independent threads of control. Alternatively, it is possible to take advantage of the large number of data elements that are independent, and assign processors to data elements. This approach is known as "**data parallelism**" [11, 33]. This approach works best for large amounts of data, and for many applications is a more natural programming approach. The Connection Machine system is a general purpose implementation of data parallelism.

The Connection Machine system is a dynamically reconfigurable computer with 65,536 processors and 32 Mbytes of memory, which can process large volumes of data at speeds exceeding one billion instructions per second (1000 MIPS). This computer is a departure from the conventional von Neumann model of computing, which has one processor with a large memory. In the Connection Machine, the processing power is distributed over the memory, so that there are many processors, each with a small amount of memory (4096 bits).

In addition to a large number of processors, a data parallel computer must have an effective means of communicating between processors. The Connection Machine system has a communications system that allows any processor to send a message to any other processor, with possibly all processors sending messages at the same time. This mechanism allows applications to dynamically reconfigure the communications topology to adapt it to the communications needs of the moment. For example, in the low level part of an image understanding system, a two dimensional grid is the most appropriate topology. At the intermediate level, such a system might want to communicate in a tree structured topology. And at the highest level, a semantic network for understanding might require an arbitrary network topology. Each of these communications topologies can be dynamically configured on the Connection Machine.

From a programming point of view, the Connection Machine system can be thought of as a parallel processing accelerator for a conventional serial computer. In fact, the Connection Machine system is made up of two parts: a front-end computer (like a Vax or a Symbolics 3600), and an array of Connection Machine processors and memory. The front-end computer can operate on the Connection Machine memory as though it were part of its own memory, or it can invoke parallel arithmetic, logical, or communications (data movement) operations on that memory. The program runs on the front-end computer, invoking parallel operations when necessary. Thus, all the program development tools of the front-end computer are available for developing Connection Machine programs.

Connection Machine programming languages are simple parallel extensions to familiar sequential languages. C* [27] is a parallel version of the C language [9], and *Lisp [21] is a parallel version of Common Lisp [32]. In each of these languages, the extensions were made in an unobtrusive manner. For example, in *Lisp, two parallel variables can be added together with +!! (the !! at the end of a operator name indicates the parallel version of that operator). The process of writing a data parallel program with a language like *Lisp is quite simple: write an algorithm as though it were operating on one data element, then use the parallel versions of the operators. In control parallelism, understanding how to do a parallel task decomposition is often an intellectually difficult task. In such a system, it is also often difficult to take an existing program and understand it. However, in data parallelism, the programming style is much closer to what programmers are used to, and it is thus much simpler to produce and understand data parallel programs.

*CFS: A Parallel Classifier System

The state of the art for Classifier Systems is represented by the CFS-C system [25], designed and implemented at the University of Michigan. This system is designed with parallelism in mind, but has been simulated on conventional serial machines, and thus has been restricted to small task domains. Serial implementations of CFS-C are relatively fast for small sets of classifiers; up to 20 cycles per second for 200 Classifiers on a one MIP (one million instructions per second) computer. However, because the match procedure (described below) requires every message to be matched against every classifier, serial implementations for large sets of classifiers are too slow to be useful.

*CFS is an implementation of CFS-C on the Connection Machine, written in *Lisp. Because of the parallel nature of *CFS on the Connection Machine, it will work with 65,000 classifiers about as fast as it works with 200 classifiers. The speed of the system does not depend on the number of classifiers and is relatively fast; up to 10 cycles per second for 65,000 Classifiers. Thus, *CFS on the Connection Machine provides a way to explore and evaluate Classifier Systems and Genetic Algorithms on large task domains.

*CFS: Overview of Operation

From the user's point of view, both CFS-C and *CFS provide the same basic structure; a message-passing rule-based system that uses Genetic Algorithms to evolve rules to solve some specified problem. Both systems are task domain independent. To define a task domain, you simply define three functions: a function to provide input messages that describe the state of the external environment on each cycle (these are called "Detector" messages); a function to analyze output messages to alter the external environment (called "Effectors"); and a function to evaluate the changes made to the environment, and supply a reward or punishment for those changes.

A "Message" is a fixed length bit string, with each bit position containing a zero, one, or "don't care" value. A "Classifier" is a rule with two conditions and an action. The conditions are message patterns which are matched with incoming messages. The action is a message pattern for production of an outgoing message.

On each cycle, the messages output from the previous cycle are combined with Detector messages describing the environment to provide the incoming message list. All Classifiers are matched with all the messages on the message list. The matching Classifiers can each post one or more new messages to the outgoing message list. The message list is limited to a small size to force the Classifiers to compete for the right to post new messages. There is a strength associated with each Classifier that is used to control this bidding process. The strength reflects how good a rule is; that is, a high strength Classifier is one that contributes to a correct solution, while a low strength Classifier is one that either does not contribute or contributes to an incorrect solution. Classifier strength is adjusted with several different mechanisms: (1) reward or punishment from the evaluator changes the strengths of all Classifiers the won the bidding competition and posted messages during that cycle; (2) Classifiers that win the bidding process pay their bid to the Classifiers in the previous cycle that produced the messages which the winning Classifiers matched (this is called the Bucket Brigade algorithm [13], and is necessary for chains of rules to form and survive); and (3) taxes are used to eliminate non-contributors and to help prevent over-general Classifiers from dominating the bidding process.

Genetic Algorithms are used periodically to replace some percentage of the population of Classifiers (generally, low strength Classifiers are replaced) with offspring from matings of other (generally, high strength) Classifiers. The two primary Genetic Algorithms used are Crossover Mating and Mutation. The Crossover algorithm considers the entire Classifier (both conditions and the action) as a chromosome, picks a random point for the crossover, and crosses two parents to produce two offspring (i.e., the high order bits up to the randomly picked point are swapped in the parents). The Mutation algorithm uses a Poisson distribution to decide whether to make zero, one, two, or three random modifications to a new offspring. The mutation rate is kept quite low, so that only a few offspring are mutated at all, and very few have more than one mutation.

142

*CFS: Parallel Data Structures and Algorithms

The inherent computational load of *CFS can be characterized as proportional to the product of the length of the message list and the number of Classifiers. Experience suggests that the message list should be restricted to a small size to promote strong competition in the Classifier population. It also appears that solving problems in large real-world task domains will require a large Classifier population. These two observations, along with the fact that the Classifiers are operated on almost entirely independently, suggest a natural data parallel approach for *CFS, which is the assignment of one processor to each Classifier.

The primary parallel data structures in *CFS are associated with Classifiers. In addition to the two conditions, action, and strength that have already been mentioned, there are about 30 other variables associated with each Classifier. Some of these variables maintain performance statistics, others are used to control various algorithms in the system. Values stored in parallel variables on the Connection Machine can be of any size needed. The parallel variables that represent a Classifier include several one bit booleans, signed integers ranging from 5 to 32 bits, and unsigned integers that are as long as the message size in the particular task domain (9 bits for the letter sequence prediction task). In the current implementation, about 850 bits are used for each Classifier, with performance statistics accounting for about half of that. That means that several Classifiers could be implemented on each physical processor on the Connection Machine (since each has 4096 bits of memory). In fact, the Connection Machine has a Virtual Processor mechanism that supports that. By selecting the right virtual processor configuration, a 65,536 processor Connection Machine can simulate a million processors, hence a million Classifiers.

The other primary data structure in *CFS is the message list, which is maintained on the front-end computer. Although all operations on Classifiers are done in parallel, the operations on messages in the message list must be done serially. However, the size of the message list is relatively small (less than 30 messages for most applications), and the number of operations that sequence through the message list is small (the match procedure, the creation of the new message list, and activation of Effectors).

To see how the parallel Classifiers and the serial message list interact, let us consider the match algorithm. Assume that each message is N bits long, and that there are at most M messages in the message list. The conditions in the Classifiers are represented as two N-bit unsigned fields, one for the bits (zeros and ones) and the other for the wildcards (the "don't care" bits). Let us allocate an M-bit "message winner" field for each condition, to represent which messages matched that condition (i.e., the m'th bit of that field will be one if the m'th message in the message list matched that condition). To match all the messages with all the Classifiers, we first sequence through the message list broadcasting each message to all Classifiers in parallel. This is the only serial part of the match, the rest of the operations are done in parallel. We compare the logical OR of the wildcard bits and the condition bits with the logical OR of the wildcard bits and the message bits. If they are the same, we set the m'th message winner bit. After sequencing through the message list, we find all Classifiers that matched by selecting all Classifiers that have non-zero message winner fields for both conditions. The whole match process takes about 3.5 milliseconds plus about 0.5 milliseconds for each message on the message list, regardless of the number of Classifiers (up to 65,536).

Parallel Genetic Algorithms In *CFS

As mentioned earlier, the critical component of Classifier Systems that drives their learning behavior is the Genetic Algorithms. In *CFS, there are currently two parallel Genetic Algorithms employed: Crossover Mating and Mutation. These algorithms are invoked periodically and replace some percentage of the population of Classifiers with offspring of matings of other Classifiers. In a typical experiment, the Genetic Algorithms might be invoked once every eleven cycles, with five percent of the population being replaced each time. The frequency of invocation of Genetic Algorithms is a prime number to avoid the effects of cyclic patterns in the test environment, which might cause strength patterns that alter the effectiveness of the Genetic Algorithms. The percent of the population being replaced is relatively low so that the Bucket Brigade and other strength adjustment algorithms have time to establish some stability.

The first step in these Genetic Algorithms is to pick a set of Classifiers to be replaced and a set of Classifiers to be parents. These two sets are the same size and a one-to-one mapping is established between them, in the form of two-way pointers between elements of each set. The parents are then copied onto the Classifiers being replaced. From that point on, the set of Classifiers being replaced is referred to as the set of offspring. Some percentage of the offspring are left as pure replications, while the rest are paired and mated with the crossover algorithm. Finally, there is a small probability that each new offspring will be changed slightly by the mutation algorithm. All of the algorithms described in this section operate at speeds that are independent of the number of Classifiers involved (up to 65,536).

Picking Parents and Classifiers to Replace

Relatively low strength Classifiers are picked to be replaced. The choice is made probabilistically, making random draws without replacement from the population with the probability of being picked proportional to the square of the inverse of the strength of the Classifier. This is done so that weak Classifiers have some small chance of not being replaced, and strong Classifiers have some small chance of being replaced. Likewise, relatively high strength Classifiers are picked as parents. This is also done probabilistically, with the probability proportional to the square of the strength.

A "Parallel Random Weighted Selection" algorithm supports the picking of parents and Classifiers to replace. Of the several approaches to implementation of this algorithm, the following has been the most successful. First, generate a random number between zero and the weight (e.g., the square of the strength) for each Classifier in parallel. Then, **Rank** those random numbers in parallel. The **Rank** operation is the first step in a parallel sort, and is done in log time on the Connection Machine using either Batcher's bitonic sort [3] or a radix sort [11]. After ranking the random numbers, the Classifier with the smallest random number will have rank 0, the Classifier with the largest random number will have rank N (the size of the population), and each rank will be unique. At this point, select the lowest five percent (or whatever percent is being replaced) of the ranked Classifiers as the Classifiers to replace, and the highest five percent of the ranked Classifiers as parents. This random weighted selection algorithm takes about 23 milliseconds on the Connection Machine.

Crossover Mating

At this point, we have identified two sets of Classifiers: a set of parents and a replacement set. Before proceeding, we need to replace the Classifiers picked for replacement with copies of their parents. The first step in this process is to make each offspring (one of the replacement set) point to a parent, and vice-versa. This is done using a "Parallel Rendezvous" algorithm, which takes three steps:

1. **Enumerate** the parent set, and **Send** the processor address of each parent to a rendezvous variable in the enumerated processors. Enumeration is another log time operation on the Connection Machine. The result of enumerating the parent set will be a unique numbering of the parents from zero to the number of parents. The **Send** from the parents to the enumerated processors will result in the rendezvous variable in processor zero containing the processor address of the first parent, in processor one the rendezvous variable will contain the processor address of the second parent, and so on. If there are N parents, then the rendezvous variable in the first N processors will contain the addresses of the parents.

2. **Enumerate** the replacement set, and have each offspring **Get** the address in the rendezvous variable from the enumerated processors. Since this enumeration will be the same as the replacement rank developed while picking the Classifiers to replace, we can use the replacement rank and skip this enumeration to save time. The **Get** will result in the first offspring obtaining the address of the first parent from the rendezvous variable in processor zero, the second offspring obtaining the address of the second parent, and so on. Now, each offspring has a pointer to its parent.

3. Offspring **Send** their processor addresses to their parents. Since offspring now have their parents' addresses, they can do this directly.

Given the pointers between parents and offspring, we now replace the offspring with copies of their parents. This is done by having parents **Send** relevant parts of themselves to their offspring using the offspring address pointers derived from the rendezvous step. Some parallel variables associated with the offspring are simply initialized, while others are copied from their parents. The strength of a new offspring is set to a value half way between its parent's strength and the average strength of the population. This allows the new offspring to participate in the bidding process quickly, without dominating the process.

The Crossover algorithm used in *CFS allows some percentage (a system parameter) of null crossovers, or pure replications. To decide which offspring will be replications, we generate a random number between 0 and 100 for each offspring. If that number is below the specified cutoff, we are done with the Crossover algorithm, since the parent has already been copied.

For the remaining offspring, we proceed with the Crossover algorithm by picking pairs to mate and

144

crossing those mates at random points. The next step is to pair the offspring (since these are now copies of parents, this is equivalent to pairing the parents). This is done by dividing the set of offspring in half (currently done by even replacement rank versus odd replacement rank), and using the rendezvous algorithm to get the even ranked offspring to point to the odd ranked offspring, and vice-versa. With this set of pointers, we can now complete the Crossover. Generate a random number between 0 and the length of the chromosome (i.e., three times the length of a message, since the chromosome contains both of the conditions and the action) for each even ranked offspring, to be used as the crossover point. Now the even ranked offspring **Get** the odd ranked offspring's chromosome (conditions and action). Now, using parallel load-byte and deposite-byte, swap the high order bits of the chromosomes up to the crossover point. Finally, store the crossed chromosomes back in the even ranked offspring and **Send** the crossed chromosomes to the odd ranked offspring.

Mutation

The Mutation algorithm uses a Poisson distribution to mutate zero, one, two, or three genes in the chromosome (bits in the conditions and action) of the new offspring. The Poisson distribution is implemented in parallel using a table (see [34]). A random number between 0 and 1000 is generated for each offspring. A match to the Poisson table indicates how many mutations to make (normally, very few mutations are done). For each mutation, a random bit position is picked, and a random new value (one, zero, or don't care) is set in that position.

Summary: Parallel Genetic Algirithms

To summarize, the parallel Genetic Algorithms used in *CFS are all independent of Classifier population size (up to 65,536). The total time for the Genetic Algorithms is around 400 milliseconds (or an average of 36 milliseconds per cycle in the experiment described above, since they were run once every 11 cycles). Very little optimization has been done on this part of the system, so the figure can probably be reduced by a factor of two or three. All these algorithms make heavy use of the communications mechanisms in the Connection Machine, both explicitly (with uses of **Send** and **Get** in parent copying and crossover) and implicitly (with uses of **Enumerate** and **Rank**). Two crucial algorithms that support the Genetic Algorithms are parallel random weighted selection (for picking parents and offspring) and par-

allel rendezvous (to establish pointers between parents and offspring and between pairs of mates in crossover).

Summary

The implementation of a parallel version of Genetic Algorithms in a Classifier System on a fine-grained massively parallel computer, the Connection Machine, provides verification that these inherently parallel algorithms can, in fact, be fully parallelized on a computer. This is best demonstrated by the speed of the system, which is independent of the number of Classifiers; and for parts of *CFS other than its Genetic Algorithms depends only on the size of the message list and is linear.

This work also provides a demonstration of the power and importance of data parallelism as a programming style. It took less than one man-month to develop the first working version of the basic *CFS system, starting only with a description of CFS-C (the documentation in [25, 26]). This also provides confirmation that the Connection Machine system is well-adapted to data parallelism and is easy to program.

Finally, parallel implementations of Classifier Systems and Genetic Algorithms, like *CFS, provide a vehicle for exploring large task domains. Ultimately, a Classifier System with a large population should be able to evolve a set of rules for any repetitive structured task for which an evaluation function can be defined. An example of a difficult task that is unlikely to ever work with a small population of Classifiers, but might work with a large population, is the game of Go. The best current Go playing program, by Wilcox [35], is only slightly better than a novice. Can we express the knowledge embedded in Wilcox's program in a set of rules and an evaluation function, and use that as the starting point for evolving rules for a really good Go player? Parallel implementations of Classifier Systems and Genetic Algorithms allow us to begin investigating such questions.

References

1. Ackley, D.H., Hinton, G.E., and Sejnowski, T.J., A Learning Algorithm for Boltzmann Machines, Cognitive Science, vol. 9, no. 1, 147-169, 1985.

2. Barto, A., Learning by Statistical Cooperation of Self-Interested Neuron-like Computing Elements, COIN Technical Report 85-11, University of Massachusetts, April 1985.

3. Batcher, K.E., Sorting Networks and their Appli-

cations. In Proc. 1968 Spring Joint Computer Conference, AFIPS, pp. 307-314, April, 1968.

4. Feldman, J.A., Dynamic Connections in Neural Networks, Fiological Cybernetics 46, 27-39, 1982.

5. Forgy, C.L., OPS5 Manual, Carnegie-Mellon University Computer Science Department Technical Report, 1981.

6. Forrest, S., Implementing Semantic Network Structures Using Classifier Systems, in J.J. Grefenstette (Ed.), Proceedings of an International Conference on Genetic Algorithms and their Applications, Carnegie-Mellon Univ., Pittsburgh, Pa., July, 1985.

7. Grossberg, S., Competition, Decision, Consensus, Journal of Mathematical Analysis and Applications, 66, 470-93, 1978.

8. Gupta, A., Parallelism in Production Systems: The Sources and the Expected Speedup, Carnegie-Mellon University Computer Science Department Technical Report CMU-CS-84-169, December 1984.

9. Harbison, S.P., and Steele, G.L., C: A Reference Manual, Prentice-Hall, New Jersey, 1984.

10. Hillis, W.D., The Connection Machine, MIT Press, 1985.

11. Hillis, W.D. and Steele, G.L., Data Parallel Algorithms, CACM, vol. 29, No. 12, pp. 1170-1183, December, 1986.

12. Hinton, G.E., Implementing Semantic Networks in Parallel Hardware, in G. Hinton and J. Anderson (Eds.), Parallel Models of Associative Memory, Hillsdale, NJ, Erlbaum, 161-187, 1981.

13. Holland, J.H., Properties of the Bucket Brigade Algorithm, in J.J. Grefenstette (Ed.), Proceedings of an International Conference on Genetic Algorithms and their Applications, Carnegie-Mellon Univ., Pittsburgh, Pa., July, 1985.

14. Holland, J.H., Escaping Brittleness: The Possibilities of General-Purpose Learning Algorithms Applied to Parallel Rule-Based Systems, in R.S. Michalski, J.G. Carbonell, and T.M. Mitchell (Eds.), Machine Learning: An Artificial Intelligence Approach, vol. II, Los Altos, California, Morgan Kaufmann Publishers, 1986.

15. Holland, J.H., Adaptation in Natural and Artificial Systems, Univ. of Michigan Press, Ann Arbor, 1975.

16. Holland, J.H., Holyoak, K.J., Nisbett, R.E., and Thagard, P.R., Induction: Processes of Inference, Learning, and Discovery, MIT Press, 1986.

17. Klopf, A.H., The Hedonistic Neuron, Washington, DC: Hemisphere, 1982.

18. Laird, J., SOAR User's Manual, Xerox PARC Internal Document, June 1985.

19. Laird, J., Rosenbloom, P., and Newell, A., Towards Chunking as a General Learning Mechinism, in Two SOAR Studies, Carnegie-Mellon University Computer Science Department Technical Report CMU-CS-85-110, January 1985.

20. Laird, J.E., Rosenbloom, P.S., and Newell, A., Chunking in Soar: The Anatomy of a General Learning Mechanism, Machine Learning, Vol. 1, No. 1, 1986.

21. Lasser, C., The Essential *Lisp Manual, Thinking Machines Technical Report, July, 1986.

22. Michalski, R., Carbonell, J., and Mitchell, T., Machine Learning, vol. II, Morgan Kauffman, 1986.

23. Minsky, M., The Society of Mind, New York, Simon and Schuster, 1986.

24. Minsky, M. and Papert, S., Perceptrons: An Introduction to Computation Geometry, MIT Press, 1969.

25. Riolo, R.L., CFS-C: A Package of Domain Independent Subroutines for Implementing Classifier Systems in Arbitrary, User-Defined Environments, Univ. of Michigan, Div. of Computer Science and Engineering, Logic of Computers Group Technical Report, January, 1986.

26. Riolo, R.L., LETSEQ: An Implementation of the CFS-C Classifier System in a Task-Domain that Involves Learning to Predict Letter Sequences, Univ. of Michigan, Div. of Computer Science and Engineering, Logic of Computers Group Technical Report, January, 1986.

27. Rose, J. and Steele, G., C* Language Quick Reference, Thinking Machines Technical Report, December, 1986.

28. Rosenblatt, F., Principles of Neurodynamics, Spartan Books, New York, 1962.

29. Rumelhart, D.E., Hinton, G.E., and Williams, R.J., Learning Internal Representations by Error Propagation, ICS Report 8506, UC San Diego, September 1985.

30. Sejnowski, T.J., NETtalk: A Parallel Network that Learns to Read Aloud, Johns Hopkins Univ. Electrical Engineering and Computer Science Technical Report JHU/EECS-86/01, January, 1986.

31. Sejnowski, T.J., Keinker, P.K., and Hinton, G.E., Symmetry Groups with Hidden Units: Beyond the Perceptron, Physica D (in press).

32. Steele, G.L., Common Lisp: The Language, Digital Press, Massachusetts, 1984.

33. Thinking Machines Corporation, Introduction to Data Level Parallelism, Thinking Machines Technical Report, April, 1986.

34. Wagner, H.M., Principles of Operations Research, Prentice-Hall, New Jersey, 1969.

35. Wilcox, B., Reflections on Building Two Go Programs, SIGART Newsletter, October 1985.

36. Wilson, S.W., Classifier System Learning of a Boolean Function, Rowland Institute for Science Research Memo RIS No. 27r, February, 1986.

37. Wilson, S.W., Knowledge Growth in an Artificial Animal, in J.J. Grefenstette (Ed.), Proceedings of an International Conference on Genetic Algorithms and their Applications, Carnegie-Mellon Univ., Pittsburgh, Pa., July, 1985.

PUNCTUATED EQUILIBRIA: A PARALLEL GENETIC ALGORITHM

by

J. P. Cohoon, S. U. Hegde, W. N. Martin, D. Richards

Department of Computer Science
University of Virginia
Charlottesville, Virginia 22903

ABSTRACT

A distributed formulation of the genetic algorithm paradigm is proposed and experimentally analyzed. Our formulation is based in part on two principles of the paleontological theory of punctuated equilibria—allopatric speciation and stasis. Allopatric speciation involves the rapid evolution of new species after being geographically separated. Stasis implies that after equilibria is reached in an environment there is little drift in genetic composition. We applied the formulation to the Optimal Linear Arrangement problem. In our experiments, the result was more than just a hardware acceleration, rather better solutions were obtained with less total work.

INTRODUCTION

The genetic algorithm paradigm has been previously proposed to generate solutions to a wide range of problems [HOLL75]. In particular, several optimization problems have been investigated. These include control systems [GOLD83], function optimization [BETH81], and combinatorial problems [COHO86, DAVI85, FOUR85, GOLD85, GREF85, SMIT85]. In all cases, serial implementations have been proposed. We will argue that there is an effective parallel realization of the genetic algorithms approach based on what evolution theorists call "punctuated equilibria." We propose a parallel implementation and present empirical evidence of its effectiveness on a combinatorial optimization problem.

While the genetic algorithm (GA) approach is easily understood, it would be difficult to glean a canonical "pseudo-code" version from published accounts. Various implementations differ and many "obvious" design decisions are omitted. In all cases, a population of solutions to the problem at hand is maintained and successive "generations" are produced by manipulating the previous generation. The population is typically kept at a fixed size. Most new solutions are formed by merging two previous ones; this is done with a "crossover" operator and suitable encodings of the solutions. Some new solutions are simply modifications of previous ones, using a "mutation" operator. Successive generations are produced with new solutions replacing some of the older ones. An ad hoc termination condition is used and the best remaining solution (or the best ever seen) is reported.

A solution is evaluated with respect to its "fitness," and of course we prefer that the most fit survive. There are two mechanisms for differential success. First, the better fit solutions are more likely to crossover, and hence propagate. Second, the less fit solutions are more likely to be replaced. It is important to realize that the GA approach is fundamentally different from, say, simulated annealing [KIRK83] which follows the "trajectory" of a single solution to a local maximum of the fitness function. With GA there are many solutions to consider and the crossover operation is so chaotic that there is no simple notion of trajectory.

How can parallelism be used with the GA approach? Initially it seems clear that the process is inherently sequential. Each generation must be produced before it can be used as the basis for the following generation; it is antithetical to the evolutionary scheme to jump forward. A simple use of parallelism is the simultaneous production of candidates for the next generation. For example, pairs of solutions could be crossed-over in parallel, along with the selection and mutation of other solutions. But algorithmic issues remain to be resolved. How are the "parents" probabilistically selected? How are the solutions that are to be replaced chosen? The simple answers to these questions, which require global information, suggest the use of shared-memory architectures. Note that this sort of parallelism does not make any fundamental contribution to the GA approach; it can be viewed simply as a "hardware accelerator".

We restrict our interest to the study of parallel algorithms for a distributed processor system without shared memory. Our reasons are threefold. First, we have access to such a system. Second, the extension of our results to massively parallel machines will be quite natural. In such a machine, the cost of connecting and distributing data is an important component in the analysis of the algorithms. We assume that the interconnection network is sparse, and hence communication between distant processors is expensive. Third, as implied above, we are interested in developing more than just a hardware accelerator. Rather we desire a distributed formulation that gives better solutions with less total work.

We feel the most natural way to distribute a genetic algorithm over the processors is to partition the population of solutions and assign one subset of the population to the local memory of each processor. Consider a straightforward implementation of the GA approach. In order to probabilistically select parents for the crossover operation, global information about the (relative) fitnesses must be used. This implies an often performed phase of data collection, processing, and broadcasting. Further, extensive data movement is required to crossover two randomly selected solutions that are on distant processors.

Considerations such as the above led us to question the wisdom of using the GA approach as it is typically presented. There are many ad hoc methods for bypassing these difficulties. For example, continuing the above examples, knowledge of the global fitness distribution can be approximated. Further, steps can be taken to artificially reduce the diameter of related computations. Instead we found a simple model that naturally maps GA onto a distributed computer system. It is drawn from the theory of punctuated equilibria, discussed in the next section.

We chose to do our initial study using the Optimal Linear Arrangement problem (OLA). It is an NP-complete combinatorial optimization problem [GARE79]. We selected it due to the practical interest in such placement problems, as well as its simple presentation. There are m objects and m positions, where the positions are arranged linearly and are separated by unit distances. For each pair of objects i and j there is a cost c_{ij}. We need to find an mapping p, where object i is assigned to position $p(i)$, that minimizes the objective function

$$\sum_{i < j} c_{ij} |p(i) - p(j)|. \qquad (1)$$

We note that OLA is related to the ubiquitous traveling salesman problem; they are both instances of the quadratic assignment problem.

PUNCTUATED EQUILIBRIA

N. Eldredge and S. J. Gould [ELDR72] presented the theory of *punctuated equilibria* (PE) to resolve certain paleontological dilemmas in the geological record. While the extent to which PE is needed to explain the data is hotly debated [ELDR85], we have found it to be an important model for understanding distributed evolutionary processes. PE is based on two principles: allopatric speciation and stasis.

Allopatric speciation involves the rapid evolution of new species after being geographically separated. The scenario involves a small subpopulation of a species, "peripheral isolates," becoming segregated into a new environment. By using latent genetic material or new mutations this subpopulation may survive and flourish in its environment. A single species may give rise to many peripheral isolates.

Stasis, or stability, of a species is simply the notion of lack of change. (This directly challenges phyletic gradualism.) It implies that after equilibria is reached in an environment there is very little drift away from the genetic composition of a species. The motivation is that "sympatric" speciation (differentiation in the same environment) is difficult since small changes can not compete with the "gene flow" of the current species. Ideally a species would persist until its environment changed (or it would drift very little).

It is instructive to define "species" in a way that relates to the concept of a solution in the GA approach. We adapt an old idea of S. Wright [WRIG32] that introduces the concept of the "adaptive landscape," which is analogous to the fitness "surface" over the space of solutions. Consider a peak of the landscape that has been discovered and populated by a subset of the gene pool. That subset (perhaps with nearby subsets) corresponds to a species. There can be many "species" in a given environment, some so distant that their mutual offspring are not adapted to the environment. The difficult question is how can a species, as a whole, leave its "niche" to migrate to an even higher peak. The concept of stasis emphasizes the problem.

PE stresses that a powerful method for generating new species is to thrust an old species into a new environment, that is, a new adaptive landscape, where change is beneficial and rewarded. For this reason we should expect a GA approach based on PE should perform better than the typical single environment scheme.

What are the implications for the GA approach? If the "environment" is unchanging then equilibrium should be rapidly attained. The resulting equivalence classes of similar solutions would correspond to species. It is possible that the highest peaks have been unexplored. Typically, when GA is used the mutation and crossover operations are relied on to eventually find the other peaks. PE indicates that a more diverse exploration of the adaptive landscape could be achieved by allopatric speciation of peripheral isolates. Therefore, subpopulations must be segregated into environments that are somehow different.

Two different schemes for changing the environment are suggested. Suppose fitness is a multi-objective function. Various low-order approximations to the true fitness could be tried at different times and places. We will not explore this further here. The second scheme simply changes the environment by throwing together previously geographically separated species. We feel that the combination of new competitors and a new gene pool would cause the desired allopatric speciation. Further, we will define fitness so that it is relative to the current local population. So a new combination of competitors will alter the fitness measure. This scheme is used in the work presented here.

GENETIC ALGORITHMS WITH PUNCTUATED EQUILIBRIA

Our basic model of parallel genetic algorithms assigns a set of n solutions to each of N processors, for a total population of size $n{\times}N$. The set assigned to each processor is its *subpopulation*. (It is a simple extension to the model to allow different and time-varying population sizes. Other extensions are discussed in Section 6.) The processors are connected by a sparse interconnection network. In practice we might expect a conventional topology to be used, such as a mesh or a hypercube, but at present the choice of topology is not considered to be important. The network should have high connectivity and small diameter to ensure adequate "mixing" as time progresses.

The overall structure of our approach is seen in Figure 1. There are E major iterations called *epochs*. During an epoch each processor, disjointly and in parallel, executes the genetic algorithm on its subpopulation. Theoretically each processor continues until it reaches equilibrium. Since we know of no adequate stopping criteria we have used a fixed number, G, of generations per epoch. This considerably simplifies the problem of "synchronizing" the processors, since each processor should be completed at nearly the same time. After each processor has stopped there is a phase during which each processor copies randomly selected subsets of its population to neighboring processors. Each processor now has acquired a surplus of solutions and must probabilistically select a set of n solutions to survive to be its initial subpopulation at the beginning of the next epoch. (The selection process is the same as the adjustment procedure used by GA proper.)

The relationship to PE should be clear. Each processor corresponds to a disjoint "environment" (as characterized by the mix of solutions residing in it). After G generations we expect to see the emergence of some very fit species. (It is not necessary or even desirable to choose G so large that only one "species" survives. Diversity must be maintained.) Then a "catastrophe" occurs and the environments change. This is simulated by having representatives of geographically adjacent environments regroup to form the new environments. By varying the amount of redistribution, that is, $S = |S_{ij}|$, we can control the amount of disruption.

There can be two types of probabilistic selection used here. The fitness of each element of a population is used for selection, where the probability of selecting an element is proportional to its fitness. When there is repeated selection from the same population it can be done either with replacement or without replacement. The decision should be based on both analogies with the natural genetic model and goals for efficiently driving the optimization process. The selection of each final (end of epoch) subpopulation is done

without replacement; the good solutions will only "propagate" at the beginning of the next epoch. (The selection of each S_{ij} is not done probabilistically. A "random", i.e. using a uniform distribution, selection is used to simulate the randomness of environment shifts.)

We present our interpretation/implementation of the GA code each processor uses in Figure 2. The *crossover rate*, $0 \le C \le 1$, determines how many new offspring are produced during each generation. "Parents" are chosen probabilistically with replacement. The crossover itself, and other details, are discussed below. Our crossover produces one offspring from two parents. The fitnesses are recalculated, relative to the new larger population. Then, probabilistically without replacement, the next population is selected. Finally, (uniform) random elements are mutated. The *mutation rate*, $0 \le M \le 1$, determines how many mutations altogether are performed.

IMPLEMENTATION DETAILS

The problem we studied, OLA, is a placement problem. Hence a solution must encode a mapping p from objects to positions. Since we may assume both objects and positions are numbered $1, 2, ..., m$, the mapping p is just a permutation. In fact, throughout we use the inverse mapping, from positions to objects, as the basis for our encodings. There are many ways to encode permutations but it is not at all clear which, if any, are suitable for the GA approach. Note that it is desirable to preserve adjacencies within groups of objects during crossover.

Several representations and crossovers have been proposed for related problems, e.g. the traveling salesman problem. Inversion vectors ("ordinal representations") are the most obvious choice since they allow "typical" crossovers (as in [HOLL75]). However the use of such crossovers with inversion vectors is quite undesirable [GREF85] since it breaks up groups of adjacent objects. Goldberg and Lingle [GOLD85] gave a "partially mapped crossover" that uses a straightforward array representation of the (inverse) mapping, where the ith entry is j if the jth object is in the ith position. Briefly, their crossover copied a contiguous portion of one parent into the offspring, while

---

```
initialize
for E iterations do
        parfor each processor i do
                run GA for G generations
        endfor
        parfor each processor i do
                for each neighbor j of i do
                        send a set of solutions,
                            S_ij, from i to j
                endfor
        endfor
        parfor each processor i do
                select an n element subpopulation
        endfor
endfor
```

Figure 1 — The parallel genetic algorithm with punctuated equilibria.

```
for G iterations do
        for n×C iterations do
                select two solutions
                crossover those solutions
                add offspring to subpopulation
        endfor
        calculate fitnesses
        select a population of n elements
        generate n×M random mutations
endfor
```

Figure 2 — The genetic algorithm used within an epoch at each processor.

---

having the other parent copy over as many other positions as possible. Smith [SMIT85] proposed a "modified crossover" for the array representation. A random division point is selected and the first "half" of one parent is copied to the offspring. The remainder of the offspring's array is filled with unused objects, while preserving their relative order within the other parent. For example, parents [7 1 3 5 6 2 4] and [3 4 2 7 1 5 6] with the division point after the third position produce the offspring [7 1 3 4 2 5 6]. We essentially used this representation and crossover but allowed the first or the second "half" of the first parent to be used. By arguments analogous to those of Goldberg and Lingle [GOLD85], we can argue that our approach has the desirable "schema-preserving" property that the GA approach exploits. However it is an open problem to give a theoretically compelling proof of that property. In any event, it is clear that our scheme tends to preserve blocks of adjacent objects.

The mutate operator was selected next. We felt that the mutations should not be too disruptive; if most adjacencies were broken then with near certainty the mutation would be immediately lost. We chose to use "inversion," the reversal of a contiguous block within the array representation. The beginning of the block was randomly selected. The length of the block was randomly chosen from an exponential distribution with mean μ. We typically kept μ small to inhibit disruption. The nature of the OLA problem encourages inversion as opposed to pairwise interchanges, which do not involve block moves.

How should fitness be calculated? With any minimization problem, such as OLA, the scores of the solutions should decrease over time. The *score* is the value of the objective function. Two simple fitness functions suggest themselves. First, the fitness could be inversely related to the score; this could cause excessive compression of the range of fitnesses. Second, the fitness could be a constant minus the score. The constant must be large enough to ensure all fitnesses are positive (since they are used in the selection process) and not too large (effectively causing compression). If such a constant was optimal initially, it would become a poor choice near equilibria. For these reasons we used a time-varying "normalized" fitness.

We chose our fitness to be a function of all the scores in the current population. We have empirically found that randomly generated solutions to the OLA problem have scores that are "normally distributed" (i.e., have a bell-shaped curve), with virtually every solution within 1 standard deviation (s.d.) of the mean, and no solutions were found more than 3 s.d.'s away. For related evidence see [COHO87, WHIT84]. Therefore we used

$$fitness(x) = \frac{(\mu_s - score(x)) + \alpha\sigma}{2\alpha\sigma} \quad (2)$$

where μ_s is the mean of the scores, σ is the s.d., and α is a small constant parameter. Note that in practice we expect $0 < fitness(x) < 1$; we use clipping to ensure it is positive. Near equilibrium the scores will not be normally distributed because the contributions from most mutations and many crossovers will almost certainly be below the mean, biasing the distribution.

Our fitness measure has several advantages. It is somewhat problem independent, so that we can reasonably compare very different instances. It also tends to control the effect of a few "outliers" on the population. A disadvantage is that it is expensive to calculate and it needs to be recomputed at regular intervals. An approximation scheme can be used where new fitnesses are calculated according to the current mean and variance. The other elements would not have their fitnesses recalculated, unless they were otherwise encountered, but the pseudo-normalization renders them comparable.

EMPIRICAL RESULTS

We performed several experiments to determine if our parallel genetic algorithm is an effective approach. The efficacy of any GA approach is determined by the design variables. Our initial experiments, reported here, have been made with the Optimal Linear Arrangement (OLA) problem as the base case. This permutation problem has a raw score (Eq. 1) that the system is to minimize for a given cost matrix. The system uses a fitness measure (Eq. 2) in selecting the elements for crossover and in determining the survivors for each generation. Remember that for both of those selection processes within a subpopulation the fitness is judged relative to that subpopulation, and that the fitness is used in a probabilistic manner.

Our current implementation is a sequential simulation of the parallel genetic algorithm with punctuated equilibria. It operates with an arbitrary configuration of the N subpopulations. Presently we are investigating "mesh" and "hyper-cube" connection topologies. Although other configurations will be analyzed, the hyper-cube topology is of particular importance to us. We plan to obtain "real" performance measures on the hyper-cube multiprocessor at the University of Virginia. In most of the initial studies described below, a mesh configuration is used with $N = 4$, i.e., each subpopulation being able to "communicate" during the inter-epoch transition with two other subpopulations.

For each experiment the number of epochs, E, is given along with the number of generations per epoch, G, and the end-of-generation subpopulation size, n. Thus, over the course of a single example the parallel system will create $N \times E \times G$ generations. If we set N and E to one, then we have a "standard" sequential GA creating G generations. While the sequential GA has a single evolutionary time line, the parallel algorithm has multiple, interrelated evolutionary time lines. The "interrelated" qualification is quite important because the parallel system does more than just create N divergent time lines. As with the sequential GA, one cannot say, a priori, how many *distinct* individuals, i.e., possible problem solutions, a particular example run of our system will examine. For our purpose here, we will use $N \times E \times G \times n$ to be an indicator of the total number of solutions created during the experiment. The remaining design variables of importance are C, the crossover rate, M, the mutation rate, S, the size of the redistribution set, α, the fitness scale factor, and μ, the mean length of the mutation block.

Results For Three Problem Instances												
I	C	M	S	μ	n	α	N	E	G	$\hat{s}$	$\bar{s}$	s^*
							4	2	50	9600	9600	
1	0.50	0.05	15	3	80	3.00	1	1	400	9600	9600	9600
							4	1	100	9600	9600	
							4	6	50	19200	19200	
2	0.50	0.05	15	3	80	3.00	1	1	1200	19200	19200	19200
							4	1	300	19200	21757	
							4	6	50	15510	15551	
3	0.50	0.05	15	3	80	3.00	1	1	1200	15540	15622	15450
							4	1	300	15540	15596	

Table 1

The Effects Of Changing The Design Variables											
C	M	S	μ	n	α	N	E	G	$\hat{s}$	$\bar{s}$	s^*
0.50	0.05	15	3	80	3.00	4	6	50	15225	15318	
0.80									15240	15315	
	0.20								15270	15311	
		40							15240	15343	
			12						15270	15360	
				50					15225	15371	15210
					1.50				15210	15258	
					0.50				15210	15225	
							12	25	15210	15266	

Table 2

Tables 1 and 2 present the results and the settings used to derive those results. In those tables the quantity, s^*, is the theoretical optimal OLA score (as opposed to the fitness measure); $\bar{s}$ is the average of the best OLA score from each example with the specified settings; and $\hat{s}$ is the score of the single best solution created during the example. In the current simulations a single random number process is used, allowing multiple examples to be generated for the same design variable setting by changing a single "seed." In the discussion below the term "average" will indicate that several examples with the same settings and inputs, but with different seeds, have been run and the resulting measures averaged. In all cases reported here, the average is taken over a minimum of four runs.

Table 1 is broken into three instances, with three rows for each instance. The first row shows the results from running the parallel genetic algorithm with punctuated equilibria, i.e., independent subpopulations *with* communication. For these results a four node mesh configuration was used. The second row shows the results from a sequential genetic algorithm. That algorithm was derived by setting N and E to one, i.e., one population creating G generations. For a comparable uniprocessors, this algorithm would require about four (N) times the amount of "wall clock" time as the parallel genetic algorithm with punctuated equilibria. The third row shows the results from a simple parallel genetic algorithm that just used four (N) independent populations *without* communication. Here each example run was derived by setting N to four and E to one, and then, at the end of the parallel operation, selecting the best overall from the best of the four populations.

For each instance, we kept $N \times E \times G \times n$ constant over all three rows. This product is indicative of the total number of OLA solutions examined by the system. By keeping the product constant we assume that approximately the same amount of total computation is required.

For these initial studies we have considered "artificial" OLA examples, which allow easy determination of the optimal score. While the examples are contrived, they exhibit natural clustering patterns. In all cases, the costs were chosen so that the identity permutation produced the optimal score; the only other optimal permutations were simple perturbations of the identity mapping. (Of course this does not make the problem any easier.) We used three types of problems, i.e., cost matrices, in our experiments.

The first type of problem instance, with unique optima, has a cost matrix of the following form:

$$
C_1(9) = \begin{bmatrix}
0 & A & B & C & D & 0 & 0 & 0 & 0 \\
A & 0 & A & B & C & D & 0 & 0 & 0 \\
B & A & 0 & A & B & C & D & 0 & 0 \\
C & B & A & 0 & A & B & C & D & 0 \\
D & C & B & A & 0 & A & B & C & D \\
0 & D & C & B & A & 0 & A & B & C \\
0 & 0 & D & C & B & A & 0 & A & B \\
0 & 0 & 0 & D & C & B & A & 0 & A \\
0 & 0 & 0 & 0 & D & C & B & A & 0
\end{bmatrix}.
$$

where $m = 9$ and $A \gg B \gg C \gg D \geq 0$. We believe the solution spaces for such problems instances to be "convex" in some sense, and therefore "easy." Instance one ($I = 1$) of Table 1 used $C_1(9)$, with $A = 1000$, $B = 100$, $C = 10$, and $D = 1$. Note that, for this instance, the parallel genetic algorithm with punctuated equilibria found the optimum solution in each example, as indicated by $\bar{s} = s^*$.

The second problem type was slightly more complex. We increased m to 18 and created a cost matrix by embedding two independent 9-element orderings as given by the following cost matrix:

$$
C_2(18) = \begin{bmatrix}
C_1(9) & 0 \\
0 & C_1(9)
\end{bmatrix}.
$$

Note that two groups of 9 are uncoupled and that this is tantamount to solving two disjoint problems. A, B, C, and D in $C_2(18)$ were as above. The settings and results for this cost matrix are shown as instance two ($I = 2$) in Table 1.

The third type of problem incorporated further complexity by embedding interrelated blocks of three elements each. For nine elements the resulting cost matrix would be

$$
C_3(9) = \begin{bmatrix}
0 & A & A & C & C & C & C & C & C \\
A & 0 & A & C & C & C & C & C & C \\
A & A & 0 & B & C & C & C & C & C \\
C & C & B & 0 & A & A & C & C & C \\
C & C & C & A & 0 & A & C & C & C \\
C & C & C & A & A & 0 & B & C & C \\
C & C & C & C & C & B & 0 & A & A \\
C & C & C & C & C & C & A & 0 & A \\
C & C & C & C & C & C & A & A & 0
\end{bmatrix}.
$$

We assume $A > B > C$. The intra-block cost, A, causes primary clustering, and the inter-block cost for adjacent blocks, B, forces an ordering of the blocks. The other costs, the C's, tend to "flatten" the search space by making all permutations have similar scores. This cost matrix pattern was extended to $C_3(18)$, i.e., eighteen objects comprised of six blocks, and we let $A = 50$, $B = 30$, and $C = 15$. The results are shown as instance three ($I = 3$) in Table 1.

The results shown in Table 2 are presented to indicate the effects of changing individual design variables. The problem instance used $C_3(18)$ with $A = 40$, $B = 30$, and

$C = 15$. Note the slight reduction in A was intended to make the optimum solution more elusive. The settings for the base case are shown in the first row. In the remaining rows we show the altered value of a particular variable and the obtained results. Again, the averages were taken over four example runs. In terms of $\bar{s}$, the most dramatic changes were due to reducing α, and due to increasing E. The effect of decreasing α is to make the fitness measure more sensitive to smaller differences between solutions that are near the current best for the subpopulation. In this way incremental improvements are given more of an opportunity to survive and create further improvements.

The increase in E effectively provides more communication opportunities between the subpopulations. The last row of Table 2 and instance three from Table 1 provide the strongest experimental results to date for the effectiveness of the parallel genetic algorithm with punctuated equilibria. These promising effects prompted an experiment combining the modifications in the last two rows of Table 2. We obtained the optimal solution in 5 out of 6 runs.

CONCLUSIONS AND EXTENSIONS

In attempting to develop parallel algorithms one always wants to obtain the simple speed-up of having more processors to do more instructions in the same "wall clock" time. However, there is evidence that in attempting to develop parallel versions of previously known algorithms one often derives a modified formulation which comprises more fundamental efficiencies. We believe this to be the case for our parallel genetic algorithm with punctuated equilibria. The partition into subpopulations specifies a simple and balanced mapping of the workload to a non-shared memory, multiprocessor system, while the intra-epoch isolation and inter-epoch communication provide a fundamental modification to the basic genetic algorithm that will generate better solutions while considering a smaller total number of individuals.

Several extensions to the model have been considered and are being attempted. For example, the use of fixed-size subpopulations is not suggested by the natural evolutionary setting. When a processor receives a surplus of very fit solutions it makes sense to retain most of them. However it is clear there should be some mechanism for limiting the size of each subpopulation as well as the total size. Varying-sized groups will create data management and coordination problems, and it is not clear they are worth the additional computational load.

Our model is essentially synchronous, though it is easily realized asynchronously with handshaking. A truly asynchronous model would allow each processor to decide for itself whether it has reached equilibrium and should begin another epoch. At that point it could poll its neighbors, asking for subsets of their current subpopulations to be sent to it. Global termination, while somewhat arbitrary before, becomes even more difficult.

ACKNOWLEDGEMENTS

The authors' work has been supported in part by the Jet Propulsion Laboratory of the California Institute of Technology under Contract 957721 to the University of Virginia. The work of James Cohoon has been supported additionally in part by the National Science Foundation through grant DMC 8505354. Their support is greatly appreciated.

REFERENCES

[BETH81] A. Bethke, *Genetic Algorithms as Function Optimizers, Ph.D. Thesis*, Department of Computer and Communication Sciences, University of Michigan, 1981.

[COHO86] J. P. Cohoon and W. D. Paris, Genetic Placement, *IEEE International Conference on Computer-Aided Design*, Santa Clara, CA, 1986, 422-425.

[COHO87] J. P. Cohoon and M. T. Roberson, *Jump Starting Simulated Annealing*, Department of Computer Science, University of Virginia, 1987.

[DAVI85] L. Davis, Job Shop Scheduling with Genetic Algorithms, *Proceedings of an International Conference on Genetic Algorithms and Their Applications*, Pittsburgh, PA, 1985, 136-140.

[ELDR72] N. Eldredge and S. J. Gould, Punctuated Equilibria: An Alternative to Phyletic Gradualism, in *Models of Paleobiology*, T. J. M. Schopf (ed.), Freeman, Cooper and Co., 1972, 82-115.

[ELDR85] N. Eldredge, *Time Frames*, Simon and Schuster, 1985.

[FOUR85] M. P. Fourman, Compaction of Symbolic Layout Using Genetic Algorithms, *Proceedings of an International Conference on Genetic Algorithms and Their Applications*, Pittsburgh, PA, 1985, 141-150.

[GARE79] M. R. Garey and D. S. Johnson, *Computers And Intractability - A Guide To The Theory Of NP-Completeness*, W. H. Freeman and Co., San Francisco, CA, 1979.

[GOLD83] D. E. Goldberg, *Computer-Aided Gas Pipeline Operation Using Genetic Algorithms and Learning Rules, Ph.D. Thesis*, Department of Civil Engineering, University of Michigan, 1983.

[GOLD85] D. E. Goldberg and R. Lingle, Jr., Alleles, Loci, and the Traveling Salesperson Problem, *Proceedings of an International Conference on Genetic Algorithms and Their Applications*, Pittsburgh, PA, 1985, 154-159.

[GREF85] J. J. Grefenstette, R. Gopal, B. J. Rosmaita and D. Van Gucht, Genetic Algorithms for the Traveling Salesperson Problem, *Proceedings of an International Conference on Genetic Algorithms and Their Applications*, Pittsburgh, PA, 1985, 160-168.

[HOLL75] J. H. Holland, *Adaptation in Natural and Artificial Systems*, University of Michigan Press, Ann Arbor, MI, 1975.

[KIRK83] S. Kirkpatrick, C. D. Gelatt and M. P. Vecchi, Optimization by Simulated Annealing, *Science 220*, 4598 (May 13, 1983), 671-680.

[SMIT85] D. Smith, Bin Packing with Adaptive Search, *Proceedings of an International Conference on Genetic Algorithms and Their Applications*, Pittsburgh, PA, 1985, 202-206.

[WHIT84] S. R. White, Concepts of Scale in Simulated Annealing, *International Conference on Computer Design: VLSI in Computers Proceedings*, Port Chester, NY, 1984, 646-651.

[WRIG32] S. Wright, The Roles of Mutation, Inbreeding, Crossbreeding, and Selection in Evolution, *Proceedings of the Sixth International Congress of Genetics 1*, (1932), 356-366.

A PARALLEL GENETIC ALGORITHM

Chrisila B. Pettey, Michael R. Leuze, and John J. Grefenstette[*]
Vanderbilt University, Nashville TN 37235

ABSTRACT

A parallel genetic algorithm (PGA) is presented as a solution to the problem of real time versus genetic search encountered in genetic algorithms with large populations. A discussion of the algorithm is followed by descriptions of experiments which were performed with the PGA and of performance measures which were collected during each experiment. The paper concludes with a discussion of experimental results.

1. Introduction

An important open question in the study of genetic algorithms (GA's) is the optimal size of a population. The problem centers around the tradeoff between the amount of genetic search that can be done and the amount of real time available. If the population size is too small, then the GA will have a, possibly improperly, constrained search space because of an insufficient number of schemata in the population. If the population size is too large, however, an inordinate amount of time will be required to perform all the evaluations. In the worst case a GA can be reduced to random search if the amount of available time is exhausted before any genetic search is performed.

Goldberg [3] has developed a theory of the optimal population size for binary-coded genetic algorithms based on the length of an individual. But, here again, the tradeoff between the amount of genetic search and the amount of real time is still evident. For instance, according to Goldberg's theory, the optimal population size for individuals of length 60 is approximately 10200. If evaluation of an individual requires 1 second, it will take approximately 2.8 hours to evaluate one generation. Since an evaluation can be as complex as solving a large queueing network model or running a simulation of processes on a multiprocessor, it is not unreasonable to believe that an evaluation could require 1 second or more. Execution times become even greater when populations with longer individuals are considered.

In order to overcome the genetic search vs. real time problem, a parallel implementation of GA's has been investigated. This class of parallel genetic algorithms (PGA's) is presented here, along with some experimental results. The implementation techniques used in this work are not restrictive to any particular multiprocessor architecture, but the results reported in this paper are from an Intel iPSC, a message-based multiprocessor system with a binary n-cube interconnection network.

2. Outline of the algorithm

A PGA operates on a very large population of several distributed groups of individuals. There is precedent for this type of population found in the idea from population genetics of a *polytypic* species [2]. A polytypic species is a species composed of different groups which are isolated from each other yet which are capable of producing offspring with each other. The human species, for example, is polytypic, in that it consists of groups isolated from each other either physically or culturally. Precedent for isolated groups in a population can also be found in Wilson's Animat [5], a classifier-based learning system, and in Schaffer's VEGA [4]. In the Animat system, each individual specifies one action, a direction for an artificial animal to move; when a parent is selected for crossover, its mate is selected from the subpopulation of individuals which specify the same action as the first parent. VEGA, on the other hand, in order to find an individual which performs well in several dimensions, performs selection by choosing subpopulations from the total population based on fitness in an individual dimension.

Research supported in part by the National Science Foundation under Grant DCR-8305693.

[*] Current address:
    Navy Center for Applied Research in AI
    Code 5510
    Naval Research Laboratory
    Washington, DC 20375-5000

A PGA consists of a group of identical "nodal GA's" (NGA's), one per node of the multiprocessor system. Each NGA maintains a small population which is a portion of the large population, and functions in much the same way as a sequential GA. The one difference between an NGA and a sequential GA is that once during each generation, an NGA communicates with its neighboring NGA's. This communication phase consists of sending the best individual in the local population to each neighbor and receiving the best individual from each neighbor's population. After the best individuals are received from the neighboring NGA's, it is necessary for an NGA to insert the new individuals into its local population. This insertion can be done by replacing random individuals, the worst individuals, or the individuals most like the incoming individuals (i.e., the smallest Hamming distance). The modified algorithm for an NGA is listed in Figure 1.

```
NGA:
    begin
        Initialization;
        Evaluation;
        while (not done)
        begin
            Communication;
            Selection;
            Recombination;
            Evaluation;
        end
    end
```

Figure 1. A Nodal Genetic Algorithm

While it is true that a PGA can be thought of as a sequential GA with a very large population, there is one major problem with this analogy. In a sequential GA an individual is selected based on its performance in the whole population, but in a PGA an individual is selected based on its performance in its local subpopulation. This difference in selection could result in premature convergence. On the other hand, this difference might lead to a slowing down of convergence and ultimately produce better results. At this time there is no theoretical basis for this type of selection.

3. Description of Experiments

Four of DeJong's testbed of functions [1]—f1, f2, f3, and f5—were used to test a PGA. For each of the four functions, an NGA maintained a population of 50 individuals and used a worst individual replacement policy. Five experiments involving different numbers of NGA's were performed. For each of the four functions, 1, 2, 4, 8, and 16 NGA's were used. Corresponding population sizes were, therefore, 50, 100, 200, 400, and 800. For each experiment the best individual performance, the online performance, and the offline performance were collected after each generation from each NGA. Each NGA was treated as a standard sequential GA, and performances were measured accordingly. From this collection of results, performances for the PGA were calculated.

4. Experimental Results

The results of the 20 experiments are graphically displayed in Figures 2 through 5. Figure 2 shows the best individual per generation for each of the four functions. Since a PGA with more NGA's has a larger initial population, it is possible for it to contain a better best individual in the initial population than a PGA with fewer NGA's. Since the addition of an NGA does not change the initial population of other NGA's, it is not possible for a PGA with more NGA's to have a worse best individual in the initial population than a PGA with fewer NGA's.

According to Goldberg's theory, the optimal population size for f1 is 116, for f2 is 51, for f3 is 2240, and for f5 is 262. The results from f1 (Figure 2a) and f5 (Figure 2d) appear to agree fairly well with the theory. Although the experiments were not run on populations of size 116 and 262, the populations of size 200 and 400 for f1 and f5, respectively, quickly found the optimum, and increasing the population size had no significant improvement. The results from f3 (Figure 2c) also tend to corroborate the theory. While a PGA was not run on a population larger than 800, the results did tend to improve with the increase of population size. Although populations of size 200 and 800 performed reasonably well on f2 (Figure 2b), the results from this function would seem to substantiate the belief that the selection performed in a PGA increases the likelihood of premature convergence. It is interesting to note that the best answer was found with a population of size 50, which is approximately the theoretical optimal population size. These data would tend to indicate that the population size for a PGA should be set with the optimal population size in mind.

Figure 3 shows the online performance of a PGA on the four functions. If it is desirable to optimize online performance, a large population should be used since a PGA's online performance is better the larger the population. However, it is not clear that online performance has any real meaning in a PGA since a PGA runs on a multiprocessor system.

Calculating the best performance and the online performance of a PGA is fairly straightforward. The offline performance, however, is a different matter. A possible offline performance measure is the average of the offline performances of each of the NGA's. Figure 4 shows the results of this measure. Perhaps more in keeping with the idea of offline performance is the measure shown in Figure 5. The offline best performance is obtained in much the same manner that offline performance is obtained in a sequential GA, with the exception that only the best individuals from each NGA are used in the measure. Therefore, the offline best performance measure is the average of the bests of the local NGA best individuals seen so far. As is to be expected, the offline best performance measure improves with an increase in population size.

It should be noted that a PGA has the desirable property that an increase in population size by the addition of another NGA should increase the execution time of a PGA only slightly. This increase in time is due to increased communication overhead among a larger set of NGA's. However, while there is no firm data as yet on increase in real time due to the addition of an NGA, experience indicates that it is negligible in comparison to the increase in real time due to a comparable increase in population size of a sequential GA.

5. Conclusions

This paper is a presentation of the initial work with a PGA. There is still much work that needs to be done with PGA's. Timing studies of the five functions on the iPSC are continuing. In the near future a PGA will be applied to the Traveling Salesman Problem and to a mapping problem (i.e., finding the appropriate placement of processes in a multiprocessor system in order to minimize the response time), and PGA's will be implemented with alternate means of communication (e.g., sending different individuals to each neighbor, sending individuals probabilistically based on their performance, etc.). Also, the selection mechanism in PGA's needs to be compared theoretically with the selection mechanism in sequential GA's. The initial work, however, indicates that a PGA is a viable means of increasing the population size of a GA since a PGA will allow the use of genetic search in problem areas where a candidate solution has a long representation and is time consuming to evaluate.

Acknowledgements

The authors would like to thank Mike Hilliard and Gunar Liepins of Oak Ridge National Laboratory for their contributions to this work.

References

[1] Kenneth A. DeJong, **An Analysis of the Behavior of a Class of Genetic Adaptive Systems**, Ph.D. Thesis, Department of Computer and Communication Sciences, University of Michigan, 1975.

[2] Theodosius Dobzhansky, **Genetics of the Evolutionary Process**, Columbia University Press, New York, 1970.

[3] David E. Goldberg, Optimal Initial Population Size for Binary-Coded Genetic Algorithms (*TCGA Report No. 85001*), Tuscaloosa: University of Alabama, The Clearinghouse for Genetic Algorithms, 1985.

[4] David J. Schaffer, **Some Experiments in Machine Learning Using Vector Evaluated Genetic Algorithms** Ph.D. Thesis, Department of Electrical Engineering, Vanderbilt University, 1984.

[5] Stewart W. Wilson, Knowledge Growth in an Artificial Animal, In *Proceedings of an International Conference on Genetic Algorithms and Their Applications*, J.J. Grefenstette, Ed., July 1985.

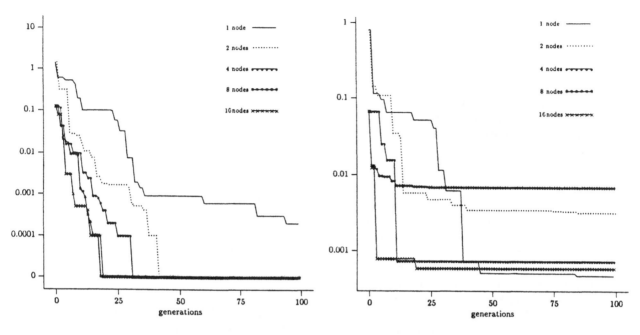

Figure 2a. Function f1

Figure 2b. Function f2

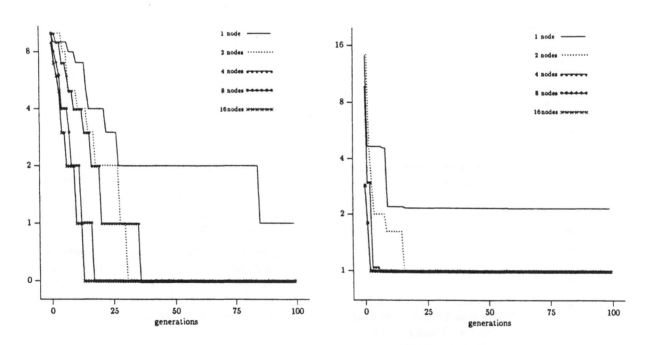

Figure 2c. Function f3

Figure 2d. Function f5

Figure 2. Best Individual Performances

158

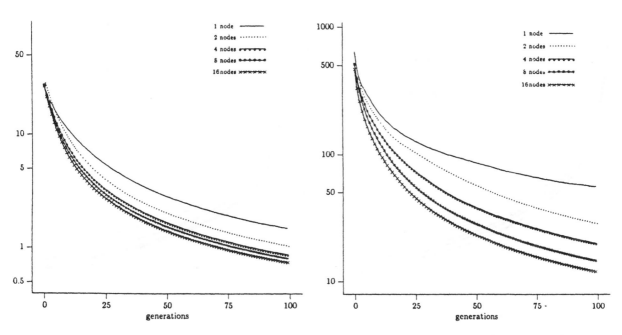

Figure 3a. Function f1

Figure 3b. Function f2

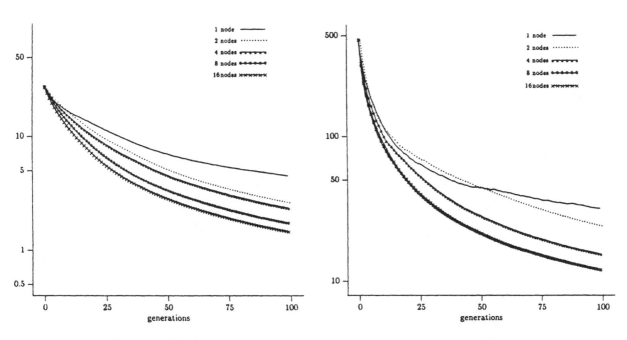

Figure 3c. Function f3

Figure 3d. Function f5

Figure 3. Online Performances

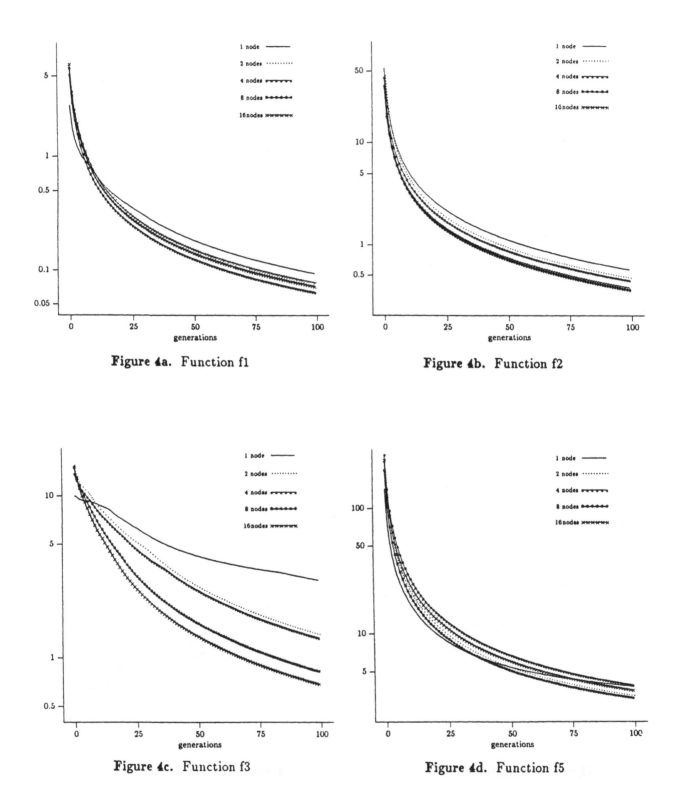

Figure 4a. Function f1

Figure 4b. Function f2

Figure 4c. Function f3

Figure 4d. Function f5

Figure 4. Offline Average Performances

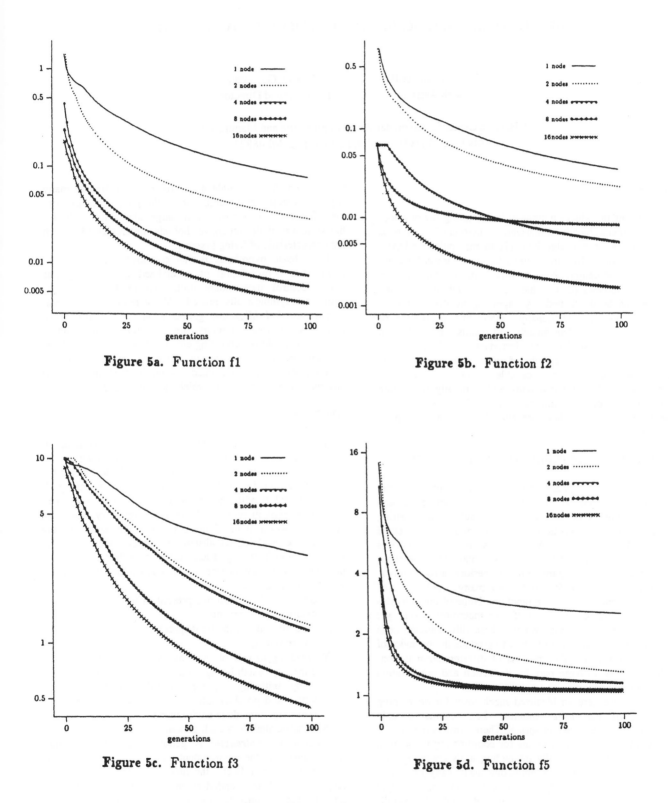

Figure 5a. Function f1

Figure 5b. Function f2

Figure 5c. Function f3

Figure 5d. Function f5

Figure 5. Offline Best Performances

GENETIC LEARNING PROCEDURES IN DISTRIBUTED ENVIRONMENTS

Adrian V. Sannier II
Research Assistant

Erik D. Goodman
Professor and Director

A.H. Case Center for Computer-Aided Engineering and Manufacturing
Michigan State University, East Lansing, MI 48823

ABSTRACT

This paper introduces a strategy for fostering the development of hierarchically organized distributed systems which uses a genetic algorithm [1] to manipulate independent, computationally limited units that work toward a common goal. The central thesis of this work is that important characteristics of the hierarchical structure of living systems can be duplicated by applying idealized genetic operators to a functionally interacting population of encoded programs. The models and results we present in this paper suggest that the introduction of functional interaction between distributed units can promote the development of a genome capable of producing a set of independent, differentiated units and implicitly organizing them into a coherent and coordinated distributed system. The results presented here are available in more complete form in [2].

AN IDEALIZED DISTRIBUTED GENETIC SYSTEM

The class of systems we have attempted to model emerges from consideration of macro-organisms composed of vast numbers of interacting, distributed units. During ontogeny, a single genetic program, or genome, represented in several strands of DNA, replicates itself, more or less exactly, millions of times. The cells containing these replicas of the original program do not all perform alike, however. Instead, they *differentiate* into many types, each of which performs a specialized function. None of the individual units operates on the scale of the macro-organism, yet together the operations which these differentiated cells perform are implicitly coordinated to produce the behavior of the larger organism. This process of differentiation is controlled, at least in large part, by the action and organization of the original genome.

We propose here an idealized mechanism for developing what we call *composite* genomes, i.e., genomes capable producing differentiated offspring. Their formation is desirable since they provide a means for coordinating the actions of independent, functionally interacting units operating in a common environment. By replicating itself many times and placing the offspring in appropriate environments, a single composite genome produces a system of implicitly coordinated independent units capable of pursuing a common objective. Furthermore, all of the information about the sys-

tem is located in a single unit, (of which there are many copies), making communication of the group strategy simple. Composite genomes are in large part responsible for the structure of the recursive, holonic hierarchies [3] which are characteristic of living systems.

Our basic hypothesis is that composite genomes arise from the consolidation of specialized genetic programs which control independent units that produce behaviors which are symbiotically related. Via a reproductive operation we call *hybridization*, genetic programs which produce distinct specialized behaviors are combined into a single genome capable of producing either behavior. Which of the encoded behaviors replicated offspring of a composite genome exhibit is determined by the internal and external environmental conditions in which they are placed.

The Basic Model

In our idealized model of the natural genetic system, an environment is defined in terms of a space, which we visualize as a two-dimensional integer grid of infinite extent, the standard setting for cellular automata. Within this grid, environmental conditions are defined in a local way, i.e., conditions exist in regions of the space and vary with time and/or the action of the living systems in the region. Living systems are modeled as abstract genomes which reside at some location in the grid and interact with the conditions present in some symmetric region surrounding them. Each genome is capable of :

1) detecting the conditions present in its immediate external environment;

2) detecting the conditions present in its internal environment;

3) reacting to sets of external and internal states, either by establishing some internal condition, or by initiating a process capable of interacting with, and possibly altering, the conditions present in its immediate environment.

Also associated with each genome in our model is a number, denoting its *strength*. A genome's strength is initially assigned by the environment and is adjusted at periodic intervals to reflect the fitness of the genome with respect to it. It is intended as an analog to the natural system, in that it provides the basis for selection. When a genome's strength falls below a certain threshold, it "dies", and is removed from the grid, but whenever its strength climbs above a somewhat higher threshold, it is able to produce an offspring. In this way, the number of offspring allocated to individuals is biased by performance. The initial strength of an offspring comes from its parents, depleting their strengths and thus restricting the frequency of individual reproduction. The principal genetic operators in the model are crossover and replication. (Augmenting these are idealized mutation and inversion operators. To simplify the presentation, their action is not discussed here; we utilize them in the standard fashion [1,4,5]).

The environmental grid mediates functional interaction between genomes. The potential for functional interaction exists wherever the processes initiated by one genome can, through the medium of a common environment, establish conditions which affect, either positively or negatively, the strength of another genome. In our model, genomes which are proximate to one another on the grid experience similar environmental conditions and can simultaneously affect their mutual environment. Since a genome's fitness is a function of its performance within its immediate environment, the fitnesses of genomes which share a common region of the grid are linked.

The grid also performs an important role in mediating reproductive interactions between genomes. In order to more accurately model the natural system, mate selection and offspring placement are spatially biased. The probability of an offspring emerging from a crossover between two parent genomes is inversely related to the distance between them. Similarly, when an offspring is placed in the grid, the probability that that offspring is found a distance x from its parents decreases inversely with the magnitude of x. These spatial dependencies appear to us to be important factors in promoting the formation of composite genomes, as we discuss below.

Structural and Spatial Coherence

In distributed populations, two kinds of groups emerge due to the action of the genetic operators and regional variations in environmental conditions. These groups derive their coherence from different properties and each serves a different function. The first of these are *structurally coherent groups*, or genotypes. The members of a genotype can be said to be structurally coherent in the sense that the structures of their programs, and hence the behaviors these programs produce, are similar. In sufficiently large, unevenly distributed populations, we expect a number of diverse genotypes to emerge due to functional specialization.

If the individual genomes in an unevenly distributed population are computationally limited, in the sense that they are incapable of responding, simultaneously, to all the demands and regularities present in their environment, then functional specialization will occur [6]. Spatially distributed genomes under selection pressure and the action of genetic operators, will begin to pursue different survival strategies and, after a time, will be separable into distinct genotypes according to their patterns of behav-

ior and the structure of the programs which encode for this behavior. As time goes on, the behaviors encoded in these specialized genotypes will become mutually exclusive, in the sense that a given genome, due to its limited computational capabilities, will be unable to adequately perform more than one of the behaviors at a time.

The second kind of grouping arises as a consequence of the spatial dependencies built into our model. Under our formulation, a collection of genomes which occupies a particular region forms a *spatially coherent group*, or sub-population. These spatial groups hold a special place in distributed systems. Not only do the individuals within them share a common context, but since mate selection and offspring placement are spatially biased, reproductive activity tends to be concentrated within them. If the population density is sufficiently low, individuals will tend to cluster in these spatially coherent groups, particularly if certain regions of the environment are more "hospitable" than others. The individuals within such "spatial niches" [7] will form isolated sub-populations whose members interact both functionally and reproductively, and tend to place their offspring back in the niche with high probability. Since the members of these groups interact functionally, if the niche contains genomes from different genotypes, the potential for symbiosis between individuals from these different types exists and is selected for.

A Reproductive Continuum

Crossovers of parents within and between the groups described above produce offspring of different characters, each of which perform a different function in the distributed system. The reproductive operations induced by the crossover operator take on the character of a continuum, producing different kinds of offspring depending on the degree of structural similarity between the crossing parents. This continuum is depicted below, linking two naturally occurring operations, replication and recombination with a third operator which we refer to as hybridization.

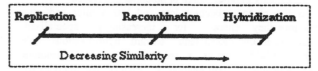

Admittedly, it may seem odd at first to assert that any kind of continuum exists between replication and recombination, since so many differences exist between them. Replication, the process by which a single composite genome produces a macro-organism composed of millions of differentiated cells, seems to have little to do with recombination, the process which produces new individuals by "mixing" two parent genomes. They occur at different levels in the biological hierarchy and the physical process which implement them are quite distinct. Nevertheless, we argue that, from an information processing perspective, replication and recombination can be considered as points on a logical continuum of reproductive operations by which new genomes can be produced from existing ones. While only certain regions of this continuum are realized in the natural genetic system, we have incorporated all of them in our model.

Replication lies at one extreme of this hypothetical continuum, occuring in our model either from the action of the replication operator or as a crossover between identical parents. The resulting offspring is an exact replica of the parental genome, but, as with all genomes in our model, its actions and responses are dictated by the state of its internal and external environment. Replication is most interesting when the parental genome is composite. When this is the case, the sections of code which become active in the offspring may differ from those which are active in the parent, due to differences in their internal and external environments. For example, a composite genome containing code for two distinct processes, each one sensitive to a distinct set of internal and external cues, can produce two differentiated types of offspring. While each is an exact genetic replica of the parent, different components of the composite genome are active in each of the offspring types, due to differences in the internal and external environments in which they have been placed. As a result the two types exhibit different behaviors.

When crossovers occur between genotypic variants, i.e., non-identical members of the same genotype, the offspring genome begins to look less like a replica of its parents and more like a mix of two similar, but distinct parents. In place of replication, we get recombination. Those familiar with genetic algorithms will recognize recombination as the standard image of crossover. Two parents, variants of the same basic genotype, cross to produce an offspring which shares sections of both parents' genetic code, and exhibits behaviors characteristic of both parents, as well as new behaviors arising from epistatic interactions between the spliced sections. Recombination has been studied extensively by a number of genetic algortihm researchers [1,4,5], and has been shown, under certain conditions, to generate individuals of increasing fitness through an intrinsically parallel search of potential genospace.

As the parents become less and less similar and the behaviors they encode for increasingly specialized, crossovers in our model tend toward hybridizations. We define hybridization as a crossover between genomes from radically different genotypes, each of which codes for a separate process activated by a distinct set of internal and external cues, which produces a new, composite genome that contains the code for both processes. It is the primary source of composite genomes in our model. In hybridization, two parent genomes, each of which codes for a different, specialized process, cross at a non-interfering point to form a composite offspring capable of exhibiting either behavior, depending on the external and internal conditions it encounters.

Composite Genomes

We see evolution in the distributed genetic system as an interaction of the operations described above. As new individual strategies emerge, recombinations between genomes which follow similar strategies produce increasingly fit individuals. When the individuals are computationally limited and spatially distributed, we expect a number of mutually exclusive strategies to emerge. If migrations occur in the space, we expect the formation of spatially coherent groups that contain genomes from more than one of these specialized genotypes.

The key to the development of successful composite genomes lies in hybridizations that occur within these structurally diverse sub-populations between symbiotically related parents. When a spatially coherent group, composed of genomes from more than one genotype, each of which exhibits a different specialized behavior, persists over time, spatial biases in mate selection and offspring placement increase the frequency of hybrid offspring, generated by parents from different genotypes within the spatial niche. Those offspring which successfully hybridize mutually beneficial behaviors will gain selective advantage. *We suggest that hybridizations which occur between the genomes in spatially coherent groups whose members are symbiotically related give rise to composite genotypes which make structurally explicit the implicit, spatial coherence that exists between the members of such groups. Replications of these composite types produce a set of independent computational units which act as an implicitly coordinated, distributed system.*

Preliminary verification of our hypothesis that successful composite genomes can form from the spatially-biased interaction of computationally limited adaptive units was provided by an experiment with the authors' software system, *Asgard*. *Asgard* is designed to simulate the behavior and adaptation of artificial animals operating under a genetic algorithm; similar systems have also been developed by Holland and Reitman [8], Booker [9], and Wilson [10]. Unlike these systems, however, the main objective of *Asgard* was the study of the evolution of a distributed population of interacting genomes, rather than the evolution of functionally isolated individuals. In the next section we describe the organization of the system and review the results of the most interesting simulation.

ASGARD

Asgard's environment is a finite, toroidal, two-dimensional grid, with a resolution of 160 x 60, which contains "food" at various locations. It is divided into 4 equal quadrants, each of which can be displayed on a Tektronix 4105 graphics terminal. The display style is similar to Wilson's [10]. The grid is "home" to a population of genomes which move about the grid in search of food. Each time step, the genomes in the grid expend one unit of strength in order to stay "alive", and each unit of food they consume increases their strength by one unit. In order for a genome to survive, then, its average food consumption must be at least one unit per time step; in order to reproduce, its average consumption must be somewhat greater than 1.

The behavior of each genome is controlled by its individual program. These programs are lists of labeled instructions of two types, **Move** and **Food?**, which specify either a movement direction or a test and transfer of control. Order of execution is controlled by a program counter that specifies which instruction in the list is to be performed next. **Move** instructions take one argument, which specifies one of eight directions of movement (N, E, SW, etc.). When executed, these instructions move the genome one unit in the specified direction. **Food?** instructions transfer control by testing the eight locations surrounding the genome for the presence of food. They take two arguments, both labels, which specify the statement to which the program counter should point given that food is or is not present in any of the surrounding locations. A short example is given below, together with a potential pattern of movement.

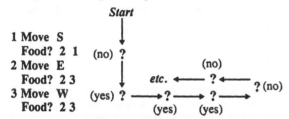

In terms of our model, each genome's immediate external environment is defined solely by the concentrations of food in its neighborhood. A genome can modify its external environment in two ways, either by consuming food or by moving to a different location in the grid. A genome's internal state is defined by the position of its program counter. By executing **Food?** instructions, the genome can detect the state of its external environment and, based on this information, can change its internal state, potentially altering its future external response pattern.

The evolution of the population is driven by an algorithm from the class of reproductive plans [1]. The algorithm starts with a population of genomes whose programs are formed at random from the set of legal instructions. Food is placed into the environment according to a pattern which may depend on time as well as the behavior of genomes in regions of the torus. The objective is to produce a population which responds to regularities in this pattern. The algorithm produces a sequence of populations whose members interact with each other through common local environments and are allocated offspring on the basis of their individual consumption. Over time, the successive populations will contain individuals adapted not only to the conditions of the artificial environment, but also to the behavior patterns of the other members of the population.

Let A(t) denote the population at time t and let **a** be any member of A(t). One iteration of the algorithm consists of the steps below :

cobegin { for all **a** in A(t) } :
  determine Loc (**a**) based on **a**'s program and
    update program counter [allows **a** one Move];
  consume food at Loc(**a**);
coend
cobegin { for all **a** in A(t) such that Str (**a**) > T_r } :

replicate a to create **a**';
begin { with probability P_c } :
  choose m at random from the set **A (t) - {a}**,
    biasing choice by distance |Loc(**a**) - Loc(**m**)|;
  crossover a' and **m**;
  replace a' with one of results of crossover;
end
choose Loc(**a**') at random, biasing the choice
  by the distance |Loc(**a**')-Loc(**a**)|;
coend
cobegin { for all **a** in A(t) such that Str (**a**) < 1 } :
  delete a from A(t);
coend
Increment t;

where:

P_c	= probability of crossover;
T_r	= reproduction threshold;
Str (**a**)	= strength of genome **a** at time t;
Food (Loc(**a**))	= number of food units present at **a**'s current grid location.

The reader will note that *Asgard*'s algorithm differs in some respects from more standard implementations, (see [1,4,5]). For example, the population size in *Asgard* is variable, governed only by the carrying capacity of the environment. Also, mate selection and offspring placement are biased by distance as our model specifies. These modifications were undertaken in order to make *Asgard* more closely resemble a community and allow for the formation of semi-isolated sub-populations. Within these sub-populations, trials are allocated to individuals and schemata in proportion to their observed fitnesses, insuring that Holland intrinsic parallelism theorems hold [1].

The Task

The task set before *Asgard*'s population is to identify and exploit the regularities present in the pattern of food placement. Although we performed experiments with a number of patterns, of various complexities, we discuss only one here, the so-called "seasonal" pattern. Under this pattern, there are three basic regularities to which the population can adapt.

1) Food can appear in only 1/8 of the space, concentrated in eight evenly-spaced fertile regions. Each genome must periodically visit one of these fertile regions in order to survive.
2) The productive capacity of each fertile region oscillates periodically between a maximum and a minimum value, (hence the term "seasonal"). Each fertile area can support many more genomes during its "summer" than its "winter", so competition for food within a particular area becomes increasingly fierce as winter approaches.

3) The amount of food actually produced during a given time step by a fertile region is linked to the amount of food consumed in the region during the previous time step. At any given time, an optimal consumption level exists for a region, and the genomes in that region can over- or under-consume with respect to this level, as a group, during a given time step, resulting in decreased food production in the next time step.

In each of the four quadrants of the grid, two 10x15 areas are established as fertile, (see figure 1a). For convenience, these areas are called farms. They are the only areas in the grid where food can be found; the rest of the grid is desert-like. Each time step, $K_i(t)$ units of food are produced by the i'th farm and distributed randomly within it, $(i = 1,..8)$. $K_i(t)$ is itself a function of two other quantities: $M_i(t)$, the seasonal productive potential of farm i; and $E_i(t)$, the consumption efficiency within farm i, a value derived from the total consumption within farm i during the previous period, $C_i(t-1)$. The exact form of these relationships is :

$$M_i(t) = A \sin((2 \Pi t / Y) + \Pi (-1)^i) + M_o, \quad A < M_o;$$

$$E_i(t+1) = \begin{cases} 1 - \dfrac{|2 C_i(t) - M_i(t)|}{M_i(t)}, & \text{for } 0 < C_i(t) < M_i(t); \\ 0, & \text{otherwise}; \end{cases}$$

$$K_i(t) = E_i(t) M_i(t)$$

where Y is the length of *Asgard*'s year.

The strength of genomes in the grid is based solely on their ability to consume; the more they consume, the stronger they become and the more offspring they have. In the absence of the factor $E_i(t)$ then, the optimal strategy for each genome would be to consume as much food as possible, at every time step. This "greedy" strategy leads to global extinction, however, when $K_i(t)$ depends on $E_i(t)$, since future food supplies are then tied to present rates of consumption. So the seasonal pattern exerts two different pressures on the members of the population. On the one hand, each genome is encouraged to compete with all the other genomes in the population for every available unit of food, in order to increase its individual strength. On the other hand, the environment gives selective advantage to groups of genomes which manage to cooperate in restricting their group consumption rate to track optimum levels.

Given the limited capabilities of each genome, however, it is clear that the forces which coordinate any group actions must come from some source outside the individual. Individuals are so limited in their range of options that they can respond to only the first two regularities of the pattern, i.e., they can seek fertile farms and, on finding them, remain near them. In order to respond to the third condition, group consumption levels must somehow be regu-

lated, and this is simply impossible from an individual perspective. The individual genomes have no way to communicate with the other members of the population, nor do they have any direct means for changing one another's behavior.

In our model, the selective pressure which the third regularity places on groups of individuals is the agent which produces coordinated action. The selective advantage given to groups of individuals which succeed in maximizing the productive efficiency of their farm assures their continued survival. Thus we expect two kinds of groups to form as a result of this pressure: spatially coherent groups of structurally similar genomes whose behaviors are nearly identical and mutually complementary and spatially coherent groups of genomes from distinct, but symbiotic genotypes, each of which performs some different, but mutually compatible behavior.

Farmers and Nomads

In studying the evolution of populations in *Asgard*, our objective was to detect the pattern and character of the changes which the population underwent over time. To this end we developed a set of tools which allowed us to study populations in *Asgard* qualitatively, as one might a colony of living bacteria, to try to categorize and account for the changing patterns of behavior and observe the evolution of the community as it developed. The interactive display thus became our primary means for studying the system.

As the size of our experiments increased, (typical population sizes were on the order of three to four hundred individuals and required almost 48 hours of CPU time on a Prime 550 to complete), observation in real-time soon proved unwieldy. In place of real-time observation, we substituted a kind of "batch" mode, which allowed more extensive study of the population at periodic intervals. A "snapshot", which preserved the complete state of the system, was taken every 300 iterations. After every "snapshot", each of the genomes in the population was automatically classified into a genotype based on similarities in program structure. Each of the genotypes' behavior patterns was then studied separately. For each genotype, *Asgard* was run interactively, using a population of representative individuals from that genotype, and their behaviors noted. After each genotype had been studied in isolation, *Asgard* was again run interactively, this time re-starting the simulation with all the data from the "snapshot", to study the behavior of the population as a whole. (In this mode, the genomes of each genotype were displayed by a different letter, thus making it possible to visually identify each genome's "species".) We give the results from one of these qualitative studies here. An initial set of 1000 individuals was constructed at random, their strengths set to S0, (see figure 1b). This initial set was entered into the grid in random locations at a graduated rate, to smooth the transient behavior of the population curve.

As the simulation begins, the programs of the initial

genomes interact with the environment to produce what look like random walks. Those which have been initially placed far from any of the farms die quickly, many without ever consuming a single unit of food. In this initial stage, selection favors those genomes with the ability to recognize and remain in the vicinity of a fertile zone. Farm efficiencies, as measured by the value $E_i(t)$, all average below .3. After 150 iterations the initial population collapse stabilizes, and the population begins to oscillate between two and three hundred individuals, evenly distributed between the four quadrants.

After 1500 iterations, (see figure 1c), the population consists of genomes which can be separated by program structure into eight different genotypes, with some slight variation in each type. Some of these genotypes are present on only one farm, while others have spread, by chance migrations and reproductions, to several of the farms in the grid. All the genomes exhibit the same basic pattern of behavior at this stage. Their programs consist of various series of **Move** instructions which cause them to drift in a particular direction, punctuated liberally with **Food?** tests. Positive values for these tests tend to halt the drift, so that the genomes wander about in various directions and, upon encountering a fertile farm, move randomly within it. Occasionally an individual will drift from one fertile farm to another, but most often those who leave a farm end up dying in the desert. Globally, the only populated areas are the regions immediately surrounding the fertile farms, the genomes there forming eight spatially coherent groups. The size of each group follows the productive capacity of the farm, climbing during the "summer", falling in "winter". In independent trials of the various genotypes, no evidence of symbiosis was found to exist between the groups. Each of the genotypes performed as well in the absence of the other groups as they did in their presence, provided population densities were maintained at approximately the same levels. Consumption efficiencies do not exceed .4, on any farm, during any season.

After 3,000 iterations however, both structurally and spatially coherent groups are present and exhibiting cooperative behavior, (see figure 1d). The two upper quadrants are completely extinct and the farms there can no longer produce food, but the lower two quadrants now sustain an average of 350 individuals, roughly the same size population as the four quadrants once maintained. Only two significant genotypes exist, each exhibiting markedly different behavior. The first group, nicknamed the Farmers, are the descendants of the genotypes present at 1,500 iterations. A group of Farmers is present at each remaining fertile farm. As individuals, they follow a fixed, circular pattern of movement, so that when placed in the neighborhood of a farm, following this pattern assures them of encountering it repeatedly. When tested in isolation, a population consisting solely of Farmers was stable and able to maintain the productive capacity of each farm in the grid. This "all Farmer" population functioned efficiently as a group, maintaining average consumption efficiencies of approximately .9 during the winter. During the summer however, the Farmers did not multiply sufficiently to keep pace with the farm's increased productive capacity and, as a result, their efficiency rating declined to around .5.

The second group, nicknamed the Nomads, are a new genotype, which exhibits a kind of migratory behavior. Each Nomad moves steadily across the screen, from left to right, in a tight, zig-zag pattern. Their rate of advance is

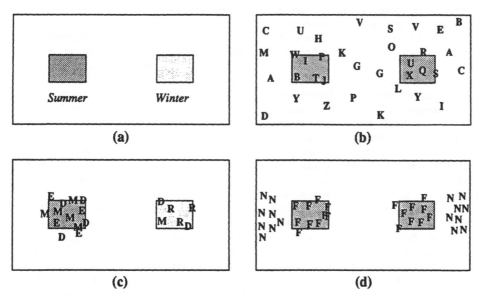

Figure 1

167

synchronized to the change of seasons, so that they strike the left edge of a farm during the farm's "spring" and move across it during its most fertile period, leaving the right-most edge of the farm as its productive potential wanes. The Nomads are found in two separate groups, which are evenly spaced between the farms in the lower two quadrants. Each group is largest as it leaves the right-most edge of a farm. As the group crosses the "desert" between farms, its numbers decrease steadily until the next farm is reached.

Unlike the Farmers, when a population of Nomads was tested in isolation, they could not survive. In following their pattern of cyclic migration, the Nomads failed to maintain consumption levels on farms during their "winter" season. As a result, only a fraction of the food available the first summer was available in the summer of the second year. Without Farmers to build up food stocks during the winter and early spring, the amount of food available to arriving groups of Nomads was gradually reduced. This decline in the summer food supply began a vicious cycle of declining numbers which ended in the extinction of the test group.

When observed together, however, the two structurally coherent groups complemented each other's efforts. With both Farmers and Nomads present in the same population, consumption efficiencies were at all times greater than .8. Recall that, operating in isolation, groups of Farmers were able to maintain near optimal consumption rates during the winter, but that during the summer their efficiency fell significantly. When Nomads and Farmers were observed together, winter consumption rates were maintained by the groups of Farmers at approximately the same level as when the Farmers were tested in isolation. (During the winter the two groups of Nomads were crossing the desert, and thus did not affect consumption rates.) When a Nomad group arrived at a farm during its "spring" though, the population influx increased the consumption rate within the farm enough to bring the value closer to the optimum. As a result, summer consumption efficiencies increased from .5 to .8.

Both structurally and spatially coherent group behaviors are present at this stage, then. The Farmers and the Nomads are both examples of structurally coherent, (or genotypic), groups. The implicitly coordinated actions of their individual members, acting on a local scale, (i.e., pursuing particular patterns of movement), add up to a group action on a global scale, i.e., the regulation of group consumption rates. And on each farm, during its summer, members of both genotypes, Farmers and Nomads, form spatially coherent groups which act together to increase farm efficiencies during that season. These increases are beneficial to both genotypes, since the increased food production allows both groups to generate more offspring. Because of spatially biased mate selection, many of these offspring are crosses between Nomad and Farmer.

Functional specialization is present in the population at this stage however, and as a result, little in the way of improvement can be expected from recombining Farmers

and Nomads. Farmer behavior is sufficiently different from Nomad behavior that an offspring which shares some of the traits of each group more often than not does a poor job at both. The Farmer and Nomad function well together, but only as separate, independent units. Each genome is limited enough in complexity that it cannot satisfactorily perform both functions. What is required is a hybridization combining the two behaviors into a single genome capable of producing both types of offspring.

A successful composite genome emerges after 4,000 iterations which consolidates the symbiotic relationship between Farmer and Nomad into a single program. At the top of this Farmer/Nomad composite is a section of code which acts as a kind of "switch". This switch is actually a series of linked **Food?** tests. When an offspring of this composite genome is placed in the grid, it tests several times for the presence of food. If two in a row of these tests turn up positive, the offspring's program counter moves to a set of statements which correspond to an infinite loop which codes for Farmer behavior; if two in a row turn up negative, the counter moves to a different set of statements, and the offspring performs an infinite loop which causes it to act like a Nomad.

The population composed entirely of composite forms performed almost exactly as the population we described at 3,000 iterations. The only difference is that the implicit link between the two groups, Farmer and Nomad, is now explicitly expressed in a single piece of code. A single copy of the composite genome, placed in fertile conditions and allowed to replicate, produces offspring which spread throughout the space and spontaneously organize themselves into the symbiotic groups of Farmers and Nomads which sustain the farms in the environment at near optimal levels.

DISCUSSION

The results of the *Asgard* experiments are encouraging. The emergence of the composite Farmer/Nomad shows that it is possible, through hybridization, to evolve a composite genome capable of producing and organizing a distributed system of independent units which work toward a common goal. *Asgard* provides another example of the versatility and adaptive power which genetic algorithms can exhibit, and as a prototypical example of the use of a genetic procedure in a distributed context, it gives insight into which facets of the natural system may be important in forming coordinated, co-adapted systems of distributed processes.

However, work with *Asgard* was hampered by a number of characteristics which made experimentation with the system unwieldy. For example, *Asgard*'s environments were extremely sensitive to slight changes in a number of internal parameters, and unforeseen interactions between environmental components often led to extinctions or population explosions. Attempts to extend *Asgard* to more useful domains proved to be exercises in frustration. Furthermore, we decided that in order to implement the distributed genetic algorithm in more realistic domains, some substitute source for the contextual clues provided by the environmental space would have to be developed.

To address some of these questions, we are currently developing a new system, *Midgard*, designed to produce an adaptive solution to the problem of balancing the load in a distributed interconnected local area network (inter-LAN). If communication costs between the nodes on an inter-LAN are sufficiently small, it is possible to achieve gains in overall efficiency by reassigning jobs between nodes in the network to exploit under utilized computing resources [11]. The algorithms which control this load balancing process are themselves typically distributed. Each node runs a scheduling process, or job scheduler, which communicates with the other schedulers in the network to determine when and how to migrate jobs between processors. *Midgard* is designed to explore the utility of a distributed, genetically based, adaptive algorithm in developing co-adapted process schedulers capable of cooperating to improve network performance.

The networks we consider are inter-LANs, in the class of systems which Fuller and Siewiorek categorize as loosely coupled [12]. The environmental grid, which in our model implicitly groups genomes operating in common contexts, is replaced in *Midgard* by explicit classes which are induced from the hierarchical structure of the network and the patterns of functional interaction which arise between its nodes. Distance is replaced by class membership as the measure of contextual proximity. Structurally coherent groups are encouraged by biasing mate selection and offspring placement to occur within a LAN cluster or processor class. Encouraging reproductive interaction within these groups fosters the formation of genotypes in the system organized according to the symmetries which exist between processors in the network.[[7]] By increasing the number of crossovers between similar machines, recombinant offspring will be generated which gradually increase the performance of the machines within clusters and within processor classes.

An analog to the spatially coherent group emerges when mate selection and offspring placement are biased to occur more often within classes induced by the occurrence of successful migrations between machines of different classes. By monitoring the patterns of successful migrations over time, reproductive interaction can be concentrated between individuals, from different genotypes, which have successfully co-operated to increase network efficiency. Favoring matings within these groups allows subpopulations working on common goals to become semi-isolated reproductively, setting the stage for successful hybridizations which explicitly capture group interdependencies.

The software to implement *Midgard* is currently under development in C on a unix-based Vax 8600. The network which the schedulers drive is implemented using C-SIM, a network simulation package developed by Schwebtman at Purdue University. Results from the experiments are expected by September of 1987.

REFERENCES

1. Holland, John H. " *Adaptation in Natural and Artificial Systems*", Ann Arbor: University of Michigan Press, 1975.
2. Sannier, A.V. ,"*Hierarchical system development in distributed genetic adaptive systems.*", Ph.D. dissertation, Michigan State University, (in preparation).
3. Koestler, Arthur. *"The Ghost in the Machine*". New York: Random House, 1976.
4. DeJong, K. A. "*An analysis of the behaviour of a class of genetic adaptive systems*". Ph.D. dissertation, University of Michigan, 1975.
5. Smith, S. F. "*A learning system based on genetic adaptive algorithms*". Ph.D. dissertation, University of Pittsburgh, 1980.
6. Grosso, P.B."*Computer simulation of genetic adaptation: Parallel subcomponent interaction in a multilocus model*". Ph.D. dissertation, University of Michigan, 1985.
7. Perry, Z. A. "*Experimental study of speciation in ecological niche theory using genetic algorithms*". Ph.D. dissertation, University of Michigan, 1984.
8. Holland, John H. & Reitman, J.S. "*Cognitive systems based on adaptive algorithms*", in Pattern Directed Inference Systems, Waterman and Hayes-Roth, Ed. New York: Academic Press, 1978.
9. Booker, Lashon. *" Intelligent behavior as an adaptation to the task environment*". Ph.D. dissertation, University of Michigan, 1982.
10. Wilson, Stewart. "*Knowledge growth in an artificial animal*", Proc. of an International Conf. on Genetic Algorithms and their Applications, July, 1985.
11. Stone, Harold S. "*Multiprocessor scheduling with the aid of network flow algorithms*",IEEE Transactions on Software Engineering, vol. SE-3, January, 1977.
12. Fuller, S.H. & Siework, D.P. "*Some observations on semi-conductor technology and the architecture of large digital modules*", Computer, vol. 6, Oct. 1973.

Parallelisation of Probabilistic Sequential Search Algorithms

Prasanna Jog

Dirk Van Gucht

Indiana University

Computer Science Department

Bloomington, IN 47405

jog@iuvax.cs.indiana.edu

vgucht@iuvax.cs.indiana.edu

Abstract

This paper explores ways of parallelising probabilistic sequential search algorithms that use a local improvement operator to generate iteratively a new candidate solution from previous candidate solution. We study the trade-off between the processors working in isolation and communicating with each other, in terms of required effort and performance achieved.

1. Introduction

This paper deals with the parallelisation of probabilistic sequential search algorithms which generate a sequence of candidate solutions (structures), each derived from the previous one by the use of a probabilistic operator. The type of operators under consideration are those that make small local changes that improve the structure. As an example, consider the probabilistic sequential search algorithm of Lin and Kernighan (the r-opt strategy) [1] used to find an approximate solution to the Traveling Salesman Problem (TSP). The TSP can be stated as follows: Given N cities, if a salesman starting from his home city is to visit each city exactly once and then return home, find the order of visits (the tour) such that the total distance traveled is minimum. In the general r-opt strategy, the operator replaces r edges in the current tour for r edges not in this tour if the resulting tour has a tour length less than the length of the previous tour. For example, the 2-opt strategy randomly selects two edges (i_1, j_1) and (i_2, j_2) from a tour (see Figure 1) and checks if

$$ED(i_1, j_1) + ED(i_2, j_2) > ED(i_1, j_2) + ED(i_2, j_1)$$

(ED stands for Euclidean distance). If this is the case, the tour is replaced by removing the edges (i_1, j_1) and (i_2, j_2) and replacing them with the edges (i_1, j_2) and (i_2, j_1) (see Figure 2).

One way of parallelising a probabilistic sequential search algorithm is to split the problem into n subproblems and let each processor work on one subproblem. Such a division is, in general, not possible. For instance, in a TSP, it is unlikely that we could make different processors attempt edge interchanges simultaneously on the same tour and hope to obtain

Figure 1. Tour with edges (i_1, j_1) and (i_2, j_2).

Figure 2. Tour with edges (i_1, j_2) and (i_2, j_1).

a legal tour. In other words, to achieve such parallelisation one has to add conflict resolution techniques, usually resulting in a degradation of the performance of the algorithm.

Another way of parallelising is to let all n processors run independently and take the best available solution at the end. We will call this the *independent strategy*. A potential problem with this strategy is that as the processors run independently, some of them may get caught in a local minima or may search sub-optimal regions of the search space, wasting valuable resource power. Intuitively, it seems likely that we might do better if we let the processors work inde-

170

pendently for some time, then exchange information about "good" candidate solutions, again work for a while, exchange new information and so on. We call such a method an *interdependent strategy* and call the time of the processing in between two information exchanges a *generation*†. Clearly, there are many ways of exchanging information about good candidate solutions. A straightforward strategy is to overwrite after each generation a certain number of "bad" candidate solutions by good candidate solutions. More sophisticated strategies could involve exchanging structural parts of good candidate solutions. Examples of such strategies are cross-over operators found in *Genetic Algorithms* (GA) [3].

In the rest of this paper, we give evidence that interdependent strategies are usually better than the independent strategy when parallelising probabilistic sequential search algorithms which use local improvement operators. In fact, we suggest that a good technique of parallelisation is to use an interdependent strategy where information exchange is done on a fairly regular basis. In Section 2, we illustrate this approach by parallelising a simple problem, the Classical Occupancy Problem [4]. Section 3 covers the parallelisation of a more complicated search algorithm: the 2-opt strategy of Lin and Kernighan for the TSP mentioned above. In Section 4, we describe experiments with a genetic algorithm for the TSP. We show that genetic algorithms can be viewed as parallel search algorithms that implement an interesting kind of interdependent strategy to achieve good, robust performance. The standard selection procedure of the GA can be viewed as a mechanism for achieving information exchange and the local improvement operator can be viewed as a recombination operator of the GA. Finally, Section 5 offers a discussion of the ideas and results given in this paper.

2. A Toy Problem: The Classical Occupancy Problem

Consider the classical occupancy problem: Given a structure of N empty cells, shoot points randomly at the cells (with a probability of $1/N$ of hitting any given cell) until all cells are filled. The time for solving this problem is the number of shots required to fill all N cells. This problem has been studied extensively by Kolchin et.al. [5]. We present here some experimental results which illustrate the advantages of an interdependent strategy over the independent strategy.

The sequential algorithm involves starting with the initial structure of N empty cells and repeatedly generating a random number between 1 and N, this is called a *trial*. If the cell was empty before, it is now assumed to be full and if not, the trial has been unsuccessful.

In the independent case, this sequential algorithm will run separately on all n processors. In this case, the time required to solve the problem is the number of shots required by the processor that finished first. In the interdependent case the algorithm would look as follows:

---

† Note that if a generation involves infinitely many trials (attempts at local improvements), the interdependent strategy reduces to the independent strategy.

assign to each processor the empty structure;
full ← 0;
generation ← 0;
while full < N do
begin
 generation ← generation + 1;
 each processor generates a number between 1 and N;
 if (at least one processor is successful) then
 begin
 randomly choose one among the successful processors;
 distribute its structure to all other processors;
 full ← full + 1;
 end;
end;

We now consider results of simulation on the classical occupancy problem with $N = 100$. First we fixed the number of processors and varied the number of trials per generation (*tpg*). As indicated by the above algorithm, after each generation the best structure was redistributed (copied) to all the processors. With the number of processors $n = 10$, we found that $tpg = 1$ resulted in the minimum number of generations. It should be noted, however, that a higher number of trials per generation also did well compared to the independent case. For $N = 100$ and $n = 10$ processors, the independent case required on average (taken over 500 experiments) 370 generations until completion. (Note that 100 is optimal). In the interdependent case, for $tpg = 1$ the processors required on average 128 generations, for $tpg = 4$ the processors required 165 generations and for $tpg = 7$ the processors required 190 generations.

Next we fixed the trials per generation and varied the number of processors. As the number of processors increased the generations required in the independent case reduced, but at a slower rate than the generations required for the interdependent case. For example, with 1 trial per generation and $N = 100$, it took 3 processors on average 221 generations to finish in the interdependent case and on average 427 generations in the independent case. With 5 processors the interdependent strategy required 166 generations while the independent case required 397 generations. With 10 processors the generations required were 128 and 370 respectively. (As the number of processors tends to infinity both strategies will require N generations). Our experiments suggest that doing less number of trials per generation and increasing the number of processors is better.

But this was a simple problem. In this problem, we know the (optimal) solution and among processors that have a successful trial, there is no one best structure, since they all have the same amount of empty cells. That is, they are all equally good. For this reason, we decided not to try a strategy of taking the k best candidate solutions with $k > 1$, although a slightly different performance may be expected. We now consider the parallelisation of a more complex problem and compare the performance of various interdependent strategies with each other and the independent strategy.

3. Experiments with a Search Algorithm for the Traveling Salesman Problem

The domain of this experiment is the Traveling Sales-man Problem (TSP). We use the operator of Lin and Kernighan (the r-opt strategy), described earlier as an example of a probabilistic operator that makes small local changes to produce new structures from old ones. The larger the value of r, the more likely it is that the final solution (when no more exchanges are possible) is optimal. However, r is usually chosen to be 2 because the possible edge interchanges is of the order of $\binom{N}{r} \times r!$†. In each generation, each processor performs a certain number of applications of the 2-opt strategy on the structure it currently holds in its local memory and after each generation the best structure was redistributed (copied) to all the processors. The domain for experiments described here is the lattice of 100 points spread over (0,0), (0,9), (9,0), (9,9) as shown in Figure 3.

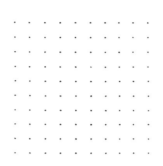

Figure 3. Lattice of 100 cities

Clearly, the optimal tour length is 100‡. We will consider the total effort, given by the number of generations times the number of trials per generation, required to get to within 10% of optimal performance as the number of trials per generation (tpg) is varied. Notice that we do not take into account the overhead involved in redistributing the structures after each generation. The algorithm is as follows:

> **for** *various values of tpg* **do**
> **begin**
>   *generation* ← 0
>   *generate a structure randomly;*
>   *copy it to all n processors;*
> **while** (*bestperformance* ≥ (1.10 ∗ *optimumvalue*))**do**
> **begin**
>   *generation* ← *generation* + 1;
>   *each processor attempts tpg local improvements;*
>   *find the structure with the best performance;*
>   *distribute this structure to all other processors;*
> **end**
> **end**

---

† It should be noted that Lin and Kernighan propose a more powerful strategy where r is varied dynamically, but the simple 2-opt strategy also gives good results and is quite efficient [2].

‡ It should be noted that similar results can be obtained for other TSPs.

The actual algorithm also keeps track of the number of successful local improvements (i.e., applications of the 2-opt operator that make the tour length smaller) and the number of experiments that got aborted (i.e. those experiments wherein the performance did not reach below 10% of optimal performance even after many generations). Figure 4 shows the graph for 10 processors. Similar graphs were obtained for different number of processors. This shows that if we have fewer trials per generation then the total effort required to get a relatively good performance is less. (As mentioned before, when tpg tends to infinity we have the independent strategy, and that clearly requires a lot more effort).

But not all trials involve successful local improvements. Those that do not perform any local improvement will take very little processor time because the tour does not need to be rearranged. Therefore, to get an idea of total time required, we plotted in Figure 5 the number of successful local improvements done on average. Again, we see that doing fewer trials per generation reduces the total time required.

There is a danger in doing too few trials per generation however. As Table I shows, out of 50 experiments for each value of tpg, some get aborted for low values of tpg. This happens when the algorithm gets caught in a local optimum, which occurs because the algorithm described above has no means of maintaining diversity of structures for low values of tpg. Note that for higher values of tpg, that is strategies closer to the independent strategy, no experiments get aborted, showing the robustness of the operator and the algorithm being used.

To avoid getting caught in a local optimum we decided to change the interdependent strategy slightly to increase the diversity of examined structures. Instead of taking the one best structure we decided to experiment with the redistribution of the k best structures after each generation. (Again as k tends to n we have the independent case). In the experiments with 10 processors we found that with $k = 4$ only 1 or 2 experiments get aborted (out of 50) for lower values of tpg. We may conclude that increasing k (i.e. maintaining diversity) makes the algorithm more robust.

There is another price we pay for exchanging information too quickly. Every time we exchange information a copy time is involved and this copy time increases as the number of trials per generation decreases. But it will decrease as k increases (for a fixed value of tpg)†. Thus, our experiments show that one obtains a good interdependent strategy by keeping tpg as low as possible to decrease the number of total trials and to use a large enough k to make the algorithm avoid getting trapped into a local minima as well as to reduce copy time.

4. Experiments using a Genetic Algorithm

Genetic Algorithms (GA) [3], introduced by Holland, have been applied with good success to function optimisation problems involving complex functions [6] as well as on some combinatorial optimisation problems [7,8,9,10,11,12,13]. A typical GA maintains a population of structures after each,

---

† It should be noted that on a parallel machine the copy time can be reduced.

generation, which consists of applying local improvement operator a certain number of times (trials) to each structure, uses a selection mechanism to produce a new population of structures for the next generation. (Thus, a trial involves a probabilistic operation that makes a small local change to the structure). The selection mechanism assigns a strength of performance measure to each structure. This measure is usually the ratio of the performance of the structure to the average performance of the population. The number of occurences of this structure in the next generation is proportional to this performance measure ‡.

A genetic algorithm can be viewed as a parallel search algorithm of the type we have been discussing in the previous sections. Whereas a sequential algorithm (using the local improvement operator) operates on one structure a GA operates on a population of n structures. If one imagines that each structure is worked on by a separate processor, the selection mechanism can now be viewed as an interdependent strategy. The n processors run separately for a while (a generation) and then exchange information (about performance) resulting in processors getting a (possibly) different structure for the next generation. This strategy is a more sophisticated version of our earlier idea which consisted of taking the k best structures from the current population.

We used a version of the genetic algorithm (GA) that uses the 2-opt local improvement operator to solve the TSP. We ran the GA for 50,000 trials, varying tpg. The population size, or alternatively the number of processors, is 50.

On the lattice of 100 points (optimum length is 100) the GA did not do well for small values of tpg (5 and 10) but did almost equally well on higher values of tpg. Table II shows the effort required for the GA to get to within 10% of the optimal performance. It should be noted that these values are close to the values obtained in our earlier interdependent strategy of taking the one best (Table I).

Next we chose the domain to be 100 points uniformly distributed between (0,0) (0,1) (1,0) (1,1). Figure 6 shows the performance versus tpg curve. The best performance is seen at about $tpg = 500$ and it worsens a little after that. Therefore using the selection mechanism of a GA as strategy of interdependency, and keeping tpg relatively small yields a fast and robust algorithm with good performance.

5. Conclusion

We have given evidence that probabilistic sequential search algorithms which operate by performing a local change on a structure to generate a new structure, can be parallelised by doing a reasonably large amount of local improvements for each structure per generation and then exchanging information about "good" structures. Doing too few trials per generation, however, may not yield good performance values as premature convergence may occur. On the other hand, we also showed that taking one best structure and redistributing it over the other processors is too simplistic a strategy since it also causes premature convergence; hence a few best should be selected for redistribution.

In fact, it turned out that the more sophisticated interdependent strategy, the selection procedure of a genetic algorithm, gave the resulted in the most robust strategy. It should be noted that we have ignored copy time in the presentation of the results. We believe however, that even if we take this overhead into account similar results concerning the independent versus interdependent strategy may be obtained.

Acknowledgements

We wish to thank the referees for helpful comments which helped in clarifying some of the ideas and results of the paper.

References
1. S. Lin and B.W. Kernighan, "An Effective Heuristic Algorithm for the Traveling Salesman Problem", *Operations Research* 1972, pp. 498-516.
2. E. L. Lawler, J.K. Lenstra, A.H.G. Rinnooy Kan and D.B. Shmoys (ED), *The Traveling Salesman Problem*, John Wiley and Sons Ltd (1985).
3. J.Holland, *Adaptation in Natural and Artificial Systems*, University of Michigan Press, 1975.
4. N.L. Johnson, S. Kotz, *Urn Models and their Applications*, Wiley and Sons, 1977.
5. V.F.Kolchin, B.A.Sevastyanov, V.P.Chistyakov, *Random Allocations*, V. H. Winston and Sons, 1978.
6. K. A. Dejong, "Adaptive system design: a genetic approach", *IEEE Trans. on System, Man and Cybernetics, Vol. SMC-10(9)*, pp 556-574 (Sept 1980).
7. J.J. Grefenstette, R. Gopal, B.J. Rosmaita and D. Van Gucht, "Genetic Algorithms for the Traveling Salesman Problem", *Proc. of an Int'l Conf. on Genetic Algorithms and Their Applications*, pp. 160-168 (July 1985).
8. J.J. Grefenstette, "Incorporating Problem Specific Knowledge into Algorithms", To appear.
9. J.Y. Suh, D. Van Gucht, "Incorporating Heuristic Information into Genetic Search", Technical Report, Indiana University, February 1987.
10. L. Davis, "Job shop scheduling with genetic algorithms", *Proc. of an Int'l Conf. on Genetic Algorithms and Their Applications*, pp. 136-140 (July 1985).
11. M.P. Fourman, "Compaction of symbolic layout using genetic algorithms", *Proc. of an Int'l Conf. on Genetic Algorithms and Their Applications* (July 1985).
12. D.E. Goldberg and R. Lingle, "Alleles, loci, and the traveling salesman problem", *Proc. of an Int'l Conf. on Genetic Algorithms and Their Applications*, pp 154-159 (July 1985).
13. D. Smith, "Bin packing with adaptive search", *Proc. of an Int'l Conf. on Genetic Algorithms and Their Applications*, pp 202-206 (July 1985).

---

‡ Most GAs also use a crossover operator that takes two structures and interchanges parts of them to produce two new structures. In this paper we ignore such operators.

tpg	total effort	success rate	total success	experiments aborted	variance
5	1505	0.030	45.009	5	0.092
10	1820	0.034	61.320	3	0.123
20	2160	0.036	77.385	3	0.093
40	2640	0.038	99.261	1	0.107
80	3360	0.035	117.112	1	0.110
160	4160	0.034	140.610	0	0.157
320	5440	0.030	160.867	0	0.245
640	6400	0.027	172.721	2	0.590
1280	7680	0.022	170.522	2	0.922
2560	10240	0.019	192.836	2	1.857
5120	15360	0.015	222.767	0	2.114

tpg - trials per generation
total effort = tpg * (generations to get to within 10%)
success rate = fraction of trials successful
total success = total number of successful improvements done
experiments aborted are out of total of 50 for each tpg

T A B L E II

tpg	total effort
5	1500
10	2058
20	2812
40	3760
80	4480
160	5600
320	6080
640	7040
1280	7680
2560	7680
5120	10240

effort for 10 processors

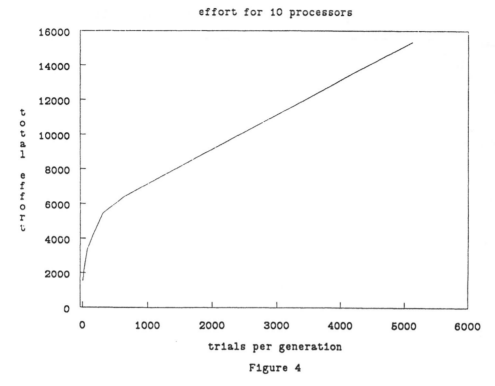

trials per generation

Figure 4

success rate for 10 processors

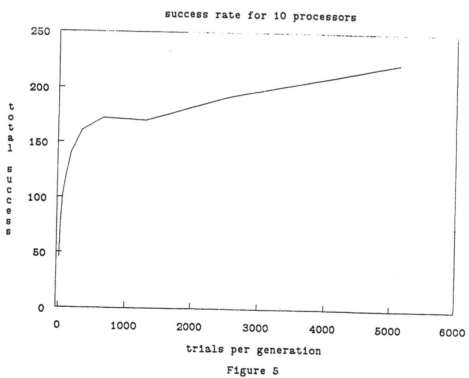

trials per generation

Figure 5

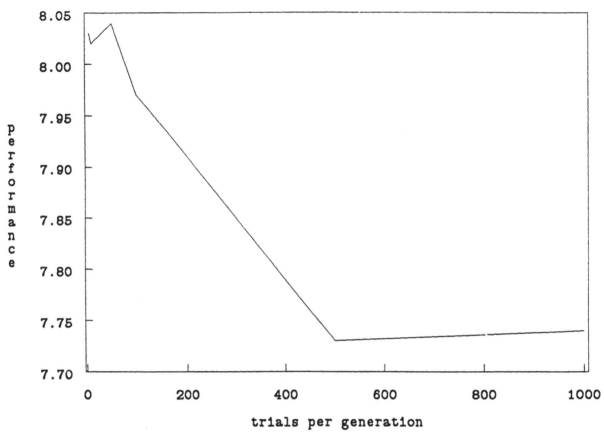

performance of 100 random cities

trials per generation

Figure 6

PARALLEL GENETIC ALGORITHM FOR A HYPERCUBE

Reiko Tanese[*]

Department of Electrical Engineering and Computer Science
University of Michigan
Ann Arbor, MI 48109-2122 USA

Abstract

This paper discusses a parallel genetic algorithm for a medium-grained hypercube computer. Each processor runs the genetic algorithm on its own sub-population, periodically selecting the best individuals from the sub-population and sending copies of them to one of its neighboring processors. The performance of the parallel algorithm on a function maximization problem is compared to the performance of the serial version. The parallel algorithm achieves comparable results with near-linear speed-up. In addition, some experiments were performed to study the effects of varying the parameters for the parallel model.

1 Introduction

The genetic algorithm, which was designed by Holland[1] in the 1960s, is applicable to a wide range of problems and its popularity is steadily increasing. In some applications, such as a simulation of natural phenomena, the algorithm requires many generations and a large number of individuals in the population. However, time limitations make it infeasible to run the algorithm with such a large population. To alleviate this, this research investigates a parallel version of the genetic algorithm on a hypercube computer. The results show that the parallel version is significantly faster than the serial one, and that nearly linear speed-up can be achieved with as many as 64 processors.

The parallelization of the algorithm involves dividing the population and placing a sub-population on each processor. A processor runs the genetic algorithm on its own sub-population, periodically selecting good individuals from the sub-population and sending copies of them to one of its neighboring prcessors. Earlier work was done by Grosso[2] studying sub-populations in the genetic algorithm on a serial computer. Grefenstette[7] has proposed several versions of

parallel adaptive algorithms for different architectures.

The next section in this paper describes the hypercube architecture and the specific hypercube computer, the NCUBE, on which this research was performed. Section 3 describes the serial and parallel algorithms studied. The algorithm's performance is measured on a function maximization problem; the function to be maximized is defined in section 4. The experiments which were conducted and their analyses are contained in section 5.

2 The Hypercube Computer

The parallel genetic algorithm presented in this paper is designed to take advantage of a parallel architecture, a medium-grained hypercube. An n-dimensional hypercube computer consists of $N = 2^n$ processors interconnected as an n-dimensional binary cube (Figure 1). Each processor is a node of the cube and has its own CPU and local memory. The communication among the processors is done via message passing. Each processor is directly connected to n other processors (its neighbors), which makes the distance between any two processors in the cube at most n communication links long. This means that information can be broadcast through the cube in n (or $\lg N$) time steps, compared to $\Theta(N^{1/2})$ in a 2-dimensional grid, another popular parallel architecture.

The specific machine used to run all the experiments in this paper is a general purpose 64-processor NCUBE/six hypercube made by NCUBE Corporation[3]. Each processor in the NCUBE/six is a powerful 32-bit custom VAX-like CPU chip with 128K bytes (soon to be 512K) of local memory. Although a quarter of this memory is needed to store the node operating system and message buffers, it is still large enough to categorize the NCUBE/six as a medium-grained hypercube computer. An 80286 host processor is used to provide the connections between the node

[*]Partially supported by Digital Equipment Corporation.

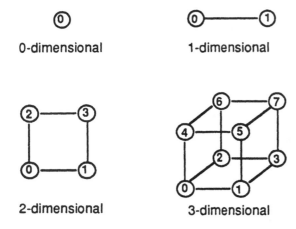

0-dimensional **1-dimensional**

2-dimensional **3-dimensional**

Figure 1: Hypercubes for $n = 0$, 1, 2, and 3

processors and the external world.

3 The Genetic Algorithm

3.1 The Serial Algorithm

The serial genetic algorithm (Figure 2) is a straight-forward implementation of a standard algorithm with two genetic operators: crossover and mutation. Two parameters, *crossover_rate* and *mutation_rate*, determine the frequency of application of these operators. *Crossover_rate* is the average number of crossovers per mating. The actual number of crossovers for any particular pair of individuals is a Poisson-distributed random variable with a mean of *crossover_rate*. That is if *crossover_rate* is 1, any pair will undergo crossover operation on the average once. Similarly, *mutation_rate* is the average number (Poisson-distributed) of mutations per individual. Notice that this differs from the traditional interpretation, in which the mutation rate represents the probability of mutation per allele. The method used here is functionally equivalent to the traditional method using *mutation_rate* / the length of a chromosome. The new method is simply more efficient, especially when there are few mutations per chromosome.

The algorithm keeps track of the best individual in the population and carries it over to the next generation. This feature, which was first used by DeJong[5], is especially helpful when solving function optimization problems, in which the environment remains unchanged over time.

Randomly generate initial population of *pop_size*.
For gen = 1 to *num_gens* do
    Compute the fitness of each individual in the
      population.
    Determine the number of offspring which each
      individual is going to have based on the
      individual's fitness.
    For i = 1 to (*pop_size* / 2) do
      Pick 2 parents randomly without replacement.
      Crossover the parents based on *crossover rate*
        to produce 2 new offspring.
      Mutate each offspring based on *mutation rate*.
    endfor
    If the best fit individual from the old population is
      not in the new population, replace one of the
      individuals in the new population with the best
      individual from the old population.
endfor

Figure 2: The serial genetic algorithm

3.2 The Parallel Algorithm

In the parallel implementation (Figure 3), each processor runs the genetic algorithm on its own sub-population, periodically selecting good individuals from its sub-population and sending copies of them to one of its neighbors. It will also receive copies of this neighbor's good individuals, with which it will replace bad individuals in its own sub-population. The neighbor with which this exchange takes place will vary over time: each exchange will take place along a different dimension of the hypercube. The frequency of exchange and the number of individuals exchanged are two new adjustable parameters.

For example, suppose there are four processors, each containing a sub-population of size 50. Suppose they are to send 10% of their good individuals to their neighbors at every 10th generation. Suppose that the processors have their identification numbers assigned as shown in Figure 1. At generation 10, processors 0 and 1 will send 5 of their good individuals to each other, and so do processors 2 and 3. At generation 20, processors 0 and 2 will exchange individuals and so do processors 1 and 3.

This exchange of individuals is designed to remedy the parallel algorithm's main difference from the serial one. In the serial algorithm, an individual can select its mate from any other individual in the population, while in the parallel version potential mates are all in

Randomly generate initial sub-population of
 sub_pop_size.
For gen = 1 to *num_gens* do
    Calculate fitness as in the serial algorithm.
    If (gen mod *frequency_of_exchange* = 0) then
        Choose *num_exchange* good individuals
            from the pool of individuals whose fitnesses
            are at least equal to the average fitness of
            the sub-population.
        Send copies of good individuals to the
            neighboring processor along one dimension
            of the hypercube.
        Receive copies of neighbor's good individuals.
        Choose *num_exchange* bad individuals
            from the pool of individuals whose fitnesses
            are no greater than the average fitness of
            the sub-population.
        Replace these individuals with the newly
            received ones.
    endif
    Allocate offspring as in the serial algorithm.
    Reproduce as in the serial algorithm.
    Keep the best fit individual from this generation
        as in the serial algorithm.
endfor

Figure 3: The parallel genetic algorithm

the same sub-population, a much smaller pool. This restriction is overcome by allowing the better fit individuals to circulate among the sub-populations, in the hope that they might prove to be "useful".

Notice that the "good" individuals to send to a neighboring processor are chosen probabilistically from the individuals whose fitnesses are at least equal to the average fitness of the sub-population. The current implementation ensures that the individual with the highest fitness has the the highest chance of being duplicated and sent to a neighboring processor. Similarly, the "bad" individuals are chosen probabilistically from the individuals whose fitnesses are no greater than the average fitness of the sub-population, giving the worst fit individual the highest chance of being replaced.

There is a limit, though, to how frequently exchanges should occur. Notice that the exchange scheme produces duplicates of the fit individuals, which is equivalent to producing more offspring. This increased fertility can, in some cases, lead to premature convergence.

Another consideration in determining the exchange frequency is the problem domain. Function optimization domain is one in which the environment is unchanging; the function values are fixed. In other domains, in which the environment may be changing, it might be better not to exchange as frequently. This is due to the fact that as the environment changes, the sub-population may undergo substantial re-adjustment. It would be best to perform exchanges only after the sub-populations have settled into quiescence, which could take a number of generations to achieve.

The parallel genetic algorithm in Figure 3 can easily be implemented on the NCUBE. The two main modifications required are: addition of an inter-processor communication routine for exchanging individuals, and addition of a host program which loads the node processors with the genetic algorithm program and establishes the I/O interface between the user and the node processors, since the node processors cannot perform direct I/O. The core of the genetic algorithm running on each processor is as in Figure 2.

4 Function Maximization

The problem of function maximization is used for preliminary demonstration of the performance of the parallel algorithm. This is because in the function optimization problem there is a clear measurement of how well the system is performing at all times, whereas in other problems performance can be harder to analyze.

The first attempt used five functions studied by DeJong in his thesis[5]. However, the serial algorithm has found the global maximum for all five functions within 200 generations, starting with a randomly generated population of 50. There is little need to parallelize problems which are quickly solvable by serial computers, so a search was made for reasonable genetically-hard functions. Bethke[4] has shown in his thesis that Walsh functions can be used to construct genetically-hard functions. This was used to define a Walsh-like function W on binary strings of length 64. The objective of the algorithm is to maximize W. W is defined as a composition function:

$$W(s) = F(Order(s))$$

where $Order(s)$ = the number of ones in the string s, $(0 \leq Order(s) \leq 64)$ and F is defined so that W has the values shown in Figure 4.

The function W has the following characteristics.

- It has many local optima and a single global op-

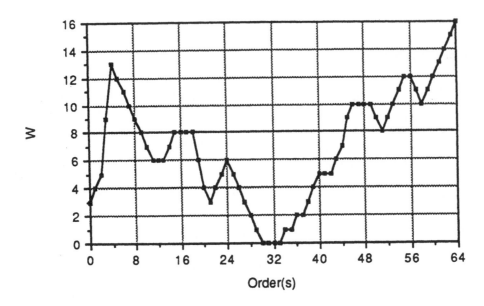

Figure 4: Function W

timum.

- The domain of W is huge, namely 2^{64}.

- The function values for neighboring points are relatively close together. This helps keep a single fit individual from taking over the population easily, thus preventing the genetic algorithm from developing a fixation.

- The global optimum is not an isolated spike which can only be found by a random search.

5 Experiments and Results

5.1 Number of Processors

Table 1 contains the results of running the parallel algorithm using various number of processors. For each dimension, the parameters are set as follows: total population size ≈ 400, *crossover_rate* $= 0.6$, *mutation_rate* $= 0.5$, and *exchange_frequency* = every 5 generations. Table 1a contains the results of runs in which 10% of sub-population is exchanged. Table 1b contains the results of runs exchanging 20% of sub-population. The runs for dimension 0, those with one processor, are equivalent to running the serial algorithm in which no exchanges occur.

Sixty-four runs were made for each dimension. Each run keeps track of the earliest generation in which the global maximum is found. The column "average gens" in Table 1 is the average of such generations over 64 runs. When a run does not find the global maximum

within 1000 generations, as seen in dimension 0, the average generation is calculated as if that run reached the global maximum in generation 1000. This is indicated in the table by ">", meaning that it took at least that many generations on average to reach the global maximum. "#runs reaching max" is the number of runs that reached the global maximum out of the 64 runs. The range column shows the earliest and the latest generations in which the global maximum is found. Since the genetic algorithm is a stochastic algorithm, this range can be quite large.

The total population size for dimension 4, 5 and 6 is kept approximately 400. This is because the parallel program handles only even sub-population sizes in the current implementation. Notice that there is no data for dimension 6, in Table 1a. This is because 10% of six individuals is less than one, so no exchanges would have taken place.

The results in Table 1 show that the parallel algorithm finds the global maximum in roughly the same number of generations as the serial algorithm.

Table 2 shows the execution times for the runs in Table 1a. The times are for complete runs of 1000 generations, regardless of when the global maximum is found. The parallel algorithm introduces two extra steps over the serial one: choosing good and bad individuals, and exchanging these individuals. From empirical observations, these steps are negligible when the sub-populations are larger than 10; typically under 1% for selection and under 2% for exchanging.

Figure 5 demonstrates the speed-up achieved by the

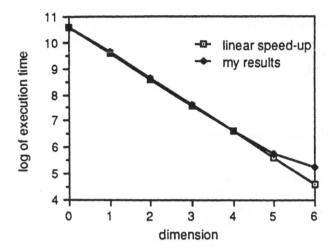

Figure 5: Dimension versus log of execution time

parallel algorithm. The graph plots the dimension of the hypercube versus the log of the execution time. Notice that for runs made on 6-dimensional hypercube, the sub-population size is only 6: consequently the communications overhead becomes a much larger factor in the execution time. It also takes longer to load all 64 processors with the program. These two factors combine to push the 6-dimensional time away from true linear speed-up.

The two results, the comparable performance and the near-linear speed-up, together demonstrate the power of the parallel algorithm.

5.2 Different Mutation and Crossover Rates

The effects of varying the mutation rate in the serial algorithm was studied by DeJong in [5]. The purpose of a mutation is to introduce a lost allele in a given bit position. When a bit position is fixed to one allele in all of the population, no amount of crossover will introduce a different allele there. Therefore, a mutation is an insurance policy which re-introduces lost alleles.

A single bit mutation of an individual can also be thought as a local search in an area surrounding that individual in a multi-dimensional space. The problem is when the population converges prematurely to a local optimum, in which case it may require more than a single mutation to get over to a new region. A high mutation rate is helpful in such situation, but it may cause too much disruption during the exploration phase.

The difficulty is in keeping the balance between the exploration and exploitation (or switching the emphasis from one to the other). Ackley[6] used a variable

mutation rate over time, in which he started out with high mutation rate to explore the search space, and gradualy lowered the rate to concentrate on a promising region. This use of the mutation rate is similar to the use of temperature in simulated annealing. Ackley used an "iterated" genetic algorithm in addition to this variable mutation rate to ensure that the algorithm would not prematurely converge to a local optimum.

The parallel algorithm shown in this paper introduces a different way to handle the exploration versus exploitation problem. Since the algorithm uses multiple processors, why not have some processors run with a high mutation rate, emphasizing exploration, and the other prcessors run with a low mutation rate, emphasizing exploitation? When a processor running with a low mutation rate exchanges individuals with a processor with a high mutation rate:

1. If any of the new individuals are less fit than the rest of the processor's sub-population, then they will eventually die off.

2. If any of the new individuals are more fit than the processor's sub-population, then they may help to focus the search in a new direction, possibly avoiding premature congergance.

Two experiments were conducted on a 3-dimensional hypercube to demonstate this point. All parameters other than *mutation_rate* were set as follows: total population size = 400, *crossover_rate* = 0.6, exchange 10% of sub-population every 5 generations. The first experiment used *mutation_rate* equal to 0.5 per individual on half of the prcessors, and 1.0 on the other half. The second experiment used *mutation_rate* of 0.5 for half of the processors, and 2.0 on the others. The results of these experiments are in lines 2 and 3 of Table 3.

Another experiment was run with different values of crossover and mutation rates on all eight processors. *Crossover_rate* is set either to 0.6 or 1.0. *Mutation_rate* can be 0.5, 1.0, 1.5, 2.0. The combination of these two parameter values makes every processor run in a different mode than the others.

The results of these runs are summarized in line 4 of Table 3. Compared to the results of the "standard" run in line 1, all three experiments found the maximum within a reasonable number of generations. These results are very encouraging in dealing with one of the main difficulties of the genetic algorithm, its sensitivity to the parameter settings. Numerous studies have dealt with this problem; the algorithm is not practical unless appropriate parameter settings can be found easily. The experiments of Table 3 suggest that the parallel algorithm can perform well even without knowing the best parameter settings.

5.3 Exchange Frequency

Table 4 shows the results of changing the frequency of exchange for runs using a 3-dimensional hypercube. The other parameters are set as follows: total population size = 400, *crossover_rate* = 0.6, *mutation_rate* = 0.5, exchange 10% of sub-population.

As the results indicate, exchanging too frequently or too infrequently may degrade the performance of the algorithm. Exchanging every 5 generations seems to be most effective for optimizing the function W.

6 Conclusion

The problems that can be solved by the genetic algorithm can be categorized in three groups:

1. Problems that work better using a large population and the serial algorithm,

2. Problems that work better using the sub-population model and the parallel algorithm,

3. Problems that work well with either using a large population and the serial algorithm, or the sub-population model and the parallel algorithm.

The function maximization problem presented in this paper belongs to the third category. Using the sub-population model for problems in this category has practical benefits, as it achieves near-linear speed-up.

The benefits of a large single population versus those of the sub-population model have been argued in the field of population genetics by Fisher and Wright[8]. According to Wright's "Shifting Balance Theory", there exist situations in population genetics in which the sub-population model succeeds but the single population model will not. It is not immediately apparent that this theory is transferable to computer science, but if it is, there may be problems which can be solved only by the parallel genetic algorithm.

Further resarch is required to identify the problems in the first category (if any), and to determine if they can benefit from other parallelization techniques.

Finally, the experiments in Table 3 suggest that the parallel algorithm may be more robust than the serial one, in that reasonable performance can be achieved by having different processors use different parameter values without determining the best possible parameter values. More investigation is required in this area, possibly studying the effects of varying other parameters in addition to mutation and crossover rates.

Acknowledgements

I would like to thank Professor Quentin Stout for his valuable advice and guidance, and Colin Underwood for his help in presenting these ideas. This work is only possible because of their enthusiasm. I also like to thank Professor John Holland for introducing me to this subject.

References

[1] J. H. Holland, *Adaptation in Natural and Artificial Systems*, University of Michigan Press, 1975.

[2] P. Grosso, *Computer Simulations of Genetic Application: Parallel Subcomponent Interaction in a Multilocus Model*, PhD Thesis, Computer and Communication Sciences, University of Michigan, 1985.

[3] J. P. Hayes, T. Mudge, Q. F. Stout, S. Colley and J. Palmer, *A Microprocessor-based Hypercube Supercomputer*, IEEE Micro, vol. 6, no. 5, Oct. 1986, pp. 6-17.

[4] A. Bethke, *Genetic Algorithms as Functional Optimizers*, PhD Thesis, Computer and Communication Sciences, University of Michigan, 1981.

[5] K. A. DeJong, *Analysis of the behavior of a class of genetic algorithms*, PhD Thesis, University of Michigan, 1975.

[6] D. H. Ackley, *Stochastic iterated genetic hillclimbing*, Carnegie-Mellon University, CMU-CS-87-107, 1987.

[7] J. J. Grefenstette, *Parallel adaptive algorithms for function optimization*, Vanderbilt University, (Preliminary Report), Technical Report CS-81-19, 1981.

[8] W. P. Provine, *Sewall Wright and Evolutionary Biology*, The University of Chicago Press, 1986.

Dim	#PEs	Sub Pop Size	(a) Exchange 10%			(b) Exchange 20%		
			Average Gens	#Runs Reaching Max	Range	Average Gens	#Runs Reaching Max	Range
0	1	400	>198	63	60-1000+	>198	63	60-1000+
1	2	200	212	64	65-615	198	64	60-675
2	4	100	201	64	55-530	>210	63	70-1000+
3	8	50	171	64	80-385	209	64	60-665
4	16	24	248	64	95-595	200	64	70-510
5	32	12	307	64	105-785	212	64	65-465
6	64	6	-	-	-	232	64	115-460

Table 1: Data for 64 runs on a hypercube with 0 to 6 dimensions

Dimension	#Processors	CPU Seconds
0	1	1548.33
1	2	787.98
2	4	393.29
3	8	199.18
4	16	98.88
5	32	54.86
6	64	37.85

Table 2: Execution times for runs of 1000 generations

Crossover Rate	Mutation Rate	Average Gens	#Runs Reaching Max	Range
0.6	0.5	171	64	80-385
0.6	0.5,1.0	150	64	45-380
0.6	0.5,2.0	199	64	65-570
0.6,1.0	0.5,1.0,1.5,2.0	153	64	65-435

Table 3: Data for 64 runs with different crossover and mutation rates (dimension=3)

Exchange Frequency (gen)	Average Gens	#Runs Reaching Max	Range
1	>222	62	70-1000+
2	>197	63	60-1000+
3	>180	63	40-1000+
5	171	64	80-385
10	>248	63	95-1000+
20	302	64	120-695

Table 4: Data for 64 runs with different frequency of exchanges (dimension=3)

Rick L. Riolo

The University of Michigan

Abstract

In Holland-type classifier systems the bucket brigade algorithm allocates strength ("credit") to classifiers that lead to rewards from environment. This paper presents results that show the bucket brigade algorithm basically works as designed—strength is passed down sequences of coupled classifiers from those classifiers that receive rewards directly from the environment to those that are stage setters. Results indicate it can take a fairly large number of trials for a classifier system to respond to changes in its environment by reallocating strength down competing sequences of classifiers that implement simple reflex and non-reflex behaviors. However, "bridging classifiers" are shown to dramatically decrease the number of times a long sequence must be executed in order reallocate strength to all the classifiers in the sequence. Bridging classifiers also were shown to be one way to avoid problems caused by sharing classifiers across competing sequences.

1 INTRODUCTION

Like all highly parallel, fine-grained, rule-based learning systems, classifier systems ([Holland, 1986a], [Burks, 1986], [Holland and Burks, 1987], [Holland, 1986b]) must solve the apportionment of credit problem. In short, the apportionment of credit problem is the problem of deciding, when many rules are active at every time step, which of those rules active at step t are necessary and sufficient for achieving some desired outcome at step $t + n$. In terms of Samuel, who first recognized the problem in the context of his checker playing program [Samuel, 1959], the problem is how to know which of the many moves (or sequences of moves) made in the early parts of a game "set the stage" for a triple jump later in the game. The problem of apportioning credit is especially difficult in complex domains in which (a) information about what is a good result is provided only occassionally, perhaps after long sequences of actions, and (b) there are millions of possible states or

state sequences, so that the system never sees the same exact sequence twice.

In classifier systems using the bucket brigade algorithm [Holland,1985], credit is allocated in the form of a value, *strength*, associated with each classifier. The strength assigned to a classifier is important for two reasons:

1. Strength determines in part what classifiers will be active at a given time step, and so controls the short term behavior of the system.

2. Strength is used by rule discovery algorithms to guide the creation and deletion of classifiers, thereby influencing the longer term learning behavior of the system.

Thus for classifier systems both to perform well and to learn, strength must be allocated properly and expeditiously by the bucket brigade algorithm.

Basically the bucket brigade algorithm acts in two ways:

1. It adjusts the strength of those classifiers that are active when a payoff is received from the environment. Each classifier's strength is changed a little at a time until it is proportional to the average of the payoffs the system receives when that classifier is active.

2. It redistributes strength from each active classifier to classifiers that posted messages that activated it. Each classifier's strength is modified a little at a time until it is proportional to the strength of the classifier(s) it activates.

Over time the bucket brigade algorithm reallocates strength from classifiers that *directly* lead to payoffs from the environment to those classifiers that *indirectly* lead to payoff, i.e., to classifiers that post messages that "set the stage" for those classifiers directly responsible for receiving payoffs.

The bucket brigade has several characteristics that make it ideal for use with highly parallel systems like classifier systems. First, the bucket brigade algorithm uses only *local* information: when adjusting the strength of a classifier,

*This work was supported by National Science Foundation Grant DCR 83-05830

it only needs to know which classifiers *directly* activated it and which classifiers it *directly* activates. There is no need for complicated book-keeping or for high-level critics to analyze sequences of actions and assign credit accordingly. Second, the bucket brigade works in a highly parallel way, changing the strength of many (or all) rules at the same time. Third, the bucket brigade acts *incrementally*, changing the strength of classifiers gradually. By changing the strength of classifiers only a small amount at a time, the classifier system tends to learn *gracefully*, without the precipitous changes in performance that may result from making a large change in response to a single, possibly anomolous, case.

One key issue for systems using the bucket brigade algorithm is how fast strength flows down long sequences of classifiers. If a whole sequence of classifiers must be activated many times in order to adjust the strength of a classifier at the beginning of the chain in response to a change in payoff associated with the last step in the sequence, the system's response to simple changes in its environment will be too slow. Wilson [Wilson, 1986] used a simple simulation to show that allocation down a sequence of classifiers can take a fairly large number of steps. (He suggested an alternative "hierarchical" bucket brigade algorithm that is designed to speed up the flow of credit down long sequences of classifiers.) Holland [Holland, 1985] mentions this problem and suggests a way to implement "bridging" classifiers that speed up the flow of strength down a long sequence of classifiers.

This paper describes some simple experiments designed to show how well the bucket brigade is able to allocate strength down long sequences of classifiers. Section 2 describes the CFS-C/FSW1 classifier system, which is used to carry out all experiments described in this paper. In Section 3, the allocation of strength down a single chain of classifiers will be examined. In Sections 4 and 5, the ability of the bucket brigade to allocate strength so that the system learns to make the proper choice at the beginning of a long sequence of steps is examined. The effects of "bridging" classifiers are also examined. In Section 6 the effect of sharing classifiers in different sequences is examined, without and with bridging classifiers.

2 THE CFS-C/FSW1 SYSTEM

All experiments described in this paper were done using the CFS-C classifier system [Riolo, 1986], set in the FSW1 ("Finite State World 1") task environment [Riolo, 1987]. This section describes the parts of the CFS-C/FSW1 system that are relevant to the experiments described in this paper. For a complete description of those systems, see the documentation cited.

Basically, the FSW1 domain is a world that is modeled as a finite Markov process, in which a *payoff* is associated with some states. The classifier system's input interface

provides a message that indicates the current state of the Markov process. The classifier's output interface provides the system with a way to alter the transition probabilities of the process, so that the system can control (in part) the path taken through the finite state world. When the classifier system visits states with non-zero payoff, that payoff is given to the system as a "reward". Thus the task for the CFS-C classifier system in the FSW1 domain is to learn to emit the appropriate signals at each step so that the Marlov process will visit states with higher payoff values as often as possible.

More formally, the FSW1 task domain is fully defined by specifying:

- A set of n states W_i, $i = 0, ..., n-1$, each with an associated payoff $\mu(W_i) \in \Re$; one state also is designated the start state.

- A set of probability transition matrices, $P(r)$, where each entry $p_{ij}(r)$ in $P(r)$ gives the probability of going to state W_j, given that the system is in state W_i and that the classifier system has emitted r as its output value ($r = 0 \ldots 15$).

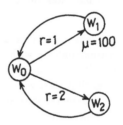

Figure 1: A simple FSW1 finite state world.

For example, consider the simple three state world shown in Figure 1. (In this and other diagrams, states are shown as circles, and arrows designate non-zero probability transitions.) W_0 is the start state. The payoff for state W_1 is 100; the payoff for the other states is 0. When the system is in state W_0, if $r = 1$ the probability of going from state W_0 to W_1 is 1.0; if $r = 2$ the probability of going from state W_0 to W_2 is 1.0. For other values of r, the probability of going from state W_0 to state W_1 or W_2 is 0. The probability of going from either W_1 or W_2 to W_0 is 1.0, no matter what the value of r. Thus if the classifier system is to maximize its payoff in this world, it must learn to set $r = 1$ whenever it is in state W_0.

The CFS-C classifier system is a standard, "Holland" type learning classifier system that consists of four basic parts:

- A *message list*, which acts as a "blackboard" for communications and short term memory. In the CFS-C classifier system, the message list has a small, maximum size.

- A *classifier list,* which consists of condition–action rules called *classifiers.* Each classifier in the CFS-C system is a two–condition classifier of the form:

$$C_1, \ C_2 \ / \ Action$$

A classifier's condition part is *satisfied* when each of the conditions C_1 and C_2 is matched by one or more messages on the message list. The second condition may be prefixed by a "~", in which case that condition is satisfied only when *no* message matches the condition C_2. A satisfied classifier produces one message for each message that matches its first condition, C_1, using the usual "pass through" procedure. Each classifier also has an associated *strength,* which is related to its usefulness in attaining rewards for the system, and a *specificity* (sometimes called its *bid ratio*), which is a measure of the generality of the classifier's conditions.

- An *input interface,* which provides the classifier system with information about its environment. In the FSW1 domain, the input interface provides one *detector* message which indicates the current state of the Markov process.

- An *output interface,* which provides a way for the classifier system to communicate with or change its environment. In the FSW1 domain, the output interface maps messages that start with a "10" (sometimes called *effector messages*) into an *effector setting,* r, $r = 0 \ldots 15$, which determines the transition probability matrix $P(r)$ used to select the next state of the Markov process.

As in other "Holland" classifier systems, messages are all strings of fixed length ℓ, built from the alphabet $\{0, 1\}$. Each condition C_i and the action part of a classifier is also a string of length ℓ, built from the alphabet $\{0, 1, \#\}$. The $\#$ acts as a "wildcard" symbol in the condition strings, and it acts as the "pass-through" symbol in the action part of a classifier.

The CFS-C/FSW1 system is run by repeatedly executing the following steps of the classifier system's "major cycle":

1. Add messages generated by the input interface to the message list. In the FSW1 domain one message, which indicates the current state $W(t)$ of the world, is added to the message list.

2. Compare all messages to all conditions of all classifiers and record all matches for classifiers that have their condition parts satisfied.

3. Generate new messsges by activating satisfied classifiers. If activating all the satisfied classifiers would produce more messages than will fit on the message list, a competition is run to determine which classifiers are to be activated. Classifiers are chosen probabilistically, without replacement, until the message list is full. The probability that a given classifier is activated is proportional to its *bid*.

4. Process the new messages through the output interface, resolving conflicts and selecting one effector setting, r, to be used for the current time step. Once r is set, the associated transition matrix $P(r)$ and the current state $W(t)$ are used to select the world state $W(t+1)$ to which the system moves.

5. Apply the bucket brigade algorithm, to redistribute strength from the environment to the system and from classifiers to other classifiers.

6. Apply *discovery algorithms,* to create new classifiers and remove classifiers that have not been useful.

7. Replace the contents of the message list with the new messages, and return to step 1.

In the CFS-C/FSW1 system, the *bid* of classifier i at step t, $B_i(t)$, is calculated as follows[1]:

$$B_i(t) = k * S_i(t) * BidRatio_i$$

k is a small constant (usually about 0.1), which acts as a "risk factor", i.e., it determines what proportion of a classifier's strength it will bid and so perhaps lose on a single step. $S_i(t)$ is the classifier's strength at step t. $BidRatio_i$ is a number between 0 and 1 that is a measure of the classifier's specificity, i.e., how many different messages it can match. A $BidRatio$ of 1 means the classifier matches exactly one message, while a $BidRatio$ of 0 means the classifier matches all messages.

When a competition is run to determine which classifiers are to be activated, the probability that a given (satisfied) classifier i will win is:

$$Prob(\ i \ wins \ ) = \beta_i(t) / \sum_j \beta_j(t)$$

The *effective bid,* $\beta_i(t)$, of a classifier i at step t, is:

$$\beta_i(t) = B_i(t)^{BidPow}$$

BidPow is a parameter that can be set to alter the shape of the probability distribution used to choose classifiers to produce messages. For example, if $BidPow = 1$ then $\beta_i(t) = B_i(t)$, i.e., a classifier's probability of producing messages is just its bid divided by the sum of bids made by all satisfied classifiers. Setting $BidPow$ to 2, 3, and so on, makes it more likely that classifiers with the highest bids

---

[1] Actually the CFS-C/FSW1 bid calculation involves other parameters not shown here, but for the experiments described in this paper, those parameters have been disabled.

will win the competition. The effects of varying $BidPow$ are considered further in section 4 of this paper.

Note that the output interface of the CFS-C/FSW1 system may have to resolve conflicts, e.g., when one classifier produces a message that says "set the effector value r to 1" and another produces a message that says "set the effector value r to 2". Since the effector can only be set to one value at a time (just as we can either lift our arm or lower it, and not both), an *effector conflict resolution mechanism* must be used. Basically, when there are conflicts the value of r is chosen probabilistically, with the probability that $r = r'$ equal to:

$$\sum_{m'} \beta_{m'}(t) / \sum_{m} \beta_{m}(t)$$

where m' ranges over the effector messages that say "set r to r'", $\beta_{m'}(t)$ is the effective bid of the classifier that posted message m', m ranges over all effector messages, and $\beta_m(t)$ is the effective bid of the classifier that posted message m. The winning r value is used to select a transition matrix $P(r)$, which in turn is used to determine to which state the system will move. Once an effector value is chosen, all messages that are inconsistent with that setting are *deleted* from the new message list.

The basis for the reallocation of strength done by the *bucket brigade algorithm* is payoffs received by the classifier system from the FSW1 environment. In the CFS-C/FSW1 system, when the Markov process enters a state W_i all classifiers that posted messages which are on the new message list (after any effector conflicts are resolved) have the *full* payoff $\mu(W_i)$ added to their strength. Thus when the activation of a classifier tends to be *directly* associated with a high reward from the environment, that classifier's strength is on average increased.

The bucket brigade algorithm also redistributes strength from classifiers to other classifiers. In particular, when a classifier posts messages, it pays the amount it bid to the classifiers that made it possible for that classifier to become active. Let $BidShare$ equal the classifier's bid, B, divided by m, number of messages that matched its conditions. Then the strength of the active classifier is decreased by $BidShare*m$ and $BidShare$ is added to the strength of each classifier that produced a message that matched the activated classifier's conditions. (If a classifier is matched by one or more "detector" messages, i.e., messages from the system's input interface, the classifier's strength is still decremented by $BidShare$ for each detector message used, but that amount is not added to the strength of any other classifier. Thus just as the environment is the ultimate source of strength, in the form of payoffs, it is also the ultimate sink for strength, when detector messages are used.)

In summary, the strength $S_i(t+1)$ of a classifier i at $t+1$ is:

$$S_i(t+1) = S_i(t) + R(t) + P_i(t) - B_i(t)$$

where $S_i(t)$ is the strength of classifier i at t, $R(t)$ is the reward from the environment during step (t), $P_i(t)$ is the sum of all payments to classifier i from classifiers that matched messages produced by i during the previous step, and $B_i(t)$ is the classifier's bid during step t. Clearly a classifier's strength reaches a fixed-point when the amount of strength it receives is equal to the amount it pays. Thus in the long run a classifier's fixed-point strength, S_{fp}, approaches:

$$S_{fp} = (R + P) / (k * BidRatio)$$

where R and P are the average amounts the classifier receives *per activation* as rewards from the environment and payments from other classifiers, respectively.

Since the focus of this paper is on the allocation of strength by the bucket brigade algorithm amoung existing classifiers, rather than the creation of new classifiers, the CFS-C/FSW1 system's rule discovery algorithms are not used in the experiments described in this paper. Instead, all classifiers are added to the initial classifier list. Those classifiers remain unchanged, except for their strengths, during the course of each experiment.

3 SIMPLE SEQUENCES OF CLASSIFIERS

To get a feel for how the bucket brigade algorithm works in the FSW1 domain, consider the finite state world shown in Figure 2. There are 13 states in this world, $W_i, i = 0, \ldots, 12$. State W_{12} has an associated payoff of 100, while the payoff for all other states is 0. The start state is W_0. The classifier system must set $r = 1$ to move from state W_0 to W_{12}; i.e., $p_{ij}(1) = 1.0$ for $j = i + 1, i = 0 \ldots 11$.

Figure 2: A single path of states leading to a reward at state W_{12}.

When the system reaches state W_{12}, it will go to state W_0 by default; i.e., $p_{ij}(0) = 1.0$ for $i = 12, j = 0$. (In this and subsequent descriptions of finite state worlds, all transitions not mentioned have probability 0.) Thus with a perfect set of classifiers, the system could achieve a reward of 100 every 13 cycles.

The CFS-C/FSW1 system was run in this world with twelve classifiers, each with a starting strength of 50. Classifier 1 was of the form:

$$d_0, d_0/e_1, r = 1$$

where each condition "d_0" matches the detector message for state W_0, and the action "$e_1, r = 1$" posts an effector message e_1 that sets the effector value r to 1. (In order to make the classifiers more readily understandable, they will be shown in an "interpreted" form rather than in terms of strings built from the $\{0, 1, \#\}$ alphabet.) Classifiers 2 through 12 are of the form:

$$e_{i-1}, e_{i-1}/e_i, r = 1$$

where the condition "e_{i-1}" matches the effector message produced by classifier $i - 1, i = 2, \ldots, 12$, and the action part of each classifier i produces an effector message e_i which sets r to 1.

In short, when the Markov process enters state W_0, classifier 1 is activated, which posts an effector message that moves the system to state W_1. Since classifier 1 is activated by detector messages, it pays its bid to the system rather than to some other classifier. At the next time step, classifier 2 is activated by the message produced by classifier 1, so classifier 2 pays its entire bid to classifier 1. Classifier 2 also posts an effector message that moves the system to state W_2. Thus the process continues, each classifier being activated by and paying its bid to the classifier that was active on the prior step. Finally the Markov process reaches state W_{12}, in which case the classifier active during that step, classifier 12, receives the payoff associated with that state (100). The system then returns to state W_0, and the cycle starts again.

Figure 3 shows the results of running the 12 classifiers described above for a period of 3000 cycles (about 230 passes through the sequence), using $k = 0.1$ and $BidPow = 1$. The strength of classifiers 1, 4, 7, 10, 11, and 12 are shown plotted against the number of time steps executed. Figure 3 clearly shows the wave of strength flowing from

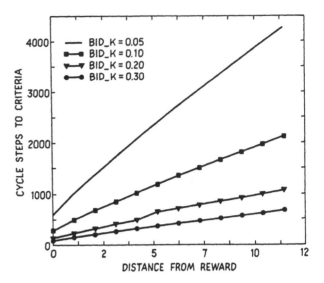

Figure 4: The number of steps required for a classifier in a chain of coupled classifiers to reach 90% of its fixed-point strength, plotted against the number of steps to the end of the chain, for $k = 0.05, 0.1, 0.2,$ and 0.3.

classifier 12, which receives the reward directly from the environment and reaches its fixed-point strength first, to classifier 1, which is farthest in the chain from the environmental reward and so reaches its fixed-point strength last. (The blips are artifacts of when strength is recorded: sometimes a classifier's strength is displayed at the end of a step in which it posted a message, so that it has just had its strength reduced by its bid but it has not yet been paid by the next classifier in the chain.)

As expected, the fixed-point strength, S_{fp}, of all the classifiers in this experiment is the same (1000), since each classifier pays its full bid to its one predecessor (or to the system for the detector message, in the case of classifier 1). The number of cycles it takes for a classifier n steps from the environmental reward to reach 90% of its S_{fp} fits the following equation:

$$t = 286 + 155n$$

where $n = 0$ for classifier 12, $n = 1$ for classifier 11, and so on. In terms of the number of passes through the sequence of states (i.e., the number of rewards received), this works out to be:

$$R = 22 + 11.9n$$

This number is in good agreement with the value arrived at in [Wilson, 1986], using a simple simulation of the bucket brigade.

One way to speed the flow of strength back through a sequence of classifiers is to increase k, the bid constant that specifies what proportion of a classifier's strength is to be risked on any one bid. Figure 4 shows a comparison of the

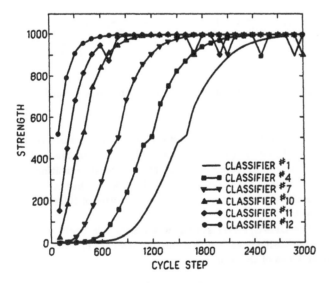

Figure 3: The flow of strength down a simple sequence of coupled classifiers. Classifier 12 leads directly to a reward, and classifier 1 is at the start of the sequence.

results obtained when the 12 classifiers described earlier were run using values of k = 0.05, 0.1, 0.2, and 0.3. The horizontal axis shows the number of steps a classifier is from the environmental reward. The vertical axis shows the number of cycles it takes for a classifier to reach 90% of its fixed-point strength. Higher values of k result in faster flow of strength down the sequence of classifiers. For example, for a classifier 10 steps from the reward, the number of passes through the sequence is 59 for $k = 0.3$, compared to 141 for $k = 0.1$.

4 CHOSING BETWEEN SIMPLE SEQUENCES OF CLASSIFIERS

Clearly one important characteristic of the bucket brigade algorithm is the number of cycles it takes for strength to flow down a chain of coupled classifiers. Another important measure of the bucket brigade algorithm's performance is the ability of the classifier system to respond to changes in the payoffs associated with states.

For example, consider the CFS-C/FSW1 world shown in Figure 5. There are 19 states in this world. The start state is W_0. When the system is in W_0, if the classifiers set the effector value r to 1, then the system goes to state W_1 with probability 1; if the classifiers set r to 2, then the system goes to W_{11}. Once the top or bottom path is chosen, the Markov process can be moved through the intervening states to W_9 or W_{19} by continuing to set r to 1 or 2, respectively. When the process reaches state W_9 or W_{19}, it always returns to state W_0.

The CFS-C/FSW1 system was run in the world described above using the follwing 18 classifiers:

$$d_0, d_0/e_1, r = 1 \qquad (1)$$
$$d_0, d_0/e_{11}, r = 2 \qquad (11)$$
$$e_{i-1}, e_{i-1}/e_i, r = 1 \qquad (i = 2 \ldots 9)$$
$$e_{i-1}, e_{i-1}/e_i, r = 2 \qquad (i = 12 \ldots 19)$$

(The numbers in parentheses on the right serve to identity the classifiers.) Each classifier has $BidRatio = 1$. Basically, the classifiers 1 and 11 compete to become active when the system is in state W_0. Those classifiers try to have the system take the top or bottom path, respectively, by (a) setting the effector value to 1 or 2, and (b) producing a message that sets the stage for the rest of the classifiers in its associated sequence to fire, one after another. (Note that 1 and 2 can't post messages at the same time, since they try to set r to different values.) For example, if classifier 1 wins the competition, its message sets r to 1, so that the system moves to state W_1. In the next step, classifier 2 is matched by the message produced by classifier 1, so classifier 2 pays its bid to classifier 1, and the system is moved to state W_2. This process continues until the system reaches state W_9 and classifier 9 receives the payoff associated with that state.

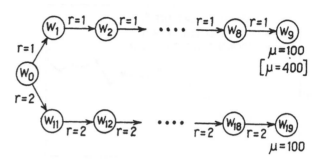

Figure 5: Two competing paths of states leading to rewards at states W_9 and W_{19}.

Suppose states W_9 and W_{19} both have a payoff of 100, and all other states have a payoff of 0. In this case it does not matter what path the system takes—the maximum payoff rate it can achieve is 100 per 10 cycles. Note that the fixed-point strength of all classifiers in both sequences is 1000 (assuming $k = 0.1$ and each classifier has a $BidRatio = 1$). In particular, classifiers 1 and 11 will have the same fixed-point strengths, so each will have a 0.50 probability of winning the competition, and so the system will go down each chain 50% of the time.

Suppose the payoff associated with state W_9 is changed to 400. In this case the optimal payoff, 400 per 10 cycles, can be achieved by always taking the top path. Thus to achieve optimal performance, the bucket brigade must reallocate strength so that classifier 1, the classifier that causes the system to go down the top path, has a higher fixed-point strength than classifier 11, the one that causes the system to go down the bottom path. The faster the system can reallocate strength, the faster the system can respond to the change in its environment.

Figure 6 shows the results of running the above classifiers in the world described above, with $\mu(W_9) = 400$ and $\mu(W_{19}) = 100$. (The results in this and the rest of the experiments described in this paper are the average of 10 runs, each started with a different seed for the system's pseudo-random number generator.) All classifiers had an initial strength of 1000, i.e., the system was started as if it had been run with $W_9 = W_{19} = 100$ until the classifiers all reached their fixed-point strengths. $BidPow$ was set to 1, i.e., a classifier's effective bid equals its bid. k was set to 0.1 in this and all the rest of the experiments described in this paper. Given that $BidRatio = 1$ for all 18 classifiers, the expected fixed-point strengths for classifiers in the top and bottom chains is 4000 and 1000, respectively. The maximum payoff rate (per 200 cycles) is 8000, and the payoff expected if the choice of path is made at random is 5000.

Figure 6 shows the marginal payoff the system received plotted against cycle steps executed. The strength of classifiers 1 and 11, the classifiers that compete to choose the

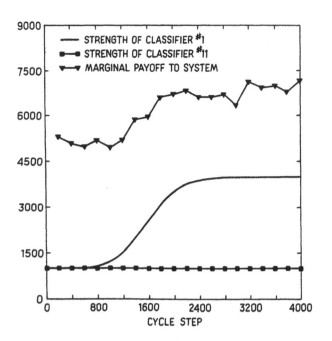

Figure 6: Marginal performance and the strength of classifiers 1 and 11 when the system is run with two competing sequences in the world shown in Figure 5. The rewards at the end of the sequences chosen by classifiers 1 and 11 were 400 and 100, respectively.

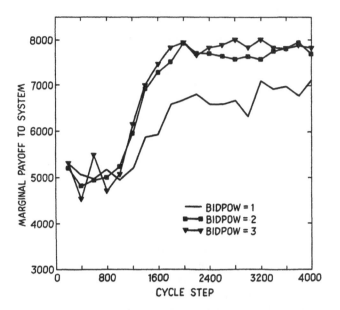

Figure 7: Marginal performance when the system was run with competing sequences of classifiers as in Figure 6, using three different values of *BidPow*.

path the system takes, is also shown. Note that as the strength of classifier 1 increases toward its fixed-point value, marginal performance also increases. Let the fixed point payoff, P_{fp}, be defined as the average marginal payoff in the last one quarter of a run. Then the average P_{fp} for the runs shown in Figure 6 was 6870, which is 85.9% of the optimal payoff rate. The system's performance is less than optimal because the competition is stochastic—the higher strength classifier has a higher probability of winning but it doesn't always win.

Also note that it takes about 1700 steps (170 trials) for the system to reach 90% of the P_{fp}. This is a little more than might be expected given the results described in the previous section; the reason for the longer observed time is that the system often traverses the lower path, in which case increased strength is not flowing down the top chain.

One way to increase the fixed-point payoff rate is to bias the effective bid in favor of high strength classifiers by setting $BidPow > 1$. The following table compares the results obtained for $BidPow = 1, 2$, and 3:

BidPow	P_{fp} (% Max)
1	85.9
2	96.7
3	98.3

As expected, increasing *BidPow* increases the payoff rate. Figure 7 shows the marginal performance obtained in these experiments plotted against the number of major-cycle steps executed by the system. Not only are the fixed-point performance levels increased by increasing *BidPow*, but the number of steps it takes the system to respond to the change in payoff is decreased somewhat. In the rest of the experiments described in this paper, *BidPow* is set to 3.

Even with $BidPow = 3$, it takes the classifier system a large number of passes down the full sequence to learn to take the path to the higher reward: as Figure 7 shows, it takes about 100–120 passes (1000–1200 cycles) to begin to respond to the change in the environment, and about 160–170 passes (1600–1700 cycles) to reach 90% of the fixed-point performance rate.

One way suggested by Holland [Holland,1985] to speed up reallocation of strength down a long sequence of classifiers is to introduce a "bridging" classifier. Basically, a bridging classifier (sometimes called an "epoch marking" or a "support" classifier) is one that is activated by a message produced by the first classifier in a sequence, and which remains active until the payoff state at the end of the sequence is reached. Since all classifiers that are active when a payoff is achieved have that payoff added to their strengths, the bridging classifier has its strength increased the first time the sequence is executed. The next time the sequence is executed, when the bridging classifier again is activated by the message produced by the first classifier in the chain, its payment to that first classifier reflects the payoff it received on the first pass down the sequence. In this way, the change in payoff at the end of a long sequence of classifiers is passed almost immediately to the classifier at the beginning of the sequence.

To test the effectiveness of bridging classifiers, the CFS-C/FSW1 system was run using the same finite state world shown in Figure 5, using the same 18 classifiers described above plus two more bridging classifiers (one for the top sequence and one for the bottom one). In particular, the bridging classifiers were:

$$(e_1 \mid m_{10}), \sim d_9/m_{10} \qquad (10)$$
$$(e_{11} \mid m_{20}), \sim d_{19}/m_{20} \qquad (20)$$

Both of the classifiers have $BidRatio = 0.5$. Classifier 10, the bridge for the top sequence, says "If the message from classifier 1 or from classifier 10 is in the message list, and the detector message for state W_9 is not in the list, then post message m_{10}". Thus if classifier 1 posts a message on step t, classifier 10 will be activated on the next step, and it will use the message it produces to activate itself until the system reaches state W_9, the end of the top path. Classifier 20 acts similarly for the bottom chain.

The starting strength for all classifiers was set to the fixed-point strength expected when the payoffs for states W_9 and W_{19} are both 100. The payoff for state W_9 was then set to 400, and the system was run for 4000 major-cycle steps.

Figure 8 compares the results obtained when the system was run with and without the bridging classifiers. Both marginal performance (per 200 steps) and the strength of classifier 1 is plotted versus cycle step. (The strength of classifier 11 doesn't change in these experiments—just the ratio of the strength of classifier 1 to 11.) Note that with the bridging classifier, the strength of classifier 1 begins to rise almost immediately, within the first 200 cycles, as does the marginal performance. On the other hand, without the bridging classifier, the strength of classifier 1 and the marginal performance doesn't begin to rise until about cycle step 1100. Similarly, with the bridging classifier marginal performance reaches 90% of its fixed-point level (98.4% of the maximum, $StdDev = 1.1\%$) in 600-700 steps, whereas without the bridging classifier it takes 1600–1700 steps.

There are many other ways to implement "bridging" classifiers. For example, the following classifiers also serve as bridges for the sequences 1–9 and 11–19:

$$e_i, e_i/m_{10} \quad i = 1 \ldots 9 \qquad (21)$$
$$e_i, e_i/m_{20} \quad i = 11 \ldots 19 \qquad (22)$$

Classifier 21 says "If the message list contains a message posted by any of the classifiers in the top sequence, then post a message". This classifier will be activated by classifier 1 and remain active until the system receives a payoff in state W_9. The difference between the this type of epoch marker and the one described earlier is that this one is activated by every classifier in a sequence, rather than just

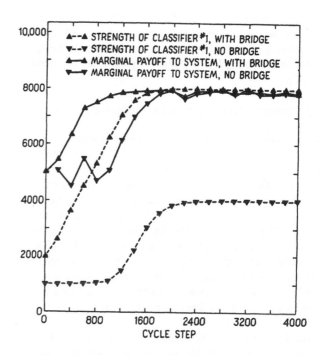

Figure 8: Marginal performance and the strength of classifier 1 observed when the system is run in the world shown in Figure 5, with and without "bridging" classifiers.

the first one in the sequence. Thus the bridging classifier passes strength to all the classifiers in the chain rather than to just the first one. (Classifier 22 acts similary for the bottom sequence.)

To test the effectiveness of the second kind of bridging classifier, the system was run in the world described in Figure 5 with the 18 classifiers described earlier and the bridging classifiers 21 and 22. The results were similar to the results obtained using the bridging classifiers 10 and 20: the strength of classifier 1 began to rise immediately, in the first 200 steps, as did the marginal performance. The system again reached 90% of its fixed-point performance rate in about 700 cycle steps.

The main difference between using the second type of bridging classifier and the first is the fixed-point strengths of the classifiers in the top sequence. With the first type of bridging classifier, the fixed-point strength of classifier 1 was changed from 2000 (for $\mu(W_9) = 100$) to 8000 (for $\mu(W_9) = 400$); the fixed-point strengths of the other classifiers in the top sequence changed from 1000 to 4000. With the second type of bridging classifier, the fixed-point strength of classifier 1 was changed from 2000 (for $\mu(W_9) = 100$) to 8000 (for $\mu(W_9) = 400$); the fixed-point strengths of the other classifiers in the to sequence changed from 1000 to values ranging from 7406 (for classifier 2) to 4000 (for classifier 9). The reason classifiers 2 through 9 have different fixed-point strengths is that the second type of bridging classifier pays some of its strength to each classifier in the sequence, but it pays more to the classifiers at the beginning of the sequence, since that is when the bridging classifier's strength is the highest (just after receiving a payoff).

5 SEQUENCES WITH MULTIPLE MESSAGE SOURCES

In the experiments described in the previous section, each classifier (except the first one) in a sequence was activated solely by the message produced by the classifier that preceded it in the sequence. Those sequences implemented something akin to a *reflex*: once the first classifier in the sequence is activiated by some signal from the environment, the rest of the classifiers in the chain are activated, one after another, until the last one fires, no matter what effect their actions are having. Since each classifier in the sequence used only messages from its predecessor, each paid its full bid to that predecessor, so that all classifiers in a sequence had the same fixed-point strength (ignoring the effects of bridging classifiers).

Another type of classifier sequence is one in which one or more classifiers after the first one in a sequence have conditions that match messages produced by sources other than their predecessors in the sequence. For example, some of the classifiers could have one condition that matches a message produced by its predecessor and a second condition that matches a detector message produced by the system's input interface. Sequences of this type are *non-reflex* sequences: the system can monitor the effects of executing each step, so that if the sequence isn't producing the expected results (as indicated by messages on the message list), the sequence can be stopped or alternatives steps can be executed.

To test the effectiveness of the bucket brigade algorithm in allocating strength down non-reflex chains, the CFS-C/FSW1 system again was run in the finite state world shown in Figure 5. In these experiments the following nine classifiers were used for the top path:

$$d_0, d_0/e_1, r = 1 \qquad (1)$$
$$e_3, d_3/e_4, r = 1 \qquad (4)$$
$$e_6, d_6/e_7, r = 1 \qquad (7)$$
$$e_{i-1}, e_{i-1}/e_i, r = 1 \qquad i = 2, 3, 5, 6, 8, 9$$

Classifier 1 is matched by state W_0. Once it is activated, classifier 2 is activated by the message produced by classifier 1, and then classifier 3 is activated by classifier 2's message. Classifier 4 is activated only if classifier 3 posted a message on the previous step *and* if the system is in state W_3. Classifiers 5 and 6 then fire reflexively, and classifier 7 fires only if the system is in state W_6. Classifiers 8 and 9 then fire reflexively.

A similar set of classifiers (11 to 19) was included for traversing the bottom path. Classifier 1 and 11 compete when the Markov process is in state W_0 to guide the system down the top or bottom path, respectively.

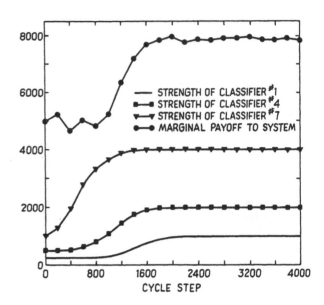

Figure 9: Marginal performance and the strength of classifiers 1, 4, and 7 when the system is run with two competing non-reflex sequences of classifiers, in which classifiers 4 and 7 each use one detector message and one message from their predecessors in the sequence.

Figure 9 shows the results of running this set of classifiers in the world shown in Figure 5, with the payoff for state $W_{19} = 100$ and the payoff for state W_9 changed from 100 to 400 at step 0. The marginal performance (per 200 steps) is plotted against the major cycle step executed. The strength of classifier's 7, 4, and 1 are also plotted. As expected, the strength of 7 begins to rise first, since it is closest in the sequence to the reward state, followed by the strength of classifier 4 and then 1. When the strength of classifier 1 begins to rise the marignal performance begins to rise, since the classifier 1 begins to win the competition with classifier 11 more often, thus leading the system down the top path to the higher payoff.

Note, however, the fixed-point strength of classifier 4 is 1/2 that of 7, and strength of classifier 1 is in turn 1/2 that of 4. The reason for this drop is that classifiers 4 and 7 pay only 1/2 of their bid to their predecessor classifiers; the other half of their bids is paid to the system for the detector messages that match those classifiers. In general, then, any sequence that has n classifiers that use messages not from their predecessors in the chain will have an exponential (in n) fall-off in strength down the sequence.

In this experiment this exponential fall-off didn't hinder the ability of the system to respond to the change in payoffs at the end of the sequences, since *both* competing sequences contain the same number of classifiers using messages from multiple sources. In other classifier structures, where the competing sequences have different number of classifiers

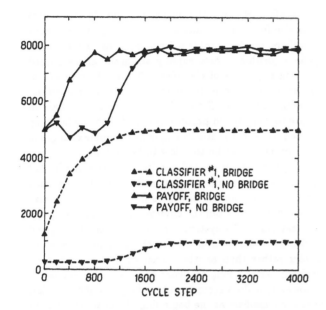

Figure 10: Marginal performance and the strength of classifier 1 when the system is run with two competing non-reflex sequences of classifiers, with and without "bridging" classifiers.

using messages from multiple sources, the results would be different.

Figure 9 also shows that the response time of the non-reflex sequence was about the same as was observed with the reflex-like sequence (described in the previous section). To see if bridging classifiers could speed up the learning rate in non-reflex sequences, the classifiers described above were run with the two bridging classifiers, 10 and 20, described in the previous section.

Figure 10 shows the results obtained for the non-reflex sequence when run with and without bridging classifiers. As with the reflex-like sequences, the rate of learning with the non-reflex sequence is greatly increased by the use of a bridging classifier like classifier 10. With the bridging classifier, the strength of classifier 1 and the system's performance began to increase immediately, in the first 200 cycles, and it reached 90% of its fixed-point performance rate in about 700 cycles. Also note that the fixed-point strength of classifier 1 is now 5000: the strength passed through the bridging classifier is able to overcome the exponential fall-off of strength observed in non-reflex chains without bridging classifiers.

6 SEQUENCES WITH SHARED PARTS

Because classifier systems exchange information through a fully open "blackboard", the message list, any classifier can be used in any context, as long as the message list contains messages that satisfy the classifier's conditions. One advantage of this architecture is that classifiers that are created

for use in one domain can be used in other domains that are similar. For example, a group of classifiers (e.g., to control a robot's "hand") that were discovered while the system was learning to do one task also could be used to solve some other task, greatly reducing the time required to learn the second task. This "knowledge sharing" not only makes it possible to learn faster, it also leads to a more economical use of classifiers, since each situation will not require its own unique classifiers.

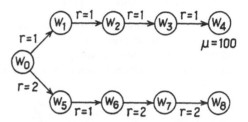

Figure 11: Paths leading to rewards at states W_4 and W_8.

In order to explore the effect of shared classifiers on the allocation of strength by the bucket brigade algorithm, the CFS-C/FSW1 system was run in the simple finite state world shown in Figure 11. There are 9 states, in this world. The start state is W_0. When the system is in W_0, if the classifiers set the effector value r to 1, then the system goes to state W_1 with probability 1; if the classifiers set r to 2, then the system goes to W_5. Once the top path is chosen, the Markov process can be moved through the intervening states to W_4 by continuing to set r to 1. If the bottom path is chosen, in order to move to W_8 the system must first set r to 1 to get to W_6 and then set r to 2 for the rest of the bottom path. When the process reaches to state W_4 or W_8, it always returns to state W_0. State W_4 has a payoff of 100; all other states have 0 payoff.

The CFS-C/FSW1 system was run in the world shown in Figure 11 with the following 8 classifiers:

$$d_0, d_0/e_1, r = 1 \qquad (1)$$
$$e_{i-1}, e_{i-1}/e_i, r = 1 \qquad (i = 2, 3, 4) \qquad (2)$$
$$d_0, d_0/e_5, r = 2 \qquad (5)$$
$$e_5, e_5/e_6, r = 1 \qquad (6)$$
$$e_{i-1}, e_{i-1}/e_i, r = 2 \qquad (i = 7, 8) \qquad$$

Classifiers 1 and 5 compete to select the path to be followed, i.e., 1 selects the top path and 5 selects the bottom. Once a path is chosen the rest of the classifiers in each sequence (2–4 or 6–8) are executed in order. Note that there are no classifiers shared between the two sequences in this case.

The system was also run with classifiers similar to those shown above, but with classifiers 2 and 6 replaced by the following single classifier:

$$e_{2,5}, e_{1,5}/e_9, r = 1 \qquad (9)$$

Classifier 9 is shared by the two sequences: it matches messages produced by either classifier 1 or classifier 5, and sets the effector value r to 1. (Classifiers 3 and 7 were modified so they both respond to to the message produced by classifier 9; "pass-through" symbols were used to ensure that classifiers 3 and 7 fire only when classifiers 1 and 5, respectively, were fired two steps before.)

The set of classifiers with the shared classifier, 9, was also run with the following bridging classifiers:

$$(e_1 \mid m_{10}), \sim d_4/m_{10} \qquad (10)$$
$$(e_5 \mid m_{11}), \sim d_8/m_{11} \qquad (11)$$

Classifier 10 serves to bridge the top sequence, and classifier 11 serves to bridge the bottom sequence.

All classifiers were started with a strength of 1000. The following table shows the results obtained for the three sets of classifiers:

	P_{fp}	$S_{fp,1}$	$S_{fp,5}$
No Sharing	3880	2048	651
Shared Classifier	1990	1075	1065
Shared, with Bridge	3913	6035	1677

When no classifiers are shared, the system basically achieves the optimal fixed-point performance (4000 per 200 steps). However, when a classifier is shared the system's performance is the about what it could achieve by choosing the path at random (2000).

The performance with shared classifiers is consistent with the fixed-point strengths of classifiers 1 and 5, which are about the same. When those classifiers compete to select a path, they each win 50% of the time. As a little thought will show, the reason classifiers 1 and 5 have the same strength when classifier 9 is shared between the chains is obvious: both 1 and 5 are paid only from classifier 9, and the fixed-point strength of classifier 9 is just the average of the payments made to it whenever it used.

Adding a bridging classifier rectifies this situation: classifier 1 now gets income from both classifier 9 and its bridge classifier, 10, and classifier 5 gets income from classifier 9 and its bridge, classifier 11. Since the bridging classifier 10 gets the 100 payoff, while classifier 11 gets 0, the strength of classifier 10 is greater than that of 11, and in turn the strength of classifier 1 is greater than that of 5. Thus adding a bridging classifier restores the fixed-point performance rate to near the maximum.

7 CONCLUSIONS

The apportionment of credit problem is the problem of deciding, when many rules are active at every time step, which of those rules active at step t are necessary and sufficient for achieving some desired outcome at step $t+n$. In classifier systems using the bucket brigade algorithm, credit is allocated in the form of a value, *strength*, associated with each classifier. Because the bucket brigade algorithm uses only local information to incrementally change the strength of classifiers, one key problem for systems using the bucket brigade algorithm is how rapidly strength can be passed down long sequences of classifiers. If a whole sequence of classifiers must be activated many times in order to adjust the strength of a classifier at the beginning of the chain in response to a change in payoff associated with the last step in the sequence, the system's response to simple changes in its environment may be too slow to be useful.

This paper has presented results that show the bucket brigade basically works as designed—strength is passed down a chain of coupled classifiers from those that receive the reward directly from the environment to those that are "stage setters". The system can thereby learn to respond to a change in the environment by choosing to activate one classifier rather than another, even when a reward is received only after a long sequence of classifiers is activated.

However, it does seem to take a large number of trials before the classifiers at the beginning of a chain reach their fixed-point strengths, and so alter the choice of paths to take. While increasing the bid constant k can speed the flow of strength, a large k means classifiers are risking a large proportion of their strength on each bid they make, so that there is not much room for classifiers to make mistakes. Increasing the *BidPow* parameter was shown to increase the fixed-point payoff rate the system will achieve, and to slightly decrease the systems response time to a change in payoff at the end of the sequence.

The bucket-brigade algorithm was shown to allocate strength down sequences that implement both "reflex" like subroutines and non-reflex like sequences. The system can respond to changes in payoff at the end of two competing non-reflex sequences just as fast as it can to changes that occur at the end of two competing reflex sequences. However, the fixed-point strengths of classifiers in non-reflex sequences fall off exponentially with each classifier that uses a message not from its predecessor in the sequence. This drop in strength could present problems for non-reflex sequences that try to compete with reflex-like sequences, and it could have effects on the creation and deletion of rules if strength is used to bias the rule discovery algorithms used by the system.

One way to ameliorate the fall of strength in non-reflex chains that use only detector messages is to change the bucket brigade algorithm so that classifiers pay less than the full *BidShare* for detector messages. This would mean that classifiers that match detector messages will in general have higher fixed-point strengths than other classifiers. The higher fixed-point strengths may bias the system's rule discovery algorithms to create more detector messages—a bias which makes some sense, since the system should put a high priority on using messages from its environment. On the other hand, such a bias in favor of classifiers that use detector messages won't solve the exponential strength fall-off problem for non-reflex sequences that use messages from other classifiers.

"Bridging" classifiers were shown to have many effects on the allocation of strength and the performance resulting from competing sequences of classifiers. Bridging classifiers lead to a dramatic decrease in the number of passes the system must make down a sequence before it can respond to a change in the environment, for both reflex and non-reflex sequences. Bridging classifiers also allocate additional strength to the earlier classifiers in non-reflex sequences, overcoming the exponential fall-off of strength seen without such bridging classifiers.

Note that classifier sequences with bridging classifiers require the same number of passes down the chain to respond to a change in payoffs at the end of the sequence, no matter how long the sequence is. For example, when the experiments described in Section 4 were repeated with sequences of 19 classifiers, the system's performance with bridging classifiers again began to increase almost immediately, within the first 15–20 trials, just as it did with sequences of 9 classifiers. Without bridging classifiers, the length 9 sequence required about 120 trials to respond, whereas the length 19 sequence required 250 trials.

One way to decrease further the response time might be to use multiple bridging classifiers for each sequence. Each bridge would pass additional strength to the first classifier in the sequence, enabling it to dominate the competition sooner.

There are many ways to implement bridging classifiers. Two ways were tried in experiments described in this paper. While each type of bridging classifier acted to decrease the system's response time, each also resulted in somewhat different distributions of strength over the classifiers in a sequence. These differences in the fixed-point strengths may have important effects on long term learning in the system if strengths are used to guide the creation and deletion of classifiers. Other types of bridging classifiers should be tried to see what effects they have.

Finally, sharing clasifiers between sequences could be a very good way to promote transfer of knowledge from one domain to another, and to economically use the same rules in more than one context. However, experiments described in this paper show that sharing classifiers can lead to problems for the allocation of strength down sequences of classifiers by the bucket brigade algorithm. Basically, sharing classifiers means the information being passed from classifier to classifier (in the form of strength) is lost, or at least greatly attenuated, when shared classifiers are involved. Simple bridging classifiers were shown to be one way to avoid the problem caused by shared classifiers.

REFERENCES

[Burks, 1986] Burks, Arthur W. "A Radically Non-Von Neumann Architecture for Learning and Discovery." In *CONPAR 86: Conference on Algorithms and Hardware for Parallel Processing, September 17-19, Proceedings.*, 1-17. Wolfgang Handler, *etal.* (Eds.). Springer-Verlag, Berlin, 1986.

[Holland,1985] Holland, J. H. "Properties of the Bucket Brigade." *Proceedings of an International Conference on Genetic Algorithms and their Applications,* 1-7. John J. Grefenstette (Ed.). Carnegie-Mellon University, Pittsburg, 1985.

[Holland, 1986a] Holland, John H. "Escaping Brittleness: The Possibilities of General-Purpose Learning Algorithms Applied to Parallel Rule-Based Systems." In *Machine Learning: An Artificial Intelligence Approach, Volume II*, Michalski, Ryszard S., Carbonell, Jamie G., and Mitchell, Tom M. (Eds). Morgan Kaufman Publishers, Inc., Los Altos, CA (1986).

[Holland and Burks, 1987] Holland, John H. and Burks, Arthur W. "Adaptive Computing System Capable of Learning and Discovery." United States patent applied for (1987).

[Holland, 1986b] Holland, John H., Holyoak, Keith J., Nisbett, Richard E. and Paul A. Thagard. *Induction. Processes of Inference, Learning, and Discovery.* The MIT Press, Cambridge, MA, 1986.

[Riolo, 1986] Riolo, Rick L. "CFS-C: A Package if Domain Independent Subroutines for Implementing Classifier Systems in Arbitrary, User-Defined Environments." Logic of Computers Group, Division of Computer Science and Engineering, University of Michigan, Ann Arbor, 1986.

[Riolo, 1987] Riolo, Rick L. "CFS-C/FSW1: An Implementation of the CFS-C Classifier System in a Domain that Involves Learning to Control a Markov Process." Logic of Computers Group, Division of Computer Science and Engineering, University of Michigan, Ann Arbor, 1987 [in prep.].

[Riolo, 1987] Riolo, Rick L. "Bucket Brigade Performance: II. Simple Default Hierarchies." [in this procedings...]

[Samuel, 1959] Samuel, A. L. "Some Studies in Machine Learning Using the Game of Checkers." *IBM Journal of Research and Development, 3,* 211-232 (1959).

[Wilson, 1986] Wilson, Stewart W. "Hierarchical Credit Allocation in a Classifier System." *Research Memo RIS No. 37r.* The Rowland Institute of Science, Cambridge MA, 1986.

BUCKET BRIGADE PERFORMANCE: II. DEFAULT HIERARCHIES

Rick L. Riolo

The University of Michigan

ABSTRACT

Learning systems that operate in environments with huge numbers of states must be able to categorize the states into equivalence classes that can be treated alike. Holland-type classifier systems can learn to categorize states by building default hierarchies of classifiers (rules). However, for default hierarchies to work properly classifiers that implement exception rules must be able to control the system when they are applicable, thus proventing the default rules from making mistakes. This paper presents results that show the standard bucket brigade algorithm does not lead to correct exception rules always winning the competition with the default rules they protect. A simple modification to the bucket brigade algorithm is suggested, and results are presented that show this modification works as desired: default hierarchies can be made to achieve payoff rates as near to optimal as desired.

1 INTRODUCTION

Any learning system that is to operate in environments with huge numbers of states must be able to *categorize* the states into equivalence classes that can be treated alike. For rule-based systems like classifier systems ([Holland, 1986a], [Burks, 1986], [Holland and Burks, 1987]) the problem involves finding a set of classifiers (condition/action rules) that induce the appropriate equivalence classes.

One approach to this problem is to try to find a set of rules that never make mistakes and that partition the whole environment. Such a set of rules in effect establishes a homomorphic model of the world. The problem with this approach is that realistic environments typically involve millions of possible states, with very complicated underlying equivalence classes, of which the system may have sampled only a small fraction. In such situations it would take a vast number of rules to establish a homomorphic model of the world.

Another approach is to implement a *default hierarchy* ([Holland, 1985], [Holland, 1986b]) of rules. A default hierarchy is a multi-level structure in which classifiers (rules) at the top levels are very general. Each general rule responds to broad set of states, so that just a few rules can cover all possible states of the world. Of course since a general rule responds in the same way to many states that don't really belong in the same category, it will often make mistakes. To correct the mistakes made by the general classifiers, lower level, *exception* rules are added to the default hierarchy. The lower level classifiers are more specific than the higher level rules: each exception rule responds to a subset of the situations covered by some more general rule.

Default hierarchies have several features that make them well suited for learning systems that must build models of very complex domains:

- Default hierarchies can be made as error-free as necessary, by adding classifiers to cover exceptions to the top level rules, to cover exceptions to the exceptions, and so on, until the required degree of accuracy is achieved.

- Default hierarchies are the basis for building *quasi-homomorphic* models of the world, which generally require far fewer rules to implement a given degree of accuracy than do equivalent homomorphic models [Holland, 1986b].

- Default hierarchies make it possible for the system to learn *gracefully*, since adding rules to cover exceptions won't cause the system's performance to change drastically, even when the new rules are incorrect.

This paper describes some simple experiments with default hierarchies implemented in the CFS-C/FSW1 classifier system [Riolo, 1987b]. These experiments show that when default hierarchies are built in a top down manner, by adding rules to cover exceptions, overall performance does improve as predicted. However, using the standard bucket brigade algorithm, the system does not achieve the performance expected. The reasons for this lower than expected performance are explained, and a modification to the bidding mechanism used in the standard bucket brigade algorithm is proposed. This modification is shown to lead to performance as close to the expected performance as desired.

---

*This work was supported by National Science Foundation Grant DCR 83-05830

2 THE CFS-C/FSW1 SYSTEM

All experiments described in this paper were done using the CFS-C classifier system [Riolo, 1986], set in the FSW1 ("Finite State World 1") task environment [Riolo, 1987a]. This section briefly describes the parts of the CFS-C/FSW1 system that are relevant to the experiments described in this paper. For more details, see [Riolo, 1987b] or the cited documentation.

Basically, the FSW1 domain is a world that is modeled as a finite Markov process, in which a non-zero *payoff* is associated with some states. The classifier system's input interface provides a message that indicates the current state of the Markov process. The classifier system's effector interface provides the system with a way to alter the transition probabilities of the process, so that the system can control (in part) the path taken through the finite state world. Basically, a message that begins with "10" is interpreted by the effector interface as a command to set the effector to some value r, $r = 0, 1, \ldots 15$, depending on the right most 4 bits of the message. The effector setting r is used to select the transition matrix $P(r)$ which specifies the probability the system will go from the current state W_i to some state W_j. When the system moves to a new state with a non-zero payoff, that payoff is given to the active classifiers as a "reward".

The CFS-C classifier system is a standard, "Holland" type learning classifier system. While the CFS-C classifiers all have two conditions, in this paper they will be treated as if they have only one condition. (This is done by making both conditions identical.)

For the experiments described in this paper, no classifiers are coupled, i.e., no classifier is satisfied by a message produced by another classifier. All classifiers match only detector messages, i.e., the classifiers are matched when the current state of the finite state process is in the set of states matched by the classifier's condition. The most important parts of the classifier system are (a) the mechanism implementing bidding and competition to post messages and to set the effectors, and (b) the allocation of payoff to classifiers from the environment.

In the CFS-C/FSW1 system the bid of classifier i at step t, $B_i(t)$, is calculated as follows:

$$B_i(t) = k * S_i(t) * BidRatio_i$$

k is a small constant (set to 0.1), which acts as a "risk factor", i.e., it determines what proportion of a classifier's strength it will bid and so perhaps lose on a single step. $S_i(t)$ is the strength of classifier i at step t. $BidRatio_i$ is a number between 0 and 1 that is a measure of the classifier's *specificity*, i.e., how many different messages it can match. A *BidRatio* of 1 means the classifier matches exactly one message, while a *BidRatio* of 0 means the classifier matches any message. Thus classifiers that implement high level, general rules in a default hierarchy will have low *BidRatios*,

while classifiers that implement lower level, exception rules will have higher *BidRatio* values.

When a competition is run to determine which classifiers are to be activated and post messages, the probability that a given (satisfied) classsifier i will win is:

$$Prob(\ i\ wins\ ) = \beta_i(t) / \sum_j \beta_j(t)$$

where j ranges over all bidding (satisfied) classifiers at t, and $\beta_i(t)$, the *effective bid* of classifier i at t, is:

$$\beta_i(t) = B_i(t)^{BidPow}$$

BidPow is a parameter that can be set to alter the shape of probability distribution used to choose classifiers to produce messages. In all experiments described in this paper, $BidPow = 3$.

Note that the output interface of the CFS-C/FSW1 system may have to resolve conflicts, e.g., when one classifier produces a message that says "set the effector value r to 1" and another produces a message that says "set the effector value r to 2". Since the effector can only be set to one value at a time (just as we can either lift our arm or lower it, and not both), an *effector conflict resolution mechanism* must be used. Basically, the value of r is chosen probabilistically, with the probability that $r = r'$ equal to:

$$\sum_{m'} \beta_{m'}(t) / \sum_m \beta_m(t)$$

where m' ranges over the effector messages that say "set r to r'", $\beta_{m'}(t)$ is the effective bid of the classifier that posted message m', and m ranges over all effector messages. Once an effector value is chosen, all messages that are inconsistent with that setting are deleted from the new message list.

When a classifier wins a competition and posts a message, its strength is decremented by the amount it bid to become active. Since there are no coupled classifiers, classifiers only receive payments from the environment when the system moves to a state with an associated non-zero payoff. In particular, the *full* payoff is added to the strength of *every* classifier that has posted a message during that time step.

Because the bids made by classifiers are not paid to other classifiers in the experiments described in this paper, the strength at step $t + 1$ of a classifier i that produced one or more messages at step t is:

$$S_i(t + 1) = S_i(t) - B_i(t) + R(t)$$

where $B_i(t)$ is the classifiers bid at step t and $R(t)$ is the reward from the enviroment at step t. Note that the fixed-point strength of classifier i, $S_{i,fp}$, is inversely proportional to its bidratio, $BidRatio_i$. In particular,

$$S_{i,fp} = I_i / (k * BidRatio_i)$$

where I_i is the average amount paid to classifier i whenever it posts messages. Other things being equal, a general classifier (with a low *BidRatio*) will have a higher fixed-point strength then a more specialized classifier (with a higher *BidRatio*).

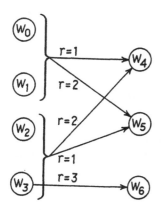

Figure 1: A simple FSW1 finite state world.

3   A SIMPLE TEST WORLD

In order to examine default hierarchies in the CFS-C/FSW1 system, consider the simple FSW1 world shown in Figure 1. There are seven states in this world, W_i, $i = 0 \ldots 6$. State W_5 is the start state. States W_4 and W_6 have payoffs of 200 and 400, respectively; all other states have zero payoff. For $i = 4$, 5, or 6, and any effector value r, $p_{ij}(r) = 0.25$, $j = 0 \ldots 3$. That is, when in state W_4, W_5, or W_6, the system has an equal chance of going to any one of the four states on the left in Figure 1, and no chance of going to a state on the right, no matter what the value of r. When in state W_0 or W_1, if $r = 1$ the system goes to W_4; if $r = 2$, the system goes to W_5. When in state W_2 or W_3, if $r = 2$ the system goes to W_4; if $r = 1$, the system goes to W_5. And when in state W_3, the system goes to W_6 only if $r = 3$. (Other values of r are not allowed in the experiments described below.)

The system can do best if it sets r to 1 when in states W_0 or W_1, sets r to 2 when in state W_2, and sets r to 3 when in state W_3. A good set of classifiers for this world would classify the states on the left into three categories and respond accordingly. (Since the system can't alter the transition probabilities when in any of the states on the right, no rules categorizing those states can be more useful than any others.) While this world is too small to show how a default hierarchy (i.e., a quasi-morphism) can require fewer classifiers than a homomorphic model, it is complex enough to show the relationship between default and exception rules.

As a simple test of the CFS-C/FSW1 system, it was run in the world shown in Figure 1 using the following three classifiers:

$$d_{0|1}/r = 1 \quad (1)$$
$$d_2/r = 2 \quad (2)$$
$$d_3/r = 3 \quad (3)$$

(The numbers in parentheses on the right serve to identify the classifiers.) The condition "$d_{0|1}$" matches two detector messages, for states W_0 or W_1. The conditions d_2 and d_3 each match one detector message, i.e., the detector messages for states W_2 and W_3, respectively. The action "$r = x$" posts an effector message that sets the effector value r to x, $x = 1$, 2, or 3.

In this and other experiments described in this paper, the system was run for 2000 major-cycle steps. In all runs classifiers reached their fixed-point strengths within the first 1000 steps. The average performance of the system over steps 1500 to 2000 is used to establish the "fixed-point" performance, P_{fp}, for one run. All results presented are the average of 10 runs (each started with a different pseudo-random number generator seed).

For the three classifiers shown above, P_{fp} was 124.4 per step (StdDev = 1.3). As can be easily calculated, the expected value is 125 (the system gets a non-zero payoff at most once every two steps). Thus these three rules perform just as expected. Of course these rules do not implement a default hierarchy: there is a general rule, 1, but it never makes mistakes, and the other rules do not cover subsets of the cases covered by the general rule. Instead, these rules implement a homomorphic model, since the rules partition the space of possible states (with respect to the 4 states on the left in Figure 1, the states the system is modeling). The next section shows how a default hierarchy can be built to cover the same states.

4   RESULTS

To test the performance of a default hierarchy in the world shown in Figure 1, the CFS-C/FSW1 system first was run with just one classifier:

$$d_{0|1|2|3}/r = 1 \quad (BidRatio = 0.56) \quad (4)$$

This general classifier clearly implements a high level default rule for this world, namely "When in any state W_i, $i = 0 \ldots 3$, set r to 1". The expected fixed-point performance for a system using just this rule is 50, since the system will get a reward only when it moves from state W_0 or W_1 to W_4, which it will do 50% of the time. The observed fixed-point performance was 49.9, or 99.8% of the expected value (StdDev = 1.9%). The classifier's fixed-point strength is 1765, which is also exactly the expected strength.

To improve the system's performance, it was run again with two rules, the above default rule, 4, and the following "exception" rule:

$$d_{2|3}/r = 2 \quad (BidRatio = 0.75) \quad (5)$$

This classifier covers a subset of the states covered by classifier 4. For that subset, it corrects a mistake made by classifier 4, since it sets r to 2, and so causes the system to go from state W_2 or W_3 to W_4 (instead of to W_5). The expected payoff for a system using the default hierarchy implemented by these two rules is 100 per step, since every other step the system should receive the 200 payoff from state W_4. The observed fixed-point payoff was 83.9, or just 83.9% of the expected rate ($StdDev = 1.8\%$). The fixed-point strengths of classifiers 4 and 5 were 2661 and 2667, respectively. Note that the strength of the default rule 4 went up as predicted [Holland, 1985] when the exception rule 5 is added to the system, but it did not go up as high as expected (to 3571).

The system also was run with an additional classifier:

$$d_3/r = 3 \quad (BidRatio = 1) \quad (6)$$

This rule covers another exception, so that the system can get to the high-payoff state W_6 whenever it is in state W_3. Together rules 4, 5, and 6 implement a complete default hierarchy for this simple world. The expected payoff for these classifiers is the same as for the original 3 perfect rules (1, 2, and 3), i.e., 125 per step. However, the observed performance was just 108.7, or 86.9% of the expected value ($StdDev = 1.3\%$). The fixed-point strengths of classifiers 4, 5, and 6 were 2860, 2667, and 4000, respectively.

Why is the performance lower than expected? First, note that the fixed-point strengths of classifiers 5 and 6 are just as expected, given the amount of payoff they receive. On the other hand, classifier 4, the top level default rule, has a fixed-point strength that is much lower than its expected value, 3571. Thus classifier 4 must be making mistakes.

To get a better idea of what is happening consider Figure 2, which shows the results of a run using just two classifiers, 4 and 5. Figure 2 shows the marginal performance of the system plotted against major-cycle steps executed. It also shows the strengths for classifiers 4 and 5.

First, note that the strength of classifier 5 stabilizes at 2667, which is the maximum strength it can reach given its maximum average income (200 per bid) and its $BidRatio$, 0.75. On the other hand, the strength of classifier 4 oscillates, and it never reaches its expected value. Instead, as soon as the strength of 4 gets much above the strength of classifier 5, performance begins to drop (as does the strength of classifier 4). This co-oscillation of the strength of classifier 4, the general default rule, and marginal performance is the key to why the performance of this default hierarchy is lower than expected.

Recall that in classifier systems there is a competition to post messages and control effectors: the higher a classifier's bid, the more likely it is to win the competition and control the system's behavior. Also recall that when a classifier loses the competition to set an effector, its messages are deleted from the message list and it does *not* pay its bid to

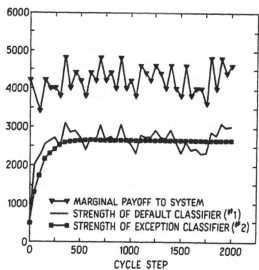

Figure 2: Performance of a default hierarchy using the standard bucket brigade algorithm.

its suppliers. Bearing these facts in mind, the reason for the oscillations and sub-expected performance are clear:

1. When the strength of an exception rule (rule 5) is greater than the strength of the default rule for which it is exception (rule 4), the exception rule tends to control behavior in the states it covers. The exception tends to protect the default from making mistakes, which allows the average income for the default rule to reach its maximum.

2. Since the default rule has a smaller $BidRatio$ than the exception rule that protects it, if the average incomes of the rules are about the same, the maximum fixed-point strength of the default rule will be greater than the maximum for the exception rule. In this example, as rule 5 protects 4, the strength of rule 4 eventually exceeds that of rule 5 (since both have a maximum income of 200 per bid).

3. As the strength of the default classifier rises, its bid and effective bid will rise. Once the effective bid of the default rule is near to or greater than the effective bid of the exception rule, the default rule will begin to win the competition. That is, the exception rule will not always win the competition in the situations it covers, which means it will not be able to stop the default rule from making mistakes.

4. Once the default rule begins making mistakes, both the system performance and the strength of the default rule will begin to fall. Eventually the system returns to the beginning of the performance oscillation, when the strength of the default rule is enough lower than that of the exception rule so that the exception

rule can again protect the default from making mistakes.

In short, the protection an exception-covering rule provides for a default rule allows the strength of the default rule to rise until the exception rule can no longer protect it. This will almost always happen in default hierarchies, since the maximal fixed-point strength of a general default classifier is in general higher than that of of more specific, exception classifier.

One way to correct this problem would be to alter the bucket brigade so that the maximum fixed-point strength of general classifiers is not higher than that for more specialized classifiers. For example, payments to classifiers could be biased so that a lower $BidRatio$ leads to a smaller share of the payment from other classifiers or from environmental rewards. Lowering the fixed-point strength of general classifiers may create some other problems, however. For instance, since default rules tend to make mistakes more often than more specialized rules, the fixed-point strength of a default rule should be relatively high, so that it can afford to make mistakes (and lose strength) without having its strength go so low that it its eliminated from the system.

Another approach is to leave the relationship between the fixed-point strengths of general versus specific classifiers the same, but to bias the *effective bid*, β, against the general classifiers. Since the effective bid only changes the probability distribution used to determine which classifiers post messages and control the systems effectors, it does not alter a classifier's *per bid* income or payment. Thus general classifiers will still have relatively high fixed-point strengths, even though specialized classifiers will tend to win the competition more often.

To test this idea, the way effective bids are calculated in the CFS-C/FSW1 system was changed by adding a factor involving a classifier's $BidRatio$. In particular, the *effective bid*, $\beta_i(t)$, of a classifier i at step t is now calculated as follows:

$$\beta_i(t) = B_i(t)^{BidPow} * BidRatio_i^{EBRPow}$$

The value of $EBRPow$ can be changed to alter the shape of probability distribution used to choose the classifiers that are to produce messages. For example, if $BidPow = 1$ and $EBRPow = 0$ then $\beta_i(t) = B_i(t)$, i.e., a classifier's probability of producing messages is just its bid divided by the sum of bids made by all satisfied classifiers. Setting $EBRPow$ equal to 1, 2, and so on, makes it less likely that general classifiers (those with lower $BidRatio$'s) will win the competition with more specific, co-active classifiers.

To test the effects of this modification, the system was run in the same finite state world described earlier, using classifiers 4, 5, and 6, which implement a simple 3 level default hierarchy. The following table shows the results obtained using various values for $EBRPow$:

EBRPow	% Expected P_{f_p} (1 StdDev)	S_{4,f_p}
0	86.9 (1.3)	2860
1	92.7 (1.3)	3104
2	95.8 (0.9)	3280
4	98.6 (1.1)	3479
6	99.5 (1.8)	3553

As can been seen, raising the $EBRPow$ parameter increases the average fixed-point performance of the system to virtually a mistake-free level. Also note that the fixed-point strength of classifier 4, the default rule, increases to almost its maximum value, 3571.

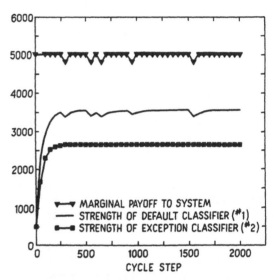

Figure 3: Performance of a default hierarchy using the modified bucket brigade algorithm with $EBRPow = 3$.

Figure 3 shows the results of repeating the experiment shown in Figure 2 with $EBRPow = 3$. The oscillations of both the marginal performance and the strength of classifier 4 are all but eliminated. Thus with a high $EBRPow$, the exception classifier 5 is able to almost always win the competition with the default rule it protects, in which case the system never makes mistakes.

The system was also run using the same three classifiers in two slightly different versions of the world shown in Figure 1. First, the system was run in a world in which setting the effector value r to 2 in states W_2 and W_3 causes the system to go to another state, W_7 which has a payoff of 100. That is, an exception rule like classifier 5 leads to a lower payoff than the default rule does when it doesn't make a mistake. In this world the expected performance (per step) is 112.5, while the observed performance with $EBRPow = 0$ was 97.7 (86.9% expected performance, $StdDev = 1.8$). However, with $EBRPow = 3$ the observed performance was 109.0 (97.5% of the expected value, $StdDev = 1.9$). Thus the default hierarchy performs just

200

as well when the exception rule leads to a lower payoff than the default rule does when it is correct.

Second, the system was run in a finite state world like that shown in Figure 1, except that various amounts of uncertainty are introduced into the transitions. For example, instead of going from state W_0 to state W_4 with probability 1.0 when r is set to 1, the system will go to that state with probability 0.92 and go to one of the other states on the right with probability 0.04 each; i.e., 8% of the time the system will go somewhere unexpected. The following table shows the results of running the three classifiers 4, 5, and 6 that implement the simple default hierachy described earlier, in worlds with increasing amounts of uncertainty (using $EBRPow = 3$):

% Un-certainty	Expected Payoff	Observed Payoff (1 StdDev)	% Optimal Payoff
0	125	122 (3.44)	97.6
8	116	115 (3.64)	99.1
16	107	105 (3.64)	98.1
32	89.0	87.5 (5.52)	98.3

As can be seen, uncertainty in the environment has little effect on the systems ability to obtain the best possible payoff rate. This is an important property for any learning system that must contend with very complex environments in which it can never completely reduce the uncertainty.

5 CONCLUSIONS

Default hierarchies are an excellent way for classifier systems to cope with very complex enviroments. However, for default hierarchies to work properly, classifiers that implement "exception" rules must be able to control the system when they are applicable, thus protecting the default rules from making mistakes. This paper has presented results that show the bucket brigade algorithm as described in [Holland, 1985] does not lead to correct exception rules always winning the competition with the default rules they protect. A simple modification to the bucket brigade algorithm is suggested, which involves biasing the calculation of the *effective bid* so that general classifiers (those with low BidRatios) have much lower effective bids than do more specific classifiers (those with high BidRatios). Results are presented that show this modification works as desired: default hierarchies can be made to achieve payoff rates as near to optimal as desired.

Since the modification to the bucket brigade algorithm only changes the effective bid made by classifiers, the allocation of strength under the bucket brigade is not altered (except insofar as the fixed-point strengths of default rules are increased to their maximum expected levels). Also, if the system does not have more specialized exception classifiers to compete with a particular default rule, that default rule will continue to control the behavior of the system. The modified bucket brigade algorithm only reduces the probability that default rules will post messages when they are competing with co-active exception rules.

The classifier system also is shown to work as expected in environments with varying amounts of uncertainty, and when the payoff received for activating a correct exception rule is less than the payoff received by the default rule it protects when the default is used in a correct situation.

REFERENCES

[Burks, 1986] Burks, Arthur W. "A Radically Non-Von Neumann Architecture for Learning and Discovery." In *CONPAR 86: Conference on Algorithms and Hardware for Parallel Processing, September 17-19, Proceedings.*, 1-17. Wolfgang Handler, *etal.* (Eds.). Springer-Verlag, Berlin, 1986.

[Holland, 1985] Holland, J. H. "Properties of the Bucket Brigade." *Proceedings of an International Conference on Genetic Algorithms and their Applications*, 1-7. John J. Grefenstette (Ed.). Carnegie-Mellon University, Pittsburg, 1985.

[Holland, 1986a] Holland, John H. "Escaping Brittleness: The Possibilities of General-Purpose Learning Algorithms Applied to Parallel Rule-Based Systems." In *Machine Learning: An Artificial Intelligence Approach, Volume II*, Michalski, Ryszard S., Carbonell, Jamie G., and Mitchell, Tom M. (Eds). Morgan Kaufman Publishers, Inc., Los Altos, CA (1986).

[Holland, 1986b] Holland, John H., Holyoak, Keith J., Nisbett, Richard E. and Paul A. Thagard. *Induction. Processes of Inference, Learning, and Discovery*. The MIT Press, Cambridge, MA, 1986.

[Holland and Burks, 1987] Holland, John H. and Burks, Arthur W. "Adaptive Computing System Capable of Learning and Discovery." United States patent applied for (1987).

[Riolo, 1986] Riolo, Rick L. "CFS-C: A Package if Domain Independent Subroutines for Implementing Classifier Systems in Arbitrary, User-Defined Environments." Logic of Computers Group, Division of Computer Science and Engineering, University of Michigan, Ann Arbor, 1986.

[Riolo, 1987a] Riolo, Rick L. "CFS-C/FSW1: An Implementation of the CFS-C Classifier System in a Domain that Involves Learning to Control a Markov Process." Logic of Computers Group, Division of Computer Science and Engineering, University of Michigan, Ann Arbor, 1987 [in prep.].

[Riolo, 1987b] Riolo, Rick L. "Bucket Brigade Performance: I. Long Sequences of Classifiers." [In these procedings.]

MULTILEVEL CREDIT ASSIGNMENT IN A GENETIC LEARNING SYSTEM

John J. Grefenstette

Navy Center for Applied Research in AI
Naval Research Laboratory
Washington, DC 20375-5000

Abstract

Genetic algorithms assign credit to building blocks based on the performance of the knowledge structures in which they occur. If the knowledge structures are rules sets, then the bucket brigade algorithm provides a means of performing additional credit assignment at the level of individual rules. This paper explores one possibility for using the fine-grained feedback provided by the bucket brigade in genetic learning systems that manipulate sets of rules.

1. Introduction

There are two distinct approaches to machine learning using Genetic Algorithms (GA's). These approaches are popularly denoted by the names of the universities where they were first elaborated. In the *Michigan approach*, first described by Holland and Reitman [Holland 78], the population comprises a single set of production rules, or *classifiers*. Each individual rule is assigned a measure, called *strength*, that indicates the utility of the rule to the system's goal of obtaining external payoff. The *bucket brigade algorithm* [Holland 86] shifts strength among the rules during the course of problem solving, so that rules achieve high strength either by obtaining direct payoff from the task environment or by setting the stage for later rules. New rules are discovered by genetic operators applied to existing rules on the basis of strength. In the *Pitt approach*, developed by De Jong and Smith at the University of Pittsburgh [Smith 80], each structure in the population maintained by the GA represents a production system program, i.e., a set of rules. Each structure is evaluated by running it through a production system interpreter in the environment of the learning task and measuring various aspects of the system's performance. As the result of each evaluation, a fitness measure is assigned to the entire program and is used to control the selection of structures for reproduction. The usual genetic search operators -- crossover, mutation and inversion -- are applied to the structures without reference to the performance of the individual rules comprising the structures.

These two approaches have provided a basis for several successful learning systems [Booker 82, Goldberg 83, Schaffer 84, Smith 80, Wilson 85], each of which incorporates significant additions to the basic outline given above. It should be emphasized that both approaches are undergoing constant evolution and that the relative merits of the two approaches is a topic of continuing interest. This paper describes the first attempt to combine the strongest features of each approach in a single learning system.

A primary strength of the Michigan approach derives from its use of the bucket brigade algorithm [Holland 85]. This elegant scheme achieves a distribution of credit among a large rule set without the need for costly bookkeeping overhead, e.g., the traces of system behavior required of some learning systems. The bucket brigade algorithm supports an important theme in massive parallelism: that effective global patterns of behavior (e.g., default hierarchies) can emerge from vast numbers of local competitions. From a GA perspective, however, the application of genetic operators in the Michigan approach is problematic. The framework described in [Holland 75] provides a theory for the evolution of co-adapted sets of alleles *within* the structures, arising as a result of competition *among* the independent structures in the population. There is no theory provided for cooperation among the members of the population, although this might be an interesting extension. As a result, instead of emerging as co-adapted alleles, co-adaptation among rules in the Michigan approach is typically achieved by additional mechanisms, e.g., triggered genetic operators and bridge classifiers [Holland 86, Riolo 87], that specifically encourage rule linkages.

In contrast, the Pitt approach corresponds more closely to the biological metaphor of evolution through natural selection. The knowledge structures in the Pitt approach correspond to chromosomes in a population of competing organisms. The performance measure corresponds to an organism's fitness to its environment. In the Pitt approach, co-adapted rules correspond to co-adapted alleles in [Holland 75]. Holland make a strong case for viewing adaptation as an optimization problem over the response surface defined by the payoff provided by the task environment and argues that GA's are suitable for performing the optimization. The Pitt approach to learning rule sets seems to be a plausible, albeit ambitious, extension of the successful use of GA's for parameter optimization problems. However, there are two primary bottlenecks in the Pitt approach to learning: computational resources and the feedback bandwidth.

Extensive computational resources are required in to evaluate thousands of complete rules sets. Two lines of current research address this issue. First, it can be shown that GA's are especially well-suited for optimization using Monte Carlo techniques in the evaluation phase [Grefenstette 87b]. This follows from the observation that even if individual structures are evaluated by probabilistic procedures, the expected error in the observed performance of hyperplanes is much less than the expected error in the the performance of the individual structures. The implication for the Pitt approach is that the amount of problem solving activity required to test individual rule sets can be fairly limited without adverse effects on the overall performance of the learning system. A second means of dealing with the computational burden of the Pitt approach is through the use of increasingly available coarse-grained parallel computers with 50 to 100 processors. It is a straightforward task to install a production system interpreter on each node of a MIMD machine and thereby perform all of the structure evaluation for a given generation in parallel. Several papers in this volume explore this approach.

The second bottleneck in the Pitt approach is the limited feedback bandwidth. In LS-1 [Smith 80] a critic provides feedback concerning the performance of each program. The critic includes not only a measure of the task level performance, but also measurements of various dynamic characteristics of the behavior during the problem solving task, such as the number of rules that fire, the number of rules suggesting external actions, and so on. All of this information is combined into a single scalar value to represent the fitness of the rule set under evaluation. Shaffer's LS-2 [Schaffer 84] expands the feedback bandwidth by allowing the critic to provide a vector of performance measures. Subpopulations are selected on the basis of each element in the performance vector, providing the equivalent of environmental niches in which specialists can evolve. Recombination in LS-2 takes place without regard to the subpopulation boundaries. The result is an effective search for Pareto-optimal regions of the search space. Yet another approach to increasing the detail of credit assignment in GA's is represented by recent attempts at the traveling-salesperson problem (TSP). In the TSP, the usual fitness measure is the overall tour length. However, this fitness measure does not provide sufficient selective pressure toward high performance tours. In one approach to this problem [Grefenstette 87a], the crossover operator takes the length of competing parental edges into account when constructing the offspring tour. This represents a low level credit assignment strategy for directly promoting high-performance first-order hyperplanes.

In this paper, we explore a similar multilevel credit assignment strategy in the context of the Pitt approach to learning production system programs. Figure 1 illustrates the overall system design. Our approach is to use the bucket brigade in the course of evaluating production sets to assign credit at the level of individual rules. The GA uses the overall performance of the rule set to guide selection, as in LS-1. But in addition, the strengths of the individual rules influences the physical representation of the structure, making it more likely that high strength rule combinations survive the crossover operation. That is, we are proposing a heuristic form of the inversion operator, called *clustering*, based on the feedback from the bucket brigade algorithm. The description of the system will proceed bottom-up: We first discuss the object level task and the representation of rules. This is followed by the descriptions of the problem solver and the learner. Experimental results are presented, followed by a discussion of future directions for this research.

2. The State Space Search Task

In the interests of obtaining general results, the object level task for our learning system is an abstract state space search characterized by the triple $< S, O, P >$, where S is a set of *states*, O is a set of state transition *operators*, and P is a mapping of *payoff* to the states. Certain states in S are *initial states*, others are *final states*. At the start of a task, a random initial state is chosen. During each problem solving step, the problem solver selects an operator that is then applied to the current state to produce the new state. A task is complete when the new state is one of the final states.

One particular problem is shown in figure 2. The set of initial states is {0, 1, 2, 3} and the set of final states is {12, 13, 14, 15}. The arcs are labeled by the operator(s) that perform the transition. In this problem, a payoff of 1000 is associated with state 13. All other states have a payoff of 0.

The object for the learning system is to learn a set of heuristic rules that select operators for the current state. The rules have the form:

IF   the current state is in the set S_i
THEN choose an operator from the set O_i

The action associated with such a rule is to choose one

of the operators in the set O_i at random.

The knowledge representation employed is an important bias for any learning system. We now describe our representation of the heuristic rules. In most state space search problems, the number of states is very large. In these cases, it is infeasible to specify arbitrary sets of states in the conditions of a heuristic rule. However, states can often be usefully characterized by a set of features. Furthermore, it is reasonable to assume that heuristic rules for selecting operators may usefully attend to some features and ignore others. In fact, Lenat cites the following as one of the central assumptions underlying the use of heuristics:

> If an action A is appropriate in situation S, then A is appropriate in most situations that are very similar to S [Lenat 83].

So the left hand sides of our rules will contain patterns that match the feature vectors of states, using the symbol # to indicate that the value of the corresponding feature is irrelevant. For ease of presentation, in this paper we identify the name of each state with its binary feature vector. On the other hand, state transition operators do not usually have features that capture their similarity. Furthermore, the number of operators is usually smaller than the number of states by several orders of magnitude. Given these considerations, it seems reasonable to permit the right hand sides to specify arbitrary sets of operators. We do so by interpreting the right hand side as a membership vector for the set of operators. In the example problem, the operator set is {a, b, c, d}. So, for example, the rule

$$0\#\#1 \rightarrow 1010$$

represents the heuristic

> IF   the current state is in the set {1, 3, 5, 7}
> THEN choose an operator from the set {a, c}

A problem solver that uses this representation is described next.

3. The Problem Solving Level

The problem solver for this system is based in part on Riolo's CFS-C system [Riolo 86]. As that system is described in detail elsewhere in this volume, we restrict our discussion to the modifications implemented for this work. At the start of each problem solving cycle, a detector message indicating the current state is posted on the message list. Each rule whose left hand sides matches the current state produces a *bid* that is proportional to the rule's strength. (The system currently ignores the specificity of the rules in computing bids.) A competition, based on bid size, is held among the bidders to see which rules get to *produce* a

message. (The maximum number of messages produced is fixed.) Effector conflicts among the resulting messages are resolved by a competition based on the total bids associated with each distinct message. Once a winning message is selected, one of the operators indicated by the message is selected at random and applied to the current state to produce the new state. Rules that produce messages consistent with the selected operator are said to be *active*. Our implementation of the bucket brigade is similar to the one in Wilson's animat system [Wilson 85]:

1) each rule producing a message has the amount of its bid deducted from its strength;

2) the total of the bids thus collected is distributed evenly among the rules active on the *previous* cycle;

3) any external reward associated with the new state is distributed evenly among the currently active rules.

Note that it is possible that no rule matches the current state. In this case, a randomly chosen operator is used to produce the next state. Since there are no active rules, no external payoff enters the system.

It is acknowledged that many of the decisions regarding our implementation of the bucket brigade are *ad hoc* and that current research may well suggest significant improvements. Nonetheless, the basic feature of even our somewhat crude version is that the strength of each rule serves as an estimator of its typical payoff.

In the example problem, it takes exactly three cycles to move from an initial state to a final state. To evaluate a given rule set, 100 traversals of the state space (300 CFS-C cycles) are performed, each traversal starting at a randomly chosen initial state. The average external payoff achieved by the rule set is returned to the learning level, along with the updated strengths of the individual rules.

4. The Learning Level

At the top level of the learning system, the GENESIS genetic algorithm system [Grefenstette 84] maintains a population of fixed-length structures, each of which is interpreted as a set of fixed length rules. For the experiments described here, each structure consists of 240 bits, interpreted as rules sets of 20 rules each. Each rule is represented by a string of 12 bits. For the left hand sides, 00 represents a "0" in the representation used by the problem solver, 11 represents a "1" and 01 and 10 both represent "#". Since the right hand sides contain no "#" symbols, only 4 bits are required to represent the right hand sides.

In addition to the usual genetic operations -- selection, crossover and mutation -- the learner also performs an additional operator, called *clustering*, described below. The *crossover* operator treats the knowledge structure as a ring, and selects two crossover points without regard for rule boundaries. Each rule in the offspring inherits the strength associated with the corresponding rule in the parent structure. (In the case of a new rule created by crossing in the middle of two rules, the new rule is assigned the average strength of the two parental rules.) The only notice that crossover pays to the rule boundaries is that duplicate rules are not included when choosing the segment from the second parent. Both offspring from crossover are kept, so that all rules in the parent structures survive in one of the offspring (with the exception of those rules in which one of the crossover points falls).

Because the performance of a knowledge structure is independent of the position of the rules within the structure, it is natural to consider the use of the *inversion* operator. Inversion typically reverses a randomly chosen portion of a structure, thereby altering the defining length of many hyperplanes. This is turn alters the probability that those hyperplanes will be disrupted by crossover. A moderate rate of inversion produces slight performance improvements in LS-1 [Smith 80]. In other studies, the effects of inversion has generally been hard to measure. One explanation is that the space being search by inversion -- the space of all possible permutations of genes -- is in general much larger than the original task space. Faced with the huge space of representation permutations, the random mutations of the representation provided by inversion cannot be expected to show much progress in the amount of time before selection pressure guides the population into convergence.

We now describe a heuristic version of inversion called *clustering*. Like inversion, clustering does not introduce any new phenotypes into the population. Rather, the intent of this new operator is to modify the physical representation of a rule set so that co-adapted sets of rules are less likely to be disrupted by crossover. Clustering is defined as follows:

1) select a rule position at random;

2) move the highest strength rule to the selected position;

3) arrange the remaining rules so that the distance from each rule to the highest strength rule is a decreasing function of the rule's strength (treating the knowledge structure as a ring for the purposes of computing distances).

An example showing the effects of clustering appears in figure 3. Clustering is performed on all structures after the selection phase and before crossover; if a given rule set is assigned multiple offspring, each offspring has a random initial position chosen for clustering. Note that the combination of clustering and crossover does not generally produce an offspring that contains all the high strength rules in each parent. In fact, experience has shown that it is usually counterproductive to impose such deterministic heuristics on genetic search. Since the strength obtained by a given rule is a function of its context in the rule set, it is possible for a group of rules to achieve low strength in one rule set and higher strength in another rule set. This is just the kind of testing of building blocks at which the GA excels.

Of course, the efficacy of the clustering heuristic depends on the assumption that co-adapted rules tend to have similar levels of strength. This is true in at least some interesting cases. For example, consider a chain of rules, e.g.,

$$R_1, R_2, ..., R_n$$

in which R_i always leads to the firing of R_{i+1}; that is, assume that R_i is $S_i \rightarrow O_i$ such that

$$o_{ij}(s_{ik}) \in S_{i+1}$$

for each $s_{ik} \in S_i$, $o_{ij} \in O_i$, and $1 \leq i < n$. If no other rules in the rule set have any states in common with S_i, for $1 \leq i < n$, then all rules in the chain converge to a common level of strength (given our rules for the bucket brigade). In this case, we expect the clustering operator to facilitate the inheritance of the chain as a group. However, the validity of the clustering heuristic in the general case certainly requires further analysis. We now describe a preliminary test of its effects in practice.

5. Experimental Results

This section describes experiments that measure the performance of the learning system with and without the clustering operator. The GA at the learning level uses parameter settings consistent with previous studies (see [De Jong 75, Grefenstette 86]):

population size = 100

crossover rate = 0.5

mutation rate = 0.001

generation gap = 1.0

scaling window = 5

Table 1 shows the average system reward for the best structures evolved during ten runs with and without clustering. Each run of the system consists of 5000 rule

205

set evaluations (50 generations). Corresponding runs start with the same initial population of knowledge structures. The performance of the learning system with clustering clearly dominates the system without clustering. (Using the Wilcoxon matched-pairs sign test, the hypothesis that both systems produce the same performance can be rejected at the 0.005 level of significance.) Figure 4 compares the payoff trajectories of the best structures in each system averaged over the ten runs. One might expect that higher performance as measured by the best structure is achieved at the expense of online performance, as is the case with a high mutation rate; for example, when the clustering operator creates an offspring containing only high strength rules, it must also create one containing only low strength rules. Figure 5 shows that this effect does not significantly harm online performance. In fact, the online performance improves with clustering. It is clear that clustering produces a significant performance advantage for this problem. Further experiments are required to validate these results on a variety of larger problems.

In two cases, the learning system with clustering evolves rule sets that achieve a perfect payoff rate. Table 2 shows the rules with above average strength in one of these perfect rule sets. The Id entry indicates the position within the knowledge structure of each rule. This rule set shows some interesting features. In practice, the sequence of states visited with this rule set is either

$$0 \rightarrow 5 \rightarrow 9 \rightarrow 13$$

or

$$\{1, 2, 3\} \rightarrow 6 \rightarrow 10 \rightarrow 13$$

It is encouraging to see that this rule set succeeds by making correct decisions early in the state space search, effectively eliminating much of the space from later consideration. There are many instances of cooperative rules. For example, even though rule 8 is overly general and would lead from state 4 to state 11 (a dead end for payoff, see fig. 2), this does no harm since state 4 is avoided by rules 4 and 9. It is also interesting to note that the rules with the highest strength occupy contiguous locations on the knowledge structure, as indicated by the Id entry. This provides support for the hypothesis that the clustering operator is partially responsible for the high level of performance.

6. Summary and Future Directions

This paper represents a preliminary study of the use of the rule level credit assignment provided by the bucket brigade in a system using the Pitt approach to genetic learning. This system shows that the information concerning the strength of individual rules can be useful in altering the physical representation of the rule sets in order to promote the linkage of co-adapted sets of rules. There are many obvious directions for further investigations. The analysis of the effects of the clustering operator on the search performed by a GA deserves closer attention. It is expected that much of the analysis applied to crossover and inversion in LS-1 [Smith 80] carries over to the clustering operator. The learning system should be extended to handle variable length structures, as in LS-1. The effects of altering the clustering rate needs to be investigated. Further experimental studies are required in order to validate the effects of clustering of larger problems. Finally, it is expected that current research on the bucket brigade will lead to improved ways to incorporate this level of feedback into genetic learning systems that evolve knowledge structures based on sets of rules.

Acknowledgements

I want to thank Lashon Booker and Ken De Jong for many simulating discussions on this topic, and Rick Riolo for providing a copy of his CFS-C software.

References

[Booker 82] L. B. Booker, *Intelligent behavior as as adaptation to the task environment*, Ph. D. Thesis, Dept. Computer and Communication Sciences, Univ. of Michigan, 1982.

[De Jong 75] K. A. De Jong, *Analysis of the behavior of a class of genetic adaptive systems*, Ph. D. Thesis, Dept. Computer and Communication Sciences, Univ. of Michigan, 1975.

[Goldberg 83] D. E. Goldberg, *Computer-aided gas pipeline operation using genetic algorithms and machine learning*, Ph. D. Thesis, Dept. Civil Eng., Univ. of Michigan, 1983.

[Grefenstette 84] J. J. Grefenstette, "A user's guide to GENESIS", Technical Report CS-83-11, Computer Science Dept., Vanderbilt Univ., 1984.

[Grefenstette 86] J. J. Grefenstette, "Optimization of control parameters for genetic algorithms", *IEEE Trans. Systems, Man, and Cybernetics*, SMC-16(1), 122-128, Jan/Feb 1986.

[Grefenstette 87a] J. J. Grefenstette, "Incorporating problem specific knowledge into genetic algorithms", to appear in **Genetic Algorithms and Simulated Annealing**, D. Davis (ed.), Pitman Series on AI, in press.

[Grefenstette 87b] J. J. Grefenstette and J. M. Fitzpatrick, "Genetic algorithms using Monte Carlo function evaluations", in preparation.

[Holland 75] J. H. Holland, **Adaptation in Natural and Artificial Systems**, Univ. Michigan Press, Ann Arbor, 1975.

[Holland 78] J. H. Holland and J. S. Reitman, "Cognitive systems based on adaptive algorithms", in **Pattern-Directed Inference Systems**, D. A. Waterman and F. Hayes-Roth (eds.), Academic Press, 1978.

[Holland 85] J. H. Holland, "Properties of the bucket brigade", *Proc. Intl. Conf. Genetic Algorithms and Their Applications*, 1-7, Pittsburgh, 1985.

[Holland 86a] J. H. Holland, "Escaping brittleness", in **Machine Learning, Vol. 2**, 593-623, R.S. Michalski, J. G. Carbonell, and T. M. Mitchell (eds.), Morgan Kaufman, 1986.

[Holland 86b] J. H. Holland, K. J. Holyoak, R. E. Nisbett and P. A. Thagard, **Induction: Processes of Inference, Learning, and Discovery**, MIT Press, Cambridge MA, 1986.

[Lenat 83] D. B. Lenat, "The role of heuristics in learning by discovery: three case studies", in **Machine Learning, An Artificial Intelligence Approach**, 243-306, R. S. Michalski, J. G. Carbonell and T. M. Mitchell (eds.), Tioga Press, Palo Alto, 1983.

[Riolo 86] R. L. Riolo, "CFS-C: A package of domain independent subroutines for implementing classifier systems in arbitrary, user-defined environments", Technical Report, Dept. of Elect. Eng. Comp. Sci., Univ. of Michigan, Jan. 1986.

[Riolo 87] R. L. Riolo, "Bucket brigade performance: long sequences of classifiers", *Proc. 2nd Intl. Conf. Genetic Algorithms and Their Applications*, Boston, 1987.

[Schaffer 84] J. D. Schaffer, *Some experiments in machine learning using vector evaluated genetic algorithms*, Ph. D. Thesis, Dept. of Electrical and Biomedical Engineering, Vanderbilt University, 1984.

[Smith 80] S. F. Smith, *A learning system based on genetic adaptive algorithms*, Ph. D. Thesis, Dept. Computer Science, Univ. of Pittsburgh, 1980.

[Wilson 85] S. W. Wilson, "Knowledge growth in an artificial animal", *Proc. Intl. Conf. Genetic Algorithms and Their Applications*, 16-23, Pittsburgh, 1985.

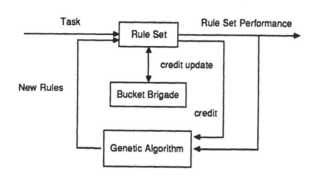

Fig. 1. Multilevel Learning System

Performance of Best Knowledge Structures		
Run	Clustering	No Clustering
1	980	880
2	920	810
3	780	790
4	1000	720
5	910	790
6	950	680
7	730	700
8	900	770
9	1000	620
10	880	770

Table 1. Effects of Clustering

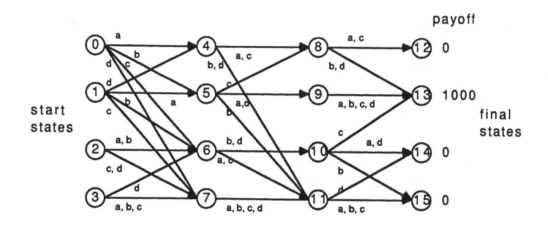

Fig. 2. An Abstract State Space Search Task

Rules with Above Average Strength				
Id	Rule			Strength
6	{3, 7}	→	{d}	10514
5	{8, 10, 12, 14}	→	{c}	9998
4	{0, 1, 8, 9}	→	{b}	4687
7	{5, 13}	→	{d}	4447
3	{5, 7, 13, 15}	→	{d}	4401
9	{0, 2}	→	{b}	3246
8	{4, 5, 6, 7}	→	{d}	3022

Fig. 3. The Clustering Operator

Table 2. A Rule Set with Perfect Payoff

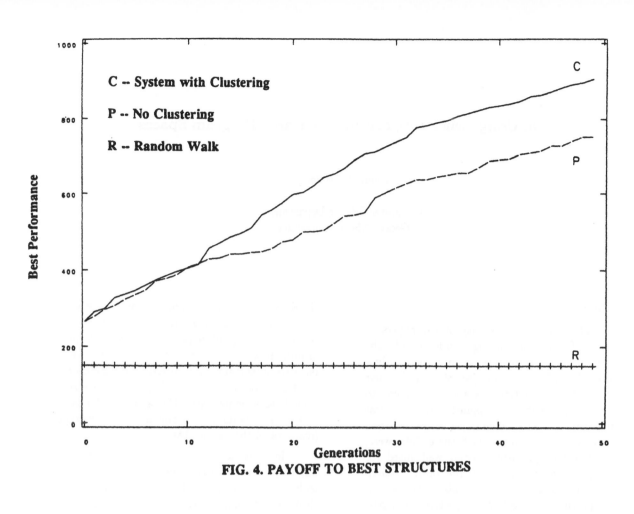

FIG. 4. PAYOFF TO BEST STRUCTURES

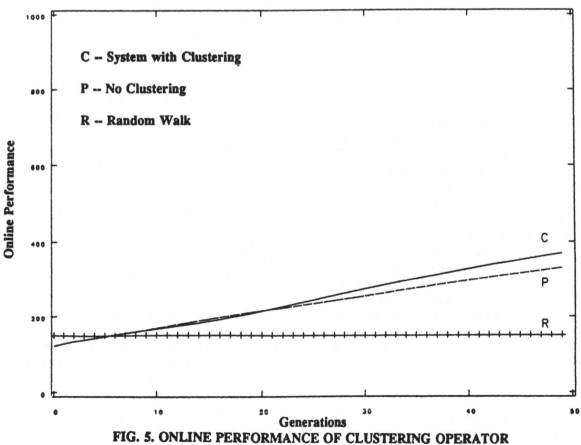

FIG. 5. ONLINE PERFORMANCE OF CLUSTERING OPERATOR

On Using Genetic Algorithms to Search Program Spaces

Kenneth De Jong

Computer Science Department
George Mason University

1. Introduction

The variety and quality of the papers in this conference is strong evidence of the dramatic increase in interest in Genetic Algorithms (GAs) both as an object of study in their own right, and in terms of the applications to which they might be applied. At our last conference, I tried to summarize where we stood in terms understanding what these GAs were, what kinds of problems seemed well-suited for GA applications, and what the open research issues appeared to be. In this paper I will attempt the same sort of perspective for a particular class of problems which is receiving considerable attention today: using GAs to search *program spaces* to quickly locate programs which are capable of performing a task at an acceptable performance level.

It has been pointed out many times that, because it has been difficult in the past to find a forum in the existing journal/conference structure for reporting GA research, there is a fairly serious gap between the "common wisdom" held by members of the GA research community and the material available in the open literature. As a consequence, those who are new to the area find it difficult to ascertain who has been doing what and frequently get involved unnecessarily in rediscovering various aspects of undocumented "wisdom" regarding the implementation and application of GAs. This seems to be particularly true when attempting to use GAs to search program spaces. So, in the following sections I'll try to summarize what we know and what the open issues are for this particular use of GAs.

2. Conceptualizing the Problem

My favorite way of conceptualizing the problem of searching program spaces is to clearly separate out the process which is executing a task program from the GAs being used to construct new (and hopefully better) task programs. If we make this separation, we can focus on two important and inter-related questions: what kind of changes to task programs are reasonable to attempt with GAs, and what kinds of task programming languages encourage (discourage) the use of GAs.

In considering what kinds of changes might be made to task programs, there appears to be a range of approaches of increasing sophistication and complexity. The simplest and most straight forward approach is to have GAs make changes to a set of parameters which control the behavior of a pre-developed, parameterized task program. The advantage to this approach is that it immediately places us on the familiar terrain of parameter optimization problems for which there is considerable understanding and guidance, and for which classical GAs can be used. It is easy at first glance to discard this approach as trivial and not at all representative of what is meant by "searching program spaces". But note that significant behavioral changes can be achieved within this simple framework. Samuel's checker player is a striking example of the power of such an approach. So, one piece of common wisdom is that, if a particular GA application permits, formulating the task modification problem as a parameter optimization problem has significant advantages.

However, there are many problems for which such a simple approach is inappropriate in the sense that "more significant" structural changes to task programs seem to be required. Frequently in these situations a more complex data structure is intimately involved in controlling the behavior of the task, and so the most natural approach is to have GAs make changes to these key structures. A good example of problems of this type occur when the task programs to be modified are designed with top level "agenda" control mechanism. Task programs for traveling salesman problems, bin packing, and scheduling problems are frequently organized in this manner and GAs are expected to construct agendas to be tested, evaluated, and subsequently used to fabricate better ones.

This approach at first glance may not seem to introduce any serious difficulties as far as using GAs, since it is usually not hard to "linearize" these data structures, map them into a string representation which can be manipulated by GAs, and then reverse the process to produce new data structures for evaluation. However, experience has taught us otherwise. Representation issues now rear their ugly heads and we can easily slip into a situation in which GAs are rendered impotent by a poor internal representation of the space to be searched. One must be careful, for example, to either choose a string representation on which the traditional genetic operators like crossover and mutation make sense, or to invent new operators better suited to the representation and which also satisfy the fundamental schema theorems. Both of these alternatives can be difficult to achieve. My favorite example of this is the amount of time and effort that has been expended in finding a "good" way to use GAs to solve traveling salesman problems. I will not dwell on these representation issues here since they are discussed in more detail in a variety of papers both in this conference and the 1985 proceedings (see, for example, [Grefenstette85], [Goldberg85], and [Davis85]).

By now the reader is probably ready to reply that neither of the approaches just discussed "really" involves searching program spaces. Rather, the reader has in mind the use of GAs to derive task programs at the more fundamental level of manipulating the executable code itself. I'm not sure that there is anything fundamentally different between interpreting an agenda and executing a Pascal program. However, I do feel that by taking such a step we are introducing an additional level of complexity as far as GA applications are concerned, and that it is important to "look before we leap". Since there is good deal of interest in such applications, the remainder of the paper will discuss these issues.

3. Choosing a Programming Language

I believe that the best way to proceed is to focus on the second of the inter-related questions posed in the introduction: what kind of programming languages encourage (discourage) the use of GAs at this level. This approach should not be surprising since we are really just raising the representation issue in yet another form.

It is quite reasonable view programs written in conventional languages like Fortran and Pascal (or even less conventional languages like Lisp and Prolog) as linear strings of symbols. This is certainly the way they are treated by editors and compilers in current program development environments. However, it is also quite obvious that this "natural" representation is a disastrous one as far as traditional GAs are concerned since standard operators like crossover and mutation seldom produce syntactically correct programs and, of those, even fewer which are semantically correct. As a consequence it should be clear that traditional GAs are not particularly effective in searching spaces in which the payoff is zero almost everywhere!

One alternative is to attempt to devise new language-specific "genetic" operators which preserve at least the syntactic (and hopefully, the semantic) integrity of the programs being manipulated. Unfortunately, the complexity of both the syntax and semantics of traditional languages makes it difficult to develop such operators. An obvious next step would be to focus on less traditional languages such as "pure" Lisp whose syntax and semantics are much simpler, leaving open the hope of developing reasonable genetic operators with the required properties. There have been a number of activities in this area including at least one paper in this conference [Fujiko87].

However, there is at least one important feature that "pure" Lisp shares with other more traditional languages: they are all procedural in nature. As a consequence most reasonable representations have the kinds of properties that cause considerable difficulty in GA applications. The two most obvious representation problems are order dependencies (interchanging two lines of code can render a program meaningless) and context sensitive interpretations (the entire meaning of a section of code can be changed by minor changes to preceding code, such as the insertion or deletion of a punctuation symbol). A more detailed discussion of these representation problems is presented in [DeJong85].

These issues are not new and were anticipated by Holland to the extent that he proposed a family of languages called classifier languages which were designed to overcome the kinds of problems being raised here [Holland75]. What is perhaps a bit surprising is that these classifier languages are a member of a broader class of languages which continues to reassert its usefulness across a broad range of activities (from compiler design to expert systems), namely, production systems (PSs) or rule-based systems. As a consequence, a good deal of time and effort has gone into studying this class of languages as a suitable language for use in searching program spaces with GAs.

4. Searching PS Program Spaces

One of the reasons that production systems have been and continue to be a favorite programming paradigm in both the expert system and machine learning communities is that PSs provide a representation of knowledge which can *simultaneously* support two kinds of activities: 1) treating knowledge as data to be manipulated as part of a knowledge acquisition and refinement process, and 2) treating knowledge as an "executable" entity to be used to perform a particular task (see, for example, [Newell77], [Buchanan78], or [Hedrick76]). This is particularly true of the "data-driven" forms of PSs (such as OPS5) in which the production rules which make up a PS program are treated as an unordered set of rules whose "left hand sides" are all independently and in parallel monitoring changes in "the environment".

It should be obvious that this same programming paradigm seems to offer significant advantages for GA applications and, in fact, has precisely the same characteristics as Holland's early classifier languages. If we focus then on PSs whose programs consist of unordered collections (sets) of rules, we can then ask how GAs can be used to search the space of PS programs for useful rule sets.

To anyone whose has read Holland's book [Holland75], the most obvious and "natural" way to proceed is to represent an entire rule set as string (individual), maintain a population of candidate rule sets, and use selection and genetic operators to produce new generations of rule sets. Historically, this was the approach taken by De Jong and his students while at the University of Pittsburgh (see, for example, [Smith80, or [Smith83]]) and has been dubbed "the Pitt approach".

However, during that same time period, Holland developed a model of cognition (classifier systems) in which the members of the population are individual rules and a rule set is represented by the entire population (see, for example, [Holland78] and [Booker82]). This quickly became known as "the Michigan approach" and initiated a continuing (friendly, but provocative) series of discussions concerning the strengths and weaknesses of the two approaches.

I think it is fair to say that most people who encounter classifier systems *after* becoming familiar with the traditional GA literature are somewhat surprised at the relatively subservient role GAs play and the emergence of a "bucket brigade" to deal with apportionment of credit issues. A reasonable explanation for this shift is that Holland was focusing on developing models of cognition rather than developing adaptive search techniques for large, complex spaces.

In any case, both approaches have produced encouraging results in quite different contexts some of which are being presented at this conference. At the same time I think it is fair to say that there is still not enough experience to understand precisely the strengths, weaknesses, and tradeoffs involved in either of the approaches. The current popular view is that the classifier approach will prove to be most useful in an on-line, real-time environment in which radical changes in behavior cannot be tolerated whereas the Pitt approach will be useful with off-line environments in which more leisurely exploration and more radical behavioral changes are acceptable.

There are also some recent developments which suggest that it might be possible to combine the two approaches in powerful and interesting ways [Grefenstette87].

5. PS Architecture Issues

Even though we have narrowed the scope of the discussion to the problem of searching PS program spaces, there are a number of PS architectural issues which still need to be addressed regardless of which (if any) of the preceding approaches are taken. In the following sections I will attempt to summarize those aspects which seem to arise most frequently.

5.1. Rule Set Sizes

If we think of rule sets as programs or knowledge bases, it seems rather silly and artificial to demand that all rule sets be the same size. However, the "path of least resistance" for GA applications leads one to precisely that point. If one adopts the Michigan approach, all implementations that I am aware of assume a fixed population size (i.e., a fixed number of classifiers). Most classical implementations of GAs as adaptive search procedures assume populations of fixed length strings. So, following the Pitt approach, using one of these implementations would require representing rule sets as fixed length strings. This issue is usually resolved (in keeping with one's philosophical and pragmatic perspectives) in one of several ways.

In classifier systems fixing the size of the rule set is viewed more in terms of setting an upper bound on the amount of classifier memory available in a cognitive model. Since humans seem to have the same sort of limitation, setting it to a reasonable, but fixed size seems to be quite justifiable (assuming mechanisms like generalization and forgetting for dealing with limited memory capabilities).

One can adopt the same view using the Pitt approach and require all rule sets (strings) to be the same fixed length. However, the justification is usually in terms of the advantages of having redundant copies of rules and having "workspace" within a rule set for new experimental building blocks without having to necessarily replace existing ones.

Historically, the strongest motivation for fixed length representations was that all the schema theorems were developed in this context. However, Smith [Smith80] was able to show that the formal results could indeed be extended to variable length strings. He complemented those results with a GA implementation which maintained a population of variable length strings and which efficiently generated variable length rule sets for a variety of tasks. One of the interesting side issues of this work was the need to provide via feedback an "incentive" to keep down the size of the rule sets by including a "bonus" for achieving the same level of performance with a shorter string.

In summary, although constraints on rule set sizes may seem at first to be too simplistic and restrictive for GA applications, this has not proven to be the case in the work to date and can be relaxed if necessary.

5.2. Rule Formats

A similar concern arises when developing the format of the rules which make up the rule sets. Requiring the rule used in an expert system shell to a conform to a rigid format consisting of a fixed number of slots on the left and right hand sides would be viewed as artificial and unduly restrictive. However, most GA-based applications do just that. Unfortunately, unlike the case of fixed length rule sets, it's much more difficult to justify such a restriction except on rather pragmatic grounds.

Whether one is treating rules or entire rule sets as individuals, one generally needs to have genetic operators like crossover and mutation occur at a finer level of granularity than just at rule boundaries. By requiring rules to be in a rigid, fixed length format, the usual genetic operators can be applied without much concern about producing syntactically or semantically meaningless offspring. If we increase the flexibility of the format by, for example, allowing a variable length left hand side, one is generally forced to modify the genetic operators to be "sensitive" to punctuation marks so that well-formed offspring are produced. However, introducing new operators means that care must be taken in ascertaining that they have the characteristics required by the schema theorems.

Most implementations of classifier systems and the more classical GA systems that I am aware of assume a fairly rigid format for reasons of simplicity. The usual (informal) arguments that are made to support the thesis that this is not a severe restriction generally take the form of: 1) the application doesn't require it or 2) one can achieve the same computational power (as the more flexible formats) by using multiple rule firings together with internal "working memory".

5.3. Working Memory

Another PS architectural dilemma revolves around the decision as to whether to use "stimulus-response" production systems in which left hand sides only "attend to" external events and right hand sides consist only of invocations of external "effectors", or whether to use the more general OPS5 model in which rules can also attend to and make changes to an internal working memory.

Arguments in favor of the latter approach involve the observation that the addition of working memory provides a more powerful computational engine which is frequently required with fixed length rule formats. The strength of this argument can be weakened somewhat by noting that in some cases the external environment *itself* can be used as working memory.

Arguments against including working memory generally fall along the lines of: 1) the application doesn't need the additional generality and complexity, 2) concerns about how one bounds the number of internal actions before generating the next external action (i.e., the halting problem), or 3) pointing out that most of the more traditional machine learning work in this area (e.g., [Michalski83]) has focused on stimulus-response models.

Most of the implementations that I am aware of provide a restricted form of internal memory, namely, a fixed format, bounded capacity message list. However, it's clear that there are plenty of uses for both architectures. I'm just happy that this choice is not imposed on us by GAs.

5.4. Pattern Matching

Many of the rule-based expert system paradigms (e.g., Mycin-like shells) and most traditional programming languages provide an IF-THEN format in which the left hand side is a boolean expression to be evaluated. This boolean sublanguage can itself become quite complex syntactically and can raise many of the representation issues discussed earlier. In particular, variable length expressions, varying types of operators and operands, and function invocations make it difficult to choose a representation and/or a set of genetic operators in which useful offspring are easily and efficiently produced.

The alternate approach used in languages like OPS5 and SNOBOL is to assume the left hand side is a pattern to be matched. Unfortunately, the pattern language can easily be as complex as boolean expressions and in many cases more complex because of the additional need to "save" objects being matched for later use in the pattern or on the right hand side.

Consequently, the GA implementor faces a fairly serious dilemma regarding the style and complexity of the left hand side of production rules. Most implementations that I am aware of have followed Holland's lead and have chosen the simple {0, 1, #} fixed length pattern language which permits a relatively direct application of traditional genetic operators. However, this choice is not without problems. The rigid fixed length nature of the patterns can lead to very complex and "creative" representations of the objects to be matched. Simple relationships like "speed > 200" may require multiple rule firings and internal memory in order to be correctly evaluated.

A favorite cognitive motivation for preferring pattern matching rather than boolean expressions is the feeling that "partial matching" is one of the powerful mechanisms that humans use to deal with the enormous variety of every day life. The observation is that we are seldom in precisely the same situation twice, but manage to function reasonably well by noting its similarity to previous experience.

This has led to some interesting discussions as to how "similarity" can be captured computationally in a natural and efficient way. Holland and other advocates of the {0, 1, #} paradigm argue that this is precisely the role that the "#" plays as patterns evolve to their appropriate level of generality. Booker and others have felt that requiring perfect matches *even* with the {0, 1, #} pattern language is still too strong and rigid a requirement, particularly as the length of the left hand side pattern increases. Rather than returning simply success or failure, they feel that the pattern matcher should return a "match score" indicating how close the pattern came to matching. An important issue here which needs to be better understood is how one computes match scores in a reasonably general, but computationally efficient manner. The interested reader can see [Booker85] for more details.

In any case we need to understand better what is involved in choosing a syntax and semantics for the left hand side of rules which balances the need for simplicity of representation and the need for expressive power. In my view this is one the most difficult and open issues in using GAs to search program spaces, and the key to successful applications.

6. Payoff Functions

In addition to choosing an appropriate representation language, careful thought must be given to the characteristics of the payoff function used to provide feedback regarding the performance of task programs. Strategies for designing effective payoff functions tend to differ somewhat depending on whether one is working with classifier systems or using the Pitt approach to evolving useful task programs.

In classifier systems the bucket brigade mechanism stands ready to distribute payoff to those rules which are deemed responsible for achieving that payoff. Because payoff is the currency of the bucket brigade economy, it is important to design a feedback function which provides a relatively steady flow of payoff rather than one in which there are long "dry spells". Wilson's "animat" environment is an excellent example of this style of payoff [Wilson85].

The situation is somewhat different in the Pitt approach in that the usual view of evaluation consists of injecting the program defined by a particular individual into a task processor and evaluating how well that program *as a whole* performed. This view can lead to some interesting considerations such as whether to reward programs which perform tasks as well as others, but use less space (rules) or time (rule firings). Smith [Smith80] found it necessary to break up the payoff function into two components: a task-specific evaluation and a task-independent measure of the program itself. Although these two components are usually combined into a single payoff, recent work by Schaffer [Schaffer85] suggests that it might be more effective to use a vector-valued payoff function in situations such as this. To my knowledge no one has explored this possibility.

However, one of the more provocative papers in this area at this conference suggests that there is an opportunity to have "the best of both worlds" with a multilevel credit assignment strategy which assigns payoff to both rule sets as well as individual rules [Grefenstette87]. This is an interesting idea which, I suspect, will generate a good deal of discussion and merits further attention.

7. Selecting Genetic Operators

It has been pointed out many times that there is nothing sacred about the traditional operators defined and analyzed by Holland. What *is* important is that we have criteria set by the schema theorems that such operators should meet. It is particularly tempting when using GAs to search program spaces to introduce new operators to deal with the complexity of the representations. One need not feel reluctant or apologetic about doing so. *However*, if changes are made to existing operators or new ones are introduced, it is important to verify that they aren't overly disruptive of the process of distribution of trials according to payoff and that they encourage the formation of building blocks. Without these basic properties, one is bound to be disappointed in the performance of GAs in searching program spaces.

8. Conclusion

So where does all this leave us? I think that it is quite clear that, as designers, if we can keep down the complexity of program spaces by using parameterized procedures or data structures which are easy to represent and manipulate with GAs, we have a much better chance for a successful GA application. If, on the other hand, the situation calls for evolving task programs at a more fundamental level, it seems equally clear that production system languages are currently the best choice for GA applications. Whether one chooses the Pitt or the Michigan approach is still a matter of individual preference. Perhaps by the time we get together again no such choice will be necessary.

References

[Booker82] Booker, L. B., "Intelligent Behavior as an Adaptation to the Task Environment", Doctoral Thesis, CCS Department, University of Michigan, 1982.

[Booker85] Booker, L. B., "Improving the Performance of Genetic Algorithms in Classifier Systems", Proc. Int'l Conference on Genetic Algorithms and their Applications, July, 1985.

[Buchanan78] Buchanan, B., Mitchell, T.M., "Model-Directed Learning of Production Rules", in *Pattern-Directed Inference Systems*, eds. Waterman and Hayes-Roth, Academic Press, 1978.

[Davis85] Davis, L. D., "Job Shop Scheduling Using Genetic Algorithms", Proc. Int'l Conference on Genetic Algorithms and their Applications, July, 1985.

[DeJong85] De Jong, K., "Genetic Algorithms: a 10 Year Perspective", Proc. Int'l Conference on Genetic Algorithms and their Applications, July, 1985.

[Fujiko87] Fujiko, C. and Dickinson, J., "Using the Genetic Algorithm to Generate Lisp Code to Solve the Prisoner's dilemma", Proc. Int'l Conference on Genetic Algorithms and their Applications, July, 1987.

[Goldberg85] Goldberg, D. and Lingle, R., Alleles, Loci, and the Traveling Salesman Problem", Proc. Int'l Conference on Genetic Algorithms and their Applications, July, 1985.

[Grefenstette85] Grefenstette, J. et al., "Genetic Algorithms for the Traveling Salesman Problem", Proc. Int'l Conference on Genetic Algorithms and their Applications, July, 1985.

[Grefenstette87] Grefenstette, J., "Multilevel Credit Assignment in a Genetic Learning System", Proc. Int'l Conference on Genetic Algorithms and their Applications, July, 1987.

[Hedrick76] Hedrick, C.L., "Learning Production Systems from Examples", Artificial Intelligence, Vol. 7, 1976.

[Holland75] J. H. Holland, *Adaptation in Natural and Artificial Systems*. University of Michigan Press, 1975.

[Holland78] Holland, J.H., Reitman, J., "Cognitive Systems Based on Adaptive Algorithms", in *Pattern-Directed Inference Systems*, eds.

Waterman and Hayes-Roth, Academic Press, 1978.

[Michalski83] Michalski, R., "A Theory and Methodology of Inductive Learning", in *Machine Learning: An Artificial Intelligence Approach*, eds. Michalski, Carbonell, and Mitchell, Tioga Publishing, 1983.

[Newell77] Newell, A., "Knowledge Representation Aspects of Production Systems", Proc. 5th IJCAI, 1977.

[Schaffer85] Schaffer, D., "Multiple Objective Optimization with Vector Evaluated Genetic Algorithms", Proc. Int'l Conference on Genetic Algorithms and their Applications, July, 1985.

[Smith80] Smith, S. F., "A Learning System Based on Genetic Adaptive Algorithms", Doctoral Thesis, Department of Computer Science, University of Pittsburgh, 1980.

[Smith83] Smith, S. F., "Flexible Learning of Problem Solving Heuristics Through Adaptive Search", Proc. 8th IJCAI, August 1983.

[Wilson85] Wilson, S., "Knowledge Growth in an Artificial Animal", Proc. Int'l Conference on Genetic Algorithms and their Applications, July, 1985.

A Genetic System for Learning Models of Consumer Choice

David Perry Greene
Stephen F. Smith

Carnegie Mellon University, Pittsburgh, PA 15213

Abstract

Consumer choice modeling can be viewed as a classification problem where the 'model' of interest is the rule that an individual uses to identify acceptable from unacceptable products in a given purchase situation. The search space of possible rules can be characterized as large, multimodal and noisy. Traditional statistical methods for generating consumer choice models are limited by the assumptions and representation they impose. A recent symbolic induction approach attempted to address these limitations but fell short in managing the complexity of the search space. It is hypothesized that probabilistic genetic search can overcome this complexity while retaining the advantages of a symbolic rule representation. This paper proposes a genetic algorithm (GA) based model generator capable of addressing these problems, describes its implementation, and compares it to alternative modeling techniques on a simulated consumer decision problem.

0. Introduction

Gaining insight into how and why a consumer chooses whether or not to buy in a specific purchase situation is of obvious interest from a marketing standpoint. An ability to identify the relevant features of a purchase situation, the relative order of importance of these features to the consumer, and the (potentially) complex relationships the consumer posits between them can provide significant leverage in both predicting product performance and focusing promotional activities. Within the marketing literature, this problem of understanding consumer behavior is referred to as consumer choice modeling. The problem can be generally stated as follows: given a collection of features that describe a specific purchase situation, and a set of examples of specific consumer choice decisions relative to this purchase situation, infer a decision rule that accounts for the consumer's behavior. Consider the situation of renting an apartment. In this case, the modeler is presented with a set of previously made rent decisions, describing each considered apartment in terms of a predefined collection of apartment features (e.g. price, distance from work, reputation of the landlord, etc.). Assuming that the consumer chooses to rent or not rent a given apartment according to some decision rule defined over these features, the goal is to construct a model of the consumer's decision rule from these examples of past choice behavior. Ideally, a model of consumer choice should demonstrate adequacy over three broad performance dimensions: 1) its ability to correctly forecast future choice decisions (or predictive validity); 2) its ability to correctly order the consumer's value for different product features (or diagnostic validity); and 3) its ability to provide insight into the consumer's decision strategy (or structural/intuitive validity). These performance dimensions provide a basis for contrasting alternative techniques for consumer choice modeling.

Traditionally, marketing researchers have relied on multiattribute statistical methods as a means of modeling consumer choice [Wilk73]. Such methods, however, are not without shortcomings. They provide limited intuition into the structure of the individual's choice rule and the assumptions that must be made concerning the structure of the solution space can sometimes result in serious predictive errors[Cury81][John85]. To overcome these limitations, a recent paper [Curr86] adopted an AI perspective of the problem, using a production rule representation and symbolic induction. While the use of production rules provided structural intuition, the representation created search difficulties which impaired the other validity measures. Genetic algorithms (GAs), because of their unique search mechanism, offer the potential of retaining the benefits of a production rule representation while overcoming the complexities of the problem space. This paper investigates the hypothesis that GA's will be able to predict decisions as well as statistical methods yet offer the representational superiority of the symbolic approach.

The remainder of this paper is divided into five sections. The first section examines the strengths and weaknesses of the conventional statistical methods. The second section considers consumer choice modeling as a symbolic learning task and describes the approach taken in [Curr86]. In the third section, an alternative approach using a genetic algorithm is developed to address the limitations in the existing methods. The next section describes a simulated problem to compare the three techniques using the three measures of validity discussed above. The fifth section presents the results followed by a brief discussion.

1. Traditional Statistical Methods

In marketing, multiattribute preference models, such as discriminant analysis and regression models, have been the traditional classification technique [Curr84]. The majority of these models represent a consumer's choices as a combination of feature weights, such as the linear regression model [Wilk73]. A major assumption in such approaches is that consumers trade-off relevant attributes of a product when forming overall evaluations. These are termed *compensatory* decision rules, because good features can compensate for the bad. Research, however, indicates the existence of non-compensatory choice strategies which do not accommodate tradeoffs [Payn76][Einh70]. Therefore one concern with these statistical models is that the presumption of compensating behavior is incorrect. Despite acknowledged robustness [Dawe74], under conditions likely to occur in a competitive market the use of compensatory models may be inappropriate and misapplication can have severe consequences[John85][Cury81].

A second concern with linear models is their limited ability to provide behavioral insights. Knowing how a person's choice strategy is constructed could provide a practical benefit by identifying targets for special emphasis or in modifying behavior [Wrig73]. Unfortunately, despite strong predictive performance, statistical methods are limited in two ways by the representational assumptions they impose. The first problem is that non-compensatory behavior is not easily identified from the feature weights. Second, the numerical coefficients offer no insight in to the configural relations among the attributes.

2. Consumer Choice Modeling as Symbolic Learning

2.1 Symbolic Representation of Choice Strategies
Production systems offer a representation which can capture the configural nature of a choice strategy in an intuitive manner. Following the terminology of [Mich80], we can represent a consumer's choice rule as a collection of elementary 'terms', where each term consists of a conjunction of attribute-value (A-V) pairs called 'selectors'. Preference for a specific apartment, for example, could be represented in the following form:

$$[rent = \$350][commute = 2 \; miles][heat\_incl. = true] \quad (1)$$

The logical union of several terms forms a disjunctive expression, leading to a disjunctive normal form (DNF) representation of more complex choice strategies. Such strategies can be classified as "compensatory" in nature since the selectors in one term can compensate for selectors in another. An example of a compensatory rule in DNF for selecting an apartment would be:

IF [rent < \$400][commute < 2miles][heat_incl. = true] (2)
or [rent < \$350][commute < 3miles][laundry_incl. = true]
THEN purchase

In contrast, a choice rule consisting of a single term (i.e. no or's) would represent a "conjunctive" choice strategy. In the consumer behavior literature the distinction between conjunctive and compensatory strategies has important implications, therefore the ability of the learning system to distinguish these structures will be an critical part of the evaluation (for this paper structure and strategy will be used interchangeably).

While behavioral researchers acknowledge the superiority of production systems as representation [Klah87], generating high validity rules is a difficult problem. As [Vali85] indicates, learning disjunctions of conjunctions is computationally complex for a reasonable number of features and becomes NP-hard in certain circumstances. If we assume only 40 binary selectors, for example, the size of the description space for a single term is 2^{40}. However, an individual is quite likely to have rules which use multiple terms ("term 1" or "term 2" or ..."term n") . For simplicity, if we restrict this compensatory decision rule to only 5 terms, the number of possible rules would be, 2^{40} x 2^{39} x 2^{38} x 2^{37} x 2^{36} or approximately 10^{58} possible combinations[1].

2.2 Concept Learning System
In a recent paper, Currim, Meyer, and Le [Curr85] identified the limitations of linear statistical models discussed in Section 1, and proposed a solution to the symbolic rule generation problem. Their approach, called the Concept Learning System (CLS), is an application of Quinlan's ID3 system [Quin84] (named after the earlier CLS system upon which ID3 is based [Hunt66]). The ID3 inductive algorithm constructs a consumer choice rule by incrementally building a classification tree that covers the training set, repeatedly adding additional selectors to underspecified branches on the basis of their estimated discriminatory power. Thus, given a training set of specific consumer judgements, with the attributes over which the judgements were rendered encoded as binary (true or false) selectors (e.g. rent < \$350, distance-from-work < 3miles), CLS searches by evaluating each selector for its ability to discriminate among the consumer's decisions. The selector which provides the best separation at each point in the search, as determined by information-theoretic measures aimed at minimizing the expected number of tests to classify an instance, becomes a new branch of the decision tree. This process continues iteratively until all training examples are correctly partitioned. The choice rule generated, then, consists of all the selectors used to build the tree (as in expression (2)).

The use of a production system formalism is an important advantage. Because of their apparent consistency with human thinking [Newe72] [Klah87] production system representation are easily understood by users. However, the use of production rules also exposes the complexity of DNF induction problems discussed earlier. The major concern in the case of CLS is that the decision tree building procedure is stepwise optimal but not necessarily globally optimal [Brei84] which means constructing a rule piece by piece will be ineffective if it is critical *combinations* of pieces which provide superior performance. A second concern is the sensitivity of the CLS inductive strategy to errors (or "noise") in the consumer choice data (which is not an uncommon occurrence in practice). As attempts are made to classify noisy training examples, the trees generated by CLS become complex and inaccurate[2]. Therefore, when conditions are less than ideal, the predictive quality of the rule may fare poorly.

3. ADAM: A Genetic Algorithm Based Model Generator

Genetic algorithms (GAs) are a class of search techniques which have demonstrated the capabilities to address such problems in a number of rule induction tasks (e.g [Smit83][Gold85][Scha85]). Accordingly, it was hypothesized that a GA would exhibit similar performance in the consumer choice modeling domain. To validate this claim, a GA-based consumer choice rule generator called ADAM (A Decision Adaptation Model) was implemented and evaluated. In the following subsections, we describe the principal components of this system. We assume familiarity with the basics of GA's and refer uninformed readers to [Holl75] [Holl86].

3.1 Representation
To simplify the comparative analysis, the binary selector coding scheme employed by CLS in formulating rules was also adopted within ADAM. Thus, a given term in a candidate rule is expressed as a string of length n over the alphabet {0,1,#} (# representing a don't care position), where n equals the number of dichotomous selectors defined and each bit position corresponds to a particular selector. A complete choice rule is then expressed as the concatenation of one or more terms. The number of terms in a given rule can vary, and there is no significance attached to the order in which terms appear. Using

---

[1] The possible combinations = $(2k)!/(2k-t)!$, where k = (the number of selectors) ,k (n \(mo {1,2,...limits of relevance}) and t = (the number of terms in a rule, t (n \(mo {1,2,..limits of cognition}), although the number of "legal" rules is a function of the independence among selectors.

[2] In [Quin86], some extensions to the CLS inductive strategy to cope with noise are proposed. These extensions were not implemented and will have to be evaluated in a later study.

implicit disjunctive normal form the rule string:

    1###1# 1##1#1 011###

would be interpreted as:

    IF   ((1) and (5))
    or ((1) and (4) and (6))
    or ((not 1) and (2) and (3) THEN choose.

If the conditions of any term are matched then the rule is active ("fired") indicating an acceptable product.

For purposes of the comparative analysis, we will assume all features describing the purchase situation to be binary attributes. Thus, there is always a one to one correspondence between purchase features and the selectors over which the term representation is defined. It should be noted, nonetheless, that the term representation is not a good one for the GA in the general case. Specifically, the representation implies that attributes which range over a continuum of values (e.g. the cost of renting an apartment) must be perceived through a set of binary selectors (e.g. [rent < = 300], [rent > 300], [rent < = 400], etc.). This yields a term representation space that includes a large number of illegal structures. However, this problem is easily resolved by simply using several string positions to recognize such attributes' values (as is routinely done in classifier systems)[3]. The need to explicitly define a set of possible selectors is specific to the CLS inductive strategy.

Assuming the above described representation of a consumer choice rule as a disjunction of one or more conjunctive terms, there are still alternatives as to the nature of the population of structures to be manipulated by the GA. On one hand, we might consider a single term to be an atomic rule of sorts, present the GA with a population of such atomic rules, and interpret the entire population as the consumer's choice rule. Adopting this approach, however, requires a means of assigning credit to the individual terms that contribute to the overall performance of the choice rule. We can bypass this problem of term credit assignment (as was done in [Smit80]) by encoding complete choice rules as individual structures in the GA population, and including discovery of term interactions as part of the GA search. In this case, the GA will manipulate variable length rule strings of the form

IF < term 1 > or < term 2 > or... < term n > THEN Choose

and the population of structures represents a collection competing choice rules. This latter approach is the approach adopted in ADAM.

3.2 Evaluation Function

The evaluation function or "critic" in ADAM contains three components. The dominant component, "prediction", measures how frequently a rule correctly predicts choice. The other two components, "specificity" and "term-count", relate to the structure of the rule. The three measure are weighted and summed to yield an overall fitness measure. Prediction is given a dominant weighting reflecting its importance in a model, however, the weights for the structural components have a critical role in determining bias, or direction of the search, toward the "true" choice strategy (eg. conjunctive or compensatory). On the whole, if two rules perform equally, the more general is preferred. Preliminary investigation showed that the GA would direct the initial search toward the appropriate structure, however, greater discrimination in the later stages was

[3] Actually, we can take advantage of the fact that with respect to many non-binary attributes we are interested in ranges of values, and define a better representation. In such situations, we have experimented with a representation that includes a <, >, or = prefix to patterns defined over such attributes, using a binary number interpretation of the attribute pattern in the case of < or > prefixes.

necessary. Some means for determining the most likely strategy was necessary to adjust the bias during the search.

3.2.1 Strategy Structures

Using Bettman's [Bett79] description of conjunctive and compensatory for a 3 attribute example, the following structures would be expected:
for conjunctive rules there would be only one term with a specific value defined at each relevant attribute:

    conjunctive: IF < A = x and B = y and C = z >
                THEN Choose,

for a linear compensatory rule the structure is disjunctions of conjunctive terms and should have many terms with fewer defined positions (low specificity, high term-count):

    compensatory: IF < A = x and B = y >
             or < A = j and C = k >
                THEN Choose.

Based on this "specificity" measures the number of don't-cares in a rule string and "term-count" measures the number of terms. Conjunctive rules would have high specificity and low term-count while compensatory rules would have the reverse.

3.2.2 Shifting Bias

Since one purpose of the rule is to infer strategy from rule structure an appropriate structural bias cannot be known a priori. Unlike traditional methods which may erroneously presume a specific structure (i.e. linear compensatory), ADAM should adapt its bias as the search progresses. Because of the GA efficiency at initially locating good structures, ADAM can use this information to adjust the evaluation function (bias) towards conjunctive or compensatory structures. That is, "fit" rules tend to acquire a specific form and the weights associated with specificity and term-count can be adjusted to favor search among rules with that form. In the later stages of the search, once a specific form becomes predominant, this bias becomes useful in discriminating among otherwise equivalent rules. Eventually this bias adjustment could be implemented as a smooth function [Berl79] based on the population average size weighted by performance, for now, the shift occurs when the size of the best structure in the population falls below the average size of the initial population (~3 terms).

3.2.3 Measuring Prediction

Predictive validity or the ability to forecast choice can be measured with a simple contingency table (Figure 1), when a rule agreed or disagreed with the training set choices.

Basic Contingency Table
("fired" implies the rule conditions were met
and so the item was acceptable)

	not fired	fired
chosen	a	b
not chosen	c	d

Fig. 1

This figure is representative of a hypothesis test, with cells b and c considered errors of omission and commission respectively. While differential penalties might be applied based on the severity (cost) of each type of error, for this paper they are considered equivalent.

3.2.4 Folding sample

One final characteristic influencing the evaluation is the segmentation of the training sample into a smaller training set. At the end of a generation a new training set was drawn starting with the element about 2/3 of the way from the previous first element. This caused a stagger or overlap of about 1/3 for each training set. The primary reason was to maintain some of the adaptive flavor of the search by providing a changing environment (the overlap of the sample allowed the change to be more gradual). One effect was to maintain diversity among the genes to prevent lost alleles. A second reason was that it requires fewer computations per generation even if the training sample size were increased. Interestingly enough, this scheme of staggering the training examples considered during evaluation appeared to lead to equal performance compared with repeated consideration of the entire training set in preliminary experiments.

3.3 Rule Generating Parameters

Based on the results of earlier studies [DeJo75] [Gref83], a population of 50 candidate choice rules is maintained by the GA in conducting its search. The initial set of rules is generated randomly with the number of terms ranging between 1 and 6, and a 33% probability of a 1, 0 or # at each individual string position. Although typically a larger percentage of #'s are used, the potential of highly specific "conjunctive" rules suggested that too general a seeding would slow the search progress.

After the evaluation function assigns a fitness to each rule the scores are normalized, and genetic operators are applied to produce a new population of candidate rules. An "elitest" strategy, as suggested by DeJong (1975), then inserts the best rule from the previous generation. The probability of crossover is set at 0.6, as originally suggested by [DeJo75]. Crossover operates at two levels (between terms and between selectors) as outlined by [Smit80] with a modification to alignment point selection to include a zero level crossover (recall that the structures being manipulated are variable length). This has the effect of permitting single terms to occur and be included in the crossover process[4]. Finally, the mutation rate was set at 0.001.

ADAM continues to search until either it finds a rule which perfectly classifies the set of choices or it reaches a prespecified number of generations. After it stops it then selects the rule with the best score. The output of this search process is a single rule used to characterize an individual's choice strategy.

4. Methodology

A simulation was constructed to perform a comparative analysis of ADAM, CLS, and a linear Logit model. The following four factors were investigated for their potential affect on performance:

1- type of "true" choice strategy (conjunctive, compensatory or mixed).
2- number of attributes on which the rule is based (3, 6, 9).
3- level of noise in representing the choice (0%, 10%, 20%).
4- sample size used for estimation (20, 100, 200) with half of each sample used as a holdout.

To provide the simulation data a table of randomly generated A-V terms was created. Each alternative consists of three, six, or nine attributes using a random number between 0 and 99. A

coding function representing a decision maker's strategy (conjunctive, compensatory or mixed) was applied resulting in a set of decisions marked as positive or negative examples. This could be thought of as a sample of products characterized by 3,6 or 9 attributes plus an indicator of whether or not the consumer thought it should be chosen.

The choice indicator was generated using the following three choice functions:

conjunctive: choice $= 1$ if $(x_1 > t_1) \therefore (x_2 > t_1) \therefore ....(x_n > t_1)$
$\qquad$ 0 otherwise

compensatory: choice $= 1$ if $(x_1 + x_2 + ... x_n) / n > t_2$
$\qquad$ 0 otherwise

mixed: choice $= 1$ if $((x_1 > t_3) \therefore (x_2 + x_3 + ... x_n) / n > t_4)$
$\qquad$ 0 otherwise

* n = number of attributes in a given experimental condition $(n \in \{3,6,9\})$
* x_i = a given attribute $(i \in \{1,2,...n\})$
* t_j = thresholds, each t will be selected a priori for each of n conditions to generate an approximately equal split between the number of "chosen" and "nonchosen" alternatives.

Noise was introduced into each coded set of examples by changing the decision indicator of any alternative in the set with a probability of 0%, 10% or 20%. This represents a severe form of misclassification since an alternative which contained acceptable attribute values is now indicated unacceptable and vice versa.

Using combinations of: choice strategy, number of attributes, and noise level, nine selection models were created representing a 3 x 3 x 3 partial factorial. Each of the nine models is applied for three different sample sizes yielding 27 (model/sample sizes). Each of these 27 conditions is repeated 5 times yielding 135 data sets. Half of each data set was used as a holdout sample meaning it represented a set of decisions not previously seen and therefore usable for evaluation. ADAM, CLS and the simulation were all programmed in PASCAL and run on an IBM-PC[5]. The Logit results were generated using Hotztrans on a VAX computer and with RATS on an IBM-PC.

5. Results

The objective of ADAM was to simulate performance under a number of conditions and to determine whether it offered any improvements with respect to the issues described in earlier sections. Performance was evaluated on the basis of the previously discussed measures of a good model: predictive, diagnostic and structural validity. These results are summarized below.

5.1 Prediction

For the simulation the ability to accurately predict is measured by how well the model's rule predicts the hold-out sample. The comparative predictive levels of the models averaged over the 5 repetitions are presented in Table 1.

[4] As suggested by Smith [Smit80], the level of crossover seems to yield better early performance when set high but better later performance when set low. In preliminary experiments staggering the crossover-level operator based on the number of generations elapsed, appeared to yield steadier increases in overall performance.

[5] The CLS code was supplied by Bob Meyer at the University of California at Los Angeles.

			sample = 10			sample = 50			sample = 100		
Strat	Atribs	Noise	GA	CLS	Logit	GA	CLS	Logit	GA	CLS	Logit
1 Conj	3	0%	100	90	92	100	100	100	100	100	100
2 Conj	6	10%	72	62	60	73	67	75	76	58	72
3 Conj	9	20%	86	73	66	80	76	80	78	66	76
4 Comp	3	10%	76	72	73	79	65	76	83	69	80
5 Comp	6	0%	75	59	83	82	68	84	78	66	82
6 Comp	9	20%	62	47	71	66	64	70	66	56	71
7 Mixd	3	20%	78	68	73	76	69	73	75	66	78
8 Mixd	6	10%	88	47	84	88	80	86	81	80	85
9 Mixd	9	0%	78	74	77	92	90	95	87	88	94

Table 1.

It is evident that ADAM, using a genetic algorithm, generated rules with equal or superior predictive ability to those of CLS across almost all the experimental conditions (the exception being 1 and 2 points difference for the mixed model with 9 attributes)[6]. In comparing ADAM to the Logit model, the major impression is how comparable and consistent their performance was. Overall ADAM predicted at 80.7% accuracy vs. Logit at 79.9%. As was expected, the performance varied across conditions. The results are shown in Table 2.

Performance Across Conditions

	overall	MODEL			NOISE			SELECTORS			SIZE		
		cnj	cmp	mxd	0%	10%	20%	3	6	9	10	50	100
Adam	80.7	85	74	83	88	82	72	85	79	77	79	82	81
Logit	79.9	80	77	83	90	79	72	83	79	78	75	82	82

Table 2.

As seen from Table 2., ADAM appears to offer a slight edge with respect to conjunctive rules and small sample sizes; areas where traditional models are expected to be weak. However none of the performance difference were found statistically significant.

A comparison of regression models using dummy variables primarily examined main effects. The results indicate significant differences ($p < .0001$) for all main effects (model type, number of attributes, %-noise, sample size) consistent with expectations. That is, increasing noise and larger attribute sets had detrimental effects on predictive accuracy, while larger samples had a positive effect. The performance of ADAM showed significant improvement over CLS. However, an F-test between regression models did not indicate significant difference over Logit at ($p < .05$) even with first order interactions included.

One explanation for the surprising strength of the logit model on conjunctive rules was the nature of the simulation environment. As several researchers have noted [Dawe74][Cury81][John85] the use of a uniform distribution in generating simulation attributes provides a best case environment for the averaging of a statistical model. However, such environments are likely to be inconsistent with a realistic market situation, where the true conditions would prove detrimental to the linear model.

Two encouraging findings were the low variance of ADAM's results across repetitions of the trials and the stability of ADAM across differences in both strategy and noise, supporting the expectations for genetic search. Note that the falloff in prediction is consistent with the increase in the noise level. Several additional runs using noise as the only experimental variable support this finding [7].

5.2 Diagnosis

When consumers make choices they frequently do not place the same weight on all the features but instead indicate that certain attributes are more important than others. Diagnostic validity measures the models ability to recover the importance of an attribute. In a regression model like Logit, attribute importance is represented by the beta coefficients or parameter weights. A comparable parameter is ADAM's relative frequency measures for each attribute. A critical question is whether production rules can provide diagnostic validity.

Diagnostic Correlation between ADAM and Logit

Correlation between Relative Frequency of Attributes in ADAM and beta coefficients from Logit.

		Sample Set Size			
Attrib	(cases)	10	50	100	
X1	(135)	0.45a	0.83a	0.78a	
X2	(135)	0.50a	0.74a	0.79a	
X3	(135)	0.41b	0.75a	0.75a	
X4	(90)	0.64a	0.65a	0.76a	
X5	(90)	0.48b	0.62a	0.65a	significance
X6	(90)	0.65a	0.58a	0.65a	a- $p < .0001$
X7	(45)	0.43	0.85a	0.61c	b- $p < .001$
X8	(45)	0.47	0.48	0.42	c- $p < .01$
X9	(45)	0.53d	0.56c	0.72b	d- $p < .05$

Table 3.

As is evidenced in Table 3., not only do the two algorithms generate equivalent predictions, but they also appear to agree as to the relative importance of attributes even across sample sizes. The correlations appear to follow increasing convergence as sample size increases although this trend was not significant ($p < .01$). This is a very interesting result since it lends support to the use of production rule models in providing useful quantitative measures as well as intuition.

5.3 Structure

Structural validity indicates the model's ability to recover the form of a given choice process, ultimately to provide insight into the individuals behavior. Doing so is a two step procedure. First, the model must find a rule that predicts well. Given that rule, the second step is to infer the underlying choice strategy based on the rule's structure. The structural elements are features such as the number of terms, the number of "don't-care" symbols (#), the distribution of usage frequency across terms, and so on. Classification is determined by specifying a

---

[6] To establish that the simulation replicated Curim et. al.'s earlier study, a t-test for difference in the pairwise results was found non-significant, t(26 df) = -0.241 , the null hypothesis that the means were equal could not be rejected. This is encouraging since it addresses the objective of extending their efforts.

[7] The slightly lower performance in compensatory rules may be attributable to the loss of information caused by encoding a 100 value random number as a dichotomous variable.

mapping from characteristics consistent with the known choice strategy to the features (structural elements) of a rule. The ability to provide structural intuition is a key advantage of ADAM over Logit. A critical issue is whether the true structure can be recovered when the data is noisy (a debilitating condition for CLS).

Structural Classification for Model by Noise%

Model:	Noise:	0%	10%	20%
	conjunctive	100%	87%	73%
	compensatory	87%	93%	60%
	mixed	60%	60%	20%

Table 4.

From the table it appears that the performance is encouragingly robust, generating misclassification within an acceptable range based on the given noise level.

5.4 Conclusion

Based on a simple simulation, the performance of ADAM was evaluated using the three validity measures. With respect to the research objectives and performance hypotheses, the following results were recorded. The GA provided superior performance to CLS across all measures especially in those areas addressing the weakness of traditional models. This suggests genetic search may offer a suitable alternative. Further, the GA performed very well with respect to the traditional strengths of the Logit model while providing the important feature of production system representation. One additional finding is that production rules can provide quantitative measures comparable to statistical coefficient. Accepting that the simulation represents a simplified situation, the results appear to provide strong support for the potential of genetic search as a method for modeling consumer choice.

6. Discussion

6.1 Review

Preference models provide intuition about how a consumer might behave and why he does so. Although the traditional tool has been the linear compensatory model, behavioral research has shown evidence of a number of situations where the use of such models is inappropriate and where misapplication can have severe consequences. A proposed alternative, based on Quinlan's classification tree building procedure, provided the necessary production system formalism, however the predictive and diagnostic performance was weak due to the complexity of the problem domain. To address the limits of earlier approaches, a classification system called ADAM was developed utilizing a GA for search. A simplified choice simulation was used to evaluate GA performance and to provide a comparison to the earlier methods. The results of the simulation support the potential of genetic search and the use of ADAM for choice modeling.

6.2 Future Directions

A model which can provide performance equal to statistical models with intuitive advantages of production systems, offers a more versatile tool for marketing professionals. However several issues need to be examined. With respect to the problem domain, it is important to look at increasing the number and type of attributes as well as different distributions of attribute sets. With respect to the representation and its influence on the solvability of a problem, two issues can be identified. The first concerns experimentation with non-binary attribute pattern representations that better facilitate the characterization of numerical ranges of values. As was mentioned in passing in Section 3.1, we have begun investigating the use of pattern prefixes in this regard. The second issue concerns the information loss that results from any discretization of the possible values that a continuous variable may assume. We are exploring techniques for dynamically rescaling (i.e. expanding or contracting) attribute ranges when performance stagnates within a specific range of values. With respect to the evaluation function the initial efforts at an adaptive bias using a shift in the evaluation function weights also appear promising. An important next step is applying an upgraded ADAM to actual consumer choice data.. Overall the positive results suggest that a much more detailed investigation of a genetic system for modeling consumer choice strategies is warranted.

References

[Berl79] Berliner,H. "On the Construction of Evaluation Functions for Large Domains", Proceedings IJCAI-79, 1979.

[Bett79] Bettman, J.R. *An Information Processing Theory of Consumer Choice*, Addison-Wesley, 1979.

[Brei84] Breiman,L. ,Friedman,J., Olshen,R. and Stone,C. *Classification and Regression Trees*, Wadsworth, Inc., 1984.

[Curr84] Currim,I. and Sarin,R.K. "A Comparative Evaluation of Multiattribute Consumer Preference Models", Management Science, vol. 30, no. 5 (May), 1984, p. 543-561.

[Curr86] Currim,I., Meyer,R.J., and Le, N., "A Concept-Learning System for the Inference of Production Models of Consumer Choice", working paper no.149, Center for Marketing Studies, UCLA , 1986.

[Cury81] Curry,D.J., Louviere,J.J. and Augustine, M.J. "On the Sensitivity of Brand-Choice Simulations to Attribute Importance Weights", Decision Sciences, vol. 12, 1981, p. 502-516.

[Dawe74] Dawes,R.M. and Corrigan,B., "Linear Models in Decision Making", Psychological Bulletin, vol. 81, no. 2, 1974, p. 95-106.

[DeJo75] DeJong,K.A. "Analysis of the Behavior of a Class of Genetic Adaptive Systems", PhD Thesis, Dept. of Computer and Communication Sciences, University of Michigan,1975.

[Einh70] Einhorn,H.J. "The Use of Nonlinear, Noncompensatory Models in Decision Making", Psychological Bulletin, vol. 73, no. 3, 1970, p. 221-230.

[Gold83] Goldberg,D. "Computer Aided Gas Pipeline Operation Using Genetic Adaptive Systems", PhD Thesis, Dept. of Civil Engineering, University of Michigan, 1983.

[Gold85] Goldberg,D. "Dynamic Systems Control Using Rule Learning and Genetic Algorithms", Proceedings of the Ninth International Joint Conference on Artificial Intelligence (Los Angeles, California) Morgan Kaufmann, 1985, p. 588-592.

[Gref83] Grefenstette,J.J. "Optimization of Genetic Search Algorithms", Tech. Rep. CS-83-14, Vanderbilt University, 1983.

[Holl75] Holland,J.H. *Adaptation in Natural and Artificial Systems*, University of Michigan Press, 1975.

[Holl86] Holland,J.H. "Escaping Brittleness: the Possibilities of General Purpose Learning Algorithms Applied to Parallel Rule-Based Systems" in *Machine Learning: An Artificial Intelligence Approach, vol. II*, R. Michalski, J. Carbonell, and T. Mitchell (Eds.), Morgan Kaufmann,1986.

[Hunt66] Hunt,E.B., Marin,J. and Stone,P.T. *Experiments in Induction*, Academic Press, 1966.

[John85] Johnson,E.J., Meyer,R.J., and Ghose,S. "When Choice Models Fail: Compensatory Models in Efficient Sets", working paper, Graduate School of Industrial Administration, Carnegie Mellon Univ., 1985.

[Klah87] Klahr,D., Langley,P. and Neches,R. *Production System Models of Learning and Development*, MIT Press, 1987.

[Mich80] Michalski,R. and Chilausky,R.L. "Knowledge acquisition by encoding expert rules versus computer induction from examples: a case study involving soybean pathology", International Journal of Man-Machine Studies, volume 12, 1980, p.63-87.

[Newe72] Newell,A. and Simon,H. (1972) *Human Problem Solving* , Prentice Hall

[Payn76] Payne, J.W. "Task Complexity and Contingent Processing in Decision Making: An Information Search and Protocol Analysis", Organizational Behavior and Human Performance, vol.16, 1976, pg. 366-387.

[Quin84] Quinlan,J.R. "Inductive Inference as a Tool for the Construction of High-Performance Programs" in *Machine Learning: An Artificial Intelligence Approach, vol. I*, R. Michalski, J. Carbonell, and T. Mitchell (Eds.), Tioga Press, 1984.

[Quin86] Quinlan,J.R. "The Effect of Noise on Concept Learning" in *Machine Learning: An Artificial Intelligence Approach, vol. II*, R. Michalski, J. Carbonell, and T. Mitchell (Eds.), Morgan Kaufmann, 1986.

[Scha85] Schaffer,J.D. "Learning Multiclass Pattern Discrimination", Proceedings of an International Conference on Genetic Algorithms and their Applications , Pittsburgh, Pa., John Grefenstette, (Ed.), 1985, p.

[Smit80] Smith,S.F. "A Learning System Based on Genetic Adaptive Algorithms", PhD Thesis, Dept. of Computer Science, University of Pittsburgh, December, 1980.

[Smit83] Smith,S.F. "Flexible Learning of Problem Solving Heuristics via Adaptive Search", Proceedings 8th International Joint Conference on AI, Karsruhe, West Germany, August, 1983.

[Vali85] Valient,L.G. "Learning Disjunctions of Conjunctions", Proceedings of the Ninth International Joint Conference on Artificial Intelligence (Los Angeles, California) Morgan Kaufmann, 1985, p. 560-566.

[Wilk73] Wilkie,W.L. and Pessemier,E. "Issues in Marketings use of Multi-Attribute Attitude Models", Journal of Marketing Research, vol. 10, November, 1973, p. 428-441.

[Wrig73] Wright,P., "Use of Consumer Judgement Models in Promotion Planning", Journal of Marketing, vol.37 , October, 1973, p. 27-33.

A STUDY OF PERMUTATION CROSSOVER OPERATORS ON THE TRAVELING SALESMAN PROBLEM

by

I.M. Oliver*, D.J. Smith†, and J.R.C. Holland‡

* Texas Instruments Ltd (Bedford UK)
†Texas Instruments Inc (Dallas TX)
‡Mullard Ltd (Malmesbury UK)

Abstract

The application of Genetic Algorithms to problems which are not ameanable to bit string representation and traditional crossover has been a growing area of interest. One approach has been to represent solutions by permutations of a list. and "permutation crossover" operators have been introduced to preserve legality of offspring. Three permutation crossovers are analyzed to characterize how they sample the o-schema space. and hence what type of problems they may be applicable to. Experiments performed on the Traveling Salesman Problem go some way to support the theoretical analysis.

Introduction

This paper is a study of three crossover operators designed to sample o-schema [GoLi85]:

* a version of Davis's "Modified" crossover [Davi85] - the Order crossover

* Goldberg and Lingle's Partially Mapped Crossover - PMX [GoLi85]

* a previously unreported crossover - the Cycle crossover.

We introduce a modified version of o-schemata and present an analysis for each of the crossovers. This is followed by experiments with the crossovers on the Euclidean Traveling Salesman Problem (TSP) [LLRS85]. The experimental results are tied back to the analytic predictions and are compared with other Genetic Algorithm (GA) approaches, a heuristic solution, a "Neural" Computation solution, and to the optimal solution.

The Crossovers

The Order Crossover

The order crossover proceeds as follows. First two cut points are chosen at random. The section of the first parent between the first and second cut points is copied whole to the offspring. The remaining places are filled using elements not occurring in this crossover section. To do this we use the order the elements are found in the second parent after the second cut point:

Parent 1	$h\,k\,c\,e\,f\,d$	$b\,l\,a$	$i\,g\,j$
Parent 2	$a\,b\,c\,d\,e\,f$	$g\,h\,i$	$j\,k\,l$
Offspring	$d\,e\,f\,g\,h\,i$	$b\,l\,a$	$j\,k\,c$

The offspring sequence, $j\,k\,c$ (return to the first position) $d\,e\,f\,g\,h\,i$, is the second parent starting at the second cut point with the elements of the crossover section of the first parent removed.

The absolute positions of some elements of the first parent are retained. Further the relative positions of some elements of the second parent are also kept.

Davis's [Davi85] 'Modified' crossover is exactly as above except that the first cut point is always at the beginning of the string.

The PMX

The PMX also proceeds by choosing two cut points at random:

| Parent 1 | $h\,k\,c\,e\,f\,d$ | $b\,l\,a$ | $i\,g\,j$ |
| Parent 2 | $a\,b\,c\,d\,e\,f$ | $g\,h\,i$ | $j\,k\,l$ |

The cut out section defines a series of swapping operations to be performed on the second parent. In the case above we must swap b with g, l with h, and a with i. Resulting in the offspring:

| Offspring | $i\,g\,c\,d\,e\,f$ | $b\,l\,a$ | $j\,k\,h$ |

The absolute positions of some elements of the both the first and second parents are preserved.

The Cycle Crossover

The cycle crossover is an answer to the question: Can we create an offspring different from the parents where every position is occupied by a corresponding element from one of the parents? The answer, in general, is yes. Every element of the offspring can come from one of the parents and usually the offspring will be different from both parents.

We wish to satisfy the following conditions:

a) Every position of the offspring must retain a value found in the corresponding position of a parent.

b) The offspring must be a permutation.

Consider again these parents:

$$\text{Parent 1} \quad h\ k\ c\ e\ f\ d\ b\ l\ a\ i\ g\ j$$
$$\text{Parent 2} \quad a\ b\ c\ d\ e\ f\ g\ h\ i\ j\ k\ l$$

Consider position one, condition a) says the offspring must contain either h or a. Suppose we choose h. Using condition b), a cannot be chosen from parent 2 since that position is now occupied by h. So a must also be chosen from parent 1.

Since a in parent 1 is above i in parent 2 we must also choose i from parent 1. Continuing the argument, having chosen h from parent 1 we must also choose $a,i,j,$ and l.

The positions of these elements are said to form a cycle, choosing any of the positions from parent 1 or 2 forces the choice of the rest if the above conditions are to hold.

The cycles are usually labelled by a number or are called unary and designated by the letter U:

$$\text{Parent 1} \quad h\ k\ c\ e\ f\ d\ b\ l\ a\ i\ g\ j$$
$$\text{Parent 2} \quad a\ b\ c\ d\ e\ f\ g\ h\ i\ j\ k\ l$$
$$\text{Cycle Label} \quad 1\ 2\ U\ 3\ 3\ 3\ 2\ 1\ 1\ 1\ 2\ 1$$

In a standard crossover operator a random crossover point or cut section is chosen. In the cycle crossover a random parent is chosen for each cycle.

Choosing cycle 1 from parent 1 and the rest from parent 2 in the above example produces the following offspring:

$$\text{Offspring} \quad h\ b\ c\ d\ e\ f\ g\ l\ a\ i\ k\ j$$
$$\text{Parent number} \quad 1\ 2\ 2\ 2\ 2\ 2\ 2\ 1\ 1\ 1\ 2\ 1$$

The absolute positions of on average half the elements of both the first and second parents are preserved.

Cycle crossover properties

Cycles have some interesting properties. Consider the cycles formed when two random parents of length L combine: (the order O of a cycle is the number elements in the cycle).

1. We can show that the probability of an element being in a cycle of order O (where $0 < O < L$)

$$= \frac{1}{L}$$

Note that this is independent of O.

2. The expected number of cycles of order O

$$= \frac{1}{L} \times \frac{L}{O} = \frac{1}{O}$$

3. The expected number of cycles formed is

$$= \sum_{O=1}^{L} \frac{1}{O}$$

4. The expected number of cycles of length 2 or greater

$$= \sum_{O=2}^{L} \frac{1}{O} \approx ln(L) - 1$$

5. If 2 parents produce $ln(L) - 1$ cycles of length 2 or greater then the number of possible ways of performing the cycle crossover to produce an offspring different from both parents is:

$$2^{ln(L)-1} - 2 = \frac{L^{ln(2)} - 4}{2}$$

In fact the expected number of different offspring for two random parents will be greater than this. This shows there are in general a good number of choices to be made, comparable with choices available when crossing over two bit strings.

O-schema Analysis

What is an o-schema ?

The analysis of the Order crossover has motivated a relaxation of the definition of an o-schema. Usually the following schema are different (where ! means do not care):

$$a\ b\ !\ !\ c\ !\ !\ !\ !\ !, \quad !\ a\ b\ !\ !\ c\ !\ !\ !\ !, \quad !\ !\ !\ !\ !\ a\ b\ !\ !\ c$$

In our scheme these are all considered equivalent to ab!!c!!!!!, the schemata has been normalized by taking the first element to be the successor of the longest string of don't care symbols. Lexical ordering of the fixed value symbols can be used to resolve don't care strings of equal length.

This definition of a schema is valid for the TSP as all the equivalent o-schema have the same value. It also has two clear advantages: there are less schemata so a given population will hold a greater percentage, and the defining length of many schemata is reduced.

For instance the following schema are equivalent:

$$b\ !\ !\ !\ !\ !\ !\ !\ !\ a, \quad a\ b\ !\ !\ !\ !\ !\ !\ !\ !$$

The first schema had a defining length of 10 but now has length 2.

Definitions

O is the order of an o-schema

D is the length of an o-schema

K is the length of a cut

L is the length of a string

Analysis method

The analysis in general follows the Goldberg and Lingle [GoLi85] analysis.

We calculate the probability of survival of o-schemata:

$$P(S) = P(S/W)P(W) + P(S/O)P(O) + P(S/C)P(C)$$

W (Within) occurs when the o-schema is entirely within the cut section.

O (Outside) occurs when the o-schema is entirely outside the cut section.

C (Cut) occurs when the o-schema contains a cut point.

$P(S/C)$, the probability of survival of an o-schema on a cut point is considered to be negligible.

Relaxing the definition of an o-schema allows for higher survival rates. However this effect is only apparent in the analysis for the Order crossover. The Cycle and PMX operators attempt to retain absolute positions in the ordering so the probability of relative movement of schemata along the string is negligible.

The Order Crossover

Let parent 1 be the parent from whom all the elements within the cut are taken.

Let parent 2 be the parent whose ordering is used to place the elements outside the cut.

The probability of the o-schema surviving from parent 1 is the probability that the o-schema is completely within the cut:

$$P(S/W)P(W) = P(W) = \frac{K - D + 1}{L}$$

The probability of the o-schema surviving from parent 2 is the probability that none of the elements of the schema have been taken from parent 1.

For large L and small D the following approximation holds:

$$P(S/O)P(O) \approx \left(1 - \frac{K}{L}\right)^D$$

Thus the probability of o-schema survival for the Order crossover is:

$$P(S) \approx \frac{K - D + 1}{L} + \left(1 - \frac{K}{L}\right)^D$$

The PMX

Let parent 1 be the parent from whom all the elements within the cut are taken.

Let parent 2 be the parent from whom all the elements outside the cut are taken, after the mapping operation has been performed.

The probability of the o-schema surviving from parent 1, is the probability that the o-schema is completely within the cut:

$$P(S/W)P(W) = P(W) = \frac{K - D + 1}{L}$$

The probability of the o-schema being completely outside the cut

$$P(O) = \frac{L - K - D + 1}{L}$$

The expected number of elements needing to be moved in the mapping operation

$$= K \times \frac{L - K}{L}$$

The probability of 1 element needing to be swapped

$$= K \times \frac{L}{L} \frac{K}{K} \times \frac{1}{L} \frac{1}{K} = \frac{K}{L}$$

For large L and small O the following approximation holds [Note 1]:

$$P(S/O) \approx \left(1 - \frac{K}{L}\right)^O$$

Thus the probability of o-schema survival for the PMX

$$P(S) \approx P(S/W)P(W) + P(S/O)P(O)$$

$$\approx \frac{K - D + 1}{L} + \frac{L - K - D + 1}{L} \times \left(1 - \frac{K}{L}\right)^O$$

The Cycle Crossover

Let N elements be taken from parent 1

Let $L - N$ elements be taken from parent 2.

(N is similar to the K factor in the Order and PMX analysis above)

The probability of o-schema surviving from parent 1 is the probability that all of the elements of the o-schema are taken from parent 1.

For large L and small O the following approximation holds

$$\approx \left(\frac{N}{L}\right)^O$$

The probability of o-schema surviving from parent 2 is the probability that all of the elements of the o-schema are taken from parent 2.

226

For for large L and small O the following approximation holds

$$\approx \left(\frac{L-N}{L}\right)^{O}$$

Thus the probability of o-schema survival for the cycle crossover

$$\approx \left(\frac{N}{L}\right)^{O} + \left(\frac{L-N}{L}\right)^{O}$$

O-schema summary

O-schema from parent 1, $P(S/W)P(W)$, have the same probability of survival with the Order crossover and PMX.

When $D = O$, the probability of survival from parent 2 is a factor of:

$$\frac{L}{L - K - D + 1}$$

more likely with the Order crossover than the PMX. However as D becomes greater than O the probability of o-schema surviving from the second parent decreases exponentially compared to the probability of survival under the PMX. Thus we would expect the order crossover to perform better than the PMX in problems where compact schemata are important. We expect the PMX would perform better than the Order crossover when compact schemata are less important.

The cycle crossover is noteworthy as the probability of an o-schema surviving is independent of its length. We would expect it to perform well in problems where the compactness of schemata is of no importance.

Experimental Method

A single 30 city problem was used for all the GA experiments, the "Neural" computation comparison, and Lin/Kernighan comparison [Note 2].

Each crossover was studied separately, no mixing of crossovers was attempted. Crossover was always applied to 80% of the population. A single mutation operator, SWAP, was used. The SWAP operator simply interchanges two positions on the string. For each crossover the SWAP operator was applied to a percentage of the population varying from 30% through 100% at intervals of 10%. Population sizes of 50, 200, and 500 were tried for each crossover with each mutation level. In all cases 50,000 tours were calculated. This gives 1,000 generations for population size 50, through 100 generations for population size 500. Roulette wheel reproduction was used with some modifications to reduce selection errors. No elitist strategy was used.

The system was written in the programming language C. One run (50,000 evaluations) takes approximately 15 minutes on an Apollo DN3000 (operating system Aegis8-Domain/IX Kernel version 9.2.5, C compiler version 4.1.6).

Experimental Results

The Order Crossover

Here we see 8 runs of the order crossover with mutations levels at 30-100%. Population size is 200. The x-axis is the *number of evaluations*, this can be thought of as the "work done", and is constant in this part of the study over all population sizes.

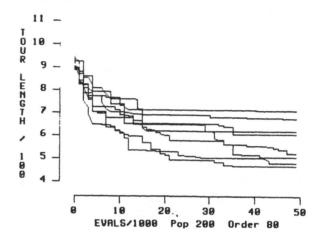

The order crossover is very sensitive to mutation levels. The difference in performance is 50% from the best (449 at 30%, pop. 500) to the worst (646 at 100%, pop. 500). There is a steady improvement in performance as mutation is decreased from 100% to 30%. This trait is common in large (500) and small (50) populations.

Performance improves slightly as population size increases. The best tour with a population of 500 (449) is 4% better than the best tour with a population of 200 (466) which is 5% better than the best tour for a population of 50 (492).

The PMX

For the PMX with population size 50 we have:

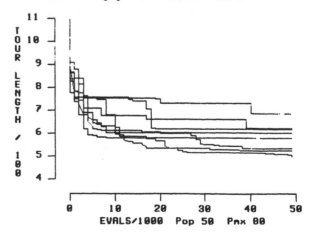

227

The PMX is sensitive (yet not so much as Order) to the mutation level. The difference in performance is 40% from the best (498 at 60%, pop 50) to the worst (687 at 100%, pop 50). The best mutation level is not as obvious as the with Order crossover, it is between 40% and 60% depending on the population size.

There is little performance variation with population size; in total a 5% difference, with populations 50, 200, and 500 giving best tours of 498, 518, and 521 respectively.

The Cycle Crossover

For the Cycle crossover with population size 50 we have:

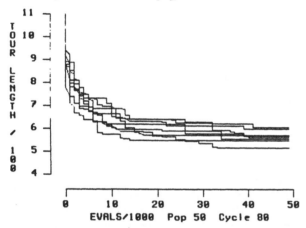

EVRLS/1000   Pop 50   Cycle 80

Cycle crossover is least sensitive to mutation levels. The variation in performance is 16% from the best (517 at 50%, pop. 50) to the worst (601 at 100%, pop. 50). The best mutation level is not clear, it varies from 50% for population 50, to 100% for population 200.

Performance was 8% better for population 50 (517) than for population 200 (559) and 500 (560).

Experiment Summary

Here we see the best runs, with a picture of the best tours, for the Order crossover, PMX, and Cycle crossover respectively.

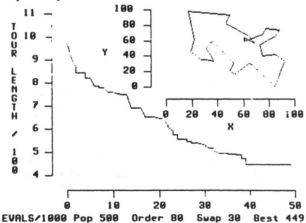

EVRLS/1000   Pop 500   Order 80   Swap 30   Best 449

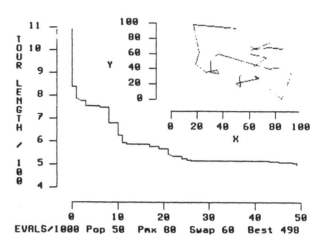

EVRLS/1000 Pop 50   Pmx 80   Swap 60   Best 498

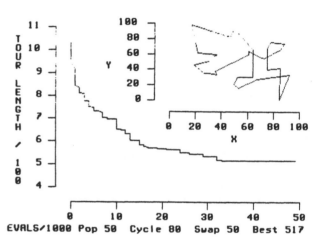

EVRLS/1000 Pop 50   Cycle 80   Swap 50   Best 517

Order does 11% better than the PMX, and 15% better than the Cycle crossover.

The o-schema analysis above ties in with these experimental results. The TSP is a problem where adjacency of particular elements (cities) is important. Thus we would expect that the Order crossover would perform best. The less sensitive behavior of the PMX and Cycle crossovers, especially the cycle crossover, can be thought of as a consequence of a built in higher level of mutation present in these operators.

It should be remembered that the experimental results are for the TSP only, and the o-schema properties of PMX and the Cycle crossover should be considered when applying permutation crossovers to other problems.

"Going for the One"

Using the results of this study, further experiments were carried out to find a very good tour for the 30 cities. The results suggested use of the Order crossover, with mutation at 30% or lower, population size 500 or larger, and more evaluations.

At population size 500, for 400 generations, with mutation at 15%, and with population size 1000, for 200 generations, with mutation at 25%, the Order crossover produced the following tour of length 425:

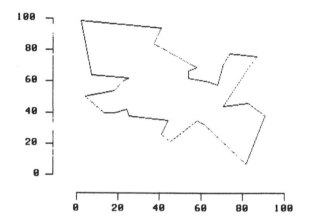

This is 5% shorter than the best tour in the comparision study.

Comparison with other approaches

We can directly compare our results the optimal tour, the Lin/Kernighan algorithm [LiKe73] and Hopfield and Tank's "Neural" computation technique {HoTa85]. Some comparison is possible with other GA results.

This is the optimal tour. Its length is 424 [Note 3]:

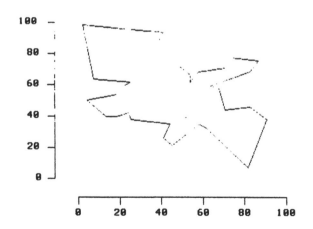

The Lin/Kernighan heuristic finds this tour. The best GA result of length 425 is within $\frac{1}{4}$% of this.

Next we see the best "Neural" computation tour. Its length is 509 [Note 4]. This is is 19% from optimal on the same 30 cities.

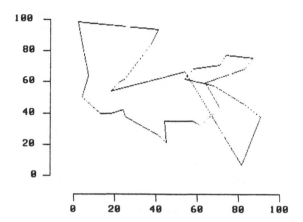

Goldberg and Lingle [GoLi85] report optimal results for 10 cities.

We have not run the same cities as Grefenstette et al [GGRG85] used, but some comparison is possible - Grefenstette et al report results within 16-27% of optimal for 50, 100, and 200 cities.

To put this work in perspective, current TSP research is on tours of tens of tousands of cities.

Summary

O-schema analysis showed that the Order crossover is superior in problems where compact schemata are important (such as the TSP). We expect the PMX to be superior when compactness is less important. The Cycle crossover preserves o-schema independent of length, and is potentially be superior in problems where compactness is not relevant.

The experimental analysis supported the theoretical prediction of good performance of the Order crossover for the TSP. Results from these experiments indicated how to the fine tune of population size and mutation level to produce results that were near optimal for the 30 cities studied.

Notes

1. Goldberg and Lingle report k+1 here, where we calculate k.

2. The coordinates of the 30 cities are: ((82 7) (91 38) (83 46) (71 44) (64 60) (68 58) (83 69) (87 76) (74 78) (71 71) (58 69) (54 62) (54 67) (37 84) (41 94) (2 99) (7 64) (22 60) (25 62) (18 54) (4 50) (13 40) (18 40) (24 42) (25 38) (41 26) (45 21) (44 35) (58 35) (62 32))

3. The optimal tour and Lin/Kernighan tour were computed by David Johnson.

4. These were not the actual coordinates used by Hopfield and Tank but were extracted from the diagrams in [HoTa85]. The extraction was quite accurate; they report 507 as the length of the "neural" tour. we calculate 509 on our points, they report 426 for the Lin/Kernighan tour, this is 426 on our points also. The

229

diagrams in [HoTa85] should be rotated through 90 degrees, laterally inverted, and scaled up by 100 to correspond with our diagrams.

References

[Davi85] Davis, Lawrence, *Applying Adaptive Algorithms to Epistatic Domains*, Proc. International Joint Conference on Artificial Intelligence, 1985.

[GGRG85] Grefenstette,J., Gopal,R., Rosmaita,B., Van Gucht,D., *Genetic Algorithms for the Traveling Salesman Problem*, Proc. International Conference on Genetic Algorithms and their Applications, 1985.

[GoLi85] Goldberg,D.E., Lingle,R., *Alleles, Loci, and the Traveling Salesman Problem*, Proc. International Conference on Genetic Algorithms and their Applications, 1985.

[HoTa85] Hopfield,J.J., Tank.D.W., *"Neural" Computation of Decisions in Optimization Problems*. Biological Cybernetics 52, 141-152, 1985.

[LiKe73] Lin.S , Kernighan.B.W., *An Effective Heuristic Algorithm for the Traveling Salesman Problem*. Operations Research 21, 498-516, 1973.

[LLRS85] Lawler.E.L., Lenstra.J.K., Rinnooy Kan.A.H.G., Shmoys.D.B., *The Traveling Salesman Problem*. John Wiley & Sons, UK, 1985.

A CLASSIFIER-BASED SYSTEM FOR DISCOVERING SCHEDULING HEURISTICS

by

M. R. Hilliard & G. E. Liepins
Oak Ridge National Laboratory, Oak Ridge, TN 37831*

Mark Palmer, Michael Morrow & Jon Richardson
University of Tennessee, Knoxville, TN 37996

ABSTRACT

A classifier system has been designed to discover heuristics for simple job shop scheduling problems. Experiments have shown that the classifier system is capable of discovering heuristics in a limited domain. We describe a new generalized version of the system and a set of experiments designed to produce more general rules based on sets of problems. Initial experiments with the generalized system indicate a potential for success.

THE NEED TO DISCOVER HEURISTICS

Constrained resources are common to many important activities. Manufacturing and distribution of goods, the mobilization and allocation of military forces, and government agencies' management of resources such as water and energy are all resource constrained. Since most optimization methods are limited either in their ability to model the constraints of the system or in their ability to solve problems of "real-world" scale, planning and scheduling in these environments requires heuristics. These heuristics may range from simple "rules of thumb" to complex algorithms based on considerable mathematical analysis; however, they all trade guarantees of optimality for speed and efficiency. The development of expert systems and other artificial intelligence techniques has led to methodologies for using heuristics to solve such problems, but the discovery of the heuristics for such a system remains a difficult task. A system which could learn heuristics based on its own experience and experimentation would provide a powerful tool for developing dynamic, responsive, and useful automated aids for planning and scheduling.

THE SCHEDULING DOMAIN

Scheduling provides a variety of increasingly complex problems to test a learning system's capabilities. We have chosen the formal structure of job shop scheduling as a model within which to work. In this model, processes must be completed in time to meet a delivery schedule as closely as possible. The processes each take a certain amount of time (run time) and may have precedence constraints (i.e., processes A and B must be complete before process C can begin). Sets of processes comprise jobs, and jobs are expected to be completed by a certain time (due date). Resources (machines) are available to complete the processes but can only be used on one process at a time. Numerous optimization based techniques have been investigated to solve this problem (including genetic algorithms [Davis, 1985]), but the most successful techniques rely on heuristics [Rinnooy Kan, 1976]. We have performed several experiments using a modification of the classifier system, on the simplest form of the problems (one process per job, no precedence constraints, one machine) using the objective of minimizing lateness, L.

$$(1) \quad L = \sum_{\text{all } i} \text{delivery\_date}_i - \text{due\_date}_i ; \quad i = \text{job 1, job 2, ..., job n}$$

This problem has a well known optimal heuristic: "Sort the jobs by increasing run time." Our experiments showed that the classifier system could find the optimal ordering of the jobs for a particular example, and, given the relative rankings of the run time, the system could develop a set of rules which said, "Do the shortest job first. Do the second shortest job second ... Do the longest job last." A recently developed extended system appears to have potential for developing more general rules.

THE PHASE I CLASSIFIER SYSTEM

The first phase of experiments with the classifier system was intended to evaluate design decisions (detectors, effectors, and feedback mechanisms). The resulting system demonstrated learning only in a limited sense; however, it provided insight into the design decisions.

The Environment

To be able to evaluate design decisions, the initial experiments with the classifier system have all considered the simplest version of the job-shop scheduling problem (as stated above). The system is presented a set of jobs with randomly generated run times and due dates, and is required to organize the jobs into a queue such that the total

* Operated by Martin Marietta Energy Systems, Inc., under contract No. DE-AC05-84OR21400 with the U. S. Department of Energy.

lateness (1) is minimized. If the jobs are renumbered by their position in the queue, then

$$(2) \quad \text{delivery date}_i = \sum_{k=1}^{i} \text{run\_time}_k.$$

It is well known [Conway, et al, 1967] that the minimum lateness schedule is achieved by organizing the jobs by increasing run time.

Classifier Representation

A system's ability to react correctly to its environment is determined in part by the adequacy of its internal representation of that environment. Within a traditional learning classifier system [Holland, 1986], there are certain representational limitations due to the use of the genetic algorithm as the primary learning mechanism [Liepins and Hilliard, 1986]. The foremost of these limitations is the necessity of encoding the environmental detector messages as strings from a small (usually binary) alphabet. The length of these detector messages determines the size of the search space for the classifier system, and a balance must be achieved to provide an internal representation of the environment which is adequate for the system to reason correctly and to develop useful classifier rules but simple enough to be searched in an acceptable period of time.

During the design of the action and reward structure, a minimal representation was necessary to provide a testbed for evaluating various decisions about the other features of the classifier system. Thus, in the Phase I experiments, the messages consisted of a single field, the rank of a job's run time in relation to other jobs in the problem. The Phase II experiments were performed using the binary representation of the run time as the message – See Table 1.

Job	Run Time	Due Date	Ranked Run Time Message List	Raw Run Time Message List
1	5	16	00	000101
2	12	22	01	001100
3	23	13	10	010111
4	50	40	11	110010

Table 1. Ranked run time and raw run time message lists.

Actions

For a classifier system to learn how to schedule jobs, it must have some means of interacting with the job queue. Interaction is accomplished through the use of effector classifiers which perturb the queue. In Phase I of the Job Shop Scheduling Classifier System, all classifiers are effector classifiers. Each of these is compared with the current detector message list (representing the current job queue with one message per job) and acts upon the matched job. A

successful classifier implementation requires that effector actions satisfy three criteria: 1) all possible orderings must be reachable by the actions; 2) the actions must be simple enough that a user can trace and analyze the steps leading to a particular queue ordering; 3) the evaluated merit of an action needs to reflect its true worth. Many possible actions were discussed including swapping jobs, moving jobs to the top of the queue, moving jobs to the top or the bottom of the queue, and moving jobs to a queue location specified by the classifier itself. Of these, we investigated moving a job to the top of the queue and moving a job to an indicated position.

The action of moving a job to the top of the queue was powerful enough to create all possible job queues and simple enough to trace and analyze (the first and second criteria). A trace of the classifiers acting in the last few cycles will indicate how the queue was formed, and any specific ordering can be achieved by placing the jobs at the top in reverse order of their run time. However, this design fails to meet the criterion of providing for an appropriate reward for action, because the system would have to learn to create a bad queue ordering in order to make a good one. This contradiction confused the classifier system and the action of moving jobs to a specific queue location was considered instead.

This second alternative — moving jobs to a specific queue location — meets all criteria. This action meets the third criterion particularly well, since the actions can be rewarded with the value of the new queue as described in the next section. Therefore, the right hand side of a rule in the Phase I experiments was the binary representation of the queue position in which to place the job matched by the left hand (detector) side.

Reward

Providing the system with feedback indicative of its performance is another major requirement of a learning classifier system implementation. Each classifier which effects a change in the system's environment must be given some reward in order to estimate the classifier's relative value within the environment and to make an appropriate decision as to which classifiers should be used in reproduction, which should be replaced during reproduction, and which should be allowed to act. The classifier system maintains a strength value for each classifier as an assessment of its relative worth within the environment. This strength is generally increased by rewards for classifiers which produce good actions and decreased by taxes and payments.

The reward within the job shop scheduling environment is based on the total lateness of the current job queue. This can be considered the learning approach to reward in contrast to the training approach where each action taken by a classifier would be evaluated and the reward would be based upon the action itself rather than the combination of its direct effects and its side effects upon the job queue. In the learning approach it is the state of the newly constructed job queue that forms the basis for the feedback to all the active classifiers and not the manner in which the new queue was formed. Thus the learning strategy permits the classifier system to develop any strategy for queue organization as long as it leads to an acceptable job queue configuration. This reward structure minimizes the amount of problem specific information in the system, and avoids encouraging myopic or "greedy" heuristics. The reward in the learning approach implicitly includes both an evaluation of the actions taken and a measure of the side effects of the actions. This approach requires that a classifier be given the opportunity to perform its action in a variety of situations (in order to separate the effect of its action from the side effects of other classifier's actions).

A successful and appropriate reward value is the actual lateness of the current queue scaled to the range [0,200]. Combining this reward strategy with the simultaneous action methodology described below created a system capable of distributing strength to a set of good classifiers.

Conflict Resolution

The conflict resolution strategy allows the system to develop sets of rules which cooperate to solve a problem. This cooperation can be based on finding niches in the environment as in Holland's default hierarchy, or it can be explicit. Our conflict resolution strategy allows for both types of operation by allowing multiple rules to compete for niches in the environment and allowing multiple rules to be active in each cycle. Each cycle proceeds through the following steps:

1. Match the detectors to the messages from the job list. Let S be the set of matching classifiers.

2. Generate a bid for each matching classifier, based of strength and add random perturbation to the bid to produce a "noisy" bid. (Bid = C*Strength + ε).

3. Select the classifier with the largest "noisy" bid. Perform the action indicated by the classifier.

4. Select the classifier with the next highest bid and (if possible) perform the action indicated by the classifier.

5. Repeat step 4 until all matching classifiers have been examined or until all slots are filled.

6. Fill any remaining slots with available jobs (maintaining their previous relative ordering).

7. Evaluate the resulting queue.

To provide more control in the experiments, there were eight jobs in the queue; therefore, the classifiers could be completely specific and did not employ #'s. The entire population of 64 possible rules (8 jobs x 8 positions) was maintained throughout the run. The classifier system established appropriate weights so that the eight optimal rules (i.e., 000/000, 001/001, ..., 111/111) dominated the population and generated an optimal queue. This was a limited demonstration of learning transferable heuristics. The system was limited by the requirement to use ranked run time (rather than raw run time) and to use specific rules.

THE GENERALIZED CLASSIFIER SYSTEM – PHASE II

Two extensions were necessary for the system to produce more general heuristics. The first is to generalize the left-hand side of the classifiers, allowing a classifier to match a set of jobs. The second extension is to reward the system for its performance on a set of problems, since appropriate generalizations require multiple examples. An analysis of the steady state of the system under different designs provided impetus for some design decisions.

Extensions

The Phase II system achieves generality in the classifier representation by using the raw run time information as in Table 1, and by incorporating a ternary representation with the third character ,#, being regarded as a "don't care" symbol and matching either 1 or 0. Thus,

100#01#   matches all of   1 0 0 0 0 1 0,
                             1 0 0 0 0 1 1,
                             1 0 0 1 0 1 0,
                             1 0 0 1 0 1 1.

Since the classifiers match sets of jobs, the conflict resolution strategy becomes more complex. Two strategies are being compared in our initial experiments, the champion strategy and the consensus strategy. In both strategies, the classifier's bid is calculated the same way bids are calculated in the all specific classifier system, except that the random perturbation is added at a different point in the process. The conflict resolution strategies view the bids through a job-position matrix. This matrix consists of cells for each job/position combination. Thus, in the case of four jobs, the matrix consists of sixteen cells and can be represented as in Figure 1.

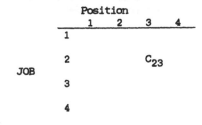

Figure 1.

Cell C_{23} contains the bids of classifiers which match job 2 and recommend placement in position 3. The champion strategy adds random perturbations to each bid in a cell and chooses the largest noisy bid to create the bid for the cell. The consensus strategy sums the bids in a cell and adds a random perturbation to the sum to create the cell's bid. In both cases the conflict resolution proceeds as in the totally specific case, with cells replacing classifiers. The reward under the champion strategy is awarded to the chosen classifier in each active cell, while the consensus strategy divides the reward equally among all classifiers bidding into an active cell. Initial experiments have shown the champion system to be superior.

The second extension, evaluating the rules on multiple problems to encourage generality, can be accomplished in two ways. In the cyclic reward implementation, the system cycles through the problems in a training suite several times in different random orders, bidding and receiving a reward for each problem. Reproduction, selection, and crossover occur intermittently throughout this cycle. In contrast, the delayed reward scheme allows the classifiers to bid, accumulates the rewards for the entire suite, and adjusts the classifier strengths based on the suite as a whole. Reproduction, selection, and crossover occur after several bidding cycles. This delayed reward is intended to prevent the most recent problem from having a stronger influence on the strengths at the time of reproduction. The two evaluation methods are being compared in Phase II.

Steady State Analysis

An analysis of the study steady equations indicates that both conflict resolution strategies tend to select more specific classifiers to act. Depending on the reward structure, selection for reproduction can tend toward general rules, specific rules, or rules with mid-level specificity. Let

S = steady state strength,
B = steady state bid,
R = average reward,
C = bid constant,
k = specificity (number of specific positions),
T = tax constant (ST paid each cycle),
n = number of jobs matched by the classifier, and
m = number of classifiers bidding into the cell.

We can consider a single classifier and a single cell. Three possible reward structures produce three different results. (See Table 2)

Steady State Value	Classifier Selection Tendency	
	Reproduction	Action
Payments = S(Ck + T) $S = \dfrac{R}{Ck + T}$	General	
$B = \dfrac{R}{1 + T/C}$		Specific
Payments = S(Ck + Tn) $S = \dfrac{R}{Ck + Tn}$	Middle	
$B = \dfrac{R}{1 + Tn/Ck}$		Specific
Payments = S(C + Tn) $S = \dfrac{R}{C + Tn}$	Specific	
$B = \dfrac{R}{1 + Tn/C}$		Specific

Table 2. Steady state analysis for the champion strategy.

The consensus strategy produces steady state values equal to the champion strategy's values divided by m. Since the bids in a cell are summed to determine the actions, the selection for actions continues to tend toward specific classifiers. Selection for reproduction, however, tends to favor classifiers occupying cells with small populations. Since the offspring tend to populate the same cell as their parents, this provides a control on overpopulation of any single cell.

Initial experiments with the systems tend to confirm these generalities, but the system is very sensitive to the value of T. If the value is too low, extremely general classifiers (#1####/010) tend to gain strength, whereas a high value tends to produce an extremely sparse matrix. A complete comparison of techniques awaits the completion of a full set of experiments. Initial analysis of the populations does reveal that once created, "good" general rules (000####/000) tend to survive.

CONCLUSIONS

Although we have not completed all the experiments in Phase II, the classifier system, when implemented with a conflict resolution scheme allowing for cooperation between classifiers, provides a mechanism which appears to be capable of generalization at a rudimentary level. The conflict resolution methods and bidding schemes developed for the simple job shop scheduling task seem to be extendible to more complex scheduling problems (precedence constraints, multiple machines, etc.) and possibly to other ordering problems. Future research will include a variety of experiments designed to help us estimate the systems ability to ignore extraneous data and the usefulness of a penalty function formulation for precedence constraints.

Acknowledgments

We wish to thank David Goldberg of the University of Alabama and Chrisila Pettey of Vanderbilt University for numerous helpful discussions and comments.

References

Conway, Richard W., William L. Maxwell, and Louis W. Miller. Theory of Scheduling. Addison-Wesley, Reading, Mass., 1967.

Davis, Lawrence, "Job Shop Scheduling with Genetic Algorithms." Proceedings of an International Conference on Genetic Algorithms and Their Applications. Pittsburgh, PA., July 24-26, 1985.

Holland, John H., "Escaping Brittleness: The Possibilities of General-Purpose Learning Algorithms Applied to Parallel Rule-Based Systems." in Machine Learning: An Artificial Intelligence Approach, Vol. II, R. S. Michalski, J. G. Carbonell, and T. M. Mitchell (Eds.), Morgan-Kaufman, Los Altos, California, 1986.

Liepins, Gunar E., and Michael R. Hilliard, "Representational Issues in Machine Learning," Proceeding of The International Symposium on Methodologies for Intelligent Systems Colloquia Program. Knoxville, Tenn., Oct. 25, 1986; ORNL-6362.

Rinnooy Kan, A. H. G., Machine Scheduling Problems: Classification, Complexity and Computations. Nijhoff, The Hague, 1976.

USING THE GENETIC ALGORITHM TO GENERATE
LISP SOURCE CODE TO SOLVE THE PRISONER'S DILEMMA

Cory Fujiki
John Dickinson
Department of Computer Science
University of Idaho
Moscow, Idaho 83843

ABSTRACT

The genetic algorithm is adapted to manipulate Lisp S-expressions. The traditional genetic operators of crossover, inversion, and mutation are modified for the Lisp domain. The process is tested using the Prisoner's Dilemma. The genetic algorithm produces solutions to the Prisoner's Dilemma as Lisp S-expressions and these results are compared to other published solutions.

INTRODUCTION

The genetic algorithm is an adaptive learning system inspired by evolution and heredity. In this particular application, the genetic algorithm will be used with a program generator to create source programs for different applications of the Prisoner's Dilemma problem.

The genetic algorithm is used to produce a set of programs (called a generation) which attempt to solve a particular problem. These programs are evaluated by a critic on how well they solve the problem and the best programs are manipulated by a set of genetic operators to create a new set of programs (the next generation). This process is repeated until a program produces an acceptable solution to the problem.

There are three genetic operators [6] traditionally used to create the new programs from existing programs: Crossover, Invert and Mutate. These genetic operators have been modified to be used with the program generator.

BACKGROUND

The initial work with the genetic algorithm manipulated a bit string representation of the solution. Smith [7] has shown that the genetic algorithm can manipulate variable length solutions that are more complex in form. Cramer [2] showed that instruction sets could be manipulated directly. Hicklin [5] showed in his work that a genetic algorithm can be applied to a program generator which creates grammatically correct LISP programs from a given set of productions [5]. The initial generation of programs were generated at random then and evaluated. Programs which rated below the average score of the entire population are replaced by new programs created from the higher rated programs. Random changes are made to programs to ensure a complete search of all possible programs. Although Hicklin's work was inspired by the genetic algorithm and Holland's work in the area, he did not use the genetic operators to develop new programs. Fujiki [4] took this work and developed genetic operators which closely approximated the traditional operators used by Holland [6].

KNOWLEDGE REPRESENTATION

A problem facing all adaptive learning systems is how to represent the knowledge being learned. In theory, the system should be flexible enough to allow unique and previously unknown solutions to be discovered. In practice, it is often necessary and even desirable to supply some built-in knowledge about a possible solution in order to speed up the search process. In Hicklin's system, the knowledge about a particular solution to a problem is represented as a program. A program is generated using a set of productions. The degree of flexibility in the system and the degree of built-in knowledge is dependent on how these productions are defined.

The types of programs generated in this study are based on the set of productions shown in Figure 1. These productions represent a subset of the productions for LISP. While not all possible LISP constructs can be generated using these productions, all of the programs generated are acceptable LISP S-expressions.

In productions 1 and 2, the symbol "Start" represents the starting symbol for the grammar. The program created are LISP functions starting with a COND command. Productions 3 and 4 are used to create any number of conditions and actions pairs.

1) Start --> (COND (T Action))
2) Start --> (COND Cond-Term (T Action))
3) Cond-Term --> (Logical Action)
4) Cond-Term --> (Logical Action) Cond-Term
5) Action --> The different actions that
   may be performed.
6) Logical --> The different possible
   conditions that can be checked.

Productions Used To Create Programs
Figure 1

Once a true condition is found, the action associated with it is performed. Only the first true condition found in a COND is used. The last condition generated is always a TRUE function with some action. This insures that the program generated will always produce some action found in the grammar no matter what conditions have been formed earlier in the program. Production 5 represents the different result productions, represented by the symbol "Action". These actions may be Lisp S-expressions or calls to specific routines. This production produces the different actions that may be desired for the problem domain being studied. Production 6 represents all of the different productions used to generate the logical condition used in the program. There can be any number of these "Logical" productions, including productions which combine the logical conditions by the use of

0. **Initialization.** Using the grammar productions, randomly create the initial populations of m Lisp expressions. All members of this initial population are considered to be mutations of the start symbol of the grammar. Whenever the grammar is used, the productions are separated into two categories; those that have only terminal symbols on the right-hand side of a production and those that have one or more variable symbols on the right-hand side. The length of the Lisp expressions is controlled by selecting productions from these two categories. A terminal percentage, t, is used to determine the probability that a production will be selected from the category that contains only terminal symbols on the right-hand side. The terminal percentage is increased as the length of the Lisp expressions increase, so that eventually the Lisp expression contains only terminal symbols.

1. **Evaluation.** All Lisp expressions are evaluated using EVAL. The value returned is used to rank each Lisp expression. Some applications may require several evaluations of a Lisp expression to obtain the actual figure of merit. For example, the prisoner.s dilemma requires several "turns"; each turn uses EVAL and the set of responses is used to calculate the figure of merit.

2. **Modify population.** A percentage, r, of the best performers in the current population is retained and the lower portion of the population is eliminated. The members eliminated are replaced by new members that are created from the remaining good performers by mutation, inversion, and crossover, that are involved according to the mutation percentage pm, the inversion percentage pi, and the crossover percentage pc.

3. **Iterate.** Go to Step 1.

Genetic Algorithm for Lisp S-expressions
Figure 2

logical "AND" and "OR" operators. An example of one complete grammar used for the Prisoner's Dilemma programs is shown in Appendix A.

GENETIC OPERATORS FOR LISP SOURCE CODE

The genetic operators must be able to change a program but at the same time keep some of the major characteristics of the program. If the operator does not change the program enough, then the search for better programs proceeds too slowly. If the operator changes the program too much, then the characteristics of the program that made it successful will be lost and little information is passed to the next generation of the programs.

The programs generated all have the same basic form in that they are all COND statements followed by one or more conditions and actions. Each condition action pair is considered to be one individual piece of information to be used by the genetic algorithm and are never broken apart by any operator. The operators used in this study were inspired by those used by Holland [6].

The crossover operator combines condition action pairs from one program with those of another program. The crossover operator divides two programs at two points picked at random in between the condition action pairs. New programs are created by combining the first part of one program with the second part of the other program. A second program is created by combining the two remaining parts of the programs. The crossover point can occur at any point in the list of conditions except after the TRUE condition found at the end of the program. A crossover after this point would be pointless since all conditions after a true statement would never be used and the program would remain the same as before. For example, a program can be represented as (Cond a b | c d) and (Cond A B C | D) where each letter is a condition action pair. Using crossover between b, c and C, D would produce the following programs: (Cond a b D) and (Cond A B C c d).

The invert operator does not change the information in a program but rather rearranges the information. When the invert operator is applied to a program, it reverses the order in which the condition action groups are evaluated, but it does not change the condition action groups themselves. The TRUE condition found at the end of the program was not included as one of the points which could be inverted. If the true condition was inverted, none of the conditions following it would be used since the program always ends after the first true condition found. If, for example, a program represented as (Cond |a b c| d) is inverted between a to c, then the resulting program would be (Cond c b a d).

The mutate operator is used to add new information to the population of programs. Once the original generation of programs has been created, the crossover operator and the invert operator can not add any new information to the programs, since they only rearrange the information that already exists. A random mutation operator is used to add new information to the programs generated.

When the mutation operator is used on a program, it removes one condition action pair picked at random in the program and replaces it with a new condition action function. This new condition action pair is created using a subset of the original grammar. Since it is desired to always have a true condition at the end of the program, the last true condition could not be changed by the mutation operator. If this condition is picked to be mutated, then only the action associated with it would be changed. For example, if a program which is represented as (Cond a b c d) is mutated at c then it would appear as (Cond a b e d) where e is a completely new condition action pair. The extent of the mutation performed on a program is determined at random.

A detailed outline description of the genetic algorithm applied to Lisp S-expressions is given in figure 2. The values for the parameters used for this work were:

(population size)	m = 80
(survival rate)	r = 25%
(terminal percentage)	t = initially 20% but increases to 100%
(mutation percentage)	pm = 25%
(inversion percentage)	pi = 25%
(crossover percentage)	pc = 25%

The percentages for the genetic operators were all set to the same value because one of the goals in Fujiki [4] was to determine the effects of the various operators.

PRISONER'S DILEMMA PROBLEM

Each program is evaluated and the highest scoring programs are used to create the next population. If two programs score the same then the smaller program is rated higher. This is done to favor the more efficient programs and remove programs with useless clauses.

The Prisoner's Dilemma problem involves two players who both must decide whether to cooperate or defect on each other. Each player is awarded points (called the payoff) depending on the action taken compared to action of the opponent. The different combinations of possible actions and the payoffs are shown in Figure 3 where R represents the payoff given to each player if both cooperate. S represents what is called the sucker payoff (i.e. the payoff for cooperating when the other player defects). T represents what is called the temptation payoff (i.e. the payoff for a player when he defects and the other player cooperates). P is called the punishment payoff when both players defect. The payoffs for each move have the following relationships in the Prisoner.s Dilemma problem, T > R > P > S. The gain for the players when both cooperate with each other is greater then when both defect. The gain for cooperating when the opponent defects is the smallest of any action. The gain for a player is greatest when he defects and the other player cooperates.

| | | Player 2 (Second Symbol) | |
		Cooperate	Defect
Player 1 (First Symbol)	Cooperate	R / R	S / T
	Defect	T / S	P / P

Points Scored in Prisoner's Dilemma
Figure 3

A second requirement for the Prisoner's Dilemma is that players can not benefit from taking turns exploiting each other. The gain from mutual cooperation must be greater than the average score for defecting and cooperating, R > (S + T)/ 2.

From the basic situation described above, several variations have been created. In this paper, the following additional requirements have been added: 1) Instead of just one round of decisions, a series of decision are to be made. Here a player could start by cooperating but decide to defect later on depending on what the other player did. 2) The strategy is used against a variety of other strategies in a round robin tournament. Here the best strategy is the one which scores the most total points at the end of the tournament. In this situation, a player may not be able to out score any other player but still win by scoring well against all of the other players.

The Prisoner's Dilemma has been used to represent a wide variety of real life situations. For example, when two businesses interact, it is usually a situation where one company would gain the most if it could get the other company to give up something for nothing, but at the same time, they have more to gain if they both cooperate than if they both try to deceive each other. Problems ranging from personnel relationships to super power negotiations have been studied using some form of the Prisoner's Dilemma problem [1].

For this study, the genetic algorithm tried to develop a strategy when having to make a series of 10 decisions against a variety of other strategies. In each situation, the program generated by the genetic algorithm was used each time a decision whether to cooperate or defect was required.

Scoring for each decision was based on the following (see Figure 4.)

| | | Player 2 (Second Value) | |
		Cooperate	Defect
Player 1 (First Value)	Cooperate	3 / 3	0 / 4
	Defect	4 / 0	1 / 1

Points Scored in Prisoner's Dilemma
Figure 4

The number of games played and the points awarded for each move was based on information from a tournament held for the Prisoner's Dilemma problem. This information was received in a file called The First Announcement of Computer Programs Tournament (of the Prisoner's Dilemma Game) on February 7, 1986. These values can be easily changed in the genetic algorithm to meet other conditions. For instance, if the grammar has no knowledge about the total number of games to be played, then a strategy for an infinite number of games can be generated.

The grammar used to generate programs had three different options it could check based on what the opponent did in the past: 1) What the opponent did on the last move, 2) what was done two moves before, and 3) if a particular action was ever done by the opponent in the past (either defect or cooperate). Other strategies could be generated by using a combination of the above checks together. The program generated could also check on the number of rounds played. While these checks were available in the grammar, there was no information about which checks to use or how to use them when creating a program. If a user was interested in other strategies then they could be added to the grammar. The actions available to program would be to either cooperate (represented by a 1) or defect (represented by a 2).

RESULTS AND CONCLUSIONS

The generation of what appear to be optimal strategies for the Prisoner's Dilemma problem came after relatively few generations in most cases. According to Axelrod's pioneering work on the Prisoner's Dilemma, the optimal strategy for the Prisoner's Dilemma under most circumstances is one he calls Tit-For-Tat [1] (there is never one optimal strategy for all cases since the best strategy depends on the other strategies being played). Tit-For-Tat cooperates on the first move and then does whatever the opponent did on the previous move (i.e. if the opponent cooperated then it cooperates, and if the opponent defected, then it defects). Axelrod states that a strategy normally has three different characteristics to be successful in a Prisoner's Dilemma tournament: Nice (i.e. does not defect first), Provocative (i.e. will defect if defected on), and Forgiving (i.e. can be made to cooperate after it has started to defect). Tit-For-Tat has all of these characteristics. This strategy is simple for the grammar to generate and therefore one would expect it to appear soon in the random generation of programs. The fact that simple strategies could produce some of the best results no doubt leads to the rapid generation of solutions.

The environment that the genetic algorithm was tested under was based on work done by Dacey and Pendegraft in their study of the Prisoner's Dilemma problem [3]. The grammar used to generate programs was designed to produce all of the different strategies studied by Dacey and Pendegraft. Other strategies were also possible with the grammar (i.e. checking two moves back), but there was no attempt at making a grammar that was all inclusive for every possible strategy. The grammar also allowed the checking of which round the program was in. The first run was played against strategies where Tit-For-Tat was thought to be optimal. The solution generated was a slight variation of Tit-For-Tat where, instead of defecting if your opponent.s last move is a defect, it defects if the opponent's last two moves are both defects. This was not one of the strategies studied by Dacey and Pendegraft and was produced by combining two strategies found in the grammar. This strategy was studied by Axelrod in his work [1] (called Tit-For-Two-Tats) and matches his contention that the best overall strategy should be nice (i.e. never defect first) and forgiving (i.e. can be made to cooperate even after being defected upon). It is also provocative, but not as much as Tit-For-Tat. When Tit-For-Tat was tried against the same environment, it was found to score lower then this new strategy. The genetic algorithm was tried against another set of strategies where Dacey and Pendegraft's work predicted Tit-For-Tat was optimal and once again Tit-For-Two-Tats won.

A third run was made against a different combination of strategies. In this environment, Dacey and Pendegraft, the strategy that was predicted to be optimal was one of cooperating with an opponent until defected upon and then defecting from that point until the end. This time, the strategy produced by the genetic algorithm matched the predicted strategy.

In the examples used above, the genetic algorithm developed a strategy against a fixed set of opponents. The fourth run was made where the programs produced by the genetic algorithm were also used as the environment that the programs were played in. Each program played all of the other programs produced each generation and then evaluated on its overall score against all of the programs. In this type of environment, a strategy may do extremely well only because it can take advantage of the other strategies currently in the population. If these strategies are replaced by different strategies, then the most successful strategies may change. This is exactly what appears to happen in this run. At first, a strategy of defecting all the time scored extremely well and begins to dominate the population. Then a small number of programs were created which had the characteristic of being both nice and provocative. These strategies, of which Tit-For-Tat is one, protects themselves from being taken advantage of by an all defecting strategy but also cooperates with other nice programs. When enough of this type of program are created, either by random mutation or by manipulating existing programs, then the all defecting strategy is no longer optimal. Eventually the strategy of cooperating until defected on, and then defecting from then on came out as the optimal strategy. This strategy appeared after approximately seventy generations and took over as the top player. Once this strategy was created no other strategy was found that scored better in over 300 generations.

In Axelrod's work on the Prisoner's Dilemma problem, he states that in a population of all-defecting players, a strategy of being nice and provocative would be the successful if a group nice and provocative players appeared in the group. But he also states that if a population of mostly all nice and provocative strategies exists, then no other type of strategy would ever be better. This is exactly what occurs in this run of the genetic algorithm. The all defecting strategy appears early in the run and appears to be the best strategy. The genetic algorithm eventually created enough programs which are nice and provocative and they are able to out score the all defecting programs. Once this occurs, this strategy is never outscored by any other strategy found by the genetic algorithm.

This strategy was not the exact one predicted by Axelrod to be the best for the general Prisoner's Dilemma tournament (i.e. Tit-For-Tat) but it does match many of the results found by Dacey and Pendegraft. It can be shown that when using only those strategies used in Dacey and Pendegraft's study, the strategy of cooperating until defected on, then permanently defecting, is the optimal one. Since it is their work that inspired the grammar producing the programs, this could be the reason why Tit-For-Tat did not win. The strategy of cooperating until defected on, then permanent defecting is considered nice and provocative but it is not forgiving. This would mean that it would do just as well or better than Tit-For-Tat in a world of nice strategies (since neither program would defect first) and both would respond when defected on. Tit-For-Tat would do better if it played against programs that tried to encourage cooperation after having defected. This type of strategy can be made by the grammar used in the genetic algorithm but it is not very common. This may be one reason why, in this particular environment, Tit-For-Tat does not appear to be optimal.

In all of the strategies developed, each one eventually learned to defect on the last move. It can be shown that in a limited number of Prisoner's Dilemma games, the optimal strategy always includes a defect on the last move. An example

of the programs generated by the genetic algorithm for the different Prisoner's Dilemma problems are shown in Appendix B.

The significance of this work is applying the genetic algorithm in the generation of real source code and showing that the genetic algorithm can be used to find optimal solutions to less then trivial problems when a proper set of productions are used.

APPENDIX A: GRAMMAR USED IN PRISONER'S DILEMMA

The following is a grammar that is used to produce the programs for the Prisoner's Dilemma problem. This grammar produces programs which can check a variety of items before returning either a 1 (which represents a cooperation move) or a 2 (which represents a defect move).

```
1)  index --> (COND (T action))
2)  index --> (COND index-cond-term (T action))
3)  index-cond-term --> (logical action)
4)  index-cond-term --> (logical action) index-cond-term
5)  action --> 1
6)  action --> 2
7)  logical --> (NOT logical)
8)  logical --> (l-op logical logical)
9)  logical --> (EQUAL NROUND 1)
10) LOGICAL --> (EQUAL NROUND 10)
11) logical --> (EQUAL OP-PLAY action)
12) logical --> (EQUAL OP2-PLAY action)
13) logical --> if-any
14) l-op --> AND
15) l-op --> OR
16) if-any --> PAST-DEF-OP
17) if-any --> PAST-COOP-OP
```

In the previous grammar, any item written in all capital letters are used in the final program. Index is the starting point for all programs. If production 1 is picked, then index becomes a COND statement with only a TRUE test (which by definition is always true). Action is a non-terminal and can be converted to either a 1 or a 2. This represents either a cooperation move or a defect move. If, in the beginning, production 2 was chosen, then a program with a COND and either one or more index-cond-term productions are used. These become some kind of logical test which must evaluate to a true statement before a corresponding action will be done. Some of the tests that can be generated in a program include: Check to see if this is round 1 of the game (production 9) or round 10 (production 10), check the last place the opponent made (production 11), check the play the opponent did two moves ago (production 12), check if the opponent ever defected in the past (production 16) or if the opponent has ever cooperated in the past (production 17). The symbols created by productions 16 and 17 are prewritten functions created for this particular problem which become true if a defect or cooperation move has ever been made. These checks can be combined using logical "AND" and "OR" statements (production 8 with productions 14 and 15).

APPENDIX B: PROGRAMS GENERATED BY GENETIC ALGORITHM

The following is an example of the programs produce by the genetic algorithm for the Prisoner's dilemma. Each program is designed to work in a LISP environment. The genetic algorithm was used to produce several different strategies for different environments for the Prisoner's Dilemma problem. The following represents two different strategies, one called Tit-For-Two-Tats by Axelrod [1] and one called Cooperation-Permanent Defection by Dacey and Pendegraft [3].

239

Tit-For-Two-Tats

```
(COND ((EQUAL NROUND 10) 2)
      ((NOT (EQUAL OP2-PLAY 2)) 1)
      ((NOT PAST-DEF-OP) 2)
      ((EQUAL OP-PLAY 2) 2)
      (T 1))
```

This strategy defects on the last move, which is when the round (stored in the variable "NROUND") is ten. If the person's action two moves ago (stored in OP2-PLAY) was not a defect (represented as a "2") then cooperate (represented as a "1"). The third condition checks to see if the opponent has ever defected (stored in PAST-DEF-OP). This condition would cause a defection if the opponent never defected. In this program, this condition is never reached since if the opponent never defected, then the opponent would not have defected two moves ago and the second condition would have been true. Therefore, the only time this program defects is if condition four is true and the conditions before it are false. Specifically, if the opponent defected two moves ago and if the last move (stored in op-play) was also a defect. Any other conditions would produce a cooperation move from the true condition in the last line of the program.

Cooperate-Permanent Defection

```
(COND (PAST-DEF-OP 2)
      (T 1))
```

This strategy is very simple to produce since one of the built-in procedures is true if the opponent has ever defected (stored in PAST-DEF-OP). This program returns a defecting move if PAST-DEF-OP is true (meaning if the opponent ever defected). Otherwise, it returns a cooperating move.

BIBLIOGRAPHY

[1] Axelrod, Robert, *Evolution of Cooperation*, Basic Books Inc, New York, 1984

[2] Cramer, Nichael Lynn, *A Representation for the Adaptive Generation of Simple Sequential Program*, Proceedings, International Conference on Genetic Algorithms and their Applications, July 1985.

[3] Dacey, Raymond; Pendegraft, Norman, *The Optimality of Tit-For-Tat*, Prepared for Presentation, International Studies Association, March 1986

[4] Fujiki, Cory, *An Evaluation of Holland's Genetic Operators Applied to a Program Generator*, Master of Science Thesis, Department of Computer Science, University of Idaho, 1986

[5] Hicklin, Joseph F, *Application of the Genetic Algorithm To Automatic Program Generation*, Master of Science Thesis, Department of Computer Science, University of Idaho, 1986

[6] Holland, John H., *Adaptation In Natural and Artificial Systems*, University of Michigan Press, Ann Arbor, 1975

[7] Smith, Stephen F., *Flexible Learning of Problem Solving Heuristics Through Adaptive Search*, Proc. 8th IJCAI,, August, 1983.

Optimal Determination of User-oriented Clusters :
An Application for the Reproductive Plan

by

Vijay V. Raghavan * and Brijesh Agarwal
The Center for Advanced Computer Studies
University of SW Louisiana
Lafayette, LA 70504-4330

Abstract

A typical Information Retrieval system is required to be able to satisfy user queries in an efficient and effective way. Furthermore, the system should be able to adapt itself to changing user patterns. Recent work in user-oriented clustering attempts to meet the above objectives by identifying document clusters that are consistent with the similarities perceived by the users, rather than those hypothesized by the designer. This paper proposes a representation framework for the application of an adaptive scheme in order to find optimal user-oriented clusters. It is shown, in particular, that the reproductive plan proposed by Holland [7] is a promising solution strategy for the optimal determination of the boundaries between clusters.

1. Introduction

Cluster analysis is an important tool employed in information retrieval to enhance both efficiency and effectiveness of the retrieval process. The retrieval strategies based on classification of documents can lead to greater efficiency by the search being restricted to just a few selected clusters; they can achieve a greater effectiveness if clusters are formed in such a way that, when the appropriate clusters are selected for retrieval (or detailed examination), the number of relevant documents obtained relative to the number of documents retrieved (or examined) is high. This implies that the clustering algorithm must ensure that documents that are likely to be relevant to the same queries are placed together in the same clusters.

Although many existing strategies for document classification consider the summarization of the data and the identification of the "natural" or "homogeneous" clusters as the primary objective, it is also attractive to specify some extrinsic criterion, based on the requirements of the application environment, according to which a placement of documents into classes is to be assessed. In the latter case, the problem of cluster analysis becomes simply an instance of combinatorial optimization problems.

When performing cluster analysis by formulating the problem as one of function optimization, one can choose from two general directions for developing a solution. On the one hand, prior knowledge of specific properties of the function to be optimized (e.g. unimodality, continuity, etc.) can be exploited in tailoring a particular strategy to the problem at hand. On the other hand, either because prior knowledge is not available or because the optimization criterion is known to be complex (and, therefore, not amenable to optimization by "standard" techniques), one could seek a solution strategy that is effective for a broad class of complex criterion functions. The classification of documents for information retrieval, in our judgement, requires the adoption of criterion functions that are quite ill-behaved. Consequently, in what follows, we develop an approach involving a robust strategy for function optimization.

By now the connection between adaptive processes and function optimization problems is well established. Several adaptive plans have been proposed and, in particular, the reproductive plan by Holland [7] has been fairly well investigated as an approach to function optimization [1-4,16]. The conclusions are that the algorithm is robust and, for the cases where the criterion functions are ill-behaved, more efficient relative to standard techniques.

Thus, there is motivation for considering the reproductive plan as an approach for performing cluster analysis. In other words, we suggest that each possible classification (a placement of objects into clusters) be considered a device and it is desired to identify progressively better performing devices vis-a-vis a clustering criterion. This view of clustering has already been investigated in Raghavan and Birchard [13]. However, in that work, certain problems of representation were not adequately resolved. The result was that the basic genetic operators such as crossover, double-crossover and mutation did not prove effective. In the current work, a framework, in which such representational problems do not exist, is identified. As a result we are able to assert that the genetic algorithm is again a promising direction to investigate.

---

* Currently on leave from University of Regina, Regina, Canada. S4S 0A2.

In the next section, the general framework that characterizes user-oriented clustering approach is presented. Then, in section 3, the definition of the problem, for which the use of the genetic algorithm is being advocated, is given. The details of the structure representation and operator specification are developed in section 4. Finally, section 5 summarizes the contributions of this work.

2. The Problem Framework

In the context of information retrieval systems, a new approach to document clustering called the user-oriented document clustering (also known as adaptive clustering) is emerging. This approach has been investigated by Yu et al. [16], and Deogun and Raghavan [14]. User-oriented clustering can be seen as a mechanism whereby the classification is based on the user perception of clusters, rather than on some similarity function perceived by the designer to represent the user criteria.

2.1 Overview of Adaptive Clustering

The adaptive clustering process is basically a two stage clustering scheme. Each document is initially assigned a position on the line ($-\infty$, ∞). In the first stage, as a query is processed, documents relevant to this query are moved closer; then some randomly selected documents are moved away from their centroid. This step is repeated for several queries. In the second stage, the clusters are identified. For the purpose of this paper, the first stage of the algorithm is adapted from Yu et. al. The second stage is based on the formulation of the problem developed by Raghavan and Deogun[14]. The important details in the algorithm are as follows:

Stage 1

1. Given documents $d_1, d_2, ..., d_N$ each document d_i is assigned an arbitrary position p_i on a real line ($-\infty$, ∞), for $1 \leq i \leq$ N.

2. Given a (next) query

   a. use the (actually) stored clusters to provide response

   b. obtain feedback from user as to which documents are relevant to the query.

   c. modify the position of documents on the line, so that the documents accessed for this query occupy positions closer to each other on the line while ensuring that points corresponding to all documents do not eventually bunch up in a small interval.

3.

   a. If the clustering based on the positions of the documents on the line (see stage 2 for details) is significantly different from the stored clusters, then reorganize the stored clusters according to the new clusters indicated.

   b. Go to step 2 (next query).

Stage 2

In this stage, optimal clusters are to be obtained by defining boundaries at suitable points on the document line.

The basic steps are:

1. Define *possible* boundary points (points on the document line where boundary between two clusters can be defined).

2. From the set of possible boundary points select some points as *actual* boundaries to obtain a particular set of clusters (a classification).

3. Evaluate the performance of this classification relative to the given set of queries, according to some performance criteria. Terminate if a sufficiently well performing classification has been obtained. Otherwise, generate a potentially better performing classification by modifying the current one. Repeat step 3.

2.2 Earlier Work on Adaptive Clustering

Several research investigations have been carried out, in the last few years, on adaptive document clustering [6,14-17].

The main emphasis of these activities have been on ways of accumulating the information gathered through user feedback (analogous to stage 1 above). In Raghavan and Sharma [15], the idea of arranging the documents on a line, proposed in [16], was retained. But the conditions under which two documents would be moved closer to or apart from each other is modified. The results indicate that the modification is computationally more efficient. The work by Deogun and Raghavan [6], in contrast, hypothesized that summarizing the usage patterns on a line is too restrictive in the sense that much useful information is lost. Consequently, an entirely new procedure that employs a weighted graph as the structure for summarizing feedback on usage patterns is proposed. The preliminary results show that this approach is effective. However, that approach has not yet been adequately compared with others existing in the literature to determine its relative performance. More recently, Oommen and Ma [11] have characterized the adaptive clustering problem within the context of certain learning automata.

Another aspect of clustering documents in this manner concerns the use of clusters so obtained during retrieval. Yu et al. do not investigate any concrete retrieval scheme. Instead they show that performance will be good if a scheme that is able to select the "best" clusters is devised. Thus, this problem is still essentially open. The difficulty is that the descriptors or properties associated with documents and queries play no part during clustering and the system, while knowing what the clusters are, has no knowledge of how documents in one cluster can be distinguished from those in another. A promising approach based on Bayesian decision theory is suggested in Deogun and Raghavan [6]. This and few other alternatives are currently under investigation.

3. The Boundary Selection Problem

Concepts such as positive, negative and boundary regions introduced by Pawlak [12] in the context of the development of the *rough set theory* are used to develop a formulation a suitable clustering criterion.

A *positive region[POS(q)]* for a query q is defined to be the set of documents in the clusters that are completely included in the relevant set of the query. Similarly, a *negative region[NEG(q)]* is defined to be a set of documents in the clusters that are completely excluded from the relevant set of the query. Documents in the remaining clusters define the *boundary region[BND(q)]*.

Clearly, an "ideal" clustering for a given set of queries will be the one in which for each query we have only positive and negative regions but no boundary regions. Therefore, in finding a clustering our motivation is to maximize the positive and negative regions collectively for all queries in the given set.

This leads us to the following function as a measure of effectiveness for a given clustering $C = \{C_1, C_2, \cdots, C_r\}$:

$$\xi_C = \sum_{i=1}^{n} w_i \frac{|POS_C(q_i)| + |NEG_C(q_i)|}{|D|},$$

where $q_1, q_2, ..., q_n$ are the queries and w_i is the weight associated with query q_i and D is the set of documents over which the partition C is defined.

The objective is to find a clustering C of document set D that maximizes ξ_C with respect to the given set of queries. Since $\sum_{i=1}^{n} w_i$ can be considered to be a constant, the objective of maximizing ξ_C is equivalent to

$$minimize \ \tau_C = \sum_{i=1}^{n} w_i \ |BND_C(q_i)|$$

τ_C can be interpreted as the cost associated with choice of clustering C.

It is not difficult to see that this cost function is biased in favor of forming many small clusters. So the following constraint is adopted:

$$\sum_{i=1}^{n} w_i * R_i \leq B,$$

where the w_is are the query weights as earlier, R_i is the number of sets among $C_1, C_2, \cdots, C_r$ such that $C_i \cap POS_C(q_i) \neq \phi$, for $1 \leq j \leq r$ and $1 \leq i \leq n$, and B is a chosen bound on the retrieval effort. Formally, the problem we want to solve is then to

find C such that

$$\tau_C = \sum_{i=1}^{n} \sum_{j,} \ w_i * |BND_C(q_i)|$$
$$C_i \bigcap BND_C(q_i) \neq \phi$$

is minimized subject to

$$\sum_{i=1}^{n} w_i * R_i \leq B.$$

This problem is called the Boundary Selection Problem (BSP)[14].

4. The Reproductive Plan

4.1 Representation

Let $b_0, b_1, ... b_m$ be the possible boundary points. We denote a classification, C, by an $(m+1)$ - dimensional binary vector $X = (x_0, x_1, ..., x_m)$, where $x_0 = 1, x_m = 1$ and, for each j, $1 \leq j < m$,

$$x_j = \begin{cases} 1, & \text{if } b_j \text{ is an actual boundary in } C \\ 0, & \text{otherwise} \end{cases}$$

Let r, $2 \leq r \leq m+1$, be the number of 1's in the solution vector X. Thus, given a bound on the retrieval effort and a set of possible boundary points, it is desired to find the X for which the cost function is a minimum.

Now each X corresponds to a solution from the search space of 2^{m-1} different solution vectors. Each X defines a classification, but some of these classifications may not be feasible (if they violate the constraint). Nevertheless, there are still a very large number of feasible solutions in the search space and no efficient procedure could possibly search the entire space exhaustively to obtain an optimal solution. Some heuristic methods, which exploit the branch-and-bound strategy, have been proposed [14]. Since the clusters interact in a non-linear way, and due to inherent parallelism and other characteristics of the reproductive plan identified in [7-10,17], effective results are likely to be obtained by adopting the basic genetic algorithm. Next, the representation of any classification as a structure and its manipulation via genetic operators are illustrated by means of examples.

Let D represent a set of 11 documents :-

$$D = \{1,2,3,4,5,6,7,8,9,10,11\}.$$

With respect to a given set of queries and their relevant sets, suppose the output of stage 1 is the following :

$$\{ (1,0.21),(2,0.27),(3,0.16),(4,1.76),(5,0.50),(6,0.60),$$
$$(7,2.11),(8,0.18),(9,0.30),(10,0.95),(11,-) \}$$

A pair (i , δ_i) in the output simply means that document d_i is at a distance δ_i from the next document on the line. This is depicted in the diagram below:

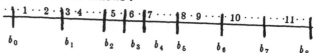

Using a suitable criterion (e.g. a threshold as to the size of a gap [see, 13]), we identify the possible boundaries as follows :-

The two extreme boundary points are always marked, by default, as actual boundaries. We now have
$X = (\ x_0, x_1, x_2, x_3, x_4, x_5, x_6, x_7, x_8\ )$ where $x_0 = 1, x_8 = 1$.

Thus, the solution space has $2^{9-2}=2^7$ different solutions. Consider one of them :

$$X = 1\,0\,1\,0\,1\,1\,0\,1\,1$$

In this case, the possible boundary points chosen as the actual partitions are

$$P = \{\ b_1, b_3, b_5, b_6, b_8, b_9\}.$$

This would result in following clustering C :

$$C = \Big\{C_1, C_2, C_3, C_4, C_5\Big\}, \text{ where}$$

$$C_1 = \Big\{1,2,3,4\Big\}\ ,\quad C_2 = \Big\{5,6\Big\}\ ,\quad C_3 = \Big\{7\Big\}\ ,\quad C_4 = \Big\{8,9,10\Big\}\ ,$$

$$C_5 = \Big\{11\Big\}.$$

Suppose that we have several structures in a population as follows :

$$\begin{aligned}X_1 &= 1\,0\,1\,1\,0\,0\,0\,1\,1\\ X_2 &= 1\,1\,0\,1\,0\,1\,0\,0\,1\\ X_3 &= 1\,1\,0\,1\,0\,0\,0\,1\,1\end{aligned}$$

A cross-over between X_1 and X_2 at position 6 will yield :-

$$\begin{array}{lll} 1\,0\,1\,1\,0\,0\,0\,1\,1 & 1\,0\,1\,1\,0\,0\,0\,0\,1 & : X_{11}\\ & \Rightarrow & \\ 1\,1\,0\,1\,0\,1\,0\,0\,1 & 1\,1\,0\,1\,0\,1\,0\,1\,1 & : X_{21} \end{array}$$

The clustering corresponding to $X_1, X_2, X_3, X_{11}, X_{21}$ are:

$$\begin{aligned}X_1 &: \{\{1,2,3,4\},\{5\},\{6,7,8,9,10\},\{11\}\}\\ X_2 &: \{\{1,2\},\{3,4,5\},\{6,7\},\{8,9,10,11\}\}\\ X_3 &: \{\{1,2\},\{3,4,5\},\{6,7,8,9,10\},\{11\}\}\\ X_{11} &: \{\{1,2,3,4\},\{5\},\{6,7,8,9,10,11\}\}\\ X_{21} &: \{\{1,2\},\{3,4,5\},\{6,7\},\{8,9,10\},\{11\}\}\end{aligned}$$

Mutation of X_3 and X_1 at positions 7 and 4 respectively would result in new structures, X_{32} and X_{12} as follows:

$$X_{32} : 1\,1\,0\,1\,0\,0\,0\,1\,1 \Rightarrow 1\,1\,0\,1\,0\,0\,1\,1\,1$$

The resulting clusters are :
$$\{\{1,2\},\{3,4,5\},\{6,7,8,9\},\{10\},\{11\}\};$$

$$X_{12} : 1\,0\,1\,1\,0\,0\,0\,1\,1 \Rightarrow 1\,0\,1\,0\,0\,0\,0\,1\,1$$

similarly, the corresponding clusters are :
$$\{\{1,2,3,4\},\{5,6,7,8,9,10\},\{11\}\}.$$

Suppose q_i is the relevant set for i^{th} query,

$$q_i = \{1, 2, 6, 7, 8, 11\}.$$

Then the associated POS, NEG, and BND regions would be :

X_1 : $POS_{X_1}(q_i) = \{11\}$; $BND_{X_1}(q_i) = \{1,2,3,4,6,7,8,9,10\}$; $NEG_{X_1}(q_i) = \{5\}$,

X_2 : $POS_{X_2}(q_i) = \{1,2,6,7\}$; $BND_{X_2}(q_i) = \{8,9,10,11\}$; $NEG_{X_2}(q_i) = \{3,4,5\}$,

X_3 : $POS_{X_3}(q_i) = \{1,2,11\}$; $BND_{X_3}(q_i) = \{6,7,8,9,10\}$;

$NEG_{X_3}(q_i) = \{3,4,5\}$,

X_{11} : $POS_{X_{11}}(q_i) = \phi$; $BND_{X_{11}}(q_i) = \{1,2,3,4,6,7,8,9,10,11\}$; $NEG_{X_{11}}(q_i) = \{5\}$,

X_{21} : $POS_{X_{21}}(q_i) = \{1,2,6,7,11\}$; $BND_{X_{21}}(q_i) = \{8,9,10\}$; $NEG_{X_{21}}(q_i) = \{3,4,5\}$,

X_{32} : $POS_{X_{32}}(q_i) = \{1,2,11\}$; $BND_{X_{32}}(q_i) = \{6,7,8,9\}$; $NEG_{X_{32}}(q_i) = \{3,4,5,10\}$,

X_{12} : $POS_{X_{12}}(q_i) = \{11\}$; $BND_{X_{12}}(q_i) = \{1,2,3,4,5,6,7,8,9,10\}$; $NEG_{X_{12}}(q_i) = \phi$.

In the original population, X_2 had the best utility with respect to q_i since its BND set was smallest. This performance could be attributed to the subunits:

Pattern 1 1 in positions 0, 1 respectively,

and 1 0 1 in positions 3, 4, 5 respectively. Notice how the offspring X_{21}, which provided these subunits, continues to perform well.

On the other hand X_1 had a low utility with respect to q_i, and subunits contributing to poor performance are :

Pattern 1 0 1 in position 0, 1, 2 respectively,

and 1 0 0 0 1 in position 3, 4, 5, 6, 7 respectively. The offsprings X_{11} and X_{12} which still have the first subunit continue to perform poorly.

Mutations generate a new classification by breaking a cluster or by merging two clusters. Crossovers help in producing new combinations of clusters.

Now we have seen how a diverse set of solutions can be generated by a few elementary operations and how the operations affect the payoff (or utility) of each structure. Also, this representation does not have the "labelling anomaly" of the previous approach [13]. Consequently, it is expected that the basic genetic operations would suffice for our application; i.e. no application-specific operators are necessary.

4.2 Discussion of the Approach

The classification scheme considered represents a novel perspective on the process of cluster analysis. When compared to approaches, for example, in pattern recognition literature, it seems to resemble paradigm-oriented classification. That is, the clusters identified depend on the feedback from users as to which documents are relevant to their queries. The fact that it resembles paradigm-oriented pattern classification gives some assurance that the use of the reproductive plan can be effective, since Cavicchio [4] has been successful in applying the algorithm to the character recognition problem.

However, the similarity of the problem addressed to paradigm-oriented classification is not that great. This can be realized by observing that the classification is not done separately for individual queries, whereby a distinction is drawn between relevant and non-relevant documents, but rather in a global sense. In other words, the clusters are required to transcend the specific queries on the basis of which they were generated and be useful in retrieving the relevant documents even for queries not encountered at any time earlier. In this context it is important that new classifications (structures) developed during the clustering process be made of up well-performing schemas (subunits). This aspect points to the fact that some sort of "homogeneous" clusters of interest to many past and potential users, are being sought. Hence, there is also some resemblance between our objectives and those of the classification strategies that fit in the class of "unsupervised" learning methods. We believe that this new perspective on classification is very useful for the retrieval environment and should be of value in other contexts as well.

It is also interesting that stages 1 and 2 of the proposed clustering strategy would be, in the terminology of Yu et. al., called adaptive document clustering. Within this broader adaptive system, we propose to apply the reproductive plan to solve the BSP. Thus, what we are developing is a layered system where on the one hand the positioning of documents on the line is being adapted in response to certain environmental influence and on the other hand the organization of these documents into clusters is adapted according to the clustering criterion. For the latter stage, the use of the genetic algorithm is advocated.

In the earlier investigation of the genetic algorithm as a way of obtaining an optimal classification [13], the concept of arranging documents on a line did not exist. Consequently, a classification was represented as a string of cluster labels: for a classification of N documents into r clusters, the string is of length N and each position on the string would be assigned a value between 0 and $r-1$ indicating the label of the cluster to which the document belonged. Thus, there was not only the problem that at each locus there would be a large number of alleles, but also that there was what we called the "labeling anomaly". That is, a cluster having label l in one structure may be totally disjoint from and unrelated to a cluster also labeled l in another structure. Such problems lead to the basic genetic operators being ineffective in generating better performing, and often even valid, structures. It is easily seen that the representation adopted here circumvents such difficulties.

The implementation of these ideas are underway.

5. Conclusion

In information retrieval, a novel approach to cluster analysis in which clusters are modified as relevance feedback from users are obtained, known as user-oriented document clustering, is actively being investigated. A combinatorial optimization problem that arises in that context requires the identification of cluster boundaries in such a way that a prescribed retrieval criterion is optimized. It is shown, by specifying a structure representation and providing examples of operator application, that the reproductive plan is a promising approach for solving this problem.

Acknowledgements

This research is supported in part by a grant from NSERC of Canada.

References

1. Bethke, A.,"Genetic Algorithms as Function Optimizers", Doctoral Thesis, CS Department, University of Michigan, 1981.

2. Brindle, A.,"Genetic Algorithms for Function Optimization", Doctoral Thesis, Department of Computing Science, University of Alberta, 1980.

3. Cavicchio, D.J., "Adaptive Search Using Simulated Evolution", TR 03296-T, Computer and Communications Dept., University of Michigan, 1970.

4. De Jong, K., "Adaptive System Design : A Genetic Approach", *IEEE Transactions on Systems, Man and Cybernetics*, pp. 566-574, vol. SMC-10, 9, Sept. 1980.

5. De Jong, K., "A Genetic Based Global Function Optimization Technique", TR 80-2, Department of Computer Science, University of Pittsburgh, 1980.

6. Deogun, J.S., and Raghavan, V.V., "User-oriented Document Clustering : A Framework for learning in Information Retrieval", *Proc. of the Ninth International ACM SIGIR Conf. on Research and Development in Information Retrieval*,pp. 157-163, Pisa, Italy, Sept. 1986.

7. Holland, J.H., "Adaptation in Natural and Artificial Systems", The University of Michigan Press, 1975.

8. Holland, J.H. et. al., "Computational Implementation of Inductive Systems", in *Induction : Process of Inference, Learning, and Discovery*, pp. 103-150, The MIT Press, 1986.

9. Mauldin, M.L., "Maintaining Diversity in Genetic Search", pp. 247-250, *Proc. AAAI-84,*August 1984.

10. Mercer, R.E. and Sampson, J.R., "Adaptive Search Using a Reproductive Meta-Plan", pp. 215-228, *Kybernetes*, vol. 7, 1978.

11. Oommen, B.J. and Ma, D., "Fast Object Partitioning Using Stochastic Learning Automata", *Proc. of the Tenth International ACM SIGIR Conf. on Research and Developing in Information Retrieval,*to appear, New Orleans, June 1987.

12. Pawlak, Z., "On Learning - A Rough Set Approach", in *Lecture Notes in Computer Science*, No. 208, Skowron A., Ed., Springer Verlag, Berlin, 1986.

13. Raghavan, V.V. and Birchard K., "A Clustering Strategy Based on a Formalism of the Reproductive Process in Natural Systems", *Proc. of the second International ACM SIGIR Conference on Information Retrieval*, pp. 10-22, Dallas, Sept. 1979.

14. Raghavan, V.V. and Deogun, J.S., "Optimal Determination of User-oriented Clusters", *Proc. of the tenth International ACM SIGIR Conf. on Research and Development in Information Retrieval* to appear, New Orleans, June 1987.

15. Raghavan, V.V. and Sharma, R.S., "A Framework and Prototype for Intelligent Organization of Information", *Canadian Journal of Information Science*, 1987, to appear.

16. Yu, C.T., Wang, Y.T. and Chen, C.H., "Adaptive Document Clustering", *Proc. of Eighth Annual International ACM SIGIR Conf. on Research and Development in Information Retrieval*, pp. 197-203, Montreal, Canada, 1985.

17. Wetzel, A., "Evaluation of the Effectiveness of Genetic Algorithms to Combinatorial Optimization", Doctoral Thesis, Department of Library and Information Science, University of Pittsburgh, 1983.

THE GENETIC ALGORITHM AND BIOLOGICAL DEVELOPMENT

by

Stewart W. Wilson

The Rowland Institute for Science, Cambridge MA 02142

Abstract

A representation for biological development is described for simulating the evolution of simple multicellular systems using the genetic algorithm. The representation consists of a set of production-like growth rules constituting the genotype, together with the method of executing the rules to produce the phenotype. Examples of development in 1-dimensional creatures are given.

1. Introduction

The genetic algorithm [1] incorporates mechanisms which resemble the mechanisms of reproduction, variation, and selection found in natural evolution, but, despite successes in several fields of application, there has been little attempt to use the algorithm as a tool to investigate, through simulation, natural evolution itself. Considerable work exists on the ontogenetic evolution of behavior, *i.e.*, learning [2-4], but relatively little on the evolution of organisms *per se* [5]. The main reason has been the absence of representations for organisms which would permit the genetic algorithm to be brought to bear. The genetic algorithm observes the genotype-phenotype distinction of biology: the algorithm's variation operators act on the genotype and its selection mechanisms apply to the phenotype. In biology, the genotype-phenotype difference is vast: the genotype is embodied in the chromosomes whereas the phenotype is the whole organism that expresses the chromosomal information. The complex decoding process that leads from one to the other is called biological development and is essential if the genotype is to be evaluated by the environment. Thus to apply the genetic algorithm to natural evolution calls for a representational scheme that both permits application of the algorithm's operators to the genotype and also defines how, based on the genotype, organisms are to be "grown", *i.e.*, their development.

The present paper outlines a few steps in the direction of such a representation [6]. The problem is addressed at the level of cells, which are treated as as "black boxes" having well-defined properties. Beginning with the fertilized egg, the cells are to divide, move, and differentiate under the control of rules so as eventually to form a mature organism. An attempt is made to respect major facts known about cells and these processes, but large compromises must occur at this point in the effort to approach algorithmic workability. The principal objective is to describe a representational framework— a sort of "developmental automaton"—sufficiently completely that randomly generated instances will grow and can be evolved under the genetic algorithm in computer experiments.

2. Evolution of Development

The problem of applying the genetic algorithm to the development of multi-cellular organisms can be divided into four parts: plan, expression, selection, and variation.

2.1 Plan

In nature, the genotype contains (1) information that is descriptive, through the action of development and the environment, of a range of possible phenotypes, and (2) information encoding the developmental process itself, *i.e.*, how to go about making a phenotype from a genotype. Both kinds of information are of course inherited and subject to variation and natural selection. Here, for simplicity, it will be assumed that only the first kind of information, termed the organism's *plan*, is heritable and subject to the genetic algorithm. The other kind, the rules for *expressing* the plan to form the phenotype, will be regarded as fixed.

What should the plan look like? Several observations on natural systems are suggestive [7]. In the first place, though individual cells can have different sizes and can change in size, growth occurs primarily through cell division: one cell becomes two "daughter" cells. Second, depending on the situation, the daughters can be phenotypically the same as the parent, they can differ from the parent but not differ from each other, or they can differ from the parent and from each other. Third, the phenotypical outcome of cell division can depend not only on the nature of the parent cell, but also on factors related to the cellular, chemical, or physical context in which the parent cell is embedded. Finally—and pivotal for this discussion—all cells in an organism are considered to contain the *same* genetic informa-

247

tion, though some of it may become in some sense "switched off" or inoperative during differentiation.

These observations have suggested the following working proposal. The plan will take the form of a so-called *production system program* (PSP) consisting of a finite number of production (condition-action) rules which will be termed *growth rules*. The growth rules have the general form

$$X + K_i \;\Rightarrow\; K_j \; K_k$$

The K's stand for cell phenotypes and X represents the local context; the symbol "+" means conjunction. In addition, each growth rule has associated with it a weight w. Every cell in the organism contains the same set of rules, or PSP.

Focussing attention on a particular rule in the PSP of a particular cell, the condition side of the rule is satisfied if that cell is (phenotypically) of type K_i and the context matches X. The action recommended by the rule is to replace the cell by two new cells, one phenotypically of type K_j, the other of type K_k. Whether or not this rule controls the parent cell's fate depends on whether the rule is selected for expression, as discussed in the next section.

The general growth rule form is open to many special cases. As in nature, the daughter cells may or may not be the same as the parent or each other. Furthermore, some rules may contain just one daughter cell, identical to the parent; such a rule, if expressed, means that cell division *does not* take place. Also, some rules may have no cell in their action parts, corresponding to dissolution of the parent cell.

Some rules may have no term corresponding to X; their condition is satisfied independent of context. In the other rules, X can take on several forms. Most simply, X can stand for the presence of a cell of a particular kind adjacent to K_i. In this case ("adjacency" type context), the spatial relation of the X cell and K_i may affect the spatial relation of the daughter cells (if there are two). Another kind of X ("signal" type) would stand for a detector for signals emitted by other cells, not necessarily in the immediate neighborhood. For present purposes, the "signal" emitted by a cell is simply a list of its phenotypical properties. The predominant direction from which matched signals are received could affect the daughter cells' spatial relation. Still another kind of X would detect aspects of the physical environment such as intercell pressure.

2.2 Expression

Since all cells contain the same "program", differential development of the system depends on the selection for expression of different rules in different cells. This is not difficult in principle, since once some differentiation occurs, the sensitivity of the rules to cell type and context will lead to further differentiation. The proposed expression mechanism consists of a *match* step and a *decision* step. Again focussing attention on a particular cell, in the match step the cell first identifies those program rules which have satisfied conditions. Then, from this *match set*, the cell chooses a single rule for expression. The chosen rule "carries out its right-hand side", *i.e.*, daughter cells are produced as prescribed and their signals are emitted.

The system's growth process is envisioned as a series of discrete time-steps. On each step, the expression mechanism operates in every cell of the current system. The operation is regarded as "parallel" in the sense that offspring of all the cells are produced simultaneously. The offspring cells then undergo, in accordance with their phenotypical properties, a process of interaction and spatial accomodation so as to form the "new" system to be input to the expression mechanism in the next time-step.

2.2.1 The decision step

The decision step of the expression mechanism makes use of the growth rule weights w and the effect of signals from nearby cells. Each growth rule in the match set has an associated weight w. If a rule's context (X) part is either absent or is of adjacency type, its *excitation* is defined to be just w. However, if a rule's context part is of signal type, the rule's excitation is defined to be the product of the weight w and the *intensity* of the received context signal. For example, suppose that a certain rule has an X which matches signals S_A emitted by nearby cells A. Suppose further that the total intensity of the signals is simply their number n_A times a constant f. Then the excitation of the rule in question would equal $f n_A w$.

The cell decides which match set rule to express using a probability distribution over the rules' excitations. That is, the probability that a particular rule will be picked is equal to its excitation divided by the sum of the excitations of the rules in the match set. The following three rules offer an interesting example.

$$
\begin{aligned}
A &\Rightarrow A \; A & w_r \\
(S_A) + A &\Rightarrow A & w_i \\
(S_A) + A &\Rightarrow 0 & w_d
\end{aligned}
$$

The first rule, termed "reproductive", takes one cell A and leaves two in its place. The second rule, termed "inhibitory", matches cell A, senses the presence of at least one A-type signal in the vicinity, and seeks, if chosen, to maintain the status quo exactly. The third rule, a deletion rule, has the same condition as the inhibitory rule, but seeks to delete the matched A cell. Each rule has a weight, as shown.

Suppose now the system consists of an aggregate of n cells of type A. In any cell, the excitations of the three rules will be:

$$e_r = w_r$$
$$e_i = w_i f n_A$$
$$e_d = w_d f n_A \quad .$$

If w_r is large and there are relatively few cells, the reproductive rule will be chosen most of the time and the aggregate will grow. As it does, however, the excitations of the inhibitory and deletion rules will increase relative to that of the reproductive rule, due to n_A. The growth rate will slow down. Eventually, an equilibrium will be reached where net growth is zero. At that point, the probability of reproduction equals the probability of deletion, or $w_r = w_d f n_A$. Solving for n_A yields the system's equilibrium size:

$$n_A^* = (1/f)(w_r/w_d) \quad .$$

The system's net growth rate dn/dt prior to equilibrium can be calculated by taking the product of n and the difference between the probabilities of reproduction and deletion. Dropping the "A" subscripts, the result is

$$\frac{dn}{dt} = n \frac{(1 - n/n^*)}{1 + (w_i/w_d + 1)(n/n^*)} \quad ,$$

showing that the system's growth rate can be "chosen" independently of its equilibrium size.

Though simple, the example is important because it illustrates one way in which the cellular program can manage the fundamental problem of bounded growth. Later examples of differentiation into finite regions of homogeneous cell type will assume the presence of growth rule sets of this or similar sort for the regions.

2.2.2 Phenotype properties

Once the decision step has picked a rule for expression, the daughter cells in the action part must be simulated, which means simulating their properties. In a real organism, each cell "type" has a myriad of physical and biochemical properties. Some of these may be more properly regarded as behavioral,

e.g., during development, cells can creep, amoeba-like to new positions. Most of the properties affect in one way or another a cell's interactions with other cells. Even if all the properties were understood, a realistic simulation would still have an enormous problem adequately representing and computing the interactions within the cell aggregate. Such a computation is necessary in order to determine the fitness, with respect to an environment, of the organism as a whole. The practical course for the present would seem to be to choose extremely simple environments, simple measures of fitness, and a very restricted range of cell properties.

2.3 Selection and variation

Because the foregoing representational framework for development takes the form of a production system program, it is straightforward to apply the genetic algorithm as the "engine" of phenotype selection and genotype variation. The application of the algorithm would be along the lines of previous work with production system programs [3,8]. One would start with a population of "egg" cells, each containing a random genotype. Each egg would undergo development and, after a standard number of timesteps, each resulting cell aggregate would be rated for fitness. The original eggs would then be copied in numbers proportional to these fitnesses to form a new population of the same size. Genetic operators would be applied to the genotypes of the new population. The cycle would be iterated through some number of generations, corresponding to evolution.

Many aspects of this scheme are quite well understood due to the research just cited and on genetic algorithms in general. However, the form of the growth rules in the genotype is somewhat unusual so some comments about coding are in order. The basic encoding would resemble that of classifiers [2]. The condition part of a rule would consist of a context taxon (for X) and a cell taxon (for K_i), each being a string of length L from $\{1, 0, \#\}$. The action part would consist of two *cell descriptions* (for K_j and K_k), both strings of length L from $\{1, 0\}$.

An *interpreter* is required to relate cell description encodings to phenotypical properties. This simply means establishing a pre-defined mapping between substrings in the cell description and properties, e.g., "110" in the 14th through 16th positions could mean the cell surface has "high stickiness", etc. To take care of rules in which one or both of the daughter cells is absent, the interpreter would simply check the setting a certain bit in each cell description: "0", say, would mean that description cell was absent and the rest of the description should be ignored. A similar system would be used to indicate the presence or absence of a context taxon and its type (adjacency, signal, or other).

A growth rule's condition would be satisfied if both (1) the cell description of the cell in which the rule finds itself matches the rule's cell taxon, and (2) at least one signal reaching the cell matches the rule's context taxon. The meaning of "match" is the same as for classifiers: the two strings must be the same at every non-# position of the taxon. The use of the "don't care" symbol # permits rule conditions to restrict their sensitivity to particular subsets of cell description and signal bits.

Calculation of the intensity of the signal matching the context taxon can be quite complex, depending on the simulation. Involved are the dependence of individual signal intensities on the distance from their sources, and also perhaps propagation delays with respect to the time-step of creation of the source cell. These factors must be predefined. In any case the total received intensity would be a sum over the individual intensities of all matched signals. As noted earlier, the net *direction* of the received signal may in some rules determine the spatial orientation of the daughter cells. The dependence would be encoded in a special bit string associated with the daughter cell descriptions.

The weight associated with a growth rule must also be encoded in order to make it, and consequently the rule's influence in the decision step, subject to the genetic algorithm. The weight would simply be concatenated, as a fixed-length binary number, with the rest of the rule string.

3. 1-D Development

As has been the case with research on cellular automata [9], the complexity of realistic three-dimensional simulations recommends initial study of one-dimensional examples. In two and three dimensions, forces between cells must lead to complicated cell movements and contortions of the "tissue". A 1-D "creature", however, could be viewed as growing inside a frictionless tube, with no forces except between adjacent cells. Cell division would lengthen the creature; deletion would shorten it. Though simple, the 1-D case can exhibit cell type configuration patterns such as symmetry, periodicity, and polarity that are analogous to patterns emerging in the development of real organisms. Some elementary examples follow.

3.1 Symmetry and periodicity

Changes in a 1-D system through time can be represented by a pyramid like the following:

$$A$$
$$B \quad B$$
$$D \quad C \quad C \quad D$$

This shows three time-steps. At first, the system consists just of cell A; then A divides to form cells B and B; then the left-hand B divides to form the (oriented) pair D C, and the right-hand B yields the pair C D. Only two growth rules are required:

$$A \Rightarrow B \ B$$
$$(B) + B \Rightarrow C \ D$$

In the second rule the context taxon is of adjacency type (indicated by the absence of "S"). This type of rule reads: "order the output cells so that the direction from the first one to the second one is the same as the direction from the context cell to the replaced cell."

Note that the pyramid diagram shows bilateral symmetry about its center line. Using additional rule sets of the self-limiting form discussed in Section 2.2.1, the C's and D's could be multiplied to yield eventually a stable symmetrical creature of finite size, D...D C...C D...D, with approximately equal groups of D cells.

The following pyramid and its rules illustrates rudimentary periodicity:

$$
\begin{array}{ll}
\begin{array}{c}
A \\
E \quad F \\
C \quad D \quad C \quad D
\end{array}
&
\begin{array}{l}
A \Rightarrow E \ F \\
(F) + E \Rightarrow D \ C \\
(E) + F \Rightarrow C \ D
\end{array}
\end{array}
$$

Again, the addition of self-limiting rule sets would result in the creature, C...C D...D C...C D...D, in which like cell groups were approximately equal in size. It is clear that quite complex structures can be built by first establishing the pattern with non-cyclic rules (in which the cell taxon will not match the output cells), and then using self-limiting rule sets which apply to the final cell types.

3.2 Polarity

An elementary polarity results from any rule in which the output cell types differ. A polarity with respect to some phenotypical *property* can be set up with non-cyclic rules as follows:

$$
\begin{array}{ll}
\begin{array}{c}
A \\
B \quad C \\
D \quad E \quad F \quad G
\end{array}
&
\begin{array}{l}
A \Rightarrow B \ C \\
(C) + B \Rightarrow E \ D \\
(B) + C \Rightarrow F \ G
\end{array}
\end{array}
$$

If in the cell descriptions of D, E, F, and G the property is, say, monotonically increasing, the amount of the property will be graded across the system. A more sophisticated gradient system occurs under the rules:

$$A \Rightarrow B\ C$$
$$(S_B) + C \Rightarrow D\ C$$
$$C \Rightarrow C\ C$$
$$(S_C) + C \Rightarrow C$$
$$(S_C) + C \Rightarrow 0$$

If B's signal loses intensity with distance, the probability that a C will change to D C will fall with distance from the left end of the structure. The result will be a decreasing distribution of D's from left to right. The last three rules are intended to control the system's overall size.

When rule sets become even slightly complicated, as in the last example, it evident that development will be difficult to predict. It can be hoped, however, that with the help of the genetic algorithm, the ability to design and analyse organisms in advance will not be necessary in order to build successful and interesting ones—just as in natural evolution it is not. What does seem essential is an adequate space of possible growth rules. The rule forms discussed include self-excitation, self-inhibition, and cross-excitation and -inhibition between different cell types. The repertoire seems fairly complete for a start, but modifications in it and in many other aspects will surely occur as the proposal is studied experimentally and analytically.

4. Conclusion

An extremely schematic representational framework for biological development has been described which may permit simulations of evolution using the genetic algorithm. Major questions that need to be addressed include the accuracy and adequacy of the representation and the problem of computing the phenotype. It is hoped that coupling "developmental automata" with genetic adaptive techniques will yield insights into biological, social, and other systems which are capable of growth.

Acknowledgement

The author thanks D.E. Goldberg for valuable comments on an earlier draft of the paper.

References

[1] Holland, J. H. *Adaptation in natural and artificial systems.* Ann Arbor: University of Michigan Press, 1975.

[2] Holland, J. H. "Escaping brittleness: the possibilities of general-purpose learning algorithms applied to parallel rule-based systems." In R. S. Michalski, J. G. Carbonell & T. M. Mitchell (Eds.), *Machine learning, an artificial intelligence approach. Volume II.* Los Altos, California: Morgan Kaufmann, 1986.

[3] Smith, S. *A learning system based on genetic algorithms.* Ph.D. Dissertation (Computer Science). University of Pittsburgh, 1980.

[4] Grefenstette, J. J. (ed.) *Proceedings of an international conference on genetic algorithms and their applications.* Pittsburgh: Carnegie-Mellon University, 1985.

[5] An important paper used mechanisms closely related to those of the genetic algorithm as defined in [1] to study the emergence of self-replication. See Holland, J. H. "Studies of the spontaneous emergence of self-replicating systems using cellular automata and formal grammars." In A. Lindenmayer & G. Rozenberg (eds.), *Automata, languages, development.* Amsterdam: North-Holland, 1976.

[6] The representation appears to share several aspects with the developmental models called L-systems. However, there do not seem to be any studies in which populations of L-systems undergo evolution. See Lindenmayer, A. "Developmental algorithms for multicellular organisms: a survey of L-systems." *J. Theor. Biol.,* **54**, 1975.

[7] For background, see Balinsky, B. I. "Development, Animal" and Waddington, C. H. "Development, Biological." *Encyclopaedia Britanica,* 15th Ed., Vol. **5**, 625-650.

[8] Schaffer, J. D. "Learning multiclass pattern discrimination." In [4].

[9] Wolfram, S. "Cellular automata as models of complexity." *Nature,* **311**, 4 October 1984, 419-424.

Genetic Algorithms and Communication Link Speed Design: Theoretical Considerations

Lawrence Davis
BBN Labs
10 Moulton Street
Cambridge, MA 02238

Susan Coombs
BBN Communications
70 Fawcett Street
Cambridge. MA 02238

Abstract

The problem of finding low-cost sets of packet switching communication network links when the network topology has been fixed is a difficult and time-consuming one. In this paper we describe the features of the problem that make it difficult, describe a genetic algorithm that solves the problem, and discuss some of the theoretical issues raised in applying genetic algorithms to this domain.

Introduction

The process of designing a packet switching communication network, as carried out at Bolt Beranek and Newman Communications Corporation (hereafter, "BBNCC"), has four major phases:

- First. information about the traffic to be carried. the customer's existing devices and communications protocols. and other customer requirements is gathered and entered into a database.

- Second, access devices are placed such that equipment and line costs are minimized and traffic from the terminals is homed to them.

- Third, packet-switching nodes are similarly placed and traffic from terminal access devices and customer hosts is homed to them.

- In the final phase, the "backbone" phase, the designer links the nodes so that they can carry the desired traffic and meet other customer requirements on speed, reliability, connectivity, and cost. (See the Figure 1 for an illustration of a backbone design.)

This process is carried out with the aid of DESIGNet[TM], BBNCC's interactive network design tool implemented in Zetalisp on Symbolics Lisp Machines.

This paper and its companion paper[1] concern a problem that occurs in the fourth phase of network design. When the designer first links nodes to create a backbone network topology, the links used are high-speed ones. The intent is to produce a topology that satisfies the customer's requirements. One such constraint imposed on the topology in figure 1 is that the net be "biconnected" — given the failure of any single network link or node, the network will still be connected.

High-speed links are very expensive. When a working topology has been found, the designer concentrates on optimizing the network cost by reducing the speeds of some or all of the network links. while satisfying the customer's design criteria. These two problems — that of choosing a topology and that of selecting low-cost, acceptable link speeds given a topology — together constitute the fourth phase of communication network design. When performed by human designers, the two processes tend to be carried out sequentially, although there is a certain amount of overlap between them.

The process of choosing link speeds given a topology is complicated by a number of factors:

- The set of allowable link speeds is determined by the available services offered by the chosen carrier(s). and often varies from network to network.

- The set of customer performance requirements varies from network to network.

- The simulator used by DESIGNet to assess the performance of a trial network is a stochastic one; understanding the effects of changing a link's speed is much more difficult when such effects change between trials.

---

[1]"Genetic Algorithms and Communication Link Speed Design: Constraints and Performance," by Susan Coombs and Lawrence Davis. in this volume

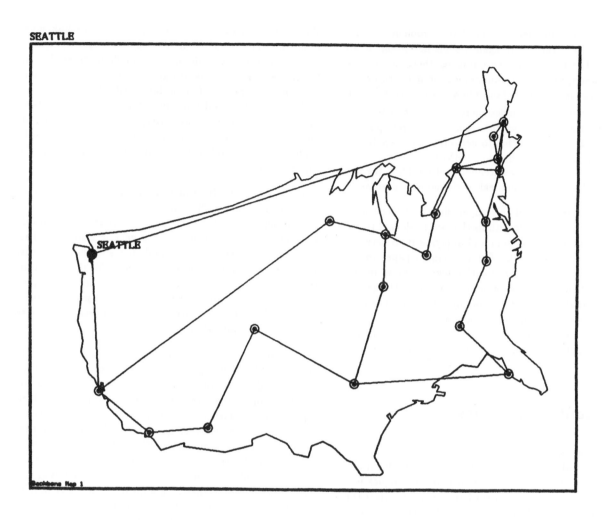

Figure 1: A Sample Backbone Topology

- The network performance constraints may be stated in stochastic terms (*e.g.* the delay of each link in the network must be below 500 milliseconds in 80% of the simulations) and it is difficult to know rapidly whether they have been satisfied.

- The differences in the costs of links of different speeds are non-linear, and often non-intuitive. They depend on the carrier and/or on the modems chosen by the customer, if analog lines are being used.

- Equivalent bandwidth of one higher-speed link between two nodes can be provided by multiple lower-speed links, generally at non-equivalent cost. The nodes treat the multiple links as one logical link when routing traffic.

- The effect of changing a link's size is difficult to predict and is highly interactive — traffic may be rerouted everywhere in the network as a result of changing the speed of a single link.

- The effect of changing a link's size may be counter-intuitive — it occasionally happens that reducing the size of one link in the network improves the entire network's performance.

- For larger backbones, the DESIGNet simulation of network performance may take a minute or more to run, leading to lengthy intervals between a designer's changes in the network and the simulation's feedback.

Given these characteristics, and the fact that a substantial amount of the cost of a packet switching communication network can be bound up in its links, the problem of finding a low-cost set of sizes for the links in a network when its topological constraints have been met is worth solving with a computer. The stochastic nature of the data and the non-linear interaction between changes in a network design make the link speed problem a difficult one to approach with heuristic and hill-climbing systems. We hypothesized that the problem would be amenable to the genetic algorithm approach, and in the fall of 1986 we applied a genetic

algorithm to a simplified version of this problem in order to measure its performance against some deterministic algorithms. The results were encouraging (they, and a more detailed description of the communication network design problem in general, are contained in an earlier paper[2]). On constraints that the human designers were using. The companion paper also describes the results of several applications of our genetic algorithm to networks that were being designed for prospective clients of BBNCC.
the basis of that work, we extended and modified the system for application to some real-world network designs.

The following sections of this paper discuss theoretical issues related to genetic algorithms that were relevant to creating our prototypical system and applying it to networks being designed at BBNCC. The companion paper to this one discusses issues concerned with integrating a wide variety of constraints on network performance into the genetic system, so that the genetic algorithm employed the same constraints that the human designers were using. The companion paper also describes the results of several applications of our genetic algorithm to networks that were being designed for prospective clients of BBNCC.

Representation Issues

Genetic algorithm researchers most frequently use bit strings as chromosomal encodings of solutions to the problem they are trying to solve. Other representation techniques have been employed, but the early work in the genetic algorithm field and most of the formal results that have been proved have been based on the bit string representation. Bit strings and their crossover, inversion, and mutation operators have been extensively studied and are fairly well understood.

We did not use bit strings in the system to be described here. Instead, our chromosomes were lists of link speeds. Each speed was keyed to a link in the backbone, and each speed was taken from the list of allowable link speeds for the design in question. This chromosome, for example, encodes link speeds for a three-link network:

$$(2400 \quad 56000 \quad 9600)$$

Evaluation of such a chromosome is carried out by assigning each link the speed encoded for it on the chromosome, simulating the resultant network's performance, and evaluating that performance against the customer's requirements.

[2] Davis, Lawrence and Susan Coombs, "Optimizing Network Link Sizes with Genetic Algorithms". To appear in *Modelling and Simulation Methodology: Knowledge Systems Paradigms*, Maurice S. Elzas, Tuncer I. Oren, and Bernard P. Ziegler, editors.

Why did we choose this representation for the link speed problem? The principal motivation was our expectation that an important genetic operator would be "creep" — altering the speed of a link upward or downward one or more steps in the hierarchy of allowable speeds. Encoding speeds with bit strings would not support this sort of operation. Interpreting a bit string as a Gray coded string would allow creeping one step up or down, but it would not easily support creeping multiple steps during the application of a single operator.

There is a potentially telling argument against our choice of representation. Other things being equal, representations using an alphabet with fewer letters and longer words will yield better performance in a genetic algorithm than representations with a larger alphabet and shorter words, since they will provide more hyperplanes for the algorithm to explore. We, on the other hand, have chosen to represent each separate link speed "word" with a single "letter". Have we discarded the basis for some important crossover effects? We do not believe so.

The performance gains acquired by using larger alphabet are derived by finding periodicities in the search space that are encoded in the longer words. Our search space is not a periodic one. When the best speeds of a link for a given topology are plotted over a number of runs, they tend to cluster in one or two regions of the link size list, rather than in periodic regions of it. While it is true that small alphabets and large words are useful for finding periodicities in a gene's values, in our domain such periodicities appear not to exist. Accordingly, we appear to have lost nothing by collapsing the representation, and it is simple for us to use the representation in implementing "creep".

Our problem space lends itself to crossover based on word values (to continue the analogy in the preceding paragraph) rather than on letter values. In the link speed domain one must find link speeds that lie in an optimal region, given the speeds of the other links. One then wishes to sample the surrounding allowable speeds, hoping to find better combinations. Complicating the search process are: the fact that evaluations in the region of the optimum may not produce monotonically decreasing evaluations as they move away from the optimal speed; the fact that the evaluation process is stochastic; and the fact that useful hyperplanes in this search space are combinations of link speeds that work well together in the context of the simulation, but these hyperplanes may not be useful if other hyperplanes are interfering with them. The crossover operator in our system operated by cutting chromosomes at two points. Despite these complicating factors, it seems to have satisfactorily detected and combined useful hyperplanes to create coadapted sets of link speeds.

Printed and bound by CPI Group (UK) Ltd, Croydon, CR0 4YY

17/10/2024

01775697-0016

The link speed problem is like the problem of optimizing parameters for a genetic or other stochastic algorithm. The task is to find a set of coadapted values for a set of parameters, under the guidance of a stochastic evaluation function (running the algorithm while using the parameter values encoded on the chromosome.) Given a fixed set of values for the other parameters, the values for a given parameter tend to lie together on the axis of possibilities, often in a standard distribution. Much of the work to be done in such domains involves finding regions of optimal values for each parameter that fit with good regions for other parameters, exploring the interactions of such regions in parallel, and settling on promising combinations of regions for further exploration. The result will be a hyperplane of coadapted values cutting across the axes of parameter values. Here, as in the link sizing problem, the task is to find reasonable combinations of contiguous values in the face of a good deal of noise and parameter interaction.

Genetic approaches to such problems have done well[3]. One question of interest for genetic algorithm researchers desiring to carry out other applications is the comparison of the performance of representations that support creep operators with representations that do not in domains with contiguous, rather than periodic, optimal parameter values.

Epistasis

At the International Conference on Genetic Algorithms and their Applications held two years ago, an interesting discussion arose concerning the status of genetic algorithms that operate in domains with high degrees of "epistasis" — suppression by one gene of other genes' effects. The problem was that John Holland's proof of the convergence of a genetic algorithm on an optimum was based on the assumption that there was a low degree of epistasis in the evaluation of the algorithm's chromosomes. In order for a genetic algorithm to carry out parallel sampling of hyperplanes when it evaluates a chromosome, it is important that each hyperplane contribute its effect to the chromosome's evaluation. This did not appear to be the case for some of the genetic systems being presented at that conference. In one example — the bin-packing system described by Derek Smith[4] — altering the position of a single rectangle to be packed in the chromosomal encoding of a packing could well alter the final position of every other rectangle in the packing! Clearly, Smith's representation led to a good deal of interaction when positions of rectangles were changed. But did it violate the low epistasis assumption? And if it did, was there a convergence proof, perhaps a weaker one,

similar to Holland's original proof, that could be proved for such domains? These questions were left open at that time, as was the question of rigorously defining the notion of epistasis.

There do not appear to have been any published answers to these questions in the interim. There is, however, a growing body of empirical evidence suggesting that genetic algorithms do indeed perform successfully in domains in which alteration of a single gene may cause tremendous divergence in a chromosome's behavior. Some of the papers on the travelling salesrep problem found in this Proceedings are examples of such successful performance. The system described in this paper is another.

We believe that applications of genetic algorithms to such problems will continue to be fruitful. In our companion paper, we describe results that support this belief. Our domain, however, appears to be an epistatic one. Consider what happens when the speed of a single link is increased in a communication network. One possibility is that the traffic in the network follows the same paths and no significant changes in delays accrue. More likely, however, is a substantial alteration in traffic patterns, as traffic that had been routed over different paths is now routed over the freer link and other traffic is re-routed in reaction to this change. It is possible to change every routing in a network by changing a single link's speed, and the resultant change in the evaluation of the network's performance can be tremendous as well. Given that the genetic algorithm performs well in this domain, we would like to raise again some of the questions raised two years ago: Is the domain we are working in intrinsically different from the domains for which convergence proofs exist with respect to epistatic effects? What is epistasis? And are there formal results that can be proved for problems like clustering, bin-packing, and capacity assignment that will help us to implement genetic algorithms in other, similar domains?

Multiple Constraints

An issue that concerned us for a good deal of time arose from the fact that the "environment" surrounding our genetic algorithm differed radically from problem to problem. It was not at all clear that we would be able in a single genetic algorithm framework to model the behavior of communication network designers with respect to the myriad constraints imposed by customers. It was also not clear that we would be able to represent those constraints in an evaluation function that a single genetic algorithm could

---

[3]See John Grefenstette, "Optimization of Control Parameters for Genetic Algorithms," in *IEEE Transactions on Systems, Man and Cybernetics*, SMC-16(1), 122-128, for a discussion of optimizing parameter values with bit string representations. Also see Lawrence Davis and Frank Ritter, "Schedule Optimization with Probabilistic Search,"

Proceedings of the 3rd IEEE Conference on Artificial Intelligence Applications, for an account of optimization of the parameters of a simulated annealer with a representation that supports a "creep" operator.

[4]Derek Smith, "Bin Packing with Adaptive Search," in Grefenstette, John J., editor, *Proceedings of the Second Conference on Genetic Algorithms and their Applications*, 1985.

use. After a period of development and experimentation the results of which are described in the companion paper, we produced a single genetic algorithm and evaluation function environment that we believe will support the application of genetic algorithms to the sort of link speed designs that are currently being carried out at BBNCC. We believe that this issue will arise frequently as genetic algorithms are developed from prototypical applications into working industrial systems. Accordingly, we have devoted our companion paper to a discussion of the techniques we used to create a genetic algorithm system capable of robust application to the link speed design problem, and to a discussion of that system's performance on actual network designs.

Conclusion

In applying genetic algorithms to the communication network link speed design problem, we made several interesting discoveries:

- Genetic algorithms perform well when applied to this domain.

- The highly stochastic and epistatic nature of the domain did not prevent the algorithm from finding and exploiting hyperplanes consisting of useful combinations of link speeds.

- Our system, based on "creep," crossover, and a non-bit string representation, performed well in this domain.

- The domain was similar in some respects to parameter optimization problems already studied by genetic algorithm researchers.

- Further research into the properties of genetic algorithms applied to such domains would be of benefit to those who will produce other, similar applications[5].

[5]The authors thank Susan Bernstein and Richard Vacca for their many helpful comments and suggestions during the preparation of this paper.

Genetic Algorithms and Communication Link Speed Design: Constraints and Operators

Susan Coombs
BBN Communications
70 Fawcett Street
Cambridge, MA 02238

Lawrence Davis
BBN Labs
10 Moulton Street
Cambridge, MA 02238

July, 1987

Abstract

In this paper we describe some novel methods for incorporating constraints into a genetic algorithm for choosing link speeds in a packet switching communications network design. We also describe the object-oriented approach we used in representing the constraints, and present the results of applying these methods to four network designs.

Introduction

Constraints play an important role in network design. A packet-switching network design typically must satisfy constraints on link utilization. connectivity, and on the maximum travel time between source and destination. In expanding a genetic algorithms approach for adjusting network link speeds from the trial network design described in Davis and Coombs (1987)[1] to actual network designs, we discovered that we needed new ways of expressing constraints to generate good designs.[2]

There are many possible varieties of constraints. Designs for two networks rarely satisfy exactly the same set of constraints. To help our genetic algorithm adapt to this fact, we implemented constraints as objects. We were particularly interested in making the constraints easy to combine and modify for each new design. By modeling constraints as objects, we also could quickly demonstrate the effects of constraints separately or in combination. Each constraint was able to annotate its behavior, making it easier to analyze the effects of the constraints on the population.

Our results were quite encouraging. We ran our genetic constraint system, LINKR, on an automatically-generated network design, as well as on three hand-optimized variations of a different network design. In both the automatically-generated and hand-optimized cases. the genetic approach improved the original design.

Constraints and Operators

In applying genetic algorithms to the link speed design problem, we implemented both constraints which impose penalties on solutions. and operators which alter the genetic representation of solutions. Examples of constraints include constraints on link utilization, node utilization, link cost. and delay. Specifically, a customer might require that the utilization of all links in a network be less than 70%. Examples of operators include crossover and "Creep".

Some constraints that we had assumed to be fixed, in particular, those modeling network routing[3], had to be formulated stochastically. We discovered other constraints, including some we had not previously considered, that were essential to designing an acceptable network. Some of these constraints took more time to evaluate than was practical, since part of our goal was to complete a network design in roughly the same amount of time as a person designing a network. Other constraints were problematic in that their evaluations fluctuated wildly under slight changes to the overall network. We developed new techniques to deal with the new kinds of constraints.

---

[1] Davis, Lawrence and Susan Coombs. "Optimizing Network Link Sizes with Genetic Algorithms," to appear in *Modelling and Simulation Methodology: Knowledge Systems Paradigms*. Maurice S. Elzas, Tuncer I. Oren. and Bernard P. Ziegler, editors.

[2] For a more complete description of the problem of adjusting network link sizes than is provided in this paper. see both our earlier paper and the companion paper being presented at this conference.

---

[3] The network routing determines how the traffic is distributed throughout the network.

Stochastic Constraints

Our attempt to model some stochastic constraints deterministically, in particular, constraints depending on network routing, proved too limiting. With deterministic routing, the genetic algorithm optimized link sizes for the particular fixed routing chosen, leading to network designs with little ability to support alternate routings, and hence low resiliency in the face of line outages. Since many of the key constraints, including link utilization, node utilization, and delay, depend on network routing, we had to overcome this limitation. To do this, we developed a strategy for modeling stochastic routing.

In modeling stochastic routing, we adopted a k-out-of-n strategy, where k "successful" routings out of n trial routings are necessary for a penalty-free solution. The success of a routing depends on the specific constraint. For example, a routing could be successful for a link-utilization constraint if all link utilizations were less than 70%. Although a strategy requiring less frequent routings would be desirable, our strategy worked acceptably in the cases we tried. By varying k, we could adjust the robustness of the routing, and by varying n, we could adjust our confidence that the routings sampled were representative.

"Ice Age" Constraints

Some constraints were problematic in that the large amount of time necessary to evaluate them made it impossible to complete a genetic design in roughly the same amount of time as a person designing a network. One constraint that proceeded at a particularly glacial pace involved checking network performance after dropping each node in the network and re-routing traffic. For this constraint we adopted a new strategy, the "Ice Age"[4] constraint strategy. An Ice Age constraint evaluates itself once every Ice Age, that is, once every n generations. An Ice Age affects an entire generation. Each member of the affected generation incorporates the Ice Age constraint's evaluation into its overall evaluation.

Many details of this approach remain to be investigated. For example, the optimal time between Ice Ages is uncertain. It cannot be too long, for then the Ice Ages have little effect on natural selection. Nor can it be too short, for then the time-saving advantage of the Ice Age approach is lost. Experimentation could also be done on whether members of non-Ice-Age generations should carry a lingering, but perhaps exponentially decreasing, penalty from the Ice Age evaluations of their ancestors.

---

[4]We are grateful to Dana Fine for suggesting the "Ice Age" approach.

"LaMarck" Operators

We observed that some constraints imposed penalties on designs which, with only slight changes, would have incurred no penalties at all. One such constraint was the constraint on mismatched line speeds. Although a network design may appear to work well with two adjacent links with widely differing speeds, in some situations one or more high-speed links funnel traffic onto the low-speed link, causing traffic to back up on the high-speed link(s). To avoid this situation, one adjusts the speeds of one or both of the links, resolving the mismatch, and eliminating the penalty the design otherwise would incur.

With the famous LaMarck, who posited the inheritance of acquired traits, in mind, we coined the "LaMarck" operator. When a LaMarck operator is evaluated, it adjusts the genetic structure of a solution as necessary to bring it into the space of legal solutions. This strategy works best when a slight, known, change to the overall network dramatically affects the evaluation of a given constraint, but does not have an appreciable effect on other constraints.

Implementation of both the Ice Age constraints and the LaMarck constraints was provisional and experimental. To begin to reap the benefits of these constraints would require further experimentation.

Bringing Object-Oriented Programming to Genetic Algorithms

One of the key elements of our implementation, which permits the application of different sets of constraints to different network designs, is the object-oriented representation we have chosen for constraints and individual members of the population. Because the constraints involved in each network design are unique, and over many network designs, potentially infinite, the structure of the genetic approach must permit reuse, adaptation, and new combinations of constraints. The object-oriented approach that we have adopted accomplishes this, and we have already built up a sizable library of constraints for use in various types of network designs.

In implementing our constraints, we first developed a small set of basic operations. To generate new members of the population after crossover, creep, or other operators are applied, we implemented a basic operation for changing link sizes. To stochastically model the routing of data traffic throughout the network, we developed a network routing operation. We then used these basic operations as building blocks in implementing specific customer constraints, such as constraints on link utilization.

Some of the constraints that we developed appear in Table 1 below. The link cost constraint sums the costs of the adjustable links in the network, and adds this cost to the overall penalty of an individual solution. The remaining constraints assign a "dollar" cost corresponding to the degree to which they are violated, and the importance of the violation. This cost contributes to the overall penalties of individual solutions.

Many of the constraints have genetic operators associated with them. Some of these operators appear in Table 2 below. The "Creep" operator, for example, uses the link-utilization constraint in determining probabilities for creeping to a higher or lower link speed. Links with high utilizations have a higher chance of creeping up, whereas links with low utilizations are more likely to creep down. The "Adjust Ports" operator is an example of a requirement that we formulated, at different times, both as a constraint imposing penalties (see Table 1), and as a LaMarck post-processor altering solutions.

Results

Applying Genetic Algorithms to an Automatically-generated Network Design

In the case of the automatically-generated network design we used, ten choices of link sizes were available, as compared to four choices in the test case described in Davis and Coombs (1987). There were 66 subnet links with adjustable sizes, as compared to 27 in the test case. Since we had little time in which to find an improved design, and since this design was significantly larger than the test design we had tried previously, we began by trying the greedy cyclic algorithm described in our earlier paper. The results from this paper show that the greedy cyclic algorithm runs significantly faster than the genetic algorithm, but does not perform as well. In this case, the greedy cyclic algorithm did not produce viable results.

We then turned to the genetic algorithm. To initialize the genetic population, we slightly increased the link speeds of the automatically-generated design in a random fashion, so the genetic algorithm would begin its search in a promising area. It found significant improvements to the design in a relatively small run: a population of 30, evolved over 20 generations. We then used a trivial post-optimization step, which consisted of attempting to lower link sizes when they were higher than in the original design. This was possible for two links. The cost savings reported in table 3 below include the effects of this post-optimization step.

Applying Genetic Algorithms to a Hand-Optimized Network Design

The three variations of the hand-optimized network design had many features in common. All three versions had roughly 26 nodes, and 37 links, with about 30 links that could be adjusted in size. Twenty choices of link speeds were available. We typically ran populations of around 30, over 20 to 50 generations.

In the first version, the network had to be reliable enough to tolerate the loss of either of two central nodes. We wrote a special constraint that worked by applying penalties when link utilizations were too high with either of the central nodes down. We experimented with making this constraint an Ice Age constraint which evaluated only once every n generations. Although people designing networks seem to use a similar approach, that is, they evaluated this time-consuming constraint sporadically rather than continually, we did not have much success with implementing this constraint as an Ice Age constraint. Perhaps a larger population would help to preserve traits that only come into play each n generations.

In the second and third versions, the primary constraint was link utilization. In the first of these, we modeled the network with twice the expected amount of traffic, and link utilizations had to be less than 100% (delay was not a factor). In the final version, the customer requested a slightly more conservative design, with link utilizations under 90%. Other constraints on these designs included link cost, modem cost, and port usage.

In analyzing the results of the genetic algorithms with the person responsible for doing the hand-optimizing of the designs, an interesting fact emerged. Two of the more important constraints to consider when designing these networks were link cost and link utilization, and these were the factors the designer concentrated on. A less crucial consideration was modem cost, since link costs usually far outweigh modem costs, and the designer did not have easy access to modem costs. In applying the genetic algorithm to these cases, however, we included a constraint for modem cost, and discovered that much of the improvement that the genetic algorithm achieved was in reducing modem costs. Apparently, genetic algorithms are able to keep track of subsidiary constraints, and to use them to advantage in finding improved solutions.

Conclusion

In the process of applying genetic algorithms to the problem of determining network link sizes, we developed novel and useful types of constraints. We also found a representation for constraints (as objects) that facilitated the rapid selection and modification of sets of constraints for individual network designs. Finally, with the successful application of genetic algorithms to the network link sizing problem, we demonstrated the value of genetic algorithms in solving design problems characterized by many differing constraints.

Constraint	Behavior
Link Cost	Sums costs for penalties
Link Utilization	Routes, sums penalties
Link Drop	Drops links each Ice Age, routes, sums penalties
Port Usage	Sums penalties

Table 1: *Constraints*

Operator	Behavior	Associated Constraint
Crossover	Combines two parents with multiple tries for different parents	
Creep	Changes a link size one step up or down	Link Utilization
Adjust Ports (LaMarck)	Adds extra ports or nodes where needed	Port Usage
Speed Mismatch (LaMarck)	Changes link sizes to correct speed mismatches	

Table 2: *Operators*

Design	Annual Cost Savings
Automatically-Generated Design	$36900
Hand-Optimized Design, Version 1	8232
Hand-Optimized Design, Version 2	45236
Hand-Optimized Design, Version 3	55716

Table 3: *Cost Savings by Design*